SWEET & MAXWELL'S

FAMILY LAW STATUTES

SECOND EDITION

EDITED BY

SWEET & MAXWELL'S
LEGAL EDITORIAL STAFF

WITH

JENNIFER TERRY, M.SC., LL.B.
*Dip.Soc.Ad., Barrister of
the Inner Temple; Social Worker*

ADVISORY EDITOR

OLIVE M. STONE
B.SC.(ECON.), LL.B., PH.D.
*of Gray's Inn, Barrister, Reader in Law,
London School of Economics*

LONDON
SWEET & MAXWELL
1976

Published in 1976 by
Sweet & Maxwell Limited of
11 New Fetter Lane, London,
and printed in Great Britain
by The Eastern Press Limited
of London and Reading

ISBN   Hardback   0421 20400 1
ISBN   Paperback   0421 20410 9

PREFACE TO SECOND EDITION

THE major problem in compiling this kind of book is what to include and, more important, what to exclude. In the six years since the first edition the shape of family law has significantly changed, and space has had to be found for over 200 pages of important new legislation, including the Matrimonial Causes and Guardianship Acts of 1973 and the Children Act 1975. As a result, many Acts of less central importance, which we would have preferred to include, had to be omitted (for example, the Equal Pay Act 1970, Maintenance Orders (Reciprocal Enforcement) Act 1972, and Sex Discrimination Act 1975).

Space was not the only problem. This second edition was originally scheduled for publication a year ago, but the promise of a new Children Act forced us to postpone the work, already at proof stage, until now. In the event, this proved something of a blessing, and the delay made it possible not only to include the vital Children Act but also to take account of an unexpectedly large number of secondary reforms and amendments which would otherwise have come too late for us to include.

The Acts now contained in this book have therefore been brought up to date to April 1, 1976, the date on which the Inheritance (Provision for Family and Dependants) Act 1975 came into force. It must be emphasised, though, that much of the Children Act 1975 will not come into force until appropriate statutory instruments have been made, and that some sections may not be implemented for several years. Only those repeals and amendments in force at April 1 have been actually made in the text; where the 1975 Act provides an amendment which is not yet in force, the object of the amendment has been left as it is, but with a footnote reference to the new provisions.

As before, the primary aim has been to present all the statutory material needed by a student for professional or university examinations on divorce and family law, but it is hoped that the final result will also be of value to legal practitioners and to members of professions associated with family law, such as social workers.

We are again greatly indebted to our Advisory Editor, Dr. Olive Stone, for her help and guidance on what to include; her patience during the extended proof stage and her unerring eye for detail made a difficult task very much easier. Responsibility for the actual editing remains, of course, entirely ours.

We would also like to extend our sincere thanks to Mrs. Jennifer Terry for her initial work in preparing the statutes in this second edition for revision, and for suggesting necessary alterations. The original index, prepared by Richard Castle, was unfortunately overtaken by events; we are extremely grateful to Robert Spicer for preparing the final one, at short notice, with his customary skill.

April 1976   SWEET & MAXWELL.

PREFACE TO FIRST EDITION

THIS volume of statutes covering family law follows the pattern set by our volumes of *Property* and *Estate Duty Statutes* being a collection of the leading Acts relevant to the subject of family law. The reader need, therefore, refer only to this volume for the up-to-date text of a statute contained in it, showing any amendments or repeals up to July 1, 1970.

In compiling this book we were faced with the problem of which statutes should be included; we were, of course, limited by the fact that it was a volume that should be of use to students, and should not, therefore, give a fully comprehensive coverage of all the statutes that might be considered relevant to family law, itself a rather loose term. We have therefore tried to present all the basic statutory material which would be needed by a student for professional examinations or at university for courses on divorce and family law. It will also be a valuable reference book for practitioners.

The contents range from the Wills Act 1837 to the Matrimonial Proceedings and Property Act and Law Reform (Miscellaneous Provisions) Act of 1970. Also included are the Matrimonial Causes Act 1967 and the Divorce Reform Act 1969, which are the two major statutes dealing with divorce law; the various statutes, starting with the Custody of Infants Act 1873 covering guardianship and maintenance of infants, as well as other important statutes which cover wills and succession, education of children, their criminal liability, legitimacy and adoption.

We have omitted, as not being of sufficiently general interest, the Royal Marriages Act 1772 and all Acts dealing with foreigners' marriages or marriages abroad; similarly procedural Acts also have been omitted and those covering nationality and citizenship.

The Acts contained in this volume have been brought up to date in relation to all Acts passed before May 1, 1970. In addition it has been possible to include the relevant portions of the Law Reform (Miscellaneous Provisions) Act 1970, Matrimonial Proceedings and Property Act 1970, and Administration of Justice Act 1970 which received the Royal Assent on May 29, 1970, and to note elsewhere in the volume the effect of these Acts. It can thus be confidently stated that the Acts passed up to July 1970 are to be found herein and this means that many Acts coming into operation on January 1, 1971, are included. The reader is warned that some repeals may only be effective when statutory instruments have been made, see, for example, Administration of Justice Act 1970 (A.J.A. 1970).

We should like to express our sincere thanks and appreciation to our Advisory Editor, Miss Olive Stone, for her help on what material should be included in this volume, and for her advice on the editing of the statutes; the responsibility for the editing of the statutes is, however, solely ours. The index was prepared by Mrs. Audrey Cozens, B.A.

July 1970.   SWEET & MAXWELL.

vi

CONTENTS

[* Those Acts marked with an asterisk are reproduced in part only.]

Wills Act 1837

(1 VICT. C. 26)

An Act for the amendment of the Laws with respect to Wills.

[3rd July 1837]

No will of a person under age valid

7. No will made by any person under the age of [eighteen] [1] years shall be valid.

Every will shall be in writing, and signed or acknowledged by the testator in the presence of two witnesses at one time, who shall attest the will

9.[2] No will shall be valid unless it shall be in writing, and executed in manner herein-after mentioned; (that is to say), it shall be signed at the foot or end thereof by the testator, or by some other person in his presence and by his direction; and such signature shall be made or acknowledged by the testator in the presence of two or more witnesses present at the same time, and such witnesses shall attest and shall subscribe the will in the presence of the testator, but no form of attestation shall be necessary.

Saving as to wills of soldiers and mariners

11.[3] Provided always, that any soldier being in actual military service, or any mariner or seaman being at sea, may dispose of his personal estate as he might have done before the making of this Act.

Wills to be revoked by marriage, except in certain cases

18.[4] Every will made by a man or woman shall be revoked by his or her marriage (except a will made in exercise of a power of appointment, when the real or personal estate thereby appointed would not in default of such appointment pass to his or her heir, customary heir, executor, or administrator, or the person entitled as his or her next of kin under the statute of distributions).

Devises of estates tail shall not lapse where inheritable issue survives, &c.

32. Where any person to whom any real estate shall be devised for an estate tail [. . .] [4a] shall die in the lifetime of the testator leaving issue who would be inheritable under such entail, and any such issue

---

[1] Eighteen was substituted for twenty-one by Family Law Reform Act 1969 (c. 46), s. 3.
[2] Provisions as to the position of signature amended by Wills Act Amendment Act 1852 (c. 24), s. 1.
[3] Explained and extended by Wills (Soldiers and Sailors) Act 1918 (c. 58), *post.*
[4] For Wills expressed to be made in contemplation of a marriage; see Law of Property Act 1925 (c. 20), s. 177.
[4a] The words in square brackets were repealed by the Statute Law Revision (Northern Ireland) Act 1973 (c. 55), Sched.

1

shall be living at the time of the death of the testator, such devise shall not lapse, but shall take effect as if the death of such person had happened immediately after the death of the testator, unless a contrary intention shall appear by the will.

Gifts to children or other issue who leave issue at the testator's death shall not lapse

33.[5] Where any person being a child or other issue of the testator to whom any real or personal estate shall be devised or bequeathed for any estate or interest not determinable at or before the death of such person shall die in the lifetime of the testator leaving issue, and any such issue of such person shall be living at the time of the death of the testator, such devise or bequest shall not lapse, but shall take effect as if the death of such person had happened immediately after the death of the testator, unless a contrary intention shall appear by the will.

Evidence Amendment Act 1853 [1]

(16 & 17 VICT. c. 83)

An Act to amend an Act of the Fourteenth and Fifteenth Victoria, Chapter Ninety-nine.   [20th August 1853.]

Husbands and wives of parties to be admissible witnesses

1. On the trial of any issue joined, or of any matter or question, or on any inquiry arising in any suit, action, or other proceeding in any court of justice, or before any person having by law or by consent of parties authority to hear, receive, and examine evidence, the husbands and wives of the parties thereto, and of the persons in whose behalf any such suit, action, or other proceeding may be brought or instituted, or opposed or defended, shall, except as herein-after excepted, be competent and compellable to give evidence, either viva voce or by deposition, according to the practice of the court, on behalf of either or any of the parties to the said suit, action, or other proceeding.

Saving as to criminal cases

2.[2] Nothing herein shall render any husband competent or compellable to give evidence for or against his wife, or any wife competent or compellable to give evidence for or against her husband, in any criminal proceeding, [. . .][3]

Husbands and wives not compellable to disclose communications

3.[4] No husband shall be compellable to disclose any communication

---

[5] Excluded by Finance Act 1958 (c. 56), ss. 29 (2), 40 (4).

[1] A husband or wife will be competent to give evidence against his or her spouse in the following cases: an action for breach of promise of marriage, Evidence Further Amendment Act 1869 (c. 68), s. 3; an indictment or other proceeding for nuisance to a public highway, river or bridge where a civil right is being enforced, Evidence Act 1877 (c. 14); a prosecution for bigamy, Criminal Justice Act 1914 (c. 58), s. 28 (3); offences under the Sexual Offences Act 1956 (c. 69), s. 39; under the National Insurance Act 1965 (c. 51), s. 94 (6), the Ministry of Social Security Act 1966 (c. 20), s. 33 (6), and the Industrial Injuries and Diseases (Old Cases) Act 1967 (c. 34), s. 11 (5).

[2] See Criminal Evidence Act 1898 (c. 36), s. 4, Sched.

[3] Words repealed by Evidence Further Amendment Act 1869 (c. 68).

[4] Section 3 of no effect, except in relation to criminal proceedings, Civil Evidence Act 1968 (c. 64), s. 16 (3).

made to him by his wife during the marriage, and no wife shall be compellable to disclose any communication made to her by her husband during the marriage

[S. 4 *repealed by S.L.R.* 1875]

Short title

5. In citing this Act in other Acts of Parliament, or in any instrument, document, or proceeding, it shall be sufficient to use the expression, " The Evidence Amendment Act 1853."

[S. 6 *repealed by S.L.R.* 1875]

Married Women's Property Act 1882

(45 & 46 VICT. C. 75)

An Act to consolidate and amend the Acts relating to the Property of Married Women.   [18th August 1882]

1–5. [*Repealed by Law Reform* (*Married Women and Tortfeasors*) *Act* 1935 (*c.* 30), *s.* 5, *Sched.* 2.]

6–9. [*Repealed by S.L.R.* 1969 (*c.* 52).]

Fraudulent investments with money of husband

10. If any investment in any such deposit or annuity as aforesaid, or in any of the public stocks or funds, or in any other stocks or funds transferable as aforesaid, or in any share, stock, debenture, or debenture stock of any corporation, company, or public body, municipal, commercial, or otherwise, or in any share, debenture, benefit, right, or claim whatsoever in, to, or upon the funds of any industrial, provident, friendly, benefit, building, or loan society, shall have been made by a married woman by means of moneys of her husband, without his consent, the Court may, upon an application under section seventeen of this Act, order such investment, and the dividends thereof, or any part thereof, to be transferred and paid respectively to the husband; and nothing in this Act contained shall give validity as against creditors of the husband, to any gift, by a husband to his wife, of any property, which, after such gift, shall continue to be in the order and disposition or reputed ownership of the husband, or to any deposit or other investment of moneys of the husband made by or in the name of his wife in fraud of his creditors: but any moneys so deposited or invested may be followed as if this Act had not passed.

Moneys payable under policy of assurance not to form part of estate of the insured

11. A married woman may [. . .][1] effect a policy upon her own life or the life of her husband for her [own benefit][1]; and the same and all benefit thereof shall enure accordingly.

A policy of assurance effected by any man on his own life, and expressed to be for the benefit of his wife, or of his children, or of his wife and children, or any of them, or by any woman on her own life,

---

[1] Words substituted and repealed by Law Reform (Married Women and Tortfeasors) Act 1935 (c. 30), s. 5, Scheds. 1, 2.

and expressed to be for the benefit of her husband, or of her children, or of her husband and children, or any of them, shall create a trust in favour of the objects therein named, and the moneys payable under any such policy shall not, so long as any object of the trust remains unperformed, form part of the estate of the insured, or be subject to his or her debts: Provided, that if it shall be proved that the policy was effected and the premiums paid with intent to defraud the creditors of the insured, they shall be entitled to receive, out of the moneys payable under the policy, a sum equal to the premiums so paid. The insured may by the policy, or by any memorandum under his or her hand, appoint a trustee or trustees of the moneys payable under the policy, and from time to time appoint a new trustee or new trustees thereof, and may make provision for the appointment of a new trustee or new trustees thereof, and for the investment of the moneys payable under any such policy. In default of any such appointment of a trustee, such policy, immediately on its being effected, shall vest in the insured and his or her legal personal representatives, in trust for the purposes aforesaid. [. . .].[2] The receipt of a trustee or trustees duly appointed, or in default of any such appointment, or in default of notice to the insurance office, the receipt of the legal personal representatives of the insured shall be a discharge to the office for the sum secured by the policy, or for the value thereof, in whole or in part.

12. [*Repealed by Law Reform (Married Women and Tortfeasors*) *Act* 1935, (*c.* 30), *s.* 5, *Sched.* 2; *Law Reform (Husband and Wife) Act* 1962 (*c.* 48), *s.* 3 (2), *Sched.*; *Theft Act* 1968 (*c.* 60), *Sched.* 3, *Pt. III.*]

13. [*Repealed by S.L.R.* 1969 (*c.* 52).]

14–15. [*Repealed by Law Reform (Married Women and Tortfeasors*) *Act* 1935 (*c.* 30), *s.* 5, *Sched.* 2.]

16. [*Repealed by Theft Act* 1968 (*c.* 60), *s.* 33 (3), *Sched.* 3, *Pt. III.*]

Questions between husband and wife as to property to be decided in a summary way

17.[3] In any question between husband and wife as to the title to or possession of property, either party, [. . .][4] may apply by summons or otherwise in a summary way to any judge of the High Court of Justice in England or in Ireland, according as such property is in England or Ireland, or (at the option of the applicant irrespectively of the value of the property in dispute) in England to the judge of the county court of the district, or in Ireland to the chairman of the civil bill court of the division in which either party resides, and the judge of the High Court of Justice or of the county court, or the chairman of the civil bill court (as the case may be) may make such order with respect to the property in dispute, and as to the costs of and consequent on the application as he thinks fit, or may direct such application to stand over from time to time, and any inquiry touching the matters in question to be made in such manner as he shall think fit: Provided always, that any such order of a judge of the High Court of Justice to be made under the provisions of this section shall be subject to appeal in the same way as an order made by the same judge in a suit pending or on an equitable plaint in

---

[2] Words repealed by S.L.R. 1969 (c. 52).
[3] Extended and explained by Matrimonial Causes (Property and Maintenance) Act 1958 (c. 35), s. 7, *post.*
[4] Words repealed by S.L.R. 1969 (c. 52).

the said court would be; and any order of a county or civil bill court under the provisions of this section shall be subject to appeal in the same way as any other order made by the same court would be, and all proceedings in a county court or civil bill court under this section in which, by reason of the value of the property in dispute, such court would not have had jurisdiction if this Act or the Married Women's Property Act 1870 had not passed, may, at the option of the defendant or respondent to such proceedings, be removed as of right into the High Court of Justice in England or Ireland (as the case may be), by writ of certiorari or otherwise as may be prescribed by any rule of such High Court; but any order made or act done in the course of such proceedings prior to such removal shall be valid, unless order shall be made to the contrary by such High Court: Provided also, that the judge of the High Court of Justice or of the county court, or the chairman of the civil bill court, if either party so require, may hear any such application in his private room. Provided also that any such bank, corporation, company, public body, or society as aforesaid, shall, in the matter of any such application for the purposes of costs or otherwise, be treated as a stakeholder only.

18–19. [*Repealed by S.L.R.* 1969 (*c.* 52).]

Married woman to be liable to the parish for the maintenance of her husband

20.[5] [. . .] [6] Where in Ireland relief is given under the provisions of the Acts relating to the relief of the destitute poor to the husband of any woman having [. . .] [7] property, the cost price of such relief is hereby declared to be a loan from the guardians of the union in which the same shall be given, and shall be recoverable from such woman as if she were a feme sole by the same actions and proceedings as money lent.

21. [*Repealed by Poor Law Act* 1927 (*c.* 14), *s.* 245, *Sched.* 11.]

22. [*Repealed by S.L.R.* 1898.]

23. [*Repealed by Law Reform (Husband and Wife) Act* 1962 (*c.* 48), *s.* 3 (2), *Sched.*]

Interpretation of terms

24. [. . .].[8] The word " property " in this Act includes a thing in action.

25. [*Repealed by S.L.R.* 1969 (*c.* 52).]

Extent of Act

26. This Act shall not extend to Scotland.

Short title

27. This Act may be cited as the Married Women's Property Act 1882.

---

[5] " Ireland " is to be construed as exclusive of Eire: see Irish Free State (Consequential adaptation of Enactments) Order 1923 (S.R. & O. 1923 No. 405).

[6] Words repealed by Poor Law Act 1927 (c. 14), s. 245, Sched. 11.

[7] Word repealed by Law Reform (Miscellaneous Provisions) Act (Northern Ireland) 1937 (c. 8) (N.I.), s. 13, Sched. 2.

[8] Words repealed by S.L.R. 1969 (c. 52).

Custody of Children Act 1891

(54 & 55 VICT. C. 3)

An Act to amend the Law relating to the Custody of Children.

[26th March 1891]

Power of Court as to production of child

1. Where the parent of a child applies to the High Court or the Court of Session for a writ or order for the production of the child, and the Court is of opinion that the parent has abandoned or deserted the child, or that he has otherwise so conducted himself that the Court should refuse to enforce his right to the custody of the child, the Court may in its discretion decline to issue the writ or make the order.

Power to Court to order repayment of costs of bringing up child

2. If at the time of the application for a writ or order for the production of the child, the child is being brought up by another person, or is boarded out by the [¹ guardians of a poor law union,] or by a [² parochial board in Scotland,] the Court may, in its discretion, if it orders the child to be given up to the parent, further order that the parent shall pay to such person, or to the guardians of such poor law union, or to such parochial board, the whole of the costs properly incurred in bringing up the child, or such portion thereof as shall seem to the Court to be just and reasonable, having regard to all the circumstances of the case.

Court in making order to have regard to conduct of parent

3. Where a parent has—
- (*a*) abandoned or deserted his child; or
- (*b*) allowed his child to be brought up by another person at that person's expense, or by the guardians of a poor law union, for such a length of time and under such circumstances as to satisfy the Court that the parent was unmindful of his parental duties;

the Court shall not make an order for the delivery of the child to the parent, unless the parent has satisfied the Court that, having regard to the welfare of the child, he is a fit person to have the custody of the child.

Power to Court as to child's religious education

4. Upon any application by the parent for the production or custody of a child, if the Court is of opinion that the parent ought not to have the custody of the child, and that the child is being brought up in a different religion to that in which the parent has a legal right to require that the child should be brought up, the Court shall have power to make such order as it may think fit to secure that the child be brought up in the religion in which the parent has a legal right to require that the child should be brought up. Nothing in this Act contained shall interfere with or affect the power of the Court to consult the wishes of the child in considering what order ought to be made, or diminish the right which any child now possesses to the exercise of its own free choice.

Definitions of " parent " and " person "

5. For the purposes of this Act the expression " parent " of a child

6

includes any person at law liable to maintain such child or entitled to his custody, and " person " includes any school or institution.

Short title

6. This Act may be cited as the Custody of Children Act 1891.

Married Women's Property Act 1893

(56 & 57 VICT. C. 63)

An Act to amend the Married Women's Property Act 1882.

[5th December 1893]

1. [*Repealed by Law Reform (Married Women and Tortfeasors) Act 1935 (c. 30), ss. 5, 8 (2), Sched. 2.*]

2. [*Repealed by Married Women (Restraint upon Anticipation) Act 1949 (c. 78), s. 1, Sched. 2.*]

Will of married woman

3. Section twenty-four of the Wills Act 1837 shall apply to the will of a married woman made during coverture whether she is or is not possessed of or entitled to any separate property at the time of making it, and such will shall not require to be re-executed or republished after the death of her husband.

4. [*Repealed by S.L.R.* 1908 (c. 49).]

Short title

5. This Act may be cited as the Married Women's Property Act 1893.

Extent

6. This Act shall not apply to Scotland.

Criminal Evidence Act 1898

(61 & 62 VICT. C. 36)

Calling of wife or husband in certain cases

4.[1]—(1) The wife or husband of a person charged with an offence under any enactment mentioned in the schedule to this Act may be called as a witness either for the prosecution or defence and without the consent of the person charged.

(2) Nothing in this Act shall affect a case where the wife or husband of a person charged with an offence may at common law be called as a witness without the consent of that person.

---

[1] Amended by Criminal Law Amendment Act 1912 (c. 20), s. 7 (6) and Criminal Justice Administration Act 1914 (c. 58), ss. 28 (3). Extended by Children and Young Persons Act 1933 (c. 12), ss. 15, 108 (6), 109 (3), Sched. 1, *post.*

Married Women's Property Act 1907

(7 EDW. 7, C. 18)

An Act to amend the Married Women's Property Act 1882.

[21st August 1907]

1. [*Repealed by Law of Property Act* 1925 (*c.* 20), *s.* 207, *Sched.* 7.]

2. [*Repealed by S.L.R.* 1969 (*c.* 52).]

Married woman entitled to prior estate to be protector of settlement alone

3.—(1) Where a married woman would, if single, be the protector of a settlement in respect of a prior estate, [. . .] [2] then she alone shall, in respect of that estate, be the protector of the settlement.

(2) This section applies to disentailing assurances and surrenders made after the thirty-first day of December one thousand eight hundred and eighty-two, and as well before as after the commencement of this Act.

Short title; construction

4.—(1) This Act may be cited as the Married Women's Property Act 1907.

[*Subs.* (2) *repealed S.L.R.* 1950 (*c.* 6).]

(3) This Act shall not extend to Scotland.

(4) This Act shall be construed with the Married Women's Property Acts 1882, 1884 and 1893, and those Acts and this Act may be cited together as the Married Women's Property Acts 1882 to 1907.

Wills (Soldiers and Sailors) Act 1918

(7 & 8 GEO. 5, C. 58)

An Act to amend the Law with respect to Testamentary Dispositions by Soldiers and Sailors.   [6th February 1918]

Explanation of s. 11 of Wills Act 1837

1. In order to remove doubts as to the construction of the Wills Act 1837, it is hereby declared and enacted that section eleven of that Act authorises and always has authorised any soldier being in actual military service, or any mariner or seaman being at sea, to dispose of his personal estate as he might have done before the passing of that Act, though under the age of [eighteen][1] years.

Extension of s. 11 of Wills Act 1837

2. Section eleven of the Wills Act 1837 shall extend to any member of His Majesty's naval or marine forces not only when he is at sea but also when he is so circumstanced that if he were a soldier he would be in actual military service within the meaning of that section.

---

[2] Words repealed by Law Reform (Married Women and Tortfeasors) Act 1935 (c. 30), ss. 5, 8 (2), Sched. 2.
[1] Eighteen substituted for twenty-one by Family Law Reform Act 1969 (c. 46), s. 3 (1).

Validity of testamentary dispositions of real property made by soldiers and sailors

3.—(1) A testamentary disposition of any real estate in England or Ireland made by a person to whom section eleven of the Wills Act 1837 applies, and who dies after the passing of this Act, shall notwithstanding that the person making the disposition was at the time of making it under [eighteen]¹ years of age or that the disposition has not been made in such manner or form as was at the passing of this Act required by law, be valid in any case where the person making the disposition was of such age and the disposition has been made in such manner and form that if the disposition had been a disposition of personal estate made by such a person domiciled in England or Ireland it would have been valid.

[*Subsection* (2) *repealed by Succession (Scotland) Act* 1964 (*c.* 41), *s.* 34 (2), *Sched.* 3.]

Power to appoint testamentary guardians

4. Where any person dies after the passing of this Act having made a will which is or which, if it had been a disposition of property, would have been rendered valid by section eleven of the Wills Act 1837, any appointment contained in that will of any person as guardian of the infant children of the testator shall be of full force and effect.

Short title and interpretation

5.—(1) This Act may be cited as the Wills (Soldiers and Sailors) Act 1918.

(2) For the purposes of section eleven of the Wills Act 1837 and this Act the expression " soldier " includes a member of the Air Force, and references in this Act to the said section eleven include a reference to that section as explained and extended by this Act.

Maintenance Orders (Facilities for Enforcement) Act 1920 ¹

(10 & 11 GEO. 5, C. 33)

An Act to facilitate the enforcement in England and Ireland of Maintenance Orders made in other parts of His Majesty's Dominions and Protectorates and vice versa.¹

[16th August 1920]

Enforcement in England and Ireland of maintenance orders made in His Majesty's dominions outside the United Kingdom

1.—(1) Where a maintenance order has, whether before or after the passing of this Act, been made against any person by any court in any part of His Majesty's dominions outside the United Kingdom to which this Act extends, and a certified copy of the order has been transmitted by the governor of that part of His Majesty's dominions to the Secretary of State, the Secretary of State shall send a copy of the order to the prescribed officer of a court in England or Ireland for registration; and on receipt thereof the order shall be registered in the prescribed manner, and shall, from the date of such registration, be of the same force and

¹ Extended by South Africa Act 1962 (c. 23), s. 2 (1), Sched. 2, para. 2, and replaced and prospectively repealed by Maintenance Orders (Reciprocal Enforcement) Act 1972 (c. 18), s. 22 (2).

effect, and, subject to the provisions of this Act, all proceedings may be taken on such order as if it had been an order originally obtained in the court in which it is so registered, and that court shall have power to enforce the order accordingly.

(2) The court in which an order is to be so registered as aforesaid shall, if the court by which the order was made was a court of superior jurisdiction, be the [Probate, Divorce and Admiralty Division] [1a] of the High Court, or in Ireland the King's Bench Division (Matrimonial) of the High Court of Justice in Ireland, and, if the court was not a court of superior jurisdiction, be a court of summary jurisdiction.

Transmission of maintenance orders made in England or Ireland

2. Where a court in England or Ireland has, whether before or after the commencement of this Act, made a maintenance order against any person, and it is proved to that court that the person against whom the order was made is resident in some part of His Majesty's dominions outside the United Kingdom to which this Act extends, the court shall send to the Secretary of State for transmission to the governor of that part of His Majesty's dominions a certified copy of the order.

Power to make provisional orders of maintenance against persons resident in His Majesty's dominions outside the United Kingdom

3.—(1) Where an application is made to a court of summary jurisdiction in England or Ireland for a maintenance order against any person, and it is proved that that person is resident in a part of His Majesty's dominions outside the United Kingdom to which this Act extends, the court may, in the absence of that person, if after hearing the evidence it is satisfied of the justice of the application, make any such order as it might have made if a summons had been duly served on that person and he had failed to appear at the hearing, but in such case the order shall be provisional only, and shall have no effect unless and until confirmed by a competent court in such part of His Majesty's dominions as aforesaid.

(2) The evidence of any witness who is examined on any such application shall be put into writing, and such deposition shall be read over to and signed by him.

(3) Where such an order is made, the court shall send to the Secretary of State for transmission to the governor of the part of His Majesty's dominions in which the person against whom the order is made is alleged to reside the depositions so taken and a certified copy of the order, together with a statement of the grounds on which the making of the order might have been opposed if the person against whom the order is made had been duly served with a summons and had appeared at the hearing, and such information as the court possesses for facilitating the identification of that person, and ascertaining his whereabouts.

(4) Where any such provisional order has come before a court in a part of His Majesty's dominions outside the United Kingdom to which this Act extends for confirmation, and the order has by that court been remitted to the court of summary jurisdiction which made the order for the purpose of taking further evidence, that court or any other court of summary jurisdiction sitting and acting for the same place shall, after giving the prescribed notice, proceed to take the evidence in like manner and subject to the like conditions as the evidence in support of the original application.

If upon the hearing of such evidence it appears to the court that the

[1a] Changed to " Family Division " by A.J.A. 1970 (c. 31), s. 1, Sched. 2, para. 2.

order ought not to have been made, the court may rescind the order, but in any other case the depositions shall be sent to the Secretary of State and dealt with in like manner as the original depositions.

(5) The confirmation of an order made under this section shall not affect any power of a court of summary jurisdiction to vary or rescind that order: Provided that on the making of a varying or rescinding order the court shall send a certified copy thereof to the Secretary of State for transmission to the governor of the part of His Majesty's dominions in which the original order was confirmed, and that in the case of an order varying the original order the order shall not have any effect unless and until confirmed in like manner as the original order.

(6) The applicant shall have the same right of appeal, if any, against a refusal to make a provisional order as he would have had against a refusal to make the order had a summons been duly served on the person against whom the order is sought to be made.

Power of court of summary jurisdiction to confirm maintenance order made out of the United Kingdom

4.—(1) Where a maintenance order has been made by a court in a part of His Majesty's dominions outside the United Kingdom to which this Act extends, and the order is provisional only and has no effect unless and until confirmed by a court of summary jurisdiction in England or Ireland, and a certified copy of the order, together with the depositions of witnesses and a statement of the grounds on which the order might have been opposed has been transmitted to the Secretary of State, and it appears to the Secretary of State that the person against whom the order was made is resident in England or Ireland, the Secretary of State may send the said documents to the prescribed officer of a court of summary jurisdiction, with a requisition that a summons be issued calling upon the person to show cause why that order should not be confirmed, and upon receipt of such documents and requisition the court shall issue such a summons and cause it to be served upon such person.

(2) A summons so issued may be served in England or Ireland in the same manner as if it had been originally issued or subsequently endorsed by a court of summary jurisdiction having jurisdiction in the place where the person happens to be.

(3) At the hearing it shall be open to the person on whom the summons was served to raise any defence which he might have raised in the original proceedings had he been a party thereto, but no other defence, and the certificate from the court which made the provisional order stating the grounds on which the making of the order might have been opposed if the person against whom the order was made had been a party to the proceedings shall be conclusive evidence that those grounds are grounds on which objection may be taken.

(4) If at the hearing the person served with the summons does not appear or, on appearing, fails to satisfy the court that the order ought not to be confirmed, the court may confirm the order either without modification or with such modifications as to the court after hearing the evidence may seem just.

(5) If the person against whom the summons was issued appears at the hearing and satisfies the court that for the purpose of any defence it is necessary to remit the case to the court which made the provisional order for the taking of any further evidence, the court may so remit the case and adjourn the proceedings for the purpose.

(6) Where a provisional order has been confirmed under this section, it may be varied or rescinded in like manner as if it had originally been made by the confirming court, and where on an application for rescission

or variation the court is satisfied that it is necessary to remit the case to the court which made the order for the purpose of taking any further evidence, the court may so remit the case and adjourn the proceedings for the purpose.

(7) Where an order has been so confirmed, the person bound thereby shall have the same right of appeal, if any, against the confirmation of the order as he would have had against the making of the order had the order been an order made by the court confirming the order.

Power of Secretary of State to make regulations for facilitating communications between courts

5. The Secretary of State may make regulations as to the manner in which a case can be remitted by a court authorised to confirm a provisional order to the court which made the provisional order, and generally for facilitating communications between such courts.

Mode of enforcing orders

6.—(1) A court of summary jurisdiction in which an order has been registered under this Act or by which an order has been confirmed under this Act, and the officers of such court, shall take all such steps for enforcing the order as may be prescribed.

(2) Every such order shall be enforceable in like manner as if the order were for the payment of a civil debt recoverable summarily:

Provided that, if the order is of such a nature that if made by the court in which it is so registered, or by which it is so confirmed, it would be enforceable in like manner as an order of affiliation, the order shall be so enforceable.

(3) A warrant of distress or commitment issued by a court of summary jurisdiction for the purpose of enforcing any order so registered or confirmed may be executed in any part of the United Kingdom in the same manner as if the warrant had been originally issued or subsequently endorsed by a court of summary jurisdiction having jurisdiction in the place where the warrant is executed.

Application of Summary Jurisdiction Acts

7. The Summary Jurisdiction Acts shall apply to proceedings before courts of summary jurisdiction under this Act in like manner as they apply to proceedings under those Acts, [. . .]²

Proof of documents signed by officers of court

8. Any document purporting to be signed by a judge or officer of a court outside the United Kingdom shall, until the contrary is proved, be deemed to have been so signed without proof of the signature or judicial or official character of the person appearing to have signed it, and the officer of a court by whom a document is signed shall, until the contrary is proved, be deemed to have been the proper officer of the court to sign the document.

Depositions to be evidence

9. Depositions taken in a court in a part of His Majesty's dominions outside the United Kingdom to which this Act extends for the purposes of this Act, may be received in evidence in proceedings before courts of summary jurisdiction under this Act.

---

² Words repealed by Justices of the Peace Act 1949 (c. 101), s. 46 (2), Sched. 7 Pt. II.

Interpretation

10. For the purposes of this Act, the expression " maintenance order " means an order other than an order of affiliation for the periodical payment of sums of money towards the maintenance of the wife or other dependants of the person against whom the order is made, and the expression " dependants " means such persons as that person is, according to the law in force in the part of His Majesty's dominions in which the maintenance order was made, liable to maintain; the expression " certified copy " in relation to an order of a court means a copy of the order certified by the proper officer of the court to be a true copy, and the expression " prescribed " means prescribed by rules of court.

Application to Ireland

11. In the application of this Act to Ireland the following modifications shall be made:—

(*a*) The Lord Chancellor of Ireland [3] may make rules regulating the procedure of courts of summary jurisdiction under this Act, and other matters incidental thereto:

(*b*) Orders intended to be registered or confirmed in Ireland shall be transmitted by the Secretary of State to the prescribed officer of a court in Ireland through the Lord Chancellor of Ireland [3]:

(*c*) The expression " maintenance order " includes an order or decree for the recovery or repayment of the cost of relief or maintenance made by virtue of the provisions of the Poor Relief (Ireland) Acts 1839 to 1914.

Extent of Act

12.[4]—(1) Where His Majesty is satisfied that reciprocal provisions have been made by the legislature of any part of His Majesty's dominions outside the United Kingdom for the enforcement within that part of maintenance orders made by courts within England and Ireland, His Majesty may by Order in Council extend this Act to that part, and thereupon that part shall become a part of His Majesty's dominions to which this Act extends.

(2) His Majesty may by Order in Council extend this Act to any British protectorate, and where so extended this Act shall apply as if any such protectorate was a part of His Majesty's dominions to which this Act extends.

Short title

13. This Act may be cited as the Maintenance Orders (Facilities for Enforcement) Act 1920.

Trustee Act 1925

(15 & 16 GEO. 5, c. 19)

Maintenance, Advancement and Protective Trusts

Power to apply income for maintenance and to accumulate surplus income during a minority

31.—(1) Where any property is held by trustees in trust for any person for any interest whatsoever, whether vested or contingent, then, subject to any prior interests or charges affecting that property—

---

[3] Office abolished by Irish Free State (Consequential Provisions) Act 1922 (c. 2), s. 2, Sched. 2 Pt. II.

[4] Extended by Maintenance Orders Act 1958 (c. 39), ss. 19, 23 (2).

(i) during the infancy of any such person, if his interest so long continues, the trustees may, at their sole discretion, pay to his parent or guardian, if any, or otherwise apply for or towards his maintenance, education, or benefit, the whole or such part, if any, of the income of that property as may, in all the circumstances, be reasonable, whether or not there is—

    (*a*) any other fund applicable to the same purpose; or

    (*b*) any person bound by law to provide for his maintenance or education; and

(ii) if such person on attaining the age of [eighteen years] [1] has not a vested interest in such income, the trustees shall thenceforth pay the income of that property and of any accretion thereto under subsection (2) of this section to him, until he either attains a vested interest therein or dies, or until failure of his interest:

Provided that, in deciding whether the whole or any part of the income of the property is during a minority to be paid or applied for the purposes aforesaid, the trustees shall have regard to the age of the infant and his requirements and generally to the circumstances of the case, and in particular to what other income, if any, is applicable for the same purposes; and where trustees have notice that the income of more than one fund is applicable for those purposes, then, so far as practicable, unless the entire income of the funds is paid or applied as aforesaid or the court otherwise directs, a proportionate part only of the income of each fund shall be so paid or applied.

(2) During the infancy of any such person, if his interest so long continues, the trustees shall accumulate all the residue of that income in the way of compound interest by investing the same and the resulting income thereof from time to time in authorised investments, and shall hold those accumulations as follows:—

(i) If any such person—

    (*a*) attains the age of [eighteen years], [1] or marries under that age, and his interest in such income during his infancy or until his marriage is a vested interest; or

    (*b*) on attaining the age of [eighteen years] [1] or on marriage under that age becomes entitled to the property from which such income arose in fee simple, absolute or determinable, or absolutely, or for an entailed interest;

the trustees shall hold the accumulations in trust for such person absolutely, but without prejudice to any provision with respect thereto contained in any settlement by him made under any statutory powers during his infancy, and so that the receipt of such person after marriage, and though still an infant, shall be a good discharge; and

(ii) In any other case the trustees shall, notwithstanding that such person had a vested interest in such income, hold the accumulations as an accretion to the capital of the property from which such accumulations arose, and as one fund with such capital for all purposes, and so that, if such property is settled land, such accumulations shall be held upon the same trusts as if the same were capital money arising therefrom;

but the trustees may, at any time during the infancy of such person if his interest so long continues, apply those accumulations, or any part thereof, as if they were income arising in the then current year.

(3) This section applies in the case of a contingent interest only if the limitation or trust carries the intermediate income of the property,

---

[1] Eighteen substituted for twenty-one by Family Law Reform Act 1969 (c. 46), s. 1 (3), Sched. 1, Pt. I.

but it applies to a future or contingent legacy by the parent of, or a person standing in loco parentis to, the legatee, if and for such period as, under the general law, the legacy carries interest for the maintenance of the legatee, and in any such case as last aforesaid the rate of interest shall (if the income available is sufficient, and subject to any rules of court to the contrary) be five pounds per centum per annum.

(4) This section applies to a vested annuity in like manner as if the annuity were the income of property held by trustees in trust to pay the income thereof to the annuitant for the same period for which the annuity is payable, save that in any case accumulations made during the infancy of the annuitant shall be held in trust for the annuitant or his personal representatives absolutely.

(5) This section does not apply where the instrument, if any, under which the interest arises came into operation before the commencement of this Act.

Power of advancement

32.—(1) Trustees may at any time or times pay or apply any capital money subject to a trust, for the advancement or benefit, in such manner as they may, in their absolute discretion, think fit, of any person entitled to the capital of the trust property or of any share thereof, whether absolutely or contingently on his attaining any specified age or on the occurrence of any other event, or subject to a gift over on his death under any specified age or on the occurrence of any other event, and whether in possession or in remainder or reversion, and such payment or application may be made notwithstanding that the interest of such person is liable to be defeated by the exercise of a power of appointment or revocation, or to be diminished by the increase of the class to which he belongs:

Provided that—

  (a) the money so paid or applied for the advancement or benefit of any person shall not exceed altogether in amount one-half of the presumptive or vested share or interest of that person in the trust property; and

  (b) if that person is or becomes absolutely and indefeasibly entitled to a share in the trust property the money so paid or applied shall be brought into account as part of such share; and

  (c) no such payment or application shall be made so as to prejudice any person entitled to any prior life or other interest, whether vested or contingent, in the money paid or applied unless such person is in existence and of full age and consents in writing to such payment or application.

(2) This section applies only where the trust property consists of money or securities or of property held upon trust for sale calling in and conversion, and such money or securities, or the proceeds of such sale calling in and conversion are not by statute or in equity considered as land, or applicable as capital money for the purposes of the Settled Land Act 1925.

(3) This section does not apply to trusts constituted or created before the commencement of this Act.

Protective trusts

33.—(1) Where any income, including an annuity or other periodical income payment, is directed to be held on protective trusts for the benefit of any person (in this section called " the principal beneficiary ")

15

for the period of his life or for any less period, then, during that period (in this section called the " trust period ") the said income shall, without prejudice to any prior interest, be held on the following trusts, namely:—

   (i) Upon trust for the principal beneficiary during the trust period or until he, whether before or after the termination of any prior interest, does or attempts to do or suffers any act or thing, or until any event happens, other than an advance under any statutory or express power, whereby, if the said income were payable during the trust period to the principal beneficiary absolutely during that period, he would be deprived of the right to receive the same or any part thereof, in any of which cases, as well as on the termination of the trust period, whichever first happens, this trust of the said income shall fail or determine;

   (ii) If the trust aforesaid fails or determines during the subsistence of the trust period, then, during the residue of that period, the said income shall be held upon trust for the application thereof for the maintenance or support, or otherwise for the benefit, of all or any one or more exclusively of the other or others of the following persons (that is to say)—

      (*a*) the principal beneficiary and his or her wife or husband, if any, and his or her children or more remote issue, if any; or

      (*b*) if there is no wife or husband or issue of the principal beneficiary in existence, the principal beneficiary and the persons who would, if he were actually dead, be entitled to the trust property or the income thereof or to the annuity fund, if any, or arrears of the annuity, as the case may be;

   as the trustees in their absolute discretion, without being liable to account for the exercise of such discretion, think fit.

(2) This section does not apply to trusts coming into operation before the commencement of this Act, and has effect subject to any variation of the implied trusts aforesaid contained in the instrument creating the trust.

(3) Nothing in this section operates to validate any trust which would, if contained in the instrument creating the trust, be liable to be set aside.

Law of Property Act 1925

(15 & 16 GEO. 5, C. 20)

Rights of husband and wife

37. A husband and wife shall, for all purposes of acquisition of any interest in property, under a disposition made or coming into operation after the commencement of this Act, be treated as two persons.

Wills in contemplation of marriage

177.—(1) A will expressed to be made in contemplation of a marriage shall, notwithstanding anything in section eighteen of the Wills Act 1837, or any other statutory provision or rule of law to the contrary, not be revoked by the solemnisation of the marriage contemplated.

(2) This section only applies to wills made after the commencement of this Act.

Administration of Estates Act 1925

(15 & 16 GEO. 5, C. 23)

PART IV

DISTRIBUTION OF RESIDUARY ESTATE

Abolition of descent to heir, curtesy, dower and escheat

45.—(1) With regard to the real estate and personal inheritance of every person dying after the commencement of this Act, there shall be abolished—

(*a*) All existing modes rules and canons of descent, and of devolution by special occupancy or otherwise, of real estate, or of a personal inheritance, whether operating by the general law or by the custom of gavelkind or borough english or by any other custom of any county, locality, or manor, or otherwise howsoever; and

(*b*) Tenancy by the curtesy and every other estate and interest of a husband in real estate as to which his wife dies intestate, whether arising under the general law or by custom or otherwise; and

(*c*) Dower and freebench and every other estate and interest of a wife in real estate as to which her husband dies intestate, whether arising under the general law or by custom or otherwise: Provided that where a right (if any) to freebench or other like right has attached before the commencement of this Act which cannot be barred by a testamentary or other disposition made by the husband, such right shall, unless released, remain in force as an equitable interest; and

(*d*) Escheat to the Crown or the Duchy of Lancaster or the Duke of Cornwall or to a mesne lord for want of heirs.

(2) Nothing in this section affects the descent or devolution of an entailed interest.

Succession to real and personal estate on intestacy

46.[1]—(1) The residuary estate of an intestate shall be distributed in the manner or be held on the trusts mentioned in this section, namely:—

(i) [If the intestate leaves a husband or wife, then in accordance with the following Table:

TABLE

If the intestate—

(1) leaves—
    (*a*) no issue, and
    (*b*) no parent, or brother or sister of the whole blood, or issue of a brother or sister of the whole blood
	the residuary estate shall be held in trust for the surviving husband or wife absolutely.

[1] The amendments to ss. 46–49 have effect as respects a person dying intestate after January 1, 1953.

17

Table—*continued*

(2) leaves issue (whether or not persons mentioned in sub-paragraph (*b*) above also survive)	the surviving husband or wife shall take the personal chattels absolutely and, in addition, the residuary estate of the intestate (other than the personal chattels) shall stand charged with the payment of a [fixed net sum],[2] free of death duties and costs, to the surviving husband or wife with interest thereon from the date of the death at the rate of four pounds per cent. per annum until paid or appropriated, and, subject to providing for that sum and the interest thereon, the residuary estate (other than the personal chattels) shall be held—

(*a*) as to one half upon trust for the surviving husband or wife during his or her life, and, subject to such life interest, on the statutory trusts for the issue of the intestate, and

(*b*) as to the other half, on the statutory trusts for the issue of the intestate.

(3) leaves one or more of the following, that is to say, a parent, a brother or sister of the whole blood, or issue of a brother or sister of the whole blood, but leaves no issue	the surviving husband or wife shall take the personal chattels absolutely and, in addition, the residuary estate of the intestate (other than the personal chattels) shall stand charged with the payment of a [fixed net sum],[3] free of death duties and costs, to the surviving husband or wife with interest thereon from the date of the death at the rate of four pounds per cent. per annum until paid or appropriated, and, subject to providing for that sum and the interest thereon, the residuary estate (other than the personal chattels) shall be held—

(*a*) as to one half in trust for the surviving husband or wife absolutely, and

(*b*) as to the other half—

(i) where the intestate leaves one parent or both parents (whether or not brothers or sisters of the intestate or their issue also survive) in trust for the parent absolutely or, as the case may be, for the two parents in equal shares absolutely

(ii) where the intestate leaves no parent, on the statu-

---

[2] Substituted by the Family Provision Act 1966, s. 1 (2) (*a*), *post.* Amount fixed at £15,000 from July 1, 1972, by S.I. 1972/916.
[3] Substituted by the Family Provision Act 1966, s. 1 (2) (*a*), *post.* Amount fixed at £40,000 from July 1, 1972, by S.I. 1972/916.

TABLE—*continued*

tory trusts for the brothers and sisters of the whole blood of the intestate.] [4]

[The fixed sums referred to in paragraphs (2) and (3) of this Table shall be of the amounts provided by or under section 1 of the Family Provision Act 1966.] [5]

(ii) If the intestate leaves issue but no husband or wife, the residuary estate of the intestate shall be held on the statutory trusts for the issue of the intestate;

(iii) If the intestate leaves [no husband or wife and] [6] no issue but both parents, then [. . .] [7] the residuary estate of the intestate shall be held in trust for the father and mother in equal shares absolutely;

(iv) If the intestate leaves [no husband or wife and] [6] no issue but one parent, then [. . .] [7] the residuary estate of the intestate shall be held in trust for the surviving father or mother absolutely;

(v) If the intestate leaves no [husband or wife and no issue and no] [8] parent, then, [. . .] [7] the residuary estate of the intestate shall be held in trust for the following persons living at the death of the intestate, and in the following order and manner, namely:—

First, on the statutory trusts for the brothers and sisters of the whole blood of the intestate; but if no person takes an absolutely vested interest under such trusts; then

Secondly, on the statutory trusts for the brothers and sisters of the half blood of the intestate; but if no person takes an absolutely vested interest under such trusts; then

Thirdly, for the grandparents of the intestate and, if more than one survive the intestate, in equal shares; but if there is no member of this class; then

Fourthly, on the statutory trusts for the uncles and aunts of the intestate (being brothers or sisters of the whole blood of a parent of the intestate); but if no person takes an absolutely vested interest under such trusts; then

Fifthly, on the statutory trusts for the uncles and aunts of the intestate (being brothers or sisters of the half blood of a parent of the intestate); [. . .] [7]

(vi) In default of any person taking an absolute interest under the foregoing provisions, the residuary estate of the intestate shall belong to the Crown or to the Duchy of Lancaster or to the Duke of Cornwall for the time being, as the case may be, as bona vacantia, and in lieu of any right to escheat.

The Crown or the said Duchy or the said Duke may (without prejudice to the powers reserved by section nine of the Civil List Act 1910, or any other powers), out of the whole or any part of the property devolving on them respectively, provide, in accordance with the existing practice, for dependants, whether kindred or not, of the intestate, and other persons for whom the intestate might reasonably have been expected to make provision.

[4] S. 46 (1) (i) was substituted by the Intestates' Estates Act 1952, *post*, s. 1 (2).
[5] Added by the Family Provision Act 1966, s. 1 (2) (*a*), *post*.
[6] Added by the Intestates' Estates Act 1952, *post*, s. 1 (3).
[7] Repealed by *ibid*.
[8] Substituted by *ibid*.

19

(2) A husband and wife shall for all purposes of distribution or division under the foregoing provisions of this section be treated as two persons.

[(3) Where the intestate and the intestate's husband or wife have died in circumstances rendering it uncertain which of them survived the other and the intestate's husband or wife is by virtue of section one hundred and eighty-four of the Law of Property Act 1925 deemed to have survived the intestate, this section shall, nevertheless, have effect as respects the intestate as if the husband or wife had not survived the intestate.

(4) The interest payable on the [fixed net sum] [9] payable to a surviving husband or wife shall be primarily payable out of income.] [10]

Statutory trusts in favour of issue and other classes of relatives of intestate

47.—(1) Where under this Part of this Act the residuary estate of an intestate, or any part thereof, is directed to be held on the statutory trusts for the issue of the intestate, the same shall be held upon the following trusts, namely: —

(i) In trust, in equal shares if more than one, for all or any the children or child of the intestate, living at the death of the intestate, who attain the age of [eighteen years] [11] or marry under that age, and for all or any of the issue living at the death of the intestate who attain the age [eighteen years] [11] or marry under that age of any child of the intestate who predeceases the intestate, such issue to take through all degrees, according to their stocks, in equal shares if more than one, the share which their parent would have taken if living at the death of the intestate, and so that no issue shall take whose parent is living at the death of the intestate and so capable of taking;

(ii) The statutory power of advancement, and the statutory provisions which relate to maintenance and accumulation of surplus income, shall apply, but when an infant marries such infant shall be entitled to give valid receipts for the income of the infant's share or interest;

(iii) Where the property held on the statutory trusts for issue is divisible into shares, then any money or property which, by way of advancement or on the marriage of a child of the intestate, has been paid to such child by the intestate or settled by the intestate for the benefit of such child (including any life or less interest and including property covenanted to be paid or settled) shall, subject to any contrary intention expressed or appearing from the circumstances of the case, be taken as being so paid or settled in or towards satisfaction of the share of such child or the share which such child would have taken if living at the death of the intestate, and shall be brought into account, at a valuation (the value to be reckoned as at the death of the intestate), in accordance with the requirements of the personal representatives;

(iv) The personal representatives may permit any infant contingently interested to have the use and enjoyment of any personal chattels in such manner and subject to such conditions (if any) as the personal representatives may consider reasonable, and without being liable to account for any consequential loss.

---

[9] Substituted by the Family Provision Act 1966, s. 1 (2) (*b*), *post*.
[10] Added by the Intestates' Estates Act 1952, s. 1 (4).
[11] Eighteen was substituted for twenty-one by Family Law Reform Act 1969 (c. 46), s. 3 (2).

(2) If the trusts in favour of the issue of the intestate fail by reason of no child or other issue attaining an absolutely vested interest—

(a) the residuary estate of the intestate and the income thereof and all statutory accumulations, if any, of the income thereof, or so much thereof as may not have been paid or applied under any power affecting the same, shall go, devolve and be held under the provisions of this Part of this Act as if the intestate had died without leaving issue living at the death of the intestate;

(b) References in this Part of this Act to the intestate " leaving no issue " shall be construed as " leaving no issue who attain an absolutely vested interest ";

(c) References in this Part of this Act to the intestate " leaving issue " or " leaving a child or other issue " shall be construed as " leaving issue who attain an absolutely vested interest."

(3) Where under this Part of this Act the residuary estate of an intestate or any part thereof is directed to be held on the statutory trusts for any class of relatives of the intestate, other than issue of the intestate, the same shall be held on trusts corresponding to the statutory trusts for the issue of the intestate (other than the provision for bringing any money or property into account) as if such trusts (other than as aforesaid) were repeated with the substitution of references to the members or member of that class for references to the children or child of the intestate.

[(4) References in paragraph (i) of subsection (1) of the last foregoing section to the intestate leaving, or not leaving, a member of the class consisting of brothers or sisters of the whole blood of the intestate and issue of brothers or sisters of the whole blood of the intestate shall be construed as references to the intestate leaving, or not leaving, a member of that class who attains an absolutely vested interest.

(5) [*Repealed by the Family Provision Act* 1966, *post, s.* 9, *Sched.* 2.*]] ¹²

[47A.¹³—(1) Where a surviving husband or wife is entitled to a life interest in part of the residuary estate, and so elects, the personal representative shall purchase or redeem the life interest by paying the capital value thereof to the tenant for life, or the persons deriving title under the tenant for life, and the costs of the transaction; and thereupon the residuary estate of the intestate **may be dealt with and distributed free from the life interest.**

(2) The said capital value shall be reckoned in accordance with the rules set out in this subsection:—

1. There shall be ascertained the annual value of the life interest to which the surviving husband or wife would be entitled if the said part of the residuary estate (whether or not yielding income) were on the date of redemption of the life interest re-invested in the two-and-a-half per cent. consolidated stock referred to in section two of the National Debt (Conversion) Act 1888.

2. There shall be ascertained the amount which, if invested on the said date in [the purchase, under the Government Annuities Act 1929, of an immediate savings bank annuity],¹⁴ would purchase an annuity for the tenant for life of the annual value ascertained under rule 1.

3. The said capital value shall, subject to rule 4, be the amount ascertained under rule 2 diminished by five per cent. thereof.

¹² Added by the Intestates' Estates Act 1952, s. 1 (3) (*c*).
¹³ Added by the Intestates' Estates Act 1952, s. 2 (*b*).
¹⁴ Words in square brackets substituted by Post Office Act 1969 (c. 48), s. 94 (2) (*c*), Sched. 6 Pt. III.

21

4. If the age of the tenant for life on the said date exceeds eighty years, a further deduction shall be made equal to five per cent. of the amount ascertained under rule 2 for each complete year by which the age exceeds eighty:

Provided that, if the effect of this rule would otherwise be that the said capital value was less than one-and-a-half times the annual value ascertained under rule 1, the said capital value shall be one-and-a-half times that annual value.

(3) An election under this section shall only be exercisable if at the time of the election the whole of the said part of the residuary estate consists of property in possession, but, for the purposes of this section, a life interest in property partly in possession and partly not in possession shall be treated as consisting of two separate life interests in those respective parts of the property.

(4) If the tenant for life dies after the exercise of the election under this section but before effect is given to that election, the date of redemption shall be taken for the purposes of subsection (2) of this section to be the date immediately before the death of the tenant for life.

(5) An election under this section shall be exercisable only within the period of twelve months from the date on which representation with respect to the estate of the intestate is first taken out:

Provided that if the surviving husband or wife satisfies the court that the limitation to the said period of twelve months will operate unfairly—

(*a*) in consequence of the representation first taken out being probate of a will subsequently revoked on the ground that the will was invalid, or

(*b*) in consequence of a question whether a person had an interest in the estate, or as to the nature of an interest in the estate, not having been determined at the time when representation was first taken out, or

(*c*) in consequence of some other circumstances affecting the administration or distribution of the estate,

the court may extend the said period.

(6) An election under this section shall be exercisable, except where the tenant for life is the sole personal representative, by notifying the personal representative (or, where there are two or more personal representatives of whom one is the tenant for life, all of them except the tenant for life) in writing; and a notification in writing under this subsection shall not be revocable except with the consent of the personal representative.

(7) Where the tenant for life is the sole personal representative an election under this section shall not be effective unless written notice thereof is given to the [principal registrar of the Family Division of the High Court] [15] within the period within which it must be made; and provision may be made by probate rules for keeping a record of such notices and making that record available to the public.

In this subsection the expression "probate rules" means rules made under section one hundred of the Supreme Court of Judicature (Consolidation) Act 1925.

(8) An election under this section by a tenant for life who is an infant shall be as valid and binding as it would be if the tenant for life were of age; but the personal representative shall, instead of paying the capital value of the life interest to the tenant for life, deal with it in the same manner as with any other part of the residuary estate to which the tenant for life is absolutely entitled.

[15] These words were substituted by the Administration of Justice Act 1970 (c. 31) s. 1 (6) and Sched. 2, Pt. 4.

(9) In considering for the purposes of the foregoing provisions of this section the question when representation was first taken out, a grant limited to settled land or to trust property shall be left out of account and a grant limited to real estate or to personal estate shall be left out of account unless a grant limited to the remainder of the estate has previously been made or is made at the same time.]

Powers of personal representative in respect of interests of surviving spouse

48.—(1) [*Repealed by the Intestates' Estates Act* 1952 (15 & 16 *Geo.* 6 & 1 *Eliz.* 2, *c.* 64), *s.* 2 (*a*).]

(2) The personal representatives may raise—

(*a*) [the fixed net sum] [16] or any part thereof and the interest thereon payable to the surviving husband or wife of the intestate on the security of the whole or any part of the residuary estate of the intestate (other than the personal chattels), so far as that estate may be sufficient for the purpose or the said sum and interest may not have been satisfied by an appropriation under the statutory power available in that behalf; and

(*b*) in like manner the capital sum, if any, required for the purchase or redemption of the life interest of the surviving husband or wife of the intestate, or any part thereof not satisfied by the application for that purpose of any part of the residuary estate of the intestate;

and in either case the amount, if any, properly required for the payment of the costs of the transaction.

Application to cases of partial intestacy

49.—(1) Where any person dies leaving a will effectively disposing of part of his property, this Part of this Act shall have effect as respects the part of his property not so disposed of subject to the provisions contained in the will and subject to the following modifications:—

[(*aa*) where the deceased leaves a husband or wife who acquires any beneficial interests under the will of the deceased (other than personal chattels specifically bequeathed) the references in this Part of this Act to the [fixed net sum] [16] payable to a surviving husband or wife, and to interest on that sum, shall be taken as references to the said sum diminished by the value at the date of death of the said beneficial interests, and to interest on that sum as so diminished, and, accordingly, where the said value exceeds the said sum, this Part of this Act shall have effect as if references to the said sum, and interest thereon, were omitted.] [17]

(*a*) The requirements [of section forty-seven of this Act] [18] as to bringing property into account shall apply to any beneficial interests acquired by any issue of the deceased under the will of the deceased, but not to beneficial interests so acquired by any other persons:

(*b*) the personal representative shall, subject to his rights and powers for the purposes of administration, be a trustee for the persons entitled under this Part of this Act in respect of the part of the estate not expressly disposed of unless it appears by the will that the personal representative is intended to take such part beneficially.

---

[16] Substituted by the Family Provision Act 1966, s. 1 (2) (*b*), *post.*
[17] Added by the Intestates' Estates Act 1952, s. 3 (2).
[18] Added by *ibid.*

[(2) References in the foregoing provisions of this section to beneficial interests acquired under a will shall be construed as including a reference to a beneficial interest acquired by virtue of the exercise by the will of a general power of appointment (including the statutory power to dispose of entailed interests), but not of a special power of appointment.

(3) For the purposes of paragraph (*aa*) in the foregoing provisions of this section the personal representative shall employ a duly qualified valuer in any case where such employment may be necessary.

(4) The references in subsection (3) of section forty-seven A of this Act to property are references to property comprised in the residuary estate and, accordingly, where a will of the deceased creates a life interest in property in possession, and the remaining interest in that property forms part of the residuary estate, the said references are references to that remaining interest (which, until the life interest determines, is property not in possession).] [19]

Section 56   SECOND SCHEDULE

[*Repealed by S.L.R. Act* 1950 (14 & 15 *Geo.* 6, *c.* 6).]

Criminal Justice Act 1925

(15 & 16 GEO. 5, c. 86)

Abolition of presumption of coercion of married woman by husband

47. Any presumption of law that an offence committed by a wife in the presence of her husband is committed under the coercion of the husband is hereby abolished, but on a charge against a wife for any offence other than treason or murder it shall be a good defence to prove that the offence was committed in the presence of, and under the coercion of, the husband.

Legitimacy Act 1926

(16 & 17 GEO. 5, c. 60)

ARRANGEMENT OF SECTIONS

An Act to amend the law relating to children born out of wedlock.
[15th December 1926]

---

[19] Added by *ibid.* s. 3 (3).

24

Legitimation by subsequent marriage of parents

1.—(1) Subject to the provisions of this section, where the parents of an illegitimate person marry or have married one another, whether before or after the commencement of this Act, the marriage shall, if the father of the illegitimate person was or is at the date of the marriage domiciled in England or Wales, render that person, if living, legitimate from the commencement of this Act,[1] or from the date of the marriage, whichever last happens.

(2) [*Repealed by the Legitimacy Act* 1959 (*c.* 73), *s.* 1 (1).]

(3) [*Repealed by Children Act* 1975 (*c.* 72), *Sched.* 4.]

(4) The provisions contained in the Schedule to this Act shall have effect with respect to the re-registration of the births of legitimated persons.

* * * * *

3-5. [*These sections were repealed by Children Act* 1975 (*c.* 72), *Sched.* 4.]

* * * * *

Right of illegitimate child and mother of illegitimate child to succeed on intestacy of the other

9. [*This section was repealed by the Family Law Reform Act* 1969 (*c.* 46), *s.* 14 (7).]

Savings

10.—(1) Nothing in this Act shall affect the succession to any dignity or title of honour or render any person capable of succeeding to or transmitting a right to succeed to any such dignity or title.

(2) Nothing in this Act shall affect the operation or construction of any disposition coming into operation before the commencement of this Act, or affect any rights under the intestacy of a person dying before the commencement of this Act.

* * * * *

Children and Young Persons Act 1933

(23 Geo. 5, c. 12) [1]

An Act to consolidate certain enactments relating to persons under the age of eighteen years. **[13th April 1933]**

PART I

PREVENTION OF CRUELTY AND EXPOSURE TO MORAL AND PHYSICAL DANGER

Offences

Cruelty to persons under sixteen

1.—(1) If any person who has attained the age of sixteen years and has the custody, charge, or care of any child or young person under that

---

[1] References to the commencement of this Act shall have effect as if they were references to the commencement of the Legitimacy Act 1959 (c. 73): *ibid.*, s. 1 (2).

[1] Extended by Shops Act 1950 (c. 28), s. 72 (1), and explained by Criminal Justice Act 1961 (c. 39), s. 14 (2), Sched. 2, para. 5.

age, wilfully assaults, ill-treats, neglects, abandons, or exposes him, or causes or procures him to be assaulted, ill-treated, neglected, abandoned, or exposed, in a manner likely to cause him unnecessary suffering or injury to health (including injury to or loss of sight, or hearing, or limb, or organ of the body, and any mental derangement), that person shall be guilty of a misdemeanour, and shall be liable—

    (*a*) on conviction on indictment, to a fine [. . .],[3a] or alternatively, [. . .],[2] or in addition thereto, to imprisonment for any term not exceeding two years;

    (*b*) on summary conviction, to a fine not exceeding [£400],[3] or alternatively, [. . .],[2] or in addition thereto, to imprisonment for any term not exceeding six months.

(2) For the purposes of this section—

    (*a*) a parent or other person legally liable to maintain a child or young person shall be deemed to have neglected him in a manner likely to cause injury to his health if he has failed to provide adequate food, clothing, medical aid or lodging for him, or if, having been unable otherwise to provide such food, clothing, medical aid or lodging, he has failed to take steps to procure it to be provided under the Acts relating to the relief of the poor;

    (*b*) where it is proved that the death of an infant under three years of age was caused by suffocation (not being suffocation caused by disease or the presence of any foreign body in the throat or air passages of the infant) while the infant was in bed with some other person who has attained the age of sixteen years, that other person shall, if he was, when he went to bed, under the influence of drink, be deemed to have neglected the infant in a manner likely to cause injury to its health.

(3) A person may be convicted of an offence under this section—

    (*a*) notwithstanding that actual suffering or injury to health, or the likelihood of actual suffering or injury to health, was obviated by the action of another person;

    (*b*) notwithstanding the death of the child or young person in question.

[*Subsection* (4) *repealed by Criminal Law Act* 1967 (*c.* 58), *s.* 10, *Scheds.* 2, *para.* 13 (1), 3, *Pt. III.*]

(5) If it is proved that a person convicted under this section was directly or indirectly interested in any sum of money accruing or payable in the event of the death of the child or young person, and had knowledge that that sum of money was accruing or becoming payable, then—

    (*a*) in the case of a conviction on indictment, [. . .][3a] and the court shall have power, in lieu of awarding any other penalty under this section, to sentence the person convicted to penal servitude for any term not exceeding five years; and

    (*b*) in the case of a summary conviction, the court in determining the sentence to be awarded shall take into consideration the fact that the person was so interested and had such knowledge.

(6) For the purposes of the last foregoing subsection—

    (*a*) a person shall be deemed to be directly or indirectly interested in a sum of money if he has any share in or any benefit from

[2] Words repealed by Children and Young Persons Act 1963 (c. 37), s. 64 (3), Sched. 5.
[3] Maximum fine raised by Children Act 1975 (c. 72), Sched. 3.
[3a] Words omitted by *ibid.*, Sched. 4.

the payment of that money, notwithstanding that he may not be a person to whom it is legally payable; and

(*b*) a copy of a policy of insurance, certified to be a true copy by an officer or agent of the insurance company granting the policy, shall be evidence that the child or young person therein stated to be insured has in fact been so insured, and that the person in whose favour the policy has been granted is the person to whom the money thereby insured is legally payable.

(7) Nothing in this section shall be construed as affecting the right of any parent, teacher, or other person having the lawful control or charge of a child or young person to administer punishment to him.

2. [*Repealed by Sexual Offences Act* 1956 (*c.* 69), *s.* 51, *Sched.* 4.]

Allowing persons under sixteen to be in brothels

3.—(1) If any person having the custody, charge or care of a child or young person who has attained the age of four years and is under the age of sixteen years, allows that child or young person to reside in or to frequent a brothel, he shall be guilty of a misdemeanour and shall be liable on conviction on indictment, or on summary conviction, to a fine not exceeding twenty-five pounds, or alternatively [. . .],[4] or in addition thereto, to imprisonment for any term not exceeding six months.

[*Subsection* (2) *repealed by Sexual Offences Act* 1956 (*c.* 69), *s.* 51, *Sched.* 4.]

Causing or allowing persons under sixteen to be used for begging

4.—(1) If any person causes or procures any child or young person under the age of sixteen years or, having the custody, charge, or care of such a child or young person, allows him to be in any street, premises, or place for the purpose of begging or receiving alms, or of inducing the giving of alms (whether or not there is any pretence of singing, playing, performing, offering anything for sale, or otherwise) he shall, on summary conviction, be liable to a fine not exceeding twenty-five pounds, or alternatively [. . .],[4] or in addition thereto, to imprisonment for any term not exceeding three months.

(2) If a person having the custody, charge, or care of a child or young person is charged with an offence under this section, and it is proved that the child or young person was in any street, premises, or place for any such purpose as aforesaid, and that the person charged allowed the child or young person to be in the street, premises, or place, he shall be presumed to have allowed him to be in the street, premises, or place for that purpose unless the contrary is proved.

(3) If any person while singing, playing, performing or offering anything for sale in a street or public place has with him a child who has been lent or hired out to him, the child shall, for the purposes of this section, be deemed to be in that street or place for the purpose of inducing the giving of alms.

Giving intoxicating liquor to children under five

5. If any person gives, or causes to be given, to any child under the age of five years any intoxicating liquor, except upon the order of a duly qualified medical practitioner, or in case of sickness, apprehended sick-

---

[4] Words repealed by Children and Young Persons Act 1963 (c. 37), s. 64 (3), Sched. 5.

ness, or other urgent cause, he shall, on summary conviction, be liable to a fine not exceeding [ten]⁵ pounds.

6. [*Repealed by Licensing Act* 1953 (*c.* 46), *s.* 168, *Sched.* 10.]

Sale of tobacco, &c., to persons under sixteen

7.—(1) Any person who sells to a person apparently under the age of sixteen years any tobacco or cigarette papers, whether for his own use or not, shall be liable, on summary conviction, in the case of a first offence to a fine not exceeding [twenty-five]⁶ pounds, in the case of a second offence to a fine not exceeding [fifty]⁶ pounds, and in the case of a third or subsequent offence to a fine not exceeding [one hundred]⁶ pounds:

Provided that a person shall not be guilty of an offence under this section in respect of any sale of tobacco otherwise than in the form of cigarettes, if he did not know and had no reason to believe that the tobacco was for the use of the person to whom it was sold.

(2) If on complaint to a court of summary jurisdiction it is proved to the satisfaction of the court that any automatic machine for the sale of tobacco kept on any premises is being extensively used by persons apparently under the age of sixteen years, the court may order the owner of the machine, or the person on whose premises the machine is kept, to take such precautions to prevent the machine being so used as may be specified in the order or, if necessary, to remove the machine, within such time as may be specified in the order, and if any person against whom such an order has been made fails to comply therewith, he shall be liable, on summary conviction, to a fine not exceeding [fifty]⁶ pounds, and to a further fine not exceeding [ten]⁶ pounds for each day during which the offence continues.

(3) It shall be the duty of a constable and of a park-keeper being in uniform to seize any tobacco or cigarette papers in the possession of any person apparently under the age of sixteen years whom he finds smoking in any street or public place, and any tobacco or cigarette papers so seized shall be disposed of, if seized by a constable, in such manner as the police authority may direct, and if seized by a park-keeper, in such manner as the authority or person by whom he was appointed may direct.

(4) Nothing in this section shall make it an offence to sell tobacco or cigarette papers to, or shall authorise the seizure of tobacco or cigarette papers in the possession of, any person who is at the time employed by a manufacturer of or dealer in tobacco, either wholesale or retail, for the purposes of his business, or is a boy messenger in uniform in the employment of a messenger company and employed as such at the time.

(5) For the purposes of this section the expression " tobacco " includes cigarettes and smoking mixtures intended as a substitute for tobacco, and the expression " cigarettes " includes cut tobacco rolled up in paper, tobacco leaf, or other material in such form as to be capable of immediate use for smoking.

8. [*Repealed by Consumer Credit Act* 1974 (*c.* 39), *Sched.* 5.]

9. [*Repealed by Scrap Metal Dealers Act* 1964 (*c.* 69), *s.* 10 (1) (2), *Sched. Pt. I.*]

---

⁵ Criminal Justice Act 1967 (c. 80), s. 92, Sched. 3 Pt. I, raised the maximum fine from £3 to £10.
⁶ Maximum fines increased by Children and Young Persons Act 1963 (c. 37), s. 32, from £2, £5, £10, £5 and £1 pound respectively.

Vagrants preventing children from receiving education

10.—(1)[7] If a person habitually wanders from place to place and takes with him any child who has attained the age of five years [or any young person who has not attained the age at which under the enactments relating to education children cease to be of compulsory school age][8] he shall, unless he proves that the child [or young person is not, by being so taken with him, prevented from receiving efficient full-time education suitable to his age, ability and aptitude, be liable on summary conviction to a fine not exceeding [ten pounds][9]].[8]

[(1A) Proceedings for an offence under this section shall not be instituted except by a local education authority; and before instituting such proceedings the authority shall consider whether it would be appropriate, instead of or as well as instituting the proceedings, to bring the child or young person in question before a juvenile court under section 1 of the Children and Young Persons Act 1969.][10]

(2) Any constable who finds a person wandering from place to place and taking a child [or young person][8] with him may, if he has reasonable ground for believing that the person is guilty of an offence under this section, apprehend him without a warrant [. . .].[11]

(3) [Where in any proceedings for an offence against this section it is proved that the parent or guardian of the child or young person is engaged in any trade or business of such a nature as to require him to travel from place to place, the person against whom the proceedings were brought shall be acquitted if it is proved that the child or young person has attended a school at which he was a registered pupil as regularly as the nature of the trade or business of the parent or guardian permits:

Provided that in the case of a child or young person who has attained the age of six years the person against whom the proceedings were brought shall not be entitled to be acquitted under this subsection unless it is proved that the child or young person has made at least two hundred attendances during the period of twelve months ending with the date on which the proceedings were instituted.][8]

(4) The Board of Education shall have power to make regulations as to the issue of certificates of attendance for the purposes of the last foregoing subsection, and any such regulations shall be laid before Parliament as soon as may be after they are made.

Exposing children under twelve to risk of burning

11. If any person who has attained the age of sixteen years, having the custody, charge or care of any child under the age of [twelve][12] years, allows the child to be in any room containing an open fire grate [or any heating appliance liable to cause injury to a person by contact therewith][12] not sufficiently protected to guard against the risk of his being burnt or scalded without taking reasonable precautions against that risk, and by reason thereof the child is killed or suffers serious injury, he shall on summary conviction be liable to a fine not exceeding ten pounds:

---

[7] Applied by Children and Young Persons Act 1969 (c. 54), s. 28 (2), *post*.
[8] Words in square brackets substituted by Education Act 1944 (c. 31), s. 120 (3), Sched. 8.
[9] Maximum fine increased from twenty shillings to ten pounds by Criminal Justice Act 1967 (c. 80), s. 92, Sched. 3 Pt. I.
[10] Inserted by Children and Young Persons Act 1969 (c. 54), s. 72 (3), Sched. 5, para. 2.
[11] Words repealed by Children and Young Persons Act 1969 (c. 54), s. 72 (4), Sched. 6.
[12] Words in square brackets substituted or added by Children and Young Persons (Amendment) Act 1952 (c. 50), ss. 8, 9, Sched.

Provided that neither this section, nor any proceedings taken there-under, shall affect any liability of any such person to be proceeded against by indictment for any indictable offence.

Failing to provide for safety of children at entertainments

12.—(1) Where there is provided in any building an entertainment for children, or an entertainment at which the majority of the persons attending are children, then, if the number of children attending the entertainment exceeds one hundred, it shall be the duty of the person providing the entertainment to station and keep stationed wherever necessary a sufficient number of adult attendants, properly instructed as to their duties, to prevent more children or other persons being admitted to the building, or to any part thereof, than the building or part can properly accommodate, and to control the movement of the children and other persons admitted while entering and leaving the building or any part thereof, and to take all other reasonable precautions for the safety of the children.

(2) Where the occupier of a building permits, for hire or reward, the building to be used for the purpose of an entertainment, he shall take all reasonable steps to secure the observance of the provisions of this section.

(3) If any person on whom any obligation is imposed by this section fails to fulfil that obligation, he shall be liable, on summary conviction, to a fine not exceeding, in the case of a first offence fifty pounds, and in the case of a second or subsequent offence one hundred pounds, and also, if the building in which the entertainment is given is licensed under the Cinematograph Act 1909, or under any of the enactments relating to the licensing of theatres and of houses and other places for music or dancing, the licence shall be liable to be revoked by the authority by whom the licence was granted.

(4) A constable may enter any building in which he has reason to believe that such an entertainment as aforesaid is being, or is about to be, provided, with a view to seeing whether the provisions of this section are carried into effect, and an officer authorised for the purpose by an authority by whom licences are granted under any of the enactments referred to in the last foregoing subsection shall have the like power of entering any building so licensed by that authority.

(5) The institution of proceedings under this section shall—

    (*a*) in the case of a building licensed by the Lord Chamberlain, or licensed by the council of a county or county borough [or the Greater London Council] [12a] under the Cinematograph Act 1909, or under the enactments relating to the licensing of theatres or houses and other places for music or dancing, be the duty of the council of the county or county borough in which the building is situated; and

    (*b*) in any other case, be the duty of the police authority.

(6) This section shall not apply to any entertainment given in a private dwelling-house.

Special Provisions as to Prosecutions for Offences specified in
First Schedule

Power to take offenders into custody

13.[13]—(1) Any constable may take into custody, without warrant—

    (*a*) any person who within his view commits any of the offences

---

[12a] Words inserted by S.I. 1970/211.
[13] This section, as applied, saved by Suicide Act 1961 (c. 60), s. 2 (4).

mentioned in the First Schedule to this Act, if the constable does not know and cannot ascertain his name and residence;

(*b*) any person who has committed, or whom he has reason to believe to have committed, any of the offences mentioned in the First Schedule to this Act, if the constable has reasonable ground for believing that that person will abscond or does not know and cannot ascertain his name and address.

(2) Where, under the powers conferred by this section, a constable arrests any person without warrant, the superintendent or inspector of police or an officer of police of equal or superior rank, or the officer in charge of the police station to which the person is brought, shall, unless in his belief the release of the person on bail would tend to defeat the ends of justice, or to cause injury or danger to the child or young person against whom the offence is alleged to have been committed, release the person arrested on his entering into such a recognisance, with or without sureties, as may in the judgment of the officer of police be required to secure his attendance upon the hearing of the charge.

Mode of charging offences and limitation of time

14.—(1) Where a person is charged with committing any of the offences mentioned in the First Schedule to this Act in respect of two or more children or young persons, the same information or summons may charge the offence in respect of all or any of them, but the person charged shall not, if he is summarily convicted, be liable to a separate penalty in respect of each child or young person except upon separate informations.

(2) The same information or summons may also charge any person as having the custody, charge, or care, alternatively or together, and may charge him with the offences of assault, ill-treatment, neglect, abandonment, or exposure, together or separately, and may charge him with committing all or any of those offences in a manner likely to cause unnecessary suffering or injury to health, alternatively or together, but when those offences are charged together the person charged shall not, if he is summarily convicted, be liable to a separate penalty for each.

[*Subsection* (3) *repealed by Children and Young Persons Act* 1963 (*c.* 37), *ss.* 21, 64 (3), *Sched.* 5.]

(4) When any offence mentioned in the First Schedule to this Act charged against any person is a continuous offence, it shall not be necessary to specify in the information, summons, or indictment, the date of the acts constituting the offence.

Evidence of husband or wife of accused person

15. As respects proceedings against any person for any of the offences mentioned in the First Schedule to this Act [otherwise than in the entry relating to the Sexual Offences Act 1956],[14] the Criminal Evidence Act 1898 shall apply as if the Schedule to that Act included references to those offences.

Supplemental

16. [*Repealed by Administration of Justice (Miscellaneous Provisions) Act* 1933 (*c.* 36), *s.* 10, *Sched.* 3.]

Interpretation of Part I

17. For the purposes of this Part of this Act—

---

[14] Words in square brackets added by Sexual Offences Act 1956 (c. 69), s. 48, Sched. 3.

Any person who is the parent or legal guardian of a child or young person or who is legally liable to maintain him shall be presumed to have the custody of him, and as between father and mother the father shall not be deemed to have ceased to have the custody of him by reason only that he has deserted, or otherwise does not reside with, the mother and the child or young person;

Any person to whose charge a child or young person is committed by any person who has the custody of him shall be presumed to have charge of the child or young person;

Any other person having actual possession or control of a child or young person shall be presumed to have the care of him.

PART II [15]

EMPLOYMENT

General Provisions as to Employment

Restrictions on employment of children

18.—(1) Subject to the provisions of this section and of any [regulations] [16] made thereunder no child shall be employed—

(a) [so long as he is under the age of thirteen years] [17]

(b) before the close of school hours on any day on which he is required to attend school; or

(c) before six o'clock in the morning or after eight o'clock in the evening on any day; or

(d) for more than two hours on any day on which he is required to attend school; or

(e) for more than two hours on any Sunday; or

(f) to lift, carry or move anything so heavy as to be likely to cause injury to him.

(2) [The Secretary of State may make regulations] [16] with respect to the employment of children, and any such [regulations] [16] may distinguish between children of different ages and sexes and between different localities, trades, occupations and circumstances, and may contain provisions—

(a) authorising—

    (i) [the employment of children under the age of thirteen years (notwithstanding anything in paragraph (a) of the last foregoing subsection) by their parents or guardians in light agricultural or horticultural work] [17];

    (ii) the employment of children (notwithstanding anything in paragraph (b) of the last foregoing subsection) for not more than one hour before the commencement of school hours on any day on which they are required to attend school;

(b) prohibiting absolutely the employment of children in any specified occupation;

(c) prescribing—

    (i) the age below which children are not to be employed;

    (ii) the number of hours in each day, or in each week, for which, and the times of day at which, they may be employed;

---

15 Extended by Children and Young Persons Act 1963 (c. 37), s. 44 (1).
16 Word(s) substituted by Employment of Children Act 1973 (c. 24), s. 1 (3), Sched. 1.
17 Words substituted by Children Act 1972 (c. 44), s. 1 (2).

(iii) the intervals to be allowed to them for meals and rest;
(iv) the holidays or half-holidays to be allowed to them;
(v) any other conditions to be observed in relation to their employment;

so, however, that no such byelaws shall modify the restrictions contained in the last foregoing subsection save in so far as is expressly permitted by paragraph (*a*) of this subsection, and any restriction contained in any such byelaws shall have effect in addition to the said restrictions.

[(*d*) prohibiting the employment of children otherwise than under and in accordance with a permit to be issued by the local education authority on application made in accordance with the regulations, and imposing on children and others requirements in connection with permits;

(*e*) requiring employers to furnish particulars with respect to children employed, or proposed to be employed, by them and to keep and produce records.] [17a]

[(3) Nothing in this section, or in any [regulation] [16] made under this section, shall prevent a child from taking part in a performance—

(*a*) under the authority of a licence granted under this Part of this Act; or

(*b*) in a case where by virtue of section 37 (3) of the Children and Young Persons Act 1963, no licence under that section is required for him to take part in the performance.] [18]

[(4) Regulations of the Secretary of State under this section shall be made by statutory instrument subject to annulment in pursuance of a resolution of either House of Parliament.] [17a]

Power of local authority to make byelaws with respect to employment of persons under eighteen other than children

19. [*Repealed by Employment of Children Act* 1973 (c. 24), *s.* 1 (5), *Sched.* 2.]

Street trading

20.[19]—(1) No person under the age of [seventeen] [20] years shall engage or be employed in street trading:

Provided that byelaws made under this section may permit young persons who have not attained the age of [seventeen] [20] years to be employed by their parents in street trading.

(2) A local authority may make byelaws regulating or prohibiting street trading by persons under the age of eighteen years, and byelaws so made may distinguish between persons of different ages and sexes and between different localities, and may contain provisions—

(*a*) forbidding any such person to engage or be employed in street trading unless he holds a licence granted by the authority, and regulating the conditions on which such licences may be granted, suspended, and revoked;

(*b*) determining the days and hours during which, and the places at which, such persons may engage or be employed in street trading;

(*c*) requiring such persons so engaged or employed to wear badges;

(*d*) regulating in any other respect the conduct of such persons while so engaged or employed.

[17a] Words added by Employment of Children Act 1973 (c. 24), s. 1 (3), Sched. 1.
[18] Words in square brackets substituted by Children and Young Persons Act 1963 (c. 37), ss. 34, 64 (1), Sched. 3, para. 4.
[19] Section modified by Children and Young Persons Act 1963 (c. 37), s. 35 (2).
[20] Words in square brackets substituted by *ibid.*, s. 35 (1).

33

[(3) No person under the age of eighteen shall on a Sunday engage or be employed in street trading of a description to which, notwithstanding section 58 of the Shops Act 1950 (which extends certain provisions to any place where a retail trade or business is carried on), those provisions do not extend.] [21]

Penalties and legal proceedings in respect of general provisions as to employment

21.—(1) If a person is employed in contravention of any of the foregoing provisions of this Part of this Act, or of the provisions of any byelaw [or regulation] [22] made thereunder, the employer and any person (other than the person employed) to whose act or default the contravention is attributable shall be liable on summary conviction to a fine not exceeding [£50] [22a] or, in the case of a second or subsequent offence, not exceeding [£100] [22a]:

Provided that, if proceedings are brought against the employer, the employer, upon information duly laid by him and on giving to the prosecution not less than three days' notice of his intention, shall be entitled to have any person (other than the person employed) to whose act or default he alleges that the contravention was due, brought before the court as a party to the proceedings, and if, after the contravention has been proved, the employer proves to the satisfaction of the court that the contravention was due to the act or default of the said other person, that person may be convicted of the offence; and if the employer further proves to the satisfaction of the court that he has used all due diligence to secure that the provisions in question should be complied with, he shall be acquitted of the offence.

(2) Where an employer seeks to avail himself of the proviso to the last foregoing subsection,

(*a*) the prosecution shall have the right to cross-examine him, if he gives evidence, and any witness called by him in support of his charge against the other person, and to call rebutting evidence; and

(*b*) the court may make such order as it thinks fit for the payment of costs by any party to the proceedings to any other party thereto.

(3) A person under the age of eighteen years, who engages in street trading in contravention of the provisions of the last foregoing section, or of any byelaw made thereunder, shall be liable on summary conviction to a fine not exceeding [ten pounds],[22b] or in the case of a second or subsequent offence, not exceeding [twenty pounds].[22b]

Entertainments and Performances

22. [*Repealed by Children and Young Persons Act* 1963 (*c.* 37), *s.* 64 (3), *Sched.* 5.]

Prohibition against persons under sixteen taking part in performances endangering life or limb

23. No person under the age of sixteen years shall take part in any [performance to which section 37 of the Children and Young Persons

---

[21] Subs. (3) added by *ibid.*, s. 35 (3).
[22] Words added by Employment of Children Act 1973 (c. 24), s. 1 (3), Sched. 1.
[22a] Maximum fines increased by Employment of Children Act 1973 (c. 24), s. 1 (3), Sched. 1.
[22b] Maximum fines increased from twenty shillings and forty shillings respectively by Children and Young Persons Act 1963 (c. 37), s. 36.

Act 1963 applies and] [23] in which his life or limbs are endangered and every person who causes or procures such a person, or being his parent or guardian allows him, to take part in such a performance, shall be liable on summary conviction to a fine not exceeding [fifty pounds] [24] or, in the case of a second or subsequent offence, not exceeding [one hundred pounds] [24] :

Provided that no proceedings shall be taken under this subsection except by or with the authority of a chief officer of police.

Restrictions on training for performances of a dangerous nature

24.—(1) No person under the age of twelve years shall be trained to take part in performances of a dangerous nature, and no person under the age of sixteen years shall be trained to take part in such performances except under and in accordance with the terms of a licence granted and in force under this section; and every person who causes or procures a person, or being his parent or guardian allows him, to be trained to take part in performances of a dangerous nature in contravention of this section, shall be liable on summary conviction to a fine not exceeding five pounds or, in the case of a second or subsequent offence, not exceeding twenty pounds.

(2) A [local authority] [25] may grant a licence for a person who has attained the age of twelve years but is under the age of sixteen years to be trained to take part in performances of a dangerous nature.

[*Subsection* (3) *repealed by Children and Young Persons Act* 1963 (*c.* 37), *ss.* 41 (2) (3), 64 (3), *Sched.* 5.]

(4) A licence under this section shall specify the place or places at which the person is to be trained and shall embody such conditions as are, in the opinion of the court, necessary for his protection, but a licence shall not be refused if the court is satisfied that the person is fit and willing to be trained and that proper provision has been made to secure his health and kind treatment.

[*Subsection* (5) *repealed by Children and Young Persons Act* 1963 (*c.* 37), *ss.* 41 (2) (3), 64 (3), *Sched.* 5.]

Employment Abroad

Restrictions on persons under eighteen going abroad for the purpose of performing for profit

25.—(1) No person having the custody, charge or care of any person under the age of eighteen years shall allow him, nor shall any person cause or procure any person under that age, to go abroad for the purpose of singing, playing, performing, or being exhibited, for profit, unless [. . .] [26] a licence has been granted in respect of him under this section:

Provided that this subsection shall not apply in any case where it is proved that the person under the age of eighteen years was only temporarily resident within [the United Kingdom].[27]

(2) A police magistrate may grant a licence in such form as the Secretary of State may prescribe, and subject to such restrictions and

---

[23] Words in square brackets substituted by Children and Young Persons Act 1963 (c. 37), s. 64 (1), Sched. 3, para. 5.

[24] Maximum fines increased from £10 and £50 respectively by Criminal Justice Act 1967 (c. 80), s. 92, Sched. 3 Pt. I.

[25] Words substituted by Children and Young Persons Act 1963 (c. 37), ss. 41 (1), 64 (1), Sched. 3, para. 6.

[26] Words repealed by Children and Young Persons Act 1963 (c. 37), s. 64 (3), Sched. 5.

[27] Words substituted by *ibid.*, ss. 42, 64 (1), Sched. 3, para. 7.

conditions as the police magistrate thinks fit, for any person who has attained the age of fourteen years but is under the age of eighteen years to go abroad for the purpose of singing, playing, performing, or being exhibited, for profit, but no such licence shall be granted in respect of any person unless the police magistrate is satisfied—

(a) that the application for the licence is made by or with the consent of his parent or guardian;

(b) that he is going abroad to fulfil a particular engagement;

(c) that he is fit for the purpose, and that proper provision has been made to secure his health, kind treatment, and adequate supervision while abroad, and his return from abroad at the expiration or revocation of the licence;

(d) that there has been furnished to him a copy of the contract of employment or other document showing the terms and conditions of employment drawn up in a language understood by him.

(3) A person applying for a licence under this section, shall, at least seven days before making the application, give to the chief officer of police for the district in which the person resides to whom the application relates, notice of the intended application together with a copy of the contract of employment or other document showing the terms and conditions of employment, and the chief officer of police shall send that copy to the police magistrate and may make a report in writing on the case to him or may appear, or instruct some person to appear, before him and show cause why the licence should not be granted, and the police magistrate shall not grant the licence unless he is satisfied that notice has been properly so given:

Provided that if it appears that the notice was given less than seven days before the making of the application, the police magistrate may nevertheless grant a licence if he is satisfied that the officer to whom the notice was given has made sufficient enquiry into the facts of the case and does not desire to oppose the application.

(4) A licence under this section shall not be granted for more than three months but may be renewed by a police magistrate from time to time for a like period, so, however, that no such renewal shall be granted, unless the police magistrate—

(a) is satisfied by a report of a British consular officer or other trustworthy person that the conditions of the licence are being complied with;

(b) is satisfied that the application for renewal is made by or with the consent of the parent or guardian of the person to whom the licence relates.

(5) A police magistrate—

(a) may vary a licence granted under this section and may at any time revoke such a licence for any cause which he, in his discretion, considers sufficient:

(b) need not, when renewing or varying a licence granted under this section, require the attendance before him of the person to whom the licence relates.

(6) The police magistrate to whom application is made for the grant, renewal or variation of a licence shall, unless he is satisfied that in the circumstances it is unnecessary, require the applicant to give such security as he may think fit (either by entering into a recognisance with or without sureties or otherwise) for the observance of the restrictions and conditions in the licence or in the licence as varied, and the recognisance may be enforced in like manner as a recognisance for the doing of some matter or thing required to be done in a proceeding before a court of summary jurisdiction is enforceable.

(7) If in any case where a licence has been granted under this section, it is proved to the satisfaction of a police magistrate that by reason of exceptional circumstances it is not in the interests of the person to whom the licence relates to require him to return from abroad at the expiration of the licence, then, notwithstanding anything in this section or any restriction or condition attached to the licence, the magistrate may by order release all persons concerned from any obligation to cause that person to return from abroad.

(8) Where a licence is granted, renewed or varied under this section, the police magistrate shall send the prescribed particulars to the Secretary of State for transmission to the proper consular officer, and every consular officer shall register the particulars so transmitted to him and perform such other duties in relation thereto as the Secretary of State may direct.

(9) In this section the expression " police magistrate " means one of the following magistrates, that is to say—

(a) the chief magistrate of the metropolitan police courts;

(b) any magistrate of the metropolitan police court in Bow Street;

(c) any stipendiary magistrate appointed by Order in Council to exercise jurisdiction under this section,

and the powers conferred by this section on a police magistrate shall in every case be exercisable by any of the magistrates aforesaid.

(10) This and the next following section extend to Scotland and to Northern Ireland.

Punishment of contraventions of last foregoing section and proceedings with respect thereto

26.—(1) If any person acts in contravention of the provisions of sub-section (1) of the last foregoing section he shall be guilty of an offence under this section and be liable, on summary conviction, to a fine not exceeding one hundred pounds, or, alternatively, [. . .],[28] or in addition thereto, to imprisonment for any term not exceeding three months:

Provided that if he procured the person to go abroad by means of any false pretence or false representation, he shall be liable on conviction on indictment to imprisonment for any term not exceeding two years.

(2) Where, in proceedings under this section against a person, it is proved that he caused, procured, or allowed a person under the age of eighteen years to go abroad and that that person has while abroad been singing, playing, performing, or being exhibited, for profit, the defendant shall be presumed to have caused, procured, or allowed him to go abroad for that purpose, unless the contrary is proved:

Provided that where the contrary is proved, the court may order the defendant to take such steps as the court directs to secure the return of the person in question to the United Kingdom, or to enter into a recognisance to make such provision as the court may direct to secure his health, kind treatment, and adequate supervision while abroad, and his return to the United Kingdom at the expiration of such period as the court may think fit.

(3) Proceedings in respect of an offence under this section or for enforcing a recognisance under this or the last foregoing section may be instituted at any time within a period of three months from the first discovery by the person taking the proceedings of the commission of the offence or, as the case may be, the non-observance of the restrictions and conditions contained in the licence, or, if at the expiration of that period the person against whom it is proposed to institute the proceedings

[28] Words repealed by *ibid.* s. 64 (3), Sched. 5.

is outside the United Kingdom, at any time within six months after his return to the United Kingdom.

(4) In any such proceedings as aforesaid, a report of any British consular officer and any deposition made on oath before a British consular officer and authenticated by the signature of that officer, respecting the observance or non-observance of any of the conditions or restrictions contained in a licence granted under the last foregoing section shall, upon proof that the consular officer, or deponent, cannot be found in the United Kingdom, be admissible in evidence, and it shall not be necessary to prove the signature or official character of the person appearing to have signed any such report or deposition.

(5) The wife or husband of a person charged with an offence under this section may be called as a witness either for the prosecution or defence, and without the consent of the person charged.

[*Subsection* (6) *repealed by Children and Young Persons Act* 1969 (*c*. 54), *s*. 72 (4), *Sched.* 6.]

Supplemental

Byelaws

27.—(1) A byelaw made under this Part of this Act shall not have effect until confirmed by the Secretary of State and shall not be so confirmed until at least thirty days after the local authority have published it in such manner as the Secretary of State directs.

(2) Before confirming such a byelaw the Secretary of State shall consider any objections thereto which may be addressed to him by persons affected or likely to be affected thereby, and may order a local enquiry to be held, and where such an enquiry is held, the person holding it shall receive such remuneration as the Secretary of State determines, and that remuneration and the expenses of the enquiry shall be paid by the local authority.

[*Subsection* (3) *repealed by Local Government Act* 1933 (*c*. 51), *ss*. 307, 308, *Sched.* 11; *London Government Act* 1939 (*c*. 40), *ss*. 207, 208, *Sched.* 8.]

Powers of entry

28.[29]—(1) If it is made to appear to a justice of the peace by the local authority, or by any constable, that there is reasonable cause to believe that the provisions of this Part of this Act, other than those relating to employment abroad, or of a byelaw [or regulation] [29a] made under the said provisions, are being contravened with respect to any person, the justice may by order under his hand addressed to an officer of the local authority, or to a constable, empower him to enter, at any reasonable time within forty-eight hours of the making of the order, any place in or in connection with which the person in question is, or is believed to be, employed, or as the case may be, in which he is, or is believed to be, taking part in [a performance],[30] or being trained, and to make enquiries therein with respect to that person.

(2) Any authorised officer of the local authority or any constable may at any time during the currency of a licence granted under section twenty-two or twenty-four of this Act enter any place where the person

[29] S. 28 applied by Education Act 1944 (c. 31), s. 59 (4).
[29a] Words added by Employment of Children Act 1973 (c. 24), s. 1 (3), Sched. 1.
[30] Words substituted by Children and Young Persons Act 1963 (c. 37), ss. 43, 64 (1), Sched. 3, para. 9.

to whom the licence relates is authorised by the licence to take part in
an entertainment or to be trained, and may make enquiries therein with
respect to that person.

(3) Any person who obstructs any officer or constable in the due
exercise of any powers conferred on him by or under this section, or who
refuses to answer or answers falsely any enquiry authorised by or under
this section to be made, shall be liable on summary conviction in respect
of each offence to a fine not exceeding twenty pounds.

Savings

29.—[*Subsections* (1) *and* (2) *repealed by Children and Young
Persons Act* 1963 (*c.* 37), *s.* 64 (3), *Sched.* 5.]

[*Subsection* (3) *repealed by Children and Young Persons Act* 1969
(*c.* 54), *s.* 72 (4), *Sched.* 6.]

(4) The said provisions shall be in addition to and not in substitution
for any enactments relating to employment in factories, workshops,
mines and quarries, or for giving effect to any international convention
regulating employment.

Interpretation of Part II

30. For the purposes of this Part of this Act and of any byelaws
[or regulations] [29a] made thereunder—
    [. . .] [31]

The expression " performance of a dangerous nature " includes all
    acrobatic performances and all performances as a contortionist;

The expression " street trading " includes the hawking of news-
    papers, matches, flowers and other articles, playing, singing or
    performing for profit, shoe-blacking and other like occupations
    carried on in streets or public places;

A person who assists in a trade or occupation carried on for profit
    shall be deemed to be employed notwithstanding that he
    receives no reward for his labour;

A chorister taking part in a religious service or in a choir practice
    for a religious service shall not, whether he receives any reward
    or not, be deemed to be employed; and

The expression " abroad " means outside Great Britain and Ireland.

PART III [32]

PROTECTION OF CHILDREN AND YOUNG PERSONS IN RELATION TO
CRIMINAL AND SUMMARY PROCEEDINGS

General Provisions as to Preliminary Proceedings

**Separation of children and young persons from adults in police stations, courts,
&c.**

31. Arrangements shall be made for preventing a child or young
person while detained in a police station, or while being conveyed to
or from any criminal court, or while waiting before or after attendance
in any criminal court, from associating with an adult (not being a

---

[31] Words repealed by Education Act 1944 (c. 31), s. 121, Sched. 9.
[32] See Children Act 1948 (c. 43), ss. 38, 39, *post.* This Part was extended by Children
and Young Persons Act 1963 (c. 37), s. 29 (2), *post,* and explained (as to London)
by London Government Act 1963 (c. 33), s. 47 (1) (2) (3).

relative) who is charged with any offence other than an offence with which the child or young person is jointly charged, and for ensuring that a girl (being a child or young person) shall while so detained, being conveyed, or waiting, be under the care of a woman.

32. [*Repealed by Children and Young Persons Act* 1969 (*c.* 54), *s.* 72 (4), *Sched.* 6.]

33. [*Repealed by Criminal Justice Act* 1948 (*c.* 58), *s.* 83, *Sched.* 10 *Pt. I.*]

Attendance at court of parent of child or young person charged with an offence, &c.

[**34.**—(1) Where a child or young person is charged with any offence or is for any other reason brought before a court, any person who is a parent or guardian of his may be required to attend at the court before which the case is heard or determined during all the stages of the proceedings, and any such person shall be so required at any stage where the court thinks it desirable, unless the court is satisfied that it would be unreasonable to require his attendance.

(2) Where a child or young person is arrested [. . .],[33] such steps shall be taken [by the person who arrested him] [34] as may be practicable to inform at least one person whose attendance may be required under this section.] [35]

35. [*Repealed by Children and Young Persons Act* 1969 (*c.* 54), *s.* 72 (4), *Sched.* 6.]

General Provisions as to Proceedings in Court

Prohibition against children being present in court during the trial of other persons

36. No child (other than an infant in arms) shall be permitted to be present in court during the trial of any other person charged with an offence, or during any proceedings preliminary thereto, except during such time as his presence is required as a witness or otherwise for the purposes of justice; and any child present in court when under this section he is not to be permitted to be so shall be ordered to be removed:

Provided that this section shall not apply to messengers, clerks, and other persons required to attend at any court for purposes connected with their employment.

Power to clear court while child or young person is giving evidence in certain cases

37.—(1) Where, in any proceedings in relation to an offence against, or any conduct contrary to, decency or morality, a person who, in the opinion of the court, is a child or young person is called as a witness, the court may direct that all or any persons, not being members or officers of the court or parties to the case, their counsel or solicitors, or persons otherwise directly concerned in the case, be excluded from the court during the taking of the evidence of that witness:

Provided that nothing in this section shall authorise the exclusion of bonâ fide representatives of a newspaper or news agency.

---

[33] Words repealed by Children and Young Persons Act 1969 (c. 54), s. 72 (4), Sched. 6.
[34] Words inserted by Children and Young Persons Act 1969 (c. 54), s. 72 (3), Sched. 5, para. 3.
[35] Section substituted by Children and Young Persons Act 1963 (c. 37), s. 25 (1).

(2) The powers conferred on a court by this section shall be in addition and without prejudice to any other powers of the court to hear proceedings in camerâ.

Evidence of child of tender years

38.—(1) Where, in any proceedings against any person for any offence, any child of tender years called as a witness does not in the opinion of the court understand the nature of an oath, his evidence may be received, though not given upon oath, if, in the opinion of the court, he is possessed of sufficient intelligence to justify the reception of the evidence, and understands the duty of speaking the truth; and his evidence, though not given on oath, but otherwise taken and reduced into writing in accordance with the provisions of section seventeen of the Indictable Offences Act 1848, or of this Part of this Act, shall be deemed to be a deposition within the meaning of that section and that Part respectively:

Provided that where evidence admitted by virtue of this section is given on behalf of the prosecution the accused shall not be liable to be convicted of the offence unless that evidence is corroborated by some other material evidence in support thereof implicating him.

(2) If any child whose evidence is received as aforesaid wilfully gives false evidence in such circumstances that he would, if the evidence had been given on oath, have been guilty of perjury, he shall be liable on summary conviction to be dealt with as if he had been summarily convicted of an indictable offence punishable in the case of an adult with imprisonment.

Power to prohibit publication of certain matter in newspapers

39.[36]—(1) In relation to any proceedings in any court [. . .],[37] the court may direct that—

(*a*) no newspaper report of the proceedings shall reveal the name, address, or school, or include any particulars calculated to lead to the identification, of any child or young person concerned in the proceedings, either as being the person [by or against][37] or in respect of whom the proceedings are taken, or as being a witness therein;

(*b*) no picture shall be published in any newspaper as being or including a picture of any child or young person so concerned in the proceedings as aforesaid;

except in so far (if at all) as may be permitted by the direction of the court.

(2) Any person who publishes any matter in contravention of any such direction shall on summary conviction be liable in respect of each offence to a fine not exceeding fifty pounds.

Special Procedure with regard to Offences specified in First Schedule

Warrant to search for or remove a child or young person

40.[38]—(1) If it appears to a justice of the peace on information

[36] " Court " includes any court in England and Wales, and the section shall apply, with necessary modifications, to sound and television broadcasts also, Children and Young Persons Act 1963 (c. 37), s. 57 (3) (4).

[37] Words deleted and substituted by Children and Young Persons Act 1963 (c. 37), ss. 57 (1), 64 (3), Sched. 5.

[38] " Cause to suspect " was explained by Children Act 1958 (c. 65), s. 8, *post*, and Adoption Act 1958 (c. 5), s. 45. This section saved by Suicide Act 1961 (c. 60), s. 2 (4), and extended by Children and Young Persons Act 1963 (c. 37), s. 23, *post*. Section also explained by Children and Young Persons Act 1969 (c. 54), s. 59 (3), *post*.

on oath laid by any person who, in the opinion of the justice, is acting in the interests of a child or young person, that there is reasonable cause to suspect—

    (*a*) that the child or young person has been or is being assaulted, ill-treated, or neglected in any place within the jurisdiction of the justice, in a manner likely to cause him unnecessary suffering, or injury to health; or

    (*b*) that any offence mentioned in the First Schedule to this Act has been or is being committed in respect of the child or young person,

the justice may issue a warrant authorising any constable named therein to search for the child or young person, and, if it is found that he has been or is being assaulted, ill-treated, or neglected in manner aforesaid, or that any such offence as aforesaid has been or is being committed in respect of him [to take him to a place of safety, or authorising any constable to remove him with or without search to a place of safety, and a child or young person taken to a place of safety in pursuance of such a warrant may be detained there],[39] until he can be brought before a juvenile court.

(2) A justice issuing a warrant under this section may by the same warrant cause any person accused of any offence in respect of the child or young person to be apprehended and brought before a court of summary jurisdiction, and proceedings to be taken against him according to law.

(3) Any constable authorised by warrant under this section to search for any child or young person, or to remove any child or young person with or without search, may enter (if need be by force) any house, building, or other place specified in the warrant, and may remove him therefrom.

(4) Every warrant issued under this section shall be addressed to and executed by a constable, who shall be accompanied by the person laying the information, if that person so desires, unless the justice by whom the warrant is issued otherwise directs, and may also, if the justice by whom the warrant is issued so directs, be accompanied by a duly qualified medical practitioner.

(5) It shall not be necessary in any information or warrant under this section to name the child or young person.

Power to proceed with case in absence of child or young person

41. Where in any proceedings with relation to any of the offences mentioned in the First Schedule to this Act, the court is satisfied that the attendance before the court of any child or young person in respect of whom the offence is alleged to have been committed is not essential to the just hearing of the case, the case may be proceeded with and determined in the absence of the child or young person.

Extension of power to take deposition of child or young person

42.—(1) Where a justice of the peace is satisfied by the evidence of a duly qualified medical practitioner that the attendance before a court of any child or young person in respect of whom any of the offences mentioned in the First Schedule to this Act is alleged to have been committed would involve serious danger to his life or health, the justice may take in writing the deposition of the child or young person on oath, and shall thereupon subscribe the deposition and add thereto a statement

---

[39] Words substituted by Children and Young Persons Act 1963 (c. 37), s. 64 (1), Sched. 3, para. 11.

of his reason for taking it and of the day when and place where it was taken, and of the names of the persons (if any) present at the taking thereof.

(2) The justice taking any such deposition shall transmit it with his statement—

(*a*) if the deposition relates to an offence for which any accused person is already committed for trial, to the proper officer of the court for trial at which the accused person has been committed; and

(*b*) in any other case, to the clerk of the court before which proceedings are pending in respect of the offence.

Admission of deposition of child or young person in evidence

43. Where, in any proceedings in respect of any of the offences mentioned in the First Schedule to this Act, the court is satisfied by the evidence of a duly qualified medical practitioner that the attendance before the court of any child or young person in respect of whom the offence is alleged to have been committed would involve serious danger to his life or health, any deposition of the child or young person taken under the Indictable Offences Act 1848, or this Part of this Act, shall be admissible in evidence either for or against the accused person without further proof thereof if it purports to be signed by the justice by or before whom it purports to be taken:

Provided that the deposition shall not be admissible in evidence against the accused person unless it is proved that reasonable notice of the intention to take the deposition has been served upon him and that he or his counsel or solicitor had, or might have had if he had chosen to be present, an opportunity of cross-examining the child or young person making the deposition.

Principles to be observed by all Courts in dealing with Children and Young Persons

General considerations

44.—(1) Every court in dealing with a child or young person who is brought before it, either as [. . .] [40] an offender or otherwise, shall have regard to the welfare of the child or young person and shall in a proper case take steps for removing him from undesirable surroundings, and for securing that proper provision is made for his education and training.

[*Subsection* (2) *repealed by Children and Young Persons Act* 1969 (*c.* 54), *s.* 72 (4), *Sched.* 6.]

Juvenile Courts

Constitution of juvenile courts

45. Courts of summary jurisdiction constituted in accordance with the provisions of the Second Schedule to this Act and sitting for the purpose of hearing any charge against a child or young person or for the purpose of exercising any other jurisdiction conferred on juvenile courts by or under this or any other Act, shall be known as juvenile courts and in whatever place sitting shall be deemed to be petty sessional courts.

[40] Words repealed by Children and Young Persons Act 1969 (c. 54), s. 72 (4), Sched. 6, *post.*

Assignment of certain matters to juvenile courts

46.—(1) Subject as hereinafter provided, no charge against a child or young person, and no application whereof the hearing is by rules made under this section assigned to juvenile courts, shall be heard by a court of summary jurisdiction which is not a juvenile court [41]:
Provided that—

(a) a charge made jointly against a child or young person and a person who has attained the age of seventeen years shall be heard by a court of summary jurisdiction other than a juvenile court; and

(b) where a child or young person is charged with an offence, the charge may be heard by a court of summary jurisdiction which is not a juvenile court if a person who has attained the age of seventeen years is charged at the same time with aiding, abetting, causing, procuring, allowing or permitting that offence; and

(c) where, in the course of any proceedings before any court of summary jurisdiction other than a juvenile court, it appears that the person to whom the proceedings relate is a child or young person, nothing in this subsection shall be construed as preventing the court, if it thinks fit so to do, from proceeding with the hearing and determination of those proceedings.

[(1A) If a notification that the accused desires to plead guilty without appearing before the court is received by the clerk of a court in pursuance of section 1 of the Magistrates' Courts Act 1957 and the court has no reason to believe that the accused is a child or young person, then, if he is a child or young person he shall be deemed to have attained the age of seventeen for the purposes of subsection (1) of this section in its application to the proceedings in question.] [42]

(2) No direction, whether contained in this or any other Act, that a charge shall be brought before a juvenile court shall be construed as restricting the powers of any justice or justices to entertain an application for bail or for a remand, and to hear such evidence as may be necessary for that purpose.

[*Subsection* (3) *repealed by Justices of the Peace Act* 1949 (c. 101), *s.* 46 (2), *Sched.* 7 *Pt. II.*]

Procedure in juvenile courts

47.—(1) Juvenile courts shall sit as often as may be necessary for the purpose of exercising any jurisdiction conferred on them by or under this or any other Act.

(2) [43] A juvenile court shall [not sit in a room in which sittings of a court other than a juvenile court are held if a sitting of that other court has been or will be held there within an hour before or after the sitting of the juvenile court] [44]; and no person shall be present at any sitting of a juvenile court except—

(a) members and officers of the court;

(b) parties to the case before the court, their solicitors and counsel, and witnesses and other persons directly concerned in that case;

(c) bona fide representatives of newspapers or news agencies;

[41] This was modified by Children and Young Persons Act 1963 (c. 37), s. 18.
[42] Subsection added by Children and Young Persons Act 1969 (c. 54), s. 72 (3), Sched. 5, para. 4.
[43] Subs. (2) excluded by Children Act 1958 (c. 65), s. 10, *post*, and Adoption Act 1958 (c. 5), s. 47.
[44] Words in square brackets substituted by Children and Young Persons Act 1963 (c. 37), s. 17 (2).

(*d*) such other persons as the court may specially authorise to be present:

[*Proviso repealed by Justices of the Peace Act* 1949 (*c.* 101), *s.* 46 (2), *Sched.* 7 *Pt. III.*]

[*Subsection* (3) *repealed by Justices of the Peace Act* 1949 (*c.* 101), *s.* 46 (2), *Sched.* 7 *Pt. II.*]

Miscellaneous provisions as to powers of juvenile courts

48.—(1) A juvenile court sitting for the purpose of hearing a charge against, [. . .],[45] a person who is believed to be a child or young person may, if it thinks fit to do so, proceed with the hearing and determination of the charge [. . .],[45] notwithstanding that it is discovered that the person in question is not a child or young person.

[(2) The attainment of the age of seventeen years by [. . .],[46] a person in whose case an order for conditional discharge has been made, shall not deprive a juvenile court of jurisdiction to enforce his attendance and deal with him in respect of [. . .][46] the commission of a further offence [. . .][47]

(3) When a juvenile court has remanded a child or young person for information to be obtained with respect to him, any juvenile court acting for the same petty sessional division or place—

(*a*) may in his absence extend the period for which he is remanded, so, however, that he appears before a court or a justice of the peace at least once in every twenty-one days;

(*b*) when the required information has been obtained, may deal with him finally;

[. . .][48]

(4) [. . .][49] . . . a juvenile court may sit on any day for the purpose of hearing and determining a charge against a child or young person in respect of an indictable offence.

(5) A juvenile court sitting in the metropolitan police court area shall have all the powers of a metropolitan police magistrate; and for the purposes of any enactment by virtue of which any powers are exercisable—

(*a*) by a court of summary jurisdiction acting for the same petty sessional division or place as a juvenile court by which some previous act has been done; or

(*b*) by a juvenile court acting for the same petty sessional division or place as a court of summary jurisdiction by which some previous act has been done,

the metropolitan police court area shall be deemed to be the place for which all metropolitan police magistrates sitting in that area and all juvenile courts sitting in that area act.

[*Subsection* (6) *repealed by Justices of the Peace Act* 1949 (*c.* 101), *s.* 46 (2), *Sched.* 7 *Pt. III.*]

Restrictions on newspaper reports of proceedings in juvenile courts

49.[50]—(1) Subject as hereinafter provided, no newspaper report of any proceedings in a juvenile court shall reveal the name, address

45 Words repealed by Children and Young Persons Act 1963 (c. 37), s. 64 (3), Sched. 5.
46 Words repealed by Children and Young Persons Act 1969 (c. 54), s. 72 (4), Sched. 6.
47 Words repealed by Criminal Justice Act 1948 (c. 58), s. 79, Sched. 9.
48 Words repealed by *ibid.*, s. 83, Sched. 10 Pt. I.
49 Words repealed by Magistrates' Courts Act 1952 (c. 55), s. 132, Sched. 6.
50 The Children and Young Persons Act 1963 (c. 37), *post*, applied this section (s. 57 (2)); explained it (s. 57 (3) (*a*)) and extended it to include sound and television broadcasts (s. 57 (4)). Amended and explained by Children and Young Persons Act 1969 (c. 54), ss. 10 (1) (2), 73 (4) (*a*), *post*.

Children and Young Persons Act 1933

or school, or include any particulars calculated to lead to the identification, of any child or young person concerned in those proceedings, either as being the person against or in respect of whom the proceedings are taken or as being a witness therein, nor shall any picture be published in any newspaper as being or including a picture of any child or young person so concerned in any such proceedings as aforesaid:

Provided that the court or the Secretary of State may in any case, if satisfied that it is in the interests of justice so to do, by order dispense with the requirements of this section to such extent as may be specified in the order.

(2) Any person who publishes any matter in contravention of this section shall on summary conviction be liable in respect of each offence to a fine not exceeding fifty pounds.

Juvenile Offenders

Age of criminal responsibility

50. It shall be conclusively presumed that no child under the age of [ten] [51] years can be guilty of any offence.

51. [*Repealed by Criminal Law Act* 1967 (*c.* 58), *s.* 10, *Sched.* 3 *Pt. III.*]

52. [*Repealed by Criminal Justice Act* 1948 (*c.* 58), *s.* 83, *Sched.* 10 *Pt. I.*]

Punishment of certain grave crimes

53.[52]—[(1) A person convicted of an offence who appears to the court to have been under the age of eighteen years at the time the offence was committed shall not, if he is convicted of murder, be sentenced to imprisonment for life, nor shall sentence of death be pronounced on or recorded against any such person; but in lieu thereof the court shall (notwithstanding anything in this or in any other Act) sentence him to be detained during Her Majesty's pleasure, and if so sentenced he shall be liable to be detained in such place and under such conditions as the Secretary of State may direct.] [53]

(2) Where a child or young person is convicted on indictment of [any offence punishable in the case of an adult with imprisonment for fourteen years or more, not being an offence the sentence for which is fixed by law],[54] and the court is of opinion that none of the other methods in which the case may legally be dealt with is suitable, the court may sentence the offender to be detained for such period as may be specified in the sentence; and where such a sentence has been passed the child or young person shall, during that period, [. . .],[55] be liable to be detained in such place and on such conditions as the Secretary of State may direct.

(3) A person detained pursuant to the directions of the Secretary of State under this section shall, while so detained, be deemed to be in legal custody.

[51] " Ten " was substituted for " eight " by Children and Young Persons Act 1963 (c. 37), s. 16 (1).
[52] Section modified by Criminal Justice Act 1967 (c. 80), ss. 61, 62 (11), and amended by Children and Young Persons Act 1969 (c. 54), s. 30 (1), *post.*
[53] Subs. (1) substituted by Murder (Abolition of Death Penalty) Act 1965 (c. 71), ss. 1 (5), 4.
[54] Words substituted by Criminal Justice Act 1961 (c. 39), ss. 2 (1), 41 (1) (3), Sched. 4.

[*Subsection* (4) *repealed by Criminal Justice Act* 1967 (*c.* 80), *s.* 103 (2), *Sched.* 7 *Pt. I.*]

54. [*Repealed by Children and Young Persons Act* 1969 (*c.* 54), *ss.* 7 (6), 72 (4), *Sched.* 6.]

Power to order parent to pay fine, &c., instead of child or young person

55.—(1) [56] Where a [. . .] [57] young person is [found guilty of] [58] any offence for the commission of which [a fine or costs may be imposed or a compensation order may be made under section 35 of the Powers of Criminal Courts Act 1973] [59] if the court is of opinion that the case would be best met by [the imposition of a fine or costs or the making of such an order], [59] whether with or without any other punishment, the court may [. . .] [57] order that [the fine, compensation or costs awarded] [59] be paid by the parent or guardian of the [. . .] [57] young person instead of by the [. . .] [57] young person, unless the court is satisfied that the parent or guardian cannot be found or that he has not conduced to the commission of the offence by neglecting to exercise due care [or control] [58] of the [. . .] young person.

[*Subsection* (2) *repealed by Children and Young Persons Act* 1969 (*c.* 54), *s.* 72 (4), *Sched.* 6.]

(3) An order under this section may be made against a parent or guardian who, having been required to attend, has failed to do so, but, save as aforesaid, no such order shall be made without giving the parent or guardian an opportunity of being heard.

[*Subsection* (4) *repealed by Administration of Justice Act* 1970 (*c.* 31), *s.* 54, *Sched.* II.]

(5) A parent or guardian may appeal against an order under this section—

(a) if made by a court of summary jurisdiction, to [the Crown Court] [60]; and

(b) if made by [the Crown Court to the Criminal Division of the Court of Appeal in accordance with Part I of the Criminal Appeal Act 1968], [61] as if the parent or guardian against whom the order was made had been convicted on indictment, and the order were a sentence passed on conviction.

Power of other courts to remit juvenile offenders to juvenile courts

56.—(1) [62] Any court by or before which a [. . .] [57] young person is found guilty of an offence other than homicide, may, [and, if it is not a juvenile court, shall unless satisfied that it would be undesirable to do so], [63] remit the case to a juvenile court acting for the place where the offender was committed for trial, or, if he was not committed for trial, to a juvenile court acting either for the same place as the remitting

---

55 Words repealed by Criminal Justice Act 1948 (c. 58), s. 83, Sched. 10 Pt. I.
56 Subs. (1) extended by Criminal Justice Act 1961 (c. 39), s. 8 (4).
57 Words repealed by Children and Young Persons Act 1969 (c. 54), s. 72 (4), Sched. 6.
58 Words added by Children and Young Persons Act 1969 (c. 54), s. 72 (3), Sched. 5, para. 5.
59 Words substituted by Criminal Justice Act 1972 (c. 71), s. 64 (1), Sched. 5. The reference to the 1973 Act was substituted by that Act, 1973 (c. 62), Sched. 5.
60 Words substituted by Courts Act 1971 (c. 23), s. 56 (1) (2), Sched. 8, para. 22, Sched. 9, Pt. I.
61 Words substituted by Criminal Appeal Act 1968 (c. 19), s. 52 (1), Sched. 5, and Courts Act 1971 (c. 23), s. 56 (1) (2), Sched. 8, para. 22, Sched. 9, Pt. I.
62 Modified by Children and Young Persons Act 1969 (c. 54), s. 7 (8), *post.*
63 Words substituted by Children and Young Persons Act 1963 (c. 37), s. 64 (1), Sched. 3, para. 14.

court or for the place where the offender [habitually resides] ⁶⁴; and, where any such case is so remitted, the offender shall be brought before a juvenile court accordingly, and that court may deal with him in any way in which it might have dealt with him if he had been tried and found guilty by that court.

(2) No appeal shall lie against an order of remission made under the last foregoing subsection, but nothing in this subsection shall affect any right of appeal against the verdict or finding on which such an order is founded [. . .].^{64a}

(3) A court by which an order remitting a case to a juvenile court is made under this section may give such directions as appear to be necessary with respect to the custody of the offender or for his release on bail until he can be brought before the juvenile court, and shall cause to be transmitted to the clerk of the juvenile court a certificate setting out the nature of the offence and stating that the offender has been found guilty thereof, and that the case has been remitted for the purpose of being dealt with under this section.

57. [*Repealed by Children and Young Persons Act 1969 (c. 54), ss. 7 (6), 72 (4), Sched. 6.*]

58. [*Repealed by Children and Young Persons Act 1969 (c. 54), s. 72 (4), Sched. 6.*]

Miscellaneous provisions as to summary proceedings against juvenile offenders

59.—(1) The words " conviction " and " sentence " shall cease to be used in relation to [. . .] ⁶⁵ young persons dealt with summarily and any reference in any enactment [whether passed before or after the " commencement of this Act "] ⁶⁶ to a person convicted, a conviction or a sentence shall, in the case of a [. . .] ⁶⁵ young person, be construed as including a reference to a person found guilty of an offence, a finding of guilt or an order made upon such a finding, as the case may be:

[*Proviso repealed by Criminal Justice Act 1948 (c. 58), s. 83, Sched. 10 Pt. I.*]

[*Subsection (2) repealed by Costs in Criminal Cases Act 1952 (c. 48), s. 18 (1), Sched.*]

60. [*Repealed by Magistrates' Courts Act 1952 (c. 55), s. 132, Sched. 6.*]

Children and Young Persons in need of Care or Protection

61. [*Repealed by Children and Young Persons Act 1963 (c. 37), ss. 2 (3), 64 (3), Sched. 5.*]

62–85. [*Repealed by Children and Young Persons Act 1969 (c. 54), s. 72 (4), Sched. 6.*]

⁶⁴ Words added by Children and Young Persons Act 1969 (c. 54), s. 72 (3), Sched. 5, para. 6.
^{64a} Words repealed by Courts Act 1971 (c. 23), s. 56 (4), Sched. 11, Pt. IV.
⁶⁵ Words repealed by Children and Young Persons Act 1969 (c. 54), s. 72 (4), Sched. 6.
⁶⁶ Words substituted by Criminal Justice Act 1948 (c. 58), s. 79, Sched. 9.

Provisions as to Contributions towards Expenses

Contributions to be made by parents, &c., of children and young persons committed to the care of fit persons, or to approved schools

86.[67]—(1) Where [a care order which is not an interim order has been made in respect of a child or young person],[68] it shall be the duty of [the persons specified in section twenty-four of the Children Act 1948] [69] to make contributions in respect of him [. . .].[69]

[*Subsection* (2) *repealed by Children and Young Persons Act* 1969 (*c.* 54), *s.* 72 (4), *Sched.* 6.]

(3) Where the child or young person has been committed to the care of a local authority [. . .],[70] the contributions shall be payable to the council of the county or county borough within which the person liable to make the contributions is for the time being residing [. . .].[70]

[*Subsection* (4) *repealed by Children and Young Persons Act* 1969 (*c.* 54), *s.* 72 (4), *Sched.* 6.]

Enforcement of duty of parent, &c., to make contributions

87.[71]—(1) Where [a care order which is not an interim order has been made in respect of a child or young person then, subject to section 62 of the Children and Young Persons Act 1969],[72] any court of summary jurisdiction having jurisdiction in the place where the person to be charged is for the time being residing may subsequently at any time, make an order (hereafter in this Act referred to as a " contribution order ") on any person who is under the last foregoing section liable to make contributions in respect of the child or young person, requiring him to contribute such weekly sum as the court having regard to his means thinks fit:

[*Proviso repealed by Children Act* 1948 (*c.* 43), *ss.* 25, 60, *Sched.* 4 *Pt. I.*]

(2) [A contribution order in respect of a child or young person may be made on the application of the local authority entitled to receive contributions in respect of him.] [72]

(3) A contribution order shall remain in force [as long as the child or young person to whom it relates is in the care of the local authority concerned].[72]

(4) Subject to the provisions of this subsection—

    (*a*) a contribution order shall be enforceable as an affiliation order and the enactments relating to the enforcement of affiliation orders shall apply accordingly, subject to any necessary modifications; and

    (*b*) section thirty of the Criminal Justice Administration Act 1914 (which contains provisions as to orders for the periodical pay-

[67] Applied by Children Act 1948 (c. 43), s. 23 (1); Children and Young Persons Act 1963 (c. 37), s. 12; applied and extended by Children and Young Persons Act 1969 (c. 54), s. 62 (1) (3). Amended by Local Government Act 1958 (c. 55), s. 62, Sched. 8, para. 2 (1) (2). Modified by Maintenance Orders Act 1950 (c. 37), s. 14, Sched. 1, *post.*
[68] Words substituted by Children and Young Persons Act 1969 (c. 54), s. 72 (3), Sched. 5, para. 8.
[69] Words substituted and deleted by Children Act 1948 (c. 43), s. 60, Sched. 3.
[70] Words repealed by Children and Young Persons Act 1969 (c. 54), s. 72 (4), Sched. 6.
[71] This section applied by Children Act 1948 (c. 43), s. 23 (1), and Children and Young Persons Act 1963 (c. 37), s. 12; modified by Maintenance Orders Act 1950 (c. 37), s. 14, Sched. 1, and Family Allowances and National Insurance Act 1956 (c. 50), s. 5 (3); extended by Maintenance Orders Act 1950 (c. 37), s. 4; and explained by Local Government Act 1958 (c. 55), s. 62, Sched. 8, para. 2 (4), and Children and Young Persons Act 1963 (c. 37), s. 30 (3).
[72] Words substituted by Children and Young Persons Act 1969 (c. 54), s. 72 (3), Sched. 5, para. 9.

ment of money made by courts of summary jurisdiction) shall apply to every contribution order whether the court which made it was, or was not, a court of summary jurisdiction;
but any powers conferred by any of the enactments aforesaid on any justices or courts of summary jurisdiction shall be exercisable, and exercisable only, by justices and courts of summary jurisdiction having jurisdiction in the place where the person liable is for the time being residing.

[*Subsection* (5) *repealed by Children and Young Persons Act* 1963 (*c.* 37), *ss.* 14 (5), 64 (3), *Sched.* 5.]

Provision as to affiliation orders

88.[73]—(1) Where a child or young person who is [the subject of a care order (other than an interim order)] [74] is illegitimate, and an affiliation order for his maintenance is in force [the court which makes the order] [74] may at the same time, and any court of summary jurisdiction having jurisdiction in the place where the putative father is for the time being residing may subsequently at any time, order the payments under the affiliation order to be paid to [the local authority who are] [74] from time to time entitled under section eighty-six of this Act to receive contributions in respect of the child or young person.

Applications for orders under this subsection may be made by [the local authorities by whom] [74] applications for contribution orders may be made.

(2) Where an order made under this section with respect to an affiliation order is in force—

(a) any powers conferred on any justices or courts of summary jurisdiction by the enactments relating to the enforcement of affiliation orders or by section thirty of the Criminal Justice Administration Act 1914 shall as respects the affiliation order in question be exercisable, and exercisable only, by justices and courts of summary jurisdiction having jurisdiction in the place where the person liable is for the time being residing;

(b) any sums received under the affiliation order shall be applied in like manner as if they were contributions received under a contribution order;

(c) if the putative father changes his address, he shall forthwith give notice thereof to the [local authority who were] [74] immediately before the change entitled to receive payments under the order and, if he fails so to do, he shall be liable on summary conviction to a fine not exceeding [ten] [75] pounds;

[*Paragraph* (d) *repealed by Magistrates' Courts Act* 1952 (*c.* 55), *s.* 132, *Sched.* 6.]

[*Subsection* (3) *repealed by Children Act* 1948 (*c.* 43), *s.* 60, *Sched.* 4 *Pt. I.*]

(4) The making of an order under this section with respect to an affiliation order shall not extend the duration of that order, and that order shall not in any case remain in force (except for the purpose of

---

[73] This section applied by Children Act 1948 (c. 43), s. 23 (1) (3), and Children and Young Persons Act 1963 (c. 37), s. 12, *post*; saved by Children Act 1948 (c. 43), s. 26 (6), and Affiliation Proceedings Act 1957 (c. 55), s. 5 (1) (a) (b); modified by Maintenance Orders Act 1950 (c. 37), s. 14, Sched. 1; and explained by Local Government Act 1958 (c. 55), s. 62, Sched. 8, para. 2 (4).
[74] Words substituted by Children and Young Persons Act 1969 (c. 54), s. 72 (3), Sched. 5, para. 10.
[75] Maximum fine increased from two pounds by Criminal Justice Act 1967 (c. 80), s. 92, Sched. 3 Pt. I.

the recovery of arrears) [after the child or young person to whom that order relates has ceased to be the subject of the care order by virtue of which the order under this section was made or, where this section applies by virtue of section 28 of the Children Act 1948, after he has ceased to be in the care of a local authority under section 1 of that Act or, in either case, if he is allowed by the local authority to be under the charge and control of a parent, guardian, relative or friend, although remaining in the care of the local authority] [74]:

Provided that, where an affiliation order would, but for the provisions of this subsection have continued in force, the mother, or any person entitled to make an application for an order under section three of the Affiliation Orders Act 1914, may apply to a court of summary jurisdiction having jurisdiction in the place where she or he is for the time being residing, for an order that the affiliation order may be revived, and that payments thereunder may until the expiration thereof be made to the applicant at such rate (not exceeding the maximum rate allowed by the law in the case of affiliation orders) as may be proper, and the court may make such an order accordingly, and where such an order is so made, any power to vary, revoke or again revive the affiliation order or any part thereof, being a power which would but for the provisions of this subsection be vested in the court which originally made the affiliation order, shall be exercisable, and exercisable only, by the court which made the order under this subsection.

Miscellaneous provisions as to contribution orders

89.[76]—[*Subsection* (1) *repealed by Children and Young Persons Act* 1969 (*c.* 54), *s.* 72 (4), *Sched.* 6.]

(2) Where, by virtue of an order made under either of the two last foregoing sections, any sum is payable to the council of a county or county borough, the council of the county or county borough in which the person liable under the order is for the time being residing shall be entitled to receive and give a discharge for, and, if necessary, enforce payment of, any arrears accrued due under the order, notwithstanding that those arrears may have accrued at a time when he was not resident in that county or county borough.

(3) In any proceedings under either of the two last foregoing sections a certificate purporting to be signed by the clerk to a council for the time being entitled to receive contributions, or by some other officer of the council duly authorised in that behalf, and stating that any sum due to the council under an order is overdue and unpaid shall be evidence of the facts stated therein.

[*Subsection* (4) *repealed by National Assistance Act* 1948 (*c.* 29), *s.* 62, *Sched.* 7 *Pt. III.*]

90, 91. [*Repealed by Children and Young Persons Act* 1969 (*c.* 54), *s.* 72 (4), *Sched.* 6.]

PART V

HOMES SUPPORTED BY VOLUNTARY CONTRIBUTIONS

Definition of voluntary homes

92. In this Part of this Act the expression " voluntary home " means any home or other institution for the boarding, care, and maintenance of

---

[76] Section modified by Maintenance Orders Act 1950 (c. 37), s. 14, Sched. 1; amended by Local Government Act 1958 (c. 55), s. 62, Sched. 8, para. 2 (5); applied by Children and Young Persons Act 1963 (c. 37), s. 12; and explained by *ibid.*, s. 30 (3).

poor children or young persons, being a home or other institution supported wholly or partly by voluntary contributions,[77] [but does not include any mental nursing home or residential home for mentally disordered persons within the meaning of Part III of the Mental Health Act 1959].[78]

Notification of particulars with respect to voluntary homes

93.[79]—(1) It shall be the duty of the person in charge of any voluntary home to send the prescribed particulars with respect to the home to the Secretary of State within three months after the commencement of this Act, or in the case of a home established after the commencement of this Act within three months from the establishment of the home and to send such particulars in every subsequent year before such date as may be prescribed.

(2) If default is made in sending the prescribed particulars with respect to any voluntary home in accordance with the requirements of this section, the person in charge of the home shall, on summary conviction, be liable to a fine not exceeding five pounds and to a further fine not exceeding twenty shillings in respect of each day during which the default continues after conviction.

94. [*Repealed by Children and Young Persons Act* 1969 (*c.* 54), *s.* 72 (4), *Sched.* 6.]

95. [*Repealed by Children Act* 1948 (*c.* 43), *s.* 60, *Sched.* 4 *Pt.* II.]

PART VI [80]

SUPPLEMENTAL

Local Authorities

Provisions as to local authorities

96.[81]—(1) Subject to the modifications hereinafter contained as to the City of London, where any powers or duties are by [Part II of this Act] [82] conferred or imposed on local authorities (by that description), those powers and duties shall [. . .] [83] be powers and duties of local education authorities [. . .] [83] and, as respects other persons, be powers and duties of councils of counties and county boroughs:

 Provided that—

  (*a*) the attainment of the age of fourteen years by a person who has previously been ordered to be sent to an approved school, or to be committed to the care of a fit person, shall not divest or relieve any local education authority for elementary education of any powers or duties in respect of him, or confer or impose any powers or duties in respect of him upon the council of any county or county borough;

  (*b*) the council of an urban district (whether a borough or not)

---

[77] Amended by Children Act 1948 (c. 43), s. 27.
[78] Words substituted by Mental Health Act 1959 (c. 72), ss. 19 (3), 149 (1), Sched. 7 Pt. I.
[79] Excluded by Children and Young Persons Act 1969 (c. 54), s. 44.
[80] Explained as regards London by London Government Act 1963 (c. 33), s. 47 (1) (3).
[81] Section amended by Acquisition of Land (Authorisation Procedure) Act 1946 (c. 49), s. 6, Sched. 4; explained as regards London by London Government Act 1963 (c. 33), s. 47 (1) and excluded by the same, s. 47 (2).
[82] Words added by Children Act 1948 (c. 43), s. 60, Sched. 3.
[83] Words repealed by Education Act 1944 (c. 31), s. 120 (3), Sched. 8.

who have under the Education Act 1921, or the Acts repealed by that Act, relinquished in favour of the council of the county all their powers and duties as a local education authority for elementary education, shall for the purposes of this Act be deemed not to be a local education authority for elementary education, and their district shall for the purposes of this Act be deemed to be part of the area of the county council.

[*Subsection* (2) *repealed by Education Act* 1944 (*c.* 31), *s.* 121, *Sched.* 9.]

(3) Expenses incurred by a local authority in connection with powers and duties which are, under this Act, exercised and performed by them as local education authorities [shall be defrayed as expenses under the enactments relating to education].[83]

(4) Expenses incurred under this Act by the council of a county or county borough, exclusive of any expenses to be defrayed [in accordance with] [83] the last foregoing subsection [. . .],[83] shall be defrayed—

[. . .] [84] as expenses for general county purposes or, as the case may be, out of the general rate.

(5) A local authority may, for the purposes of their functions under this Act, acquire, dispose of, or otherwise deal with land—

[*Paragraph* (*a*) *repealed* (*except London*) *by Local Government Act* 1933 (*c.* 51), *ss.* 307, 308, *Sched.* 11; (*London*) *by London Government Act* 1939 (*c.* 40), *ss.* 207, 208, *Sched.* 8.]

(*b*) in the case of the council of a county borough or urban district, in like manner as for the purposes of the Public Health Act 1875, and sections one hundred and seventy-five to one hundred and seventy-eight of that Act shall apply accordingly.

[*Subsection* (6) *repealed by London Government Act* 1963 (*c.* 33), *s.* 93 (1), *Sched.* 18 *Pt.* II.]

(7) [Subject to the provisions of section thirty-nine of the Children Act 1948 (which requires certain matters to be referred to the children's committee and restricts the reference of other matters to that committee).] [84] Subject to the provisions of section four of the Education Act 1921 (which require certain matters to be referred to education committees) a local authority may refer to a committee appointed for the purposes of this Act, or to any committee appointed for the purposes of any other Act, any matter relating to the exercise by the authority of any of their powers under this Act and may delegate any of the said powers (other than any power to borrow money) to any such committee.

(8) A local authority, or a committee to whom any powers of a local authority under this Act have been delegated, may by resolution empower the clerk or the chief education officer of the authority to exercise in the name of the authority in any case which appears to him to be one of urgency any powers of the authority or, as the case may be, of the committee with respect to the institution of proceedings under this Act.

Modifications of last foregoing section as to City of London

97. The last foregoing section shall, in its application to the City of London, have effect subject to the modifications that the powers and duties of a local authority under this Act [. . .] [85] as respects street trading and employment, shall be powers and duties of the Common Council and any expenses of the Common Council shall be defrayed out of the general rate:

---

[84] Words repealed by National Assistance Act 1948 (c. 29), s. 62, Sched. 7 Pt. III.
[85] Words repealed by Children Act 1948 (c. 43), s. 60, Sched. 3.

Provided that—

(a) the powers and duties of a local authority with respect to the granting of licences for children to take part in entertainments shall be powers and duties of the [. . .] [86] local education authority [. . .] [87]; and

(b) nothing in this section shall exempt the City of London from the liability to contribute towards the expenses incurred by the London County Council as local authority under this Act [. . .] [85]

Institution of proceedings by local or poor law authorities

[**98.** Without prejudice to the provisions of the last foregoing section, a local education authority may institute proceedings for any offence under Part I or Part II of this Act.] [88]

Supplementary Provisions as to Legal Proceedings

Presumption and determination of age

99.[89]—(1) Where a person, whether charged with an offence or not, is brought before any court otherwise than for the purpose of giving evidence, and it appears to the court that he is a child or young person, the court shall make due inquiry as to the age of that person, and for that purpose shall take such evidence as may be forthcoming at the hearing of the case, but an order or judgment of the court shall not be invalidated by any subsequent proof that the age of that person has not been correctly stated to the court, and the age presumed or declared by the court to be the age of the person so brought before it shall, for the purposes of this Act, be deemed to be the true age of that person, and, where it appears to the court that the person so brought before it has attained the age of seventeen years, that person shall for the purposes of this Act be deemed not to be a child or young person.

(2) Where in any charge or indictment for any offence under this Act or any of the offences mentioned in the First Schedule to this Act [except as provided in that Schedule],[90] it is alleged that the person by or in respect of whom the offence was committed was a child or young person or was under or had attained any specified age, and he appears to the court to have been at the date of the commission of the alleged offence a child or young person, or to have been under or to have attained the specified age, as the case may be, he shall for the purposes of this Act be presumed at that date to have been a child or young person or to have been under or to have attained that age, as the case may be, unless the contrary is proved.

(3) Where, in any charge or indictment for any offence under this Act or any of the offences mentioned in the First Schedule to this Act, it is alleged that the person in respect of whom the offence was committed was a child or was a young person, it shall not be a defence to prove that the person alleged to have been a child was a young person or the person alleged to have been a young person was a child in any case where the acts constituting the alleged offence would equally have been an offence if committed in respect of a young person or child respectively.

[86] Words repealed by London Government Act 1963 (c. 33), s. 93 (1), Sched. 18 Pt. II.
[87] Words repealed by Education Act 1944 (c. 31), s. 121, Sched. 9.
[88] Section substituted by Children Act 1948 (c. 43), s. 60, Sched. 3, and saved by Children and Young Persons Act 1963 (c. 37), s. 56 (1).
[89] Section applied by Mental Health Act 1959 (c. 72), s. 80 (8), and extended by Children and Young Persons Act 1969 (c. 54), s. 70 (3).
[90] Words substituted by Sexual Offences Act 1956 (c. 69), s. 48, Sched. 3.

(4) Where a person is charged with an offence under this Act in respect of a person apparently under a specified age it shall be a defence to prove that the person was actually of or over that age.

Evidence of wages of defendant

100. In any proceedings under this Act a copy of an entry in the wages book of any employer of labour, or if no wages book be kept a written statement signed by the employer or by any responsible person in his employ, shall be evidence that the wages therein entered or stated as having been paid to any person, have in fact been so paid.

Application of Summary Jurisdiction Acts

101.—(1) Subject to the provisions of this Act, all orders of a court of summary jurisdiction, whether a petty sessional court or not, under this Act shall be made, and all proceedings in relation to any such orders shall be taken, in manner provided by the Summary Jurisdiction Acts [. . .] [90a]

[*Subsection (2) repealed by Justices of the Peace Act 1949 (c. 101), s. 46 (2), Sched. 7 Pt. II.*]

Appeals to quarter sessions

102.—(1) Appeals to [the Crown Court] [90b] from orders of a court of summary jurisdiction under this Act may be brought in the following cases and by the following persons, that is to say—

[*Paragraphs (a) (b) repealed by Children and Young Persons Act 1969 (c. 54), s. 72 (4), Sched. 6.*]

(c) [91] in the case of an order requiring a person to contribute in respect of [himself or any other person],[92] by the person required to contribute;

(d) in the case of an order requiring all or any part of the payments accruing due under an affiliation order to be paid to some other person, by the person who would but for the order be entitled to the payments;

(e) in the case of an order requiring the owner of an automatic machine for the sale of tobacco or the person on whose premises such a machine is kept, to take precautions to prevent the machine being extensively used by persons apparently under the age of sixteen years or to remove the machine, by any person aggrieved;

[*Proviso (f) repealed by Children Act 1948 (c. 43), s. 60, Sched. 4 Pt. II.*]

and, in relation to an appeal from a refusal to make an order under the said subsection (2), the refusal shall be deemed to be an order.

(2) Nothing in this section shall be construed as affecting [. . .] [93] any other right of appeal conferred by this or any other Act.

103, 104. [*Repealed by Children and Young Persons Act 1969 (c. 54), s. 72 (4), Sched. 6.*]

[90a] Words repealed by Justices of the Peace Act 1949 (c. 101), s. 46 (2), Sched. 7 Pt. II.
[90b] Words substituted by Courts Act 1971 (c. 23), s. 56 (2), Sched. 9, Pt. I.
[91] Explained by Children and Young Persons Act 1963 (c. 37), s. 30 (3).
[92] Words substituted by Children Act 1948 (c. 43), s. 60, Sched. 3.
[93] Words repealed by Children and Young Persons Act 1969 (c. 54), s. 72 (4), Sched. 6.

General

Variation of Orders in Council

105. An Order in Council under this Act may be revoked or varied by any subsequent Order in Council.

Provisions as to documents, &c.

106.[94]—(1) An order or other act of the Secretary of State under this Act may be signified under the hand of the Secretary of State or an Under-Secretary of State or an Assistant Under-Secretary.

(2) A document purporting to be a copy—

> (a) of an order made by a court under or by virtue of any of the provisions contained in sections fifty-six, [eighty-seven and eighty-eight of] [95] this Act; or
>
> [*Paragraph (b) repealed by Education Act* 1944 (*c.* 31), *s.* 121, *Sched.* 9.]
>
> (c) of an affiliation order referred to in an order under section eighty-eight of this Act,

shall, if it purports to be certified as a true copy by the clerk of the court, be evidence of the order.

[*Subsections* (3)–(5) *repealed by Children and Young Persons Act* 1969 (*c.* 54), *s.* 72 (4), *Sched.* 6.]

Interpretation

107.—(1) In this Act, unless the context otherwise requires, the following expressions have the meanings hereby respectively assigned to them, that is to say,—

> [" Care order " and " interim order " have the same meaning as in the Children and Young Persons Act 1969].[96]
>
> [*Definitions repealed by Children and Young Persons Act* 1969 (*c.* 54), *s.* 72 (4), *Sched.* 6.]
>
> " Chief officer of police " [as regards England has the same meaning as in the Police Act 1964],[96a] as regards Scotland has the same meaning as in the Police (Scotland) Act 1890 and as regards Northern Ireland means a district inspector of the Royal Ulster Constabulary;
>
> " Child " means a person under the age of fourteen years;
>
> " Guardian," in relation to a child or young person, includes any person who, in the opinion of the court having cognisance of any case in relation to the child or young person or in which the child or young person is concerned, has for the time being the charge of or control over the child or young person;
>
> [*Definition repealed by Children and Young Persons Act* 1963 (*c.* 37), *s.* 64 (3), *Sched.* 5.]
>
> " Intoxicating liquor " [has the same meaning as in the Licensing Act 1964].[97]
>
> " Legal guardian " in relation to a child or young person, means a person appointed, according to law, to be his guardian by deed or will, or by order of a court of competent jurisdiction;

---

[94] Power to apply this section in Criminal Justice Act 1948 (c. 58), s. 49 (2); it was also extended by Children and Young Persons Act 1963 (c. 37), s. 11 (2) (4), *post.*

[95] Words substituted by Children and Young Persons Act 1969 (c. 54), s. 72 (3), Sched. 5 para. 11.

[96] Words added by Children and Young Persons Act 1969 (c. 54), s. 72 (3), Sched. 5 para. 12 (1) (2).

[96a] Words substituted by Police Act 1964 (c. 48), s. 63, Sched. 9.

[97] Words substituted by Finance Act 1967 (c. 54), s. 5 (1) (e).

[*Definition repealed by Children and Young Persons Act* 1969 (*c.* 54), *s.* 72 (4), *Sched.* 6.]
" Metropolitan police court area " means the area consisting of the police court divisions for the time being constituted under the Metropolitan Police Courts Acts 1839 and 1840 [and the City of London] [1];
" Place of safety " means [a community home provided by a local authority or a controlled community home, any] [2] police station, or any hospital, surgery, or any other suitable place, the occupier of which is willing temporarily to receive a child or young person;
[*Definition repealed by Police Act* 1964 (*c.* 48), *s.* 64 (3), *Sched.* 10 *Pt. I.*]
[*Definition repealed by National Assistance Act* 1948 (*c.* 29), *s.* 62, *Sched.* 7 *Pt. III.*]
" Prescribed " means prescribed by regulations made by the Secretary of State;
" Public place " includes any public park, garden, sea beach or railway station, and any ground to which the public for the time being have or are permitted to have access, whether on payment or otherwise;
" Street " includes any highway and any public bridge, road, lane, footway, square, court, alley or passage, whether a thoroughfare or not;
" Young person " means a person who has attained the age of fourteen years and is under the age of seventeen years.
[*Subsection* (2) *repealed by Children and Young Persons Act* 1969 (*c.* 54), *s.* 72 (3) (4), *Sched.* 5 *para.* 12 (3), *Sched.* 6.]
(3) References in this Act to any enactment or to any provision in any enactment shall, unless the context otherwise requires, be construed as references to that enactment or provision as amended by any subsequent enactment including this Act.

Transitory provisions

108.—(1) Without prejudice to the provisions of the Interpretation Act 1889 with respect to repeals, the transitory provisions set out in the Fifth Schedule to this Act shall have effect for the purposes of the transition to the provisions of this Act from the provisions of the enactments repealed by the Children and Young Persons Act 1932 and by this Act.
[*Subsections* (2) (3) *repealed by Children and Young Persons Act* 1969 (*c.* 54), *s.* 72 (4), *Sched.* 6.]
(4) References in any Act or other document to juvenile courts under the Children Act 1908 shall be construed as including references to such courts under this Act.
(5) References in any Act or other document to any enactment repealed and re-enacted with or without modifications by this Act (except references in Part VI of the Children Act 1908 or Part VI of the Children and Young Persons Act 1932) shall be construed as including references to the corresponding provision of this Act.
(6) The reference in the First Schedule to this Act to any offence under sections one, two, three, eleven or twenty-three of this Act shall be construed as including a reference to any offence under the Dangerous Performances Acts 1879 and 1897 or under Part II of the Children Act 1908.

[1] Children and Young Persons Act 1963 (c. 37), s. 64 (1), Sched. 3 para. 24.
[2] Words substituted by Children and Young Persons Act 1969 (c. 54), s. 72 (3), Sched. 5 para. 12 (1) (2).

Short title, commencement, extent and repeals

109.—(1) This Act may be cited as the Children and Young Persons Act 1933.

[Subsection (2) repealed by S.L.R. 1950.]

(3) Save as therein otherwise expressly provided, this Act shall not extend to Scotland or Northern Ireland.

[Subsection (4) repealed by S.L.R. 1950.]

SCHEDULES

FIRST SCHEDULE [3]

OFFENCES AGAINST CHILDREN AND YOUNG PERSONS, WITH RESPECT TO WHICH SPECIAL PROVISIONS OF THIS ACT APPLY

The murder or manslaughter of a child or young person.

Infanticide.

Any offence under sections twenty-seven, [. . .],[4] or fifty-six of the Offences against the Person Act 1861, and any offence against a child or young person under sections five, forty-two, forty-three [. . .][4] of that Act, [. . .][4] [. . .][4]

Any offence under sections one, [. . .],[4] three, four, eleven or twenty-three of this Act.

[Any offence against a child or young person under any of the following sections of the Sexual Offences Act 1956, that is to say, sections two to seven, ten to sixteen, nineteen, twenty, twenty-two to twenty-six and twenty-eight, and any attempt to commit against a child or young person an offence under section two, five, six, seven, ten, eleven, twelve, twenty-two or twenty-three of that Act :

Provided that for the purposes of subsection (2) of section ninety-nine of this Act this entry shall apply so far only as it relates to offences under sections ten, eleven, twelve, fourteen, fifteen, sixteen, twenty and twenty-eight of the Sexual Offences Act 1956, and attempts to commit offences under sections ten, eleven and twelve of that Act.] [5]

Any other offence involving bodily injury to a child or young person.

SECOND SCHEDULE

[Repealed and substituted by Children and Young Persons Act 1963 (c. 37), ss. 17 (1), 64 (3), Scheds. 2, 5.]

THIRD SCHEDULE

[Repealed by Magistrates' Courts Act 1952 (c. 55), s. 132, Sched. 6.]

FOURTH SCHEDULE

[Repealed by Children and Young Persons Act 1969 (c. 54), s. 72 (4), Sched. 6.]

. . . . . .

SIXTH SCHEDULE

[Repealed by S.L.R. 1950.]

---

[3] Amended by Suicide Act 1961 (c. 60), s. 2 (3), Sched. 1 Pt. I, and amended with saving by Indecency with Children Act 1960 (c. 33), s. 1 (3).
[4] Words repealed by Sexual Offences Act 1956 (c. 69), s. 51, Sched. 4.
[5] Added by Sexual Offences Act 1956 (c. 69), s. 48, Sched. 3.

Law Reform (Married Women and Tortfeasors) Act 1935

(25 & 26 GEO. 5, c. 30)

An Act to amend the law relating to the capacity, property, and liabilities of married women, and the liabilities of husbands; and to amend the law relating to proceedings against, and contribution between, tort-feasors.   [2nd August 1935.]

PART I

CAPACITY, PROPERTY, AND LIABILITIES OF MARRIED WOMEN; AND LIABILITIES OF HUSBANDS

Capacity of married women

1. Subject to the provisions of this Part of this Act [. . .],[1] a married woman shall—

(a) be capable of acquiring, holding and disposing of, any property; and

(b) be capable of rendering herself, and being rendered, liable in respect of any tort, contract, debt, or obligation; and

(c) be capable of suing and being sued, either in tort or in contract or otherwise; and

(d) be subject to the law relating to bankruptcy and to the enforcement of judgments and orders,

in all respects as if she were a feme sole.

Property of married women

2.—(1) Subject to the provisions of this Part of this Act all property which—

(a) immediately before the passing of this Act was the separate property of a married woman or held for her separate use in equity; or

(b) belongs at the time of her marriage to a woman married after the passing of this Act; or

(c) after the passing of this Act is acquired by or devolves upon a married woman,

shall belong to her in all respects as if she were a feme sole and may be disposed of accordingly:

[*Proviso and subsections* (2) *and* (3) *repealed by Married Women (Restraint upon Anticipation) Act* 1949 (*c.* 78), *s.* 1, *Sched.* 2.]

Abolition of husband's liability for wife's torts and ante-nuptial contracts, debts and obligations

3. Subject to the provisions of this Part of this Act, the husband of a married woman shall not, by reason only of his being her husband, be liable—

(a) in respect of any tort committed by her whether before or after the marriage, or in respect of any contract entered into, or debt or obligation incurred, by her before the marriage; or

(b) to be sued, or made a party to any legal proceeding brought, in respect of any such tort, contract, debt, or obligation.

---

[1] Words repealed by Law Reform (Husband and Wife) Act 1962 (c. 48), s. 3 (2), Sched.

Savings

4.—(1) Nothing in this Part of this Act shall—

 (*a*) during coverture which began before the first day of January eighteen hundred and eighty-three, affect any property to which the title (whether vested or contingent, and whether in possession, reversion, or remainder) of a married woman accrued before that date, except property held for her separate use in equity;

 (*b*) affect any legal proceeding in respect of any tort if proceedings had been instituted in respect thereof before the passing of this Act;

 (*c*) enable any judgment or order against a married woman in respect of a contract entered into, or debt or obligation incurred, before the passing of this Act, to be enforced in bankruptcy or to be enforced otherwise than against her property.

(2) For the avoidance of doubt it is hereby declared that nothing in this Part of this Act—

 (*a*) renders the husband of a married woman liable in respect of any contract entered into, or debt or obligation incurred, by her after the marriage in respect of which he would not have been liable if this Act had not been passed;

 (*b*) exempts the husband of a married woman from liability in respect of any contract entered into, or debt or obligation (not being a debt or obligation arising out of the commission of a tort) incurred, by her after the marriage in respect of which he would have been liable if this Act had not been passed;

 (*c*) prevents a husband and wife from acquiring, holding, and disposing of, any property jointly or as tenants in common, or from rendering themselves, or being rendered, jointly liable in respect of any tort, contract, debt or obligation, and of suing and being sued either in tort or in contract or otherwise, in like manner as if they were not married;

 (*d*) prevents the exercise of any joint power given to a husband and wife.

Consequential amendments and repeals

5.—(1) The enactments mentioned in the first column of the First Schedule to this Act shall have effect subject to the amendments specified in the second column of that Schedule.

[*Subsection* (2) *repealed by S.L.R.* 1950.]

PART II [2]

PROCEEDINGS AGAINST, AND CONTRIBUTION BETWEEN, TORTFEASORS

Proceedings against and contribution between, joint and several tortfeasors

6.[3]—(1) Where damage is suffered by any person as a result of a tort (whether a crime or not)—

 (*a*) [3a] judgment recovered against any tort-feasor liable in respect of

---

[2] Part II applied by Crown Proceedings Act 1947 (c. 44), s. 4 (2).

[3] Applied by Law Reform (Contributory Negligence) Act 1945 (c. 28), s. 1 (3), and Public Utilities Street Works Act 1950 (c. 39), s. 19 (4); restricted by Limitation Act 1963 (c. 47), s. 4 (1) (2), and excluded by Carriage of Goods by Road Act 1965 (c. 37), s. 5.

[3a] Excluded by Carriage by Railways Act 1972 (c. 33), s. 6 (2).

that damage shall not be a bar to an action against any other person who would, if sued, have been liable as a joint tortfeasor in respect of the same damage;

(b) if more than one action is brought in respect of that damage by or on behalf of the person by whom it was suffered, or for the benefit of the estate, or of the [dependants] [4] of that person, against tort-feasors liable in respect of the damage (whether as joint tort-feasors or otherwise) the sums recoverable under the judgments given in those actions by way of damages shall not in the aggregate exceed the amount of the damages awarded by the judgment first given; and in any of those actions, other than that in which judgment is first given, the plaintiff shall not be entitled to costs unless the court is of opinion that there was reasonable ground for bringing the action;

(c) any tort-feasor liable in respect of that damage may recover contribution from any other tort-feasor who is, or would if sued have been, liable in respect of the same damage, whether as a joint tort-feasor or otherwise, so, however, that no person shall be entitled to recover contribution under this section from any person entitled to be indemnified by him in respect of the liability in respect of which the contribution is sought.

(2) In any proceedings for contribution under this section the amount of the contribution recoverable from any person shall be such as may be found by the court to be just and equitable having regard to the extent of that person's responsibility for the damage; and the court shall have power to exempt any person from liability to make contribution, or to direct that the contribution to be recovered from any person shall amount to a complete indemnity.

(3) For the purposes of this section—

[(a) the expression " dependants " means the persons for whose benefit actions may be brought under the Fatal Accidents Acts 1846 to 1959; and] [4]

(b) the reference in this section to " the judgment first given " shall, in a case where that judgment is reversed on appeal, be construed as a reference to the judgment first given which is not so reversed and, in a case where a judgment is varied on appeal, be construed as a reference to that judgment as so varied.

(4) Nothing in this section shall—

(a) apply with respect to any tort committed before the commencement of this Part of this Act; or

(b) affect any criminal proceedings against any person in respect of any wrongful act; or

(c) render enforceable any agreement for indemnity which would not have been enforceable if this section had not been passed.

7. [*Repealed by S.L.R.* 1950.]

PART III

SUPPLEMENTARY

Short title, extent and construction of references

8.—(1) This Act may be cited as the Law Reform (Married Women and Tortfeasors) Act 1935.

(2) This Act shall not extend to Scotland or to Northern Ireland.

---

[4] Words substituted by Fatal Accidents Act 1959 (c. 65), s. 1 (4).

(3) Any reference in this Act to any other enactment or to any provision of any other enactment shall, unless the context otherwise requires, be construed as a reference to that enactment, or that provision, as the case may be, as amended by any subsequent enactment including this Act.

SCHEDULES

FIRST SCHEDULE

CONSEQUENTIAL AMENDMENTS EFFECTED BY PART I OF ACT

Enactments to be Amended	Amendment
The Married Women's Property Act 1882	In section seven for the words "her separate estate" there shall be substituted the word "she." In section eleven, for the words "separate use" there shall be substituted the words "own benefit." In section twelve for the words "such property belonged to her as" there shall be substituted the words "she were."
The Larceny Act 1916 - - - -	In subsection (1) of section thirty-six, for the words "such property belonged to her as" there shall be substituted the words "she were."
The Supreme Court of Judicature (Consolidation) Act 1925.	[*Repealed by Matrimonial Causes Act 1950 (c. 25), s. 34, Sched.*]

SECOND SCHEDULE

[*Repealed by S.L.R. 1950.*]

Education Act 1944

(7 & 8 GEO. 6, C. 31)

Compulsory Attendance at Primary and Secondary Schools

Compulsory school age

35.[1] In this Act the expression [" compulsory school age " [2]] means any age between five years and fifteen years, and accordingly a person shall be deemed to be of compulsory school age if he has attained the age of five years and has not attained the age of fifteen years and a person shall be deemed to be over compulsory school age as soon as he has attained the age of fifteen years:

---

[1] Amended Education Act 1962 (c. 12), s. 9 (5)–(7).
[2] Previously explained Education Act 1946 (c. 50), s. 8 (1) (2). See now Education Act 1962 (c. 12), s. 9.

Provided that, as soon as the Minister is satisfied that it has become practicable to raise to sixteen the upper limit of the compulsory school age, he shall lay before Parliament the draft of an Order in Council directing that the foregoing provisions of this section shall have effect as if for references therein to the age of fifteen years there were substituted references to the age of sixteen years; and unless either House of Parliament, within the period of forty days beginning with the day on which any such draft as aforesaid is laid before it, resolves that the draft be not presented to His Majesty, His Majesty may by Order in Council direct accordingly.[2a]

In reckoning any such period of forty days, no account shall be taken of any time during which Parliament is dissolved or prorogued or during which both Houses are adjourned for more than four days.

Duty of parents to secure the education of their children

36.[3] It shall be the duty of the parent of every child of compulsory school age to cause him to receive efficient full-time education suitable to his age, ability, and aptitude, either by regular attendance at school or otherwise.

School attendance orders

37. (1) If it appears to a local education authority that the parent of any child of compulsory school age [4] in their area is failing to perform the duty imposed on him by the last foregoing section, it shall be the duty of the authority to serve upon the parent a notice requiring him, within such time as may be specified in the notice not being less than fourteen days from the service thereof, to satisfy the authority that the child is receiving efficient full-time education suitable to his age,[4] ability, and aptitude either by regular attendance at school or otherwise.

(2) If, after such a notice has been served upon a parent by a local education authority, the parent fails to satisfy the authority in accordance with the requirements of the notice that the child to whom the notice relates is receiving efficient full-time education suitable to his age, ability, and aptitude, then, if in the opinion of the authority it is expedient that he should attend school, the authority shall serve upon the parent an order in the prescribed form (hereinafter referred to as a " school attendance order ") requiring him to cause the child to become a registered pupil at a school named in the order :

[" Provided that—

(*a*) no such order shall be served by the authority upon the parent until the expiration of the period of fourteen days beginning with the day next following that on which they have served upon him a written notice of their intention to serve the order stating that if, before the expiration of that period, he selects a school at which he desires the child to become a registered pupil, that school will, unless the Minister otherwise directs, be named in the order; and

(*b*) if, before the expiration of that period, the parent selects such a school as aforesaid, that school shall, unless the Minister otherwise directs, be so named."] [5]

(3) If the local education authority are of opinion that the school selected by the parent as the school to be named in a school attendance

---

[2a] Such an Order was made on March 22, 1972, and came into force on September 1, 1972 (S.I. 1972/444).
[3] Excluded by Education (Miscellaneous Provisions) Act 1948 (c. 40), s. 4 (2).
[4] As to onus of proof of age, see *ibid.* s. 9.
[5] Added by Education (Miscellaneous Provisions) Act 1953 (c. 33), s. 10.

order is unsuitable to the age, ability or aptitude of the child with respect to whom the order is to be made, or that the attendance of the child at the school so selected would involve unreasonable expense to the authority, the authority may, after giving to the parent notice of their intention to do so, apply to the Minister for a direction determining what school is to be named in the order.

(4) If at any time while a school attendance order is in force with respect to any child the parent of the child makes application to the local education authority by whom the order was made requesting that another school be substituted for that named in the order, or requesting that the order be revoked on the ground that arrangements have been made for the child to receive efficient full-time education suitable to his age, ability, and aptitude otherwise than at school, the authority shall amend or revoke the order in compliance with the request unless they are of opinion that the proposed change of school is unreasonable or inexpedient in the interests of the child, or that no satisfactory arrangements have been made for the education of the child otherwise than at school, as the case may be; and if a parent is aggrieved by a refusal of the authority to comply with any such request, he may refer the question to the Minister, who shall give such direction thereon as he thinks fit.

(5) If any person upon whom a school attendance order is served fails to comply with the requirements of the order, he shall be guilty of an offence against this section unless he proves that he is causing the child to receive efficient full-time education suitable to his age, ability, and aptitude otherwise than at school.

(6) If in proceedings against any person for a failure to comply with a school attendance order that person is acquitted, the court may direct that the school attendance order shall cease to be in force, but without prejudice to the duty of the local education authority to take further action under this section if at any time the authority are of opinion that having regard to any change of circumstances it is expedient so to do.

(7) Save as provided by the last foregoing subsection, a school attendance order made with respect to any child shall, subject to any amendment thereof which may be made by the local education authority, continue in force so long as he is of compulsory school age unless revoked by that authority.

Additional provisions as to compulsory attendance at special schools

38. (1) While the upper limit of the compulsory school age is, in relation to other children, less than sixteen, a person who is a registered pupil at a special school shall nevertheless be deemed to be of compulsory school age until he attains the age of sixteen years and shall not be deemed to be over compulsory school age until he has attained that age.

(2) A child who has under arrangements made by a local education authority become a registered pupil at a special school shall not be withdrawn from the school without the consent of that authority; but if the parent of any such child is aggrieved by a refusal of the authority to comply with an application made by the parent requesting such consent, he may refer the question to the Minister, who shall give such direction thereon as he thinks fit.

(3) No direction given by the Minister under the last foregoing subsection or under subsection (3) or subsection (4) of the last foregoing section shall be such as to require a pupil to be a registered pupil at a special school unless either the parent consents to his attending such a school or there is in force a certificate issued by a medical officer of the

local education authority showing that the child is suffering from some disability of mind or body of such a nature and extent that, in the opinion of the Minister, it is expedient that the child should attend a special school.

Duty of parents to secure regular attendance of registered pupils

39. (1) If any child of compulsory school age [4] who is a registered pupil at a school fails to attend regularly thereat, the parent of the child shall be guilty of an offence against this section.

(2) In any proceedings for an offence against this section in respect of a child who is not a boarder at the school at which he is a registered pupil, the child shall not be deemed to have failed to attend regularly at the school by reason of his absence therefrom with leave or—

(a) at any time when he was prevented from attending by reason of sickness or any unavoidable cause;

(b) on any day exclusively set apart for religious observance by the religious body to which his parent belongs;

(c) if the parent proves that the school at which the child is a registered pupil is not within walking distance of the child's home, and that no suitable arrangements have been made by the local education authority either for his transport to and from the school or for boarding accommodation for him at or near the school or for enabling him to become a registered pupil at a school nearer to his home.

(3) Where in any proceedings for an offence against this section it is proved that the child has no fixed abode, paragraph (c) of the last foregoing subsection shall not apply, but if the parent proves that he is engaged in any trade or business of such a nature as to require him to travel from place to place and that the child has attended at a school at which he was a registered pupil as regularly as the nature of the trade or business of the parent permits, the parent shall be acquitted:

Provided that, in the case of a child who has attained the age of six years, the parent shall not be entitled to be acquitted under this subsection unless he proves that the child has made at least two hundred attendances during the period of twelve months ending with the date on which the proceedings were instituted.

(4) In any proceedings for an offence against this section in respect of a child who is a boarder at the school at which he is a registered pupil, the child shall be deemed to have failed to attend regularly at the school if he is absent therefrom without leave during any part of the school term at a time when he was not prevented from being present by reason of sickness or any unavoidable cause.

(5) In this section the expression " leave " in relation to any school means leave granted by any person authorised in that behalf by the managers, governors or proprietor of the school, and the expression " walking distance " means, in relation to a child who has not attained the age of eight years two miles, and in the case of any other child three miles, measured by the nearest available route.

Enforcement of school attendance

40. (1) Subject to the provisions of this section, any person guilty of an offence against section thirty-seven or section thirty-nine of this Act shall be liable on summary conviction, in the case of a first offence against that section to a fine not exceeding one pound,[6] in the case of a second

---

[6] Maximum fines increased by Criminal Justice Act 1967 (c. 80), s. 92, Sched. 3 Pt. I, to £10 for a first offence against the relevant section and £20 for a second or subsequent offence against that section.

Education Act 1944

offence against that section to a fine not exceeding five pounds,[6] and in the case of a third or subsequent offence against that section to a fine not exceeding ten pounds [6] or to imprisonment for a term not exceeding one month or to both such fine and such imprisonment.

[(2) Proceedings for such offences as aforesaid shall not be instituted except by a local education authority; and before instituting such proceedings the authority shall consider whether it would be appropriate, instead of or as well as instituting the proceedings, to bring the child in question before a juvenile court under section 1 of the Children and Young Persons Act 1969.

(3) The court by which a person is convicted of an offence against section 37 of this Act or before which a person is charged with an offence against section 39 of this Act may if it thinks fit direct the authority who instituted the proceedings to bring the child to whom the proceedings relate before a juvenile court under the said section 1; and it shall be the duty of the authority to comply with the direction.

(4) Where a child in respect of whom a school attendance order is in force is brought before a juvenile court by a local education authority under the said section 1 and the court finds that the condition set out in subsection (2) (e) of that section is not satisfied with respect to him, the court may direct that the order shall cease to be in force.] [7]

40A. [*Repealed by Children and Young Persons Act* 1969 (c. 54), s. 72 (4), Sched. 6.]

National Assistance Act 1948

(11 & 12 GEO. 6, c. 29)

Recovery of Expenses

Liability to maintain wife or husband, and children

42.—(1) For the purposes of this Act—

    (a) a man shall be liable to maintain his wife and his children, and

    (b) a woman shall be liable to maintain her husband and her children.

(2) The reference in paragraph (a) of the last foregoing subsection to a man's children includes a reference to children of whom he has been adjudged to be the putative father, and the reference in paragraph (b) of that subsection to a woman's children includes a reference to her illegitimate children.

(3) In the application of subsection (2) of this section to Scotland, for the reference to children of whom a man has been adjudged to be the putative father there shall be substituted a reference to children his paternity of whom has been admitted or otherwise established.

Recovery of cost of assistance from persons liable for maintenance

43.[1]—(1) Where assistance is given or applied for by reference to the requirements of any person (in this section referred to as a person assisted), [. . .] [2] the local authority concerned may make a complaint

---

[7] Substituted by Children and Young Persons Act 1969 (c. 54), s. 72 (3), Sched. 5, para. 13.
[1] Extended by Maintenance Orders Act 1950 (c. 37), ss. 4, 9, *post*, and Ministry of Social Security Act 1966 (c. 20), s. 25 (1).
[2] Words repealed by Ministry of Social Security Act 1966 (c. 20), s. 39 (3), Sched. 8.

to the court against any other person who for the purposes of this Act is liable to maintain the person assisted.

(2) On a complaint under this section the court shall have regard to all the circumstances and in particular to the resources of the defendant, and may order the defendant to pay such sum, weekly or otherwise, as the court may consider appropriate.

(3) For the purposes of the application of the last foregoing subsection to payments in respect of assistance given before the complaint was made, a person shall not be treated as having at the time when the complaint is heard any greater resources than he had at the time when the assistance was given.

(4) In this section the expression " assistance " means [. . .] [2] the provision of accommodation under Part III of this Act (hereinafter referred to as " assistance under Part III of this Act "); and the expression " the court " means a court of summary jurisdiction having jurisdiction in the place where the assistance was given or applied for.

(5) Payments under subsection (2) of this section shall be made—

(a) to [. . .] [2] the local authority concerned, in respect of the cost of assistance, whether given before or after the making of the order, or

(b) to the applicant for assistance or any other person being a person assisted, or

(c) to such other person as appears to the court expedient in the interests of the person assisted,

or as to part in one such manner and as to part in another, as may be provided by the order.

[*Subsection (6) repealed by Ministry of Social Security Act 1966 (c. 20), s. 39 (3), Sched. 8.*]

Affiliation orders

44.[3]—(1) The following provisions of this section shall have effect where—

[*Paragraph (a) repealed by Ministry of Social Security Act 1966 (c. 20), s. 39 (3), Sched. 8.*]

(b) accommodation is provided for an illegitimate child by, or by arrangement with, a local authority under Part III of this Act,

and the provisions of the last foregoing section shall not apply in relation to the father of the child.

(2) If no affiliation order is in force, the [. . .] [4] local authority may within three years from the time when the [. . .] [4] accommodation was provided make application to a court of summary jurisdiction having jurisdiction in the place where the mother of the child resides for a summons to be served under section three of the Bastardy Laws Amendment Act 1872.

(3) In any proceedings on an application under the last foregoing subsection the court shall hear such evidence as the [. . .] [4] local authority may produce [. . .] [5] and shall in all other respects, but subject to the provisions of the next following subsection, proceed as on an application made by the mother under the said section three.

(4) An order under section four of the said Act of 1872 made on an application under subsection (2) of this section may be made so as to provide that the payments, or a part of the payments, to be made thereunder shall, in lieu of being made to the mother or a person

---

[3] Extended by Maintenance Orders Act 1950 (c. 37), ss. 3 (1) (3), 8, and saved by Affiliation Proceedings Act 1957 (c. 55), s. 5 (1) (2) (c).

[4] Words repealed by Ministry of Social Security Act 1966 (c. 20), s. 39 (3), Sched. 8.

[5] Words repealed by Affiliation Proceedings (Amendment) Act 1972 (c. 49), s. 1 (4) (a).

appointed to have the custody of the child, be made to the [. . .] [4] local authority or to such other person as the court may direct.

(5) On an application by the [. . .] [4] local authority in any proceedings under the said section three brought by the mother of the child an order under the said section four may be made so as to provide as aforesaid.

(6) Any order under the said section four, whether made before or after the commencement of this Act, may on the application of the [. . .] [4] local authority be varied so as to provide as aforesaid; and any order under the said section four which provides as aforesaid may on the application of the mother of the child be varied so as to provide that the payments thereunder shall be made to the mother or a person appointed to have the custody of the child.

(7) In the application of this section to Scotland, subsection (1) shall have effect as if all the words after " Part III of this Act " were omitted and the following provisions shall have effect in substitution for the five last foregoing subsections:

(a) [. . .] [4] Board or the local authority shall have the like right as the mother to raise an action of affiliation and aliment concluding for payment of aliment for the child;

(b) where in any action of affiliation and aliment in respect of the child, whether at the instance of [. . .] [4] Board or the local authority under the last foregoing paragraph or at the instance of the mother, the court grants or has granted decree against any person for payment of aliment for the child, the court may, at the time of granting the decree or at any subsequent time, on the application of the Board or the local authority, order that the sums due under the decree or any part thereof shall in lieu of being paid to the mother of the child be paid to the Board or the local authority or such other person as the court may direct;

(c) the Board, or local authority or other person in whose favour any such order as aforesaid is made shall have the like right to enforce the decree (so far as relating to the said sums) by diligence, including the right to take proceedings under the Civil Imprisonment (Scotland) Act 1882, as if the decree were a decree in favour of the Board or authority or person.

[*Subsection* (8) *repealed by Ministry of Social Security Act* 1966 (*c.* 20), *s.* 39 (3), *Sched.* 8.]

[*Subsection* (9) *repealed by Justices of the Peace Act* 1949 (*c.* 101), *s.* 46 (2), *Sched.* 7 *Pt. II.*]

Failure to maintain

51.—(1) Where a person persistently refuses or neglects to maintain himself or any person whom he is liable to maintain for the purposes of this Act, and in consequence of his refusal or neglect [. . .] [4] accommodation under Part III thereof is provided for, himself or any other person, he shall be guilty of an offence.

(2) For the purposes of this section, a person shall not be deemed to refuse or neglect to maintain himself or any other person by reason only of anything done or omitted in furtherance of a trade dispute.

(3) A person guilty of an offence under this section shall be liable on summary conviction—

(a) where [. . .] [4] the accommodation was provided for him, to imprisonment for a term not exceeding three months;

(b) in any other case, to a fine not exceeding fifty pounds or to imprisonment for a term not exceeding three months or to both such imprisonment and such fine.

Children Act 1948 [1]

(11 & 12 GEO. 6, C. 43)

An Act to make further provision for the care or welfare, up to the age of eighteen and, in certain cases, for further periods, of boys and girls when they are without parents or have been lost or abandoned by, or are living away from, their parents, or when their parents are unfit or unable to take care of them, and in certain other circumstances; to amend the Children and Young Persons Act 1933, the Children and Young Persons (Scotland) Act 1937, the Guardianship of Infants Act 1925 and certain other enactments relating to children; and for purposes connected with the matters aforesaid. [30th June 1948.]

PART I

DUTY OF LOCAL AUTHORITIES TO ASSUME CARE OF CHILDREN

Duty of local authority to provide for orphans, deserted children, etc.

1.[2]—(1) Where it appears to a local authority with respect to a child in their area appearing to them to be under the age of seventeen—

(a) that he has neither parent nor guardian or has been and remains abandoned by his parents or guardian or is lost; or

(b) that his parents or guardian are, for the time being or permanently, prevented by reason of mental or bodily disease or infirmity or other incapacity or any other circumstances from providing for his proper accommodation, maintenance and upbringing; and

(c) in either case, that the intervention of the local authority under this section is necessary in the interests of the welfare of the child,

it shall be the duty of the local authority to receive the child into their care under this section.

(2) Where a local authority have received a child into their care under this section, it shall, subject to the provisions of this Part of this Act, be their duty to keep the child in their care so long as the welfare of the child appears to them to require it and the child has not attained the age of eighteen.

(3) Nothing in this section shall authorise a local authority to keep a child in their care under this section if any parent or guardian desires to take over the care of the child, and the local authority shall, in all cases where it appears to them consistent with the welfare of the child so to do, endeavour to secure that the care of the child is taken over either—

(a) by a parent or guardian of his, or

(b) by a relative or friend of his, being, where possible, a person of the same religious persuasion as the child or who gives an undertaking that the child will be brought up in that religious persuasion.

---

[1] Explained, as regards London, by the London Government Act 1963 (c. 33), s. 47 (1) (3).

[2] Extended by Children Act 1958 (c. 65), s. 7 (4) and Adoption Act 1958 (c. 5), s. 43 (3); explained by Mental Health Act 1959 (c. 72), s. 9 (3). See now Children Act 1975 (c. 72), ss. 56, 95. *post*.

(4) Where a local authority receive a child into their care under this section who is then ordinarily resident in the area of another local authority,—

(a) that other local authority may at any time not later than three months after the determination (whether by agreement between the authorities or in accordance with the following provisions of this subsection) of the ordinary residence of the child, or with the concurrence of the first-mentioned authority at any subsequent time, take over the care of the child; and

(b) the first-mentioned authority may recover from the other authority any expenses duly incurred by them under Part II of this Act in respect of him (including any expenses so incurred after he has ceased to be a child and, if the other authority take over the care of him, including also any travelling or other expenses incurred in connection with the taking-over).

Any question arising under this subsection as to the ordinary residence of a child shall be determined by the Secretary of State.

(5) In determining for the purposes of the last foregoing subsection the ordinary residence of any child, any period during which he resided in any place as an inmate of a school or other institution, or in accordance with the requirements of a supervision order or probation order or the conditions of a recognisance, or while boarded out under this Act, the Poor Law Act 1930, the Children and Young Persons Act 1933, the Poor Law (Scotland) Act 1934, or the Children and Young Persons (Scotland) Act 1937, by a local authority or education authority shall be disregarded.

Assumption by local authority of parental rights

2.[3]—(1) Subject to the provisions of this Part of this Act, a local authority may resolve with respect to any child in their care under the foregoing section in whose case it appears to them—

(a) that his parents are dead and that he has no guardian; or

(b) that a parent or guardian of his (hereinafter referred to as the person on whose account the resolution was passed) has abandoned him or suffers from some permanent disability rendering the said person incapable of caring for the child, or is of such habits or mode of life as to be unfit to have the care of the child,

that all the rights and powers which the deceased parents would have if they were still living, or, as the case may be, all the rights and powers of the person on whose account the resolution was passed, shall vest in the local authority.

(2) In the case of a resolution passed by virtue of paragraph (b) of the last foregoing subsection, unless the person on whose account the resolution was passed has consented in writing to the passing of the resolution, the local authority, if the whereabouts of the said person are known to them, shall forthwith after the passing of the resolution serve on him notice in writing of the passing thereof; and if, not later than one month after such a notice is served on him, the person on whose account the resolution was passed serves a notice in writing on the local authority objecting to the resolution, the resolution shall, subject to the provisions of subsection (3) of this section, lapse on the expiration of fourteen days from the service of the notice of objection.

Every notice served by a local authority under this subsection shall

---

[3] Amended, modified and explained by Children and Young Persons Act 1963 (c. 37), ss. 48 (1) (2), 50, *post*. Modified also by Guardianship of Minors Act 1971 (c. 3), s. 5 (2). See now new s. 2 to be substituted by Children Act 1975 (c. 72), s. 57, *post*.

inform the person on whom the notice is served of his right to object to the resolution and of the effect of any objection made by him.

(3) Where a notice has been served on a local authority under subsection (2) of this section, the authority may not later than fourteen days from the receipt by them of the notice complain to a juvenile court, or in Scotland the sheriff, having jurisdiction in the area of the authority, and in that event the resolution shall not lapse by reason of the service of the notice until the determination of the complaint, and the court or sheriff may, on the hearing of the complaint, order that the resolution shall not lapse by reason of the service of the notice:

Provided that the court or sheriff shall not so order unless satisfied that the child had been, and at the time when the resolution was passed remained, abandoned by the person who made the objection or that that person is unfit to have the care of the child by reason of [mental disorder within the meaning of the Mental Health Act 1959] [4] or by reason of his habits or mode of life.

(4) Any notice under this section may be served by post, so however that a notice served by a local authority under subsection (2) of this section shall not be duly served by post unless it is sent in a registered letter.

Effect of assumption by local authority of parental rights

3.[4a]—(1) While a resolution passed by virtue of paragraph (*a*) of subsection (1) of section two of this Act is in force with respect to a child, all rights and powers which the deceased parents would have if they were still living shall, in respect of the child, be vested in the local authority in accordance with the resolution.

(2) While a resolution passed by virtue of paragraph (*b*) of the said subsection (1) is in force with respect to a child, all rights and powers of the person on whose account the resolution was passed shall, in respect of the child, be vested in the local authority in accordance with the resolution, and subsection (3) of section one of this Act shall not in respect of the child apply in relation to the person on whose account the resolution was passed.

[*Subsections (3)–(5) repealed by Children and Young Persons Act* 1969 (*c.* 54), *s.* 72 (4), *Sched.* 6.]

(6) A resolution under the said section two shall not relieve any person from any liability to maintain, or contribute to the maintenance of, the child.

(7) A resolution under the said section two shall not authorise a local authority to cause a child to be brought up in any religious creed other than that in which he would have been brought up but for the resolution.

[(8) Any person who—
  (*a*) knowingly assists or induces or persistently attempts to induce a child to whom this subsection applies to run away, or
  (*b*) without lawful authority takes away such a child, or
  (*c*) knowingly harbours or conceals such a child who has run away or who has been taken away or prevents him from returning,
shall be liable on summary conviction to a fine not exceeding [£400] [4b] or to imprisonment for a term not exceeding [three months] [4b] or to both.

This subsection applies to any child in the care of a local authority under section 1 of this Act with respect to whom a resolution is in force

---

[4] Words substituted by Mental Health Act 1959 (c. 72), s. 149 (1), Sched. 7, Pt. I.
[4a] See Children Act 1975 (c. 72), ss. 95–96, *post.*
[4b] Substituted by Children Act, 1975 (c. 72), Sched. 3.

under section 2 thereof and for whom accommodation (whether in a home or otherwise) is being provided by the local authority in pursuance of Part II of this Act; and references in this subsection to running away or taking away or to returning are references to running away or taking away from, or to returning to, a place where accommodation is or was being so provided.] [5]

Duration and rescission of resolutions under section two

4.[5a]—(1) Subject to the provisions of this Part of this Act, a resolution under section two of this Act shall continue in force until the child with respect to whom it was passed attains the age of eighteen.

(2) A resolution under the said section two may be rescinded by resolution of the local authority if it appears to them that the rescinding of the resolution will be for the benefit of the child.

(3) On complaint being made—

    (*a*) in the case of a resolution passed by virtue of paragraph (*a*) of subsection (1) of the said section two, by a person claiming to be a parent or guardian of the child;

    (*b*) in the case of a resolution passed by virtue of paragraph (*b*) thereof, by the person on whose account the resolution was passed,

a juvenile court, or in Scotland the sheriff, having jurisdiction where the complainant resides, if satisfied that there was no ground for the making of the resolution or that the resolution should in the interests of the child be determined, may by order determine the resolution, and the resolution shall thereupon cease to have effect:

[*Proviso repealed by Children and Young Persons Act* 1969 (*c.* 54), *s.* 72 (3) (4), *Sched.* 5, *para.* 14, *Sched.* 6,]

5. [*Repealed by Children and Young Persons Act* 1969 (*c.* 54), *s.* 72 (4), *Sched.* 6.*]

Application of preceding provisions to children already subject, or becoming subject, to orders of court

6.—(1) The reception of a child into their care by a local authority under section one of this Act, and the passing of a resolution with respect to him under section two of this Act, shall not affect any supervision order or probation order previously made with respect to him by any court.

(2) Where an order of any court is in force giving the custody of a child to any person, the foregoing provisions of this Part of this Act shall have effect in relation to the child as if for references to the parents or guardian of the child or to a parent or guardian of his there were substituted references to that person.

[*Subsections* (3) (4) *repealed by Children and Young Persons Act* 1969 (*c.* 54), *s.* 72 (4), *Sched.* 6.]

7. [*Repealed by Children and Young Persons Act* 1969 (*c.* 54), *s.* 72 (4), *Sched.* 6.]

8.[*Repealed by Mental Health Act* 1959 (*c.* 72), *s.* 149 (2), *Sched.* 8, *Pt. II.*]

---

[5] Subsection added by Children and Young Persons Act 1963 (c. 37), ss. 49, 64 (1), Sched. 2, para. 38.

[5a] New ss. 4A and 4B are to be added in by Children Act 1975 (c. 72), s. 58, Sched. 3, para. 5, *post.*

Meaning of " parents or guardian "

9. Save as expressly provided in section six of this Act, any reference in this Part of this Act to the parents or guardian of a child shall be construed as a reference to all the persons who are parents of the child or who are guardians of the child.

Duty of parents to maintain contact with local authorities having their children in care

10.—(1) The parent of a child who [. . .] [6] is in the care of a local authority under section one of this Act shall secure that the appropriate local authority are informed of the parent's address for the time being.

(2) Where under subsection (4) of section one of this Act a local authority take over the care of a child from another local authority, that other authority shall where possible inform the parent of the child that the care of the child has been so taken over.

(3) For the purposes of subsection (1) of this section, the appropriate local authority shall be the authority in whose care the child is for the time being:

Provided that where under subsection (4) of section one of this Act a local authority have taken over the care of a child from another authority, then unless and until a parent is informed that the care of a child has been so taken over the appropriate local authority shall in relation to that parent continue to be the authority from whom the care of the child was taken over.

(4) Any parent who knowingly fails to comply with subsection (1) of this section shall be liable on summary conviction to a fine not exceeding [ten pounds] [7]:

Provided that it shall be a defence in any proceedings under this subsection to prove that the defendant was residing at the same address as the other parent of the child, and had reasonable cause to believe that the other parent had informed the appropriate authority that both parents were residing at that address.

PART II [8]

TREATMENT OF CHILDREN IN CARE OF LOCAL AUTHORITIES

Children to whom Part II applies

11. Except where the contrary intention appears, any reference in this Part of this Act to a child who is or was in the care of a local authority is a reference to a child who is or was in the care of the authority under section 1 of this Act or by virtue of a care order within the meaning of the Children and Young Persons Act 1969 or a warrant under section 23 (1) of that Act (which relates to remands in the care of local authorities).] [9]

General duty of local authority

12. [(1) In reaching any decision relating to a child in their care, a local authority shall give first consideration to the need to safeguard and

---

[6] Words repealed by Children and Young Persons Act 1963 (c. 37), s. 64 (3), Sched. 5.
[7] Maximum fine increased from five pounds by Criminal Justice Act 1967 (c. 80), ss. 92, 106 (2), Sched. 3, Pt. I.
[8] Applied by Matrimonial Proceedings (Magistrates' Courts) Act 1960 (c. 48), s. 3 (2), *post*; Matrimonial Causes Act 1965 (c. 72), s. 36 (1) (5), *post*; extended by Family Law Reform Act 1969 (c. 46), s. 7 (2) (3), *post*.
[9] Substituted, and excluded as substituted, by Children and Young Persons Act 1969 (c. 54), s. 27 (1).

promote the welfare of the child throughout his childhood; and shall so far as practicable ascertain the wishes and feelings of the child regarding the decision and give due consideration to them, having regard to his age and understanding.

(1A) If it appears to the local authority that it is necessary, for the purpose of protecting members of the public, to exercise their powers in relation to a particular child in their care in a manner which may not be consistent with their duty under the foregoing subsection, the authority may, notwithstanding that duty, act in that manner.] [10]

(2) In providing for a child in their care, a local authority shall make such use of facilities and services available for children in the care of their own parents as appears to the local authority reasonable in his case.

Provision of accommodation and maintenance for children in care

[13.—(1) A local authority shall discharge their duty to provide accommodation and maintenance for a child in their care in such one of the following ways as they think fit, namely,—

(a) by boarding him out on such terms as to payment by the authority and otherwise as the authority may, subject to the provisions of this Act and regulations thereunder, determine; or

(b) by maintaining him in a community home or in any such home as is referred to in section 64 of the Children and Young Persons Act 1969; or

(c) by maintaining him in a voluntary home (other than a community home) the managers of which are willing to receive him;

or by making such other arrangements as seem appropriate to the local authority.

(2) [11] Without prejudice to the generality of subsection (1) of this section, a local authority may allow a child in their care, either for a fixed period or until the local authority otherwise determine, to be under the charge and control of a parent, guardian, relative or friend.

(3) The terms, as to payment and other matters, on which a child may be accommodated and maintained in any such home as is referred to in section 64 of that Act shall be such as the Secretary of State may from time to time determine.] [12]

Regulations as to boarding-out

14.—(1) The Secretary of State may by regulations make provision for the welfare of children boarded out by local authorities under paragraph (a) of subsection (1) of the last foregoing section.

(2) Without prejudice to the generality of the last foregoing subsection, regulations under this section may provide—

(a) for the recording by local authorities of information relating to persons with whom children are boarded out as aforesaid and persons who are willing to have children so boarded out with them;

(b) for securing that children shall not be boarded out in any household unless that household is for the time being approved by such local authority as may be prescribed by the regulations;

(c) for securing that where possible the person with whom any child is to be boarded out is either of the same religious persuasion as the child or gives an undertaking that the child will be brought up in that religious persuasion;

[10] Substituted by Children Act 1975 (c. 72), s. 59.
[11] Extended and modified by *ibid.* ss. 22 (4), 26 (3), *post.*
[12] Substituted by Children and Young Persons Act 1969 (c. 54), s. 49.

(d) for securing that children boarded out as aforesaid, and the premises in which they are boarded out, will be supervised and inspected by a local authority and that the children will be removed from those premises if their welfare appears to require it.

15, 16. [*Repealed by Children and Young Persons Act* 1969 (*c.* 54), *s.* 72 (4), *Sched.* 6.]

Power of local authorities to arrange for emigration of children

17.—(1) A local authority may, with the consent of the Secretary of State, procure or assist in procuring the emigration of any child in their care.

(2) The Secretary of State shall not give his consent under this section unless he is satisfied that emigration would benefit the child, and that suitable arangements have been or will be made for the child's reception and welfare in the country to which he is going, that the parents or guardian of the child have been consulted or that it is not practicable to consult them, and that the child consents:

Provided that where a child is too young to form or express a proper opinion on the matter, the Secretary of State may consent to his emigration notwithstanding that the child is unable to consent thereto in any case where the child is to emigrate in company with a parent, guardian or relative of his, or is to emigrate for the purpose of joining a parent, guardian, relative or friend.

(3) In the last foregoing subsection the expression " parents or guardian " shall be construed in accordance with the provisions of section nine of this Act.

Burial or cremation of deceased children

18.[13]—(1) A local authority may cause to be buried or cremated the body of any deceased child who immediately before his death was in the care of the authority:

Provided that the authority shall not cause the body to be cremated where cremation is not in accordance with the practice of the child's religious persuasion.

(2) Where a local authority exercise the powers referred to in subsection (1) of this section, they may if at the time of his death the child had not attained the age of sixteen years recover from any parent of the child any expenses incurred by them under [the said subsection (1), less any amount received by the authority by way of death grant in respect of that death under section 32 of the Social Security Act 1975].

(3) Any sums recoverable by a local authority under subsection (2) of this section shall, without prejudice to any other method for the recovery thereof, be recoverable summarily as a civil debt.

(4) Nothing in this section shall affect any enactment regulating or authorising the burial, cremation or anatomical examination of the body of a deceased person.

Accommodation of persons over school age in convenient community home

[**19.** A local authority may provide accommodation in a community home for any person who is over compulsory school age but has not attained the age of twenty-one if the community home is provided for children who are over compulsory school age and is near the place where

---

13 Amended by National Insurance Act (1957 c. 26), s. 7 (2). The words in square brackets in subs. (2) were substituted by Social Security Act 1973 (c. 38), Sched. 27, and 1975 (c. 18), Sched. 1.

that person is employed or seeking employment or receiving education or training.] [14]

Financial assistance towards expenses of maintenance, education or training of persons over eighteen

20.—(1) A local authority may make contributions to the cost of the accommodation and maintenance of [any person over compulsory school age but under the age of twenty-one who is, or has at any time after ceasing to be of compulsory school age been, in the care of a local authority] [15] being [either a person who has attained the age of seventeen but has ceased to be in the care of a local authority, or] [16] a person who has attained the age of eighteen, in any place near the place where he may be employed, or seeking employment, or in receipt of education or training.

(2) A local authority may make grants to persons who have attained the age of [seventeen] [16] but have not attained the age of twenty-one and who [at or after the time when they attained the age of seventeen] [16] were in the care of a local authority, to enable them to meet expenses connected with their receiving suitable education or training.

(3) Where a person—

(a) is engaged in a course of education or training at the time when he attains the age of twenty-one; or

(b) having previously been engaged in a course of education or training which has been interrupted by any circumstances, resumes the course as soon as practicable,

then if a local authority are at the said time, or were at the time when the course was interrupted, as the case may be, making any contributions or grants in respect of him under any of the foregoing provisions of this section, their powers under those provisions shall continue with respect to him until the completion of the course.

Allocation of functions as between local authority and local education authority

21. The Secretary of State and the Minister of Education, or in Scotland the Secretary of State, may make regulations for providing, where a local authority under this Part of this Act and a local education authority as such have concurrent functions, by which authority the functions are to be exercised, and for determining as respects any functions of a local education authority specified in the regulations whether a child in the care of a local authority is to be treated as a child of parents of sufficient resources or a child of parents without resources.

Power of local authority to defray expenses of parents, etc., visiting children or attending funerals

22. A local authority may make payments to any parent or guardian of, or other person connected with, a child in their care in respect of travelling, subsistence or other expenses incurred by the parent, guardian or other person in visiting the child or attending his funeral, if it appears to the authority that the parent, guardian or other person would not otherwise be able to visit the child or attend the funeral without undue hardship and that the circumstances warrant the making of the payments.

[14] Substituted by Children and Young Persons Act 1969 (c. 54), s. 50.
[15] Words substituted by Children and Young Persons Act 1969 (c. 54), s. 72 (3), Sched. 5, para. 15.
[16] Words substituted by Children and Young Persons Act 1963 (c. 37), s. 46.

PART III [17]

CONTRIBUTIONS TOWARDS MAINTENANCE OF CHILDREN

Contributions in respect of children in care of local authority

23.[18]—(1) Subject to the provisions of this Part of this Act, sections eighty-six to eighty-eight of the Children and Young Persons Act 1933 and sections ninety to ninety-two of the Children and Young Persons (Scotland) Act 1937 [. . .] [19] shall apply to children received into the care of a local authority under section one of this Act as they apply to children [in the care of a local authority by virtue of such an order as is mentioned in subsection (1) of the said section 86].[20]

(2) Subject to the provisions of this Part of this Act, to the provisions of the said Acts of 1933 and 1937 as to appeals and to the provisions of the said Act of 1937 as to revocation or variation; a contribution order in respect of a child in the care of a local authority under section one of this Act shall remain in force so long as he remains in the care of a local authority under the said section one.

[*Subsection (3) repealed by Children and Young Persons Act 1969 (c. 54), s. 72 (4), Sched. 6.*]

Persons liable to make contributions

24.[21]—(1) The persons liable under section eighty-six of the said Act of 1933 or section ninety of the said Act of 1937 to make contributions shall be the persons specified in that behalf in the following provisions of this section, and no others.

(2) The father and the mother of a child shall be liable to make contributions in respect of the child, but only so long as the child has not attained the age of sixteen; and no payments shall be required to be made under a contribution order made on the father or mother of a child in respect of any period after the child has attained that age.

(3) A person who has attained the age of sixteen and is engaged in remunerative full-time work shall be liable to make contributions in respect of himself.

25. [*Repealed by Children and Young Persons Act 1969 (c. 54), s. 72 (4), Sched. 6.*]

Affiliation orders

26.[19]—(1) In England or Wales, where—

    (*a*) an illegitimate child is in the care of a local authority under section one of this Act, or

    [(*b*) an illegitimate child is in the care of a local authority by virtue of such an order as is mentioned in section 86 (1) of the Children and Young Persons Act 1933, or] [20]

    [*Paragraph repealed by Children and Young Persons Act 1969 (c. 54), s. 72 (4), Sched. 6.*]

and no affiliation order has been made in respect of the child, the local authority whose area includes the place where the mother of the child

---

[17] Applied by Matrimonial Proceedings (Magistrates' Courts) Act 1960 (c. 48), s. 3 (2).
[18] Section saved by Affiliation Proceedings Act 1957 (c. 55), s. 5 (2) (*b*).
[19] Words repealed by Children and Young Persons Act 1969 (c. 54), s. 72 (4), Sched. 6.
[20] Words substituted by *ibid.*, s. 72 (3), Sched. 5, para. 16.
[21] Excluded by Children and Young Persons Act 1963 (c. 37), s. 13.
[19] Extended and modified by Maintenance Orders Act 1950 (c. 37), ss. 3 (1) (3), 8, 14, Sched. 1; saved by Affiliation Proceedings Act 1957 (c. 55), s. 5 (1) (2) (*d*).
[20] Substituted by Children and Young Persons Act 1969 (c. 54), s. 72 (3), Sched. 5 para. 17.

resides may make application to a court of summary jurisdiction having jurisdiction in that place for a summons to be served under section three of the Bastardy Laws Amendment Act 1872:

Provided that no application shall be made under this subsection—

(i) in a case falling within paragraph (*a*) of this subsection, after the expiration of three years from the time when the child was received or last received into the care of the local authority or of another local authority from whom the care of the child was taken over by the first-mentioned authority;

(ii) in a case falling within paragraph (*b*) of this subsection, after the expiration of three years from the coming into force of the order mentioned in the said paragraph (*b*) or, as the case may be, the time when the local authority began to maintain the child [. . .].[21]

(2) In any proceedings on an application under the last foregoing subsection the court shall hear such evidence as the local authority may produce [. . .] [21a] and shall in all other respects, but subject to the provisions of the next following subsection, proceed as on an application made by the mother under the said section three.

(3) An order made under section four of the said Act of 1872 on an application under subsection (1) of this section shall provide that the payments to be made under the order shall, in lieu of being made to the mother or a person appointed to have the custody of the child, be made to the [local authority who are] [20] from time to time entitled under section eighty-six of the said Act of 1933 to receive contributions in respect of the child.

(4) Where in accordance with subsection (4) of section eighty-eight of the Children and Young Persons Act 1933 (which limits the duration of affiliation orders) an affiliation order has ceased to be in force, and but for that subsection the order would still be in force, then if the condition specified in paragraph (*a*), [or (*b*)] [20] of subsection (1) of this section is fulfilled, the local authority whose area includes the place where the putative father of the child resides may make application to a court of summary jurisdiction having jurisdiction in that place—

(a) for the affiliation order to be revived, and

(b) for payments thereunder to be made to the [local authority who are] [20] from time to time entitled under section eighty-six of the said Act of 1933 to receive contributions in respect of the child,

and the court may make an order accordingly.

(5) Part IV of the said Act of 1933 shall apply in relation to an order made on an application under subsection (1) of this section or to an affiliation order revived under the last foregoing subsection as if it were an affiliation order in respect of which an order had been made under subsection (1) of section eighty-eight of that Act.

[*Subsection* (6) *repealed by Magistrates Courts Act* 1952 (*c.* 55), *s.* 132, *Sched.* 6.]

[*Subsection* (7) *repealed by Justices of the Peace Act* 1949 (*c.* 101), *s.* 46 (2), *Sched.* 7 *Pt.* II.]

(8) In Scotland, where the condition specified in paragraph (*a*), (*b*) or (*c*) of subsection (1) of this section is fulfilled and no decree for aliment has been granted in respect of the child—

(a) the local authority shall have the like right as the mother to raise an action of affiliation and aliment concluding for payment of aliment for the child;

---

[21] Words repealed by *ibid.* s. 72 (4), Sched. 6.
[21a] Words repealed by Affiliation Proceedings (Amendment) Act 1972 (c. 49), s. 1 (4) (*a*).

(b) where in an action of affiliation and aliment raised under the last foregoing paragraph, the court grants decree against any person for aliment of the child, Part V of the said Act of 1937 shall apply to payments under the decree as if they were payments in respect of which an order had been made under subsection (1) of section ninety-two of that Act;

(c) the local authority or other person in whose favour any such order as aforesaid is made shall have the like right to enforce the decree (so far as relating to the said sums) by diligence, including the right to take proceedings under the Civil Imprisonment (Scotland) Act 1882 as if the decree were a decree in favour of the authority or person.

In this subsection, references to the local authority include, where the context so requires, references to the education authority, and the reference to paragraph (c) of subsection (1) of this section shall be construed accordingly.

PART IV

VOLUNTARY HOMES AND VOLUNTARY ORGANISATIONS

Provisions as to voluntary homes to extend to homes supported wholly or partly by endowments

27. Section ninety-two of the Children and Young Persons Act 1933 and section ninety-six of the Children and Young Persons (Scotland) Act 1937 (which define the expression " voluntary home ") shall have effect as if to the reference therein to a home or other institution supported wholly or partly by voluntary contributions there were added a reference to a home or other institution supported wholly or partly by endowments, not being a school within the meaning of the Education Act 1944 or the Education (Scotland) Act 1946.

Extension of age limits in provisions relating to voluntary homes

28. A person shall not be deemed for the purposes of Part V of the Children and Young Persons Act 1933 or Part VI of the Children and Young Persons (Scotland) Act 1937 to cease to be a young person until he attains the age of eighteen, and accordingly references to young persons in the said Part V or the said Part VI, or any other enactment in so far as it relates to the said Part V or the said Part VI, shall be construed as including references to all persons over the age of fourteen who have not attained the age of eighteen.

Registration of voluntary homes

29.[22]—(1) After the end of the year nineteen hundred and forty-eight no voluntary home shall be carried on unless it is for the time being registered in a register to be kept for the purposes of this section by the Secretary of State.

(2) Application for registration under this section shall be made by the persons carrying on or intending to carry on the home to which the application relates, and shall be made in such manner, and accompanied by such particulars, as the Secretary of State may by regulations prescribe.

(3) On an application duly made under the last foregoing subsection—
[. . .] [23] the Secretary of State may either grant or refuse the applica-

[22] Ss. 29 to 32 excluded by Children and Young Persons Act 1969 (c. 54), s. 44.
[23] Words repealed by S.L.R. 1953.

tion, as he thinks fit, but where he refuses the application he shall give the applicant notice in writing of the refusal.

(4) Where at any time after the end of the year nineteen hundred and forty-eight it appears to the Secretary of State that the conduct of any voluntary home is not in accordance with regulations made or directions given under section thirty-one of this Act or is otherwise unsatisfactory, he may, after giving to the persons carrying on the home not less than twenty-eight days' notice in writing of his proposal so to do, remove the home from the register.

(5) Any person who carries on a voluntary home in contravention of the provisions of subsection (1) of this section shall be guilty of an offence and liable on summary conviction to a fine not exceeding fifty pounds and to a further fine not exceeding two pounds in respect of each day during which the offence continues after conviction.

(6) Where—

(*a*) a voluntary home is carried on in contravention of the provisions of subsection (1) of this section; or

(*b*) notice of a proposal to remove a voluntary home from the register is given under subsection (4) thereof,

the Secretary of State may, notwithstanding that the time for any appeal under the next following section has not expired or that such an appeal is pending, notify the local authority in whose area the home is situated, and require them forthwith to remove from the home and receive into their care under section one of this Act all or any of the children for whom accommodation is being provided in the home; and the local authority shall comply with the requirement whether or not the circumstances of the children are such that they fall within paragraphs (*a*) to (*c*) of subsection (1) of the said section one and notwithstanding that any of the children may appear to the local authority to be over the age of seventeen.

For the purpose of carrying out the duty of the local authority under this subsection, any person authorised in that behalf by the local authority may enter any premises in which the home in question is being carried on.

(7) Where the Secretary of State registers a home under this section or removes a home from the register, he shall notify the local authority in whose area the home is situated.

(8) Any notice under this section required to be given by the Secretary of State to the persons carrying on, or intending to carry on, a voluntary home may be given to those persons by being delivered personally to any one of them, or being sent by post in a registered letter to them or any one of them.

For the purposes of section twenty-six of the Interpretation Act 1889 (which defines " service by post ") a letter enclosing a notice under this section to the persons carrying on a voluntary home or any one of them shall be deemed to be properly addressed if it is addressed to them or him at the home.

(9) Section ninety-five of the Children and Young Persons Act 1933 and section ninety-nine of the Children and Young Persons (Scotland) Act 1937 are hereby repealed as from the first day of January, nineteen hundred and forty-nine.

Appeals

30.—(1) Where under the last foregoing section application for the registration of a voluntary home is refused, or it is proposed to remove a voluntary home from the register, the persons intending to carry on or carrying on the home, as the case may be, may within fourteen days from the giving of the notice under subsection (3) or subsection (4) of that section appeal against the refusal or proposal; and where the appeal is brought against a proposal to remove a home from the register, the home shall not be removed therefrom before the determination of the appeal.

(2) An appeal under this section shall be brought by notice in writing addressed to the Secretary of State requiring him to refer the refusal or proposal to an appeal tribunal constituted in accordance with the provisions of Part I of the First Schedule to this Act.

(3) On an appeal under this section the appeal tribunal may confirm the refusal or proposal of the Secretary of State or may direct that the home shall be registered or, as the case may be, shall not be removed from the register, and the Secretary of State shall comply with the direction.

(4) The Lord Chancellor may with the concurrence of the Lord President of the Council make rules as to the practice and procedure to be followed with respect to the constitution of appeal tribunals for the purposes of this section, as to the manner of making appeals to such tribunals, and as to proceedings before such tribunals and matters incidental to or consequential on such proceedings; and without prejudice to the generality of the foregoing provisions of this subsection such rules may make provision as to the particulars to be supplied by or to the Secretary of State of matters relevant to the determination of the appeal, and as to representation before such tribunals, whether by counsel or solicitor or otherwise.

(5) The Secretary of State may out of moneys provided by Parliament—

    (*a*) pay to members of tribunals constituted for the purposes of this section such fees and allowances as he may with the consent of the Treasury determine,

    (*b*) defray the expenses of such tribunals up to such amount as he may with the like consent determine.

(6) The provisions of the Arbitration Acts 1889 to 1934 shall not apply to any proceedings before a tribunal constituted for the purposes of this section except so far as any provisions thereof may be applied thereto with or without modifications by rules made under this section.

(7) In the application of this section to Scotland, for the reference to Part I of the First Schedule to this Act there shall be substituted a reference to Part II of that Schedule, and for the references to the Lord Chancellor and the Lord President of the Council there shall respectively be substituted references to the Lord President of the Court of Session and to the Secretary of State; and rules made under subsection (4) of this section may make provision for a reference to the Court of Session, by way of stated case, of any question of law arising in such proceedings.

Regulations as to conduct of voluntary homes

31.—(1) The Secretary of State may make regulations as to the conduct of voluntary homes and for securing the welfare of the children therein, and regulations under this section may in particular—

    (*a*) impose requirements as to the accommodation and equipment to be provided in homes, authorise the Secretary of State to give directions prohibiting the provision for the children in any home of clothing of any description specified in the directions, and impose requirements as to the medical arrangements to be made for protecting the health of the children in the homes;

    (*b*) require the furnishing to the Secretary of State of information as to the facilities provided for the parents and guardians of children in the homes to visit and communicate with the children, and authorise the Secretary of State to give directions as to the provision of such facilities;

(c) authorise the Secretary of State to give directions limiting the number of children who may at any one time be accommodated in any particular home;

(d) provide for consultation with the Secretary of State as to applicants for appointment to the charge of a home and empower the Secretary of State to prohibit the appointment of any particular applicant therefor except in the cases (if any) in which the regulations dispense with such consultation by reason that the person to be appointed possesses such qualifications as may be prescribed by the regulations;

(e) require notice to be given to the Secretary of State of any change of the person in charge of a home; and

(f) impose requirements as to the facilities which are to be given for children to receive a religious upbringing appropriate to the persuasion to which they belong,

and may contain different provisions for different descriptions of cases and as respects different descriptions of homes.

(2) Where any regulation under this section provides that this subsection shall have effect in relation thereto, any person who contravenes or fails to comply with the regulation or any requirement or direction thereunder shall be liable on summary conviction to a fine not exceeding fifty pounds.

Provisions where particulars to be sent of voluntary homes are varied

32.—(1) Where the Secretary of State by regulations made under section ninety-three of the Children and Young Persons Act 1933 or section ninety-seven of the Children and Young Persons (Scotland) Act 1937 varies the particulars which are to be sent by persons in charge of voluntary homes—

(a) the person in charge of such a home shall send the prescribed particulars to the Secretary of State within three months from the date of the making of the regulations;

(b) where any such home was established before, but not more than three months before, the making of the regulations, compliance with the last foregoing paragraph shall be sufficient compliance with the requirement of the said section ninety-three or ninety-seven to send the prescribed particulars within three months from the establishment of the home;

(c) in the year in which the particulars are varied, compliance with paragraph (a) of this subsection by the person in charge of any voluntary home shall be sufficient compliance with the requirement of the said section ninety-three or ninety-seven to send the prescribed particulars before the prescribed date in that year.

(2) Any default in complying with the requirements of paragraph (a) of the last foregoing subsection shall be deemed to be such a default as is mentioned in subsection (2) of the said section ninety-three or in subsection (3) of the said section ninety-seven, as the case may be.

Powers of Secretary of State as to voluntary organisations

33.[23a]—(1) The Secretary of State may by regulations control the

23a See now Children Act 1975 (c. 72), s. 56, *post.*

making and carrying out by voluntary organisations of arrangements for the emigration of children.

(2) Any such regulations may contain such consequential and incidental provisions as appear to the Secretary of State to be necessary or expedient, including, in particular, provisions for requiring information to be given to the Secretary of State as to the operations or intended operations of the organisation and for enabling the Secretary of State to be satisfied that suitable arrangements have been or will be made for the children's reception and welfare in the country to which they are going.

(3) The power conferred by Part II of this Act on the Secretary of State to make regulations as to the boarding-out of children by local authorities shall extend also to the boarding-out of children by voluntary organisations:

Provided that in the provisions of the said Part II conferring that power any reference to the supervision and inspection by a local authority of boarded-out children and the premises in which they are boarded out shall, in relation to children boarded out by voluntary organisations, be deemed to be a reference to supervision and inspection either by a local authority or, where it is so provided by or under the regulations, by a voluntary organisation.

(4) Where any regulation under this section provides that this subsection shall have effect in relation thereto, any person who contravenes or fails to comply with the regulation shall be liable on summary conviction to a fine not exceeding fifty pounds.

After-care of children formerly in care of local authorities or voluntary organisations

34.—(1) Where it comes to the knowledge of a local authority that there is in their area any child over compulsory school age who at the time when he ceased to be of that age or at any subsequent time was, but is no longer,—

(a) in the care of a local authority under section one of this Act, or

(b) in the care of a voluntary organisation,

then, unless the authority are satisfied that the welfare of the child does not require it, they shall be under a duty so long as he has not attained the age of eighteen to advise and befriend him:

Provided that where in a case falling within paragraph (b) of this subsection the local authority are satisfied that the voluntary organisation have the necessary facilities for advising and befriending him, the local authority may make arrangements whereby, while the arrangements continue in force, he shall be advised and befriended by the voluntary organisation instead of by the local authority.

(2) Where a child over compulsory school age—

(a) ceases to be in the care of a local authority under section one of this Act and proposes to reside in the area of another local authority, or

(b) ceases to be in the care of a voluntary organisation, the authority or organisation shall inform the local authority for the area in which the child proposes to reside.

(3) Where it comes to the knowledge of a local authority or a voluntary organisation that a child whom they have been advising and befriending in pursuance of this section proposes to transfer or has transferred his residence to the area of another local authority, the first-mentioned local authority or, as the case may be, the voluntary organisation, shall inform the said other local authority.

PART V

35-37. [*Repealed by Children Act 1958 (c. 65), s. 40 (2), Sched. 3.*]

PART VI

ADMINISTRATIVE AND FINANCIAL PROVISIONS

Local authorities

38.—(1) In England and Wales, the local authorities for the purposes of this Act and of Parts III [. . .] [24] IV of the Children and Young Persons Act 1933 [and of Part I of the Children Act 1958 [and of Parts I and III of the Children and Young Persons Act 1963] [25] shall be the councils of counties [24] [other than metropolitan counties, of metropolitan districts and London boroughs and the Common Council of the City of London].[26-31]

(2) In Scotland, the local authorities for the purposes of this Act shall be the councils of counties and large burghs.

Children's committee

39-42. [*Repealed by Local Authority Social Services Act 1970 (c. 42), s. 14 (2), Sched. 3, except in relation to Scotland.*]

Advisory Council on Child Care

43.—(1) There shall be a council, to be known as the Advisory Council on Child Care, for the purpose of advising the Secretary of State on matters connected with the discharge of his functions in England and Wales under this Act, [the Children and Young Persons Act 1933 to 1969, the Adoption Act 1958] [32] [The Adoption Act 1968 and the Children Act 1975].[32a]

(2) The said council shall consist of such persons, to be appointed by the Secretary of State, as the Secretary of State may think fit, being persons specially qualified to deal with matters affecting the welfare of children and persons having such other qualifications as the Secretary of State considers requisite.

Among the persons appointed under this subsection there shall be persons having experience in local government.

(3) The Secretary of State shall appoint a person to be chairman, and a person to be the secretary, of the said council.

(4) It shall be the duty of the said council to advise the Secretary of State on any matter which the Secretary of State may refer to them, being such a matter as is mentioned in subsection (1) of this section, and they may also, of their own motion, make representations to the Secretary of State as respects any such matter as is mentioned in that subsection.

(5) The Secretary of State may make out of moneys provided by Parliament such payments to the members of the said council in respect of travelling, subsistence and other expenses as he may with the consent of the Treasury determine.

[24] Repealed and substituted by Children Act 1958 (c. 65), s. 40 (1), Sched. 2; amended by Children and Young Persons Act 1969 (c. 54), s. 63.
[25] Words added by Children and Young Persons Act 1963 (c. 37), s. 64 (1), Sched. 3, para. 40.
[26-31] Words substituted by Local Government Act 1972 (c. 70), s. 195 (6), Sched. 23, para. 3.
[32] Words repealed and added by Children and Young Persons Act 1969 (c. 54), s. 72 (3), Sched. 5 para. 19.
[32a] Added by Children Act 1975 (c. 72), Sched. 3, para. 6.

Advisory Council on Child Care for Scotland

44.—(1) There shall be a separate Advisory Council on Child Care for Scotland, for the purpose of advising the Secretary of State on matters connected with the discharge of his functions under this Act, Parts [. . .] [33] V and VI of the Children and Young Persons (Scotland) Act 1937, [. . .] [33] [section 1 of the Children and Young Persons Act 1963] [34] [or any of the enactments specified in paragraphs (*b*) and (*c*) of subsection (1) of section thirty-nine of this Act, except subsection (3) of section thirty-two of the Adoption Act 1958] [33] and the provisions of subsections (2) to (4) of the last foregoing section shall apply accordingly.

(2) The Secretary of State may require the Advisory Council to appoint, and the council with the approval of the Secretary of State shall have power to appoint, committees to deal with any matter mentioned in the last foregoing subsection.

(3) Any committee appointed under the last foregoing subsection shall include such persons as may be nominated by the Secretary of State, being persons, other than members of the council, having special knowledge or experience of the subject with which the committee is required to deal.

(4) A report of any such committee shall be submitted to the Secretary of State by the council, who may make such comments thereon as they think fit.

(5) The Secretary of State may make out of moneys provided by Parliament such payments to the members of the said council and to the members of any committees appointed under the provisions of this section, in respect of travelling, subsistence and other expenses as he may with the consent of the Treasury determine.

Grants for training in child care

45.—(1) The Secretary of State with the consent of the Treasury may out of moneys provided by Parliament defray or contribute towards any fees or expenses incurred by persons undergoing training approved by the Secretary of State with a view to, or in the course of, their employment for the purposes of any of the enactments specified in [subsection (1A) of this section], [34a] or their employment by a voluntary organisation for similar purposes, and may defray or contribute towards the cost of maintenance of persons undergoing such training.

[(1A) The enactments referred to in subsection (1) of this section are—

(*a*) Parts III and IV of the Children and Young Persons Act 1933;

(*b*) this Act;

(*c*) the Children Act 1958;

(*d*) the Adoption Act 1958;

(*e*) section 2 (1) (*f*) of the Matrimonial Proceedings (Magistrates' Courts) Act 1960, section 37 of the Matrimonial Causes Act 1965 and section 7 (4) of the Family Law Reform Act 1969;

(*f*) the Children and Young Persons Act 1963, except Part II and section 56; and

(*g*) the Children and Young Persons Act 1969.] [34a]

(2) The Secretary of State may out of moneys provided by Parliament make grants of such amounts, and subject to such conditions, as he may with the consent of the Treasury determine towards expenses incurred

---

[33] Words repealed and added by Adoption Act 1958 (c. 5), s. 58 (1), Sched. 4.

[34] Words added by Children and Young Persons Act 1963 (c. 37), s. 64 (1), Sched. 3 para. 43.

[34a] Words substituted by Local Authority Social Services Act 1970 (c. 42), s. 14 (1), Sched 2, para. 5.

by any body of persons in providing courses suitable for persons undergoing training as aforesaid.

Grants to voluntary organisations

46.[35]—(1) The Secretary of State may make out of moneys provided by Parliament grants of such amounts, and subject to such conditions, as he may with the consent of the Treasury determine towards expenses incurred or to be incurred by voluntary organisations, in circumstances such that it appears to the Secretary of State requisite that the grants should be made, for improving premises in which voluntary homes are being carried on or the equipment of voluntary homes, or for securing that voluntary homes will be better provided with qualified staff.

(2) A local authority may [. . .][36] make contributions to any voluntary organisation the object or primary object of which is to promote the welfare of children.

47. [*Repealed by Local Government Act* 1958 (*c.* 55), *s.* 67, *Sched.* 9 Pt. II.]

Administrative expenses of Secretary of State

48. The administrative expenses incurred by the Secretary of State under this Act shall be defrayed out of moneys provided by Parliament.

49. [*Repealed by Local Government Act* 1972 (*c.* 70), *s.* 272 (1), *Sched.* 30.]

PART VII

MISCELLANEOUS AND GENERAL

50. [*Repealed by Guardianship of Minors Act* 1971 (*c.* 3), *s.* 18 (2), *Sched.* 2, *in relation to England and Wales.*]

Provisions as to places of safety

51.—(1) Local authorities shall make provision, in [community homes provided by them or in controlled community homes] [37-39] for the reception and maintenance of children removed to a place of safety under the Children and Young Persons Act 1933, the Children and Young Persons (Scotland) Act 1937, [Part I of the Children Act 1958, or Part IV of the Adoption Act 1958] [40] [or sections 2 (5), 16 (3) or 28 of the Children and Young Persons Act 1969 and of children detained by them in pursuance of arrangements under section 29 (3) of that Act].[37-39]

[*Subsection* (2) *repealed by Children and Young Persons Act* 1969 (*c.* 54), *s.* 72 (4), *Sched.* 6.]

(3)[41] Where under any of the enactments mentioned in subsection (1) of this section a child is removed to a place of safety not being a [community home provided by a local authority or a controlled community home][39] and not being a hospital vested in the Minister of Health or the Secretary of State, the expenses of the child's maintenance there shall be recoverable from the local authority within whose area the child was immediately before his removal.

---

[35] Restricted by Children and Young Persons Act 1969 (c. 54), s. 65 (2), *post.*
[36] Words repealed by Local Government Act 1958 (c. 55), s. 67, Sched. 9 Pt. II.
[37-39] Words substituted and added by Children and Young Persons Act 1969 (c. 54), s. 72 (3), Sched. 5, para. 20.
[40] Words substituted by Adoption Act 1958 (c. 5), s. 58 (1), Sched. 4.
[41] Explained by Children and Young Persons Act 1963 (c. 37), s. 59 (2), *post.*

52. [*Subsection* (1) *repealed by S.L.R.* 1965.]

(2) Subsection (1) of this section shall have effect both as respects England and Wales and as respects Scotland.

(3) For the avoidance of doubt it is hereby declared that references in the said section eleven to an order or resolution made or passed under any enactment include references to an order or resolution which by virtue of any other provision is deemed to be made or passed under the said enactment.

53. [*Repealed by Guardianship of Minors Act* 1971 (*c.* 3), *s.* 18 (2), *Sched.* 2, *in relation to England and Wales.*]

Provisions as to entry and inspection

54. [*Subsections* (1) *and* (2) *repealed by Children and Young Persons Act* 1969 (*c.* 54), *s.* 72 (4), *Sched.* 6.]

(3) It shall be the duty of local authorities from time to time to cause children in voluntary homes in their area [other than community homes] [42] to be visited in the interests of the wellbeing of the children, and any person authorised in that behalf by a local authority may enter any [such] [42] voluntary home in the area of the authority for the purpose of visiting the children in the home.

(4) Any person authorised in that behalf by a local authority may enter any voluntary home outside the area of the authority for the purpose of visiting children in the home who are in the care of the authority under section one of this Act or are for the time being committed to the care of the authority [by a care order within the meaning of the Children and Young Persons Act 1969 or by a warrant under section 23 (1) of that Act].[42]

(5) Nothing in the two last foregoing subsections shall apply to a voluntary home which, otherwise than by virtue of [section 58 of the Children and Young Persons Act 1969] [42] or section ninety-eight of the said Act of 1937, is as a whole subject to inspection by, or under the authority of, a Government department.

(6) A person who proposes to exercise any power of entry or inspection conferred by this Act shall if so required produce some duly authenticated document showing his authority to exercise the power.

(7) Any person who obstructs the exercise of any such power as aforesaid shall be guilty of an offence and liable on summary conviction to a fine not exceeding five pounds in the case of a first offence or twenty pounds in the case of a second or any subsequent offence.

Prosecution of offences

55.—(1) In England and Wales, a local authority may institute proceedings for any offence under this Act, the provisions of the Children and Young Persons Act 1933, other than the provisions of Parts I and II thereof, [. . .].[43]

[*Subsection* (2) *repealed by S.L.R.* 1953.]

Acquisition of land

56.[44]—(1) The council of a county borough may be authorised by

---

[42] Words substituted by Children and Young Persons Act 1969 (c. 54), s. 72 (3), Sched. 5 para. 21.

[43] Words repealed by Children Act 1958 (c. 65), s. 40 (2), Sched. 3.

[44] Powers of the Ministry of Health now exercised by Ministry of Housing and Local Government—S.I. 1951/753; functions as to Wales transferred to Secretary of State—S.I. 1965/319, art. 2, Sched. 1; functions transferred to Secretary of State—S.I. 1967/486, art. 2 (6), Sched. 2.

the Minister of Health to purchase compulsorily any land, whether situated within or outside the area of the council, for the purpose of any of their functions under this Act; and the council of a county or large burgh in Scotland may be authorised by the Secretary of State to purchase compulsorily any land, whether situated within or outside the county or burgh, for the purpose of any of their functions under this Act.

(2) The Acquisition of Land (Authorisation Procedure) Act 1946, shall apply in relation to the compulsory purchase of land under this section by the council of a county borough as, by virtue of subsection (1) of section one hundred and fifty-nine of the Local Government Act 1933, it applies to the compulsory purchase of land by a county council for the purpose of their functions under this Act; and accordingly for the purposes of the said Act of 1946 subsection (1) of this section shall be deemed to have been in force immediately before the commencement of that Act.

(3) Section two of the said Act of 1946 (which confers temporary powers for the speedy acquisition of land in urgent cases) shall not apply to the acquisition of land for the purposes of this Act, whether by a county council or by a county borough council.

(4) The Acquisition of Land (Authorisation Procedure) (Scotland) Act 1947 (other than section two thereof) shall apply in relation to the compulsory purchase of land under this section as if subsection (1) thereof had been in force immediately before the commencement of the said Act.

Transfer, superannuation and compensation of officers

57.—(1) The Secretary of State may by regulations provide—

(*a*) for the transfer to a local authority of officers employed immediately before the commencement of this Act by the Common Council of the City of London or the council of a metropolitan borough or county district solely or mainly for the purposes of functions transferred by this Act from that council to the said local authority;

(*b*) for enabling the Common Council of the City of London and the council of any metropolitan borough or county district in the case of any officer of the council who is a contributory employee or local Act contributor within the meaning of the Local Government Superannuation Act 1937 and is transferred under the regulations to secure, by resolution passed in respect of him not later than three months after his transfer under the regulations, that for the purposes of the said Act of 1937 any non-contributing service of his shall be reckonable as contributing service and, in the case of any such officer on whom if he had remained in their employment a similar benefit could have been conferred by the council on his becoming entitled to a superannuation allowance, that the length of his service shall be deemed for the purposes of the said Act of 1937 or, as the case may be, the local Act in question, to be increased by such period as may be specified in the resolution;

(*c*) for granting to persons who immediately before being transferred under the regulations were, by virtue of the employment from which they are so transferred, entitled to participate in superannuation benefits, an option either to participate, by virtue of their employment by the local authority to which they are transferred under the regulations, in superannuation benefits under a superannuation scheme of the local authority specified in the regulations or to retain rights corresponding with those previously enjoyed by them;

(d) for the payment by local authorities, subject to such exceptions or conditions (if any) as may be prescribed by the regulations, of compensation to persons of such descriptions as may be so prescribed who immediately before such date as may be so prescribed were employed by the Common Council of the City of London, the council of a metropolitan borough or the council of a county district in such full-time work as may be prescribed by the regulations and who suffer loss of employment or loss or diminution of emoluments which is attributable to the passing of this Act;

(e) for extending any provision made under paragraph (d) of this subsection to persons of such descriptions as may be prescribed by the regulations who, having before such date as aforesaid been employed as aforesaid and being persons who would have been so employed immediately before that date but for any national service (as defined in the regulations) in which they have been engaged, lose the prospect of their re-employment in any such work as a consequence of the passing of this Act;

(f) for such matters supplementary to and consequential on the matters aforesaid as appear to the Secretary of State to be necessary.

(2) Regulations under this section may provide for the determination by the Secretary of State of all questions arising under the regulations and may make different provisions for different classes of cases.

Regulations and orders

58.—(1) Any power to make regulations or orders conferred on a Minister by this Act shall be exercisable by statutory instrument.

(2) Any statutory instrument made in the exercise of any power to make regulations conferred by this Act shall be subject to annulment in pursuance of resolution of either House of Parliament.

Interpretation

59.—(1) In this Act, except where the context otherwise requires, the following expressions have the meanings hereby assigned to them respectively:—

[*Definition repealed by Children and Young Persons Act 1969 (c. 54), s. 72 (4), Sched. 6.*]

" child " means a person under the age of eighteen years [and any person who has attained that age and is the subject of a care order within the meaning of the Children and Young Persons Act 1969] [45];

" complain " in relation to Scotland means to make an application, and the expressions " complaint " and " complainant " shall be construed accordingly;

"compulsory school age " has in England and Wales the same meaning as in the Education Act 1944 and in Scotland means school age as defined in the Education (Scotland) Act 1946;

" contribution order " means in England or Wales a contribution order under section eighty-seven of the Children and Young Persons Act 1933 and in Scotland a contribution order under

---

[45] Words added by Children and Young Persons Act 1969 (c. 54), s. 72 (3), Sched. 5 para. 22.

section ninety-one of the Children and Young Persons (Scotland) Act 1937;

" functions " includes powers and duties;

" guardian " means a person appointed by deed or will or by order of a court of competent jurisdiction to be the guardian of a child;

" hospital " has the meaning assigned to it by section seventy-nine of the National Health Service Act 1946, or, as respects Scotland, section eighty of the National Health Service (Scotland) Act 1947;

" Large burgh " has the same meaning as in the Local Government (Scotland) Act 1947;

" local education authority " means a local education authority for the purposes of the Education Act 1944, or in Scotland an education authority for the purposes of the Education (Scotland) Act 1946;

" parent "—

> (a) [*Repealed by Children Act* 1975 (*c.* 72), *Sched.* 4.
> (b) in relation to a child who is illegitimate, means his mother, to the exclusion of his father;

" precept for a rate ", in relation to Scotland, means requisition for a rate;

" recognisance ", in relation to Scotland, means bond;

" recoverable summarily as a civil debt ", in relation to Scotland, means recoverable as a civil debt;

" relative " [46] has, throughout Great Britain, the meaning assigned to it by section two hundred and twenty of the Public Health Act 1936;

" voluntary home " has the same meaning as in Part V of the Children and Young Persons Act 1933 or, as respects Scotland, Part VI of the Children and Young Persons (Scotland) Act 1937;

" voluntary organisation " means a body the activities of which are carried on otherwise than for profit, but does not include any public or local authority.

[*Subsection* (2) *repealed by Children and Young Persons Act* 1969 (*c.* 54), *s.* 72 (4), *Sched.* 6.]

(3) References in this Act to any enactment shall, except where the context otherwise requires, be construed as references to the enactment as amended by or under any other enactment, including this Act.

(4) As respects Scotland any reference in this Act to a county or to the council thereof shall be construed, in relation to counties combined for the purposes mentioned in subsection (1) of section one hundred and eighteen of the Local Government (Scotland) Act 1947, as a reference to the combined county or the joint county council.

(5) A small burgh, as defined in the said Act of 1947, shall for the purposes of this Act be deemed to be included in the county in the area of which it is situated.

Transitional provisions, minor amendments and repeals

60.—(1) The transitional provisions set out in the Second Schedule to this Act shall have effect for the purposes of this Act.

(2) The enactments specified in the Third Schedule to this Act shall have effect subject to the amendments specified therein, being minor amendments and amendments consequential on the provisions of this Act.

---

[46] Definition amended by Adoption of Children Act 1949 (c. 98), s. 13, to include adopted and illegitimate children.

[*Subsection* (3) *repealed by S.L.R.* 1950.]

Application to Isles of Scilly

61. This Act shall, in its application to the Isles of Scilly, have effect subject to such exceptions, adaptations and modifications as may be prescribed by order of the Secretary of State, and any such order may be revoked or varied by a subsequent order.

Short title, commencement and extent

62.—(1) This Act may be cited as the Children Act 1948.
[*Subsection* (2) *repealed by S.L.R.* 1950.]
(3) This Act shall not extend to Northern Ireland.

SCHEDULES

FIRST SCHEDULE

APPEAL TRIBUNALS

PART I

CONSTITUTION OF APPEAL TRIBUNALS FOR ENGLAND AND WALES

1. For the purpose of enabling appeal tribunals to be constituted as occasion may require, there shall be appointed two panels, that is to say—

(*a*) a panel (hereinafter referred to as the "legal panel") appointed by the Lord Chancellor, of persons who will be available to act when required as chairman of any such tribunal; and

(*b*) a panel (hereinafter referred to as the "welfare panel") appointed by the Lord President of the Council, of persons who will be available to act when required as members of any such tribunal.

2.—(1) No person shall be qualified to be appointed to the legal panel unless he possesses such legal qualifications as the Lord Chancellor considers suitable, and no person shall be qualified to be appointed to the welfare panel unless he has had such experience in children's welfare work as the Lord President of the Council considers suitable.

(2) An officer of any Government department shall be disqualified from being appointed to either of the said panels.

3. Any person appointed to be a member of either of the said panels shall hold office as such subject to such conditions as to the period of his membership and otherwise as may be determined by the Lord Chancellor or the Lord President of the Council, as the case may be.

4. Where any appeal is required to be determined by a tribunal constituted in accordance with this Part of this Schedule, the tribunal shall consist of a chairman being a member of the legal panel and two other members being members of the welfare panel, and the chairman and other members of the tribunal shall be impartial persons appointed from those panels by the Lord Chancellor and the Lord President of the Council respectively.

PART II

CONSTITUTION OF APPEAL TRIBUNALS FOR SCOTLAND

5. For the purpose of enabling appeal tribunals to be constituted as occasion may require, there shall be appointed by the Secretary of State a panel (hereinafter referred to as the "welfare panel") of persons to act when required as members of any such tribunal.

6. No officer of any Government department shall be qualified to be appointed to the welfare panel.

7. Any person appointed to be a member of the welfare panel shall hold office for such period and subject to such conditions as may be determined by the Secretary of State.

8. Where any appeal is required to be determined by a tribunal constituted in accordance with this Schedule, the tribunal shall consist of a sheriff (or, if he is unable to act, a person qualified for appointment as sheriff nominated by the Lord President of the Court of Session), who shall be chairman, and two other members being impartial persons who shall be appointed from the welfare panel by the Secretary of State.

9. In this Part of this Schedule the expression "sheriff" does not include sheriff-substitute, and means the sheriff of the county in which the voluntary home to which the appeal relates is situated or is proposed to be established.

. . . .

FOURTH SCHEDULE

[*Repealed by* S.L.R. 1950.]

Marriage Act 1949 [1]

(12 & 13 GEO. 6, C. 76)

An Act to consolidate certain enactments relating to the solemnization and registration of marriages in England with such corrections and improvements as may be authorised under the Consolidation of Enactments (Procedure) Act 1949.

[24th November 1949.]

PART I

RESTRICTIONS ON MARRIAGE

Marriages within prohibited degrees

1.—(1) A marriage solemnized between a man and any of the persons mentioned in the first column of Part I of the First Schedule to this Act, or between a woman and any of the persons mentioned in the second column of the said Part I, shall be void.

[*Subsections* (2) (3) *repealed by Marriage (Enabling) Act* 1960 (*c.* 29), *s.* 1 (4), *Sched.*]

Marriages of persons under sixteen

2. A marriage solemnized between persons either of whom is under the age of sixteen shall be void.

Marriages of persons under twenty-one

3.[2]—(1) Where the marriage of an infant, not being a widower or widow, is intended to be solemnized on the authority of a certificate issued by a superintendent registrar under Part III of this Act, whether by licence or without licence, the consent of the person or persons specified in the Second Schedule to this Act shall be required:

---

[1] Amended S.I. 1952/991; power to amend granted by Public Expenditure and Receipts Act 1968 (c. 14), s. 5 (1), Sched. 3; explained by Pastoral Measure 1968 (No. 1), s. 29 (2), and applied by Sharing of Church Buildings Act 1969 (c. 38), s. 6, Sched. 1.

[2] Extended by Family Law Reform Act 1969 (c. 46), s. 2 (3), and Marriage (Registrar General's Licence) Act 1970 (c. 34), s. 3 (*b*). See now Children Act 1975 (c. 72), Sched. 3, para. 7, *post.*

Provided that—

    (*a*) if the superintendent registrar is satisfied that the consent of any person whose consent is so required cannot be obtained by reason of absence or inaccessibility or by reason of his being under any disability, the necessity for the consent of that person shall be dispensed with, if there is any other person whose consent is also required; and if the consent of no other person is required, the Registrar General may dispense with the necessity of obtaining any consent, or the court may, on application being made, consent to the marriage, and the consent of the court so given shall have the same effect as if it had been given by the person whose consent cannot be so obtained;

    (*b*) if any person whose consent is required refuses his consent, the court may, on application being made, consent to the marriage, and the consent of the court so given shall have the same effect as if it had been given by the person whose consent is refused.

(2) The last foregoing subsection shall apply to marriages intended to be solemnized on the authority of a common licence, with the substitution of references to the ecclesiastical authority by whom the licence was granted for references to the superintendent registrar, and with the substitution of a reference to the Master of the Faculties for the reference to the Registrar General.

(3) Where the marriage of an infant, not being a widower or widow, is intended to be solemnized after the publication of banns of matrimony then, if any person whose consent to the marriage would have been required under this section in the case of a marriage intended to be solemnized otherwise than after the publication of the banns, openly and publicly declares or causes to be declared, in the church or chapel in which the banns are published, at the time of the publication, his dissent from the intended marriage, the publication of banns shall be void.

(4) A clergyman shall not be liable to ecclesiastical censure for solemnizing the marriage of an infant after the publication of banns without the consent of the parents or guardians of the infant unless he had notice of the dissent of any person who is entitled to give notice of dissent under the last foregoing subsection.

(5) For the purposes of this section, " the court " means the High Court [, the county court of the district in which any applicant or respondent resides],³ or a court of summary jurisdiction [having jurisdiction in the place in which any applicant or respondent resides],³ and rules of court may be made for enabling applications under this section—

    (*a*) if made to the High Court, to be heard in chambers;

    (*b*) if made to the county court, to be heard and determined by the registrar subject to appeal to the judge;

    (*c*) if made to a court of summary jurisdiction, to be heard and determined otherwise than in open court,

and shall provide that, where an application is made in consequence of a refusal to give consent, notice of the application shall be served on the person who has refused consent.

(6) Nothing in this section shall dispense with the necessity of obtaining the consent of the High Court to the marriage of a ward of court.

Hours for solemnization of marriages

4. A marriage may be solemnized at any time between the hours of eight in the forenoon and six in the afternoon.

---

³ Words substituted and added by Marriage (Registrar General's Licence) Act 1970, c. 34).

PART II [4]

MARRIAGE ACCORDING TO RITES OF THE CHURCH OF ENGLAND

Preliminary

Methods of authorising marriages

5. A marriage according to the rites of the Church of England may be solemnized—

(*a*) after the publication of banns of matrimony;

(*b*) on the authority of a special licence of marriage granted by the Archbishop of Canterbury or any other person by virtue of the Ecclesiastical Licences Act 1533 (in this Act referred to as a " special licence ");

(*c*) on the authority of a licence of marriage (other than a special licence) granted by an ecclesiastical authority having power to grant such a licence (in this Act referred to as a " common licence "); or

(*d*) [4a] on the authority of a certificate issued by a superintendent registrar under Part III of this Act.

Marriage by banns

Place of publication of banns

6.[5]—(1) Subject to the provisions of this Act, where a marriage is intended to be solemnized after the publication of banns of matrimony, the banns shall be published—

(*a*) if the persons to be married reside in the same parish, in the parish church of that parish;

(*b*) if the persons to be married do not reside in the same parish, in the parish church of each parish in which one of them resides:

Provided that if either of the persons to be married resides in a chapelry or in a district specified in a licence granted under section twenty of this Act, the banns may be published in an authorised chapel of that chapelry or district instead of in the parish church of the parish in which that person resides.

(2) In relation to a person who resides in an extra-parochial place, the last foregoing subsection shall have effect as if for references to a parish there were substituted references to that extra-parochial place, and as if for references to a parish church there were substituted references to an authorised chapel of that place.

(3) For the purposes of this section, any parish in which there is no parish church or chapel belonging thereto or no church or chapel in which divine service is usually solemnized every Sunday, and any extra-parochial place which has no authorised chapel, shall be deemed to belong to any adjoining parish or chapelry.

(4) Banns of matrimony may be published in any parish church or authorised chapel which is the usual place of worship of the persons to be married or of one of them although neither of those persons resides in the parish or chapelry to which the church or chapel belongs:

Provided that the publication of banns by virtue of this subsection shall be in addition to and not in substitution for the publication of banns required by subsection (1) of this section.

---

[4] Applied by Sharing of Church Buildings Act 1969 (c. 38), s. 6 (2).

[4a] Extended by Marriage (Registrar General's Licence) Act 1970 (c. 34), s. 1.

[5] Extended by Pastoral Measure 1968 (No. 1), s. 29 (2).

Time and manner of publication of banns

7.—(1) Subject to the provisions of section nine of this Act, banns of matrimony shall be published on three Sundays preceding the solemnization of the marriage during morning service or, if there is no morning service on a Sunday on which the banns are to be published, during evening service.

(2) Banns of matrimony shall be published in an audible manner and in accordance with the form of words prescribed by the rubric prefixed to the office of matrimony in the Book of Common Prayer, and all the other rules prescribed by the said rubric concerning the publication of banns and the solemnization of matrimony shall, so far as they are consistent with the provisions of this Part of this Act, be duly observed.

(3) The parochial church council of a parish shall provide for every church and chapel in the parish in which marriages may be solemnized, a register book of banns made of durable materials and marked in the manner directed by section fifty-four of this Act for the register book of marriages, and all banns shall be published from the said register book of banns by the officiating clergyman, and not from loose papers, and after each publication the entry in the register book shall be signed by the officiating clergyman, or by some person under his direction.

(4) Any reference in the last foregoing subsection to a parochial church council shall, in relation to an authorised chapel in an extra-parochial place, be construed as a reference to the chapel warden or other officer exercising analogous duties in the chapel or, if there is no such officer, such person as may be appointed in that behalf by the bishop of the diocese.

Notice to clergyman before publication of banns

8. No clergyman shall be obliged to publish banns of matrimony unless the persons to be married, at least seven days before the date on which they wish the banns to be published for the first time, deliver or cause to be delivered to him a notice in writing, dated on the day on which it is so delivered, stating the christian name and surname and the place of residence of each of them, and the period during which each of them has resided at his or her place of residence.

Persons by whom banns may be published

9.—(1) Subject to the provisions of this section and of section fourteen of this Act, it shall not be lawful for any person other than a clergyman to publish banns of matrimony.

(2) Where on any Sunday in any church or other building in which banns of matrimony may be published a clergyman does not officiate at the service at which it is usual in that church or building to publish banns, the banns may be published—

(*a*) by a clergyman at some other service at which banns of matrimony may be published; or

(*b*) by a layman during the course of a public reading authorised by the bishop of the diocese of a portion or portions of the service of morning or evening prayer, the public reading being at the hour when the service at which it is usual to publish banns is commonly held or at such other hour as the bishop may authorise:

Provided that banns shall not be published by a layman unless the incumbent or minister in charge of the said church or building, or some other clergyman nominated in that behalf by the bishop, has made or authorised to be made the requisite entry in the register book of banns of the said church or building.

(3) Where a layman publishes banns of matrimony by virtue of this section the layman shall sign the register book of banns provided under section seven of this Act and for that purpose shall be deemed to be the officiating clergyman within the meaning of that section.

Publication of banns commenced in one church and completed in another

10.[6]—(1) Where the publication of banns of matrimony has been duly commenced in any church, the publication may be completed in the same church or in any other church which, by virtue of the Union of Benefices Measure 1923 or the New Parishes Measure 1943, has at the time of the completion taken the place of the first-mentioned church for the purpose of publication of banns of matrimony either generally or in relation to the parties to the intended marriage.

(2) Where the publication of banns of matrimony has been duly commenced in any building which by virtue of a reorganisation scheme under the Reorganisation Areas Measure 1944 ceases to be a parish church or, as the case may be, ceases to be licensed for marriages, the publication may be completed in such other building, being either a parish church or a building licensed for marriages, as may be directed by the bishop of the diocese to take the place of the first-mentioned building for the purposes of the publication of banns.

Certificates of publication of banns

11.—(1) Where a marriage is intended to be solemnized after the publication of banns of matrimony and the persons to be married do not reside in the same parish or other ecclesiastical district, a clergyman shall not solemnize the marriage in the parish or district in which one of those persons resides unless there is produced to him a certificate that the banns have been published in accordance with the provisions of this Part of this Act in the parish or other ecclesiastical district in which the other person resides.

(2) Where a marriage is intended to be solemnized in a church or chapel of a parish or other ecclesiastical district in which neither of the persons to be married resides, after the publication of banns therein by virtue of subsection (4) of section six of this Act, a clergyman shall not solemnize the marriage unless there is produced to him—

(a) if the persons to be married reside in the same parish or other ecclesiastical district, a certificate that the banns have been published in accordance with the provisions of this Part of this Act in that parish or district; or

(b) if the persons to be married do not reside in the same parish or other ecclesiastical district, certificates that the banns have been published as aforesaid in each parish or district in which one of them resides.

(3) Where banns are published by virtue of subsection (3) of section six of this Act in a parish or chapelry adjoining the parish or extra-parochial place in which the banns would otherwise be required to be published, a certificate that the banns have been published in that parish or chapelry shall have the like force and effect as a certificate that banns have been published in a parish in which one of the persons to be married resides.

(4) Any certificate required under this section shall be signed by the incumbent or minister in charge of the building in which the banns were published or by a clergyman nominated in that behalf by the bishop of the diocese.

6 Amended by Pastoral Measure 1968 (No. 1), s. 29 (2), Sched. 3 para. 14 (1).

Solemnization of marriage after publication of banns

12.—(1) Subject to the provisions of this Part of this Act, where banns of matrimony have been published, the marriage shall be solemnized in the church or chapel or, as the case may be, one of the churches or chapels in which the banns have been published.

(2) Where a marriage is not solemnized within three months after the completion of the publication of the banns, that publication shall be void and no clergyman shall solemnize the marriage on the authority thereof.

Publication of banns in Scotland, Northern Ireland or Republic of Ireland

13. Where a marriage is intended to be solemnized in England, after the publication of banns of matrimony, between parties of whom one is residing in England and the other is residing in Scotland, Northern Ireland or the Republic of Ireland, then, if banns have been published or proclaimed in any church of the parish or place in which that other party is residing according to the law or custom there prevailing, a certificate given in accordance with that law or custom that the banns have been so published or proclaimed shall as respects that party be sufficient for the purposes of section eleven of this Act, and the marriage shall not be void by reason only that the banns have not been published in the manner required for the publication of banns in England.

Publication of banns on board His Majesty's ships

14.—(1) Where a marriage is intended to be solemnized in England, after the publication of banns of matrimony, between parties of whom one is residing in England and the other is an officer, seaman or marine borne on the books of one of His Majesty's ships at sea, the banns may be published on three successive Sundays during morning service on board that ship by the chaplain, or, if there is no chaplain, by the captain or other officer commanding the ship, and, where banns have been so published, the person who published them shall, unless the banns have been forbidden on any of the grounds on which banns may be forbidden, give a certificate of publication.

(2) A certificate issued under this section shall be in such form as may be prescribed by the Admiralty and shall, as respects the party who is an officer, seaman or marine as aforesaid, be sufficient for the purposes of section eleven of this Act, and all provisions of this Act (including penal provisions) relating to the publication of banns and certificates thereof and all rules required by section seven of this Act to be observed shall apply in the case of banns published under this section subject to such adaptations therein as may be made by His Majesty by Order in Council.

Marriage by Common Licence

Places in which marriages may be solemnized by common licence

15.[7]—(1) Subject to the provisions of this Part of this Act, a common licence shall not be granted for the solemnization of a marriage in any church or chapel other than—

    (a) the parish church of the parish, or an authorised chapel of the ecclesiastical district, in which one of the persons to be married

[7] Extended by Pastoral Measure 1968 (No. 1), s. 29 (2).

has had his or her usual place of residence for fifteen days immediately before the grant of the licence; or

(*b*) a parish church or authorised chapel which is the usual place of worship of the persons to be married or of one of them.

(2) For the purposes of this section, any parish in which there is no parish church or chapel belonging thereto or no church or chapel in which divine service is usually solemnized every Sunday, and any extra-parochial place which has no authorised chapel, shall be deemed to belong to any adjoining parish or chapelry.

Provisions as to common licences

16.—(1) A common licence shall not be granted unless one of the persons to be married has sworn before a person having authority to grant such a licence—

(*a*) that he or she believes that there is no impediment of kindred or alliance or any other lawful cause, nor any suit commenced in any court, to bar or hinder the solemnization of the marriage in accordance with the licence;

(*b*) that one of the persons to be married has had his or her usual place of residence in the parish or other ecclesiastical district in which the marriage is to be solemnized for fifteen days immediately before the grant of the licence or that the parish church or authorised chapel in which the marriage is to be solemnized is the usual place of worship of those persons or of one of them;

(*c*) where one of the persons to be married is an infant and is not a widower or widow, that the consent of the person or persons whose consent to the marriage is required under section three of this Act has been obtained, that the necessity of obtaining any such consent has been dispensed with under that section, that the court has consented to the marriage under that section, or that there is no person whose consent to the marriage is so required.

(2) If any caveat is entered against the grant of a common licence, the caveat having been duly signed by or on behalf of the person by whom it is entered and stating his place of residence and the ground of objection on which the caveat is founded, no licence shall be granted until the caveat or a copy thereof is transmitted to the ecclesiastical judge out of whose office the licence is to issue, and the judge has certified to the registrar of the diocese that he has examined into the matter of the caveat and is satisfied that it ought not to obstruct the grant of the licence, or until the caveat is withdrawn by the person who entered it.

(3) Where a marriage is not solemnized within three months after the grant of a common licence, the licence shall be void and no clergyman shall solemnize the marriage on the authority thereof.

(4) No surrogate deputed by an ecclesiastical judge who has power to grant common licences shall grant any such licence until he has taken an oath before that judge, or a commissioner appointed under the seal of that judge, faithfully to execute his office according to law, to the best of his knowledge, and has given security by his bond in the sum of one hundred pounds to the bishop of the diocese for the due and faithful execution of his office.

Marriage under superintendent registrar's certificate

Marriage under superintendent registrar's certificate

17. A marriage according to the rites of the Church of England may be solemnized on the authority of a certificate of a superintendent registrar in force under Part III of this Act in any church or chapel in which banns of matrimony may be published:

Provided that a marriage shall not be solemnized as aforesaid in any such church or chapel without the consent of the minister thereof or by any person other than a clergyman.

Publication of banns and solemnization of marriages during disuse of churches

Publication of banns and solemnization of marriages during repair and rebuilding of churches

18.—(1) Where any church or chapel in which banns may be published and marriages solemnized is being rebuilt or repaired, and on that account is not being used for divine service, banns of matrimony which could otherwise have been published therein and marriages which could otherwise have been solemnized therein may be published or solemnized, as the case may be,—

(*a*) in any building licensed by the bishop of the diocese for the performance of divine service during the disuse of the church or chapel, being a building within the parish or other ecclesiastical district in which the disused church or chapel is situated; or

(*b*) if no building has been licensed as aforesaid, in any such consecrated chapel as the bishop of the diocese may in writing direct, being a chapel within the said parish or district; or

(*c*) if no building has been licensed as mentioned in paragraph (*a*) of this subsection and no direction has been given by the bishop under the last foregoing paragraph, in a church or chapel of any adjoining parish or other ecclesiastical district, being a church or chapel in which banns may be published and marriages solemnized.

(2) Any fees paid in respect of marriages solemnized by virtue of paragraph (*b*) of the last foregoing subsection in a consecrated chapel specified in a direction given by the bishop of the diocese under that paragraph shall be applied as the bishop, with the consent of the incumbent of the disused church or chapel, may in writing direct.

(3) Any marriage solemnized by virtue of the said subsection in any licensed building or consecrated chapel or in the church or chapel of an adjoining parish or district shall be deemed for the purposes of Part IV of this Act to have been solemnized in the disused church or chapel and shall accordingly be registered in the marriage register books kept by the incumbent of the disused church or chapel.

Publication of banns and solemnization of marriage where church injured by war damage

19. Where an order made by the Church Commissioners under section three of the Diocesan Reorganisation Committees Measure 1941 (which enables orders to be made deferring the restoration of churches injured by war damage) is in force as respects any church, banns of matrimony of persons entitled to be married in that church may be published, and marriages of such persons may be solemnized, in such other church, chapel or place of worship within the diocese as the bishop of the diocese shall in writing direct.

*Licensing of chapels for publication of banns and
solemnization of marriages*

**Licensing of chapels for publication of banns and solemnization of marriages for
persons residing in specified district**

20.[8]—(1) Subject to the provisions of this section, the bishop of the
diocese in which a public chapel is situated may—

    (a) if he thinks it necessary so to do for the due accommodation and
convenience of the inhabitants of any district; and

    (b) if the patron and incumbent of the church of the parish in which
the public chapel is situated have signified their consent under
their respective hands and seals,

authorise by a licence under his hand and seal the publication of banns
and the solemnization of marriages in that public chapel between parties
both or either of whom reside or resides within a district of which the
limits shall be specified in the licence; and any such licence may include
such provisions concerning the amount, appropriation or apportionment
of dues and such other particulars as the bishop thinks fit.

(2) Notwithstanding anything in the last foregoing subsection, the
bishop of the diocese may grant a licence under this section without the
consent of the patron and incumbent of the church of the parish in
which the public chapel is situated after two months notice in writing
given to the patron and incumbent by the registrar of the diocese:

Provided that where any patron or incumbent who refuses or withholds his consent to the grant of a licence under this section delivers to
the bishop under his hand and seal a statement of the reasons for
which the consent has been refused or withheld, no licence shall be
granted by the bishop until he has inquired into the reasons contained
in the statement.

(3) Where a bishop grants a licence under this section without the
consent of the patron and incumbent, the patron or incumbent may,
within one month from the grant of the licence, appeal to the archbishop
of the province who shall hear the appeal in a summary manner, and
shall make such order confirming, revoking or varying the licence as
seems to him expedient.

(4) Any licence granted or order made under this section may at any
time be revoked in writing under the hand and seal of the bishop of
the diocese with the consent in writing of the archbishop of the province;
and the registrar of the diocese shall notify the revocation in writing
to the minister officiating in the chapel concerned and shall give public
notice of the revocation by advertisement in some newspaper circulating
within the county in which the chapel is situated and in the London
Gazette.

(5) There shall be displayed in some conspicuous part of the interior
of any chapel licensed under this section the words " Banns may be
published and marriages may be solemnized in this chapel ".

(6) Every consent of a patron or incumbent delivered under subsection (1) of this section, a copy of every notice given by the registrar
of a diocese under subsection (2) of this section, every statement of
reasons delivered by a patron or incumbent under the said subsection (2),
together with the bishop's decision thereon under his hand and seal, every
order made by an archbishop under subsection (3) of this section and
every revocation and consent made or given under subsection (4) of
this section, shall be registered in the registry of the diocese.

(7) The district specified in a licence granted under this section may

[8] Applied by Sharing of Church Buildings Act 1969 (c. 38), s. 61 (2) (b).

be taken out of more than one parish; and where any such licence specifies a district taken out of more than one parish the expressions " patron " and " incumbent " shall for the purposes of this section mean the patron or incumbent, as the case may be, of the church of every parish out of which the district so specified is taken.

(8) In this section the expression " public chapel " means any public chapel with or without a chapelry annexed thereto, or any chapel duly licensed for the celebration of divine service according to the rites and ceremonies of the Church of England, or any chapel the minister of which is duly licensed to officiate therein according to the rites and ceremonies of the Church of England.

Authorising of publication of banns and solemnization of marriages in churches and chapels of extra-parochial places

21.[9]—(1) Where any extra-parochial place has belonging to it or within it any church or chapel of the Church of England, the bishop of the diocese in which the church or chapel is situated may, if he thinks fit, authorise in writing under his hand and seal the publication of banns and the solemnization of marriages by banns or licence in that church or chapel between parties both or either of whom reside or resides in that extra-parochial place.

(2) Every authorisation given under the last foregoing subsection shall be registered in the registry of the diocese.

Miscellaneous Provisions

Witnesses

22. All marriages solemnized according to the rites of the Church of England shall be solemnized in the presence of two or more witnesses in addition to the clergyman by whom the marriage is solemnized.

Benefices held in plurality

23.[10] Where two or more benefices are held in plurality under the Pastoral Reorganisation Measure 1949, the bishop of the diocese in which the benefices are situated or, during a vacancy in the see, the guardian of the spiritualities thereof, may in writing direct where banns of matrimony of persons entitled to be married in any church of those benefices may be published and where marriages of those persons may be solemnized:

Provided that—

    (a) nothing in this section shall deprive a person of the right to be married in any church in which he would have been entitled to be married if no directions had been given under this section; and

    (b) a person may be married in a church in which he would have been entitled to be married as aforesaid notwithstanding that the banns of matrimony have, by virtue of this section, been published only in some other church.

Proof of residence not necessary to validity of marriage by banns or common licence

24.—(1) Where any marriage has been solemnized after the publication of banns of matrimony, it shall not be necessary in support of the

[9] Applied by *ibid.*, s. 6 (4).
[10] Applied and extended by Pastoral Measure 1968 (No. 1), ss. 27 (3), 29 (2), Sched. 3, para. 14 (3).

marriage to give any proof of the residence of the parties or either of them in any parish or other ecclesiastical district in which the banns were published, and no evidence shall be given to prove the contrary in any proceedings touching the validity of the marriage.

(2) Where any marriage has been solemnized on the authority of a common licence, it shall not be necessary in support of the marriage to give any proof that the usual place of residence of one of the parties was for fifteen days immediately before the grant of the licence in the parish or other ecclesiastical district in which the marriage was solemnized, and no evidence shall be given to prove the contrary in any proceedings touching the validity of the marriage.

Void marriages

25. If any persons knowingly and wilfully intermarry according to the rites of the Church of England (otherwise than by special licence)—

(a) in any place other than a church or other building in which banns may be published;

(b) without banns having been duly published, a common licence having been obtained, or a certificate having been duly issued under Part III of this Act by a superintendent registrar to whom due notice of marriage has been given; or

(c) on the authority of a publication of banns which is void by virtue of subsection (3) of section three or subsection (2) of section twelve of this Act, on the authority of a common licence which is void by virtue of subsection (3) of section sixteen of this Act, or on the authority of a certificate of a superintendent registrar which is void by virtue of subsection (2) of section thirty-three of this Act;

(d) in the case of a marriage on the authority of a certificate of a superintendent registrar, in any place other than the church or other building specified in the notice of marriage and certificate;

or if they knowingly and wilfully consent to or acquiesce in the solemnization of the marriage by any person who is not in Holy Orders, the marriage shall be void.

PART III

MARRIAGE UNDER SUPERINTENDENT REGISTRAR'S CERTIFICATE

Issue of certificates

Marriages which may be solemnized on authority of superintendent registrar's certificate

26.[10a]—(1) Subject to the provisions of this Part of this Act, the following marriages may be solemnized on the authority of a certificate of a superintendent registrar—

(a) a marriage in a registered building according to such form and ceremony as the persons to be married see fit to adopt;

(b) a marriage in the office of a superintendent registrar;

(c) a marriage according to the usages of the Society of Friends (commonly called Quakers);

(d) a marriage between two persons professing the Jewish religion according to the usages of the Jews;

(e) a marriage according to the rites of the Church of England.

(2) [11] A marriage on the authority of a certificate of a superintendent

---

[10a] Extended by Marriage (Registrar General's Licence) Act 1970 (c. 34), s. 1.
[11] Excluded by Sharing of Church Buildings Act 1969 (c. 38), s. 6 (3).

registrar may be either by a licence issued by the superintendent registrar or without a licence:

Provided that a superintendent registrar shall not issue a licence for a marriage in any church or chapel in which marriages may be solemnized according to the rites of the Church of England, or in any church or chapel belonging to the Church of England or licensed for the celebration of divine worship according to the rites and ceremonies of the Church of England.

Notice of marriage

27.—(1) Where a marriage is intended to be solemnized on the authority of a certificate of a superintendent registrar without licence, notice of marriage in the prescribed form shall be given—

(a) if the persons to be married have resided in the same registration district for the period of seven days immediately before the giving of the notice, by either of those persons to the superintendent registrar of that district;

(b) if the persons to be married have not resided in the same registration district for the said period of seven days as aforesaid, by either of those persons to the superintendent registrar of each registration district in which one of them has resided for that period.

(2) Where a marriage is intended to be solemnized as aforesaid by licence, then, whether the persons to be married reside in the same or in different registration districts, notice of marriage in the prescribed form shall be given by either of those persons to the superintendent registrar of the registration district in which one of them has resided for the period of fifteen days immediately before the giving of the notice, and it shall not be required that notice of marriage shall be given to more than one superintendent registrar.

(3) A notice of marriage shall state the name and surname, marital status, occupation and place of residence of each of the persons to be married and the church or other building in which the marriage is to be solemnized and—

(a) in the case of a marriage intended to be solemnized without licence, shall state the period, not being less than seven days, during which each of the persons to be married has resided in his or her place of residence;

(b) in the case of a marriage intended to be solemnized by licence, shall state the period, not being less than fifteen days, during which one of the persons to be married has resided in the district in which notice of marriage is given:

Provided that if either of the persons to be married has resided in the place stated in the notice for more than one month, the notice may state that he or she has resided there for more than one month.

(4) The superintendent registrar shall file all notices of marriage and keep them with the records of his office, and shall also forthwith enter the particulars given in every such notice, together with the date of the notice and the name of the person by whom the notice was given, in a book (in this Act referred to as " the marriage notice book ") furnished to him for that purpose by the Registrar General, and the marriage notice book shall be open for inspection free of charge at all reasonable hours.

(5) If the persons to be married wish to be married in the presence of a registrar in a registered building for which an authorised person has been appointed, they shall, at the time when notice of marriage is given

---

to the superintendent registrar under this section, give notice to him that they require a registrar to be present at the marriage.

(6) The superintendent registrar shall be entitled to a fee of [£1·00] [12] for every entry made in the marriage notice book under this section.

Declaration to accompany notice of marriage

28.—(1) No certificate or licence for marriage shall be issued by a superintendent registrar unless the notice of marriage is accompanied by a solemn declaration in writing, in the body or at the foot of the notice, made and signed at the time of the giving of the notice by the person by whom the notice is given and attested as mentioned in subsection (2) of this section—

(a) that he or she believes that there is no impediment of kindred or alliance or other lawful hindrance to the marriage;

(b) in the case of a marriage intended to be solemnized without licence, that the persons to be married have for the period of seven days immediately before the giving of the notice had their usual places of residence within the registration district or registration districts in which notice is given, or, in the case of a marriage intended to be solemnized by licence, that one of the persons to be married has for the period of fifteen days immediately before the giving of the notice had his or her usual place of residence within the registration district in which notice is given;

(c) where one of the persons to be married is an infant and is not a widower or widow, that the consent of the person or persons whose consent to the marriage is required under section three of this Act has been obtained, that the necessity of obtaining any such consent has been dispensed with under that section, that the court has consented to the marriage under that section, or that there is no person whose consent to the marriage is so required.

(2) Any such declaration as aforesaid shall be signed by the person giving the notice of marriage in the presence of the superintendent registrar to whom the notice is given or his deputy, or in the presence of a registrar of births and deaths or of marriages for the registration district in which the person giving the notice resides or his deputy, and that superintendent registrar, deputy superintendent registrar, registrar or deputy registrar, as the case may be, shall attest the declaration by adding thereto his name, description and place of residence.

Caveat against issue of certificate or licence

29.—(1) Any person [. . .] [13] may enter a caveat with the superintendent registrar against the issue of a certificate or licence for the marriage of any person named therein.

(2) If any caveat is entered as aforesaid, the caveat having been signed by or on behalf of the person by whom it was entered and stating his place of residence and the ground of objection on which the caveat is founded, no certificate or licence shall be issued until the superintendent registrar has examined into the matter of the caveat and is satisfied that it ought not to obstruct the issue of the certificate or licence, or until the caveat has been withdrawn by the person who entered it; and if the superintendent registrar is doubtful whether to issue a certificate or licence he may refer the matter of the caveat to the Registrar General.

[12] Fee raised by S.I. 1972/911.
[13] Words repealed by S.I. 1968/1242.

(3) Where a superintendent registrar refuses, by reason of any such caveat as aforesaid, to issue a certificate or licence, the person applying therefor may appeal to the Registrar General who shall either confirm the refusal or direct that a certificate or licence shall be issued.

(4) Any person who enters a caveat against the issue of a certificate or licence on grounds which the Registrar General declares to be frivolous and to be such that they ought not to obstruct the issue of the certificate or licence, shall be liable for the costs of the proceedings before the Registrar General and for damages recoverable by the person against whose marriage the caveat was entered.

(5) For the purpose of enabling any person to recover any such costs and damages as aforesaid, a copy of the declaration of the Registrar General purporting to be sealed with the seal of the General Register Office shall be evidence that the Registrar General has declared the caveat to have been entered on grounds which are frivolous and such that they ought not to obstruct the issue of the certificate or licence.

Forbidding of issue of certificate

30. Any person whose consent to a marriage intended to be solemnized on the authority of a certificate of a superintendent registrar is required under section three of this Act may forbid the issue of such a certificate by writing, at any time before the issue of the certificate, the word " forbidden " opposite to the entry of the notice of marriage in the marriage notice book, and by subscribing thereto his name and place of residence and the capacity, in relation to either of the persons to be married, in which he forbids the issue of the certificate; and where the issue of a certificate has been so forbidden, the notice of marriage and all proceedings thereon shall be void:

Provided that where, by virtue of paragraph (b) of the proviso to subsection (1) of the said section three, the court has consented to a marriage and the consent of the court has the same effect as if it had been given by a person whose consent has been refused, that person shall not be entitled to forbid the issue of a certificate for that marriage under this section, and the notice of marriage and the proceedings thereon shall not be void by virtue of this section.

Marriage under certificate without licence

31.—(1) Where a marriage is intended to be solemnized on the authority of a certificate of a superintendent registrar without licence, the superintendent registrar to whom notice of marriage has been given shall suspend or affix in some conspicuous place in his office, for twenty-one successive days next after the day on which the notice was entered in the marriage book, the notice of marriage, or an exact copy signed by him of the particulars thereof as entered in the marriage notice book.

(2) At the expiration of the said period of twenty-one days the superintendent registrar, on the request of the person by whom the notice of marriage was given, shall issue a certificate in the prescribed form unless—

(a) any lawful impediment to the issue of the certificate has been shown to the satisfaction of the superintendent registrar; or

(b) the issue of the certificate has been forbidden under the last foregoing section by any person authorised in that behalf.

(3) Every such certificate shall set out the particulars contained in the notice of marriage and the day on which the notice was entered in the marriage notice book and shall contain a statement that the issue of the certificate has not been forbidden as aforesaid.

(4) No marriage shall be solemnized on the production of a certificate

of a superintendent registrar without licence until after the expiration of the said period of twenty-one days.

(5) Where a marriage is to be solemnized in a registered building for which an authorised person has been appointed and no notice requiring a registrar to be present at the marriage has been given to the superintendent registrar under subsection (5) of section twenty-seven of this Act, the superintendent registrar shall, when issuing a certificate under this section, give to one of the persons to be married printed instructions in the prescribed form for the due solemnization of the marriage.

[*Subsection* (6) *repealed by* S.I. 1968/1242.]

Marriage under certificate by licence

32.—(1) Where a marriage is intended to be solemnized on the authority of a certificate of a superintendent registrar by licence, the person by whom notice of marriage is given shall state in the notice that the marriage is intended to be solemnized by licence, and the notice shall not be suspended in the office of the superintendent registrar.

(2) Where a notice of marriage containing such a statement as aforesaid has been received by a superintendent registrar, then, after the expiration of one whole day next after the day on which the notice was entered in the marriage notice book, the superintendent registrar, on the request of the person by whom the notice was given, shall issue a certificate and a licence in the prescribed form unless—

(*a*) any lawful impediment to the issue of the certificate has been shown to the satisfaction of the superintendent registrar; or

(*b*) the issue of the certificate has been forbidden under section thirty of this Act by any person authorised in that behalf.

(3) Every such certificate shall set out the particulars contained in the notice of marriage and the day on which the notice was entered in the marriage notice book, and shall contain a statement that the issue of the certificate has not been forbidden as aforesaid.

(4) Where a marriage is to be solemnized in a registered building for which an authorised person has been appointed and no notice requiring a registrar to be present at the marriage has been given to the superintendent registrar under subsection (5) of section twenty-seven of this Act, the superintendent registrar shall, when issuing a certificate and licence under this section, give to one of the persons to be married printed instructions in the prescribed form for the due solemnization of the marriage.

(5) A superintendent registrar shall be entitled to receive [. . .] [14] for every licence so issued the sum of [£5·00] [14a] over and above the amount paid for the stamps necessary on the issue of the licence.

(6) A superintendent registrar shall not issue a licence under this section until he has given security by his bond in the sum of one hundred pounds to the Registrar General for the due and faithful execution of his office.

Period of validity of certificate and licence

33.—(1) A marriage may be solemnized on the authority of a certificate of a superintendent registrar, whether by licence or without licence, at any time within three months from the day on which the notice of marriage was entered in the marriage notice book.

(2) If the marriage is not solemnized within the said period of three months, the notice of marriage and the certificate, and any licence which

[14] Words repealed by S.I. 1968/1242.
[14a] Fee raised by S.I. 1972/911.

may have been granted thereon, shall be void, and no person shall solemnize the marriage on the authority thereof.

Marriages normally to be solemnized in registration district in which one of parties resides

34. Subject to the provisions of the next following section, a superintendent registrar shall not issue a certificate for the solemnization of a marriage in a building which is not within a registration district in which one of the persons to be married has resided, in the case of a marriage without licence, for the period of seven days immediately before the giving of the notice of marriage or, in the case of a marriage by licence, for the period of fifteen days immediately before the giving of that notice.

Marriages in registration district in which neither party resides

35.—(1) A superintendent registrar may issue a certificate, or if the marriage is to be by licence, a certificate and a licence, for the solemnization of a marriage in a registered building which is not within a registration district in which either of the persons to be married resides, where the person giving the notice of marriage declares by endorsement thereon in the prescribed form—

[(*a*) that the persons to be married desire the marriage to be solemnized, according to a specified form, rite or ceremony, being a form, rite or ceremony of a body or denomination of christians or other persons meeting for religious worship to which one of them professes to belong.] [15]

(*b*) that, to the best of his or her belief, there is not within the registration district in which one of them resides any registered building in which marriage is solemnized according to that form, rite or ceremony;

(*c*) the registration district nearest to the residence of that person in which there is a registered building in which marriage may be so solemnized; and

(*d*) the registered building in that district in which the marriage is intended to be solemnized;

and where any such certificate or certificate and licence is issued, the marriage may be solemnized in the registered building stated in the notice.

[(2) A superintendent registrar may issue a certificate or, if the marriage is to be by licence, a certificate and a licence, for the solemnization of a marriage in a registered building which is the usual place of worship of the persons to be married, or of one of them, notwithstanding that the building is not within a registration district in which either of those persons resides.] [15]

(3) A superintendent registrar may issue a certificate for the solemnization of a marriage in any parish church or authorised chapel which is the usual place of worship of the persons to be married, or of one of them, notwithstanding that the church or chapel is not within a registration district in which either of those persons resides.

(4) A superintendent registrar may issue a certificate or, if the marriage is to be by licence, a certificate and a licence, for the solemnization of a marriage according to the usages of the Society of Friends or in accordance with the usages of persons professing the Jewish religion, notwithstanding that the building or place in which the marriage is to be solemnized is not within a registration district in which either of the persons to be married resides.

[15] Substituted by Marriage Act 1949 (Amendment) Act 1954 (c. 47), ss. 1, 2. And see Marriage (Registrar General's Licence) Act 1970 (c. 34).

(5) Where a marriage is intended to be solemnized on the authority of a certificate of a superintendent registrar issued under subsection (2) or subsection (3) of this section, the notice of marriage given to the superintendent registrar and the certificate issued by the superintendent registrar shall state, in addition to the description of the registered building or, as the case may be, the parish church or authorised chapel, in which the marriage is to be solemnized, that it is the usual place of worship of the persons to be married or of one of them and, in the latter case, shall state the name of the person whose usual place of worship it is.

Superintendent registrar to issue licences only for marriages to be solemnized in his registration district

36. Subject to the provisions of the last foregoing section, a superintendent registrar shall not issue a licence for the solemnization of a marriage—

    (*a*) in a registered building which is not within his registration district;

    (*b*) in the office of any other superintendent registrar.

One party resident in Scotland

37.—(1) Where a marriage is intended to be solemnized in England on the authority of a certificate of a superintendent registrar without licence between parties of whom one is residing in Scotland and the other is residing in England the following provisions shall have effect—

    (*a*) the party residing in Scotland may, subject to and in accordance with the provisions of section seven of the Marriage Notice (Scotland) Act 1878, give notice of the intended marriage as if the parties were residing in different parishes or districts in Scotland and as if the marriage were intended to be contracted or celebrated in Scotland, and the provisions of that Act relating to notices of intended marriages and the granting of certificates of due publication thereof shall apply accordingly,

    (*b*) the party residing in England may, subject to and in accordance with the provisions of sections twenty-seven and twenty-eight of this Act, give notice of the intended marriage as if both parties were residing in different registration districts in England, and the provisions of this Part of this Act relating to notices of marriage and the issue of certificates for marriage shall apply accordingly;

    (*c*) a certificate of due publication of a notice of the intended marriage granted in Scotland by virtue of paragraph (*a*) of this subsection shall, for the purposes of the marriage, have the like force and effect in all respects as a certificate for marriage issued by a superintendent registrar under this Part of this Act;

    (*d*) for the purposes of section thirty-three of this Act the notice given in Scotland shall be deemed to have been entered in a marriage notice book by a superintendent registrar in England on the day on which it was given.

(2) Where a marriage is intended to be solemnized as aforesaid between parties of whom one is residing in Scotland and the other is residing in England and a certificate of proclamation of banns in Scotland has been issued under the hand of the minister or session clerk of the parish in which the proclamation was made—

    (*a*) the superintendent registrar of the registration district in which the party residing in England is residing may accept notice of marriage given by that party, subject to and in accordance with the provisions of sections twenty-seven and twenty-eight of this Act, as if both parties were residing in different registration districts in England, and the provisions of this Part of this Act relating to notices of marriage and the issue of certificates for marriage shall apply accordingly;

(b) the production of the certificate of proclamation of banns to the person by whom the marriage is to be solemnized shall be as valid for authorising that person to solemnize the marriage as the production of a certificate for marriage of a superintendent registrar of a registration district in England would be in the case of a person residing in that district.

One party resident in Northern Ireland

38.—(1) Where a marriage is intended to be solemnized in England on the authority of a certificate of a superintendent registrar without licence between parties of whom one is residing in Northern Ireland and the other is residing in England, the party residing in Northern Ireland may give notice of marriage in the form used for that purpose in Northern Ireland or to the like effect to the registrar of the district in Northern Ireland in which he or she has resided for not less than seven days immediately before the giving of the notice.

(2) Any such notice as aforesaid shall state the name and surname, marital status, occupation, age and place of residence of each of the persons to be married and the period, not being less than seven days, during which each of them has resided in that place and the church or other building in which the marriage is to be solemnized:

Provided that if either of the persons to be married has resided in the place stated in the notice for more than one month, the notice may state that he or she has resided there for more than one month.

(3) Any such notice as aforesaid shall be dealt with, and a certificate for marriage issued by the registrar, in the manner prescribed by the Marriages (Ireland) Act 1844, as amended by the Marriages (Ireland) Act 1846, and the Marriage Law (Ireland) Amendment Act 1863:

Provided that the registrar shall not issue a certificate until the expiration of twenty-one days from the day on which the notice was entered in the marriage notice book required to be kept under the said Marriages (Ireland) Act 1844.

(4) The production to the person by whom the marriage is to be solemnized of a certificate issued under the last foregoing subsection shall be as valid for authorising that person to solemnize the marriage as the production of a certificate for marriage of a superintendent registrar of a registration district in England would be in the case of a person residing in that district.

Issue of certificates on board His Majesty's ships

39.—(1) Where a marriage is intended to be solemnized in England on the authority of a certificate of a superintendent registrar without licence between parties of whom one is residing in England and the other is an officer, seaman, or marine borne on the books of one of His Majesty's ships at sea, the last-mentioned party may give notice of his intention to the captain or other officer commanding the ship, together with the name and address of the other party to the marriage, and such other information as may be necessary to enable the captain or other officer to fill up a certificate under this section, and shall at the same time make and sign such a declaration as is required by section twenty-eight of this Act, and the captain or officer may attest the declaration and thereupon issue a certificate to the officer, seaman or marine giving the notice.

(2) A certificate issued under this section shall be in such form as may be prescribed by the Admiralty and shall have the like force and effect as a certificate issued by a superintendent registrar under this Part of this Act, and all provisions of this Act (including penal provisions) relating to notices and declarations for obtaining certificates from superintendent registrars and to such certificates shall apply in the case of certificates issued under this section, subject to such adaptations therein as may be made by His Majesty by Order in Council.

(3) Where a marriage is intended to be solemnized in England as aforesaid and a certificate has been issued to one of the parties under this section, the superintendent registrar of the registration district in which the other party is residing may accept notice of marriage given by that party, subject to and in accordance with the provisions of sections twenty-seven and twenty-eight of this Act, as if both parties were residing in different registration districts in England, and the provisions of this Part of this Act relating to notices of marriage and the issue of certificates for marriage shall apply accordingly.

Forms of certificates to be furnished by Registrar General

40.—(1) The Registrar General shall furnish to every superintendent registrar a sufficient number of forms of certificates for marriage.

(2) In order to distinguish the certificates to be issued for marriages by licence from the certificates to be issued for marriages without licence, a watermark in the form of the word " licence," in Roman letters, shall be laid and manufactured in the substance of the paper on which the certificates to be issued for marriage by licence are written or printed, and every certificate to be issued for marriage by licence shall be printed with red ink and every certificate to be issued for marriage without licence shall be printed with black ink, and such other distinctive marks between the two kinds of certificates as the Registrar General may from time to time think fit shall be used.

Marriages in registered buildings
Registration of buildings

41.—(1) Any proprietor or trustee of a separate building, which has been certified as required by law as a place of religious worship may apply to the superintendent registrar of the registration district in which the building is situated for the building to be registered for the solemnization of marriages therein.

[(2) Any person making such an application as aforesaid shall deliver to the superintendent registrar a certificate, signed in duplicate by at least twenty householders and dated not earlier than one month before the making of the application, stating that the building is being used by them as their usual place of public religious worship and that they desire that the building should be registered as aforesaid, and both certificates shall be countersigned by the proprietor or trustee by whom they are delivered.] [16]

(3) The superintendent registrar shall send both certificates delivered to him under the last foregoing subsection to the Registrar General who shall register the building in a book to be kept for that purpose in the General Register Office.

(4) The Registrar General shall endorse on both certificates sent to him as aforesaid the date of the registration, and shall keep one certificate with the records of the General Register Office and shall return the other certificate to the superintendent registrar who shall keep it with the records of his office.

[16] Substituted by Marriage Acts Amendment Act 1958 (c. 29), s. 1 (1).

(5) On the return of the certificate under the last foregoing subsection, the superintendent registrar shall—

(a) enter the date of the registration of the building in a book to be provided for that purpose by the Registrar General;

(b) give a certificate of the registration signed by him, on durable materials, to the proprietor or trustee by whom the certificates delivered to him under subsection (2) of this section were countersigned; and

(c) give public notice of the registration of the building by advertisement in some newspaper circulating in the county in which the building is situated and in the London Gazette.

(6) For every entry, certificate and notice made or given under the last foregoing subsection the superintendent registrar shall be entitled to receive, at the time of the delivery of the certificates under subsection (2) of this section, the sum of [six pounds].[17]

[(7) For the purpose of being registered for the solemnization of marriages under this section, any building used for public religious worship as a Roman Catholic chapel exclusively shall be deemed to be a separate building notwithstanding that it is under the same roof as another building or forms part only of a building.] [16]

Cancellation of registration and substitution of another building

42.—(1) Where, on an application made by or through the superintendent registrar of the registration district in which the building is situated, it is shown to the satisfaction of the Registrar General that a registered building is no longer used for the purpose of public religious worship by the congregation on whose behalf it was registered, he shall cause the registration to be cancelled, [. . .].[18]

[*Subsection* (2) *repealed by Marriage Acts Amendment Act* 1958 (*c.* 29), *s.* 1 (1).]

(3) Where the Registrar General cancels the registration of any building, [. . .] [18] under this section, he shall inform the superintendent registrar who shall enter that fact and the date thereof in the book provided for the registration of buildings, and shall certify and publish the cancellation, [. . .] [18] in the manner provided by subsection (5) of the last foregoing section in the case of the [. . .] [18] registration of a building.

[*Subsection* (4) *repealed by Marriage Acts Amendment Act* 1958 (*c.* 29), *s.* 1 (1).]

(5) Where the registration of any building has been cancelled, [. . .] [18] under this section, it shall not be lawful to solemnize any marriage in the disused building, unless the building has been registered again in accordance with the provisions of this Part of this Act.

Appointment of authorised persons

43.—(1) For the purpose of enabling marriages to be solemnized in a registered building without the presence of a registrar, the trustees or governing body of that building may authorise a person to be present at the solemnization of marriages in that building and, where a person is so authorised in respect of any registered building, the trustees or governing body of that building shall, within the prescribed time and in the prescribed manner, certify the name and address of the person so authorised to the Registrar General and to the superintendent registrar of the registration district in which the building is situated.

[Provided that, in relation to a building which becomes registered

---

[17] Fee raised by S.I. 1972/911.
[18] Words repealed by Marriage Acts Amendment Act 1958 (c. 29) s. 1 (1).

after the thirty-first day of December, nineteen hundred and fifty-eight, the power conferred by this subsection to authorise a person to be present as aforesaid shall not be exercisable before the expiration of one year from the date of registration of the building or, where the congregation on whose behalf the building is registered previously used for the purpose of public religious worship another building of which the registration has been cancelled not earlier than one month before the date of registration, aforesaid, one year from the date of registration of that other building.] [19]

(2) Any person whose name and address have been certified as aforesaid is in this Act referred to as an " authorised person ".

(3) Nothing in this section shall be taken to relate or have any reference to marriages solemnized according to the usages of the Society of Friends or of persons professing the Jewish religion.

Solemnization of marriage in registered building

44.—(1) Subject to the provisions of this section, where a notice of marriage and certificate issued by a superintendent registrar state that a marriage between the persons named therein is intended to be solemnized in a registered building, the marriage may be solemnized in that building according to such form and ceremony as those persons may see fit to adopt:

Provided that no marriage shall be solemnized in any registered building without the consent of the minister or of one of the trustees, owners, deacons or managers thereof, or in the case of a registered building of the Roman Catholic Church, without the consent of the officiating minister thereof.

(2) Subject to the provisions of this section, a marriage solemnized in a registered building shall be solemnized with open doors in the presence of two or more witnesses and in the presence of either—

(*a*) a register of the registration district in which the registered building is situated, or

(*b*) an authorised person whose name and address have been certified in accordance with the last foregoing section by the trustees or governing body of that registered building or of some other registered building in the same registration district.

(3) Where a marriage is solemnized in a registered building each of the persons contracting the marriage shall, in some part of the ceremony and in the presence of the witnesses and the registrar or authorised person, make the following declaration:—

" I do solemnly declare that I know not of any lawful impediment why I, *AB*, may not be joined in matrimony to *CD* " and each of them shall say to the other:—

" I call upon these persons here present to witness that I, *AB*, do take thee, *CD*, to be my lawful wedded wife [*or* husband] ":

Provided that if the marriage is solemnized in the presence of an authorised person without the presence of a registrar, the persons to be married, instead of saying each to the other the last-mentioned form of words, may say:—

" I, *AB*, do take thee, *C.D.*, to be my wedded wife [*or* husband] ".

(4) A marriage shall not be solemnized in a registered building without the presence of a registrar until duplicate marriage register books have been supplied by the Registrar General under Part IV of this Act to the authorised person or to the trustees or governing body of the building.

---

[19] Proviso added by *ibid.*, s. 1 (2).

(5) If the Registrar General is not satisfied with respect to any building registered or proposed to be registered for the solemnization of marriages therein that sufficient security exists for the due registration of marriages by an authorised person under Part IV of this Act and for the safe custody of marriage register books, he may in his discretion attach to the continuance of the registration, or to the registration, of the building a condition that no marriage may be solemnized therein without the presence of a registrar.

Marriages in register offices

Solemnization of marriage in register office

45.—(1) Where a marriage is intended to be solemnized on the authority of a certificate of a superintendent registrar, the persons to be married may state in the notice of marriage that they wish to be married in the office of the superintendent registrar or one of the superintendent registrars, as the case may be, to whom notice of marriage is given, and where any such notice has been given and the certificate or certificate and licence, as the case may be, has or have been issued accordingly, the marriage may be solemnized in the said office, with open doors, in the presence of the superintendent registrar and a registrar of the registration district of that superintendent registrar and in the presence of two witnesses, and the persons to be married shall make the declarations and use the form of words set out in subsection (3) of the last foregoing section in the case of marriages in registered buildings in the presence of a registrar.

(2) No religious service shall be used at any marriage solemnized in the office of a superintendent registrar.

Register office marriage followed by religious ceremony

46.—(1) If the parties to a marriage solemnized in the office of a superintendent registrar desire to add the religious ceremony ordained or used by the church or persuasion of which they are members, they may present themselves, after giving notice of their intention so to do, to the clergyman or minister of the church or persuasion of which they are members, and the clergyman or minister, upon the production of a certificate of their marriage before the superintendent registrar and upon the payment of the customary fees (if any), may, if he sees fit, read or celebrate in the church or chapel of which he is the regular minister the marriage service of the church or persuasion to which he belongs or nominate some other minister to do so.

(2) Nothing in the reading or celebration of a marriage service under this section shall supersede or invalidate any marriage previously solemnized in the office of a superintendent registrar, and the reading or celebration shall not be entered as a marriage in any marriage register book kept under Part IV of this Act.

(3) No person who is not entitled to solemnize marriages according to the rites of the Church of England shall by virtue of this section be entitled to read or celebrate the marriage service in any church or chapel of the Church of England.

Marriages according to usages of Society of Friends

Marriages according to usages of Society of Friends

47.—(1) No person who is not a member of the Society of Friends shall be married according to the usages of that Society unless he or she is authorised to be so married under or in pursuance of a general rule of the said Society in England.

(2) A marriage solemnized according to the said usages shall not be valid unless either—

    (*a*) the person giving notice of marriage declares, either verbally or, if so required, in writing, that each of the parties to the marriage is either a member of the Society of Friends or is in profession with or of the persuasion of that Society; or

    (*b*) there is produced to the superintendent registrar, at the time when notice of marriage is given, a certificate purporting to be signed by a registering officer of the Society of Friends in England to the effect that any party to the marriage who is not a member of the Society of Friends or in profession with or of the persuasion of that Society, is authorised to be married according to the said usages under or in pursuance of a general rule of the said Society in England.

(3) Any such certificate as aforesaid shall be for all purposes conclusive evidence that any person to whom it relates is authorised to be married according to the usages of the said Society, and the entry of the marriage in a marriage register book under Part IV of this Act, or a certified copy thereof made under the said Part IV, shall be conclusive evidence of the production of such a certificate.

(4) A copy of any general rule of the Society of Friends purporting to be signed by the recording clerk for the time being of the said Society in London shall be admitted as evidence of the general rule in all proceedings touching the validity of any marriage solemnized according to the usages of the said Society.

Miscellaneous Provisions

Proof of certain matters not necessary to validity of marriages

48.—(1) Where any marriage has been solemnized under the provisions of this Part of this Act, it shall not be necessary in support of the marriage to give any proof—

    (*a*) that before the marriage either of the parties thereto resided, or resided for any period, in the registration district stated in the notice of marriage to be that of his or her place of residence;

    (*b*) that any person whose consent to the marriage was required by section three of this Act had given his consent;

    (*c*) that the registered building in which the marriage was solemnized had been certified as required by law as a place of religious worship;

    (*d*) that that building was the usual place of worship of either of the parties to the marriage; or

    (*e*) that the facts stated in a declaration made under subsection (1) of section thirty-five of this Act were correct:

nor shall any evidence be given to prove the contrary in any proceedings touching the validity of the marriage.

(2) A marriage solemnized in accordance with the provisions of this Part of this Act in a registered building which has not been certified as required by law as a place of religious worship shall be as valid as if the building had been so certified.

Void marriages

49. If any persons knowingly and wilfully intermarry under the provisions of this Part of this Act—

    (*a*) without having given due notice of marriage to the superintendent registrar;

    (*b*) without a certificate for marriage having been duly issued by the superintendent registrar to whom notice of marriage was given;

(c) without a licence having been so issued, in a case in which a licence is necessary;

(d) on the authority of a certificate which is void by virtue of subsection (2) of section thirty-three of this Act;

(e) in any place other than the church, chapel, registered building, office or other place specified in the notice of marriage and certificate of the superintendent registrar;

(f) in the case of a marriage in a registered building (not being a marriage in the presence of an authorised person), in the absence of a registrar of the registration district in which the registered building is situated; or

(g) in the case of a marriage in the office of a superintendent registrar, in the absence of the superintendent registrar or of a registrar of the registration district of that superintendent registrar;

the marriage shall be void.

Person to whom certificate to be delivered

50.—(1) Where a marriage is intended to be solemnized on the authority of a certificate of a superintendent registrar, the certificate or, if notice of marriage has been given to more than one superintendent registrar, the certificates shall be delivered to the following person, that is to say:—

(a) if the marriage is to be solemnized in a registered building in the presence of a registrar, that registrar;

(b) if the marriage is to be solemnized in a registered building without the presence of a registrar, the authorised person in whose presence the marriage is to be solemnized;

(c) if the marriage is to be solemnized in the office of a superintendent registrar, the registrar in whose presence the marriage is to be solemnized;

(d) if the marriage is to be solemnized according to the usages of the Society of Friends, the registering officer of that Society for the place where the marriage is to be solemnized;

(e) if the marriage is to be solemnized according to the usages of persons professing the Jewish religion, the officer of a synagogue by whom the marriage is required to be registered under Part IV of this Act;

(f) if the marriage is to be solemnized according to the rites of the Church of England, the officiating clergyman.

(2) In the application of the last foregoing subsection to a marriage solemnized otherwise than according to the rites of the Church of England, the reference therein to a certificate shall, if the marriage is by licence, be construed as a reference to the certificate and licence.

(3) Where a marriage is solemnized in a registered building without the presence of a registrar, the certificate or certificate and licence, as the case may be, shall be kept in the prescribed custody and shall be produced with the marriage register books kept by the authorised person under Part IV of this Act as and when required by the Registrar General.

Fees of registrars for attending marriages

51. A registrar shall be entitled to receive from persons married under this Part of this Act in his presence the sum of [£1·50] [20] if the marriage is by licence and, in any other case, the sum of [£1·50].[20]

Provision for marriages in Welsh language

52. The Registrar General shall furnish to every registrar in Wales

[20] Fees raised by S.I. 1972/911.

and in every place in which the Welsh language is commonly used a true and exact translation into the Welsh language of the declaration and form of words required to be used under section forty-four of this Act, and the said translation may be used in any place in which the Welsh language is commonly used in the same manner as is prescribed by the said section forty-four for the use of the declaration and form of words in the English language.

PART IV

REGISTRATION OF MARRIAGES

Persons by whom marriages are to be registered

53.[20a] Subject to the provisions of Part V of this Act, a marriage shall be registered in accordance with the provisions of this Part of this Act by the following person, that is to say,—

    (*a*) in the case of a marriage solemnized according to the rites of the Church of England, by the clergyman by whom the marriage is solemnized;

    (*b*) in the case of a marriage solemnized according to the usages of the Society of Friends, by the registering officer of that Society appointed for the district in which the marriage is solemnized;

    (*c*) in the case of a marriage solemnized according to the usages of persons professing the Jewish religion, by the secretary of the synagogue of which the husband is a member;

    (*d*) in the case of a marriage solemnized in a registered building in the presence of a registrar, by that registrar;

    (*e*) in the case of a marriage solemnized in a registered building without the presence of a registrar, by the authorised person in whose presence the marriage is solemnized;

    (*f*) in the case of a marriage solemnized in the office of a superintendent registrar, by the registrar in whose presence the marriage is solemnized.

Provision of marriage register books by Registrar General

54.—(1) The Registrar General shall furnish to the rector, vicar or curate in charge of every church and chapel in which marriages may be solemnized according to the rites of the Church of England (hereafter in this Part of this Act referred to as the " incumbent ") and to every registering officer of the Society of Friends, secretary of a synagogue and registrar and, in the case of a registered building for which an authorised person has been appointed, to the authorised person or to the trustees or governing body of the building, such number of register books for making entries of marriages in the prescribed form, and such number of forms for making certified copies of those entries, as may be required for the purposes of this Part of this Act.

(2) Marriage register books furnished as aforesaid shall be of durable materials, and the heads of information required to be known and registered in relation to marriages shall be printed on each side of every leaf thereof; and every page of a marriage register book, and every place of entry therein, shall be numbered progressively from the beginning to the end of the book, beginning with the number one, and every entry shall be divided from the following entry by a printed line.

[20a] Extended by Marriage (Registrar General's Licence) Act 1970 (c. 34), s. 14.

Manner of registration of marriages

55.[20b]—(1) Every person who is required under this Part of this Act to register a marriage shall, immediately after the solemnization of the marriage, or, in the case of a marriage according to the usages of the Society of Friends, as soon as conveniently may be after the solemnization of the marriage, register in duplicate in two marriage register books the particulars relating to the marriage in the prescribed form:

Provided that—

(a) where a registrar is required to register a marriage as aforesaid, the said particulars need not be registered in duplicate;

(b) before registering a marriage in accordance with the provisions of this Part of this Act, a registering officer of the Society of Friends and a secretary of a synagogue shall, whether or not he was present at the marriage, satisfy himself that the proceedings in relation to the marriage were conformable to the usages of the said Society or of persons professing the Jewish religion, as the case may be.

(2) Every entry made in a marriage register book by virtue of this section by a clergyman, registering officer, secretary or authorised person shall be signed by the clergyman, registering officer, secretary or authorised person, as the case may be, and by the parties to the marriage and two witnesses, and every entry so made by a registrar shall be signed by the person by or before whom the marriage was solemnized, if any, and by the registrar, the parties to the marriage and two witnesses.

(3) Every entry made in a marriage register book by virtue of this section shall be made in consecutive order from the beginning to the end of each book and, in the case of an entry made otherwise than by a registrar, the number of the entry shall be the same in each duplicate marriage register book.

Power to ask for particulars of marriage

56. Every person who is required under this Part of this Act to register a marriage may ask the parties to the marriage the particulars relating to the marriage which are required to be entered in the marriage register book.

Quarterly returns to be made to superintendent registrar

57.—(1) Every incumbent, registering officer of the Society of Friends, secretary of a synagogue, authorised person and registrar shall in the months of January, April, July and October—

(a) make and deliver to the superintendent registrar, on forms supplied by the Registrar General, a true copy certified by him under his hand of all entries of marriages made in the marriage register book kept by him during the period of three months ending with the last day of the month immediately before the month in which the copy is required by this subsection to be made; or

(b) if no marriage has been registered in the said book during that period, deliver to the superintendent registrar a certificate of that fact under his hand, on a form supplied by the Registrar General.

(2) The certified copies and certificates required to be delivered by a registrar under the last foregoing subsection shall be delivered to the superintendent registrar on such days in the months of January, April,

[20b] Extended by Marriage (Registrar General's Licence) Act 1970 (c. 34), s. 15.

July and October as may be appointed by the Registrar General, and shall be certified by the registrar in the prescribed form.

(3) Any incumbent and any authorised person who is required by subsection (1) of this section to deliver to the superintendent registrar a certified copy of entries in the marriage register book or a certificate that no marriage has been registered, may deliver the copy or certificate to any registrar who is under the superintendence of that superintendent registrar, and every registrar who receives such a certified copy or certificate shall deliver it to the superintendent registrar; and a superintendent registrar may direct the registrars under his superintendence quarterly or more often, if he thinks fit or is ordered so to do by the Registrar General, to collect any such certified copies or certificates from every incumbent and authorised person within his registration district.

(4) The superintendent registrar shall pay or cause to be paid to every incumbent and authorised person by whom a certified copy is delivered under subsection (1) of this section the sum of [25p] [21] for every entry contained in the certified copy; [and that sum shall be reimbursed to the superintendent registrar—

(a) in the case of a registration district in the City of London, the Inner Temple and the Middle Temple, by the Common Council of the City of London;

(b) in any other case, by the council of the non-metropolitan county, metropolitan district or London borough in which his registration district is situated].[21a]

(5) Where a certified copy is delivered to the superintendent registrar by a registrar under subsection (1) of this section, the superintendent registrar shall verify the copy and, if the copy is found to be correct, shall certify it under his hand to be a true copy; and where a certificate that no marriage has been registered is so delivered, the superintendent registrar shall countersign the certificate.

[*Subsection (6) repealed by Registration Service Act* 1953 (c. 37), *s.* 23 (2), *Sched.* 2.]

Quarterly returns to be made by superintendent registrar to Registrar General

58.—(1) Every superintendent registrar shall, four times in every year on such days as may be appointed by the Registrar General, send to the Registrar General all certified copies of entries in marriage register books which he has received during the three months immediately before the days so appointed respectively, and if it appears, by interruption of the regular progression of numbers or otherwise, that the copy of any part of any book has not been duly delivered to him, the superintendent registrar shall as far as possible procure, consistently with the provisions of this Part of this Act, that the deficiency is remedied.

(2) The certified copies sent to the Registrar General under the last foregoing subsection shall be kept in the General Register Office in such order and such manner as the Registrar General, under the direction of the Minister of Health, may think fit [. . . .].[22]

Custody of register books

59. Every incumbent, registering officer of the Society of Friends, secretary of a synagogue, authorised person and registrar shall keep marriage register books safely until they are filled, so however that any register book kept by an authorised person shall be kept in accordance

---

[21] Fee raised by S.I. 1972/911.
[21a] Words substituted by Local Government Act 1972 (c. 70), s. 251 (2), Sched. 29, para. 40.
[22] Words repealed by Registration Service Act 1953 (c. 37), s. 23, Scheds. 1, 2.

with regulations made under section seventy-four of this Act and any register book kept by a registrar shall, when not in use, be kept in the register box provided for the purpose by the Registrar General [. . .].²²

Filled register books

60.—(1) Where any marriage register book required to be kept in duplicate under this Part of this Act is filled, one copy thereof shall be delivered to the superintendent registrar and the other copy—

(*a*) in the case of a register book kept by an incumbent, shall remain in the custody of the incumbent and be kept by him with the registers of baptisms and burials of the parish or other ecclesiastical district in which the marriages registered therein have been solemnized;

(*b*) in the case of a register book kept by a registering officer of the Society of Friends or by the secretary of a synagogue, shall remain in the custody of the members of the Society of Friends or of persons professing the Jewish religion, as the case may be, to be kept with the other registers and records of the said Society or of the said persons, and shall, for the purposes of this Act, be deemed to be in the keeping of the registering officer or secretary for the time being, as the case may be;

(*c*) in the case of a register book kept by an authorised person, shall be kept in prescribed custody.

(2) Where a marriage register book kept by a registrar is filled, the registrar shall deliver it to the superintendent registrar to be kept by him with the records of his office.

Correction of errors in register book

61.—(1) A person required to register a marriage under this Part of this Act who discovers an error in the form or substance of an entry made in a marriage register book kept by him shall not be liable to any penalty by reason only that, within one month after the discovery of the error, he corrects the erroneous entry in the presence of the parties to the marriage to which the entry relates or, in the case of the death or absence of either of those parties, in the presence of the superintendent registrar and two other credible witnesses, by entry in the margin of the register book, without any alteration of the original entry.

(2) Any such marginal entry as aforesaid shall be signed by the person by whom the entry is made and shall be attested by the persons in whose presence the entry is required to be made under the last foregoing subsection, and the person by whom the entry is made shall add the date when it is made.

(3) Where any such marginal entry is made by a person who is required to register marriages in duplicate under this Part of this Act, that person shall make the like entry, attested in the like manner, in the duplicate marriage register book.

(4) Any person who makes any such marginal entry as aforesaid shall make the like entry in the certified copy of the register book required to be made by him under this Part of this Act or, if a certified copy has already been delivered to the superintendent registrar, shall make and deliver to the superintendent registrar a separate certified copy of the original erroneous entry and of the marginal correction made therein.

(5) Where a marriage to which an erroneous entry in a marriage register relates has been solemnized according to the rites of the Church of England and either of the parties to the marriage is dead or absent, the reference in subsection (1) of this section to the superintendent registrar and two other credible witnesses shall be construed as a refer-

ence either to those persons or to the church wardens or chapel warden of the church or chapel in which the marriage was solemnized.

Disposal of register books on church ceasing to be used for solemnization of marriages

62.—(1) Where any church or chapel of the Church of England ceases to be used for the solemnization of marriages, whether by reason of demolition, revocation of a licence or otherwise, any marriage register books in the custody of the incumbent of that church or chapel shall forthwith be delivered to the incumbent of the church which is, or becomes, the parish church of the parish in which the disused church or chapel is situated.

(2) Any incumbent to whom any marriage register books have been delivered under the last foregoing subsection—

(a) shall, when he next delivers to the superintendent registrar under this Part of this Act a certified copy of the entries in the marriage register books of marriages solemnized in the parish church, deliver also a copy of all entries which have been made in the first mentioned marriage register books after the date of the last entry therein of which a certified copy has already been delivered to the superintendent registrar; and

(b) shall, unless the said first mentioned marriage register books are the only register books in use for the parish, forward such of the said books as have not been filled to the Registrar General in order that they may be formally closed.

Searches in register books

63.—(1) Every incumbent, registering officer of the Society of Friends, secretary of a synagogue and registrar by whom a marriage register book is kept shall at all reasonable hours allow searches to be made in any marriage register book in his keeping, and shall give a copy certified under his hand of any entry in such a book, on payment of the following fee, that is to say—

[*Paragraph (a) repealed by S.I.* 1968/1242.]

[(a) to [50p] [22a] where application for a copy is made—
   (i) at the time of registering the marriage or
   (ii) to a registrar by whom the book containing the entry is kept, and
(b) to [75p] in any other case.] [23]

(2) The last foregoing subsection shall apply in the case of a registered building for which an authorised person has been appointed with the substitution for the reference to the incumbent of a reference to the person having the custody of a marriage register book in accordance with regulations made under section seventy-four of this Act.

Searches of indexes kept by superintendent registrars

64.—(1) Every superintendent registrar shall cause indexes of the marriage register books in his office to be made and to be kept with the other records of his office, and the Registrar General shall supply to every superintendent registrar suitable forms for the making of such indexes.

(2) Any person shall be entitled [at any time when the register office is required to be open for the transaction of public business] [24] to search the said indexes, and to have a certified copy of any entry in the said marriage register books under the hand of the superintendent registrar,

[22a] Fee raised by S.I. 1972/911.
[23] Paragraphs added by S.I. 1968/1242.
[24] Amended by Registration Service Act 1953 (c. 37), s. 23 (1), Sched. 1, para. 14.

on payment to the superintendent registrar of the following fee, that
is to say:—

(a) for every general search, the sum of [£3·00] [25];

[*Paragraph (b) repealed by S.I.* 1968/1242.]

(c) for every certified copy, the sum of [75p]. [25]

Searches of indexes kept by Registrar General

65.—(1) The Registrar General shall cause indexes of all certified
copies of entries in marriage register books sent to him under this Part
of this Act to be made and kept in the General Register Office.

(2) Any person shall be entitled to search the said indexes [at any
time when the General Register Office is open for that purpose], [26] and to
have a certified copy of any entry in the said certified copies of marriage
register books, on payment to the Registrar General or to such other
person as may be appointed to act on his behalf of the following fee,
that is to say:—

[*Paragraphs (a) (b) repealed by S.I.* 1968/1242.]

(c) for every certified copy, the sum of [75p]. [25]

(3) The Registrar General shall cause all certified copies of entries
given in the General Register Office to be sealed or stamped with the
seal of that Office; and any certified copy of an entry purporting to be
sealed or stamped with the said seal shall be received as evidence of
the marriage to which it relates without any further or other proof of
the entry, and no certified copy purporting to have been given in the
said Office shall be of any force or effect unless it is sealed or stamped as
aforesaid.

[*Subsection (4) repealed by Registration Service Act* 1953 (c. 37), s.
23 (1), *Sched.* 1, *para.* 15.]

Sending documents by post

66. Any certificate, return or other document required by this Part
of this Act to be delivered or sent to the Registrar General, a superintendent registrar or a registrar may be sent by post.

Interpretation of Part IV

67. In this Part of this Act, except where the context otherwise
requires, the following expressions have the meanings hereby respectively
assigned to them, that is to say:—

" general search " means a search conducted during any number of
successive hours not exceeding six, without the object of the
search being specified;

" incumbent " has the meaning assigned to it by section fifty-four of
this Act;

" particular search " means a search of the indexes covering a period
not exceeding five years for a specified entry;

" registering officer of the Society of Friends " means a person whom
the recording clerk of the Society of Friends certifies in writing
under his hand to the Registrar General to be a registering officer
in England of that Society;

" secretary of a synagogue " means—

(a) a person whom the President of the London Committee
of Deputies of the British Jews certifies in writing to the
Registrar General to be the secretary of a synagogue in
England of persons professing the Jewish religion;

---

[25] Fees raised by S.I. 1972/911.
[26] Amended by Registration Service Act 1953 (c. 37), s. 23 (1), Sched. 1, para. 15.

(b) the person whom twenty householders professing the Jewish religion and being members of the West London Synagogue of British Jews certify in writing to the Registrar General to be the secretary of that Synagogue;

[(c) the person whom twenty householders professing the Jewish religion and being members of the Liberal Jewish Synagogue, St. John's Wood, certify in writing to the Registrar General to be the secretary of that Synagogue;

(d) a person whom the secretary of either the West London Synagogue of British Jews or the Liberal Jewish Synagogue, St. John's Wood, certifies in writing to be the secretary of some other synagogue of not less than twenty householders professing the Jewish religion, being a synagogue which is connected with the said West London Synagogue or with the said Liberal Jewish Synagogue, St. John's Wood, as the case may be, and has been established for not less than one year.] [27]

" superintendent registrar " means—

(a) in the case of a marriage registered by a clergyman, the superintendent registrar of the registration district in which the church or chapel in which the marriage was solemnized is situated;

(b) in the case of a marriage registered by a registering officer of the Society of Friends, the superintendent registrar of the registration district which is assigned by the Registrar General to that registering officer;

(c) in the case of a marriage registered by the secretary of a synagogue, the superintendent registrar of the registration district which is assigned by the Registrar General to that secretary;

(d) in the case of a marriage registered by an authorised person, the superintendent registrar of the registration district in which the registered building in which the marriage was solemnized is situated;

(e) in the case of a marriage registered by a registrar, the superintendent registrar of the registration district within which that registrar was appointed to act.

PART V

MARRIAGES IN NAVAL, MILITARY, AND AIR FORCE CHAPELS

Solemnization of marriages in naval, military, and air force chapels

68.[28]—(1) The use of any chapel to which this Part of this Act applies for the publication therein of banns of marriages to which this Part of this Act applies, and for the solemnization therein, whether according to the rites of the Church of England or otherwise, of such marriages, may be authorised under and subject to the provisions of this Part of this Act.

(2) This Part of this Act shall apply only to chapels which are certified by the Admiralty to be naval chapels and to chapels which are certified by a Secretary of State to be military or air force chapels, and shall apply only to marriages between parties of whom one at least is a qualified person, that is to say a person who, at the relevant date—

(a) is serving in the Royal Navy, the Royal Marines, the Regular Land Forces or the Regular Air Forces; or

(b) has served in any force mentioned in the last foregoing paragraph otherwise than with a commission granted or under an engage-

---

[27] Substituted by Marriage (Secretaries of Synagogues) Act 1959 (c. 13), s. 1.
[28] Extended by S.I. 1965/1536, art. 12 (2), Sched. 3.

ment entered into only for the purpose of a war or other national emergency; or

(c) is, as a member of a reserve of officers, a reserve force, the Territorial Army or the Auxiliary Air Force, called out on actual or permanent service or embodied; or

(d) is a woman actually employed in any capacity specified in the Third Schedule to this Act, as amended by any Order in Council for the time being in force under this section, in the service of any force mentioned in the foregoing paragraphs of this sub-section; or

(e) is a daughter of a person qualified under any of the foregoing paragraphs of this subsection.

(3) For the purposes of the last foregoing subsection, the expression " relevant date " means—

(a) in a case where notice is given under section eight of this Act before publications of banns, the date of the notice;

(b) in a case where banns are published without such notice, the date of the first publication of banns;

(c) in a case where an oath is taken under section sixteen of this Act for the purpose of obtaining a common licence, the date of taking the oath;

(d) in any other case, the date when notice of marriage is given to the superintendent registrar under section twenty-seven of this Act;

and the expression " daughter " [. . .] [28a] does not include a step-daughter.

(4) His Majesty may by Order in Council direct that subject to any exceptions specified in the Order, there shall be added to Part I, Part II or Part III of the Third Schedule to this Act, women in the service of any of His Majesty's naval, military or air forces respectively in such capacities as may be specified in the Order.

(5) An Order in Council made under the last foregoing subsection may be varied or revoked by a subsequent Order in Council.

(6) Nothing in this Part of this Act shall be taken to confer upon any person a right to be married in a chapel to which this Part of this Act applies.

Licensing of chapels for marriages according to rites of Church of England

69.—(1) With respect to marriages according to the rites of the Church of England, the bishop of the diocese in which any chapel to which this Part of this Act applies is situated may, on the application of the Admiralty, in the case of a naval chapel, or of a Secretary of State, in the case of any other chapel, by licence authorise the publication of banns of marriages to which this Part of this Act applies, and the solemnization of such marriages, in the chapel, and while any such licence in respect of the chapel is in force—

(a) any such banns or marriages which could lawfully be published or solemnized in the parish church of the parish in which the chapel is situated may be published or solemnized in the chapel; and

(b) the foregoing provisions of this Act relating to marriages according to the rites of the Church of England (excluding the provisions specified in Part I of the Fourth Schedule to this Act) shall apply in relation to the chapel, and in relation to the publication of banns therein, and in relation to marriages solemnized or intended to be solemnized therein according to those rites, as if the chapel were a parish church:

28a Words repealed by Children Act 1975 (c. 72), Sched. 4.

Provided that the provisions of this Act specified in Part II of the said Schedule shall apply subject to the modifications specified in that Part.

(2) Where a licence has been issued in respect of a chapel under this section, the bishop of the diocese in which the chapel is situated may at any time, and shall on the application of the Admiralty or a Secretary of State, revoke the licence.

(3) Upon the issue or revocation of a licence under this section, the registrar of the diocese shall register that fact and give notice thereof in writing to the Admiralty or a Secretary of State, as the case may be, who shall cause a copy of the notice to be published in the London Gazette and in some newspaper circulating in the diocese and to be sent to the Registrar General.

(4) The Admiralty or any person authorised by them, in the case of a naval chapel licensed under this section, and a Secretary of State or any person authorised by him, in the case of any other chapel so licensed, shall appoint one or more clergymen for the purpose of registering marriages solemnized in the chapel according to the rites of the Church of England, and no marriage shall be solemnized in the chapel according to those rites except in the presence of a clergyman so appointed.

(5) The provisions of this Act, and of any regulations made under section seventy-four of this Act, relating to the registration of marriages by authorised persons shall apply in relation to marriages solemnized according to the rites of the Church of England in a chapel licensed under this section as they apply in relation to marriages solemnized in a registered building without the presence of a registrar, subject to the following modifications:—

> (a) for any reference in those provisions to an authorised person there shall be substituted a reference to a clergyman appointed under this section, and
>
> (b) for any reference in those provisions to the trustees or governing body of a registered building there shall be substituted a reference to the Admiralty or any person authorised by them, in the case of a naval chapel, and a reference to a Secretary of State or any person authorised by him, in the case of any other chapel.

Registration of chapels for marriages otherwise than according to rites of Church of England

70.—(1) With respect to marriages otherwise than according to the rites of the Church of England, the Registrar General shall, on the application of the Admiralty, in the case of a naval chapel, or of a Secretary of State, in the case of any other chapel, register any chapel to which this Part of this Act applies for the solemnization therein of marriages to which this Part of this Act applies, and while any chapel is so registered—

> (a) any such marriages which could lawfully be solemnized in a registered building situated in the same registration district as the chapel, may be solemnized in the chapel; and
>
> (b) the foregoing provisions of this Act relating to marriages otherwise than according to the rites of the Church of England and to the registration of such marriages (excluding the provisions specified in Part III of the Fourth Schedule to this Act) shall apply in relation to the chapel, and in relation to marriages solemnized or intended to be solemnized therein otherwise than according to those rites, as if the chapel were a registered building:

Provided that the provisions of this Act specified in Part IV of the said Schedule shall apply subject to the modifications specified in that Part.

(2) The Registrar General shall, on the application of the Admiralty or a Secretary of State, as the case may be, cancel the registration of any chapel registered by him under this section.

(3) Immediately after registering, or cancelling the registration of, any chapel under this section, the Registrar General shall cause notice of that fact to be published in the London Gazette and in some newspaper circulating in the registration district in which the chapel is situated and to be given to the superintendent registrar of that district, who shall record the registration or cancellation in such manner as may be prescribed by the Registrar General.

Evidence of marriages under Part V

71. Where a marriage has been solemnized under this Part of this Act, it shall not be necessary, in support of the marriage, to give any proof—

(*a*) that the chapel in which the marriage was solemnized was certified or licensed or registered in accordance with this Part of this Act; or

(*b*) that either of the parties was a qualified person within the meaning of this Part of this Act; or

(*c*) in the case of a marriage according to the rites of the Church of England, that the marriage was solemnized in the presence of a clergyman duly appointed under this Part of this Act for the purpose of registering marriages;

and no evidence shall be given to prove the contrary in any proceedings touching the validity of any such marriage.

PART VI

GENERAL

Supplementary provisions as to marriages in usual places of worship

72.[29]—(1) For the purposes of the following provisions of this Act, that is to say, subsection (4) of section six, paragraph (*b*) of subsection (1) of section fifteen and subsection (3) of section thirty-five, no parish church or authorised chapel shall be deemed to be the usual place of worship of any person unless he is enrolled on the church electoral roll of the area in which that church or chapel is situated, and where any person is enrolled on the church electoral roll of an area in which he does not reside that enrolment shall be sufficient evidence that his usual place of worship is a parish church or authorised chapel in that area.

(2) Persons intending to be married shall have the like but no greater right of having their banns published and marriage solemnized by virtue of the said provisions in a parish church or authorised chapel which is the usual place of worship of one or both of them as they have of having their banns published and marriage solemnized in the parish church or public chapel of the parish or chapelry in which they or one of them resides.

(3) Where any marriage has been solemnized by virtue of the said provisions it shall not be necessary in support of the marriage to give any proof of the actual enrolment of the parties or of one of them on the church electoral roll of the area in which the parish church or authorised chapel in which the marriage was solemnized was situated, nor shall any

[29] Amended by Marriage (Wales and Monmouthshire) Act 1962 (c. 32), s. 1 (2).

evidence be given to prove the contrary in any proceedings touching the validity of the marriage.

(4) In this section the expression " church electoral roll " means a church electoral roll provision for which is made in the Rules for the Representation of the Laity contained in the Schedule to the Representation of the Laity Measure 1929.

Lists of licensed chapels and registered buildings

73.—(1) The registrar of every diocese shall, within fifteen days after the first day of January in every year, make out and send by post to the Registrar General at his office a list of all chapels within that diocese in which marriages may be solemnized according to the rites of the Church of England (being chapels which belong to the Church of England or have been licensed under Part V of this Act), and shall distinguish in that list which chapels have a parish, chapelry or other recognised ecclesiastical division annexed to them, which are chapels licensed under section twenty of this Act and which are chapels licensed under the said Part V, and, in the case of chapels licensed under the said section twenty, shall state in the list the district for which each chapel is licensed according to the description thereof in the licence.

(2) The Registrar General shall in every year make out and cause to be printed a list of all chapels included in any list sent to him under the last foregoing subsection and of all registered buildings and shall state in that list the county and registration district within which each chapel or registered building is situated and the names and places of residence of the superintendent registrars, registrars and deputy registrars of each district.

(3) A copy of every list made by the Registrar General under the last foregoing subsection shall be sent to every registrar and superintendent registrar.

Regulations

74. The Registrar General, with the approval of the Minister of Health, may by statutory instrument make regulations—

    (a) prescribing the duties of [. . .] [30] authorised persons under this Act;

    (b) prescribing any thing which by this Act is required to be prescribed.

Offences relating to solemnization of marriages

75.—(1) Any person who knowingly and wilfully—

    (a) solemnizes a marriage at any other time than between the hours of eight in the forenoon and six in the afternoon (not being a marriage by special licence, a marriage according to the usages of the Society of Friends or a marriage between two persons professing the Jewish religion according to the usages of the Jews);

    (b) solemnizes a marriage according to the rites of the Church of England without banns of matrimony having been duly published (not being a marriage solemnized on the authority of a special licence, a common licence or a certificate of a superintendent registrar);

    (c) solemnizes a marriage according to the said rites (not being a marriage by special licence) in any place other than a church or other building in which banns may be published;

[30] Words repealed by Registration Service Act 1953 (c. 37), s. 23 (2), Sched. 2.

(*d*) solemnizes a marriage according to the said rites falsely pretending to be in Holy Orders;

shall be guilty of felony and shall be liable to imprisonment for a term not exceeding fourteen years.

(2) Any person who knowingly and wilfully—

(*a*) solemnizes a marriage (not being a marriage by special licence, a marriage according to the usages of the Society of Friends or a marriage between two persons professing the Jewish religion according to the usages of the Jews) in any place other than—

(i) a church or other building in which marriages may be solemnized according to the rites of the Church of England, or

(ii) the registered building or office specified in the notice of marriage and certificate required under Part III of this Act;

(*b*) solemnizes a marriage in any such registered building as aforesaid (not being a marriage in the presence of an authorised person) in the absence of a registrar of the district in which the registered building is situated;

(*c*) solemnizes a marriage in the office of a superintendent registrar in the absence of a registrar of the district in which the office is situated;

(*d*) solemnizes a marriage on the authority of a certificate of a superintendent registrar (not being a marriage by licence) within twenty-one days after the day on which the notice of marriage was entered in the marriage notice book; or

(*e*) solemnizes a marriage on the authority of a certificate of a superintendent registrar after the expiration of three months from the said day on which the notice of marriage was entered as aforesaid;

shall be guilty of felony and shall be liable to imprisonment for a term not exceeding five years.

(3) A superintendent registrar who knowingly and wilfully—

(*a*) issues any certificate for marriage (not being a marriage by licence) before the expiration of twenty-one days from the day on which the notice of marriage was entered in the marriage notice book, or issues a certificate for marriage by licence before the expiration of one whole day from the said day on which the notice was entered as aforesaid;

(*b*) issues any certificate or licence for marriage after the expiration of three months from the said day;

(*c*) issues any certificate the issue of which has been forbidden under section thirty of this Act by any person entitled to forbid the issue of such a certificate; or

(*d*) solemnizes or permits to be solemnized in his office any marriage which is void by virtue of any of the provisions of Part III of this Act;

shall be guilty of felony and shall be liable to imprisonment for a term not exceeding five years.

(4) No prosecution under this section shall be commenced after the expiration of three years from the commission of the offence.

(5) Any reference in subsection (2) of this section to a registered building shall be construed as including a reference to any chapel registered under section seventy of this Act.

Offences relating to registration of marriages

76.—(1) Any person who refuses or without reasonable cause omits to register any marriage which he is required by this Act to register, and any person having the custody of a marriage register book or a certified copy of a marriage register book or part thereof who carelessly loses or injures the said book or copy or carelessly allows the said book or copy to be injured while in his keeping, shall be liable on summary conviction to a fine not exceeding fifty pounds.

(2) Where any person who is required under Part IV of this Act to make and deliver to a superintendent registrar a certified copy of entries made in the marriage register book kept by him, or a certificate that no entries have been made therein since the date of the last certified copy, refuses to deliver any such copy or certificate, or fails to deliver any such copy or certificate during any month in which he is required to do so, he shall be liable on summary conviction to a fine not exceeding [twenty pounds].[31]

(3) Any registrar who knowingly and wilfully registers any marriage which is void by virtue of any of the provisions of Part III of this Act shall be guilty of felony and shall be liable to imprisonment for a term not exceeding five years.

(4) The balance of any sum paid or recovered on account of a fine imposed under subsection (1) or subsection (2) of this section, after making any such payments in respect of court or police fees as are mentioned in paragraphs (*a*), (*b*) and (*c*) of subsection (1) of section five of the Criminal Justice Administration Act 1914, shall be paid—

(*a*) in the case of a fine imposed under subsection (1) of this section, into the Exchequer; and

(*b*) in the case of a fine imposed under subsection (2) of this section, to the Registrar General or such other person as may be appointed by the Treasury, for the use of His Majesty.

(5) Subject as may be prescribed, a superintendent registrar may prosecute any person guilty of an offence under either of the said subsections committed within his district, and any costs incurred by the superintendent registrar in prosecuting such a person, being costs which are not otherwise provided for, shall be defrayed out of moneys provided by Parliament.

(6) No prosecution under subsection (3) of this section shall be commenced after the expiration of three years from the commission of the offence.

Offences by authorised persons

77. Any authorised person who refuses or fails to comply with the provisions of this Act or of any regulations made under section seventy-four thereof shall be guilty of an offence against this Act, and, unless the offence is one for which a specific penalty is provided under the foregoing provisions of this Part of this Act, shall be liable, on summary conviction, to a fine not exceeding ten pounds or, on conviction on indictment, to imprisonment for a term not exceeding two years or to a fine not exceeding fifty pounds, and shall upon conviction cease to be an authorised person.

Interpretation

78.[32]—(1) In this Act, except where the context otherwise requires, the following expressions have the meanings hereby respectively assigned to them, that is to say—

" authorised chapel " means—

(*a*) in relation to a chapelry, a chapel of the chapelry in

[31] Maximum fine raised from £10 by Criminal Justice Act 1967 (c. 80), s. 92, Sched. 3 Pt. I.
[32] Explained by Marriage (Wales and Monmouthshire) Act 1962 (c. 32), s. 2.

which banns of matrimony could lawfully be published immediately before the passing of the Marriage Act 1823, or in which banns may be published and marriages may be solemnized by virtue of section two of the Marriages Confirmation Act 1825, or of an authorisation given under section three of the Marriage Act 1823;

(*b*) in relation to an extra-parochial place, a church or chapel of that place in which banns may be published and marriages may be solemnized by virtue of section two of the Marriages Confirmation Act 1825, or of an authorisation given under section three of the Marriage Act 1823, or section twenty-one of this Act;

(*c*) in relation to a district specified in a licence granted under section twenty of this Act, the chapel in which banns may be published and marriages may be solemnized by virtue of that licence;

" authorised person " has the meaning assigned to it by section forty-three of this Act;

" brother " includes a brother of the half blood;

" clergyman " means a clerk in Holy Orders of the Church of England;

" common licence " has the meaning assigned to it by section five of this Act;

" ecclesiastical district," in relation to a district other than a parish, means a district specified in a licence granted under section twenty of this Act, a chapelry or an extra-parochial place;

" infant " means a person under the age of [eighteen years] [32a];

" marriage notice book " has the meaning assigned to it by section twenty-seven of this Act;

" parish " means an ecclesiastical parish and includes a district constituted under the Church Building Acts 1818 to 1884, notwithstanding that the district has not become a new parish by virtue of section fourteen of the New Parishes Act 1856 or section five of the New Parishes Measure 1943, being a district to which Acts of Parliament relating to the publication of banns of matrimony and the solemnization of marriages were applied by the said Church Building Acts as if the district had been an ancient parish, and the expression " parish church " shall be construed accordingly;

" prescribed " means prescribed by regulations made under section seventy-four of this Act;

" registered building " means a building registered under Part III of this Act;

" registrar " means a registrar of marriages;

" Registrar General " means the Registrar General of Births, Deaths and Marriages in England;

" registration district " means the district of a superintendent registrar;

" sister " includes a sister of the half blood;

" special licence " has the meaning assigned to it by section five of this Act;

" superintendent registrar " means a superintendent registrar of births, deaths and marriages;

" trustees or governing body," in relation to Roman Catholic registered buildings, includes a bishop or vicar general of the diocese.

(2) Any reference in this Act to the Church of England shall, unless

[32a] Amended by Family Law Reform Act 1969 (c. 46), s. 2 (1) (c).

the context otherwise requires, be construed as including a reference to the Church in Wales.

Repeals and savings

79.—(1) The Acts specified in Part I of the Fifth Schedule to this Act, and the Measures of the Church Assembly specified in Part II of that Schedule, are hereby repealed to the extent specified in relation thereto in the third column of that Schedule.

(2) Any banns published, licence or certificate issued, notice, consent, authorisation or direction given, Order in Council, rules, order, declaration, return, appointment or entry made, registration effected, caveat entered or other thing done under any enactment repealed by this Act shall, if in force at the commencement of this Act, continue in force, and have effect as if published, issued, given, made, effected, entered or done under the corresponding provision of this Act.

(3) Where a period of time specified in any enactment repealed by this Act is current at the commencement of this Act, this Act shall have effect as if the corresponding provision thereof had been in force when that period began to run.

(4) Any document referring to an enactment repealed by this Act shall be construed as referring to the corresponding provision of this Act.

(5) Nothing in this Act shall affect any law or custom relating to the marriage of members of the Royal Family.

(6) Nothing in this Act shall affect the right of the Archbishop of Canterbury or any other person by virtue of the Ecclesiastical Licences Act 1533 to grant special licences to marry at any convenient time or place, or affect the validity of any marriage solemnized on the authority of such a licence.

(7) Nothing in this Act shall affect the validity of any marriage solemnized before the commencement of this Act.

(8) Nothing in this Act shall affect any authority given under section three of the Marriage Act 1823 before the repeal thereof for the publication of banns and the solemnization of marriages in any chapel, or affect the operation of section four of that Act in relation to that chapel.

(9) Nothing in this Act shall affect any right, title, estate, interest, will, claim, payment, commutation, composition, discharge, settlement or other thing, or the devolution or distribution of any property which, by virtue of section two of the Deceased Wife's Sister's Marriage Act 1907; was not affected by the Marriage (Prohibited Degrees of Relationship) Acts 1907 to 1931.

(10) Nothing in this Act shall enable any proceedings to be taken in an ecclesiastical court which could not have been taken if this Act had not been passed.

(11) Nothing in this Act shall require any caution or security to be given which would not have required to be given if this Act had not been passed.

(12) Nothing in this Act shall affect any power to extend a Measure of the Church Assembly to the Channel Islands or affect any such Measure which has been so extended.

(13) Nothing in the foregoing provisions of this section shall be taken as prejudicing the operation of section thirty-eight of the Interpretation Act 1889 (which relates to the effect of repeals).

Short title, extent and commencement

80.—(1) This Act may be cited as the Marriage Act 1949.

(2) Save as is otherwise expressly provided, this Act shall not extend to Scotland or to Northern Ireland.

(3) The provisions of this Act specified in the Sixth Schedule to this Act shall not extend to Wales or Monmouthshire.

(4) This Act shall come into force on the first day of January, nineteen hundred and fifty.

SCHEDULES

FIRST SCHEDULE

KINDRED AND AFFINITY

Part I

Prohibited degrees of relationship

Mother [adoptive mother or former adoptive mother][33]	Father [adoptive father or former adoptive father][33]
Daughter [adoptive daughter or former adoptive daughter][33]	Son [adoptive son or former adoptive son][33]
Father's mother	Father's father
Mother's mother	Mother's father
Son's daughter	Son's son
Daughter's daughter	Daughter's son
Sister	Brother
Wife's mother	Husband's father
Wife's daughter	Husband's son
Father's wife	Mother's husband
Son's wife	Daughter's husband
Father's father's wife	Father's mother's husband
Mother's father's wife	Mother's mother's husband
Wife's father's mother	Husband's father's father
Wife's mother's mother	Husband's mother's father
Wife's son's daughter	Husband's son's son
Wife's daughter's daughter	Husband's daughter's son
Son's son's wife	Son's daughter's husband
Daughter's son's wife	Daughter's daughter's husband
Father's sister	Father's brother
Mother's sister	Mother's brother
Brother's daughter	Brother's son
Sister's daughter	Sister's son

Part II

[*Repealed by Marriage (Enabling) Act* 1960 (*c.* 29), *s.* 1 (4), *Sched.*]

SECOND SCHEDULE

CONSENTS REQUIRED TO THE MARRIAGE OF AN INFANT BY COMMON LICENCE OR SUPERINTENDENT REGISTRAR'S CERTIFICATE

I. Where the Infant is Legitimate

Circumstances	*Person or Persons whose consent is required*
1. Where both parents are living:	
(*a*) if parents are living together;	Both parents.
(*b*) if parents are divorced or separated by order of any court or by agreement;	The parent to whom the custody of the infant is committed by order of the court or by the agreement, or, if the custody of the infant is so committed to one parent during part of the year and to the other parent during the rest of the year, both parents.

[33] Words added by Children Act 1975 (c. 72), Sched. 3, para. 8.

I. Where the Infant is Legitimate—*continued*

Circumstances	*Person or Persons whose consent is required*
1. Where both parents are living—*cont.*	
(c) if one parent has been deserted by the other;	The parent who has been deserted.
(d) if both parents have been deprived of custody of infant by order of any court.	The person to whose custody the infant is committed by order of the court.
2. Where one parent is dead:	The surviving parent.
(a) if there is no other guardian;	
(b) if a guardian has been appointed by the deceased parent [or by the court under section 3 of the Guardianship of Minors Act 1971] [33]	The surviving parent and the guardian if acting jointly, or the surviving parent or the guardian if the parent or guardian is the sole guardian of the infant.
3. Where both parents are dead.	The guardians or guardian appointed by the deceased parents or by the court under [section 3 or 5 of the Guardianship of Minors Act 1971].[34]

II. Where the Infant is Illegitimate

Circumstances	*Person whose consent is required*
If the mother of the infant is alive.	The mother, or if she has by order of any court been deprived of the custody of the infant, the person to whom the custody of the infant has been committed by order of the court.
If the mother of the infant is dead.	The guardian appointed by the mother.

THIRD SCHEDULE

CAPACITIES REFERRED TO IN SECTION 68 (2) (d) OF THIS ACT

Part I

Naval Forces

Employment with the medical branch of the Royal Navy as an officer.
Member of the Women Royal Naval Service.
Member of Queen Alexandra's Royal Naval Nursing Service, or its reserve.

Part II

Military Forces

Employment with the Royal Army Medical Corps as an officer.
Member of Queen Alexandra's Imperial Military Nursing Service, or its reserve.
Member of the Auxiliary Territorial Service.

Part III

Air Forces

Employment with the medical branch of the Royal Air Force as an officer.
Member of Princess Mary's Royal Air Force Nursing Service, or its reserve.
Member of the Women's Auxiliary Air Force.

[33a] Words substituted by Guardianship of Minors Act 1971 (c. 3), s. 18 (1), Sched. 1, in relation to England and Wales.

. . . . . .

SIXTH SCHEDULE

PROVISIONS OF ACT WHICH DO NOT EXTEND TO WALES

[. . .] 35

Section ten.

[. . .] 35

Section nineteen.

Subsection (7) of section twenty.

Section twenty-three.

[. . .] 35

. . . . . .

Married Women (Restraint upon Anticipation) Act 1949

(12, 13 & 14 GEO. 6, c. 78)

An Act to render inoperative any restriction upon anticipation or alienation attached to the enjoyment of property by a woman.

[16th December 1949.]

Abolition of restraint upon anticipation, and consequential amendments and repeals

1.—(1) No restriction upon anticipation or alienation attached, or purported to be attached, to the enjoyment of any property by a woman which could not have been attached to the enjoyment of that property by a man shall be of any effect after the passing of this Act.

(2) The preceding subsection shall have effect whatever is the date of the passing, execution or coming into operation of the Act or instrument containing the provision by virtue of which the restriction was attached or purported to be attached, and accordingly in section two of the Law Reform (Married Women and Tortfeasors) Act 1935, the proviso to subsection (1) and subsections (2) and (3) (which make provision differentiating as to the operation of such a restriction between an Act passed before the passing of that Act or an instrument executed before the date mentioned in the said proviso on the one hand and an instrument executed on or after that date on the other hand) are hereby repealed.

(3) The enactments mentioned in the first column of the First Schedule to this Act shall have effect subject to the amendments specified in the second column of that Schedule.

[*Subsection (4) repealed by S.L.R.* 1953.]

Short title and extent

2.—(1) This Act may be cited as the Married Women (Restraint upon Anticipation) Act 1949.

(2) This Act shall not extend to Scotland or to Northern Ireland.

35 Repealed by Marriage (Wales and Monmouthshire) Act 1962 (c. 32), s. 1 (1).

SCHEDULES

FIRST SCHEDULE

CONSEQUENTIAL AMENDMENTS

The Married Women's Property Act 1882 (45 & 46 Vict. c. 75).	In section nineteen, the words from "or shall interfere" to "before marriage" shall be repealed, and the word "but" shall be substituted for the word "and" where it occurs immediately after the said repealed words.

[Paragraph repealed by Matrimonial Causes Act 1950 (c. 25), s. 34, Sched.]

SECOND SCHEDULE
[Repealed by S.L.R. 1953.]

Law Reform (Miscellaneous Provisions) Act 1949

(12, 13 & 14 GEO. 6, c. 100)

An Act to amend the law relating to divorce and other matrimonial proceedings, the admissibility of evidence as to access, the charge and payment of percentage under the Lunacy Act 1890 and to wards of court; and for purposes connected therewith.
[16th December 1949.]

Wards of court

9.—(1) Subject to the provisions of this section, no infant shall be made a ward of court except by virtue of an order to that effect made by the court.

(2) Where application is made for such an order in respect of an infant, the infant shall become a ward of court on the making of the application, but shall cease to be a ward of court at the expiration of such period as may be prescribed by rules of court unless within that period an order has been made in accordance with the application.

(3) The court may, either upon an application in that behalf or without such an application, order that any infant who is for the time being a ward of court shall cease to be a ward of court.

Maintenance Orders Act 1950 [1]

(14 GEO. 6, c. 37)

An Act to enable certain maintenance orders and other orders relating to married persons and children to be made and enforced throughout the United Kingdom. [26th October, 1950.]

---

[1] Explained by Children and Young Persons Act 1963 (c. 37), s. 30 (3), *post.*

Part I

Jurisdiction

Jurisdiction of English Courts

1. [*Repealed by Matrimonial Proceedings (Magistrates' Courts) Act* 1960 (*c.* 48), *s.* 18 (1), *Sched.*]

Jurisdiction of English summary courts to make orders for custody and maintenance of infants

2.[2]—[*Subsections* (1) *and* (2) *repealed by Guardianship of Minors Act* 1971 (*c.* 3), *ss.* 18 (2), 20 (4) (*a*), *Sched.* 2.]

(3) Where proceedings for an order under [. . .] [2a] section four of the Summary Jurisdiction (Married Women) Act 1895 relating to the custody of an infant are brought in a court of summary jurisdiction in England by a woman residing in Scotland or Northern Ireland, that court shall have jurisdiction to make any order in respect of the infant under the said section five upon the application of the defendant in the proceedings.

Jurisdiction of English courts to make affiliation orders

3.[3]—(1) A court in England shall have jurisdiction in proceedings under the Bastardy Laws Amendment Act 1872, or under section forty-four of the National Assistance Act 1948, or section twenty-six of the Children Act 1948, for an affiliation order against a man residing in Scotland or Northern Ireland, if the act of intercourse resulting in the birth of the child or any act of intercourse between the parties which may have resulted therein took place in England.

(2) Where the mother of a child resides in Scotland or Northern Ireland, and the person alleged to be the father in England, a court of summary jurisdiction having jurisdiction in the place in which the person alleged to be the father resides shall have jurisdiction in proceedings by the mother for an affiliation order against him under the Bastardy Laws Amendment Act 1872.

(3) A court in England by which an affiliation order has been made under any of the enactments mentioned in subsection (1) of this section shall have jurisdiction in proceedings by or against a person residing in Scotland or Northern Ireland for the revocation, revival or variation of that order.

(4) Notwithstanding anything in section three of the Bastardy Laws Amendment Act 1872, an application under that section for an affiliation order in respect of a child born before the commencement of this Act may be made to a court having jurisdiction by virtue of subsection (1) of this section at any time within one year after the commencement of this Act, if—

(*a*) the person alleged to be the father of the child ceased to reside in England before the expiration of one year from the birth of the child; and

(*b*) the circumstances are such that if that person had become resident in England immediately before the application, the court would have had jurisdiction in proceedings under the said section three apart from the provisions of this section.

---

[2] Explained by Legitimacy Act 1959 (c. 73), s. 3 (1), *post.*

[2a] Words repealed by Guardianship of Minors Act 1971 (c. 3), ss. 18 (2), 20 (4) (*a*), Sched. 2.

[3] Saved by Affiliation Proceedings Act 1957 (c. 55), s. 3 (2); and amended by Ministry of Social Security Act 1966 (c. 20), s. 24 (9).

Contributions under Children and Young Persons Act 1933 and National Assistance Act 1948

4.[4]—(1) A court of summary jurisdiction in England shall have jurisdiction in proceedings against a person residing in Scotland or Northern Ireland—

(a) for a contribution order under section eighty-seven of the Children and Young Persons Act 1933 (which provides for the recovery from parents of sums in respect of children and young persons who are committed to the care of a fit person or otherwise dealt with under that Act or the Children Act 1948);

(b) for an order under section forty-three of the National Assistance Act 1948 (which provides for the recovery from spouses or parents of sums in respect of assistance given under that Act).

(2) A court in England by which an order has been made under the said section eighty-seven or the said section forty-three shall have jurisdiction in proceedings by or against a person residing in Scotland or Northern Ireland for the revocation, revival or variation of that order.

5. [*Repealed, with saving, by Matrimonial Proceedings (Magistrates' Courts) Act 1960 (c. 48), s. 18 (1), Sched.*]

Jurisdiction of Scottish Courts

Jurisdiction of the sheriff in certain actions of aliment

6.—(1) The sheriff shall have jurisdiction in an action at the instance of a married woman against her husband concluding for the payment of aliment to herself and any child of the marriage if—

(a) the husband resides in England or Northern Ireland; and

(b) the parties last ordinarily resided together as man and wife in Scotland; and

(c) the pursuer resides within the jurisdiction of the sheriff.

(2) In this section the expression " an action concluding for the payment of aliment " means [. . .],[4a] an action of adherence and aliment or an action of interim aliment.

Jurisdiction of the sheriff to make orders for custody and maintenance of pupil children

7.[5] An order under the Guardianship of Infants Acts 1886 and 1925, giving the custody of a pupil child [to a person resident in Scotland],[5a] whether with or without an order [requiring payments to be made][5a] towards the maintenance of the pupil child, may be made, if [one parent] resides in England or Northern Ireland and [the other parent][5a] and the pupil child reside in Scotland, by the sheriff within whose jurisdiction [the other parent][5a] resides.

Jurisdiction of the sheriff in certain actions of affiliation and aliment

8.[6]—(1) Subject to the provisions of this section, the sheriff shall have jurisdiction in an action of affiliation and aliment (whether at the instance of the mother of the child or at the instance of the National Assistance

[4] Amended by Ministry of Social Security Act 1966 (c. 20), s. 23 (6), and applied by Merchant Shipping Act 1970 (c. 36), s. 17 (7).
[4a] Words repealed by Domicile and Matrimonial Proceedings Act 1973 (c. 45), s. 17 (2), Sched. 6.
[5] Explained by Legitimacy Act 1959 (c. 73), s. 3 (1), *post.*
[5a] Words substituted by Guardianship Act 1973 (c. 29), s. 11 (6), Sched. 4.
[6] Amended by Ministry of Social Security Act 1966 (c. 20), s. 24 (10) (d).

Board or of a local authority under section forty-four of the National
Assistance Act 1948 or section twenty-six of the Children Act 1948) if—

   (a) the person alleged to be the father resides in England or Northern
   Ireland; and

   (b) the act of intercourse resulting in the birth of the child or any
   act of intercourse between the parties which may have resulted
   therein took place in Scotland; and

   (c) the mother resides within the jurisdiction of the sheriff.

(2) The sheriff shall not by virtue of the foregoing subsection have
jurisdiction in such an action as aforesaid in relation to a child born
before the commencement of this Act unless—

   (a) the child was born within one year before the commencement
   of this Act; or

   (b) the person alleged to be the father of the child made payment of
   any sums in respect of aliment of the child within one year from
   the birth of the child; or

   (c) the person alleged to be the father of the child has not at any
   time since the birth of the child been subject to the jurisdiction
   of any sheriff court in Scotland and the action is commenced
   within twelve months after the commencement of this Act.

Contributions under Children and Young Persons (Scotland) Act 1937 and National Assistance Act 1948

9.[7]—(1) A court in Scotland shall have jurisdiction in proceedings
against a person residing in England or Northern Ireland—

   (a) for a contribution order under section ninety-one of the Children
   and Young Persons (Scotland) Act 1937 (which provides for the
   recovery from parents of sums in respect of children and young
   persons who are committed to the care of a fit person or otherwise dealt with under that Act or the Children Act 1948);

   (b) for an order under section forty-three of the National Assistance
   Act 1948 (which provides for the recovery from spouses or parents
   of sums in respect of assistance given under that Act).

(2) A court in Scotland by which an order has been made under the
said section ninety-one or the said section forty-three shall have jurisdiction in proceedings against a person residing in England or Northern
Ireland for the revocation or variation of that order.

Jurisdiction of Northern Ireland Courts

Jurisdiction of Northern Ireland courts to make orders under the Summary Jurisdiction (Separation and Maintenance) Act (Northern Ireland) 1945

10.—(1) Subject to the following provisions of this section, a court of
summary jurisdiction in Northern Ireland shall have jurisdiction to make
an order under section three or section four of the Summary Jurisdiction
(Separation and Maintenance) Act (Northern Ireland) 1945 in proceedings
against a man residing in England or Scotland, if the applicant in the
proceedings resides in Northern Ireland and the parties last ordinarily
resided together as man and wife in Northern Ireland.

(2) It is hereby declared that a court in Northern Ireland has jurisdiction—

   (a) in proceedings under the said Act by a woman residing in England
   or Scotland against a man residing in Northern Ireland;

---

[7] Amended by Ministry of Social Security Act 1966 (c. 20), s. 23 (6), and applied by
Merchant Shipping Act 1970 (c. 36), s. 17 (7).

(*b*) in proceedings under section five of the said Act by or against a person residing in England or Scotland for the variation, discharge or suspension of an order made under section three or section four of the said Act.

(3) The reference in this section to the discharge of an order made under section three or section four of the Summary Jurisdiction (Separation and Maintenance) Act (Northern Ireland) 1945 includes a reference to the making of a new order under subsection (2) of section five of that Act.

(4) Nothing in this section shall be construed as enabling a court to make a separation order under paragraph (*a*) of subsection (1) of section three of the Summary Jurisdiction (Separation and Maintenance) Act (Northern Ireland) 1945 against a person residing in England or Scotland.

Jurisdiction of Northern Ireland courts to make affiliation orders

11.—(1) A court in Northern Ireland shall have jurisdiction in proceedings under the Illegitimate Children (Affiliation Orders) Act (Northern Ireland) 1924, section twenty-one of the National Assistance Act (Northern Ireland) 1948, section twelve of the Welfare Services Act (Northern Ireland) 1949, or section one hundred and twenty-four of the Children and Young Persons Act (Northern Ireland) 1950, for an affiliation order against a man residing in England or Scotland, if the act of intercourse resulting in the birth of the child or any act of intercourse between the parties which may have resulted therein took place in Northern Ireland.

(2) Where the mother of a child resides in England or Scotland and the person alleged to be the father in Northern Ireland, a court of summary jurisdiction for the petty sessions district in which the person alleged to be the father resides shall have jurisdiction in proceedings by the mother for an affiliation order against him under the Illegitimate Children (Affiliation Orders) Act (Northern Ireland) 1924.

(3) A court in Northern Ireland shall have jurisdiction in proceedings by or against a person residing in England or Scotland for the revocation, revival or variation of an affiliation order made under any of the enactments mentioned in subsection (1) of this section.

(4) Notwithstanding anything in subsection (3) of section two of the Illegitimate Children (Affiliation Orders) Act (Northern Ireland) 1924, an application under that Act for an affiliation order in respect of a child born before the commencement of this Act may be made to a court having jurisdiction by virtue of subsection (1) of this section at any time within one year after the commencement of this Act if—

(*a*) the person alleged to be the father of the child ceased to reside in Northern Ireland before the expiration of one year from the birth of the child; and

(*b*) the circumstances are such that if that person had become resident in Northern Ireland immediately before the application, the court would have had jurisdiction in proceedings under the said Act apart from the provisions of this section.

Contributions under enactments relating to children, national assistance and welfare services

12.[7a]—(1) A court of summary jurisdiction in Northern Ireland shall have jurisdiction in proceedings against a person residing in England or Scotland—

(*a*) for a contribution order under section one hundred and twenty-

---

[7a] Applied by Merchant Shipping Act 1970 (c. 36), s. 17 (7).

two of the Children and Young Persons Act (Northern Ireland) 1950 (which provides for the recovery from parents of sums in respect of children and young persons received into care or otherwise dealt with under that Act);

(*b*) for an order under section twenty of the National Assistance Act (Northern Ireland) 1948 or section eleven of the Welfare Services Act (Northern Ireland) 1949 (which provide for the recovery from spouses or parents of sums in respect of assistance or accommodation given or provided under those Acts).

(2) A court of summary jurisdiction in Northern Ireland shall have jurisdiction in proceedings by or against a person residing in England or Scotland for the variation or rescission of any contribution order made under the said section one hundred and twenty-two [or of any order made under the said section 20 or the said section 11].[8]

Transfer of proceedings in Northern Ireland

13.—(1) Proceedings begun against a defendant residing in England or Scotland in a court having jurisdiction by virtue of subsection (1) of section ten of this Act, not being a court having jurisdiction in the place where the parties last ordinarily resided together as man and wife, may be removed, upon application made by the defendant in accordance with rules made by the Lord Chief Justice of Northern Ireland, into a court of summary jurisdiction having jurisdiction in that place.

(2) The Lord Chief Justice of Northern Ireland shall have power to make rules for the purposes of this section.

Supplemental
Modification of enactments relating to children and young persons

14. The provisions of the enactments specified in the First Schedule to this Act shall have effect subject to the modifications set out in that Schedule, being modifications consequential on the foregoing provisions of this Part of this Act.

Services of process

15.[9]—(1) Where proceedings are begun in a court having jurisdiction under or by virtue of this Part of this Act [or section 15 of the Guardianship of Minors Act 1971][9a] against a person residing in another part of the United Kingdom, any summons or initial writ addressed to him in the proceedings may, if endorsed in accordance with the provisions of this section in that part of the United Kingdom, be served within that part of the United Kingdom as if it had been issued or authorised to be served, as the case may be, by the endorsing authority.

(2) A summons or writ may be endorsed under this section, in England by a justice of the peace, in Scotland by a sheriff, and in Northern Ireland by a resident magistrate; and the endorsement shall be made in the form numbered 1 in the Second Schedule to this Act, or any form to the like effect.

(3) In any proceedings in which a summons or writ is served under this section, the service may be proved by means of a declaration made

---

[8] Words added by Supplementary Benefits Act 1966 (c. 20), s. 39 (1), Sched. 6, para. 14.
[9] Applied by Maintenance Orders Act 1958 (c. 39), s. 20 (3) *post*; further applied by Attachment of Earnings Act 1971 (c. 32), s. 20 (2); and extended by Matrimonial Proceedings (Magistrates' Courts) Act 1960 (c. 48), s. 14 (1), *post.* See now also Children Act 1975 (c. 72), Sched. 3, para. 10, *post.*
[9a] Words added by Guardianship of Minors Act 1971 (c. 3), ss. 18 (1), 20 (4) (*a*), Sched. 1, in relation to England and Wales.

in the form numbered 2 in the Second Schedule to this Act, or any form to the like effect, before a justice of the peace, sheriff, or resid!ent magistrate, as the case may be.

(4) Nothing in this section shall be construed as authorising the service of a summons or writ otherwise than personally.

(5) Section four of the Summary Jurisdiction (Process) Act 1881 shall not apply to any process which may be served under this section; and nothing in this section or in any other enactment shall be construed as authorising the execution in one part of the United Kingdom of a warrant for the arrest of a person who fails to appear in answer to any such process issued in another part of the United Kingdom.

PART II

ENFORCEMENT

Application of Part II

16.[10]—(1) Any order to which this section applies (in this Part of this Act referred to as a maintenance order) made by a court in any part of the United Kingdom may, if registered in accordance with the provisions of this Part of this Act in a court in another part of the United Kingdom, be enforced in accordance with those provisions in that other part of the United Kingdom.

(2) This section applies to the following orders, that is to say—

    (*a*) an order for alimony, maintenance or other payments made or deemed to be made by a court in England under any of the following enactments:—

        (i) [sections 15 to 17, 19 to 22, 30, 34 and 35 of the Matrimonial Causes Act 1965, and sections 22, 23 (1) (2) and (4) and 27 of the Matrimonial Causes Act 1973;] [10a]

        (ii) the Summary Jurisdiction (Separation and Maintenance) Acts 1895 to 1949;

        (iii) [section 9 (2), 10 (1), or 12 (2) of the Guardianship of Minors Act 1971] [10b] [or section 2 (3) or 2 (4) (a) of the Guardianship Act 1973;] [10c]

        (iv) section four of the Bastardy Laws Amendment Act 1872, section forty-four of the National Assistance Act 1948, or section twenty-six of the Children Act 1948;

        (v) section eighty-seven of the Children and Young Persons Act 1933 or section forty-three of the National Assistance Act 1948;

    (*b*) a decree for payment of aliment granted by a court in Scotland, including—

        (i) an order for the payment of an annual or periodical allowance under section two of the Divorce (Scotland) Act 1938;

        (ii) an order for the payment of weekly or periodical sums under subsection (2) of section three or subsection (4) of section five of the Guardianship of Infants Act 1915;

        (iii) an order for the payment of sums in respect of

[10] Amended by Matrimonial Proceedings (Children) Act 1958 (c. 40), s. 17, *post*, to include orders made under Act; Matrimonial Causes Act 1965 (c. 72), s. 38, *post*; Ministry of Social Security Act 1966 (c. 20), ss. 23 (6), 24 (9), (10) (d); and extended by Family Law Reform Act 1969 (c. 46), ss. 4 (5) (a), 6 (7), 28 (4) (c), *post*. See now also Children Act 1975 (c. 72), Sched. 3, para. 11, *post*.
[10a] Words substituted by Matrimonial Causes Act 1973 (c. 18), s. 54 (1) (a), Sched 2.
[10b] Words substituted by Guardianship of Minors Act 1971 (c. 3), ss. 18 (1), 20 (4) (a), Sched. 1, in relation to England and Wales.
[10c] Words added by Guardianship Act 1973 (c. 29), s. 9 (2), in relation to England and Wales.

aliment under subsection (3) of section one of the Illegitimate Children (Scotland) Act 1930;

(iv) a decree for payment of aliment under section forty-four of the National Assistance Act 1948 or under section twenty-six of the Children Act 1948; and

(v) a contribution order under section ninety-one of the Children and Young Persons (Scotland) Act 1937 or an order under section forty-three of the National Assistance Act 1948;

(c) an order for alimony, maintenance or other payments made by a court in Northern Ireland under or by virtue of any of the following enactments:—

(i) subsection (2) of section seventeen, subsections (2) to (7) of section nineteen, subsection (2) of section twenty, section. twenty-two or subsection (1) of section twenty-eight of the Matrimonial Causes Act (Northern Ireland) 1939;

(ii) the Summary Jurisdiction (Separation and Maintenance) Act (Northern Ireland) 1945;

(iii) section one of the Illegitimate Children (Affiliation Orders) Act (Northern Ireland) 1924, section twenty-one of the National Assistance Act (Northern Ireland) 1948, section twelve of the Welfare Services Act (Northern Ireland) 1949, or section one hundred and twenty-four of the Children and Young Persons Act (Northern Ireland) 1950;

(iv) section one hundred and twenty-two of the Children and Young Persons Act (Northern Ireland) 1950, section twenty of the National Assistance Act (Northern Ireland) 1948, or section eleven of the Welfare Services Act (Northern Ireland) 1949;

(v) [any enactment of the Parliament of Northern Ireland containing provisions corresponding with section 22 (1), 34 or 35 of the Matrimonial Causes Act 1965, with section 22, 23 (1) (2) or (4) or 27 of the Matrimonial Causes Act 1973, or with section 12 (2) of the Guardianship of Minors Act 1971.] [10a]

(3) For the purposes of this section, any order made before the commencement of the Matrimonial Causes Act (Northern Ireland) 1939, being an order which, if that Act had been in force, could have been made under or by virtue of any provision of that Act, shall be deemed to be an order made by virtue of that provision.

Procedure for registration of maintenance orders

17.—(1) An application for the registration of a maintenance order under this Part of this Act shall be made in the prescribed manner to the appropriate authority, that is to say—

(a) where the maintenance order was made by a court of summary jurisdiction in England, a justice or justices acting for the same place as the court which made the order;

(b) where the maintenance order was made by a court of summary jurisdiction in Northern Ireland, a resident magistrate acting for the same petty sessions district as the court which made the order;

(c) in every other case, the prescribed officer of the court which made the order.

(2) If upon application made as aforesaid by or on behalf of the person entitled to payments under a maintenance order it appears that the person liable to make those payments resides in another part of the

United Kingdom, and that it is convenient that the order should be enforceable there, the appropriate authority shall cause a certified copy of the order to be sent to the prescribed officer of a court in that part of the United Kingdom in accordance with the provisions of the next following subsection.

(3) The court to whose officer the certified copy of a maintenance order is sent under this section shall be—

(a) where the maintenance order was made by a superior court, the Supreme Court of Judicature in England, the Court of Session or the Supreme Court of Judicature of Northern Ireland, as the case may be;

(b) in any other case, a court of summary jurisdiction acting for the place in England or Northern Ireland in which the defendant appears to be, or, as the case may be, the sheriff court in Scotland within the jurisdiction of which he appears to be.

(4) Where the prescribed officer of any court receives a certified copy of a maintenance order sent to him under this section, he shall cause the order to be registered in that court in the prescribed manner, and shall give notice of the registration in the prescribed manner to the prescribed officer of the court which made the order.

(5) The officer to whom any notice is given under the last foregoing subsection shall cause particulars of the notice to be registered in his court in the prescribed manner.

(6) Where the sums payable under a maintenance order, being an order made by a court of summary jurisdiction in England or Northern Ireland, are payable to or through an officer of any court, that officer shall, if the person entitled to the payments so requests, make an application on behalf of that person for the registration of the order under this Part of this Act; but the person at whose request the application is made shall have the same liability for costs properly incurred in or about the application as if the application had been made by him.

(7) An order which is for the time being registered under this Part of this Act in any court shall not be registered thereunder in any other court.

Enforcement of registered orders

18.—(1) Subject to the provisions of this section, a maintenance order registered under this Part of this Act in a court in any part of the United Kingdom may be enforced in that part of the United Kingdom in all respects as if it had been made by that court and as if that court had had jurisdiction to make it; and proceedings for or with respect to the enforcement of any such order may be taken accordingly.

(2) Every maintenance order registered under this Part of this Act in a court of summary jurisdiction in England [. . .] [11] shall be enforceable as if it were an affiliation order made by that court under the Bastardy Laws Amendment Act 1872 and the provisions of any enactment with respect to the enforcement of affiliation orders (including enactments relating to the accrual of arrears and the remission of sums due) shall apply accordingly.

(3) Every maintenance order registered under this Part of this Act in a court of summary jurisdiction in Northern Ireland [. . .] [11] shall be enforceable as if it were an order made by that court under the Summary Jurisdiction (Separation and Maintenance) Act (Northern Ireland) 1945 and the provisions of section six of that Act shall apply accordingly.

[*Subsection* (4) (5) *repealed by Ministry of Social Security Act* 1966 (c. 20), s. 39 (3), *Sched.* 8.]

[11] Words repealed by Supplementary Benefits Act 1966 (c. 20), s. 39 (3), Sched. 8.

(6) Except as provided by this section, no proceedings shall be taken for or with respect to the enforcement of a maintenance order which is for the time being registered in any court under this Part of this Act.

Functions of collecting officer, etc.

19.[12]—(1) Where a maintenance order made in England or Northern Ireland by a court of summary jurisdiction is registered in any court under this Part of this Act, any provision of the order by virtue of which sums payable thereunder are required to be paid through or to any officer or person on behalf of the person entitled thereto shall be of no effect so long as the order is so registered.

(2) Where a maintenance order is registered under this Part of this Act in a court of summary jurisdiction in England or Northern Ireland, the court shall, unless it is satisfied that it is undesirable to do so, order that all payments to be made under the maintenance order (including any arrears accrued before the date of the registration) shall be made through the collecting officer of the court or the collecting officer of some other court of summary jurisdiction in England or Northern Ireland, as the case may be.

(3) An order made by a court of summary jurisdiction under subsection (2) of this section may be varied or revoked by a subsequent order.

(4) Where by virtue of the provisions of this section or any order made thereunder payments under a maintenance order cease to be or become payable through or to any officer or person, the person liable to make the payments shall, until he is given the prescribed notice to that effect, be deemed to comply with the maintenance order if he makes payments in accordance with the maintenance order and any order under this section of which he has received such notice.

(5) In any case where, by virtue of an order made under this section by a court in Northern Ireland, payments under a maintenance order are required to be made through the collecting officer of any court—

(*a*) subsections (3) and (4) of section eight of the Illegitimate Children (Affiliation Orders) Act (Northern Ireland) 1924 (which regulate the functions of collecting officers in relation to affiliation orders) shall apply as if the maintenance order were an affiliation order within the meaning of that section and as if the order under this section were made under that Act, and references in those subsections to the mother and the putative father shall be construed accordingly; and

(*b*) subsection (2) of section seven of the Summary Jurisdiction (Separation and Maintenance) Act (Northern Ireland) 1945 (which relates to the remuneration of persons through whom weekly sums are paid under that Act) shall have effect as if money paid in accordance with the order under this section were paid in pursuance of an order made under that Act.

Arrears under registered maintenance orders

20.—(1) Where application is made for the registration of a maintenance order under this Part of this Act, the applicant may lodge with the appropriate authority—

(*a*) if the payments under the order are required to be made to or through an officer of any court, a certificate in the prescribed form, signed by that officer, as to the amount of any arrears due under the order;

---

[12] Applied by Maintenance Orders Act 1958 (c. 39), ss. 2 (6), 5 (5), *post.*

(*b*) in any other case, a statutory declaration or affidavit as to the amount of those arrears;

and if a certified copy of the maintenance order is sent to the prescribed officer of any court in pursuance of the application, the certificate, declaration or affidavit shall also be sent to that officer.

(2) In any proceedings for or with respect to the enforcement of a maintenance order which is for the time being registered in any court under this Part of this Act, a certificate, declaration or affidavit sent under this section to the appropriate officer of that court shall be evidence, and in Scotland sufficient evidence, of the facts stated therein.

(3) Where a maintenance order made by a court in England or Northern Ireland is registered in a court in Scotland, a person shall not be entitled, except with the leave of the last-mentioned court, to enforce, whether by diligence or otherwise, the payment of any arrears accrued and due under the order before the commencement of this Act; and on any application for leave to enforce the payment of any such arrears, the court may refuse leave, or may grant leave subject to such restrictions and conditions (including conditions as to the allowing of time for payment or the making of payment by instalments) as the court thinks proper, or may remit the payment of such arrears or of any part thereof.

Discharge and variation of maintenance orders registered in superior courts

21.—(1) The registration of a maintenance order in a superior court under this Part of this Act shall not confer on that court any power to vary or discharge the order, or affect any jurisdiction of the court in which the order was made to vary or discharge the order.

(2) Where a maintenance order made in Scotland is for the time being registered under this Part of this Act in a superior court, the person liable to make payments under the order may, upon application made to that court in the prescribed manner, adduce before that court any evidence upon which he would be entitled to rely in any proceedings brought before the court by which the order was made for the variation or discharge of the order.

(3) A court before which evidence is adduced in accordance with the foregoing subsection shall cause a transcript or summary of that evidence, signed by the deponent, to be sent to the prescribed officer of the court by which the order was made; and in any proceedings before the last-mentioned court for the variation or discharge of the order, the transcript or summary shall be evidence of the facts stated therein.

Discharge and variation of maintenance orders registered in summary or sheriff courts

22.—(1) Where a maintenance order is for the time being registered under this Part of this Act in a court of summary jurisdiction or sheriff court, that court may, upon application made in the prescribed manner by or on behalf of the person liable to make payments under the order or the person entitled to those payments, by order make such variation as the court thinks fit in the rate of the payments under the maintenance order; but no such variation shall impose on the person liable to make payments under the maintenance order a liability to make payments in excess of the maximum rate (if any) authorised by the law for the time being in force in the part of the United Kingdom in which the maintenance order was made.

(2) For the purposes of subsection (1) of this section, a court in any part of the United Kingdom may take notice of the law in force in any other part of the United Kingdom.

(3) Section fifteen of this Act shall apply to the service of process for the purposes of this section as it applies to the service of process in

proceedings begun in a court having jurisdiction by virtue of Part I of this Act.

(4) Except as provided by subsection (1) of this section, no variation shall be made in the rate of the payments under a maintenance order which is for the time being registered under this Part of this Act in a court of summary jurisdiction or sheriff court, but without prejudice to any power of the court which made the order to discharge it or vary it otherwise than in respect of the rate of the payments thereunder.

(5) Where a maintenance order is for the time being registered under this Part of this Act in a court of summary jurisdiction or sheriff court—

(a) the person entitled to payments under the order or the person liable to make payments under the order may, upon application made in the prescribed manner to the court by which the order was made, or in which the order is registered, as the case may be, adduce in the prescribed manner before the court in which the application is made any evidence on which he would be entitled to rely in proceedings for the variation or discharge of the order;

(b) the court in which the application is made shall cause a transcript or summary of that evidence, signed by the deponent, to be sent to the prescribed officer of the court in which the order is registered or of the court by which the order was made, as the case may be; and in any proceedings for the variation or discharge of the order the transcript or summary shall be evidence of the facts stated therein.

Notice of variation, etc.

23.—(1) Where a maintenance order registered under this Part of this Act in any court is varied by that court, the prescribed officer of that court shall give notice of the variation in the prescribed manner to the prescribed officer of the court by which the order was made.

(2) Where a maintenance order registered under this Part of this Act in any court is discharged or varied by any other court, the prescribed officer of the last-mentioned court shall give notice of the discharge or variation in the prescribed manner to the prescribed officer of the court in which the order is registered.

(3) The officer to whom any notice is given under this section shall cause particulars of the notice to be registered in his court in the prescribed manner.

Cancellation of registration

24.—(1) At any time while a maintenance order is registered under this Part of this Act in any court, an application for the cancellation of the registration may be made in the prescribed manner to the prescribed officer of that court by or on behalf of the person entitled to payments under the order; and upon any such application that officer shall (unless proceedings for the variation of the order are pending in that court), cancel the registration, and thereupon the order shall cease to be registered in that court.

(2) Where, after a maintenance order has been registered under this Part of this Act in a court of summary jurisdiction in England or Northern Ireland or a sheriff court in Scotland, it appears to the appropriate authority (as defined by section seventeen of this Act), upon application made in the prescribed manner by or on behalf of the person liable to make payments under the order, that that person has ceased to reside in England, Northern Ireland or Scotland, as the case may be, the appropriate authority may cause a notice to that effect to be sent to the prescribed officer of the court in which the order is registered; and where such a notice is sent the prescribed officer shall cancel the

Maintenance Orders Act 1950

registration of the maintenance order, and thereupon the order shall cease to be registered in that court.

(3) Where the prescribed officer of any court cancels the registration of a maintenance order under this section, he shall give notice of the cancellation in the prescribed manner to the prescribed officer of the court by which the order was made and the last-mentioned officer shall cause particulars of the notice to be registered in his court in the prescribed manner.

(4) Except as provided by subsection (5) of this section, the cancellation of the registration of a maintenance order shall not affect anything done in relation to the maintenance order while it was registered.

(5) On the cancellation of the registration of a maintenance order, any order made in relation thereto under subsection (2) of section nineteen of this Act shall cease to have effect; but until the person liable to make payments under the maintenance order receives the prescribed notice of the cancellation, he shall be deemed to comply with the maintenance order if he makes payments in accordance with any order under the said subsection (2) which was in force immediately before the cancellation.

(6) Where, by virtue of an order made under subsection (2) of section nineteen of this Act, sums payable under a maintenance order registered in a court of summary jurisdiction in England or Northern Ireland are payable through the collecting officer of any court, that officer shall, if the person entitled to the payments so requests, make an application on behalf of that person for the cancellation of the registration.

Rules as to procedure of courts of summary jurisdiction

25.—(1) The power of the Lord Chancellor to make rules under section fifteen of the Justices of the Peace Act 1949 shall include power to make rules for regulating the practice to be followed in courts of summary jurisdiction in England under this Part of this Act.

(2) The Lord Chief Justice of Northern Ireland shall have power to make rules for regulating the practice to be followed in courts of summary jurisdiction in Northern Ireland under this Part of this Act.

(3) Rules made for the purposes of this Part of this Act may require that any order or other matter required under this Part of this Act to be registered in a court of summary jurisdiction in England or Northern Ireland shall be registered—

(a) in England, by means of a memorandum entered and signed by the prescribed officer of the court in the register kept pursuant to section twenty-two of the Summary Jurisdiction Act 1879;

(b) in Northern Ireland, by means of an entry made and signed by the prescribed officer of the court in the order book kept pursuant to section twenty-one of the Petty Sessions (Ireland) Act 1851.

PART III

GENERAL

Proof of declarations, etc.

26.—(1) Any document purporting to be a declaration made under section fifteen of this Act, or to be a certified copy, statutory declaration, affidavit, certificate, transcript or summary made for the purposes of this Act or of any rules made thereunder shall, unless the contrary is shown, be deemed without further proof to be the document which it purports to be, and to have been duly certified, made or signed by or before the person or persons by or before whom it purports to have been certified, made or signed.

(2) Paragraph 7 of the Second Schedule to the Emergency Laws

146

(Miscellaneous Provisions) Act 1947 (which relates to the proof of affiliation orders and maintenance orders and of orders for the discharge or variation of such orders) shall apply to the registration of orders under Part II of this Act, and to the cancellation of such registration, as it applies to the variation of orders; and for the purposes of that paragraph—

(*a*) a maintenance order registered under the said Part II in a court of summary jurisdiction; and

(*b*) any proceeding under the said Part II relating to a maintenance order made by or registered in such a court, being a proceeding of which a memorandum is required to be entered in the register kept by the clerk of that court pursuant to section twenty-two of the Summary Jurisdiction Act 1879,

shall be deemed to be an order made by that court.

General provisions as to jurisdiction

27.—(1) Nothing in this Act shall be construed as derogating from any jurisdiction exercisable, apart from the provisions of this Act, by any court in any part of the United Kingdom.

(2) It is hereby declared that any jurisdiction conferred by Part I of this Act, or any enactment therein referred to, upon a court in any part of the United Kingdom is exercisable notwithstanding that any party to the proceedings is not domiciled in that part of the United Kingdom; and any jurisdiction so conferred in affiliation proceedings shall be exercisable notwithstanding that the child to whom the proceedings relate was not born in that part of the United Kingdom.

(3) For the avoidance of doubt it is hereby declared that in relation to proceedings in which the sheriff has jurisdiction by virtue of the provisions of this Act there are the same rights of appeal and of remit to the Court of Session as there are in relation to the like proceedings in which the sheriff has jurisdiction otherwise than by virtue of the said provisions.

Interpretation

28.—(1) In this Act the following expressions have the meanings hereby assigned to them, that is to say—

" certified copy ", in relation to an order of any court, means a copy certified by the proper officer of the court to be a true copy of the order or of the official record thereof;

" collecting officer ", in relation to a court of summary jurisdiction in England, means the person authorised to act as such under section twenty-one of the Justices of the Peace Act 1949, and in relation to a court of summary jurisdiction in Northern Ireland, means the officer appointed under subsection (1) of section eight of the Illegitimate Children (Affiliation Orders) Act (Northern Ireland) 1924;

[*Definition repealed by National Insurance Act* 1962 (*c.* 30), *s.* 30 (2), *Sched.* 4 *Part IV.*]

" enactment " includes any order, rule or regulation made in pursuance of any Act;

" England " includes Wales;

" prescribed " means, in relation to a court of summary jurisdiction in England or Northern Ireland, prescribed by rules made under section fifteen of the Justices of the Peace Act 1949 or by rules made by the Lord Chief Justice of Northern Ireland under this Act, as the case may be, and in relation to any other court means prescribed by rules of court.

147

(2) References in this Act to parts of the United Kingdom are references to England, Scotland and Northern Ireland.

(3) Any reference in this Act to any enactment shall be construed as a reference to that enactment as amended by any subsequent enactment, including this Act.

29.—[*Repealed by National Insurance Act* 1955 (*c.* 8), *s.* 6 (3), *Sched.*]

30.—[*Repealed by S.L.R.* 1953.]

Special provisions relating to Northern Ireland

31. [*Subsection* (1) *repealed by Northern Ireland Constitution Act* 1973 (*c.* 36), *Sched.* 6.]

(2) Any reference in this Act to an enactment of the Parliament of Northern Ireland, or to an enactment which that Parliament has power to amend, shall be construed, in relation to Northern Ireland, as a reference to that enactment as amended by any Act of that Parliament, whether passed before or after this Act, and to any enactment of that Parliament passed after this Act and re-enacting the said enactment with or without modifications.

Short title and commencement

32.—(1) This Act may be cited as the Maintenance Orders Act 1950.

(2) This Act shall come into force on the first day of January, nineteen hundred and fifty-one.

SCHEDULES

FIRST SCHEDULE

MODIFICATION OF CERTAIN ENACTMENTS

The Children and Young Persons Act 1933, 23 & 24 Geo. 5. c. 12.

Section eighty-six ... Where the person liable to make contributions in respect of a child or young person is for the time being residing in Scotland or Northern Ireland, subsection (3) shall have effect as if for references to the council of the county or county borough in which the person liable as aforesaid is for the time being residing there were substituted references to the local authority having the care of the child or young person [. . .].[13]

Section eighty-seven ... Where the person to be charged under a contribution order resides in Scotland or Northern Ireland, subsection (1) shall have effect as if for the reference to a court of summary jurisdiction having jurisdiction in the place where the said person is for the time being residing there were substituted a reference to a court of summary jurisdiction having jurisdiction in the place in which the person entitled under section eighty-six to receive the contributions resides or, if

[13] Words repealed by Children and Young Persons Act 1969 (c. 54), s. 72 (4), Sched. 6.

The Children and Young Persons Act 1933—*continued*

Section eighty-seven—
cont.

that person is a local authority, having jurisdiction within the area of that authority.

Where the person on whom a contribution order has been made is for the time being residing in Scotland or Northern Ireland, subsection (4) shall have effect as if the words from "but any powers" to the end of the subsection were omitted.

Section eighty-eight   ...

Where the putative father of an illegitimate child or young person resides in Scotland or Northern Ireland, subsection (1) shall have effect as if for the reference to the place where the putative father is for the time being residing there were substituted a reference to the place where the mother of the child is for the time being residing.

Where the person liable under an affiliation order in respect of which an order under section eighty-eight is in force is for the time being residing in Scotland or Northern Ireland, paragraph (*a*) of subsection (2) shall not apply.

Section eighty-nine   ...

Where the person liable under a contribution order made under section eighty-seven, or under an affiliation order in respect of which an order under section eighty-eight is in force, is for the time being residing in Scotland or Northern Ireland, subsection (2) shall have effect as if for the reference to the council of the county or county borough in which the person liable under the order is for the time being residing there were substituted a reference to the local authority to whom sums are payable under the order and as if for the words "when he was not resident in the county or county borough" there were substituted the words "when that authority were not entitled to sums payable under the order".

The Children and Young Persons (Scotland) Act 1937, 1 Edw. 8 & 1 Geo. 6. c. 37.—

Section ninety-one   ...

[*Repealed by Social Work (Scotland) Act* 1968 (*c.* 49), *s.* 95 (2), *Sched.* 9 Pt. I.]

The Children Act 1948, 11 & 12 Geo. 6. c. 43.

Section twenty-six   ...

Where the putative father of a child in respect of whom an order has been made under section eighty-eight of the Children and Young Persons Act 1933 is for the time being residing in Scotland or Northern Ireland, subsection (4) shall have effect as if for references to the local authority whose area includes the place where the putative father of the child resides, and to a court of summary jurisdiction having jurisdiction in that place, there were substituted references to the local authority who, if the affiliation order were still in force, would be entitled to payments thereunder, and to a court of summary jurisdiction having jurisdiction within the area of that authority.

The Children and Young Persons Act (Northern Ireland) 1950 c. 5.

Section one hundred and twenty-one

Where the person liable to make contributions in respect of a child or young person who is ordered to be sent to a training school resides in England or Scotland, paragraph (*b*) of subsection (5) shall have effect as if for the reference to the council of the county or county borough in which the person liable as aforesaid

The Children and Young Persons Act (Northern Ireland) 1950—*continued*

Section one hundred and twenty-one—*cont.*	is for the time being residing there were substituted a reference to the local authority named in the training school order under subsection (2) of section seventy-four.
Section one hundred and twenty-two	Where the person liable to make contributions in respect of a child or young person resides in England or Scotland, subsections (1) (2) and (6) shall have effect as if for the references to a court of summary jurisdiction acting for the petty sessions district in which the person liable to make contributions or the contributor resides there were substituted references to a court of summary jurisdiction acting for the petty sessions district in which the person entitled under section one hundred and twenty-one to receive the contributions resides or, if that person is a welfare authority or local authority, a court of summary jurisdiction having jurisdiction within the area of that authority.
Section one hundred and twenty-three	Where the putative father of an illegitimate child or young person resides in England or Scotland, subsection (2) shall have effect as if for the reference to a court of summary jurisdiction acting for the petty sessions district in which the putative father is for the time being residing there were substituted a reference to a court of summary jurisdiction acting for the petty sessions district in which the applicant for the order under that subsection resides or, if the applicant is a welfare authority or local authority, a court of summary jurisdiction having jurisdiction within the area of that authority.
Section one hundred and twenty-five	Where the person liable under an order made under section one hundred and twenty-two or section one hundred and twenty-four, or under an affiliation order in respect of which an order under section one hundred and twenty-three is in force, is for the time being residing in England or Scotland, subsection (2) shall have effect as if for the reference to the council of the county or county borough in which the person liable under the order is for the time being residing there were substituted a reference to the welfare authority or local authority to whom sums are payable under the order, and as if for the words " when he was not resident in that county or county borough " there were substituted the words " when that authority were not entitled to sums payable under the order ".

SECOND SCHEDULE
FORMS

FORM No. 1: ENDORSEMENT OF SUMMONS

I, A. B., a justice of the peace [sheriff] [resident magistrate] for the [county] of   , hereby authorise the service of this summons [writ] in England [Scotland] [Northern Ireland] under section fifteen of the Maintenance Orders Act 1950.

Given under my hand this

day of   , 19 .

FORM No. 2: DECLARATION AS TO SERVICE

I, C. D. of   hereby declare that on the   day
of   19   , I served E. F. of   with the
summons [writ] now shown to me and marked " A " by delivering a true copy to
him.

(*Signed*) C. D.

Declared before me this
day of   , 19   .

A. B.
Justice of the Peace [sheriff] [resident
magistrate] for the [county] of

.   .   .   .   .   .

Children and Young Persons (Amendment) Act 1952

(15 & 16 GEO. 6 and 1 ELIZ. 2, c. 50)

An Act to amend the Children and Young Persons Act 1933 and
section twenty-seven of the Criminal Justice Act 1948; and for
purposes connected therewith.   [1st August 1952.]

1. [*Repealed by Children and Young Persons Act 1963 (c. 37), s. 64
(3), Sched. 5.*]

2–5. [*Repealed by Children and Young Persons Act 1969 (c. 54),
s. 72 (4), Sched. 6.*]

6, 7. [*Repealed by Children and Young Persons Act 1963 (c. 37),
s. 64 (3), Sched. 5.*]

Exposing children under twelve to risk of burning

8. Section eleven of the principal Act shall be amended as follows:—
    (*a*) by the substitution of the word " twelve " for the word
        " seven "; and
    (*b*) by inserting after the words " fire grate " the words " or any
        heating appliance liable to cause injury to a person by contact
        therewith ".

Consequential amendments of enactments

9. The enactments specified in the Schedule to this Act shall have
effect subject to the amendments respectively specified in that Schedule,
being amendments consequential on the foregoing provisions of this Act.

Interpretation

10.—(1) In this Act the expression " the principal Act " means the
Children and Young Persons Act 1933.

(2) Save in so far as the context otherwise requires, any reference
in this Act to any other enactment shall be construed as a reference to
that enactment as amended by or under any other enactment, including
this Act.

(3) Subject to the foregoing provisions of this section, this Act shall

be construed as one with the Children and Young Persons Acts 1933 and 1938.

Short title, citation, extent and commencement

11.—(1) This Act may be cited as the Children and Young Persons (Amendment) Act 1952, and this Act and the Children and Young Persons Acts 1933 and 1938 may be cited together as the Children and Young Persons Acts 1933 to 1952.

(2) This Act shall not extend to Scotland or Northern Ireland.

(3) This Act shall come into operation on the first day of October, nineteen hundred and fifty-two.

. . . . . .

Magistrates' Courts Act 1952

(15 & 16 Geo. 6 and 1 Eliz. 2, c. 55)

Affiliation orders and orders for periodical payment

51.—[*Repealed by Affiliation Proceedings Act* 1957 (*c.* 55), *s.* 12 (1), *Sched.*]

Periodical payment through justices' clerk

52.[1]—(1) Where a magistrates' court orders money to be paid periodically by one person to another, the court may order that the payment shall be made to the clerk of the court or the clerk of any other magistrates' court.

(2) Where the order is an affiliation order, an order under the Summary Jurisdiction (Separation and Maintenance) Acts 1895 to 1949, or an order under [the Guardianship of Minors Acts 1971 and 1973],[1a] the court shall, unless upon representations expressly made in that behalf by [the person to whom the payments under the order fell to be made][2] it is satisfied that it is undesirable to do so, exercise its power under the preceding subsection:

[*Proviso repealed by Matrimonial Proceedings (Magistrates' Courts) Act* 1960 (*c.* 48), *s.* 18 (1), *Sched.*]

(3) [Where periodical payments under an order of any court are required to be paid to or through the clerk of a magistrates' court],[3] and any sums payable under the order are in arrear, the clerk shall, if the person for whose benefit the payment should have been made so requests in writing, and unless it appears to the clerk that it is unreasonable in the circumstances to do so, proceed in his own name for the recovery of those sums; but the said person shall have the same liability for all the costs properly incurred in or about the proceedings as if the proceedings had been taken by him.

(4) Nothing in this section shall affect any right of a person to proceed in his own name for the recovery of sums payable on his behalf under [an order of any court].[3]

---

[1] Saved by Affiliation Proceedings Act 1957 (c. 55), s. 5 (5); and Matrimonial Proceedings (Magistrates' Courts) 1960 (c. 48), s. 13 (2).

[1a] Words substituted by Guardianship Act 1973 (c. 29), s. 9, in relation to England and Wales.

[2] Modified by Matrimonial Proceedings (Magistrates' Courts) Act 1960 (c. 48), s. 13 (2), *post.*

[3] Words substituted by Maintenance Orders Act 1958 (c. 39), s. 20 (6).

Revocation, variation, etc., of orders for periodical payment

53.[4] Where a magistrates' court has made an order for the periodical payment of money, the court may, by order on complaint, revoke, revive or vary the order.

Domestic proceedings and constitution of courts

56.[5]—(1) In this Act the expression " domestic proceedings " means proceedings—

    (*a*) under [the Guardianship of Minors Acts 1971 and 1973) [1a];

    (*b*) under the Summary Jurisdiction (Separation and Maintenance) Acts 1895 to 1949;

    (*c*) under section three or section four of the Maintenance Orders (Facilities for Enforcement) Act 1920;

    (*d*) under subsection (3) of section four of the Family Allowances Act 1945, or under that subsection as applied by subsection (2) of section nineteen of the National Insurance Act 1946;

    (*e*) under section three of the Marriage Act 1949,

other than proceedings for the enforcement of an order made under any of the enactments mentioned in paragraphs (*a*) and (*b*) of this subsection, or for the variation of any provision for the payment of money contained in an order made under any of those enactments, or in an order made or confirmed under the enactments mentioned in paragraph (*c*) of this subsection.

(2) A magistrates' court when hearing domestic proceedings shall be composed of not more than three justices of the peace, including, so far as practicable, both a man and a woman.

Sittings of magistrates' courts for domestic proceedings

57.—(1) The business of magistrates' courts shall, so far as is consistent with the due dispatch of business, be arranged in such manner as may be requisite for separating the hearing and determination of domestic proceedings from other business.

(2) No person shall be present during the hearing and determination by a magistrates' court of any domestic proceedings, except—

    (*a*) officers of the court;

    (*b*) parties to the case before the court, their solicitors and counsel, witnesses and other persons directly concerned in the case, and other persons whom either party desires to be present;

    (*c*) solicitors and counsel in attendance for other cases;

    (*d*) representatives of newspapers or news agencies;

    (*e*) any other person whom the court may permit to be present, so, however, that permission shall not be withheld from a person who appears to the court to have adequate grounds for attendance.

(3) When hearing domestic proceedings, a magistrates' court may, if it thinks it necessary in the interest of the administration of justice or of public decency, direct that any persons, not being officers of the court or parties to the case, the parties' solicitors or counsel, or other persons directly concerned in the case, be excluded during the taking of any indecent evidence.

---

[4] Extended by Affiliation Proceedings Act 1957 (c. 55), s. 7 (1) and Matrimonial Proceedings (Magistrates' Courts) Act 1960 (c. 48), s. 8 (1).

[5] Excluded by Matrimonial Proceedings (Magistrates' Courts) Act 1960 (c. 48), s. 8 (3), *post*; and Administration of Justice Act 1964 (c. 42), s. 11 (1); amended by Legitimacy Act 1959 (c. 73), s. 5 (1), *post*; and Supplementary Benefits Act 1966 (c. 20), ss. 23 (5), 24 (8), 25 (2); extended by Affiliation Proceedings (Amendment) Act 1972 (c. 49), s. 3 (1) (2), to include proceedings under that Act. See also now Children Act 1975 (c. 72), Sched. 3, para. 12, *post*.

(4) Where the same parties are parties to domestic proceedings and to proceedings for the enforcement of an order made under the Summary Jurisdiction (Separation and Maintenance) Acts 1895 to 1949 or [the Guardianship of Minors Acts 1971 and 1973],[5a] or made or confirmed under the Maintenance Orders (Facilities for Enforcement) Act 1920, or for the variation of any provision for the payment of money contained in an order made or confirmed under any of those Acts, and the proceedings are heard together by a magistrates' court, the provisions of the last two preceding subsections shall, unless the court otherwise determines, have effect as if the whole of those proceedings were domestic proceedings.

(5) The powers conferred on a magistrates' court by this section shall be in addition and without prejudice to any other powers of the court to hear proceedings *in camera*.

(6) Nothing in this section shall affect the exercise by a magistrates' court of the power to direct that witnesses shall be excluded until they are called for examination.

Newspaper reports of domestic proceedings

58.—(1) It shall not be lawful for the proprietor, editor or publisher of a newspaper or periodical to print or publish, or cause or procure to be printed or published, in it any particulars of domestic proceedings in a magistrates' court other than the following, that is to say—

(*a*) the names, addresses and occupations of the parties and witnesses;

(*b*) the grounds of the application, and a concise statement of the charges, defences and counter-charges in support of which evidence has been given;

(*c*) submissions on any point of law arising in the course of the proceedings and the decision of the court on the submissions;

(*d*) the decision of the court, and any observations made by the court in giving it.

(2) Any person acting in contravention of this section shall be liable on summary conviction to imprisonment for a term not exceeding four months or a fine not exceeding one hundred pounds or both.

(3) No prosecution for an offence under this section shall be begun without the consent of the Attorney General.

(4) Nothing in this section shall prohibit the printing or publishing of any matter in a newspaper or periodical of a technical character *bona fide* intended for circulation among members of the legal or medical professions.

Report by probation officer on attempted conciliation

59.—(1) Where in any domestic proceedings under the Summary Jurisdiction (Separation and Maintenance) Acts 1895 to 1949 a magistrates' court has requested a probation officer or any other person to attempt to effect a conciliation between the parties, the probation officer or that other person may, if the attempt has proved unsuccessful and he thinks fit in the circumstances of the case to do so, furnish to the court a report made in the prescribed form and containing—

(*a*) the allegations made by the complainant and defendant respectively; and

(*b*) information about such other matters relating to the proceedings or to the parties as may be prescribed:

Provided that no allegation made by a party shall be included in a report made under this subsection without his or her consent in writing.

(2) Where a probation officer or other person furnishes a report to

---

[5a] Words substituted by Guardianship Act 1973, (c. 29) s. 9 (2), in relation to England and Wales.

the court under this section he shall cause copies of it to be delivered to the complainant and the defendant, or sent by post addressed to each of them at his or her last or usual place of abode.

(3) Where a report made by a probation officer or other person has been furnished to the court and delivered or sent to the complainant and the defendant under this section, the court may, if it thinks fit, make use of the report for the purpose of putting or causing to be put questions to any witness; so, however, that nothing contained in the report shall be received by the court as evidence.

Report by probation officer on means of parties

60.[6]—(1) Where in any domestic proceedings in which an order may be made for the periodical payment of money by any person, or in any proceedings for the enforcement or variation of any such order, or in any proceedings in any matter of bastardy, a magistrates' court has requested a probation officer to investigate the means of the parties to the proceedings, the court may direct the probation officer to report the result of his investigation to the court in accordance with the provisions of this section:

Provided that in the case of any such domestic proceedings [. . .] [7] no direction to report to the court shall be given to a probation officer under this subsection until the court has determined all issues arising in the proceedings other than the amount to be directed to be paid by such an order.

(2) Where the court directs a probation officer under this section to report to the court the result of any such investigation as aforesaid, the court may require him—

  (a) to furnish to the court a statement in writing about his investigation, which shall be read aloud in the presence of such parties to the proceedings as may be present at the hearing; or

  (b) to make an oral statement to the court about his investigation.

(3) Immediately after the statement of the probation officer has been read aloud or made, as the case may be, under the last preceding subsection, the court shall ask each party to the proceedings whether he or she objects to anything contained in the statement; and where objection is made the court shall require the probation officer to give evidence on oath about his investigation.

(4) Any statement made by a probation officer in a statement furnished or made by him under subsection (2) of this section, or any evidence which he is required to give under subsection (3) of this section, may be received by the court as evidence, notwithstanding anything to the contrary in any enactment or rule of law relating to the admissibility of evidence.

Examination of witnesses by court

61. Where in any domestic proceedings, or in any proceedings for the enforcement or variation of an order made in domestic proceedings, or in proceedings in any matter of bastardy, it appears to a magistrates' court that any party to the proceedings who is not legally represented is unable effectively to examine or cross-examine a witness, the court shall ascertain from that party what are the matters about which the witness may be able to depose or on which the witness ought to be cross-examined, as the case may be, and shall put, or cause to be put, to the witness such questions in the interests of that party as may appear to the court to be proper.

---

[6] Excluded by Matrimonial Proceedings (Magistrates' Courts) Act 1960 (c. 48), s. 4 (8), *post.*
[7] Repealed by Legitimacy Act 1959 (c. 73), s. 5 (2).

Religion of probation officer

62. Where a magistrates' court determines to request a probation officer or other person to attempt to effect conciliation between parties to any domestic proceedings under the Summary Jurisdiction (Separation and Maintenance) Acts 1895 to 1949, the court shall have regard to the religious persuasion of the parties, and, if the court determines to request a probation officer to attempt to effect conciliation, it shall, where the religious persuasion of both parties is the same, select for that purpose a probation officer of that religious persuasion if such a probation officer is available.

Arrears under affiliation order, etc.

Complaint for arrears

74.[8]—(1) Where default is made in paying a sum ordered to be paid by an affiliation order or order enforceable as an affiliation order, the court shall not enforce payment of the sum under section sixty-four of this Act except by an order made on complaint.

(2) A complaint under this section shall be made not earlier than the fifteenth day after the making of the order for the enforcement of which it is made; but subject to this such a complaint may be made at any time notwithstanding anything in this or any other Act.

[(3) In relation to complaints under this section, section forty-seven of this Act shall not apply and section forty-eight thereof shall have effect as if the words " if evidence has been received on a previous occasion " were omitted.

(4) Where at the time and place appointed for the hearing or adjourned hearing of a complaint under this section the complainant appears but the defendant does not, the court may proceed in his absence:

Provided that the court shall not begin to hear the complaint in the absence of the defendant unless either it is proved to the satisfaction of the court, on oath, or in such other manner as may be prescribed, that the summons was served on him within what appears to the court to be a reasonable time before the hearing or adjourned hearing or the defendant has appeared on a previous occasion to answer the complaint.

(5) If a complaint under this section is substantiated on oath, any justice of the peace acting for the same petty sessions area as a court having jurisdiction to hear the complaint may issue a warrant for the defendant's arrest, whether or not a summons has been previously issued.

(6) A magistrates' court shall not impose imprisonment in respect of a default to which a complaint under this section relates unless the court has inquired in the presence of the defendant whether the default was due to the defendant's wilful refusal or culpable neglect, and shall not impose imprisonment as aforesaid if it is of opinion that the default was not so due; and, without prejudice to the foregoing provisions of this subsection, a magistrates' court shall not impose imprisonment as aforesaid—

    (a) in a case in which the court has power to make an attachment of earnings order [under the Maintenance Orders Act 1958,] [8a] unless the court is of opinion that it is inappropriate to make such an order;

    (b) in any case, in the absence of the defendant.

(7) Notwithstanding anything in subsection (3) of section sixty-four of this Act, the period for which a defendant may be committed to prison

8 Extended by Criminal Justice Act 1967 (c. 80), s. 79 (3).
8a Words repealed by A.J.A. 1970 (c. 31), s. 54, Sched. 11.

under a warrant of commitment issued in pursuance of a complaint under this section shall not exceed six weeks.

(8) The imprisonment or other detention of a defendant under a warrant of commitment issued as aforesaid shall not operate to discharge the defendant from his liability to pay the sum in respect of which the warrant was issued.] [9]

Effect of committal on arrears

75. Where a person is committed to custody under this Part of this Act for failure to pay a sum due under an affiliation order or order enforceable as an affiliation order, then, unless the court that commits him otherwise directs, no arrears shall accrue under the order while he is in custody.

Power to remit arrears

76. On the hearing of a complaint for the enforcement, revocation, revival, variation or discharge of an affiliation order or an order enforceable as an affiliation order, the court may remit the whole or any part of the sum due under the order.

Limitation of time

Limitation of time

104.[10] Except as otherwise expressly provided by an enactment, a magistrates' court shall not try an information or hear a complaint unless the information was laid, or the complaint made, within [three years] [11] from the time when the offence was committed, or the matter of complaint arose:

Provided that this section shall not restrict any power to try summarily an indictable offence under section nineteen, twenty or twenty-one of this Act, or under the provisions of any enactment not contained in this Act whereby an indictable offence may be tried summarily with the consent of the accused but not otherwise.

---

[9] Substituted by Maintenance Orders Act 1958 (c. 39), s. 16 (1).

[10] Excluded by Restrictive Trade Practices Act 1956 (c. 68), s. 17 (2); Solicitors Act 1957 (c. 27), ss. 24, 37 (2), 39 (4); Dentists Act 1957 (c. 28), s. 34 (3); Maintenance Orders Act 1958 (c. 39), s. 20 (7); Obscene Publications Act 1959 (c. 66), s. 2 (2); Finance Act 1960 (c. 44), s. 55 (1); Films Act 1960 (c. 57), s. 45 (3); Protection of Depositors Act 1963 (c. 16), s. 23 (3); Plant Varieties and Seeds Act 1964 (c. 14), ss. 23 (2), 28 (1); Licensing Act 1964 (c. 26), s. 48 (3); Housing Act 1964 (c. 56), s. 17 (6); Building Control Act 1966 (c. 27), s. 1 (8); Industrial Development Act 1966 (c. 34), s. 8 (10); Criminal Justice Act 1967 (c. 80), s. 90 (2); Companies Act 1967 (c. 81), s. 49 (3); Firearms Act 1968 (c. 27), s. 51 (4); Trade Descriptions Act 1968 (c. 29), s. 19 (2); Medicines Act 1968 (c. 67), s. 125 (1); Transport Act 1968 (c. 73), s. 32 (6), Sched. 8 para 8; Development of Tourism Act 1969 (c. 51), s. 12 (3), Sched. 2 para. 3 (2); Children and Young Persons Act 1969 (c. 54), s. 57 (2), *post*; Auctions (Bidding Agreements) Act 1969 (c. 56), s. 1 (2); Attachment of Earnings Act 1971 (c. 32), s. 19 (5); Industry Act 1972 (c. 63), ss. 4 (3), 11 (8), Sched. 1, para. 4 (2). Modified by Food and Drugs Act 1955 (c. 16), s. 108 (1).

[11] Substituted by Historic Buildings and Ancient Monuments Act 1953 (c. 49), s. 15 (1), and Finance Act 1965 (c. 25), s. 92 (7).

Intestates' Estates Act 1952

(15 & 16 GEO. 6 & 1 ELIZ. 2, c. 64)

An Act to amend the law of England and Wales about the property of persons dying intestate; to amend the Inheritance (Family Provision) Act 1938; and for purposes connected therewith.

[30th October 1952.]

PART I

AMENDMENTS OF LAW OF INTESTATE SUCCESSION

1–4. [*These sections amend the Administration of Estates Act 1925, ss. 46–49, ante, pp. 22–28.*]

Rights of surviving spouse as respects the matrimonial home

5. The Second Schedule to this Act shall have effect for enabling the surviving husband or wife of a person dying intestate after the commencement of this Act to acquire the matrimonial home.

6. [*Interpretation and construction.*]

PART II

AMENDMENTS OF INHERITANCE (FAMILY PROVISION) ACT 1938

7. [*Repealed by Inheritance (Provision for Family and Dependants) Act 1975 (c. 63), Sched.*]

8. [*Repealed by the Family Provision Act 1966 (c. 35), Sched. 2.*]

PART III

GENERAL

Short title and commencement

9.—(1) This Act may be cited as the Intestates' Estates Act 1952.

(2) This Act shall come into operation on the first day of January, nineteen hundred and fifty-three.

SCHEDULES

FIRST SCHEDULE

[*This Schedule sets out ss. 46–49 of the Administration of Estates Act 1925, ante, pp. 22–28, as amended by Part I of this Act.*]

Section 5　　　　　　　　SECOND SCHEDULE

RIGHTS OF SURVIVING SPOUSE AS RESPECTS THE MATRIMONIAL HOME

1.—(1) Subject to the provisions of this Schedule, where the residuary estate of the intestate comprises an interest in a dwelling-house in which the surviving husband or wife was resident at the time of the intestate's death, the surviving husband or wife may require the personal representative, in exercise of the power conferred by section forty-one of the principal Act (and with due regard to the requirements of that section as to valuation) to appropriate the said interest in the dwelling-house in or towards satisfaction of any absolute interest of the surviving husband or wife in the real and personal estate of the intestate.

(2)[1] The right conferred by this paragraph shall not be exercisable where the interest is—

(a) a tenancy which at the date of the death of the intestate was a tenancy which would determine within the period of two years from that date; or

(b) a tenancy which the landlord by notice given after that date could determine within the remainder of that period.

(3) Nothing in subsection (5) of section forty-one of the principal Act (which requires the personal representative, in making an appropriation to any person under that section, to have regard to the rights of others) shall prevent the personal representative from giving effect to the right conferred by this paragraph.

(4) The reference in this paragraph to an absolute interest in the real and personal estate of the intestate includes a reference to the capital value of a life interest which the surviving husband or wife has under this Act elected to have redeemed.

(5) Where part of a building was, at the date of the death of the intestate, occupied as a separate dwelling, that dwelling shall for the purposes of this Schedule be treated as a dwelling-house.

2. Where—

(a) the dwelling-house forms part of a building and an interest in the whole of the building is comprised in the residuary estate; or

(b) the dwelling-house is held with agricultural land and an interest in the agricultural land is comprised in the residuary estate; or

(c) the whole or a part of the dwelling-house was at the time of the intestate's death used as a hotel or lodging house; or

(d) a part of the dwelling-house was at the time of the intestate's death used for purposes other than domestic purposes,

the right conferred by paragraph 1 of this Schedule shall not be exercisable unless the court, on being satisfied that the exercise of that right is not likely to diminish the value of assets in the residuary estate (other than the said interest in the dwelling-house) or make them more difficult to dispose of, so orders.

3.—(1) The right conferred by paragraph 1 of this Schedule—

(a) shall not be exercisable after the expiration of twelve months from the first taking out of representation with respect to the intestate's estate;

(b) shall not be exercisable after the death of the surviving husband or wife;

(c) shall be exercisable, except where the surviving husband or wife is the sole personal representative, by notifying the personal representative (or, where there are two or more personal representatives of whom one is the surviving husband or wife, all of them except the surviving husband or wife) in writing.

(2) A notification in writing under paragraph (c) of the foregoing sub-paragraph shall not be revocable except with the consent of the personal representative; but the surviving husband or wife may require the personal representative to have the said interest in the dwelling-house valued in accordance with section forty-one of the principal Act and to inform him or her of the result of that valuation before he or she decides whether to exercise the right.

(3) Subsection (9) of the section forty-seven A added to the principal Act by section two of this Act shall apply for the purposes of the construction of the reference in this paragraph to the first taking out of representation, and the proviso to subsection (5) of that section shall apply for the purpose of enabling the surviving husband or wife to apply for an extension of the period of twelve months mentioned in this paragraph.

4.—(1) During the period of twelve months mentioned in paragraph 3 of this Schedule the personal representative shall not without the written consent of the surviving husband or wife sell or otherwise dispose of the said interest in the dwelling-house except in the course of administration owing to want of other assets.

[1] This sub-paragraph shall not apply in certain cases: Leasehold Reform Act 1967 (c. 88), s. 7 (8).

(2) An application to the court under paragraph 2 of this Schedule may be made by the personal representative as well as by the surviving husband or wife, and if, on an application under that paragraph, the court does not order that the right conferred by paragraph 1 of this Schedule shall be exercisable by the surviving husband or wife, the court may authorise the personal representative to dispose of the said interest in the dwelling-house within the said period of twelve months.

(3) Where the court under sub-paragraph (3) of paragraph 3 of this Schedule extends the said period of twelve months, the court may direct that this paragraph shall apply in relation to the extended period as it applied in relation to the original period of twelve months.

(4) This paragraph shall not apply where the surviving husband or wife is the sole personal representative or one of two or more personal representatives.

(5) Nothing in this paragraph shall confer any right on the surviving husband or wife as against a purchaser from the personal representative.

5.—(1) Where the surviving husband or wife is one of two or more personal representatives, the rule that a trustee may not be a purchaser of trust property shall not prevent the surviving husband or wife from purchasing out of the estate of the intestate an interest in a dwelling-house in which the surviving husband or wife was resident at the time of the intestate's death.

(2) The power of appropriation under section forty-one of the principal Act shall include power to appropriate an interest in a dwelling-house in which the surviving husband or wife was resident at the time of the intestate's death partly in satisfaction of an interest of the surviving husband or wife in the real and personal estate of the intestate and partly in return for a payment of money by the surviving husband or wife to the personal representative.

6.—(1) Where the surviving husband or wife is a person of unsound mind or a defective, a requirement or consent under this Schedule may be made or given on his or her behalf by the committee or receiver, if any, or, where there is no committee or receiver, by the court.

(2) A requirement or consent made or given under this Schedule by a surviving husband or wife who is an infant shall be as valid and binding as it would be if he or she were of age; and, as respects an appropriation in pursuance of paragraph 1 of this Schedule, the provisions of section forty-one of the principal Act as to obtaining the consent of the infant's parent or guardian, or of the court on behalf of the infant, shall not apply.

7.—(1) Except where the context otherwise requires, references in this Schedule to a dwelling-house include references to any garden or portion of ground attached to and usually occupied with the dwelling-house or otherwise required for the amenity or convenience of the dwelling-house.

(2) This Schedule shall be construed as one with Part IV of the principal Act.

THIRD SCHEDULE

[*Repealed by the Inheritance (Provision for Family and Dependants) Act 1975 (c. 63), Sched.*]

FOURTH SCHEDULE

[*Repealed by the Family Provision Act 1966, (c. 35), Sched. 2.*]

Affiliation Proceedings Act 1957

(5 & 6 ELIZ. 2, c. 55)

An Act to consolidate the enactments relating to bastardy, with corrections and improvements made under the Consolidation of Enactments (Procedure) Act 1949.   [31st July, 1957]

Commencement of affiliation proceedings

1.[1] A single woman who is with child, or who has been delivered of an illegitimate child, may apply by complaint to a justice of the peace for a summons to be served on the man alleged by her to be the father of the child.

Time for application for summons

2.—(1) A complaint under section one of this Act, where the complainant has been delivered of an illegitimate child, may be made—

(a) at any time within [three years] [1a] from the child's birth, or

(b) at any subsequent time, upon proof that the man alleged to be the father of the child has within the [three years] [1a] next after the birth paid money for its maintenance, or

(c) at any time within the twelve months next after the man's return to England, upon proof that he ceased to reside in England within the [three years] [1a] next after the birth.

(2) A single woman who has been delivered of a child may, upon proof that—

(a) before the birth she was a party to a marriage which would have been valid but for provisions of an Act of Parliament making it void on account of her, or the other party to the marriage, being under the age of sixteen, and

(b) the said other party had access to her within twelve months before the birth,

make at any time a complaint under section one of this Act against that party, notwithstanding that he may not within the [three years] [1a] next after the birth have paid money for the child's maintenance.

Venue and procedure

3.—(1) A complaint under section one of this Act—

(a) shall not be made except to a justice of the peace acting for the petty sessions area (within the meaning of the Magistrates' Courts Act 1952) in which the mother of the child resides,

(b) if made before the birth of the child, shall be substantiated on oath,

and the magistrates' court which, under the summons, is to hear the complaint shall be a magistrates' court for the said petty sessions area.

(2) The foregoing subsection shall have effect subject to subsection (2) of section three of the Maintenance Orders Act 1950 (which relates to a complaint by a person residing in Scotland or Northern Ireland).

(3) If the justice to whom a complaint under section one of this Act has been made dies, or ceases to be a justice, or is unable to act, the summons may be issued by any other justice acting for the same petty sessions area.

Powers of court on hearing of complaint

4.—[(1) On the hearing of a complaint under section 1 of this Act the court may adjudge the defendant to be the putative father of the child, but shall not do so, in a case where evidence is given by the mother, unless her evidence is corroborated in some material particular by other evidence to the court's satisfaction.] [1b]

(2) [Where the court has adjudged the defendant to be the putative

---

[1] Explained by Legitimacy Act 1959 (c. 73), s. 4, *post*; and extended by Ministry of Social Security Act 1966 (c. 20), s. 24 (2).

[1a] Words substituted by Affiliation Proceedings (Amendment) Act 1972 (c. 49), s. 2 (1).

[1b] Words substituted by Affiliation Proceedings (Amendment) Act 1972 (c. 49) s. 1 (1)·

father of the child it may also] [1c] if it thinks fit in all the circumstances of the case, proceed to make against him an order (referred to in this Act as " an affiliation order ") for the payment by him of—

    (*a*) a sum of money weekly, [. . .],[2] for the maintenance and education of the child,

    (*b*) the expenses incidental to the birth of the child, and

    (*c*) if the child has died before the making of the order, the child's funeral expenses.

(3) Where a complaint under section one of this Act is made before or within two months after the birth of the child, any weekly sum ordered to be paid under paragraph (*a*) of the last foregoing subsection may, if the court thinks fit, be calculated from the date of the birth.

Persons entitled to payments under affiliation order

5.[2a]—(1) Subject to the provisions of this section and of the enactments mentioned in the following subsection, the person entitled to any payments to be made under an affiliation order shall be the child's mother, and the order shall make provision accordingly.

(2) The enactments referred to above are—

    (*a*) section eighty-eight of the Children and Young Persons Act 1933 (which provides that, where an illegitimate child is committed to the care of a [local authority] [3] the person entitled to receive contributions in respect of the child under section eighty-six of that Act may be given the benefit of payments under an affiliation order in respect of the child);

    (*b*) the said section eighty-eight as extended by section twenty-three of the Children Act 1948 (which applies the former section to children received into the care of a local authority under section one of the Act of 1948);

    (*c*) section forty-four of the National Assistance Act 1948 (under which [. . .] [4] a local authority giving assistance in respect of an illegitimate child may obtain an affiliation order providing for payments thereunder being made to the [. . .] [4] authority, or may apply for an existing order to be varied so as to provide as aforesaid); and

    (*d*) section twenty-six of the Children Act 1948 (which makes provision corresponding to the said section forty-four for the benefit of a local authority having an illegitimate child in their care [. . .]).[5]

(3) An affiliation order may, on the application of a person other than the child's mother who for the time being has the custody of the child, either legally or by any arrangement approved by the court, be made or varied by a magistrates' court so as to entitle that person to any payments to be made under the order.

(4) Where an affiliation order for the time being provides for the child's mother to be entitled to any payments to be made under the order the payments shall be due under the order in respect of such time and so long as she is living and of sound mind and is not in prison, and if the mother has died, or is of unsound mind, or is in prison, any two justices of the peace may by order from time to time appoint some person (with his consent) to have the custody of the child; and a person appointed as guardian under this subsection shall be entitled to any

[1c] Words substituted by *ibid.*, s. 1 (2).
[2] Words repealed by Maintenance Orders Act 1968 (c. 36), s. 1, Sched.
[2a] See Children Act 1975 (c. 72), Sched. 3, para. 14 *post*.
[3] Words substituted by Children and Young Persons Act 1969 (c. 54), s. 72 (3), Sched. 5, para. 28 (1).
[4] Words repealed by Ministry of Social Security Act 1966 (c. 20), s. 39 (3), Sched. 8.
[5] Words repealed by Children and Young Persons Act 1969 (c. 54), s. 72 (4), Sched. 6.

payments to be made under the affiliation order and may make application for the recovery of any payments due thereunder in the same manner as the mother might have done.

Any two justices of the peace may revoke an appointment made under this subsection and appoint another person thereunder in place of the person formerly appointed.

(5) An affiliation order shall, in any case where payments to be made thereunder are not ordered to be made to the clerk of a magistrates' court under section fifty-two of the Magistrates' Courts Act 1952, provide for the payments to be made to the person for the time being entitled thereto in accordance with the provisions of this Act.

Duration of orders

6. Subject to the provisions of this Act, an affiliation order shall not, except for the purpose of recovering money previously due under the order, be of any force or validity after the child has attained the age of sixteen years or has died; and payments under the order shall not be required to be made in respect of any period after the child has attained the age of thirteen years unless the order contains a direction that payments to be made under it are to continue until the child attains the age of sixteen years

Continuance of payments in certain cases

7.—(1) The power under section fifty-three of the Magistrates' Courts Act 1952 to vary or revive an affiliation order shall, notwithstanding anything in the last foregoing section, include power to vary or revive it in accordance with the following provisions of this section.

(2) [6] If, on the application of the child's mother, it appears to the court that the child is or will be engaged in a course of education or training after attaining the age of sixteen years, and that it is expedient for that purpose for payments to be made under the order after the child attains that age, then subject to the two next following subsections the court may by order direct that payments shall be so made for such period, not exceeding two years from the date of the order, as may be specified in the order.

(3) Subject to the next following subsection, the period specified in an order made by virtue of the foregoing provisions of this section may from time to time be extended by a subsequent order so made, but shall not in any case extend beyond the date when the child attains the age of twenty-one.

(4) Notwithstanding anything in the foregoing provisions of this section or in any order made by virtue of this section, an affiliation order shall not operate, after the child has attained the age of sixteen,—

[(a) subject to the next following subsection, so as to require payments thereunder to be made in respect of any period when the child is in the care of a local authority under section 1 of the Children Act 1948 or by virtue of a care order (other than an interim order) within the meaning of the Children and Young Persons Act 1969;] [7]

(b) so as to entitle any person other than the child's mother to the payments.

(5) [. . .] [8] paragraph (a) of the last foregoing subsection shall not apply to any part of such a period as is there mentioned during which the child is permitted to reside with his mother.

[6] Subsections (2) (3) extended by Family Law Reform Act 1969 (c. 46), s. 5 (2).
[7] Words substituted by Children and Young Persons Act 1969 (c. 54), s. 72 (3), Sched. 5 para. 28 (2) (3).
[8] Words repealed by *ibid.* s. 72 (4), Sched. 6.

(6) Any reference in this section to a child's mother shall be taken as including a reference to any person for the time being having the custody of the child either legally or by any arrangement approved by the court, except that it shall not be taken as referring to a local authority in whose care the child is under section one of the Children Act 1948 or [by virtue of such a care order as aforesaid].[7]

Appeal

8.—(1) An appeal shall lie to [the Crown Court] [8a] from the making of an order under this Act, or from any refusal by a magistrates' court to make such an order, or from the revocation, revival or variation by a magistrates' court of such an order.

(2) On an appeal against an order under section four of this Act by the person adjudged to be the putative father (as well as on an appeal against a refusal to make an order under that section) the court shall [hear any evidence given by or on behalf of either party but shall not confirm the order appealed against (or reverse the refusal to make an order), in a case where evidence is given by the mother, unless her evidence is corroborated in some material particular by other evidence to the court's satisfaction.] [8b]

Duty of putative father to notify change of address

9.—(1) A person against whom an affiliation order has been made—

(a) shall, if he changes his address and he is required to make any payment under the order to the clerk of a magistrates' court, give notice of the change to the clerk of that court;

(b) shall, in a case where the foregoing paragraph does not apply and he is required under the order to make any payments (including payments of costs) to any person, give notice of any change of address to such person (if any) as may be specified in the order.

(2) Any person failing without reasonable excuse to give a notice which he is required by this section to give shall be liable on summary conviction to a fine not exceeding [ten pounds].[9]

10. [*Repealed by Maintenance Orders Act 1958 (c. 39), s. 23 (4).*]

Misconduct by guardian of illegitimate child

11. If any person appointed under subsection (4) of section five of this Act to have the custody of an illegitimate child—

(a) misapplies any money paid by the putative father for the child's support, or

(b) withholds proper nourishment from, or otherwise abuses or mal-treats, the child,

he shall be liable on summary conviction to a fine not exceeding ten pounds.

Repeals and savings

12. [*Subsection (1) repealed by Statute Law (Repeals) Act 1974 (c. 22), Sched., Pt. XI.*]

(2) Any application, order, appointment or other thing made or having effect under or for the purposes of an enactment repealed by this

[8a] Words substituted by Courts Act 1971 (c. 23), s. 56 (2), Sched. 9, Pt. I.
[8b] Words substituted by Affiliation Proceedings (Amendment) Act 1972 (c. 49), s. 1 (3).
[9] Maximum fine increased from two pounds by Criminal Justice Act 1967 (c. 80), s. 92, Sched. 3, Pt. I.

Act and pending or in force immediately before the commencement of this Act shall be deemed to have been made under or for the purposes of the corresponding enactment in this Act; and any proceeding or other thing begun under any enactment so repealed may be continued under this Act, as if begun thereunder.

(3) So much of any enactment or document as refers expressly or by implication to any enactment repealed by this Act shall, if and so far as the nature of the subject-matter of the enactment or document permits, be construed as referring to this Act or the corresponding enactment therein, as the case may require.

(4) Nothing in this section shall be taken as prejudicing the general application of section thirty-eight of the Interpretation Act 1889 with regard to the effect of repeals.

Short title, extent and commencement

13.—(1) This Act may be cited as the Affiliation Proceedings Act 1957.

(2) This Act shall not extend to Scotland or Northern Ireland.

(3) This Act shall come into force on the first day of April, nineteen hundred and fifty-eight.

SCHEDULE

[*Repealed by Statute Law (Repeals) Act* 1974 (*c.* 22), *Sched., Pt. XI.*]

Matrimonial Causes (Property and Maintenance) Act 1958

(6 & 7 ELIZ. 2, C. 35)

An Act to enable the power of the court in matrimonial proceedings to order alimony, maintenance or the securing of a sum of money to be exercised at any time after a decree; to provide for the setting aside of dispositions of property made for the purpose of reducing the assets available for satisfying such an order; to enable the court after the death of a party to a marriage which has been dissolved or annulled to make provision out of his estate in favour of the other party; and to extend the powers of the court under section seventeen of the Married Women's Property Act 1882.   [7th July 1958]

1–6. [*Repealed by Matrimonial Causes Act* 1965 (*c.* 72), *s.* 45, *Sched.* 2.]

Extension of s. 17 of Married Women's Property Act 1882

7.—(1) Any right of a wife, under section seventeen of the Married Women's Property Act 1882 to apply to a judge of the High Court or of a county court, in any question between husband and wife as to the title to or possession of property, shall include the right to make such an application where it is claimed by the wife that her husband has had in his possession or under his control—

    (*a*) money to which, or to a share of which, she was beneficially
        entitled (whether by reason that it represented the proceeds of
        property to which, or to an interest in which, she was beneficially
        entitled, or for any other reason), or
    (*b*) property (other than money) to which, or to an interest in which,
        she was beneficially entitled,

and that either that money or other property has ceased to be in his
possession or under his control or that she does not know whether it is
still in his possession or under his control.

(2) Where, on an application made to a judge of the High Court or
of a county court under the said section seventeen, as extended by the
preceding subsection, the judge is satisfied—

    (*a*) that the husband has had in his possession or under his control
        money or other property as mentioned in paragraph (*a*) or
        paragraph (*b*) of the preceding subsection, and
    (*b*) that he has not made to the wife, in respect of that money or
        other property, such payment or disposition as would have been
        appropriate in the circumstances,

the power to make orders under that section shall be extended in
accordance with the next following subsection.

(3) Where the last preceding subsection applies, the power to make
orders under the said section seventeen shall include power for the
judge to order the husband to pay to the wife—

    (*a*) in a case falling within paragraph (*a*) of subsection (1) of this
        section, such sum in respect of the money to which the applica-
        tion relates, or the wife's share thereof, as the case may be, or
    (*b*) in a case falling within paragraph (*b*) of the said subsection (1),
        such sum in respect of the value of the property to which the
        application relates, or the wife's interest therein, as the case
        may be,

as the judge may consider appropriate.

(4) Where on an application under the said section seventeen as
extended by this section it appears to the judge that there is any
property which—

    (*a*) represents the whole or part of the money or property in
        question, and
    (*b*) is property in respect of which an order could have been made
        under that section if an application had been made by the
        wife thereunder in a question as to the title to or possession of
        that property,

the judge (either in substitution for or in addition to the making of
an order in accordance with the last preceding subsection) may make
any order under that section in respect of that property which he could
have made on such an application as is mentioned in paragraph (*b*)
of this subsection.

(5) The preceding provisions of this section shall have effect in
relation to a husband as they have effect in relation to a wife, as if
any reference to the husband were a reference to the wife and any
reference to the wife were a reference to the husband.

(6) Any power of a judge under the said section seventeen to direct
inquiries or give any other directions in relation to an application under
that section shall be exercisable in relation to an application made
under that section as extended by this section; and the provisos to
that section (which relate to appeals and other matters) shall apply

in relation to any order made under the said section seventeen as extended by this section as they apply in relation to an order made under that section apart from this section.

(7) For the avoidance of doubt it is hereby declared that any power conferred by the said section seventeen to make orders with respect to any property includes power to order a sale of the property.

Interpretation

8.—(1) In this Act, except in so far as the context otherwise requires, the following expressions have the meanings hereby assigned to them respectively, that is to say:—

" disposition " does not include any provision contained in a will, but, with that exception, includes any conveyance, assurance or gift of property of any description, whether made by an instrument or otherwise;

" property " means any real or personal property, any estate or interest in real or personal property, any money, any negotiable instrument, debt or other chose in action, and any other right or interest whether in possession or not;

" will " includes a codicil.

(2) Except in so far as the context otherwise requires, any reference in this Act to an enactment shall be construed as a reference to that enactment as amended by or under any other enactment.

Short title, commencement and extent

9.—(1) This Act may be cited as the Matrimonial Causes (Property and Maintenance) Act 1958.

(2) This Act shall come into operation on such day as may be appointed by the Lord Chancellor by an order made by statutory instrument.

(3) This Act shall not extend to Scotland or to Northern Ireland.

SCHEDULE

[*Repealed by Matrimonial Causes Act* 1965 (c. 72), *s.* 45, *Sched.* 2.]

Maintenance Orders Act 1958 [1]

(6 & 7 Eliz. 2, c. 39)

An Act to make provision for the registration in the High Court or a magistrates' court of certain maintenance orders made by the order of those courts or a county court and with respect to the enforcement and variation of registered orders; to make provision for the attachment of sums falling to be paid by way of wages, salary or other earnings or by way of pension for the purpose of enforcing certain maintenance

[1] Explained by Children and Young Persons Act 1963 (c. 37), s. 30 (3).

orders; to amend section seventy-four of the Magistrates' Courts Act 1952; to make provision for the review of committals to prison by magistrates' courts for failure to comply with maintenance orders; to enable Orders in Council under section twelve of the Maintenance Orders (Facilities for Enforcement) Act 1920 to be revoked or varied; and for purposes connected with the matters aforesaid.

[7th July 1958]

Part I

Registration, enforcement and variation of certain maintenance orders

Application of Part I

1.—(1) The provisions of this Part of this Act shall have effect for the purpose of enabling maintenance orders to which this Part of this Act applies to be registered—

(a) in the case of an order made by the High Court or a county court, in a magistrates' court; and

(b) in the case of an order made by a magistrates' court, in the High Court,

and, subject to those provisions, while so registered—

(i) to be enforced in like manner as an order made by the court of registration; and

(ii) in the case of an order registered in a magistrates' court, to be varied by a magistrates' court.

(2) This Part of this Act applies to maintenance orders made by the High Court, a county court or a magistrates' court, other than orders registered under Part II of the Maintenance Orders Act 1950.

(3) Without prejudice to the provisions of section twenty-one of this Act, in this Part of this Act, unless the context otherwise requires, the following expressions have the following meanings—

" High Court order ", " county court order " and " magistrates' court order " mean an order made by the High Court, a county court or a magistrates' court, as the case may be;

" order " means a maintenance order to which this Part of this Act applies;

" original court " and " court of registration ", in relation to an order, mean the court by which the order was made or, as the case may be, the court in which the order is registered;

" registered " means registered in accordance with the provisions of this Part of this Act, and " registration " shall be construed accordingly;

and for the purposes of this Part of this Act an order for the payment by the defendant of any costs incurred in proceedings relating to a maintenance order, being an order for the payment of costs made while the maintenance order is not registered, shall be deemed to form part of that maintenance order.

Registration of orders

2.—(1) A person entitled to receive payments under a High Court or county court order may apply for the registration of the order to the original court, and the court may, if it thinks fit, grant the application.

(2) Where an application for the registration of such an order is granted—

    (*a*) no proceedings shall be begun, and no writ, warrant or other process shall be issued, for the enforcement of the order before the registration of the order or the expiration of the prescribed period from the grant of the application, whichever first occurs; and

    (*b*) the orignal court shall, on being satisfied within the period aforesaid by the person who made the application that no such proceedings or process begun or issued before the grant of the application remain pending or in force, cause a certified copy of the order to be sent to the clerk of the magistrates' court acting for the petty sessions area in which the defendant appears to be;

but if at the expiration of the period aforesaid the original court has not been so satisfied, the grant of the application shall become void.

(3) A person entitled to receive payments under a magistrates' court order who considers that the order could be more effectively enforced if it were registered may apply for the registration of the order to the original court, and the court shall grant the application on being satisfied in the prescribed manner that, at the time when the application was made, an amount equal to not less, in the case of an order for weekly payments, than four or, in any other case, than two of the payments required by the order was due thereunder and unpaid.

(4) Where an application for the registration of a magistrates' court order is granted—

    (*a*) no proceedings for the enforcement of the order shall be begun before the registration takes place and no warrant or other process for the enforcement thereof shall be issued in consequence of any such proceedings begun before the grant of the application;

    (*b*) any warrant of commitment issued for the enforcement of the order shall cease to have effect when the person in possession of the warrant is informed of the grant of the application, unless the defendant has then already been detained in pursuance of the warrant; and

    (*c*) the orignal court shall, on being satisfied in the prescribed manner that no process for the enforcement of the order issued before the grant of the application remains in force, cause a certified copy of the order to be sent to the prescribed officer of the High Court.

(5) The officer or clerk of a court who receives a certified copy of an order sent to him under this section shall cause the order to be registered in that court.

(6) Subsections (1) to (4) of section nineteen of the Maintenance Orders Act 1950 (which provide for the suspension, while a magistrates' court order is registered under Part II of that Act, of any provision of the order requiring payments to be made through a third party, for ordering payments under an order so registered in a magistrates' court to be paid through a collecting officer, and for authorising a person to make payments otherwise than in accordance with the requirements of that section until he has notice of those requirements) shall have effect for the purposes of this Part of this Act as if for any reference in that section to the said Part II and a maintenance order there were substituted

a reference to this Part of this Act and a maintenance order to which this Part of this Act applies.

(7) In this section " certified copy " in relation to an order of a court means a copy certified by the proper officer of the court to be a true copy of the order or of the official record thereof.

Enforcement of registered orders

3.—(1) Subject to the provisions of this section, a registered order shall be enforceable in all respects as if it had been made by the court of registration and as if that court had had jurisdiction to make it; and proceedings for or with respect to the enforcement of a registered order may be taken accordingly.

(2) Subject to the provisions of the next following subsection, an order registered in a magistrates' court shall be enforceable as if it were an affiliation order; and the provisions of any enactment with respect to the enforcement of affiliation orders (including enactments relating to the accrual of arrears and the remission of sums due) shall apply accordingly.

In this subsection " enactment " includes any order, rule or regulation made in pursuance of any Act.

(3) Where an order remains or becomes registered after the discharge of the order, no proceedings shall be taken by virtue of that registration except in respect of arrears which were due under the order at the time of the discharge and have not been remitted.

(4) Except as provided by this section, no proceedings shall be taken for or with respect to the enforcement of a registered order.

Variation of orders registered in magistrates' courts

4.—(1) The provisions of this section shall have effect with respect to the variation of orders registered in magistrates' courts, and references in this section to registered orders shall be construed accordingly.

(2) Subject to the following provisions of this section—

    (*a*) the court of registration may exercise the same jurisdiction to vary any rate of payments specified by a registered order (other than jurisdiction in a case where a party to the order is not present in England when the application for variation is made) as is exercisable, apart from this subsection, by the original court; and

    (*b*) a rate of payments specified by a registered order shall not be varied except by the court of registration or any other magistrates' court to which the jurisdiction conferred by the foregoing paragraph is extended by rules of court.

[(3) A rate of payments specified by a registered order shall not be varied by virtue of the last foregoing subsection so as to exceed [the rate of payments specified by the order as made or last varied by the original court].²] ²ᵃ

(4) If it appears to the court to which an application is made by virtue of subsection (2) of this section for the variation of a rate of payments specified by a registered order that, by reason of the limitations imposed on the court's jurisdiction by the last foregoing subsection or for any other reason, it is appropriate to remit the application to the original court, the first-mentioned court shall so remit the application, and the original court shall thereupon deal with the application as if the order were not registered.

(5) Nothing in subsection (2) of this section shall affect the jurisdic-

---

² Words substituted by Maintenance Orders Act 1968 (c. 36), s. 1, Sched.
²ᵃ Subs. (3) repealed by A.J.A. 1970 (c. 31), s. 54, Sched. 11.

tion of the original court to vary a rate of payments specified by a registered order if an application for the variation of that rate is made to that court—

(a) in proceedings for a variation of provisions of the order which do not specify a rate of payments; or

(b) at a time when a party to the order is not present in England.

(6) No application for any variation of a registered order shall be made to any court while proceedings for any variation of the order are pending in any other court.

(7) Where a magistrates' court, in exercise of the jurisdiction conferred by subsection (2) of this section, varies or refuses to vary a registered order, an appeal from the variation or refusal shall lie to the High Court; and so much of subsection (1) of section sixty-three of the Supreme Court of Judicature (Consolidation) Act 1925 as requires an appeal from any court to the High Court to be heard and determined by a divisional court shall not apply to appeals under this subsection.

Cancellation of registration

5.—(1) If a person entitled to receive payments under a registered order desires the registration to be cancelled, he may give notice under this section.

(2) Where the original court varies or discharges an order registered in a magistrates' court, the original court may, if it thinks fit, give notice under this section.

(3) Where a magistrates' court discharges an order registered in the High Court and it appears to the magistrates' court, whether by reason of the remission of arrears by that court or otherwise, that no arrears under the order remain to be recovered, the magistrates' court shall give notice under this section.

(4) Notice under this section shall be given to the court of registration; and where such notice is given—

(a) no proceedings for the enforcement of the registered order shall be begun before the cancellation of the registration and no writ, warrant or other process for the enforcement thereof shall be issued in consequence of any such proceedings begun before the giving of the notice;

(b) where the order is registered in a magistrates' court, any warrant of commitment issued for the enforcement of the order shall cease to have effect when the person in possession of the warrant is informed of the giving of the notice, unless the defendant has then already been detained in pursuance of the warrant; and

(c) the court of registration shall cancel the registration on being satisfied in the prescribed manner—

(i) that no process for the enforcement of the registered order issued before the giving of the notice remains in force; and

(ii) in the case of an order registered in a magistrates' court, that no proceedings for the variation of the order are pending in a magistrates' court.

(5) On the cancellation of the registration of a High Court or county court order, any order made in relation thereto under subsection (2) of section nineteen of the Maintenance Orders Act 1950, as applied by subsection (6) of section two of this Act, shall cease to have effect, but until the defendant receives the prescribed notice of the cancellation he shall be deemed to comply with the High Court or county court order if he makes payments in accordance with any order under the said subsection (2) as so applied which was in force immediately before the cancellation and of which he has notice.

ATTACHMENT OF EARNINGS ORDERS

Powers of courts to make orders attaching earnings of defaulters under maintenance orders

6–8. [*Repealed by Administration of Justice Act* 1970 (c. 31), s. 54, Sched. 11.]

Variation and discharge etc. of attachment of earnings orders

9. [*Repealed by Attachment of Earnings Act* 1971 (c. 32), s. 29 (2), Sched. 6.]

Liabilities of persons to whom attachment of earnings orders are directed

10–15. [*Repealed by Administration of Justice Act* (c. 31), s. 54, Sched. 11.]

PART III [4-5]

MISCELLANEOUS AND SUPPLEMENTAL

Miscellaneous

Amendment of Magistrates' Courts Act 1952

16.—(1) Section seventy-four of the Magistrates' Courts Act 1952 (which relates to the enforcement of payments under affiliation orders and orders enforceable as affiliation orders) shall have effect, in relation to complaints under that section made on or after the date on which this section comes into operation and to proceedings in pursuance of such complaints, as if for subsections (3) to (7) thereof there were substituted the following subsections, that is to say—

" (3) In relation to complaints under this section, section forty-seven of this Act shall not apply and section forty-eight thereof shall have effect as if the words " if evidence has been received on a previous occasion " were omitted.

(4) Where at the time and place appointed for the hearing or adjourned hearing of a complaint under this section the complainant appears but the defendant does not, the court may proceed in his absence:

Provided that the court shall not begin to hear the complaint in the absence of the defendant unless either it is proved to the satisfaction of the court, on oath, or in such other manner as may be prescribed, that the summons was served on him within what appears to the court to be a reasonable time before the hearing or adjourned hearing or the defendant has appeared on a previous occasion to answer the complaint.

(5) If a complaint under this section is substantiated on oath, any justice of the peace acting for the same petty sessions area as a court having jurisdiction to hear the complaint may issue a warrant for the defendant's arrest, whether or not a summons has been previously issued.

(6) A magistrates' court shall not impose imprisonment in respect of a default to which a complaint under this section relates unless the court has inquired in the presence of the defendant whether the default was due to the defendant's wilful refusal or culpable neglect, and shall not impose imprisonment as aforesaid if it is of opinion that the default was not so due; and, without prejudice to the fore-

---

[3] Applied by Criminal Justice Act 1967 (c. 80), ss. 46 (2), 79 (7), Sched. 1.
[4-5] Applied in part by Criminal Justice Act 1967 (c. 80), ss. 46 (2), 79 (7), Sched. 1.

going provisions of this subsection, a magistrates' court shall not impose imprisonment as aforesaid—

(a) in a case in which the court has power to make an attachment of earnings order under the Maintenance Orders Act 1958 unless the court is of opinion that it is inappropriate to make such an order;

(b) in any case, in the absence of the defendant.

(7) Notwithstanding anything in subsection (3) of section sixty-four of this Act, the period for which a defendant may be committed to prison under a warrant of commitment issued in pursuance of a complaint under this section shall not exceed six weeks.

(8) The imprisonment or other detention of a defendant under a warrant of commitment issued as aforesaid shall not operate to discharge the defendant from his liability to pay the sum in respect of which the warrant was issued."

(2) Subsections (7) and (8) of the said section seventy-four as amended by the foregoing subsection shall have effect in relation to a warrant of commitment issued on or after the date on which this section comes into operation in pursuance of a complaint under that section made before that date (not being a warrant of which the issue was postponed before that date by virtue of section sixty-five of the said Act of 1952) as those subsections have effect in relation to a warrant of commitment issued in pursuance of such a complaint made after that date.

Prohibition of committal more than once in respect of same arrears

17.[6] Where a defendant has been imprisoned or otherwise detained under an order or warrant of commitment issued in respect of his failure to pay a sum due under a maintenance order, then, notwithstanding anything in this Act, no such order or warrant (other than a warrant of which the issue has been postponed under paragraph (ii) of subsection (5) of the next following section) shall thereafter be issued in respect of that sum or any part thereof.

Powers of magistrates to review committals, etc.

18.—(1) Where, for the purpose of enforcing a maintenance order, a magistrates' court has exercised its power under subsection (2) of section sixty-five of the Magistrates' Courts Act 1952 or this section to postpone the issue of a warrant of commitment and under the terms of the postponement the warrant falls to be issued, then—

(a) the warrant shall not be issued except in pursuance of subsection (2) or paragraph (a) of subsection (3) of this section; and

(b) the clerk of the court shall give notice to the defendant stating that if the defendant considers there are grounds for not issuing the warrant he may make an application to the court in the prescribed manner requesting that the warrant shall not be issued and stating those grounds.

(2) If no such application is received by the clerk of the court within the prescribed period, any justice of the peace acting for the same petty sessions area as the court may issue the warrant of commitment at any time after the expiration of that period; and if such an application is so received any such justice may, after considering the statements contained in the application—

(a) if he is of opinion that the application should be further considered, refer it to the court;

(b) if he is not of that opinion, issue the warrant forthwith;

[6] Sections 17 and 18 extended by Criminal Justice Act 1967 (c. 80), s. 79 (3), and applied by A.J.A. 1970 (c. 31), s. 43 (2), Sched. 10, para. 5.

and when an application is referred to the court under this subsection, the clerk of the court shall give to the defendant and the person in whose favour the maintenance order in question was made notice of the time and place appointed for the consideration of the application by the court.

(3) On considering an application referred to it under the last foregoing subsection the court shall, unless in pursuance of subsection (6) of this section it remits the whole of the sum in respect of which the warrant could otherwise be issued, either—

(a) issue the warrant; or

(b) further postpone the issue thereof until such time and on such conditions, if any, as the court thinks just; or

(c) if in consequence of any change in the circumstances of the defendant the court considers it appropriate so to do, order that the warrant shall not be issued in any event.

(4) A defendant who is for the time being imprisoned or otherwise detained under a warrant of commitment issued by a magistrates' court for the purpose of enforcing a maintenance order, and who is not detained otherwise than for the enforcement of such an order, may make an application to the court in the prescribed manner requesting that the warrant shall be cancelled and stating the grounds of the application; and thereupon any justice of the peace acting for the same petty sessions area as the court may, after considering the statements contained in the application—

(a) if he is of opinion that the application should be further considered, refer it to the court;

(b) if he is not of that opinion, refuse the application;

and when an application is referred to the court under this subsection, the clerk of the court shall give to the person in charge of the prison or other place in which the defendant is detained and the person in whose favour the maintenance order in question was made notice of the time and place appointed for the consideration of the application by the court.

(5) On considering an application referred to it under the last foregoing subsection, the court shall, unless in pursuance of the next following subsection it remits the whole of the sum in respect of which the warrant was issued or such part thereof as remains to be paid, either—

(a) refuse the application; or

(b) if the court is satisfied that the defendant is unable to pay, or to make any payment or further payment towards, the sum aforesaid and if it is of opinion that in all the circumstances of the case the defendant ought not to continue to be detained under the warrant, order that the warrant shall cease to have effect when the person in charge of the prison or other place aforesaid is informed of the making of the order;

and where the court makes an order under paragraph (b) of this subsection, it may if it thinks fit also—

(i) fix a term of imprisonment in respect of the sum aforesaid or such part thereof as remains to be paid, being a term not exceeding so much of the term of the previous warrant as, after taking into account any reduction thereof by virtue of the next following subsection, remained to be served at the date of the order; and

(ii) postpone the issue of a warrant for the commitment of the defendant for that term until such time and on such conditions, if any, as the court thinks just.

(6) On considering an application under this section in respect of a warrant or a postponed warrant, the court may, if the maintenance order in question is an affiliation order or an order enforceable as an affiliation order, remit the whole or any part of the sum due under the

order; and where the court remits the sum or part of the sum in respect of which the warrant was issued or the postponed warrant could have been issued, section sixty-seven of the Magistrates' Courts Act 1952 (which provides that on payment of the sum for which imprisonment has been ordered by a magistrates' court the order shall cease to have effect and that on payment of part of that sum the period of detention shall be reduced proportionately) shall apply as if payment of that sum or part had been made as therein mentioned.

(7) Where notice of the time and place appointed for the consideration of an application is required by this section to be given to the defendant or the person in whose favour the maintenance order in question was made and the defendant or, as the case may be, that person does not appear at that time and place, the court may proceed with the consideration of the application in his absence.

(8) A notice required by this section to be given by the clerk of a magistrates' court to any person shall be deemed to be given to that person if it is sent by registered post addressed to him at his last known address, notwithstanding that the notice is returned as undelivered or is for any other reason not received by that person.

Revocation and variation of Orders in Council under Maintenance Orders (Facilities for Enforcement) Act 1920

19. Her Majesty may by Order in Council revoke or vary any Order in Council made under section twelve of the Maintenance Orders (Facilities for Enforcement) Act 1920 (which provides for the extension of that Act by Order in Council to certain oversea territories), and an Order under this section may contain such incidental, consequential and transitional provisions as Her Majesty considers expedient for the purposes of that Act.

Supplemental

Special provisions as to magistrates' courts

20. [6a]—(1) Notwithstanding anything in this Act, the clerk of magistrates' court who is entitled to receive payments under a maintenance order for transmission to another person shall not apply for the registration of the maintenance order under Part I of this Act or give notice in relation to the order in pursuance of subsection (1) of section five thereof, unless he is requested in writing to do so by a person entitled to receive the payments through him; and where the clerk is requested as aforesaid—

    (i) he shall comply with the request unless it appears to him unreasonable in the circumstances to do so;

    (ii) the person by whom the request was made shall have the same liabilities for all the costs properly incurred in or about any proceedings taken in pursuance of the request as if the proceedings had been taken by that person.

(2) An application to a magistrates' court by virtue of subsection (2) of section four of this Act for the variation of a maintenance order shall be made by complaint.

(6) In subsection (3) of section fifty-two of the Magistrates' Courts Act 1952 (which provides for the clerk through whom payments under a magistrates' court order are required to be made to proceed in his own name for the recovery of arrears under the order) for the words " Where an order under subsection (1) of this section requires the payments to

---

[6a] Reprinted as amended (except subsection (6)) by Attachment of Earnings Act 1971 (c. 32), s. 27 (1), Sched. 5.

be made weekly " there shall be substituted the words " **Where periodical** payments under an order of any court are required to be paid to or through the clerk of a magistrates' court "; and in subsection (4) of that section (which provides that nothing in that section shall affect any right of a person to proceed in his own name for the recovery of sums payable on his behalf under any order under subsection (1) of that section) for the words " any order under subsection (1) of this section " there shall be substituted the words " an order of any court."

(8) For the avoidance of doubt it is hereby declared that a complaint may be made to enforce payment of a sum due and unpaid under a maintenance order notwithstanding that a previous complaint has been made in respect of that sum or a part thereof and whether or not an order was made in pursuance of the previous complaint.

Interpretation, etc.

21.[7]—(1) In this Act, unless the context otherwise requires, the following expressions have the following meanings—

" affiliation order ", " magistrates' court " and " petty sessions area " have the meanings assigned to them by the Magistrates' Courts Act 1952, and for the purposes of the definition of a magistrates' court the reference to that Act in subsection (2) of section one hundred and twenty-four thereof shall be construed as including a reference to this Act;

[. . .] [8];

" defendant ", in relation to a maintenance order or a related attachment of earnings order, means the person liable to make payments under the maintenance order;

[. . .] [8];
[. . .] [8];

" England " includes Wales;

[. . .] [8];
[. . .] [8];

" prescribed " means prescribed by rules of court;
" proper officer ", in relation to a magistrates' court, means the clerk of the court;
" rules of court ", in relation to a magistrates' court, means rules under section fifteen of the Justices of the Peace Act 1949.

(2) Any reference in this Act to a person entitled to receive payments under a maintenance order is a reference to a person entitled to receive such payments either directly or through another person or for transmission to another person.

(3) Any reference in this Act to proceedings relating to an order includes a reference to proceedings in which the order may be made.

(4) Any reference in this Act to costs incurred in proceedings relating to a maintenance order shall be construed, in the case of a maintenance order made by the High Court, as a reference to such costs as are included in an order for costs relating solely to that maintenance order.

(5) Any earnings which, in pursuance of a scheme under the Dock Workers (Regulation of Employment) Act 1946, fall to be paid to a defendant by a body responsible for the local administration of the scheme acting as agent for the defendant's employer or as delegate of the body responsible for the general administration of the scheme shall be treated for the purposes of this Act as falling to be paid to the defendant by the last-mentioned body acting as a principal.

[7] Amended by Ministry of Social Security Act 1966 (c. 20), ss. 23 (6), 24 (9); and Family Law Reform Act 1969 (c. 46), ss. 4 (5) (b), 6 (7).
[8] Words repealed by A.J.A. 1970 (c. 31), s. 54, Sched. 11.

(6) Any reference in this Act to any enactment is a reference to that enactment as amended by or under any subsequent enactment.

22. [*Repealed by Northern Ireland Constitution Act* 1973 (*c.* 36), *Sched.* 6.]

Short title, extent, commencement and repeals

23.—(1) This Act may be cited as the Maintenance Orders Act 1958.

(2) This Act [. . .] [9] shall not extend to Scotland or, except section nineteen, the said paragraph (*a*) [. . .] [10] to Northern Ireland.

(3) This Act shall come into operation on such date as the Secretary of State may by order, made by statutory instrument, appoint; and different dates may be so appointed for the purposes of different provisions of this Act.

(4) Subsection (2) of section eight of the Guardianship of Infants Act 1925 and section ten of the Affiliation Proceedings Act 1957 are hereby repealed; but nothing in this subsection shall affect any order in force or deemed to be in force under either of those provisions at the commencement of this subsection, and any such order may be discharged or varied as if this subsection had not been passed.

SCHEDULE

Schedule repealed by A.J.A. 1970 (*c.* 31), *s.* 54, *Sched.* 11.

Children Act 1958 [1]

(6 & 7 Eliz. 2, c. 65)

An Act to make fresh provision for the protection of children living away from their parents; to amend the law relating to the adoption of children; and for purposes connected with the matters aforesaid.   [1st August 1958]

PART I [2]

CHILD PROTECTION

Duty of local authorities to ensure well-being of foster children

1. [3] It shall be the duty of every local authority to satisfy themselves as to the well-being of children within their area who are foster children within the meaning of this Part of this Act and, for that purpose, to secure that, so far as appears to the authority to be appropriate, the children are visited from time to time by officers of the authority and that such advice is given as to the care and maintenance of the children as appears to be needed.

[9] Words repealed by Attachment of Earnings Act 1971 (c. 32), s. 29 (2), Sched. 6.
[10] Words repealed by Northern Ireland Constitution Act 1973 (c. 36), Sched. 6.
[1] Explained by London Government Act 1963 (c. 33), s. 47 (1) (3).
[2] Sections 1–6, 14 reprinted as amended by Children and Young Persons Act 1969 (c. 54), s. 72 (5), Sched. 7.
[3] Substituted by *ibid*. s. 51.

Meaning of " foster child "

2.[3a]—(1) In this Part of this Act " foster child " means, subject to the following provisions of this section, a child below the upper limit of the compulsory school age whose care and maintenance are undertaken [. . .] [4] by a person who is not a relative or guardian of his.

(2) A child is not a foster child within the meaning of this Part of this Act while he is in the care of a local authority or a voluntary organisation or is boarded cut by [. . .] [4] a local health authority or a local education authority (or, in Scotland, an education authority).

(3) A child is not a foster child within the meaning of this Part of this Act while he is in the care of any person—

(a) in premises in which any parent, adult relative or guardian of his is for the time being residing;

(b) in any voluntary home within the meaning of Part V of the Children and Young Persons Act 1933, or in any residential establishment within the meaning of the Social Work (Scotland) Act 1968;

(c) in any school within the meaning of the Education Acts 1944 to 1953, or the Education (Scotland) Acts 1939 to 1956 [in which he is receiving full-time education] [5];

(d) in any hospital or in any nursing home registered or exempted from registration under Part VI of the Public Health Act 1936, Part XI of the Public Health (London) Act 1936, or the Nursing Homes Registration (Scotland) Act 1938; or

(e) in any home or institution not specified in this section but maintained by a public or local authority.

[(3A) A child is not a foster child within the meaning of this Part of this Act at any time while his care and maintenance are undertaken by a person, other than a relative or guardian of his, if at that time—

(a) that person does not intend to, and does not in fact, undertake his care and maintenance for a continuous period of more than six days; or

(b) that person is not a regular foster parent and does not intend to, and does not in fact, undertake his care and maintenance for a continuous period of more than twenty-seven days;

and for the purposes of this subsection a person is a regular foster parent if, during the period of twelve months immediately preceding the date on which he begins to undertake the care and maintenance of the child in question, he had, otherwise than as a relative or guardian, the care and maintenance of one or more children either for a period of, or periods amounting in the aggregate to, not less than three months or for at least three continuous periods each of which was of more than six days.] [6]

(4) A child is not a foster child within the meaning of this Part of this Act while he is in the care of any person in compliance with a [supervision order within the meaning of the Children and Young Persons Act 1969 or a] [7] probation order or supervision requirement or by virtue of a fit person order or while he is in an approved school or is deemed for the purposes of [. . .] [8] the Children and Young Persons (Scotland) Act 1937 to be under the care of the managers of an approved school or while he is liable to be detained or subject to guardianship under the Mental Health Act 1959 or the Mental Health (Scotland) Act 1960, or is resident in a residential home for mentally disordered persons within the meaning

3a See now Children Act 1975 (c. 72), Sched. 3, para. 16, *post.*
4 Words repealed by *ibid.* ss. 52 (1), 72 (4), Sched. 6.
5 Words added by *ibid.* s. 52 (2).
6 Subsection added by *ibid.* s. 52 (3).
7 Substituted by *ibid.* s. 72 (3), Sched. 5, para. 29.
8 Words repealed by *ibid.* s. 72 (4), Sched. 6.

of Part III of the Mental Health Act 1959, or in a residential home for persons suffering from mental disorder within the meaning of Part III of the Mental Health (Scotland) Act 1960.

[(4A) A child is not a foster child for the purposes of this Part of this Act while he is placed in the care and possession of a person who proposes to adopt him under arrangements made by such a local authority or registered adoption society as is referred to in Part II of the Adoption Act 1958 or while he is a protected child within the meaning of Part IV of that Act.] [9]

[Subsections (6) (7) repealed by Children and Young Persons Act 1969 (c. 54), s. 72 (4), Sched. 6.]

Duty of persons maintaining foster children to notify local authority

3.—(1) [Subject to the following provisions of this section,] [9] a person who proposes to maintain as a foster child a child not already in his care shall give written notice thereof to the local authority not less than two weeks and not more than four weeks before he receives the child, unless he receives him in an emergency; and a person who maintains a foster child whom he received in an emergency or who became a foster child while in his care shall give written notice thereof to the local authority not later than forty-eight hours after he receives the child or, as the case may be, after the child becomes a foster child.

(2) Every such notice shall specify [the date on which it is intended that the child should be received or, as the case may be, on which the child was in fact received or became a foster child and] [10] the premises in which the child is to be or is being kept and shall be given to the local authority for the area in which those premises are situated.

[(2A) A person shall not be required to give notice under subsection (1) of this section in relation to a child if—

(a) he has on a previous occasion given notice under that subsection in respect of that or any other child, specifying the premises at which he proposes to keep the child in question; and

(b) he has not, at any time since that notice was given, ceased to maintain at least one foster child at those premises and been required by virtue of the following provisions of this section to give notice under subsection (5A) of this section in respect of those premises.] [11]

(3) Where a person who is maintaining [one or more foster children] [12] changes his permanent address or the premises in which the child is, or the children are, kept he shall, not less than two weeks [and not more than four weeks] [12] before the change or, if the change is made in an emergency, not later than [forty-eight hours] [12] after the change, give written notice to the said local authority, specifying the new address or premises, and if the new premises are in the area of another local authority, the authority to whom the notice is given shall inform that other local authority and give them such of the particulars mentioned in subsection (7) of this section as are known to them.

(4) If a foster child dies [. . .] [13] the person who was maintaining him shall, within forty-eight hours thereof, give to the local authority and to the person from whom the child was received notice in writing of the death [. . .].[13]

---

[9] Subsection added by *ibid.* s. 52 (5). An alternative sub (4A) is provided for Scotland by Children Act 1975 (c. 72), Sched. 3, para. 17, *post.*
[10] Words added by *ibid.* s. 53 (2) (3).
[11] Section added by *ibid.* s. 53 (4).
[12] Substituted by *ibid.* s. 53 (5).
[13] Amended and repealed by *ibid.* ss. 53 (6), 72 (4), Sched. 6.

(5) Where a foster child [is removed or removes himself from the care of the person maintaining him, that person shall at the request of the local authority give them the name and address, if known, of the person (if any) into whose care the child has been removed].[13]

[(5A) Subject to the provisions of the following subsection, where a person who has been maintaining one or more foster children at any premises ceases to maintain foster children at those premises and the circumstances are such that no notice is required to be given under subsection (3) or subsection (4) of this section, that person shall, within forty-eight hours after he ceases to maintain any foster child at those premises, give notice in writing thereof to the local authority.

(5B) A person need not give the notice required by the preceding subsection in consequence of his ceasing to maintain foster children at any premises if, at the time he so ceases, he intends within twenty-seven days again to maintain any of them as a foster child at those premises; but if he subsequently abandons that intention or the said period expires without his having given effect to it he shall give the said notice within forty-eight hours of that event.] [14]

[*Subsection* (6) *repealed by Children and Young Persons Act* 1969 (*c.* 54), *s.* 72 (4), *Sched.* 6.]

(7) A person maintaining or proposing to maintain a foster child shall at the request of the local authority give them the following particulars, so far as known to him, that is to say, the name, sex, and date and place of birth of the child, and the name and address of every person who is a parent or guardian or acts as a guardian of the child or from whom the child has been or is to be received.

Power to inspect premises, impose conditions, or prohibit the keeping of foster children

4.—(1) Any officer of a local authority authorised to visit foster children may, after producing, if asked to do so, some duly authenticated document showing that he is so authorised, inspect any premises in the area of the authority in [the whole or any part of] [15] which foster children are to be or are being kept.

[(1A) If it is shown to the satisfaction of a justice of the peace on sworn information in writing—

(a) that there is reasonable cause to believe that a foster child is being kept in any premises, or in any part thereof; and

(b) that admission to those premises or that part thereof has been refused to a duly authorised officer of the local authority or that such a refusal is apprehended or that the occupier is temporarily absent,

the justice may by warrant under his hand authorise an officer of the local authority to enter the premises if need be by force, at any reasonable time within forty-eight hours of the issue of the warrant, for the purpose of inspecting the premises.] [16]

(2) Where a person is keeping or proposes to keep foster children in premises used (while foster children are kept therein) wholly or [partly] [17] for that purpose, the local authority may impose on him requirements, to be complied with, after such time as the authority may specify, whenever a foster child is kept in the premises, as to—

(a) the number, age and sex of the foster children who may be kept at any one time in the premises or any part thereof;

---

14 Sections substituted by *ibid.* s. 53 (7).
15 Words added by *ibid.* s. 54 (1).
16 Subsection added by *ibid.* s. 54 (2).
17 Substituted by *ibid.* s. 55 (1) (3).

(b) the accommodation and equipment to be provided for the children;

(c) the medical arrangements to be made for protecting the health of the children;

(d) the giving of particulars of the person for the time being in charge of the children;

(e) the number, qualifications or experience of the persons employed in looking after the children;

(f) the keeping of records;

[(g) the fire precautions to be taken in the premises;

(h) the giving of particulars of any foster child received in the premises and of any change in the number or identity of the foster children kept therein;] [18]

but any such requirement may be limited to a particular class of foster children kept in the premises and any requirement imposed under paragraphs (b) to (h) of this subsection may be limited by the authority so as to apply only when the number of foster children kept in the premises exceeds a specified number.

[(3) Where a person proposes to keep a foster child in any premises and the local authority are of the opinion that—

(a) the premises are not suitable premises in which to keep foster children; or

(b) that person is not a suitable person to have the care and maintenance of foster children; or

(c) it would be detrimental to that child to be kept by that person in those premises;

the local authority may impose a prohibition on that person under subsection (3A) of this section.

(3A) A prohibition imposed on any person under this subsection may—

(a) prohibit him from keeping any foster child in premises specified in the prohibition; or

(b) prohibit him from keeping any foster child in any premises in the area of the local authority; or

(c) prohibit him from keeping a particular child specified in the prohibition in premises so specified.

(3B) Where a local authority have imposed a prohibition on any person under subsection (3A) of this section, the local authority may, if they think fit, cancel the prohibition, either of their own motion or on an application made by that person on the ground of a change in the circumstances in which a foster child would be kept by him.] [19]

(4) Where a local authority impose a requirement on any person under subsection (2) of this section as respects any premises, they may prohibit him from keeping foster children in the premises after the time specified for compliance with the requirement unless the requirement is complied with.

(5) Any requirement or prohibition imposed under this section shall be imposed by notice in writing addressed to the person on whom it is imposed.

Appeal to juvenile court against requirement or prohibition imposed under section four

5.—(1) Any person aggrieved by any requirement or prohibition imposed under section four of this Act may, within fourteen days from the date on which he is notified of the requirement or prohibition [or,

---

[18] Added by *ibid.* s. 55 (2).
[19] Substituted by *ibid.* s. 55 (4).

in the case of a prohibition imposed under subsection (3A) of that section within fourteen days from the refusal by the local authority to accede to an application by him for the cancellation of the prohibition],[20] appeal to a juvenile court, and where the appeal is against such a requirement the requirement shall not have effect while the appeal is pending.

(2) Where the court allows such an appeal it may, instead of cancelling the requirement or prohibition, vary the requirement or allow more time for compliance with it or, where an absolute prohibition has been imposed, substitute for it a prohibition to use the premises after such time as the court may specify unless such specified requirements as the local authority had power to impose under section four of this Act are complied with.

(3) Any notice by which a requirement or prohibition is imposed on any person under section four of this Act shall contain a statement informing him of his right to appeal against the requirement or prohibition and of the time within which he may do so.

(4) Any requirement or prohibition specified or substituted under this section by the court shall be deemed for the purposes of this Part of this Act other than this section to have been imposed by the local authority under section four of this Act.

(5) In the application of this section to Scotland, for references to a juvenile court there shall be substituted references to the sheriff.

Disqualification for keeping foster children

6.—(1) A person shall not maintain a foster child if—
> (a) an order has been made against him under this Part of this Act removing a child from his care;
> (b) an order has been made under the Children and Young Persons Act 1933, [the Children and Young Persons Act 1969] [21] or the Children and Young Persons (Scotland) Act 1937, or a supervision requirement has been made under the Social Work (Scotland) Act 1968 and by virtue of the order or requirement a child was removed from his care;
> (c) he has been convicted of any offence specified in the First Schedule to the said Act of 1933 or the First Schedule to the said Act of 1937 [or has been placed on probation or discharged absolutely or conditionally for any such offence] [20];
> (d) his rights and powers with respect to a child have been vested in a local authority under section two of the Children Act 1948 [or under section 16 of the Social Work (Scotland) Act 1968] [20];
> (e) a local health authority or in Scotland a local authority have made an order under subsection (3) or (4) of section one of the Nurseries and Child-Minders Regulation Act 1948 refusing, or an order under section five of that Act cancelling, the registration of any premises occupied by him or his registration;
> [(f) an order has been made under section 43 of the Adoption Act 1958 for the removal of a protected child who was being kept or was about to be received by him,] [20]

unless he has disclosed that fact to the local authority and [obtained their written consent.] [21a]

[(2) Where this section applies to any person, otherwise than by virtue of this subsection, it shall apply also to any other person who lives

---

[20] Words added by *ibid.* s. 55 (5).
[21] Added by *ibid.* ss. 56 (1) (2), 73 (4) (a).
[21a] Words substituted by Children Act 1975 (c. 72), Sched. 3, para. 18.

in the same premises as he does or who lives in premises at which he is employed.] [20]

Removal of foster children kept in unsuitable surroundings

7.[22]—(1) If a juvenile court is satisfied, on the complaint of a local authority, that a foster child is being kept or is about to be received by any person who is unfit to have his care, or in contravention of the last foregoing section or of any prohibition imposed by a local authority under section four of this Act, or in any premises or any environment detrimental or likely to be detrimental to him, the court may make an order for his removal to a place of safety until he can be restored to a parent, relative or guardian of his, or until other arrangements can be made with respect to him; and on proof that there is imminent danger to the health or well-being of the child the power to make an order under this section may be exercised by a justice of the peace acting on the application of a person authorised to visit foster children.

(2) An order under this section may be executed by any person authorised to visit foster children or by any constable and may, [. . .] [23] be executed on a Sunday.

(3) An order under this section made on the ground that a prohibition of a local authority under section four of this Act has been contravened may require the removal from the premises of all the foster children kept there.

(4) A local authority may receive into their care under section one of the Children Act 1948 any child removed under this section, whether or not the circumstances of the child are such that they fall within paragraphs (a) to (c) of subsection (1) of the said section one and notwithstanding that he may appear to the local authority to be over the age of seventeen.

(5) Where a child is removed under this section the local authority shall, if practicable, inform a parent or guardian of the child, or any person who acts as his guardian.

(6) In the application of this section to Scotland, for references to a juvenile court there shall be substituted references to the sheriff [or, as the case may be, Part II of the Social Work (Scotland) Act 1968].[24]

Extension of power to issue warrants to search for and remove a child

8. For the purposes of section forty of the Children and Young Persons Act 1933 or section forty-seven of the Children and Young Persons (Scotland) Act 1937 (which enable a warrant authorising the search for and removal of a child to be issued on suspicion of unnecessary suffering caused to, or certain offences committed against, the child), any refusal to allow the visiting of a foster child or the inspection of any premises by a person authorised to do so under this Part of this Act shall be treated as giving reasonable cause for such a suspicion.

Avoidance of insurances on lives of foster children

9. A person who maintains a foster child [for reward] [25] shall be deemed for the purposes of the Life Assurance Act 1774 to have no interest in the life of the child.

[22] Extended by Children and Young Persons Act 1963 (c. 37), s. 23.
[23] Words repealed by S.L.R. 1969.
[24] Words added by Social Work (Scotland) Act 1968 (c. 49), s. 95 (1), Sched. 8, para. 46.
[25] Words added by Children and Young Persons Act 1969 (c. 54), s. 72 (3), Sched. 5, para. 30.

Sittings of juvenile courts in proceedings under Part I

10. Subsection (2) of section forty-seven of the Children and Young Persons Act 1933 (which restricts the time and place at which a sitting of a juvenile court may be held and the persons who may be present at such a sitting) shall not apply to any sitting of a juvenile court in any proceedings under this Part of this Act.

Appeal to the Crown Court

11. An appeal shall lie to [the Crown Court] [25a] from any order made under this Part of this Act by a juvenile court or any other magistrates' court within the meaning of the Magistrates' Courts Act 1952.

Extension of Part I to certain school children during holidays

12.—(1) Where a child below the upper limit of the compulsory school age resides during school holidays in a school to which this section applies, then, if he so resides for a period exceeding [two weeks],[26] the provisions of this Part of this Act shall apply in relation to him as if paragraph (c) of subsection (3) of section two of this Act were omitted, but subject to the modifications specified in the next following subsection.

(2) Where this Part of this Act applies to a child by virtue of the foregoing subsection—

(a) subsections (1) to (6) of section three, subsections (2) to (5) of section four, and section thirteen of this Act shall not apply; but

(b) the person undertaking the care and maintenance of children in the school during the school holidays shall, not less than two weeks before this Part of this Act first applies to a child in that school during those holidays, give written notice to the local authority that children to whom this Part of this Act applies will reside in the school during those holidays, and any such notice shall state the estimated number of the children.

(3) A local authority may exempt any person from the duty of giving notices under this section, and any such exemption may be granted for a specified period or indefinitely and may be revoked at any time by notice in writing served on that person.

(4) This section applies to any school within the meaning of the Education Acts 1944 to 1953 which is not a school maintained by a local education authority.

Extension of Part I to certain children above compulsory school age

13. Where a child is a foster child on attaining the upper limit of the compulsory school age this Part of this Act shall apply in relation to him as it applies in relation to a foster child, until the earliest of the following events, that is to say, until—

(a) he would, apart from that limit, have ceased to be a foster child;

(b) he reaches the age of eighteen; or

(c) he lives elsewhere than with the person with whom he was living when he attained the said limit.

Offences

14.—(1) A person shall be guilty of an offence if—

(a) being required, under any provision of this Part of this Act, to give any notice or information, he fails to give the notice within the time specified in that provision or fails to give the

---

[25a] Words substituted by Courts Act 1971 (c. 23), s. 56 (2), Sched. 9, Pt. I.
[26] Words substituted by Children and Young Persons Act 1969 (c. 54), s. 72 (3), Sched. 5, para. 31.

information within a reasonable time, or knowingly makes or causes or procures another person to make any false or misleading statement in the notice or information;

(b) he refuses to allow the visiting of any foster child by a duly authorised officer of a local authority or the inspection, under the power conferred by subsection (1) of section four of this Act, of any premises [or wilfully obstructs a person entitled to enter any premises by virtue of a warrant under subsection (1A) of that section] [27];

(c) he fails to comply with any requirement imposed by a local authority under this Part of this Act or keeps any foster child in any premises in contravention of a prohibition so imposed;

(d) he maintains a foster child in contravention of section six of this Act; or

(e) he refuses to comply with an order under this Part of this Act for the removal of any child or obstructs any person in the execution of such an order.

[(1A) Where section 6 of this Act applies to any person by virtue only of subsection (2) of that section, he shall not be guilty of an offence under paragraph (d) of subsection (1) of this section if he proves that he did not know, and had no reasonable ground for believing, that a person living or employed in the premises in which he lives was a person to whom that section applies.] [28]

(2) A person guilty of an offence under this section shall be liable on summary conviction to imprisonment for a term not exceeding six months or a fine not exceeding [£400] [28a] or both.

[(2A) If any person who is required, under any provision of this Part of this Act, to give a notice fails to give the notice within the time specified in that provision, then, notwithstanding anything in section 104 of the Magistrates' Courts Act 1952 (time limit for proceedings) proceedings for the offence may be brought at any time within six months from the date when evidence of the offence came to the knowledge of the local authority.] [28]

(3) In England and Wales, a local authority may institute proceedings for an offence under this section.

Service of notices by post

15. Any notice or information required to be given under this Part of this Act may be given by post.

16. [*Repealed by Trustee Investments Act* 1961 (c. 62), s. 16 (2), *Sched.* 5.]

Interpretation of Part I

17. In this Part of this Act the following expressions have the meanings hereby respectively assigned to them, that is to say,—

["approved school" has the same meaning as in the Children and Young Persons (Scotland) Act 1937;] [29]

"child" means a person under the age of eighteen;

"compulsory school age" has, in England and Wales, the same meaning as in the Education Acts 1944 to 1953 and, in Scotland, means school age within the meaning of the Education (Scotland) Acts 1939 to 1956;

[27] Words added by *ibid.* s. 54 (3).
[28] Subsections added by *ibid.* ss. 57 (1) (2), 73 (4) (a).
[28a] Words substituted by Children Act 1975 (c. 72), Sched. 3, para. 19.
[29] Added and amended by Children and Young Persons Act 1969 (c. 54), s. 72 (3), Sched. 5, para. 32.

" fit person order " means an order under [. . .] [30] the Children and Young Persons (Scotland) Act 1937 committing a child to the care of a fit person;

" local authority " means, in England and Wales, the council of a county or county borough and, in Scotland, the council of a [region or islands area] [30a]

[*definition repealed by Children Act 1975 (c. 72), Sched. 4.*]

" place of safety " means a [community home] [29] provided by a local authority [a controlled community] [29] home, police station, or any hospital, surgery or other suitable place the occupier of which is willing temporarily to receive a child;

" relative " has the same meaning as in the [Adoption Act 1958] [31];

" voluntary organisation " means a body the activities of which are carried on otherwise than for profit.

18–36. [*Repealed by Adoption Act 1958 (c. 5), s. 59 (2), Sched. 6.*]

PART III
MISCELLANEOUS AND GENERAL

Prohibition of anonymous advertisements offering to undertake care of children

37.—(1) No advertisement indicating that a person will undertake, or will arrange for, the care and maintenance of a child shall be published, unless it truly states that person's name and address.

(2) A person who causes to be published or knowingly publishes an advertisement in contravention of this section shall be guilty of an offence, and liable on summary conviction to imprisonment for a term not exceeding six months or a fine not exceeding [£400] [32] or both.

(3) In England and Wales, a local authority may institute proceedings for an offence under this section.

38. [*Repealed by S.L.R. 1969.*]

Expenses

39. There shall be paid out of moneys provided by Parliament any increase attributable to this Act in the sums payable out of moneys so provided—

(a) under section forty-seven of the Children Act 1948; or

(b) under Part I of the Local Government Act 1948 or the Local Government (Financial Provisions) (Scotland) Act 1954, as amended by the Valuation and Rating (Scotland) Act 1956.

Minor and consequential amendments and repeals

40.—(1) The enactments described in the first column of the Second Schedule to this Act shall have effect subject to the amendments set out in the second column of that Schedule, being minor amendments and amendments consequential on the foregoing provisions of this Act.

[*Subsection (2) repealed by S.L.R. 1969.*]

Short title, construction, commencement and extent

41.—(1) This Act may be cited as the Children Act 1958.

(2) Any reference in this Act to any other enactment is a reference thereto as amended, and includes a reference thereto as applied, by or

[30] Words repealed by *ibid.* s. 72 (4), Sched. 6.
[30a] Words substituted by Local Government (Scotland) Act 1973 (c. 65), Sched. 27.
[31] Words substituted by Adoption Act 1958 (c. 5), s. 58 (1), Sched. 4.
[32] Words substituted by Children Act 1975 (c. 72), Sched. 3, para. 20.

under any subsequent enactment, including, except where the context otherwise requires, this Act.

(3) This Act shall come into force on the first day of April, nineteen hundred and fifty-nine.

(4) This Act does not extend to Northern Ireland.

SCHEDULES

FIRST SCHEDULE

[Repealed by Adoption Act 1958 (c. 5), s. 59 (2), Sched. 6.]

SECOND SCHEDULE

MINOR AND CONSEQUENTIAL AMENDMENTS

Enactment	Amendment
The Children Act 1948. 11 & 12 Geo. 6. c. 43.	In section thirty-eight, in subsection (1), the word " and ", in the second place where that word occurs, shall be omitted and for the words from " and the welfare authorities " to the end of the subsection there shall be substituted the words " and of Part I of the Children Act 1958 shall be the councils of counties and county boroughs ".

[Paragraphs repealed by Adoption Act 1958 (c. 5), s. 59 (2), Sched. 6.]

[Paragraph repealed by Children and Young Persons Act 1969 (c. 54), s. 72 (4), Sched. 6.]

The Nurseries and Child-Minders Regulation Act 1948. 11 & 12 Geo. 6. c. 53.	In section eight, in subsection (1), for the words from " section two hundred and nineteen " to the end of the subsection, there shall be substituted the words " section two of the Children Act 1958 ". In section thirteen, in subsection (2), in the definition of " child life protection enactments ", for the words from " relating to child life protection " to the end of the definition there shall be substituted the words " of Part I of the Children Act 1958 ".

[Paragraphs repealed by Adoption Act 1958 (c. 5), s. 59 (2), Sched. 6.]

THIRD SCHEDULE

[Repealed by S.L.R. 1969.]

Adoption Act 1958 [1]

(7 & 8 ELIZ. 2, c. 5)

An Act to consolidate the enactments relating to the adoption of children. [18th December 1958]

---

[1] Explained as regards London, by London Government Act 1963 (c. 33), s. 47 (1) (3); and extended by Adoption Act 1964 (c. 57), s. 1, and Adoption Act 1968 (c. 53), ss. 2, 4, 8. References throughout the Act to " Adoption Rules ", " infant " and " infants " and " care and possession " were replaced by " Rules ", " child " and " children ", and " actual custody " respectively, by the Children Act 1975 (c. 72), Sched. 3, para. 21, *post.*

PART I

ADOPTION ORDERS

Making of adoption orders

Power to make adoption orders

1.[2]—(1) Subject to the provisions of this Act, the court may, upon an application made in the prescribed manner by a person domiciled in England or Scotland, make an order (in this Act referred to as an adoption order) authorising the applicant to adopt [a child].

(2) An adoption order may be made on the application of two spouses authorising them jointly to adopt [a child]; but an adoption order shall not in any other case be made authorising more than one person to adopt [a child].

(3) An adoption order may be made authorising the adoption of [a child] by the mother or father of the [child], either alone or jointly with her or his spouse.

(4) An adoption order may be made in respect of [a child] who has already been the subject of an adoption order under this Act or the Adoption Act 1950 or any enactment repealed by that Act; and in relation to an application for an adoption order in respect of such [a child], the adopter or adopters under the previous or last previous adoption order shall be deemed to be the parent or parents of the [child] for all the purposes of this Act.

(5) An adoption order shall not be made in England unless the applicant and the [child] reside in England and shall not be made in Scotland unless the applicant and the [child] reside in Scotland, subject however to section twelve of this Act.

Age and sex of applicant

2.—(1) Subject to subsection (2) of this section, an adoption order shall not be made in respect of [a child] unless the applicant—

(a) is the mother or father of the [child];

(b) is a relative of the [child], and has attained the age of twenty-one years; or

(c) has attained the age of twenty-five years.

(2) An adoption order may be made in respect of [a child] on the joint application of two spouses—

(a) if either of the applicants is the mother or father of the [child]; or

(b) if the condition set out in paragraph (b) or paragraph (c) of subsection (1) of this section is satisfied in the case of one of the applicants, and the other of them has attained the age of twenty-one years.

(3) An adoption order shall not be made in respect of [a child] who is a female in favour of a sole applicant who is a male, unless the court is satisfied that there are special circumstances which justify as an exceptional measure the making of an adoption order.

[Actual custody] of [children] before adoption, and notification of local authority

3.—(1) An adoption order shall not be made in respect of any [child] unless he has been continuously in the [actual custody] of the applicant for at least three consecutive months immediately preceding the date of the order, not counting any time before the date which appears to the court to be the date on which the [child] attained the age of six weeks.

---

[2] Extended by Adoption Act 1968 (c. 53), s. 10 (3).

(2) Except where the applicant or one of the applicants is a parent of the [child], an adoption order shall not be made in respect of [a child] who at the hearing of the application is below the upper limit of the compulsory school age unless the applicant has, at least three months before the date of the order, given notice in writing to the local authority within whose area he was then resident of his intention to apply for an adoption order in respect of the [child].

Consents

4.[3]—(1) Subject to section five of this Act, an adoption order shall not be made—

(a) in any case, except with the consent of every person who is a parent or guardian of the [child];

(b) on the application of one of two spouses, except with the consent of the other spouse;

and shall not be made in Scotland in respect of [a child] who is a minor except with the consent of the [child].

(2) The consent of any person to the making of an adoption order in pursuance of an application (not being the consent of the [child]) may be given [. . .] [3a] without knowing the identity of the applicant for the order.

(3) The reference in paragraph (a) of subsection (1) of this section to a parent of [a child] does not include a reference to any person having the rights and powers of a parent of the [child] by virtue of any of the following enactments, that is to say—

[(a) section 24 of the Children and Young Persons Act 1969 (which relates to the powers and duties of local authorities with respect to persons committed to their care in pursuance of that Act)] [4];

[*Paragraph (b) repealed by Social Work (Scotland) Act 1968 (c. 49), ss. 95, 97 (1), Sched. 8, para. 37, 9 Pt. I.*]

(c) section three of the Children Act 1948 (which applies to children in respect of whom the local authority have assumed parental rights by resolution under section two of that Act);

[(d) section 17 of the Social Work (Scotland) Act 1968 (which makes corresponding provision for Scotland).] [5]

Power to dispense with consent

5.[6]—(1) The court may dispense with any consent required by paragraph (a) of subsection (1) of section four of this Act if it is satisfied that the person whose consent is to be dispensed with—

(a) has abandoned, neglected or persistently ill-treated the [child]; or

(b) cannot be found or is incapable of giving his consent or is withholding his consent unreasonably.

(2) If the court is satisfied that any person whose consent is required by the said paragraph (a) has persistently failed without reasonable cause to discharge the obligations of a parent or guardian of the [child], the court may dispense with his consent whether or not it is satisfied of the matters mentioned in subsection (1) of this section.

(3) Where a person who has given his consent to the making of an adoption order without knowing the identity of the applicant therefor subsequently withdraws his consent on the ground only that he does not

---

[3] Excluded by Adoption Act 1968 (c. 53), s. 2 (4).

[3a] Words repealed by Children Act 1975 (c. 72), Sched. 4.

[4] Substituted by Children and Young Persons Act 1969 (c. 54), ss. 72 (3), 73 (4) (c), Sched. 5, para. 33.

[5] Added by Social Work (Scotland) Act 1968 (c. 49), ss. 95 (1), 97 (1), Sched. 8, para. 37.

[6] Excluded by Adoption Act 1968 (c. 53), s. 2 (4).

know the identity of the applicant, his consent shall be deemed for the purposes of this section to be unreasonably withheld.

(4) The court may dispense with the consent of the spouse of an applicant for an adoption order if it is satisfied that the person whose consent is to be dispensed with cannot be found or is incapable of giving his consent or that the spouses have separated and are living apart and that the separation is likely to be permanent.

Evidence of consent of parent or guardian

6.[7]—(1) Where a parent or guardian of [a child] does not attend in the proceedings on an application for an adoption order for the purpose of giving his consent to the making of the order, then, subject to subsection (2) of this section, a document signifying his consent to the making of such an order shall, if the person in whose favour the order is to be made is named in the document or (where the identity of that person is not known to the consenting party) is distinguished therein in the prescribed manner, be admissible as evidence of that consent, whether the document is executed before or after the commencement of the proceedings; and where any such document is attested as mentioned in subsection (3) of this section, it shall be admissible as aforesaid without further proof of the signature of the person by whom it is executed.

(2) A document signifying the consent of the mother of [a child] shall not be admissible under this section unless—

(a) the [child] is at least six weeks old on the date of the execution of the document; and

(b) the document is attested on that date as mentioned in subsection (3) of this section.

(3) Any reference in this section to a document being attested as mentioned in this subsection is, if the document is executed in the United Kingdom, a reference to its being attested by either a justice of the peace or—

(a) if it is executed in England, an officer of a county court appointed for the purposes of section eighty-four of the County Courts Act 1934 or a justices' clerk within the meaning of section twenty-one of the Justices of the Peace Act 1949;

(b) if it is executed in Scotland, the sheriff;

and, if it is executed outside the United Kingdom, a reference to its being attested by a person of any such class as may be prescribed.

(4) For the purposes of this section a document purporting to be attested as mentioned in subsection (3) of this section shall be deemed to be so attested, and to be executed and attested on the date and at the place specified in the document, unless the contrary is proved.

(5) In the application of this section to Scotland, for the words " admissible as evidence " and the word " admissible " there shall be substituted the words " sufficient evidence ".

Functions of court as to adoption orders

7.—(1) The court before making an adoption order shall be satisfied—

(a) that every person whose consent is necessary under this Act, and whose consent is not dispensed with, has consented to and understands the nature and effect of the adoption order for which application is made, and in particular in the case of any parent understands that the effect of the adoption order will be permanently to deprive him or her of his or her parental rights;

(b) [*Repealed by Children Act* 1975 (c. 72), *Sched.* 4.]

[7] Excluded by Adoption Act 1968 (c. 53), s. 2 (4).

(c) that the applicant has not received or agreed to receive, and that no person has made or given or agreed to make or give to the applicant, any payment or other reward in consideration of the adoption except such as the court may sanction.

(2) [*Subsection repealed by Children Act 1975 (c. 72), Sched. 4.*]

(3) The court in an adoption order may impose such terms and conditions as the court may think fit, and in particular may require the adopter by bond or otherwise to make for the [child] such provision (if any) as in the opinion of the court is just and expedient.

Interim orders

8.—(1) Subject to the provisions of this section, the court may, upon any application for an adoption order, postpone the determination of the application and make an interim order giving the custody of the [child] to the applicant for a period not exceeding two years by way of a probationary period upon such terms as regards provision for the maintenance and education and supervision of the welfare of the [child] and otherwise as the court may think fit.

(2) All such consents as are required to an adoption order shall be necessary to an interim order but subject to a like power on the part of the court to dispense with any such consent.

(3) An interim order shall not be made in any case where the making of an adoption order would be unlawful by virtue of section three of this Act.

(4) Where an interim order has been made giving the custody of [a child] to the applicant for a period of less than two years, the court may by order extend that period, but the total period for which the custody of the [child] is given to the applicant under the order as varied under this subsection shall not exceed two years.

(5) An interim order shall not be deemed to be an adoption order within the meaning of this Act.

Jurisdiction and procedure in England

9.—(1) An application for an adoption order may be made in England to the High Court or, at the option of the applicant but subject to Adoption Rules, to any county court or magistrates' court within the jurisdiction of which the applicant or the [child] resides at the date of the application.

(2) In this Act " Rules " means rules made under subsection (3) of this section or made by virtue of this section under section fifteen of the Justices of the Peace Act 1949.

(3) [8] Rules in regard to any matter to be prescribed under [the relevant provisions] [7a] and dealing generally with all matters of procedure and incidental matters arising out of [the relevant provisions] [7a] and for carrying [the relevant provisions] [7a] into effect shall be made in England by the Lord Chancellor.

[In this subsection " the relevant provisions " means this Part, Part III and Part V of this Act and Part I of the Children Act 1975.] [7a]

(4) Subsection (3) of this section does not apply in relation to proceedings before magistrates' courts, but the power to make rules conferred by section fifteen of the Justices of the Peace Act 1949, shall include power to make provision as to any of the matters mentioned in that subsection.

(5) [8] [Rules] may provide for applications for adoption orders being heard and determined otherwise than in open court and, where the

[7a] Words amended by Children Act 1975 (c. 72), Sched. 3, para. 22.
[8] Amended by Children and Young Persons Act 1963 (c. 37), s. 54 (1).

application is made to a magistrates' court, for the hearing and determination of the application in a juvenile court, and may make provision for excluding or restricting the jurisdiction of any court where a previous application made by the same applicant in respect of the same [child] has been refused by that or any other court.

(6) [Rules] made as respects magistrates' courts may provide for enabling any fact tending to establish the identity of [a child] with [a child] to whom a document relates to be proved by affidavit and for excluding or restricting in relation to any facts that may be so proved the power of a justice of the peace to compel the attendance of witnesses.

(7) For the purpose of any application in England for an adoption order, the court shall, subject to [Rules], appoint some person to act as guardian ad litem of the [child] upon the hearing of the application with the duty of safeguarding the interests of the [child] before the court.

(8) Where the person so appointed is an officer of a local authority the court may authorise the authority to incur any necessary expenditure; but nothing in this section shall be deemed to authorise the court to appoint an officer of a local authority to act as guardian ad litem except with the consent of that authority.

Appeals from magistrates' courts in England

10.—(1) Where, on an application made in England to a magistrates' court, the court makes or refuses to make an adoption order, an appeal shall lie to the High Court.

(2) So much of subsection (1) of section sixty-three of the Supreme Court of Judicature (Consolidation) Act 1925 as requires an appeal from any court or person to the High Court to be heard and determined by a divisional court shall not apply to appeals under this section.

Jurisdiction and procedure in Scotland

11.[9]—(1) An application for an adoption order may be made in Scotland to the Court of Session or to the sheriff court [. . .] [10] within whose jurisdiction the applicant or the [child] resides at the date of the application.

(2) In Scotland, provision shall be made by act of sederunt with regard to any matter to be prescribed under [the relevant provisions],[7a] and generally with regard to all matters of procedure and incidental matters arising out of [the relevant provisions] [7a] and for carrying [the relevant provisions] [7a] into effect.

(3) Any such act of sederunt may provide for applications for adoption orders to be heard and determined otherwise than in open court and may make provision for excluding or restricting the jurisdiction of any court where a previous application made by the same applicant in respect of the same [child] has been refused by that or any other court.

(4) For the purposes of any application in Scotland for an adoption order, the court shall, subject to any act of sederunt under this section, appoint some person to act as curator ad litem of the [child] upon the hearing of the application with the duty of safeguarding the interests of the [child] before the court.

(5) Where the person so appointed is an officer or servant of a local authority and appointed as such, the court may authorise the authority to incur any necessary expenditure; but nothing in this section shall be deemed to authorise the court to appoint an officer or servant of a local authority to act as curator ad litem of [a child] except with the consent of that authority.

---

[9] Amended by Children and Young Persons Act (c. 37), s. 54.
[10] Words repealed by Social Work (Scotland) Act 1968 (c. 49), s. 95 (2), Sched. 9 Pt. I.

Modification of foregoing provisions in the case of applicants not ordinarily resident in Great Britain

12.—(1) An adoption order may, notwithstanding anything in this Act, be made on the application of a person who is not ordinarily resident in Great Britain; and in relation to such an application—

(a) subsection (5) of section one of this Act does not apply; and

(b) subsection (2) of section three of this Act applies with the substitution of the word " living " for the word " resident ".

(2) Subsection (1) of section nine and subsection (1) of section eleven of this Act do not apply in relation to an application for an adoption order by a person not ordinarily resident in Great Britain, but such an application may be made, in England to the High Court or the county court, and in Scotland to the Court of Session or the sheriff court.

(3) Where an application for an adoption order is made jointly by spouses who are not, or one of whom is not, ordinarily resident in Great Britain, the notice required by subsection (2) of section three of this Act (as modified by subsection (1) of this section) may be given by either of the applicants; and the provisions of subsection (1) of that section shall be deemed to be complied with if they are complied with in the case of one of the applicants and the applicants have been living together in Great Britain for at least one of the three months mentioned in that subsection.

(4) This section does not affect the construction of subsection (1) of the said section three in its application to any joint application to which subsection (3) of this section does not apply.

Effects of adoption orders

13, 14. [*These sections were repealed by Children Act* 1975 (c. 72), *Sched.* 4].

Affiliation orders, etc.

15.[11]—(1)-(3) [*Subsections repealed by Children Act* 1975 (c. 72), *Sched.* 4.]

(4) Where an adoption order is made in respect of an infant in respect of whom a resolution is in force under section two of the Children Act 1948 [or section 16 of the Social Work (Scotland) Act 1968 (which sections provide] [12] for the assumption by local authorities of parental rights in certain circumstances) the resolution shall cease to have effect.

(5) The references in this section to an adoption order include references to an order authorising an adoption made under the Adoption of Children Act (Northern Ireland) 1950 or any enactment of the Parliament of Northern Ireland for the time being in force.

16, 17. [*These sections were repealed by Children Act* 1975 (c. 72), *Sched.* 4.]

18. [*Subsection* (1) *repealed by Children Act* 1975 (c. 72), *Sched.* 4.]
[*Subsections* (2) (3) (4) *repealed by Succession (Scotland) Act* 1964 (c. 41), ss. 24 (4), 34 (2), *Sched.* 3.]

---

11 Extended by Adoption Act 1964 (c. 57), s. 1 (2); Adoption Act 1968 (c. 53), s. 4 (2)
12 Words substituted by Social Work (Scotland) Act 1968 (c. 49), s. 95 (1), Sched. 8, para. 38.

Citizenship

19.[13]—(1) Where an adoption order is made in respect of [a child] who is not a citizen of the United Kingdom and Colonies, then, if the adopter, or in the case of a joint adoption the male adopter, is a citizen of the United Kingdom and Colonies, the [child] shall be a citizen of the United Kingdom and Colonies as from the date of the order.

(2) The references in this section to an adoption order include references to an order authorising an adoption under the Adoption of Children Act (Northern Ireland) 1950 or any enactment of the Parliament of Northern Ireland for the time being in force.

Registration

Adopted Children Register (England)

20.[14]—(1) The Registrar General shall maintain at the General Register Office a register, to be called the Adopted Children Register, in which shall be made such entries as may be directed to be made therein by adoption orders, but no other entries.

(2) In England, a certified copy of an entry in the Adopted Children Register, if purporting to be sealed or stamped with the seal of the General Register Office, shall, without any further or other proof of that entry, be received as evidence of the adoption to which it relates and, where the entry contains a record of the date of the birth or the country or the district and sub-district of the birth of the adopted person, shall also be received as aforesaid as evidence of that date or country or district and sub-district in all respects as if the copy were a certified copy of an entry in the Registers of Births.

(3) The Registrar General shall cause an index of the Adopted Children Register to be made and kept in the General Register Office; and every person shall be entitled to search that index and to have a certified copy of any entry in the Adopted Children Register in all respects upon and subject to the same terms, conditions and regulations as to payment of fees and otherwise as are applicable under the Births and Deaths Registration Act 1953 and The Registration Service Act 1953 in respect of searches in other indexes kept in the General Register Office and in respect of the supply from that office of certified copies of entries in the certified copies of the Registers of Births and Deaths.

(4) The Registrar General shall, in addition to the Adopted Children Register and the index thereof, keep such other registers and books, and make such entries therein, as may be necessary to record and make traceable the connection between any entry in the Registers of Births which has been marked " Adopted " [. . .] [15] and any corresponding entry in the Adopted Children Register.

(5) The registers and books kept under subsection (4) of this section shall not be, nor shall any index thereof be, open to public inspection or search, and the Registrar General shall not furnish any person with any information contained in or with any copy or extract from any such registers or books except under an order of any of the following courts, that is to say—

    (*a*) the High Court;

    (*b*) the Westminster County Court or such other county court as may be prescribed; and

---

[13] Extended by Adoption Act 1964 (c. 57), ss. 1 (3), 4 (4); and Adoption Act 1968 (c. 53), s. 4 (2); saved by Adoption Act 1968 (c. 53), ss. 9 (5), 13, 14 (3).
[14] Extended by Adoption Act 1964 (c. 57), s. 2 (1). See now Children Act 1975 (c. 72), s. 26, *post*.
[15] Words repealed by Children Act 1975 (c. 72), Sched. 4.

(c) the court by which an adoption order was made in respect of the person to whom the information, copy or extract relates.

(6) In relation to an adoption order made by a magistrates' court, the reference in paragraph (c) of subsection (5) of this section to the court by which the order was made includes a reference to a court acting for the same petty sessions area.

Registration of English adoptions

21.[16]—(1) Every adoption order made by a court in England shall contain a direction to the Registrar General to make in the Adopted Children Register an entry in [such form as the Registrar General may by regulations specify].[17]

(2) For the purposes of compliance with the requirements of the last foregoing subsection,—

(a) where the precise date of the [child's] birth is not proved to the satisfaction of the court, the court shall determine the probable date of his birth and the date so determined shall be specified in the order as the date of his birth;

(b) where the country of birth of the [child] is not proved to the satisfaction of the court, then, if it appears probable that the [child] was born within the United Kingdom, the Channel Islands or the Isle of Man, he shall be treated as having been born in England, and in any other case the particulars of the country of birth may be omitted from the order and from the entry in the Adopted Children Register;

and the names to be specified in the order as the name and surname of the [child] shall be the name or names and surname stated in that behalf in the application for the adoption order, or, if no name or surname is so stated, the original name or names of the [child] and the surname of the applicant.

(3) [Repealed by Children Act 1975 (c. 72), Sched. 4.]

(4) Whereupon any application to a court in England for an adoption order in respect of [a child] (not being [a child] who has previously been the subject of an adoption order made by a court in England under this Act or any enactment at the time in force) there is proved to the satisfaction of the court the identity of the [child] with a child to whom an entry in the Registers of Birth relates, any adoption order made in pursuance of the application shall contain a direction to the Registrar General to cause the entry in the Registers of Births to be marked with the word " Adopted ".

(5) Where an adoption order is made by a court in England in respect of [a child] who has previously been the subject of an adoption order made by such a court under this Act or any enactment at the time in force, the order shall contain a direction to the Registrar General to cause the previous entry in the Adopted Children Register to be marked with the word " Readopted ".

(6) Where an adoption order is made by a court in England, the prescribed officer of the court shall cause the order to be communicated in the prescribed manner to the Registrar General, and upon receipt of the communication the Registrar General shall cause compliance to be made with the directions contained in the order.

Adopted Children Register (Scotland)

22.[18]—(1) The Registrar General for Scotland shall maintain at the

---

16 Modified by Adoption Act 1964 (c. 57), s. 3 (1); and Adoption Act 1968 (c. 53), s. 8.
17 Words substituted by Children Act 1975 (c. 72), Sched. 3, para. 24.
18 Extended by Adoption Act 1964 (c. 57), s. 2 (1). See now Children Act 1975 (c. 72), s. 27, post.

[General Register Office] [19] a register, to be called the Adopted Children Register, in which shall be made such entries as may be directed to be made therein by adoption orders, but no other entries.

(2) In Scotland, an extract of any entry in the Adopted Children Register maintained under this section, if purporting to be sealed or stamped with the seal of the [General Register Office],[19] shall, without any further or other proof of the entry, be received as evidence of the adoption to which it relates and, where the entry contains a record of the date of the birth or the country of the birth of the adopted person, shall also be received as aforesaid as evidence of that date or country in all respects as if the extract were an extract of an entry in the Register of Births.

(3) The Registrar General for Scotland shall cause an index of the Adopted Children Register maintained under this section to be made and kept in the [General Register Office] [19]; and every person shall be entitled to search that index and to have an extract of any entry in the said register in all respects upon and subject to the same terms, conditions and regulations as to payment of fees and otherwise as are applicable under the Registration of Births, Deaths and Marriages (Scotland) [Act 1965] [19] in respect of searches in other indexes kept in the [General Register Office] [19] and in respect of the supply from that office of extracts of entries in the Registers of Births, Deaths and Marriages.

(4) The Registrar General for Scotland shall, in addition to the Adopted Children Register and the index thereto, keep such other registers and books, and make such entries therein, as may be necessary to record and make traceable the connection between any entry in the Register of Births which has been marked " Adopted " pursuant to the next following section or any enactment at the time in force, and any corresponding entry in the Adopted Children Register maintained under this section; but the registers and books kept under this subsection shall not be, nor shall any index thereof be, open to public inspection or search, nor, except under an order of the Court of Session or a sheriff, shall the Registrar General furnish any information contained in or any copy or extract from any such registers or books to any person other than an adopted person who has attained the age of seventeen years and to whom that information, copy or extract relates.

(5) Regulations made under the Registration of Births, Deaths and Marriages (Scotland) [Act 1965],[19] may make provision as to the duties to be performed by Registrars of Births, Deaths and Marriages in the execution of this and the next following section.

(6) The provisions of the Registration of Births, Deaths and Marriages (Scotland) [Act 1965],[19] [. . .] [20] with regard to the alteration of erroneous entries shall apply to the Adopted Children Register maintained by the Registrar General for Scotland and to registration therein in like manner as they apply to any register of births and to registration therein.

Registration of Scottish adoptions

23.[21]—(1) Every adoption order made by a court in Scotland shall contain a direction to the Registrar General for Scotland to make in the Adopted Children Register maintained by him an entry recording the adoption in [such form as the Registrar General for Scotland may by regulations specify].[22]

[19] Words substituted by Registration of Births, Deaths and Marriages (Scotland) Act 1965 (c. 49), s. 58 (1), Sched. 1, paras. 7, 8.
[20] Words repealed by *ibid.* s. 58 (2), Sched. 2.
[21] Modified by Adoption Act 1964 (c. 57), s. 3 (1); extended by Adoption Act 1968 (c. 53), s. 8 (5) (*b*).
[22] Words substituted by Children Act 1975 (c. 72), Sched. 3, para. 25.

(2) For the purposes of compliance with the requirements of the foregoing subsection,—

(a) where the precise date of the [child's] birth is not proved to the satisfaction of the court, the court shall determine the probable date of his birth and the date so determined shall be specified in the order as the date of his birth;

(b) where the country of birth of the [child] is not proved to the satisfaction of the court, then, if it appears probable that the [child] was born within the United Kingdom, the Channel Islands or the Isle of Man, he shall be treated as having been born in Scotland, and in any other case the particulars of the country of birth may be omitted from the order and from the entry in the Adopted Children Register;

and the names to be specified in the order as the name and surname of the [child] shall be the name or names and surname stated in that behalf in the application for the adoption order, or, if no name or surname is so stated, the original name or names of the [child] and the surname of the applicant.

(3) There shall be produced with every application to a court in Scotland for an adoption order in respect of [a child] whose birth has been registered under the Registration of Births, Deaths and Marriages (Scotland) Acts 1854 to 1938 [or under the Registration of Births, Deaths and Marriages (Scotland) Act 1965],[19] an extract of the entry of the birth.

(4) Where upon any application to a court in Scotland for an adoption order in respect of [a child] (not being [a child] who has previously been the subject of an adoption order made by a court in Scotland under this Act or any enactment at the time in force) there is proved to the satisfaction of the court the identity of the [child] with a child to whom an entry in the Register of Births relates, any adoption order made in pursuance of the application shall contain a direction to the Registrar General for Scotland to cause the entry in that register to be marked with the word " Adopted."

(5) Where an adoption order is made by a court in Scotland in respect of [a child] who has previously been the subject of an adoption order made by such a court under this Act or any enactment at the time in force, the order shall contain a direction to the Registrar General for Scotland to cause the previous entry in the Adopted Children Register maintained by him to be marked with the word " Re-adopted."

(6) Where an adoption order is made by a court in Scotland, the clerk of the court shall cause the order to be communicated to the Registrar General for Scotland, and upon receipt of the communication the Registrar General shall cause compliance to be made with the directions contained in the order.

Amendment of orders and rectification of Registers

24.—(1) The court by which an adoption order has been made may, on the application of the adopter or of the adopted person, amend the order by the correction of any error in the particulars contained therein, and may—

(a) if satisfied on the application of the adopter or of the adopted person that within one year beginning with the date of the order any new name has been given to the adopted person (whether in baptism or otherwise), or taken by him, either in lieu of or in addition to a name specified in the particulars required to be entered in the Adopted Children Register in pursuance of the order, amend the order by substituting or adding that name in those particulars, as the case may require;

(b) if satisfied on the application of any person concerned that a direction for the marking of an entry in the Registers of Births, the Register of Births or the Adopted Children Register included in the order in pursuance of subsection (4) or subsection (5) of section twenty-one or subsection (4) or subsection (5) of section twenty-three of this Act was wrongly so included, revoke that direction.

(2) Where an adoption order is amended or a direction revoked under subsection (1) of this section, the prescribed officer of the court or, in Scotland, the clerk of the court, shall cause the amendment to be communicated in the prescribed manner to the Registrar General or, as the case may be, the Registrar General for Scotland, who shall as the case may require,—

(a) cause the entry in the Adopted Children Register to be amended accordingly; or

(b) cause the marking of the entry in the Registers of Births, the Register of Births or the Adopted Children Register to be cancelled.

(3) Where an adoption order is quashed or an appeal against an adoption order allowed by any court, the court shall give directions to the Registrar General or the Registrar General for Scotland to cancel any entry in the Adopted Children Register, and any marking of an entry in that Register, the Registers of Births or the Register of Births, as the case may be, which was effected in pursuance of the order.

(4) Where the Registrar General is notified by the Registrar General for Scotland that an adoption order has been made by a court in Scotland in respect of [a child] to whom an entry in the Registers of Births or the Adopted Children Register relates, the Registrar General shall cause the entry to be marked " Adopted (Scotland) " or, as the case may be, " Re-adopted (Scotland) "; and where, after an entry has been so marked, the Registrar General is notified as aforesaid that the adoption order has been quashed, or that an appeal against the adoption order has been allowed, he shall cause the marking to be cancelled.

(5) Where the Registrar General for Scotland is notified by the Registrar General that an adoption order has been made by a court in England in respect of [a child] to whom an entry in the Register of Births or the Adopted Children Register maintained by the Registrar General for Scotland relates, the Registrar General for Scotland shall cause the entry to be marked " Adopted (England) " or, as the case may be, " Re-adopted (England) "; and where, after an entry has been so marked, the Registrar General for Scotland is notified as aforesaid that the adoption order has been quashed, or that an appeal against the adoption order has been allowed, he shall cause the marking to be cancelled.

(6) Where an adoption order has been amended, any certified copy of the relevant entry in the Adopted Children Register which may be issued pursuant to subsection (3) of section twenty of this Act shall be a copy of the entry as amended, without the reproduction of any note or marking relating to the amendment or of any matter cancelled pursuant thereto; and a copy or extract of an entry in any register, being an entry the marking of which has been cancelled, shall be deemed to be an accurate copy if and only if both the marking and the cancellation are omitted therefrom.

(7) In relation to an adoption order made by a magistrates' court, the reference in subsection (1) of this section to the court by which the order has been made includes a reference to a court acting for the same petty sessions area.

25. [*Section repealed by Children Act 1975 (c. 72), Sched. 4.*]

Legitimation following adoption

Legitimation: revocation of adoption orders and cancellations in Registers

26.[23]—(1) Where any person adopted by his father or mother alone has subsequently become a legitimated person on the marriage of his father and mother, the court by which the adoption order was made may, on the application of any of the parties concerned, revoke that order.

(2) Where an adoption order is revoked under this section, the prescribed officer of the court or, in Scotland, the clerk of the court, shall cause the revocation to be communicated in the prescribed manner to the Registrar General or, as the case may be, the Registrar General for Scotland, who shall cause to be cancelled—

(*a*) the entry in the Adopted Children Register relating to the adopted person; and

(*b*) the marking with the word " Adopted " (or, as the case may be, with that word and the word " (Scotland) " or " (England) ") of any entry relating to him in the Registers of Births or the Register of Births;

and a copy or extract of an entry in any register, being an entry the marking of which is cancelled under this section, shall be deemed to be an accurate copy if and only if both the marking and the cancellation are omitted therefrom.

(3) In relation to an adoption order made by a magistrates' court, the reference in subsection (1) of this section to the court by which the order was made includes a reference to a court acting for the same petty sessions area.

Legitimation: marking of entries on re-registration of births

27. Without prejudice to the provisions of section twenty-six of this Act, where, after an entry in the Registers of Births or the Register of Births has been marked with the word " Adopted " (with or without the addition of the word " (Scotland) " or " (England) ") the birth is re-registered under section fourteen of the Births and Deaths Registration Act 1953 or [section 20 of the Registration of Births, Deaths and Marriages (Scotland) Act 1965 (which provide for re-registration of births in certain cases)],[24] the entry made on the re-registration shall be marked in the like manner.

PART II

LOCAL AUTHORITIES AND ADOPTION SOCIETIES

Local authorities

28.—(1) The local authorities for the purposes of this Act are, in England, the councils of counties [other than metropolitan counties, of metropolitan districts and London boroughs and the Common Council of the City of London][25] and, in Scotland, the councils of [regions and islands areas].[26]

---

23 Extended by Adoption Act 1960 (c. 59), s. 1 (3), *post.* See Children Act 1975 (c. 72), Sched. 3, para. 26, *post.*

24 Amended by Registration of Births, Deaths and Marriages (Scotland) Act 1975 (c. 49), s. 58 (1), Sched. 1, para. 9.

25 Words substituted by Local Government Act 1972 (c. 70), s. 195 (5), Sched. 23, para. 8.

26 Words substituted by Local Government (Scotland) Act 1973 (c. 65), Sched. 27.

(2) Every such local authority have power to make and participate in arrangements for the adoption of children.

Restriction on making arrangements for adoption

29.[27]—(1) It shall not be lawful for any body of persons to make any arrangements for the adoption of [a child] unless that body is a registered adoption society or a local authority.

(2) It shall not be lawful for a registered adoption society or local authority by whom arrangements are made for the adoption of [a child] to place him in the [actual custody] of a person who proposes to adopt him if an adoption order in respect of the [child] could not lawfully be made in favour of that person.

(3) Every person who—

    (*a*) takes any part in the management or control of a body of persons which exists wholly or in part for the purpose of making arrangements for the adoption of [children] and which is not a registered adoption society or a local authority; or

    (*b*) is guilty of a contravention of subsection (1) or subsection (2) of this section;

shall be liable on summary conviction to imprisonment for a term not exceeding six months or to a fine not exceeding one hundred pounds or to both.

(4) In any proceedings for an offence under paragraph (*a*) of subsection (3) of this section, proof of things done or of words written, spoken or published (whether or not in the presence of any party to the proceedings) by any person taking part in the management or control of a body of persons, or in making arrangements for the adoption of [children] on behalf of the body, shall be admissible as evidence of the purpose for which that body exists.

(5) The court by which a person is convicted of a contravention of subsection (2) of this section may order the [child] in respect of whom the offence was committed to be returned to his parent or guardian or to the registered adoption society or local authority.

Registration of adoption societies

30.[28]—(1) Subject to the following provisions of this Part of this Act, where an application is made in the prescribed manner by or on behalf of an adoption society to the local authority in whose area the administrative centre of the society is situated and there is furnished therewith the prescribed information relating to the activities of the society, the local authority shall, on payment by the society of such fee (not exceeding [two pounds] [29]) as may be prescribed, register the society under this Part of this Act.

(2) Any question where the administrative centre of an adoption society is situated shall be determined by the Secretary of State, whose determination shall be final.

(3) A local authority shall not register an adoption society under this Part of this Act unless the authority are satisfied, by such evidence as the authority may reasonably require, that the society are a charitable association.

---

[27] See now Children Act 1975 (c. 72), s. 28, *post*.
[28] Power to amend contained in Local Government Act 1966 (c. 42), s. 35 (2), Sched. 3, Pt. II. See now approval provisions in Children Act 1975 (c. 72), s. 4.
[29] Fee increased from one pound by S.I. 1968/170.

(4) A local authority may refuse to register an adoption society under this Part of this Act, if it appears to the authority—

(a) that the activities of the society are not controlled by a committee of members of the society who are responsible to the members of the society;

(b) that any person proposed to be employed, or employed, by the society for the purpose of making any arrangements for the adoption of children on behalf of the society is not a fit and proper person to be so employed;

(c) that the number of competent persons proposed to be employed, or employed, by the society for the purpose aforesaid is, in the opinion of the authority, insufficient having regard to the extent of the activities of the society in connection with that purpose; or

(d) that any person taking part in the management or control of the society or any member of the society has been convicted of an offence under this Part of this Act, Part II of the Adoption Act 1950, or the Adoption of Children (Regulation) Act 1939, or of a breach of any regulations made under this Part of this Act, the said Part II, or the said Act of 1939.

(5) A local authority may at any time cancel the registration of an adoption society on any ground which would entitle the authority to refuse an application for the registration of the society, or on the ground that the society are no longer a charitable association, or on the ground that the administrative centre of the society is no longer situated in the area of the authority.

Procedure and right of appeal

31.—(1) Where a local authority propose to refuse an application for registration made to them by or on behalf of an adoption society or to cancel the registration of an adoption society, the local authority shall give to the society not less than fourteen days' notice in writing of their intention to do so.

(2) Every such notice shall state the grounds on which the authority intend to refuse the application or to cancel the registration, as the case may be, and shall contain an intimation that, if within fourteen days after the receipt of the notice the society inform the authority in writing that they desire to do so, the authority will, before refusing the application or cancelling the registration, as the case may be, give to the society an opportunity of causing representations to be made to the authority by or on behalf of the society.

(3) If the local authority, after giving to the society an opportunity of causing such representations as aforesaid to be made, decide to refuse the application for registration or to cancel the registration, as the case may be, they shall give to the society notice in writing of their decision.

(4) Any adoption society aggrieved by the refusal of an application for registration, or by the cancellation of their registration, by a local authority may—

(a) in England, appeal to [the Crown Court] [30] by a notice of appeal given within twenty-one days after notice in writing of the decision has been given to the society;

(b) in Scotland, appeal to the sheriff within whose jurisdiction the administrative centre of the society is situated within the said twenty-one days.

[*Subsection (5) repealed by Courts Act 1971 (c. 23), s. 56 (4), Sched. 11, Pt. IV.*]

[30] Words substituted by Courts Act 1971 (c. 23), s. 56 (2), Sched. 9, Pt. I.

(6) Where the registration of an adoption society is cancelled by a local authority, the adoption society shall, for the purposes of this Part of this Act, be deemed to be registered under this Part of this Act during the period within which an appeal against the cancellation may be brought under this section and, if such an appeal is brought, until the determination or abandonment of the appeal.

Adoption societies regulations, etc.

32.—(1) The Secretary of State may make regulations for any of the purposes set out in the Third Schedule to this Act and for prescribing anything which by this Part of this Act (including that Schedule) is authorised or required to be prescribed.

(2) Any person who contravenes or fails to comply with the provisions of regulations made under subsection (2) of this section shall be liable on summary conviction to a fine not exceeding [£400].[31]

(3) The Secretary of State may make regulations with respect to the exercise by local authorities of their functions of making or participating in arrangements for the adoption of children, and such regulations may make provision, in relation to local authorities who exercise those functions, for purposes corresponding with the purposes for which the Secretary of State has power under subsection (1) of this section to make regulations in relation to registered adoption societies.

Inspection of books, etc., of registered adoption societies

33.[32]—(1) A local authority may at any time give notice in writing to any registered adoption society which has been registered by the authority under this Part of this Act, or to any officer of such a society, requiring that society or officer to produce to the authority such books, accounts and other documents relating to the performance by the society of the function of making arrangements for the adoption of [children] as the authority may consider necessary for the exercise of the powers conferred on the authority by subsection (5) of section thirty of this Act.

(2) Any such notice may contain a requirement that any information to be furnished in accordance with the notice shall be verified by statutory declaration.

(3) Any person who fails to comply with the requirements of a notice under this section shall be liable on summary conviction to imprisonment for a term not exceeding three months or to a fine not exceeding fifty pounds or to both.

PART III

[ACTUAL CUSTODY] OF [CHILDREN] AWAITING ADOPTION

Restriction on removal by parent or guardian after giving consent

34.[33] While an application for an adoption order in respect of [a child] is pending in any court, a parent or guardian of the [child] who has signified his consent to the making of an adoption order in pursuance of the application shall not be entitled, except with the leave of the court, to remove the [child] from the [actual custody] of the applicant, and in considering whether to grant or refuse such leave the court shall have regard to the welfare of the [child].

[31] Words substituted by Children Act 1975 (c. 72), Sched. 3.
[32] See now *ibid*, para. 28, *post*.
[33] See now *ibid*, s. 29, *post*.

Return of [children] placed by adoption societies and local authorities

35.[34]—(1) Subject to subsection (2) of this section, at any time after [a child] has been delivered into the [actual custody] of any person in pursuance of arrangements made by a registered adoption society or local authority for the adoption of the [child] by that person, and before an adoption order has been made on the application of that person in respect of the [child]—

(a) that person may give notice in writing to the society or authority of his intention not to retain the [actual custody] of the [child]; or

(b) the society or authority may cause notice in writing to be given to that person of their intention not to allow the [child] to remain in his [actual custody].

(2) After an application has been made for an adoption order in the case of [a child], no notice shall be given in respect of that [child] under paragraph (b) of subsection (1) of this section except with the leave of the court.

(3) Where a notice is given to an adoption society or local authority by any person, or by such a society or authority to any person, under subsection (1) of this section, or where an application for an adoption order made by any person in respect of [a child] placed in his care and possession by such a society or authority is refused by the court or withdrawn, that person shall, within seven days after the date on which notice was given or the application refused or withdrawn, as the case may be, cause the [child] to be returned to the society or authority, and the society or authority shall receive the [child].

(4) Where the period specified in an interim order made under section eight of this Act (whether as originally made or as varied under subsection (4) of that section) expires without an adoption order having been made in respect of the [child], subsection (3) of this section shall apply as if the application for an adoption order upon which the interim order was made had been refused at the expiration of that period.

(5) It shall be sufficient compliance with the requirements of subsection (3) of this section if the [child] is delivered to, and is received by, a suitable person nominated for the purpose by the adoption society or local authority.

(6) Any person who contravenes the provisions of this section shall be liable on summary conviction to imprisonment for a term not exceeding [three][31] months or to a fine not exceeding [£400][31] or to both; and the court by which the offender is convicted may order the infant in respect of whom the offence is committed to be returned to his parent or guardian or to the registered adoption society or local authority.

Further provisions as to adoption of children in care of local authorities

36.[35]—(1) Where notice of intention to apply for an adoption order is given in pursuance of subsection (2) of section three of this Act in respect of [a child] who is for the time being in the care of a local authority, not being [a child] who was delivered into the [actual custody] of the person by whom the notice is given in pursuance of such arrangements as are mentioned in subsection (1) of section thirty-five of this Act, the said section thirty-five shall apply as if the [child] had been so delivered, except that where the application is refused by the court or withdrawn the [child] need not be returned to the local authority unless the local authority so require.

[34] See now *ibid*, s. 31, *post*.
[35] See now *ibid*, Sched. 3, para. 30, *post*.

(2) Where notice of intention is given as aforesaid in respect of any [child] who is for the time being in the care of a local authority then, until the application for an adoption order has been made and disposed of, any right of the local authority to require the [child] to be returned to them otherwise than in pursuance of the said section thirty-five shall be suspended; and while the [child] remains in the [actual custody] of the person by whom the notice is given—

    (a) no contribution shall be payable (whether under a contribution order or otherwise) in respect of the [child] by any person liable under section eighty-six of the Children and Young Persons Act 1933 [or section 78 of the Social Work (Scotland) Act 1968],[36] to make contributions in respect of him (but without prejudice to the recovery of any sum due at the time the notice is given); and

[*Paragraph (b) repealed by S.L.R.* 1965.]

unless twelve weeks have elapsed since the giving of the notice without the application being made or the application has been refused by the court or withdrawn.

(3) Where notice of intention to apply for an adoption order is given as aforesaid in respect of any [child] who is for the time being in the care of a local authority, and is given to a local authority other than the local authority in whose care the [child] is, the authority to whom the notice is given shall inform that other authority of the receipt of the notice.

PART IV

SUPERVISION OF CHILDREN AWAITING ADOPTION OR PLACED WITH STRANGERS

Meaning of protected child

37.[37]—(1) Subject to the following provisions of this section, where—

    (a) arrangements are made for placing a child below the upper limit of the compulsory school age in the [actual custody] of a person who is not a parent, guardian or relative of his [but who proposes to adopt him],[38] and another person, not being a parent or guardian of his, takes part in the arrangements; or

    (b) notice of intention to apply for an adoption order in respect of a child is given under subsection (2) of section three of this Act,

then, while the child is in the [actual custody] of the person first mentioned in paragraph (a) of this subsection or, as the case may be, of the person giving the notice mentioned in paragraph (b) thereof [. . .],[39] he is a protected child within the meaning of this Part of this Act.

(2) A child is not a protected child [. . .][39] while the child is in the care of any person in any of the circumstances mentioned in subsections (2) [or (4)][40] of section two of the Children Act 1958, or paragraphs (b) to (e) of subsection (3) of that section.

(3) A child is not a protected child by reason of any such notice as is mentioned in paragraph (b) of subsection (1) of this section while he is

---

[36] Words substituted by Social Work (Scotland) Act 1968 (c. 49), s. 95 (1), Sched. 8, para. 39.
[37] See now Children Act 1975 (c. 72), Sched. 3, para. 31, *post.*
[38] Words added by Children and Young Persons Act 1969 (c. 54), s. 52 (4) (a).
[39] Words repealed by *ibid.* s. 72 (4), Sched. 6.
[40] Words substituted by *ibid.* ss. 72 (3), 73 (4) (c), Sched. 5, para. 35.

[. . .] [39] in the care of any person in any such school, home or institution as is mentioned in subsection (3) [. . .] [40] of section two of the Children Act 1958 [nor while he is liable to be detained, subject to guardianship or resident as mentioned in subsection (4) of that section].[41]

(4) A protected child ceases to be a protected child on the making of an adoption order in respect of him or on his attaining the age of eighteen, whichever first occurs.

(5) A child in the [actual custody] of two spouses one of whom is a parent, relative or guardian of his shall be deemed for the purposes of this Part of this Act to be in the [actual custody] of that one of them.

Duty of local authority to secure well-being of protected children

38. It shall be the duty of every local authority to secure that protected children within their area are visited from time to time by officers of the authority, who shall satisfy themselves as to the well-being of the children and give such advice as to their care and maintenance as may appear to be needed.

Power to inspect premises

39. Any officer of a local authority authorised to visit protected children may, after producing, if asked to do so, some duly authenticated document showing that he is so authorised, inspect any premises in the area of the authority in which such children are to be or are being kept.

Notices and information to be given to local authorities

40.[42]—(1) Subject to subsection (2) of this section, where arrangements are made for the placing of a child in the [actual custody] of any person and by reason of the arrangements the child would be a protected child while in the [actual custody] of that person, every person taking part in the arrangements shall give notice in writing of the arrangements to the local authority for the area in which the person in whose [actual custody] the child is to be placed is living.

(2) A notice under subsection (1) of this section need not be given by the person in whose [actual custody] the child is to be placed, nor by a parent or guardian of the child.

(3) A notice under subsection (1) of this section shall be given not less than two weeks before the child is placed as mentioned in that subsection, except that where the child is so placed in an emergency, the notice may be given not later than one week after the child is so placed.

(4) Where a person who has a protected child in his [actual custody] changes his permanent address he shall, not less than two weeks before the change, or, if the change is made in an emergency, not later than one week after the change, give written notice specifying the new address to the local authority in whose area his permanent address is before the change, and if the new address is in the area of another local authority, the authority to whom the notice is given shall inform that other local authority and give them such of the particulars mentioned in subsection (6) of this section as are known to them.

(5) If a protected child dies, the person in whose [actual custody] he was at his death shall within forty-eight hours of the death give to the local authority notice in writing of the death.

(6) A person who has or proposes to have a protected child in his [actual custody] shall at the request of the local authority give them

---

40 Words repealed by Mental Health (Scotland) Act 1960 (c. 61), ss. 19 (3), 113 (2), Sched. 5.
41 Words added by Mental Health Act 1959 (c. 72), ss. 19 (3), 149 (1), Sched. 7, Pt. II.
42 See now Children Act 1975 (c. 72), Sched. 3, para. 32, *post*.

the following particulars, so far as known to him, that is to say, the name, sex and date and place of birth of the child, and the name and address of every person who is a parent or guardian or acts as a guardian of the child or from whom the child has been or is to be received.

Power of local authority to prohibit placing of child

41. Where arrangements are made for the placing of a child in the [actual custody] of any person, and by reason of the arrangements the child would be a protected child while in the [actual custody] of that person, then, if neither a registered adoption society nor a local authority took part in the arrangements and it appears to the authority to whom notice is to be given under the last foregoing section that it would be detrimental to the child to be kept by that person in the premises in which he proposes to keep him, they may by notice in writing given to that person prohibit him from receiving the child in those premises.

Appeal to juvenile court against prohibition under section 41

42.—(1) A person aggrieved by a prohibition imposed under the last foregoing section may, within fourteen days from the date on which he is notified of the prohibition, appeal to a juvenile court.

(2) The notice by which a prohibition is imposed under that section shall contain a statement informing the person on whom it is imposed of his right to appeal against the prohibition and of the time within which he may do so.

(3) In the application of this section to Scotland, for the reference to a juvenile court there shall be substituted a reference to the sheriff.

Removal of protected children from unsuitable surroundings

43.[43]—(1) If a juvenile court is satisfied, on the complaint of a local authority, that a protected child is being kept or is about to be received by any person who is unfit to have his care, or in contravention of any prohibition imposed by the local authority under section forty-one of this Act, or in any premises or any environment detrimental or likely to be detrimental to him, the court may make an order for his removal to a place of safety until he can be restored to a parent, relative or guardian of his, or until other arrangements can be made with respect to him; and on proof that there is imminent danger to the health or well-being of the child the power to make an order under this section may be exercised by a justice of the peace acting on the application of a person authorised to visit protected children.

(2) An order under this section may be executed by any person authorised to visit protected children or by any constable and may, [. . .],[44] be executed on a Sunday.

(3) A local authority may receive into their care under section one of the Children Act 1948 [or as the case may be, section 15 of the Social Work (Scotland) Act 1968][45] any child removed under [the said section 1 or, as the case may be, the said section 15][45] whether or not the circumstances of the child are such that they fall within paragraphs (a) to (c) of subsection (1) of that section and notwithstanding that he may appear to the local authority to be over the age of seventeen.

(4) Where a child is removed under this section the local authority shall, if practicable, inform a parent or guardian of the child, or any person who acts as his guardian.

[43] Extended by Children and Young Persons Act 1963 (c. 37), s. 23.
[44] Words repealed by S.L.R. 1969.
[45] Words added by Social Work (Scotland) Act 1968 (c. 49), ss. 95 (1), 97 (1) Sched. 8, para. 40.

(5) In the application of this section to Scotland, for references to a juvenile court there shall be substituted references to the sheriff.

Offences under Part IV

44.—(1) A person shall be guilty of an offence if—

(*a*) being required, under any provision of this Part of this Act, to give any notice or information, he fails to give the notice within the time specified in that provision or fails to give the information within a reasonable time, or knowingly makes or causes or procures another person to make any false or misleading statement in the notice or information;

(*b*) he refuses to allow the visiting of a protected child by a duly authorised officer of a local authority or the inspection, under the power conferred by section thirty-nine of this Act, of any premises;

(*c*) he keeps any child in any premises in contravention of a prohibition imposed under this Part of this Act;

(*d*) he refuses to comply with an order under this Part of this Act for the removal of any child or obstructs any person in the execution of such an order.

(2) A person guilty of an offence under this section shall be liable on summary conviction to imprisonment for a term not exceeding [three] [46] months or a fine not exceeding [£400] or both.

Extension of power to issue warrants to search for and remove a child

45. For the purposes of section forty of the Children and Young Persons Act 1933, or section forty-seven of the Children and Young Persons (Scotland) Act 1937 (which enable a warrant authorising the search for and and removal of a child to be issued on suspicion of unnecessary suffering caused to, or certain offences committed against, the child), any refusal to allow the visiting of a protected child or the inspection of any premises by a person authorised to do so under this Part of this Act shall be treated as giving reasonable cause for such a suspicion.

Avoidance of insurances on lives of protected children

46. A person who maintains a protected child shall be deemed for the purposes of the Life Assurance Act 1774 to have no interest in the life of the child.

Sittings of juvenile courts in proceedings under Part IV

47. Subsection (2) of section forty-seven of the Children and Young Persons Act 1933 (which restricts the time and place at which a sitting of a juvenile court may be held and the persons who may be present at such a sitting) shall not apply to any sitting of a juvenile court in any proceedings under this Part of this Act.

Appeal to the Crown Court

48. An appeal shall lie to [the Crown Court] [47] from any order made under this Part of this Act by a juvenile court or any other magistrates' court within the meaning of the Magistrates' Courts Act 1952.

49.[*Section repealed by Children Act 1975 (c. 72), Sched. 4.*]

[46] Words substituted by Children Act 1975 (c. 72), Sched. 3.
[47] Words substituted by Courts Act 1971 (c. 23), s. 56 (2), Sched. 9, Pt. I.

PART V

MISCELLANEOUS AND GENERAL

Prohibition of certain payments

50.[48]—(1) Subject to the provisions of this section, it shall not be lawful to make or give to any person any payment or reward for or in consideration of—

(*a*) the adoption by that person of [a child];

(*b*) the grant by that person of any consent required in connection with the adoption of [a child];

(*c*) the transfer by that person of the [actual custody] of [a child] with a view to the adoption of the [child]; or

(*d*) the making by that person of any arrangements for the adoption of [a child].

(2) Any person who makes or gives, or agrees or offers to make or give, any payment or reward prohibited by this section, or who receives or agrees to receive or attempts to obtain any such payment or reward, shall be liable on summary conviction to imprisonment for a term not exceeding [three] [46] months or to a fine not exceeding [£400] [46] or to both; and the court may order any [child] in respect of whom the offence was committed to be removed to a place of safety until he can be restored to his parents or guardian or until other arrangements can be made for him.

(3) This section does not apply to any payment made to an adoption society or local authority by a parent or guardian of [a child] or by a person who adopts or proposes to adopt [a child], being a payment in respect of expenses reasonably incurred by the society or authority in connection with the adoption of the [child], or to any payment or reward authorised by the court to which an application for an adoption order in respect of [a child] is made.

Restriction upon advertisements

51.—(1) It shall not be lawful for any advertisement to be published indicating—

(*a*) that the parent or guardian of [a child] desires to cause the [child] to be adopted; or

(*b*) that a person desires to adopt [a child]; or

(*c*) that any person (not being a registered adoption society or a local authority) is willing to make arrangements for the adoption of [a child].

(2) Any person who causes to be published or knowingly publishes an advertisement in contravention of the provisions of this section shall be liable on summary conviction to a fine not exceeding [£400].[46]

Restriction on removal of infants for adoption outside British Islands

52.[49]—(1) Except under the authority of an order under section fifty-three of this Act, it shall not be lawful for any person to take or send [a child] who is a British subject out of Great Britain to any place outside the British Islands with view to the adoption of the [child] [. . .] [50] by any person not being a parent or guardian or relative of the [child]; and any person who takes or sends [a child] out of Great Britain to any place in contravention of this subsection, or makes or takes part in any arrangements for transferring the care and

---

[48] See Children Act 1975 (c. 72), s. 32, *post*.

[49] Excluded by Children and Young Persons Act 1963 (c. 37), s. 55.

[50] Words repealed by Children Act 1975 (c. 72), Sched. 4.

possession of [a child] to any person for that purpose, shall be liable on summary conviction to imprisonment for a term not exceeding [three] months or to a fine not exceeding [£400] [46] or to both.

(2) In any proceedings under this section, a report by a British consular officer or a deposition made before a British consular officer and authenticated under the signature of that officer shall, upon proof that the officer or the deponent cannot be found in the United Kingdom, be admissible as evidence of the matters stated therein, and it shall not be necessary to prove the signature or official character of the person who appears to have signed any such report or deposition.

(3) In this section " the British Islands " means the United Kingdom, the Channel Islands and the Isle of Man.

(4) In the application of this section to Scotland, for the words " admissible as evidence " there shall be substituted the words " sufficient evidence ".

Provisional adoption by persons domiciled outside Great Britain

53.[51]—(1) If the court is satisfied, upon an application being made by a person who is not domiciled in England or Scotland, that the applicant intends to adopt [a child] under the law of or within the country in which he is domiciled, and for that purpose desires to remove the infant from Great Britain either immediately or after an interval, the court may, subject to the provisions of this section, make an order (in this section referred to as a provisional adoption order) authorising the applicant to remove the [child] for the purpose aforesaid, and giving to the applicant the custody of the [child] pending his adoption as aforesaid.

(2) An application for a provisional adoption order may be made, in England to the High Court or the county court, and in Scotland to the Court of Session or the sheriff court.

(3) A provisional adoption order may be made in any case where, apart from the domicile of the applicant, an adoption order could be made in respect of the [child] under Part I of this Act, but shall not be made in any other case.

(4) Subject to the provisions of this section, the provisions of this Act, other than this section and sections sixteen, seventeen and nineteen, shall apply in relation to a provisional adoption order as they apply in relation to an adoption order, and references in those provisions to adoption, to an adoption order, to an application or applicant for such an order and to an adopter or a person adopted or authorised to be adopted under such an order shall be construed accordingly.

(5) In relation to a provisional adoption order section three of this Act shall have effect as if for the word " three ", both where it occurs in subsection (1) and where it occurs in subsection (2), there were substituted the word " six ".

(6) Any entry in the Registers of Births, the Register of Births or the Adopted Children Register which is required to be marked in consequence of the making of a provisional adoption order shall, in lieu of being marked with the word " Adopted " or " Re-adopted " (with or without the addition of the word " (Scotland) " or " (England) ") be marked with the words " Provisionally adopted " or " Provisionally re-adopted ", as the case may require.

Offences

54.—(1) Where any offence under Part II, Part III, Part IV or Part V of this Act committed by a body corporate is proved to have been

[51] Modified by Adoption Act 1964 (c. 57), s. 3 (3).

committed with the consent or connivance of, or to be attributable to any neglect on the part of, any director, manager, member of the committee, secretary or other officer of the body, he, as well as the body, shall be deemed to be guilty of that offence and shall be liable to be proceeded against and punished accordingly.

(2) Proceedings for an offence under Part II, Part III, Part IV or Part V of this Act may, in England, be taken by a local authority.

Service of notices, etc.

55.[52] Any notice or information required to be given under this Act may be given by post.

[Rules and Regulations

56.—(1) Any power to make rules or regulations conferred by this Act on the Lord Chancellor, the Secretary of State, the Registrar General or the Registrar General for Scotland shall be exercisable by statutory instrument which shall be subject to annulment in pursuance of a resolution of either House of Parliament.

(2) The Registrar General shall not make regulations under section 20A or 21 of this Act except with the approval of the Secretary of State.

(3) The Registrar General for Scotland shall not make regulations under section 23 of this Act except with the approval of the Secretary of State.

(4) The Statutory Instruments Act 1946 shall apply to a statutory instrument containing regulations made for the purposes of this Act by the Registrar General for Scotland as if the regulations had been made by a Minister of the Crown.] [46]

Interpretation

57.—(1) In this Act, unless the context otherwise requires, the following expressions have the meanings hereby respectively assigned to them, that is to say—

" adoption order " has the meaning assigned to it by section one of this Act;

" Adoption Rules " has the meaning assigned to it by subsection (2) of section nine of this Act;

" adoption society " means a body of persons whose functions consist of or include the making of arrangements for the adoption of children;

" body of persons " means any body of persons, whether incorporated or unincorporated;

[" child ", except where used to express a relationship, means a person who has not attained the age of 18;

" Convention adoption order " has the same meaning as in the Children Act 1975;] [46]

" charitable association " means a body of persons which exists only for the purpose of promoting a charitable, benevolent or philanthropic object, whether or not the object is charitable within the meaning of any rule of law, and which applies the whole of its profits (if any) or other income in promoting the objects for which it exists;

" compulsory school age ", in relation to England, has the same meaning as in the Education Acts 1944 to 1953 and, in relation to Scotland, means school age as defined in the Education (Scotland) Acts 1939 to 1956;

[52] See now Children Act 1975 (c. 72), Sched. 3, para. 37, *post.*

" court " means a court having jurisdiction to make adoption orders;

" England " includes Wales;

" father ", in relation to an illegitimate [child], means the natural father;

[" guardian " means—

> (a) a person appointed by deed or will in accordance with the provisions of the Guardianship of Infants Acts 1886 and 1925 or the Guardianship of Minors Act 1971 or by a court of competent jurisdiction to be the guardian of the child, and
>
> (b) in the case of an illegitimate child, includes the father where he has custody of the child by virtue of an order under section 9 of the Guardianship of Minors Act 1971, or under section 2 of the Illegitimate Children (Scotland) Act 1930;] [46]

" place of safety " means a [community home] [53] provided by a local authority [a controlled community] [53] home, police station, or any hospital, surgery or other suitable place the occupier of which is willing temporarily to receive a child [and in Scotland has the same meaning as in the Social Work (Scotland) Act 1968] [54];

" prescribed ", in Part I of this Act, means prescribed by Adoption Rules or an act of sederunt under section eleven of this Act, and except in Part I of this Act, means prescribed by regulations made by the Secretary of State;

" registered adoption society " means an adoption society registered under Part II of this Act;

" Registrar General for Scotland " means the Registrar General of Births, Deaths and Marriages in Scotland;

" relative ", in relation to [a child], means a grandparent, brother, sister, uncle or aunt, whether of the full blood or half blood or by affinity, and includes—

> (a) [*repealed by Children Act 1975 (c. 72), Sched. 4.*]
>
> (b) where the [child] is illegitimate, the father of the [child] and any person who would be a relative of the [child] within the meaning of this definition if the [child] were the legitimate child of his mother and father.

[" voluntary organisation " means a body other than a public or local authority the activities of which are not carried on for profit.

(1A) In this Act, in relation to Scotland, unless the context otherwise requires " actual custody " means care and possession.] [46]

(2) For the purposes of this Act, a person shall be deemed to make arrangements for the adoption of [a child] or to take part in arrangements for the placing of a child in the [actual custody] of another person, if (as the case may be)—

> (a) he enters into or makes any agreement or arrangement for, or for facilitating, the adoption of the [child] by any other person, whether the adoption is effected, or is intended to be effected, in pursuance of an adoption order or otherwise; or
>
> (b) he enters into or makes any agreement or arrangement for, or facilitates, the placing of the child in the [actual custody] of that other person;

or if he initiates or takes part in any negotiations of which the purpose or effect is the conclusion of any agreement or the making of any arrangement therefor, or if he causes another to do so.

(3) This Act applies to citizens of the Republic of Ireland as it applies

---

[53] Words substituted by the Children and Young Persons Act 1969 (c. 54), s. 72 (3), Sched. 5, para. 36.

[54] Words added by Social Work (Scotland) Act 1968 (c. 49), ss. 95 (1), 92 (1), Sched. 8, para. 41.

to British subjects, and references in this Act to British subjects shall be construed accordingly.

(4) Any reference in this Act to any other enactment shall be construed as a reference to that enactment as amended by any subsequent enactment.

Amendment and adaptation of enactments

58.—(1) The amendments specified in the Fourth Schedule to this Act, being amendments consequential on the provisions of this Act, shall be made in the enactments mentioned in that Schedule (and shall, in so far as those enactments have been amended by the Second Schedule to the Children Act 1958, have effect in substitution for the amendments so made).

[*Subsections (2) and (3) repealed by Children Act 1975 (c. 72), Sched. 4.*]

Transitional provisions and repeals

59.—(1) This Act has effect subject to the transitional provisions set out in the Fifth Schedule to this Act.

[*Subsection (2) repealed by Statute Law (Repeals) Act 1974 (c. 22), Sched., Pt. XI.*]

(3) The mention of particular matters in the Fifth Schedule to this Act shall be without prejudice to the general application of section thirty-eight of the Interpretation Act 1889 (which relates to the effect of repeals).

Short title, extent and commencement

60.—(1) This Act may be cited as the Adoption Act 1958.

(2) This Act (except section nineteen, and so much of section fifty-eight as repeals section sixteen of the Adoption Act 1950) does not extend to Northern Ireland.

(3) This Act comes into force on the first day of April, nineteen hundred and fifty-nine.

SCHEDULES

[*Schedules 1 and 2 repealed by Children Act 1975 (c. 72), Sched. 4.*]

THIRD SCHEDULE

PURPOSES FOR WHICH ADOPTION SOCIETIES REGULATIONS MAY BE MADE

1. For regulating the conduct of negotiations entered into by or on behalf of registered adoption societies with persons who, having the [actual custody] of [children], are desirous of causing the [children] to be adopted, and in particular for securing—

(a) that, where the parent or guardian of [a child] proposes to place the [child] at the disposition of the society with a view to the [child] being adopted, he shall be furnished with a memorandum in the prescribed form explaining, in ordinary language, the effect, in relation to his rights as a parent or guardian, of the making of an adoption order in respect of the [child], and calling attention to the provisions of this Act and of any rules made thereunder relating to the consent of a parent or guardian to the making of such an order, and to the provisions of this Act relating to the sending or taking of [children] abroad; and

(b) that, before so placing the [child] at the disposition of the society, the parent or guardian shall sign a document in the prescribed form certifying that he has read and understood the said memorandum.

2. For requiring that the case of every [child] proposed to be delivered by or on behalf of a registered adoption society into the [actual custody] of a person

proposing to adopt him shall be considered by a committee (to be called a "case committee") appointed by the society for the purpose and consisting of not less than three persons.

3. For prescribing, in the case of every such [child] as aforesaid, the inquiries which must be made and the reports which must be obtained by the society in relation to the [child] and the person proposing to adopt him for the purpose of ensuring, so far as may be, the suitability of the [child] and the person proposing to adopt him respectively, and, in particular, for requiring that a report on the health of the [child] signed by a fully registered medical practitioner must be obtained by the society.

4. For securing that no such [child] shall be delivered into the [actual custody] of a person proposing to adopt him by or on behalf of the society until that person has been interviewed by the case committee or by some person on their behalf, until a representative of the committee has inspected any premises in Great Britain in which the person proposing to adopt the [child] intends that the infant should reside permanently, and until the committee have considered the prescribed reports.

5. For requiring a registered adoption society to furnish to the registration authority by whom the society was registered the prescribed accounts and the prescribed information relating to the activities of the society.

6. For making provision for the care and supervision of [children] who have been placed by their parents or guardians at the disposition of adoption societies.

7. For prohibiting or restricting the disclosure of records kept by registered adoption societies and making provision for the safe keeping of such records when they are no longer required.

FOURTH SCHEDULE

[*Amendments to Children Act* 1948 *ante, pp.* 76–103, *and Children Act* 1958 *ante, pp.* 201–211.]

SIXTH SCHEDULE

[*Repealed by Statute Law (Repeals) Act* 1974 (*c.* 22), *Sched., Pt. XI.*]

Mental Health Act 1959

(7 & 8 Eliz. 2, c. 72)

. . . .

Children and young persons in care of local authority

50. In any case where the rights and powers of a parent of a patient, being a child or young person, are vested in a local authority or other person by virtue of—

[(*a*) section 24 of the Children and Young Persons Act 1969 (which relates to the powers and duties of local authorities with respect to persons committed to their care in pursuance of that Act).] [1]

[*Paragraph* (*b*) *repealed by Social Work (Scotland) Act* 1968 (*c.* 49), *ss.* 95 (2), 97 (1), *Sched.* 9 *Pt. II.*]

(*c*) section three of the Children Act 1948 (which relates to children in respect of whom parental rights have been assumed under section two of that Act), [or

(*d*) section 17 of the Social Work (Scotland) Act 1968 (which makes
     corresponding provision for Scotland)] [2]
that authority or person shall be deemed to be the nearest relative of the
patient in preference to any person except the patient's husband or wife
(if any) and except, in a case where the said rights and powers are vested
in a local authority by virtue of subsection (2) of the said section three,
any parent of the patient not being the person on whose account the
resolution mentioned in that subsection was passed.

Nearest relative of infant under guardianship, etc.

51.—(1) Where a patient who has not attained the age of [eighteen] [3]
years—

(*a*) is, by virtue of an order made by a court in the exercise of
     jurisdiction (whether under any enactment or otherwise) in
     respect of the guardianship of infants (including an order under
     section thirty-eight of the Sexual Offences Act 1956), or by virtue
     of a deed or will executed by his father or mother, under the
     guardianship of a person not being his nearest relative under
     the foregoing provisions of this Act, or is under the joint
     guardianship of two persons of whom one is such a person as
     aforesaid; or

(*b*) is, by virtue of an order made by a court in the exercise of such
     jurisdiction as aforesaid or in matrimonial proceedings, or by
     virtue of a separation agreement between his father and mother,
     in the custody of any such person,
the person or persons having the guardianship or custody of the patient
shall, to the exclusion of any other person, be deemed to be his nearest
relative.

(2) Subsection (4) of section forty-nine of this Act shall apply in
relation to a person who is, or who is one of the persons, deemed to be
the nearest relative of a patient by virtue of this section as it applies
in relation to a person who would be the nearest relative under subsection (3) of that section.

(3) A patient shall be treated for the purposes of this section as being
in the custody of another person if he would be in that other person's
custody apart from section thirty-four of this Act.

(4) In this section " court " includes a court in Scotland or Northern
Ireland, and " enactment " includes an enactment of the Parliament of
Northern Ireland.

Legitimacy Act 1959

(7 & 8 Eliz. 2, c. 73)

An Act to amend the Legitimacy Act 1926 to legitimate the children
of certain void marriages, and otherwise to amend the law
relating to children born out of wedlock.   [29th July 1959]

---

[1] Paragraph substituted by Children and Young Persons Act 1969 (c. 54), s. 72 (3),
    Sched. 5, para. 39.
[2] Paragraph added by Social Work (Scotland) Act 1968 (c. 49), ss. 95 (1), 97 (1),
    Sched. 8, para. 49.
[3] Eighteen substituted for twenty-one by Family Law Reform Act 1969 (c. 46), s. 1 (3),
    Sched. 1 Pt. I.

Amendment of Legitimacy Act 1926

1.—(1) Subsection (2) of section one of the Legitimacy Act 1926 (which excludes the operation of that Act in the case of an illegitimate person whose father or mother was married to a third person at the time of the birth) is hereby repealed.

(2) In relation to an illegitimate person to whom it applies by virtue of this section, the Legitimacy Act 1926 shall have effect as if for references to the commencement of that Act there were substituted references to the commencement of this Act.

Legitimacy of children of certain void marriages

2.—(1) Subject to the provisions of this section, the child of a void marriage, whether born before or after the commencement of this Act, shall be treated as the legitimate child of his parents if at the time of the act of intercourse resulting in the birth (or at the time of the celebration of the marriage if later) both or either of the parties reasonably believed that the marriage was valid.

(2) This section applies, and applies only, where the father of the child was domiciled in England at the time of the birth or, if he died before the birth, was so domiciled immediately before his death.

(3) This section, so far as it affects the succession to a dignity or title of honour, or the devolution of property settled therewith, applies only to children born after the commencement of this Act.

(4) This section does not affect any rights under the intestacy of a person who died before the commencement of this Act, and does not (except so far as may be necessary to avoid the severance from a dignity or title of honour of property settled therewith) affect the operation or construction of any disposition coming into operation before the commencement of this Act.

(5) In this section the following expressions have the meanings hereby assigned to them, that is to say—

" void marriage " means a marriage, not being voidable only, in respect of which the High Court has or had jurisdiction to grant a decree of nullity, or would have or would have had such jurisdiction if the parties were domiciled in England;

" disposition " has the same meaning as in the Legitimacy Act 1926;

and any reference in this section to property settled with a dignity or title of honour is a reference to any real or personal property, or any interest in such property, which is limited by any disposition (whether subject to a preceding limitation or charge or not) in such a way as to devolve with the dignity or title as nearly as the law permits, whether or not the disposition contains an express reference to the dignity or title and whether or not the property or some interest in the property may in some event become severed from it.

[*Subsection* (6) *repealed by Matrimonial Causes Act* 1965 (*c.* 72), *s.* 45, *Sched.* 2.]

Custody and guardianship of illegitimate infants

3. [*Section* 3 *repealed by Guardianship of Minors Act* 1971 (*c.* 3), *s.* 18 (2), *Sched.* 2, *in relation to England and Wales.*]

Applications, etc., under s. 1 of Affiliation Proceedings Act 1957

4. An application under section one of the Affiliation Proceedings

Act 1957 may be made by a woman who was a single woman at the date of the birth of the child whether or not she is a single woman at the time of the application and the reference to a single woman in section two of that Act (which relates to the time within which such application may be made) shall be construed accordingly.

Procedure on applications for affiliation orders

5. [*Subsection* (1) *repealed by Affiliation Proceedings (Amendment) Act* 1972 (*c.* 49), *s.* 3 (3).]

(2) In subsection (1) of section sixty of the Magistrates' Courts Act 1952, the words " or of proceedings for an affiliation order " are hereby repealed.

Extent, short title, commencement, and saving

6.—(1) This Act shall not apply to Scotland or Northern Ireland.

(2) This Act may be cited as the Legitimacy Act 1959.

(3) This Act shall come into force on the expiration of three months beginning with the day on which it is passed.

(4) It is hereby declared that nothing in this Act affects the Succession to the Throne.

Marriage (Enabling) Act 1960

(8 & 9 Eliz. 2, c. 29)

An Act to enable a person to marry certain kin of a former spouse.
[13th April 1960]

Certain marriages not to be void

1.—(1) No marriage hereafter contracted (whether in or out of Great Britain) between a man and a woman who is the sister, aunt or niece of a former wife of his (whether living or not), or was formerly the wife of his brother, uncle or nephew (whether living or not), shall by reason of that relationship be void or voidable under any enactment or rule of law applying in Great Britain as a marriage between persons within the prohibited degrees of affinity.

(2) In the foregoing subsection words of kinship apply equally to kin of the whole and of the half blood.

(3) This section does not validate a marriage, if either party to it is at the time of the marriage domiciled in a country outside Great Britain, and under the law of that country there cannot be a valid marriage between the parties.

(4) The enactments mentioned in the Schedule to this Act are hereby repealed to the extent specified in the third column of the Schedule.

Short title, citation and extent

2.—(1) This Act may be cited as the Marriage (Enabling) Act 1960, and this Act and the Marriage Acts 1949 to 1958 may be cited together as the Marriage Acts 1949 to 1960.

(2) This Act shall not apply to Northern Ireland.

SCHEDULE

ENACTMENTS REPEALED

Session and Chapter	Short Title	Extent of Repeal
7 Edw. 7. c. 47.	The Deceased Wife's Sister's Marriage Act 1907.	The whole Act.
11 & 12 Geo. 5. c. 24.	The Deceased Brother's Widow's Marriage Act 1921.	The whole Act.
21 & 22 Geo. 5. c. 31.	The Marriage (Prohibited Degrees of Relationship) Act 1931.	The whole Act.
12, 13 & 14 Geo. 6. c. 76.	The Marriage Act 1949.	Subsections (2) and (3) of section one; Part II of the First Schedule.

Matrimonial Proceedings (Magistrates' Courts) Act 1960 [1]

(8 & 9 ELIZ. 2, c. 48)

An Act to amend and consolidate certain enactments relating to matrimonial proceedings in magistrates' courts and to make in the case of other proceedings the same amendments as to the maximum weekly rate of the maintenance payments which may be ordered by a magistrates' court as are made in the case of matrimonial proceedings.   [29th July 1960]

Jurisdiction of magistrates' court in matrimonial proceedings

1.—(1) A married woman or a married man may apply by way of complaint to a magistrates' court for an order under this Act against the other party to the marriage on any of the following causes of complaint arising during the subsistence of the marriage, that is to say, that the defendant—

(*a*) has deserted the complainant; or

(*b*) has been guilty of persistent cruelty to—

    (i) the complainant; or

    (ii) an infant child of the complainant; or

    (iii) an infant child of the defendant who, at the time of the cruelty, was a child of the family; or

(*c*) has been found guilty—

    (i) on indictment, of any offence which involved an assault upon the complainant; or

    (ii) by a magistrates' court, of an offence against the complainant under section twenty, forty-two, forty-three or forty-seven of the Offences against the Person Act 1861, being, in the case of the said section forty-two, an offence for which the defendant has been sentenced to imprisonment or any other form of detention for a term of not less than one month; or

---

[1] Explained, as regards England, by Matrimonial Causes Act 1965 (c. 72), s. 42 (2), and extended by Matrimonial Proceedings (Polygamous Marriages) Act 1972 (c. 38), s. 1 (1) (*f*).

      (iii) of, or of an attempt to commit, an offence under any
of sections one to twenty-nine of the Sexual Offences Act 1956,
or under section one of the Indecency with Children Act 1960,
against an infant child of the complainant, or against an infant
child of the defendant who, at the time of the commission of or
attempt to commit the offence, was a child of the family; or

(*d*) has committed adultery; or

(*e*) while knowingly suffering from a venereal disease has insisted on,
or has without the complainant being aware of the presence of
that disease permitted, sexual intercourse between the complainant and the defendant; or

(*f*) is for the time being an habitual drunkard or a drug addict; or

(*g*) being the husband, has compelled the wife to submit herself to
prostitution or has been guilty of such conduct as was likely to
result and has resulted in the wife's submitting herself to prostitution; or

(*h*) being the husband, has wilfully neglected to provide reasonable
maintenance for the wife or for any child of the family who is,
or would but for that neglect have been, a dependant; or

(*i*) being the wife, has wilfully neglected to provide, or to make a
proper contribution towards, reasonable maintenance for the
husband or for any child of the family who is, or would but for
that neglect have been, a dependant, in a case where, by reason
of the impairment of the husband's earning capacity through
age, illness, or disability of mind or body, and having regard to
any resources of the husband and the wife respectively which are,
or should properly be made, available for the purpose, it is reasonable in all the circumstances to expect the wife so to provide or
contribute.

(2) A magistrates' court shall [subject to section 11 of the Administration of Justice Act 1964, and any determination of the committee of
magistrates thereunder] [2] have jurisdiction to hear a complaint under
this section—

(*a*) if at the date of the making of the complaint either the complainant or the defendant ordinarily resides within the petty sessions
area for which that court acts; or

(*b*) except in the case of a complaint by virtue of paragraph (*c*) of
the foregoing subsection, if the cause of complaint arose wholly
or partly within the said petty sessions area; or

(*c*) in the case of a complaint by virtue of the said paragraph (*c*), if
the offence or attempt to which the complaint relates occurred
within the said petty sessions area.

(3) The jurisdiction conferred by the last foregoing subsection—

(*a*) shall be exercisable notwithstanding that the defendant resides
in Scotland or Northern Ireland if the complainant resides in
England and the parties last ordinarily resided together as
man and wife in England; and

(*b*) is hereby declared to be exercisable where the complainant
resides in Scotland or Northern Ireland if the defendant resides
in England:

Provided that nothing in this subsection shall be construed as enabling
a court to include in an order under this Act against a person residing in
Scotland or Northern Ireland a provision such as is mentioned in paragraph (*a*) of subsection (1) of section two of this Act.

[2] Words added by Administration of Justice Act 1964 (c. 42), s. 39 (2), Sched. 3 Pt. II,
para. 27.

Order by magistrates' court in matrimonial proceedings

2.—(1) Subject to the proviso to subsection (3) of section one of this Act and to the provisions of this section and of section four of this Act, on hearing a complaint under the said section one by either of the parties to a marriage the court may make an order (in this Act referred to as a " matrimonial order ") containing any one or more of the following provisions, namely—

(a) a provision that the complainant be no longer bound to cohabit with the defendant (which provision while in force shall have effect in all respects as a decree of judicial separation);

(b) a provision that the husband shall pay to the wife such weekly sum [. . .] [3] as the court considers reasonable in all the circumstances of the case;

(c) where, by reason of the impairment of the husband's earning capacity through age, illness, or disability of mind or body, it appears to the court reasonable in all the circumstances so to order, a provision that the wife shall pay to the husband such weekly sum [. . .] [3] as the court considers reasonable in all the circumstances of the case;

(d) a provision for the legal custody of any child of the family who is under the age of sixteen years;

(e) if it appears to the court that there are exceptional circumstances making it impracticable or undesirable for any such child as aforesaid to be entrusted to either of the parties or to any other individual, a provision committing the care of the child to a specified local authority, being the [local social services authority for the area] [3a] in which the child was, in the opinion of the court, resident immediately before being so committed;

(f) [3b] if, in the case of any child committed by the order to the legal custody of any person, it appears to the court that there are exceptional circumstances making it desirable that the child should be under the supervision of an independent person, a provision that the child be under the supervision—

　(i) of a probation officer appointed for or assigned to the petty sessions area in which in the opinion of the court the child is or will be resident; or

　(ii) of a specified local authority, being [a local social services authority] [3a]

(g) a provision for access to any child of the family by either of the parties or by any other person who is a parent of that child, in a case where the child is committed by the order to the legal custody of a person other than that party or parent;

(h) a provision for the making by the defendant or by the complainant or by each of them, for the maintenance of any child of the family, of [weekly payments] [3] being—

　(i) if and for so long as the child is under the age of sixteen years, payments to any person to whom the legal custody of the child is for the time being committed by the order, or by any other order made by a court in England and for the time being in force, or, during any period when the child is in the care of a local authority under the order, to that local authority;

---

[3] Words repealed and substituted by Maintenance Orders Act 1968 (c. 36), s. 1, Sched.
[3a] Words substituted by Local Government Act 1972 (c. 70), s. 195 (6), Sched. 23, para. 10.
[3b] The supervision of a child subject to a court order under s. 2 (1) (f) (ii) of this Act is conferred as a function of social services committee by Local Authority Social Services Act 1970 (c. 42), s. 2 (1), Sched. 1.

        (ii) if it appears to the court that the child is, or will be, or if such payments were made would be, a dependant though over the age of sixteen years, and that it is expedient that such payments should be made in respect of that child while such a dependant, payments to such person (who may be the child or, during any such period as aforesaid, the local authority) as may be specified in the order, for such period during which the child is over that age but under the age of twenty-one years as may be so specified.

(2) Where, on a complaint under section one of this Act, the court makes a matrimonial order on the ground that the defendant is for the time being an habitual drunkard or a drug addict, and the order contains such a provision as is mentioned in paragraph (*a*) of the foregoing subsection, then, if in all the circumstances, and after giving each party to the proceedings an opportunity of making representations, the court thinks it proper so to do, the court may include in that order—

    (*a*) if the complainant is the husband, a provision such as is mentioned in paragraph (*b*) of the foregoing subsection; or

    (*b*) if the complainant is the wife, a provision such as is mentioned in paragraph (*c*) of that subsection;

but save as aforesaid the said paragraph (*b*) or (*c*) shall not authorise the court to require any payment such as is therein mentioned to be made by the complainant.

(3) The court hearing a complaint under section one of this Act shall not make a matrimonial order containing a provision such as is mentioned in paragraph (*a*), (*b*) or (*c*) of subsection (1) of this section—

    (*a*) on the ground that the defendant has committed an act of adultery, unless the court is satisfied that the complainant has not condoned or connived at, or by wilful neglect or misconduct conduced to, that act of adultery; or

    (*b*) where the complainant is proved to have committed an act of adultery during the subsistence of the marriage, unless the court is satisfied that the defendant has condoned or connived at, or by wilful neglect or misconduct conduced to, that act of adultery.

(4) The court shall not make an order containing—

    (*a*) such a provision as is mentioned in paragraph (*d*) or (*e*) of subsection (1) of this section in respect of any child with respect to whose custody an order made by a court in England is for the time being in force;

    (*b*) such a provision as is mentioned in paragraph (*e*), (*f*) or (*g*) of the said subsection (1) in respect of any child who is already for the purposes of Part II of the Children Act 1948 in the care of a local authority;

    (*c*) such a provision as is mentioned in the said paragraph (*f*) or (*g*) in respect of any child in respect of whom the order contains such a provision as is mentioned in the said paragraph (*e*).

(5) In considering whether any, and if so what, provision should be included in a matrimonial order by virtue of paragraph (*h*) of subsection (1) of this section for payments by one of the parties in respect of a child who is not a child of that party, the court shall have regard to the extent, if any, to which that party had, on or after the acceptance of the child as one of the family, assumed responsibility for the child's maintenance, and to the liability of any person other than a party to the marriage to maintain the child.

Supplementary provisions with respect to order for care or supervision of child

    3.—(1) Before including in a matrimonial order a provision committing a child to the care of a local authority, the court shall inform the authority of their proposal so to do and hear any representations from the authority, including any representations as to the inclusion in the order by virtue of paragraph (*h*) of subsection (1) of section two of this Act of provision for payments to the authority.

(2) Upon the inclusion in a matrimonial order of a provision committing a child as aforesaid—

(*a*) Part II of the Children Act 1948 (which relates to the treatment of children in the care of a local authority) except section seventeen thereof (which relates to arrangements for the emigration of such children); and

(*b*) for the purposes only of contributions by the child himself at a time when he has attained the age of sixteen and is engaged in remunerative full-time work, Part III of that Act (which relates to contributions towards the maintenance of children in the care of a local authority),

shall apply as if the child had been received by the local authority into their care under section one of that Act.

(3) While such a provision as aforesaid remains in force with respect to any child, the child shall continue in the care of the local authority notwithstanding any claim by a parent or other person.

(4) Any such provision as aforesaid shall cease to have effect as respects any child when the child attains the age of eighteen years.

(5) Each parent or guardian of any child for the time being in the care of a local authority under a matrimonial order shall give notice to the authority of any change of address of that parent or guardian, and any person who without reasonable excuse fails to comply with this subsection shall be liable on summary conviction to a fine not exceeding [ten pounds].[4]

(6) Where a matrimonial order provides for a child to be under the supervision of a probation officer, that officer shall be selected in like manner as if the order were a probation order.

[(7) Where a matrimonial order provides for a child to be under the supervision of a local authority, the functions of the authority under that order shall be deemed to be included among the functions specified in subsection (1) of section thirty-nine of the Children Act 1948 (being the functions for the purposes of which a local authority are required to establish a children's committee), and any duties falling to be discharged by the authority by virtue of the order shall be discharged through an officer of the authority employed in connection with functions specified as aforesaid.][4a]

(8) For the purposes of any matrimonial order providing for a child to be under the supervision of a probation officer or of a local authority, without prejudice to section eight of this Act, provision may be made by rules for substituting from time to time a probation officer appointed for or assigned to a different petty sessions area, or, as the case may be, a different local authority, if in the opinion of the court the child is or will be resident in that petty sessions area or, as the case may be, in the area of that authority.

(9) Any provision of a matrimonial order that a child be under the supervision of a probation officer or local authority shall cease to have effect as respects any child when the child attains the age of sixteen years.

[4] Maximum fine increased from five pounds by Criminal Justice Act 1967 (c. 80), s. 92, Sched. 3 Pt. I.

[4a] Subsection repealed by Local Authority Social Services Act 1970 (c. 42).

Special powers and duties with respect to children

4.—(1) Where the court has begun to hear a complaint—

    (*a*) under section one of this Act; or

    (*b*) for the variation of a matrimonial order—

        (i) by the revocation, addition or alteration of provision for the legal custody of a child; or

        (ii) by the revocation of a provision committing a child to the care of a local authority or a provision that a child be under the supervision of a probation officer or local authority; or

    (*c*) for the revocation of a matrimonial order consisting of or including any such provision as aforesaid,

then, whether or not the court makes the order for which the complaint is made, but subject to subsections (4) and (5) of section two of this Act and subsection (6) of this section, the court may make a matrimonial order containing, or, as the case may be, vary the matrimonial order so that it contains, any provision such as is mentioned in paragraphs (*d*) to (*h*) of subsection (1) of the said section two which, after giving each party to the proceedings an opportunity of making representations, the court thinks proper in all the circumstances; and the court shall not dismiss or make its final order on any complaint in a case where the powers conferred on the court by this subsection are or may be exercisable until it has decided whether or not, and if so how, those powers should be exercised.

(2) Where, on hearing such a complaint as aforesaid or a complaint for the variation of a matrimonial order by the revocation, addition or alteration of provision for access to a child, the court, after it has made any decision which falls to be made on the complaint with respect to any provision such as is mentioned in paragraphs (*a*) to (*c*) of subsection (1) of section two of this Act, is of the opinion that it has not sufficient information to make the decision required by the foregoing subsection or, as the case may be, to make a decision as to access to the child, the court may call for a report, either oral or in writing, by a probation officer, [or by such an officer of a local authority as is mentioned in subsection (7)] [4b] of section three of this Act, with respect to such matters as the court may specify, being matters appearing to the court to be relevant to that decision [or for such a report by an officer of a local authority employed in connection with functions of the authority under the Children and Young Persons Acts 1933 to 1969.] [4c]

(3) A report made in pursuance of subsection (2) of this section shall be made to the court at a hearing of the complaint unless it is in writing in which case—

    (*a*) a copy of the report shall be given to each party to the proceedings or to his counsel or solicitor either before or during a hearing of the complaint; and

    (*b*) if the court thinks fit, the report, or such parts of the report as the court requires, shall be read aloud at a hearing of the complaint.

(4) The court may and, if requested to do so at the hearing by a party to the proceedings or his counsel or solicitor, shall, require the officer by whom the report was made to give evidence on or with respect to the matters referred to in the report and if the officer gives such evidence, any party to the proceedings may give or call evidence on or with

---

[4b] Words in square brackets repealed by Guardianship Act 1973 (c. 29), s. 8, in relation to England and Wales.

[4c] Words added by *ibid.*, in relation to England and Wales.

respect to any such matter or any matter referred to in the officer's evidence.

(4A) Subject to the next following subsection, the court may take account of—

    (*a*) any statement contained in a report made at a hearing of the complaint or of which copies have been given to the parties or their representatives in accordance with subsection (3) (*a*) of this section; and

    (*b*) any evidence given by the officer under subsection (4) of this section,

in so far as the statement or evidence relates to the matters specified by the court under subsection (2) of this section, notwithstanding any enactment or rule of law to the contrary.] [4d]

(5) A report in pursuance of subsection (2) of this section shall not include anything said by either of the parties to a marriage in the course of an interview which took place with, or in the presence of, a probation officer with a view to the reconciliation of those parties, unless both parties have consented to its inclusion; and if anything so said is included without the consent of both those parties as part of any statement made or read aloud under subsection (3) of this section, then, unless both these parties agree otherwise, that part of the statement shall, for the purposes of the giving of evidence under the said subsection (3) and for the purposes of [subsections 4 and 4A] [4d] of this section, be deemed not to be contained in the statement.

(6) On the hearing of a complaint under section one of this Act in the case of which there is a child of the family who is not a child of both the parties, other than a child with respect to whose custody an order made by a court in England is for the time being in force—

    (*a*) subsections (1) and (3) of this section shall have effect as if any person who, though not a party to the proceedings, is a parent of that child and who is present or represented by counsel or solicitor at the hearing were a party to the proceedings; and

    (*b*) if any such person is not so present or represented, the court shall not make a matrimonial order on the complaint unless it is proved to the satisfaction of the court, on oath or in such other manner as may be prescribed by rules, that such steps have been taken as may be so prescribed with a view to giving notice to that person of the making of the complaint and of the time and place appointed for the hearing:

Provided that nothing in paragraph (*b*) of this subsection shall require notice to be given to any person as the father of an illegitimate child unless that person has been adjudged by a court to be the father of that child.

(7) Where for the purposes of this section the court adjourns the hearing of any complaint, then, subject to subsection (2) of section forty-six of the Magistrates' Courts Act 1952 (which requires adequate notice of the time and place of the resumption of the hearing to be given to the parties), the court may resume the hearing at the time and place appointed notwithstanding the absence of both or all of the parties.

(8) In any proceedings in which the powers conferred on the court by subsection (1) of this section are or may be exercisable, the question whether or not, and if so how, those powers should be exercised shall be excepted from the issues arising in the proceedings which, under the proviso to subsection (1) of section sixty of the Magistrates' Courts Act 1952, must be determined by the court before the court may direct a probation officer to make to the court under that section a report on the means of the parties.

[4d] Substituted by Children Act 1975 (c. 72), s. 91.

Refusal of order in case more suitable for High Court

5. Where on hearing any complaint under section one of this Act a magistrates' court is of the opinion that any of the matters in question between the parties would be more conveniently dealt with by the High Court, the magistrates' court may refuse to make a matrimonial order on the complaint, and no appeal shall lie from that refusal; but if in any proceedings in the High Court relating to or comprising the same subject matter as that complaint the High Court so orders, the complaint shall be re-heard and determined by a magistrates' court acting for the same petty sessions area as the first-mentioned court.

Interim order by magistrates' court or High Court

6.—(1) Where in the case of any complaint made to a magistrates' court under section one of this Act—

 (*a*) the magistrates' court, at any time before making its final order on the complaint, adjourns the hearing of the complaint for any period exceeding one week; or

 (*b*) the magistrates' court refuses by virtue of section five of this Act to make a matrimonial order on the complaint; or

 (*c*) after such a refusal by the magistrates' court as aforesaid, or on an appeal under section eleven of this Act from, or from the refusal of, a matrimonial order on the complaint, the High Court by virtue of the said section five or eleven orders that the complaint shall be re-heard by a magistrates' court,

then, in a case falling within paragraph (*a*) or (*b*) of this subsection the magistrates' court, or in a case falling within paragraph (*c*) thereof the High Court, may make an order under this section (in this Act referred to as an " interim order ").

 (2) An interim order may contain—

 (*a*) any such provision as is mentioned in paragraph (*b*), (*c*) or (*h*) of subsection (1) of section two of this Act; and

 (*b*) where by reason of special circumstances the court thinks it proper, but subject to subsection (4) of the said section two, any provision such as is mentioned in paragraph (*d*) or (*g*) of that subsection;

and for the purposes of paragraph (*a*) of this subsection the reference in sub-paragraph (i) of the said paragraph (*h*) to any person to whom the legal custody of a child is for the time being committed by an order shall be construed as including a reference to any person, being one of the parties or a parent of the child, who for the time being has the care of the child; and an appeal against an interim order shall not lie if the appeal relates only to such a provision of the order as is mentioned in paragraph (*a*) of this subsection.

 (3) Without prejudice to sections seven, eight and eleven of this Act, an interim order in connection with any complaint shall cease to be in force on whichever of the following dates occurs first, that is to say—

 (*a*) the date, if any, specified for the purpose in the interim order;

 (*b*) the date of the expiration of the period of three months beginning with the date of—

  (i) the making of the interim order; or

  (ii) if the interim order is one of two or more such orders made with respect to the same complaint by virtue of the same paragraph of subsection (1) of this section, the making of the first of those interim orders;

 (*c*) the date of the making of a final order on, or the dismissal of, the complaint by a magistrates' court.

 (4) An interim order made by the High Court under this section on ordering that a complaint be re-heard by a magistrates' court shall, for

the purposes of its enforcement and for the purposes of section eight of this Act, be treated as if it were an order of that magistrates' court and not of the High Court.

(5) The powers conferred on the High Court by this section shall be without prejudice to the powers of that court on an appeal under section eleven of this Act from the refusal of an interim order by a magistrates' court.

Suspension or cessation of orders

7.—(1) Where a matrimonial or interim order is made while the parties to the marriage in question are cohabiting—

(a) the order shall not be enforceable and no liability shall accrue thereunder until they have ceased to cohabit; and

(b) if in the case of a matrimonial order they continue to cohabit for the period of three months beginning with the date of the making of the order, the order shall cease to have effect at the expiration of that period:

Provided that, unless the court in making the order directs otherwise, this subsection shall not apply to any provision of the order—

(i) committing a child to the legal custody of a person other than one of the parties, or for access to that child by either of the parties or by any other person who is a parent of the child; or

(ii) committing a child to the care of a local authority or providing for a child to be under the supervision of a probation officer or local authority; or

(iii) for the making by either or each of the parties to a person other than one of the parties of payments for the maintenance of a child.

(2) Without prejudice to section eight of this Act, any provision of a matrimonial or interim order other than such a provision as is referred to in the proviso to the foregoing subsection shall cease to have effect upon the parties to the marriage in question resuming cohabitation.

(3) Where after the making by a magistrates' court of—

(a) a matrimonial order consisting of or including a provision such as is mentioned in paragraph (b), (c) or (h) of subsection (1) of section two of this Act; or

(b) an interim order,

proceedings between, and relating to the marriage of, the parties to the proceedings in which that order was made have been commenced in the High Court [or the county court,] [4e] [the court in which the proceedings or any application made therein are or is pending] [4f] may, if it thinks fit, direct that the said provision or, as the case may be, the interim order shall cease to have effect on such date as [may be specified in the direction].[4f]

[(4) Where after the making by a magistrates' court of a matrimonial order consisting of or including a provision such as is mentioned in paragraph (b) or (c) of section 2 (1) of this Act the marriage of the parties to the proceedings in which that order was made is dissolved or annulled but the order continues in force, then, subject to subsection (5) of this section, that order or, as the case may be, that provision thereof shall cease to have effect on the remarriage of the party in whose favour it was made, except in relation to any arrears due under it on the date of such remarriage and shall not be capable of being revived.

(5) Subsection (4) of this section shall not apply where the party in whose favour such an order as is therein mentioned was made remarried

[4e] Words added by Matrimonial Proceedings and Property Act 1970 (c. 45), s. 33.
[4f] Words substituted by *ibid.*

before the commencement of the Matrimonial Proceedings and Property Act 1970.

(6) For the avoidance of doubt it is hereby declared that references in this section to remarriage include references to a marriage which is by law void or voidable.] [4g]

Revocation, revival and variation of orders

8.—(1) Subject to section four of this Act, section fifty-three of the Magistrates' Courts Act 1952 (which provides for the revocation, revival or variation, by order on complaint, of an order of a magistrates' court for the periodical payment of money) and the proviso to subsection (1) of section fifty-five of that Act (which relates to costs on the hearing of such a complaint) shall apply for the purpose of the revocation, revival or variation of any matrimonial or interim order as if that order were an order for the periodical payment of money, whether or not it is in fact such an order; and a complaint for the said purpose may be heard whatever the time at which it is made; and for the avoidance of doubt it is hereby declared that for the purposes of this Act the expression " variation " in relation to any order includes the addition to that order of any provision authorised by this Act to be included in such an order:

Provided that, without prejudice to the powers and duties of the court under section four of this Act, nothing in this section shall authorise the making of a complaint—

(a) for the variation of an order by the addition of a provision committing a child to the care of a local authority or providing for a child to be under the supervision of a probation officer or local authority; or

(b) for the revival of any such provision as aforesaid which has ceased to be in force; or

(c) for the variation of a provision committing a child to the care of a local authority.

(2) Where on a complaint for the revocation of a matrimonial order it is proved that the parties to the marriage in question have resumed cohabitation or that the party on whose complaint the order was made has during the subsistence of the marriage committed an act of adultery, the court shall revoke the order:

Provided that—

(a) the court shall not be bound by reason of such a resumption of cohabitation to revoke any provision of the order such as is mentioned in the proviso to subsection (1) of section seven of this Act;

(b) the court shall not revoke the order by reason of such an act of adultery as aforesaid—

(i) except at the request of the person who was the defendant to the proceedings in which the order was made; or

(ii) if the court is of the opinion that the person aforesaid has condoned or connived at, or by wilful neglect or misconduct conduced to, that act of adultery,

and shall not be bound by reason of that act of adultery to revoke any provision of the order included therein by virtue of paragraphs (d) to (h) of subsection (1) of section two of this Act.

(3) The court before which there fall to be heard any proceedings for the variation of a provision for the payment of money contained in a matrimonial or interim order may, if it thinks fit, order that those

[4g] Subsections (4) (5) and (6) added by *ibid.*, s. 30 (1).

proceedings and any other proceedings being heard therewith shall be treated for the purposes of the Magistrates' Courts Act 1952, as domestic proceedings; and that Act shall thereupon have effect accordingly notwithstanding anything in subsection (1) of section fifty-six thereof; and no appeal shall lie from, or from the refusal of, an order under this subsection.

Complaint for variation, etc., by or against person outside England

9.—(1) It is hereby declared that any jurisdiction conferred on a court by virtue of section eight of this Act is exercisable notwithstanding that the proceedings are brought by or against a person residing outside England:

Provided that a matrimonial order shall not be varied by the addition of such a provision as is mentioned in paragraph (*a*) of subsection (1) of section two of this Act if the defendant to the complaint for the variation resides outside England.

(2) Where, at the time and place appointed for the hearing of a complaint by virtue of section eight of this Act, the defendant does not appear but—

(*a*) the court is satisfied that there is reason to believe that the defendant has been outside the United Kingdom during the whole of the period beginning one month before the making of the complaint and ending with the date of the hearing; and

(*b*) it is proved to the satisfaction of the court, on oath or in such other manner as may be prescribed by rules, that such steps have been taken as may be so prescribed with a view to giving notice to the defendant of the making of the complaint and of the time and place aforesaid,

the court may, if it thinks it reasonable in all the circumstances so to do, proceed to hear and determine the complaint at the time and place appointed for the hearing or for any adjourned hearing in like manner as if the defendant had appeared at that time and place.

(3) Where a complaint for the revocation or variation of any provision for the making of payments by the complainant to the defendant is heard by virtue of subsection (2) of this section in the absence of the defendant, and the court is satisfied that there is reason to believe that during the period of six months immediately preceding the making of the complaint the defendant was continuously outside the United Kingdom or was not in the United Kingdom on more than thirty days, then, if in all the circumstances, and having regard to any communication to the court in writing purporting to be from the defendant, the court thinks it reasonable so to do, the court may make the order for which the complaint is made or make such variation in that provision by way of reducing the amount of the payments as the court thinks fit.

(4) For the purposes of the hearing by virtue of subsection (2) of this section, in the absence of the defendant, of a complaint for the revocation or variation of a matrimonial order under which payments fall to be made by the complainant to the defendant through the clerk of a magistrates' court, a certificate in writing by that clerk dated not earlier than ten days before the date of the hearing and stating that, during the period mentioned in paragraph (*a*) of subsection (2) of this section (or so much thereof as precedes the date of the certificate) or, as the case may be, during the period mentioned in subsection (3) of this section—

(*a*) every payment made under the order has been forwarded by the clerk to an address outside the United Kingdom; and

(*b*) the defendant has not to the knowledge of the clerk been in the United Kingdom at any time or, in the case of the period mentioned in the said subsection (3), on more than thirty days, shall be sufficient evidence that there is reason to believe as mentioned in paragraph (*a*) of the said subsection (2) or, as the case may be, in the said subsection (3).

(5) Nothing in this section shall be construed as authorising the making of an order by virtue of section eight of this Act against a person residing outside England for the inclusion in a matrimonial or interim order of any provision requiring payments to be made by that person exceeding in amount those, if any, required to be made by him under the order sought to be varied, unless the order by virtue of the said section eight is made at a hearing at which either that person appears or the requirements of subsection (3) of section forty-seven of the Magistrates' Courts Act 1952 with respect to proof of service of summons or appearance on a previous occasion are satisfied in respect of that person.

Parties to complaint for variation, etc.

10.—(1) A complaint by virtue of section eight of this Act for the revocation, revival or variation of a matrimonial or interim order may be made in the following cases by the following persons in addition to the parties to the marriage in question, that is to say—

(*a*) where a child of the family is not a child of both the parties to the marriage, a complaint relating to any provision with respect to the child such as is mentioned in paragraph (*d*) or (*g*) of subsection (1) of section two of this Act may be made by any person who, though not one of the parties to the marriage, is a parent of the child;

(*b*) a complaint relating to payments under the order such as are mentioned in paragraph (*h*) of the said subsection (1) may be made by any person to whom such payments fall, or upon the making of the order for which the complaint is made would fall, to be made;

(*c*) where under the order a child is for the time being committed to the legal custody of some person other than one of the parents or to the care of a local authority, a complaint relating to any provision with respect to the child such as is mentioned in the said paragraph (*d*) or (*g*) may be made by any person to whose legal custody the child is committed by the order or who seeks the legal custody of the child by the complaint;

(*d*) where under the order a child is for the time being under the supervision of a probation officer or local authority, the probation officer or local authority may make a complaint relating to any provision with respect to the child such as is mentioned in the said paragraphs (*d*), (*g*) and (*h*);

(*e*) a complaint for the revocation of a provision of the order committing a child to the care of a local authority may be made by that local authority or by any person to whose legal custody the child is for the time being committed by the order or who by the same complaint also seeks the legal custody of the child;

(*f*) a complaint for the variation or revocation of a provision of the order that a child be under the supervision of a probation officer or local authority may be made by that probation officer or local authority, or by any person to whose legal custody the child is for the time being committed by the order or who by the same complaint also seeks the legal custody of the child.

(2) Provision may be made by rules as to what persons shall be made defendants to any such complaint as aforesaid; and where in the case of any such complaint there are two or more defendants, the powers of the court under subsection (1) of section fifty-five of the Magistrates'

Courts Act 1952 shall be deemed to include power, whatever adjudication the court makes on the complaint, to order any of the parties to pay the whole or part of the costs of all or any of the other parties.

Appeals

11.—(1) Subject to section five, subsection (2) of section six and subsection (3) of section eight of this Act, an appeal shall lie to the High Court from, and from the refusal or revocation of, or a refusal to revoke, a matrimonial or interim order by a magistrates' court.

(2) Subject to subsection (3) of this section, any order of the High Court on an appeal under this section shall for the purposes of the enforcement of the order and for the purposes of section eight of this Act be treated as if it were an order of the magistrates' court from which the appeal was brought and not of the High Court.

(3) The last foregoing subsection shall not apply to an order directing that a complaint shall be re-heard by a magistrates' court or, without prejudice to the provisions of subsection (4) of section six of this Act, to an order to which the said subsection (4) applies.

Time limit for complaint on ground of adultery

12.—(1) A complaint under section one of this Act on the ground of the commission of an act of adultery by the defendant may be heard if it is made within six months of the date when that act of adultery first became known to the complainant.

(2) Such a complaint as aforesaid shall not be dismissed by reason only that it was not made within the six months allowed by the foregoing subsection if the court is satisfied that the complainant—

(*a*) during the said six months or any part thereof was serving outside the United Kingdom in Her Majesty's forces, or as the master or a member of the crew of a British ship or of a ship for the time being chartered on behalf of Her Majesty; and

(*b*) on the date of the making of the complaint, had not been in the United Kingdom for a continuous period of three months since the date of his return to the United Kingdom after the expiration of the said six months or, if he was in the United Kingdom at the expiration of those six months, the date of his last return to the United Kingdom during those six months.

(3) For the purposes of the last foregoing subsection—

(*a*) a certificate purporting to be signed by an officer designated for the purpose by the [Defence Council] [5] that the complainant during any period or periods was serving outside the United Kingdom in Her Majesty's naval, military or air forces, as the case may be; and

(*b*) a certificate purporting to be signed by a person designated for the purpose by the Minister of Transport that the complainant during any period or periods was serving outside the United Kingdom as the master or a member of the crew of a British ship or of a ship for the time being chartered on behalf of Her Majesty,

shall be evidence of the facts so certified and that the complainant was not in the United Kingdom during any such period or periods.

Enforcement, etc.

13.—(1) The payment of any sum of money directed to be paid by

[5] Words substituted by S.I. 1964/488.

an order made by virtue of this Act may be enforced in the same manner as the payment of money is enforced under an affiliation order.

(2) Without prejudice to section fifty-two of the Magistrates' Courts Act 1952 (which relates to the power of the court to direct payments to be made through the clerk of a magistrates' court), the court making an order by virtue of this Act for payment of a periodical sum by one person to another may direct that it shall be paid to some third party on that other person's behalf instead of directly to that other person; and, for the purposes of any order made by virtue of this Act, the said section fifty-two shall have effect as if, in subsection (2) thereof, for the words " the applicant for the order " in the first place where those words occur there were substituted the words " the person to whom the payments under the order fall to be made ".

(3) Where an order made by virtue of this Act contains a provision committing a child to the legal custody of any person, or to the care of a local authority, a copy of the order may be served on any other person in whose actual custody the child for the time being is; and thereupon that provision may, without prejudice to any other remedy which may be available, be enforced under subsection (3) of section fifty-four of the Magistrates' Courts Act 1952 as if it were an order of the court requiring that other person to give up the child to the person to whom the legal custody of the child is committed or, as the case may be, to the local authority.

(4) Any person for the time being under an obligation to make payments under any order made in proceedings brought by virtue of this Act shall give notice to such persons, if any, as may be specified in the order of any change of address; and any person who without reasonable excuse fails to comply with this subsection shall be liable on summary conviction to a fine not exceeding [ten pounds].[6]

[(5) A person shall not be entitled to enforce through the High Court or any county court the payment of any arrears due under an order made by virtue of this Act without the leave of that court if those arrears became due more than twelve months before proceedings to enforce the payment of them are begun.

(6) The court hearing an application for the grant of leave under subsection (5) of this section may refuse leave, or may grant leave subject to such restrictions and conditions (including conditions as to the allowing of time for payment or the making of payment by instalments) as that court thinks proper, or may remit the payment of such arrears or any part thereof.

(7) An application for the grant of leave under the said subsection (5) shall be made in such manner as may be prescribed by rules of court.] [7]

[13A.—(1) Where—

    (*a*) an order to which this section applies or a provision thereof has ceased to have effect by reason of the remarriage of the person entitled to payments under the order, and

    (*b*) the person liable to make payments under the order made payments in accordance with it in respect of a period after the date of such remarriage in the mistaken belief that the order or provision was still subsisting,

no proceedings in respect of a cause of action arising out of the circumstances mentioned in paragraphs (*a*) and (*b*) above shall be maintainable by the person so liable or his or her personal representatives against the person so entitled or her or his personal representatives, but on an

[6] Maximum fine increased from five pounds by Criminal Justice Act 1967 (c. 80), s. 92, Sched. 3 Pt. I.

[7] Words added by Matrimonial Proceedings and Property Act 1970 (c. 45), s. 32.

application made under this section the court may exercise the powers conferred on it by the following subsection.

This section applies to an order in relation to which subsection (4) of section 7 of this Act, as amended by the Matrimonial Proceedings and Property Act 1970, applies.

(2) The court may order the respondent to an application made under this section to pay to the applicant a sum equal to the amount of the payments made in respect of the period mentioned in subsection (1) (*b*) of this section or, if it appears to the court that it would be unjust to make that order, it may either order the respondent to pay to the applicant such lesser sum as it thinks fit or dismiss the application.

(3) An application under this section may be made by the person liable to make payments under an order to which this section applies or his or her personal representatives and may be made against the person entitled to payments under the order or her or his personal representatives.

(4) An application under this section may be made in proceedings in the High Court or a county court for leave to enforce, or the enforcement of, the payment of arrears under an order to which this section applies, but except as aforesaid such an application shall be made to a county court, and accordingly references in this section to the court are references to the High Court or a county court, as the circumstances require.

(5) An order under this section for the payment of any sum may provide for the payment of that sum by instalments of such amount as may be specified in the order.

(6) The jurisdiction conferred on a county court by this section shall be exercisable by a county court notwithstanding that by reason of the amount claimed in an application under this section the jurisdiction would not but for this subsection be exercisable by a county court.

(7) Section 13 (1) and (2) of this Act shall not apply to an order under this section.

(8) The clerk of a magistrates' court to whom any payments under an order to which this section applies are required to be made, and the collecting officer under an attachment of earnings order made to secure payments under the first mentioned order, shall not be liable—

   (*a*) in the case of that clerk, for any act done by him in pursuance of the first mentioned order after the date on which that order or a provision thereof ceased to have effect by reason of the remarriage of the person entitled to payments under it, and

   (*b*) in the case of the collecting officer, for any act done by him after that date in accordance with any enactment or rule of court specifying how payments made to him in compliance with the attachment of earnings order are to be dealt with,

if, but only if, the act was one which he would have been under a duty to do had the first mentioned order or a provision thereof not ceased to have effect as aforesaid and the act was done before notice in writing of the fact that the person so entitled had remarried was given to him by or on behalf of that person, the person liable to make payments under the first mentioned order or the personal representatives of either of those persons.

(9) In this section " collecting officer ", in relation to an attachment of earnings order, means the officer of the High Court, the registrar of a county court or the clerk of a magistrates' court to whom a person makes payments in compliance with the order.] [8]

---

[8] Section added by *ibid.*, s. 31.

Parties resident or domiciled outside England

14.—(1) Section fifteen of the Maintenance Orders Act 1950 (which relates to the service of process on a person residing in Scotland or Northern Ireland) shall have effect as if subsection (3) of section one and subsection (1) of section nine of this Act were included in Part I of that Act.

(2) Nothing in either of the said subsections shall be construed as derogating from any jurisdiction exercisable by any court apart from the provisions of those subsections.

(3) It is hereby declared that any jurisdiction conferred on a magistrates' court by this Act is exercisable notwithstanding that any party to the proceedings is not domiciled in England.

15. [*Repealed by Maintenance Orders Act* 1968 (*c.* 36), *s.* 3 (4).]

Interpretation

16.—(1) In this Act, save where the context otherwise requires, the following expressions have the following meanings respectively, that is to say—

" child ", in relation to one or both of the parties to a marriage, includes an illegitimate [. . .] [8a] child of that party or, as the case may be, or both parties, [. . .] [8a] and " parent ", in relation to any child, shall be construed accordingly; [. . .] [8a]

" child of the family ", in relation to the parties to a marriage, means—

(a) any child of both parties; and

(b) any other child of either party who has been accepted as one of the family by the other party;

" dependant " means a person—

(a) who is under the age of sixteen years; or

(b) who, having attained the age of sixteen but not of twenty-one years, is either receiving full-time instruction at an educational establishment or undergoing training for a trade, profession or vocation in such circumstances that he is required to devote the whole of his time to that training for a period of not less than two years; or

(c) whose earning capacity is impaired through illness or disability of mind or body and who has not attained the age of twenty-one years;

" drug addict " means a person (not being a mentally disordered person within the meaning of the Mental Health Act 1959) who, by reason of the habitual taking or using, otherwise than upon medical advice, of [any controlled drug within the meaning of the Misuse of Drugs Act 1971] [9]—

(a) is at times dangerous to himself or to others, or incapable of managing himself or his affairs; or

(b) so conducts himself that it would not be reasonable to expect a spouse of ordinary sensibilities to continue to cohabit with him;

" habitual drunkard " means a person (not being a mentally disordered person within the meaning of the Mental Health Act 1959) who, by reason of habitual intemperate drinking of intoxicating liquor—

(a) is at times dangerous to himself or to others, or incapable of managing himself or his affairs; or

---

[8a] Words repealed by Children Act 1975 (c. 72), Sched. 4.
[9] Words substituted by Misuse of Drugs Act 1971 (c. 38), s. 34.

  (*b*) so conducts himself that it would not be reasonable to expect a spouse of ordinary sensibilities to continue to cohabit with him;

" interim order " means an order under section six of this Act and includes any order made by virtue of section eight of this Act varying or reviving an order under the said section six;

[" local social services authority " means the council of a non-metropolitan county or a metropolitan district or London borough, or the common council of the City of London.] [10]

" matrimonial order " means an order under section two of this Act and includes any order made by virtue of section eight of this Act varying or reviving an order under the said section two;

" petty sessions area " has the same meaning as in the Magistrates' Courts Act 1952;

" rules " means rules made under section fifteen of the Justices of the Peace Act 1949.

(2) Save where the context otherwise requires, any reference in this Act to any enactment shall be construed as a reference to that enactment as amended by or under any subsequent enactment, including this Act.

Expenses

17. There shall be defrayed out of moneys provided by Parliament any increase attributable to this Act in the sums payable out of moneys so provided under any other enactment.

Repeals and savings

18.—(1) [. . .] [11] the repeal by this subsection of section five of the Maintenance Orders Act 1950 shall not affect the validity of any rules made by virtue of that section.

(2) Any application, complaint or order made, or other thing done, under or by virtue of any of the enactments repealed by this Act shall, so far as pending or in force immediately before the commencement of this Act, continue to have effect as if made or done under or by virtue of the corresponding enactment in this Act; and anything begun under any of the said enactments may be continued under this Act as if begun under this Act.

(3) So much of any enactment or document as refers expressly or by implication to any enactment repealed by this Act shall, if and so far as the context permits, be construed as referring to this Act or the corresponding enactment therein.

(4) Nothing in this section shall be taken as affecting the general application of section thirty-eight of the Interpretation Act 1889 with regard to the effect of repeals.

Short title, extent and commencement

19.—(1) This Act may be cited as the Matrimonial Proceedings (Magistrates' Courts) Act 1960.

(2) This Act, except for subsection (1) of section fourteen and the repeal of sections one and five of the Maintenance Orders Act 1950, shall not extend to Scotland or to Northern Ireland.

(3) This Act shall come into force on such day as the Secretary of State may by order made by statutory instrument appoint.

SCHEDULE

[*Repealed by Statute Law (Repeals) Act* 1974 (*c.* 22), *Sched., Pt. XI.*]

---

[10] Definition added by Local Government Act 1972 (c. 70), s. 195 (6), Sched. 23, para. 10.
[11] Words repealed by Statute Law (Repeals) Act 1974 (c. 22), Sched., Pt. XI.

Adoption Act 1960

(8 & 9 ELIZ. 2, c. 59)

An Act to amend the law with respect to the revocation of adoption orders in cases of legitimation, and to make further provision in connection with the revocation of such orders under section twenty-six of the Adoption Act 1958.

[29th July 1960]

Further provision for revocation of adoption orders in cases of legitimation

1.—(1) Where any person legitimated by virtue of section one of the Legitimacy Act 1959 had been adopted by his father and mother before the commencement of that Act, the court by which the adoption order was made may, on the application of any of the parties concerned, revoke that order.

(2) [*Repealed by Children Act* 1975 (*c.* 72), Sched. 4.]

(3) This section shall be construed as one with section twenty-six of the Adoption Act 1958; and any reference in that Act to that section or to subsection (1) of that section shall be construed as including a reference to subsection (1) of this section.

Short title and extent

2.—(1) This Act may be cited as the Adoption Act 1960.
(2) This Act does not extend to Northern Ireland.

Education Act 1962

(10 & 11 ELIZ. 2, c. 12)

School leaving dates

School leaving dates in England and Wales

9.[1]—(1) The provision of subsections (2) to (4) of this section shall have effect in relation to any person who on a date when either—

(*a*) he is a registered pupil at a school, or
(*b*) not being such a pupil, he has been a registered pupil at a school within the preceding period of twelve months,

attains an age which (apart from this section) would in his case be the upper limit of the compulsory school age.

(2) If he attains that age on any date from the beginning of September to the end of January, he shall be deemed not to have attained that age until the end of the appropriate spring term at his school.

(3) If he attains that age on any date on or after the beginning of February but before the end of the appropriate summer term at his school, he shall be deemed not to have attained that age until the end of that summer term.

(4) If he attains that age on any date between the end of the appropriate summer term at his school and the beginning of September next following the end of that summer term (whether another term has then

[1] Saved by Family Allowances Act 1965 (c. 53), s. 2 (2).

begun or not) he shall be deemed to have attained that age at the end of that summer term.

(5) The provisions of this section shall have effect for the purposes of the Act of 1944, and for the purposes of any enactment whereby the definition of compulsory school age in that Act is applied or incorporated; and for references in any enactment to section eight of the Education Act 1946 there shall, in relation to compulsory school age, be substituted references to this section:

Provided that for the purposes of any enactment relating to family allowances [. . . social security] [2] the provisions of this section shall have effect as if subsection (4) thereof were omitted.

(6) This section shall not apply where the date referred to in subsection (1) thereof is a date before the beginning of September, nineteen hundred and sixty-three.

(7) In this section " the appropriate spring term ", in relation to a person, means the last term at his school which ends before the month of May next following the date on which he attains the age in question, and " the appropriate summer term ", in relation to a person, means the last term at his school which ends before the month of September next following that date; and any reference to a person's school is a reference to the last school at which he is a registered pupil for a term ending before the said month of May or month of September (as the case may be) or for part of such a term.

Law Reform (Husband and Wife) Act 1962

(10 & 11 ELIZ. 2, C. 48)

An Act to amend the law with respect to civil proceedings between husband and wife.   [1st August 1962]

Actions in tort between husband and wife

1.—(1) Subject to the provisions of this section, each of the parties to a marriage shall have the like right of action in tort against the other as if they were not married.

(2) Where an action in tort is brought by one of the parties to a marriage against the other during the subsistence of the marriage, the court may stay the action if it appears—

(a) that no substantial benefit would accrue to either party from the continuation of the proceedings; or

(b) that the question or questions in issue could more conveniently be disposed of on an application made under section seventeen of the Married Women's Property Act 1882 (determination of questions between husband and wife as to the title to or possession of property);

and without prejudice to paragraph (b) of this subsection the court may, in such an action, either exercise any power which could be exercised on an application under the said section seventeen, or give such directions as it thinks fit for the disposal under that section of any question arising in the proceedings.

(3) Provision shall be made by rules of court for requiring the court to consider at an early stage of the proceedings whether the power to

[2] Words substituted by Social Security Act 1973 (c. 38), Sched. 27, as amended by Social Security (Consequential Provisions) Act 1975 (c. 18), Sched. 1.

stay an action under subsection (2) of this section should or should not
be exercised; and rules under the County Courts Act 1959 may confer
on the registrar any jurisdiction of the court under that subsection.

(4) This section does not extend to Scotland.

Proceedings between husband and wife in respect of delict

2.—(1) Subject to the provisions of this section, each of the parties
to a marriage shall have the like right to bring proceedings against the
other in respect of a wrongful or negligent act or omission, or for
the prevention of a wrongful act, as if they were not married.

(2) Where any such proceedings are brought by one of the parties to
a marriage against the other during the subsistence of the marriage,
the court may dismiss the proceedings if it appears that no substantial
benefit would accrue to either party from the continuation thereof;
and it shall be the duty of the court to consider at an early stage of the
proceedings whether the power to dismiss the proceedings under this
subsection should or should not be exercised.

(3) This section extends to Scotland only.

Short title, repeal, interpretation, saving and extent

3.—(1) This Act may be cited as the Law Reform (Husband and
Wife) Act 1962.

[*Subsection (2) repealed by Statute Law (Repeals) Act 1974 (c. 22),
Sched., Pt. XI.*]

(3) The references in subsection (1) of section one and subsection (1)
of section two of this Act to the parties to a marriage include references
to the persons who were parties to a marriage which has been dissolved.

(4) This Act does not apply to any cause of action which arose, or
would but for the subsistence of a marriage have arisen, before the
commencement of this Act.

(5) This Act does not extend to Northern Ireland.

SCHEDULE

[*Repealed by Statute Law (Repeals) Act 1974 (c. 22), Sched., Pt. XI.*)

Children and Young Persons Act 1963

(1963 c. 37)

An Act to amend the law relating to children and young persons;
and for purposes connected therewith. [31st July 1963]

PART I

CARE AND CONTROL OF CHILDREN AND YOUNG PERSONS

Welfare powers of local authorities

Extension of power to promote welfare of children

1.[1]—(1) It shall be the duty of every local authority to make available
such advice, guidance and assistance as may promote the welfare of

---

[1] Applied by Children and Young Persons Act 1969 (c. 54), s. 68 (1).

children by diminishing the need to receive children into or keep them in care under the Children Act 1948, the principal Act or the principal Scottish Act or to bring children before a juvenile court; and any provisions made by a local authority under this subsection may, if the local authority think fit, include provision for giving assistance in kind or, in exceptional circumstances, in cash.

(2) In carrying out their duty under subsection (1) of this section a local authority may make arrangements with voluntary organisations or other persons for the provision by those organisations or other persons of such advice, guidance or assistance as is mentioned in that subsection.

(3) Where any provision which may be made by a local authority under subsection (1) of this section is made (whether by that or any other authority) under any other enactment the local authority shall not be required to make the provision under this section but shall have power to do so.

[Subsection (4) repealed by Children and Young Persons Act 1969 (c. 54), s. 72 (4), Sched. 6.]

(5) In this section " child " means a person under the age of eighteen.

Children and young persons in need of care, protection or control

2. [Repealed by Children and Young Persons Act 1969 (c. 54), s. 72 (4), Sched. 6.]

Children and young persons beyond control

3.—(1) No child or young person shall be brought before a juvenile court by his parent or guardian on the ground that he is unable to control him; but where the parent or guardian of a child or young person has, by notice in writing, requested the local authority within whose area the child or young person resides to bring him before a juvenile court under [section 1 of the Children and Young Persons Act 1969] [2] and the local authority refuse to do so or fail to do so within twenty-eight days from the date on which the notice is given the parent or guardian may apply by complaint to a juvenile court for an order directing them to do so.

(2) Where a complaint has been made under this section for an order against a local authority, the local authority shall make available to the court such information as to the home surroundings, school record, health and character of the child or young person as appears to them likely to assist the court and shall for that purpose make such investigations as may be necessary.

(3) On the hearing of a complaint under this section the child or young person shall not be present.

4-9. [Repealed by Children and Young Persons Act 1969 (c. 54), s. 72 (4), Sched. 6.]

10. [Repealed by Children and Young Persons Act 1969 (c. 54), ss. 72 (4), 73 (4) (d), Sched. 6.]

11-15. [Repealed by Children and Young Persons Act 1969 (c. 54), s. 72 (4), Sched. 6.]

[2] Words substituted by ibid. s. 72 (3), Sched. 5, para. 47.

Juvenile courts and proceedings in connection with children and young persons

Offences committed by children

16.—(1) Section 50 of the principal Act shall be amended by substituting therein the word " ten " for the word " eight ".

(2) In any proceedings for an offence committed or alleged to have been committed by a person of or over the age of twenty-one, any offence of which he was found guilty while under the age of fourteen shall be disregarded for the purposes of any evidence relating to his previous convictions; and he shall not be asked, and if asked shall not be required to answer, any question relating to such an offence, notwithstanding that the question would otherwise be admissible under section 1 of the Criminal Evidence Act 1898.

Constitution and place of sitting of juvenile courts

17.—(1) For Schedule 2 to the principal Act (which relates to the constitution of juvenile courts) there shall be substituted Schedule 2 to this Act.

(2) In section 47 (2) of the principal Act (which relates to sittings of juvenile courts) for the words from " subject as hereinafter provided " to " other courts are held " there shall be substituted the words " not sit in a room in which sittings of a court other than a juvenile court are held if a sitting of that other court has been or will be held there within an hour before or after the sitting of the juvenile court ".

Jurisdiction of magistrates' courts in certain cases involving children and young persons

18. Notwithstanding section 46 (1) of the principal Act (which restricts the jurisdiction of magistrates' courts which are not juvenile courts in cases where a child or young person is charged with an offence) a magistrates' court which is not a juvenile court may hear an information against a child or young person if he is charged—

   (*a*) with aiding, abetting, causing, procuring, allowing or permitting an offence with which a person who has attained the age of seventeen is charged at the same time; or

   (*b*) with an offence arising out of circumstances which are the same as or connected with those giving rise to an offence with which a person who has attained the age of seventeen is charged at the same time.

19. [*Repealed by Courts Act* 1971 (*c.* 23), *s.* 56 (4), *Sched.* 11, *Pt. IV.*]

20. [*Repealed by Administration of Justice Act* 1964 (*c.* 42), *s.* 41 (8), *Sched.* 5.*]*

21. [*Repealed by Statute Law (Repeals) Act* 1974 (*c.* 22), *Sched., Pt. XI.*]

22. [*Repealed by Children and Young Persons Act* 1969 (*c.* 54), *s.* 72 (4), *Sched.* 6.]

Children and young persons detained in places of safety

23.—(1) A court or justice of the peace—

   [*Paragraph* (*a*) *repealed by Children and Young Persons Act* 1969 (*c.* 54), *s.* 72 (4), *Sched.* 6.]

(b) issuing a warrant under section 40 of [the principal Act] [3-4] authorising a constable to take a child or young person to a place of safety; or

(c) ordering the removal of a child or young person to a place of safety under section 7 of the Children Act 1958 or section 43 of the Adoption Act 1958;

shall specify in the warrant, [. . .] [5] or order a period, which shall not exceed twenty-eight days, beyond which the child or young person must not be detained in a place of safety without being brought before a juvenile court; and accordingly the child or young person shall be brought before a juvenile court not later than the end of that period unless he has been released or received into the care of a local authority.

[*Subsection* (2) *repealed by Children and Young Persons Act* 1969 (*c.* 54), *s.* 72 (4), *Sched.* 6.]

(3) A child or young person required to be brought before a juvenile court or a justice of the peace under subsection (1) [. . .] [5] of this section shall (if not otherwise brought before the court or justice) be brought before the court or justice by the local authority in whose area the place of safety is situated; and the person occupying or in charge of a place of safety not provided by that local authority shall as soon as practicable notify that local authority whenever a child or young person [. . .] [5] is taken there as mentioned in subsection (1) [. . .] [5] of this section.

(4) Notwithstanding anything in the preceding provisions of this section, where the person to be brought before a court or justice is under the age of five or cannot be brought before the court or justice by reason of illness or accident, the duty to bring him before the court or justice may be discharged by the making of an application for an order under subsection (5) of this section.

(5) Where a person is brought before a juvenile court or justice of the peace in pursuance of subsection (3) of this section or an application is made in respect of any person to a juvenile court or justice of the peace in pursuance of subsection (4) thereof, the court or justice may either order him to be released or make an interim order [within the meaning of the Children and Young Persons Act 1969].[3-4]

[*Subsections* (6) *to* (8) *repealed by Children and Young Persons Act* 1969 (*c.* 54), *s.* 72 (4), *Sched.* 6.]

24. [*Repealed by Children and Young Persons Act* 1969 (*c.* 54), *s.* 72 (4), *Sched.* 6.]

25. [*Subsection* (1) *amends section* 34 *of the Children and Young Persons Act* 1933, *see ante, pp.* 37–73.]

[*Subsection* (2) *repealed by Children and Young Persons Act* 1969 (*c.* 54), *s.* 72 (4), *Sched.* 6.]

Medical evidence by certificate

26. In any proceedings, other than proceedings for an offence, before a juvenile court, and on any appeal from a decision of a juvenile court in any such proceedings, any document purporting to be a certificate of a fully registered medical practitioner as to any person's physical or mental condition shall be admissible as evidence of that condition.

Evidence of children in committal proceedings for sexual offences

27.—(1) In any proceedings before a magistrates' court inquiring into a sexual offence as examining justices—

[3-4] Words substituted by Children and Young Persons Act 1969 (c. 54), s. 72 (3), Sched. 5, para. 48.
[5] Words repealed by *ibid.* s. 72 (4), Sched. 6.

(*a*) a child shall not be called as a witness for the prosecution; but

(*b*) any statement made in writing by or taken in writing from the child shall be admissible in evidence of any matter of which his oral testimony would be admissible;

except in a case where the application of this subsection is excluded under subsection (2) of this section.

(2) Subsection (1) of this section shall not apply—

(*a*) where at or before the time when such a statement is tendered in evidence the defence objects to the application of that subsection; or

(*b*) where the prosecution requires the attendance of the child for the purpose of establishing the identity of any person; or

(*c*) where the court is satisfied that it has not been possible to obtain from the child a statement that may be given in evidence under this section; or

(*d*) where the inquiry into the offence takes place after the court has discontinued to try it summarily and the child has given evidence in the summary trial.

(3) Section 23 of the Magistrates' Courts Act 1952 (which, in a case where an inquiry into an offence is followed by summary trial, treats evidence given for the purposes of the inquiry as having been given for the purposes of the trial) shall not apply to any statement admitted in pursuance of subsection (1) of this section.

(4) In this section " sexual offence " means any offence under the Sexual Offences Act 1956, or the Indecency with Children Act 1960, or any attempt to commit such an offence.

Form of oath for use in juvenile courts and by children and young persons in other courts

28.—(1) Subject to subsection (2) of this section, in relation to any oath administered to and taken by any person before a juvenile court or administered to and taken by any child or young person before any other court, section 2 of the Oaths Act 1909 shall have effect as if the words " I promise before Almighty God " were set out in it instead of the words " I swear by Almighty God that ".

(2) Where in any oath otherwise duly administered and taken either of the forms mentioned in this section is used instead of the other, the oath shall nevertheless be deemed to have been duly administered and taken.

Provisions as to persons between the ages of 17 and 18

29.—(1) Where proceedings in respect of a young person are begun [under section 1 of the Children and Young Persons Act 1969 or for an offence] [6] and he attains the age of seventeen before the conclusion of the proceedings, the court may [. . .] [7] deal with the case and make any order which it could have made if he had not attained that age.

[*Subsection* (2) *repealed by Children and Young Persons Act* 1969 (*c.* 54), *s.* 72 (3) (4), *Sched.* 5, *para.* 49, *Sched.* 6.]

Recovery of arrears of contributions

Recovery of arrears of contributions

30.—(1) Where during any period (in this section referred to as " the period of default ")—

[6] Words added by Children and Young Persons Act 1969 (c. 54), s. 72 (3), Sched. 5, para. 49.
[7] Words repealed by *ibid.* s. 72 (4), Sched. 6.

(a) a person was liable to make contributions in respect of a child; but

(b) no order was in force requiring him to make the contributions; a magistrates' court acting for the petty sessions area where he is for the time being residing may, on the application of [the local authority who] [8] would have been entitled to receive payment under such an order, make an order (in this section referred to as an " arrears order ") requiring him to pay such weekly sum, for such period, as the court, having regard to his means, thinks fit; but the aggregate of the payments required to be made by any person under an arrears order shall not exceed the aggregate that, in the opinion of the court, would have been payable by him under a contribution order in respect of the period of default or, if it exceeded three months, the last part thereof, less the aggregate of the payments (if any) made by him in respect of his liability during that period or, as the case may be, the last part thereof.

For the purposes of this subsection the last part of the period of default shall be taken to be the last three months thereof and such time, if any, preceding the last three months as is equal to the time during which it continued after the making of the application for the arrears order.

(2) No application for an arrears order shall be made later than three months after the end of the period of default.

(3) An arrears order shall be treated as a contribution order, and payments under it as contributions, for the purposes of the following enactments, that is to say—

in the principal Act, [subsection (3)] [8] of section 86, sections 87 (4), 89 and 102 (1) (c),
the Maintenance Orders Act 1950,
the Maintenance Orders Act 1958,
paragraph 2 of Schedule 8 to the Local Government Act 1958,
[section 62 of the Children and Young Persons Act 1969.] [8]

(4) Where the person who was liable to make contributions resides in Scotland or Northern Ireland, subsection (1) of this section shall have effect as if for the magistrates' court therein mentioned there were substituted [a magistrates' court acting for the area or part of the area of the local authority which is the applicant].[8]

(5) A person liable to make payments under an arrears order shall, except at a time when he is under a duty to give information of his address under section [24 (8) of the Children and Young Persons Act 1969 keep the local authority] [8] to whom the payments are to be made informed of his address; and if he fails to do so he shall be liable on summary conviction to a fine not exceeding [ten pounds].[9]

(6) In this section—

" child " has the same meaning as in the Children Act 1948,
" contributions " means contributions under section 86 of the principal Act, and
" contribution order " means an order under section 87 of the principal Act.

Increase of certain penalties

Increase of penalty for cruelty

31. In section 1 of the principal Act (cruelty to persons under sixteen) paragraph (b) of subsection (1) (which provides for a fine not exceeding

[8] Words substituted by ibid. s. 72 (3), Sched. 5, para. 50.
[9] Maximum fine increased from five pounds by Criminal Justice Act 1967 (c. 80), s. 92, Sched. 3. Pt. I.

twenty-five pounds on summary conviction) shall be amended, as respects offences committed after the commencement of this Act, by the substitution for the words " twenty-five pounds " of the words " one hundred pounds ".

Increase of penalty for sales of tobacco, etc., to persons under 16

32. Section 7 of the principal Act and section 18 of the principal Scottish Act (which, in subsection (1), prohibit the sale of tobacco and cigarette papers to persons apparently under the age of sixteen and, in subsection (2), enable a court to order measures to be taken to prevent the use by such persons of automatic machines for the sale of tobacco) shall each be amended, as respects offences committed after the commencement of this Act, by substituting—

(a) in subsection (1) (which provides for fines not exceeding two, five and ten pounds on a first, second or subsequent conviction) for the words " two ", " five " and " ten " the words " twenty-five ", " fifty " and " one hundred ", respectively; and

(b) in subsection (2) (which provides for fines not exceeding five pounds for failure to comply with the order of the court and further fines not exceeding one pound for each day during which the offence continues) for the words " five " and " one " the words " fifty " and " ten ", respectively.

New appeals

33. [*Repealed by Children and Young Persons Act 1969 (c. 54), s. 72 (4), Sched. 6.*]

PART II

EMPLOYMENT OF CHILDREN AND YOUNG PERSONS

General provisions as to employment

Hours of employment

34. For paragraph (c) of section 18 (1) of the principal Act (which prohibits the employment of children before six o'clock in the morning or after eight o'clock in the evening) and for paragraph (c) of section 28 (1) of the principal Scottish Act (which prohibits such employment before six o'clock in the morning or after seven o'clock in the evening, or at certain times of the year eight o'clock in the evening) there shall be substituted the following paragraph:—

" (c) before seven o'clock in the morning or after seven o'clock in the evening on any day; or ".

Street trading

35.—(1) In section 20 (1) of the principal Act (which, subject to certain exceptions, prohibits persons under the age of sixteen from engaging or being employed in street trading) for the word " sixteen ", in both places where it occurs, there shall be substituted the word " seventeen ".

(2) Nothing in the said section 20 or section 30 of the principal Scottish Act or in any byelaw made under either of those sections shall restrict the engagement or employment of any person in the carrying on in any place of a retail trade or business (within the meaning of the Shops Act 1950) on any occasion on which it is customary for retail trades or businesses to be carried on in that place.

(3) At the end of the said section 20 there shall be added the following subsection :—

" (3) No person under the age of eighteen shall on a Sunday engage or be employed in street trading of a description to which, notwithstanding section 58 of the Shops Act 1950 (which extends certain provisions to any place where a retail trade or business is carried on), those provisions do not extend."

Increase of certain penalties

36. Section 21 of the principal Act and section 31 of the principal Scottish Act (which impose penalties for contraventions of the general provisions of those Acts as to employment) shall each be amended, as respects offences committed after the commencement of this Act, as follows :—

  (a) in subsection (1) (which provides for fines not exceeding five pounds and twenty pounds for first and subsequent offences respectively) for the words " five pounds " there shall be substituted the words " twenty pounds " and for the words " twenty pounds " the words " fifty pounds "; and

  (b) in subsection (3) (which provides for fines of twenty shillings and forty shillings for first and subsequent offences respectively) for the words " twenty shillings " there shall be substituted the words " ten pounds " and for the words " forty shillings " the words " twenty pounds ".

Entertainment

Restriction on persons under 16 taking part in public performances, etc.

37.—(1) Subject to the provisions of this section, a child shall not take part in a performance to which this section applies except under the authority of a licence granted by the local authority in whose area he resides or, if he does not reside in Great Britain, by the local authority in whose area the applicant or one of the applicants for the licence resides or has his place of business.

  (2) This section applies to—

  (a) any performance in connection with which a charge is made (whether for admission or otherwise);

  (b) any performance in licensed premises within the meaning of the Licensing Act 1953 or the Licensing (Scotland) Act 1959 or in premises in respect of which a club is registered under the said Act of 1959 or the Licensing Act 1961;

  (c) any broadcast performance;

  (d) any performance recorded (by whatever means) with a view to its use in a broadcast or in a film intended for public exhibition;

and a child shall be treated for the purposes of this section as taking part in a performance if he takes the place of a performer in any rehearsal or in any preparation for the recording of the performance.

  (3) A licence under this section shall not be required for any child to take part in a performance to which this section applies if—

  (a) in the six months preceding the performance he has not taken part in other performances to which this section applies on more than three days; or

  (b) the performance is given under arrangements made by a school (within the meaning of the Education Act 1944 or the Education (Scotland) Act 1962) or made by a body of persons approved for the purposes of this section by the Secretary of State or by the local authority in whose area the performance takes place, and no payment in respect of the child's taking part in the performance is made, whether to him or to any other person, except for defraying expenses;

but the Secretary of State may by regulations made by statutory instrument prescribe conditions to be observed with respect to the hours of work, rest or meals of children taking part in performances as mentioned in paragraph (*a*) of this subsection.

(4) The power to grant licences under this section shall be exercisable subject to such restrictions and conditions as the Secretary of State may by regulations made by statutory instrument prescribe and a local authority shall not grant a licence for a child to take part in a performance or series of performances unless they are satisfied that he is fit to do so, that proper provision has been made to secure his health and kind treatment and that, having regard to such provision (if any) as has been or will be made therefor, his education will not suffer; but if they are so satisfied, in the case of an application duly made for a licence under this section which they have power to grant, they shall not refuse to grant the licence.

(5) Regulations under this section may make different provision for different circumstances and may prescribe, among the conditions subject to which a licence is to be granted, conditions requiring the approval of a local authority and may provide for that approval to be given subject to conditions imposed by the authority.

(6) Without prejudice to the generality of the preceding subsection, regulations under this section may prescribe, among the conditions subject to which a licence may be granted, a condition requiring sums earned by the child in respect of whom the licence is granted in taking part in a performance to which the licence relates to be paid into the county court (or, in Scotland, consigned in the sheriff court) or dealt with in a manner approved by the local authority.

(7) A licence under this section shall specify the times, if any, during which the child in respect of whom it is granted may be absent from school for the purposes authorised by the licence; and for the purposes of the enactments relating to education a child who is so absent during any times so specified shall be deemed to be absent with leave granted by a person authorised in that behalf by the managers, governors or proprietor of the school or, in Scotland, with reasonable excuse.

(8) Any statutory instrument made under this section shall be subject to annulment in pursuance of a resolution of either House of Parliament.

Restriction on licences for performances by children under 13

38.—(1) A licence under the preceding section in respect of a child under the age of thirteen shall not be granted unless—

  (*a*) the licence is for acting and the application therefor is accompanied by a declaration that the part he is to act cannot be taken except by a child of about his age; or

  (*b*) the licence is for dancing in a ballet which does not form part of an entertainment of which anything other than ballet or opera also forms part and the application for the licence is accompanied by a declaration that the part he is to dance cannot be taken except by a child of about his age; or

  (*c*) the nature of his part in the performance is wholly or mainly musical and either the nature of the performance is also wholly or mainly musical or the performance consists only of opera and ballet.

(2) On the extension of the compulsory school age (or, in Scotland, school age) to sixteen years, that is to say—

(a) in England and Wales, on the coming into force of an Order in Council under section 35 of the Education Act 1944; and

(b) in Scotland, on the coming into force of regulations under section 32 of the Education (Scotland) Act 1962;

subsection (1) of this section shall have effect as if for the word " thirteen " there were substituted the word " fourteen ".

Supplementary provisions as to licences under section 37

39.—(1) A licence under section 37 of this Act may be varied on the application of the person holding it by the local authority by whom it was granted or by any local authority in whose area the performance or one of the performances to which it relates takes place.

(2) The local authority by whom such a licence was granted, and any local authority in whose area the performance or one of the performances to which it relates takes place, may vary or revoke the licence if any condition subject to which it was granted is not observed or they are not satisfied as to the matters mentioned in subsection (4) of the said section 37, but shall, before doing so, give to the holder of the licence such notice (if any) of their intention as may be practicable in the circumstances.

(3) Where a local authority grant such a licence authorising a child to take part in a performance in the area of another local authority they shall send to that other authority such particulars as the Secretary of State may by regulations made by statutory instrument prescribe; and where a local authority vary or revoke such a licence which was granted by, or relates to a performance in the area of, another local authority, they shall inform that other authority.

(4) A local authority proposing to vary or revoke such a licence granted by another local authority shall, if practicable, consult that other authority.

(5) The holder of such a licence shall keep such records as the Secretary of State may by regulations made by statutory instrument prescribe and shall on request produce them to an officer of the authority who granted the licence, at any time not later than six months after the performance or last performance to which it relates.

(6) Where a local authority refuse an application for a licence under section 37 of this Act or revoke or, otherwise than on the application of the holder, vary such a licence they shall state their grounds for doing so in writing to the applicant or, as the case may be, the holder of the licence; and the applicant or holder may appeal to a magistrates' court or, in Scotland, the sheriff, against the refusal, revocation or variation, and against any condition subject to which the licence is granted or any approval is given, not being a condition which the local authority are required to impose.

(7) Any statutory instrument made under this section shall be subject to annulment in pursuance of a resolution of either House of Parliament.

Offences

40.—(1) If any person—

(a) causes or procures any child or, being his parent or guardian, allows him, to take part in any performance in contravention of section 37 of this Act; or

(b) fails to observe any condition subject to which a licence under that section is granted, or any condition prescribed under subsection (3) of that section; or

(c) knowingly or recklessly makes any false statement in or in connection with an application for a licence under that section;

he shall be liable on summary conviction to a fine not exceeding one hundred pounds or imprisonment for a term not exceeding three months or both.

(2) If any person fails to keep or produce any record which he is required to keep or produce under section 39 of this Act, he shall be liable on summary conviction to a fine not exceeding fifty pounds or imprisonment for a term not exceeding three months or both.

(3) The court by which the holder or one of the holders of a licence under section 37 of this Act is convicted of an offence under this section may revoke the licence.

(4) In any proceedings for an offence under this section alleged to have been committed by causing, procuring or allowing a child to take part in a performance without a licence under section 37 of this Act it shall be a defence to prove that the accused believed that the condition specified in paragraph (*a*) of subsection (3) of that section was satisfied and that he had reasonable grounds for that belief.

Licences for training persons between 12 and 16 for performances of a dangerous nature

41.—(1) The power to grant licences under section 24 of the principal Act (which relates to the training of persons under the age of sixteen to take part in performances of a dangerous nature) shall be exercisable by the local authority for the area or one of the areas in which the training is to take place instead of by a magistrates' court.

(2) A licence under the said section 24 or under section 34 of the principal Scottish Act (which makes provision in Scotland similar to that made in England and Wales by the said section 24 as amended by subsection (1) of this section) may be revoked or varied by the authority who granted it if any of the conditions embodied therein are not complied with or if it appears to them that the person to whom the licence relates is no longer fit and willing to be trained or that proper provision is no longer being made to secure his health and kind treatment.

(3) Where an authority refuse an application for such a licence or revoke or vary such a licence they shall state their grounds for doing so in writing to the applicant, or, as the case may be, to the holder of the licence, and the applicant or holder may appeal to a magistrates' court or, in Scotland, to the sheriff, against the refusal, revocation or variation.

Licences for children and young persons performing abroad

42.—(1) Section 25 of the principal Act (which prohibits persons under eighteen from going abroad for the purpose of performing for profit except under the authority of a licence granted under that section) and section 26 of that Act (which imposes penalties for contraventions) shall have effect as if the words " singing, playing, performing or being exhibited " included taking part in any such performance as is mentioned in paragraph (*c*) or (*d*) of section 37 (2) of this Act.

(2) A licence under the said section 25 may be granted in respect of a person notwithstanding that he is under the age of fourteen if—

  (*a*) the engagement which he is to fulfil is for acting and the application for the licence is accompanied by a declaration that the part he is to act cannot be taken except by a person of about his age; or

  (*b*) the engagement is for dancing in a ballet which does not form part of an entertainment of which anything other than ballet or opera also forms part and the application for the licence is accompanied by a declaration that the part he is to dance cannot be taken except by a child of about his age; or

(c) the engagement is for taking part in a performance the nature of which is wholly or mainly musical or which consists only of opera and ballet and the nature of his part in the performance is wholly or mainly musical.

Extended powers of entry

43. For subsection (2) of section 28 of the principal Act and for subsection (2) of section 36 of the principal Scottish Act there shall be substituted the following subsection:—

" (2) Any authorised officer of the said authority or any constable may—

(a) at any time enter any place used as a broadcasting studio or film studio or used for the recording of a performance with a view to its use in a broadcast or in a film intended for public exhibition and make inquiries therein as to any children taking part in performances to which section 37 of the Children and Young Persons Act 1963 applies;

(b) at any time during the currency of a licence granted under the said section 37 or under the provisions of this Part of this Act relating to training for dangerous performances enter any place (whether or not it is such a place as is mentioned in paragraph (a) of this subsection) where the person to whom the licence relates is authorised by the licence to take part in a performance or to be trained, and may make inquiries therein with respect to that person."

Construction of Part II

Construction of Part II

44.—(1) This Part of this Act, in its application to England and Wales, and, as regards section 42, in its application elsewhere, shall be construed, and Part II of the principal Act shall have effect, as if this Part were included in that Part.

(2) This Part of this Act, except section 42, shall, in its application to Scotland, be construed as if it were included in Part III of the principal Scottish Act and as if references to a local authority were references to an education authority; and the said Part III shall have effect as if this Part of this Act (except section 42) were included in it.

PART III

MISCELLANEOUS AND GENERAL

Research and financial

Research

45.—(1) The Secretary of State may conduct or assist other persons in conducting research into any matter connected with his functions or the functions of local authorities under the Children and Young Persons Acts 1933 to 1956, [. . .] [10] the Children Act 1948, the Children Act 1958 [the Children and Young Persons Act 1969] [11] or this Act, or any matter connected with the adoption of children.

(2) Any local authority may conduct or assist other persons in conducting research into any matter connected with their functions

[10] Words repealed by Social Work (Scotland) Act 1968 (c. 49), ss. 95 (2), 97 (1), Sched. 9, Pt. II.
[11] Words added by Children and Young Persons Act 1969 (c. 54), s. 72 (3), Sched. 5, para. 51.

under the enactments mentioned in subsection (1) of this section or their functions connected with the adoption of children.

Financial assistance under s. 20 of Children Act 1948

46.—(1) In subsection (1) of section 20 of the Children Act 1948 (which authorises a local authority to contribute towards the cost of accommodation and maintenance of certain persons over the age of eighteen who have been in the care of a local authority) after the word " being " there shall be inserted the words " either a person who has attained the age of seventeen but has ceased to be in the care of a local authority, or ".

(2) In subsection (2) of the said section 20 (which authorises a local authority to make grants towards the education or training of certain persons over the age of eighteen who immediately before they attained that age were in the care of a local authority) for the word " eighteen ", in the first place where it occurs, there shall be substituted the word " seventeen " and for the words " immediately before they attained the age of eighteen " there shall be substituted the words " at or after the time when they attained the age of seventeen ".

Power of local authority to guarantee apprenticeship deeds etc. of persons in their care

47. While a person is in the care of a local authority under the principal Act, the principal Scottish Act or the Children Act 1948 or by virtue of an order under the Matrimonial Proceedings (Children) Act 1958 or the Matrimonial Proceedings (Magistrates' Courts) Act 1960, the local authority may undertake any obligation by way of guarantee under any deed of apprenticeship or articles of clerkship entered into by that person; and where the local authority have undertaken any such obligation under any deed or articles they may at any time (whether or not the person concerned is still in their care) undertake the like obligation under any deed or articles supplemental thereto.

Children in respect of whom parental rights may be or have been assumed by local authority

Extension of power of local authority to assume parental rights

48.—(1) Where, after a child has been received into the care of a local authority under section 1 of the Children Act 1948, the whereabouts of any parent or guardian of his have remained unknown for not less than twelve months, then, for the purposes of section 2 of that Act (which enables a local authority in certain circumstances to assume parental rights) the parent or guardian shall be deemed to have abandoned the child.

(2) The power of a local authority under paragraph (b) of section 2 (1) of the Children Act 1948 to resolve that all rights and powers of a parent or guardian shall vest in them may be exercised, as well as in the cases mentioned in that paragraph, in any case where it appears to them—

(a) that the parent or guardian suffers from a mental disorder (within the meaning of the Mental Health Act 1959 or the Mental Health (Scotland) Act 1960) which renders him unfit to have the care of the child; or

(b) that the parent or guardian has so persistently failed without reasonable cause to discharge the obligations of a parent or guardian as to be unfit to have the care of the child;

and the power of the court or sheriff, under subsection (3) of that section, to order that the resolution shall not lapse may also be exercised if the court or sheriff is satisfied that the person who objected to the resolution is unfit to have the care of the child by reason of his persistent failure to discharge the obligations of a parent or guardian.

(3) In this section " child " has the same meaning as in the Children Act 1948.

Harbouring or concealing child required to return to local authority

49.—(1) Where a local authority have, in accordance with [section 13 (2)] [12] of the Children Act 1948, allowed any person to take over the care of a child with respect to whom a resolution under section 2 of that Act is in force and have by notice in writing required that person to return the child at a time specified in the notice (which, if that person has been allowed to take [charge] [12] of the child for a fixed period, shall not be earlier than the end of that period) any person who harbours or conceals the child after that time or prevents him from returning as required by the notice shall be liable on summary conviction to a fine not exceeding twenty pounds or to imprisonment for a term not exceeding two months or to both.

(2) In this section " child " has the same meaning as in the Children Act 1948.

Extension of power to appoint guardian

50. [*Repealed by Guardianship of Minors Act* 1971 (*c.* 3), *s.* 18 (2), *Sched.* 2, *in relation to England and Wales.*]

Persons under supervision changing country of residence

51, 52. [*Repealed by Social Work (Scotland) Act* 1968 (*c.* 49), *ss.* 95 (2), 97 (1), *Sched.* 9 *Pts.* I, II.]

Children and young persons escaping to other parts of British Islands

Arrest in one part of British Islands of children or young persons escaping in other part

53. [*Subsections* (1) (2) *repealed by Children and Young Persons Act* 1969 (*c.* 54), *ss.* 72 (4), 73 (4) (*d*), *Sched.* 6.]

(3) Every person who is authorised by the managers of a training school within the meaning of the Children and Young Persons Act (Northern Ireland) 1950 to arrest a person under their care and bring him back to his school shall, for the purpose of acting on that authority, have all the powers, protection and privileges—

(*a*) in Great Britain or the Isle of Man, of a constable;
(*b*) in Jersey, of a member of the police;
(*c*) in any other part of the Channel Islands, of an officer of police within the meaning of section 43 of the Larceny (Guernsey) Law 1958, or any corresponding law for the time being in force.

Amendment of Adoption Act 1958

54. [*Repealed by Children Act* 1975 (*c.* 72), *Sched.* 4.]

Emigration with consent of Secretary of State

55. Section 52 of the Adoption Act 1958 (which, subject to excep-

[12] Words substituted by Children and Young Persons Act 1969 (c. 54), s. 72 (3), Sched. 5, para. 52.

tions, requires the authority of a provisional adoption order for the taking or sending abroad for adoption of infants who are British subjects) shall not apply in the case of any infant emigrating under the authority of the Secretary of State given under [. . .] [13] [. . .] [14] [. . .] [13] section 17 of the Children Act 1948 [or section 23 of the Social Work (Scotland) Act 1968] [14] [. . .].[13]

Miscellaneous
Prosecution of offences under Part I or Part II of principal Act

56.—(1) Without prejudice to section 98 of the principal Act (which authorises a local education authority to institute proceedings for an offence under Part I or Part II of that Act) any such proceedings may be instituted by the council of a county or county borough, whether or not the council are the local education authority, and may, where the council are the local education authority, be instituted by them otherwise than in that capacity.

(2) So much of subsection (5) of section 85 of the Local Government Act 1933 and [subsection (1) of section 3 of the Local Authority Social Services Act 1970] [14a] as restricts the matters that may be referred to or dealt with by committees established under [the said section 85 and section 2 of the said Act of 1970] [14a] respectively shall not apply in relation to any functions exercisable by a council in pursuance of this section.

Newspaper and broadcast reports of proceedings involving children and young persons

57.—(1) In section 39 of the principal Act and in section 46 of the principal Scottish Act (which empower a court to prohibit the publication in newspapers of pictures or matter leading to the identification of children and young persons concerned in certain proceedings) the words " which arise out of any offence against, or any conduct contrary to, decency or morality " shall be omitted and for the word " against " in paragraph (*a*) there shall be substituted the words " by or against ".

(2) Section 49 of the principal Act and section 54 of the principal Scottish Act (which restrict newspaper reports of proceedings in juvenile courts) shall, with the necessary modifications, apply in relation to any proceedings on appeal from a juvenile court (including an appeal by case stated or, in Scotland, stated case) as they apply in relation to proceedings in a juvenile court.

[(3) The said sections 39 and 49 shall extend to Scotland and the said sections 46 and 54 shall extend to England and Wales, but—

(*a*) references to a court in the said sections 39 and 49 shall not include a court in Scotland; and

(*b*) references to a court in the said sections 46 and 54 shall not include a court in England or Wales.] [15]

(4) The said sections 39 and 49 and the said sections 46 and 54 shall, with the necessary modifications, apply in relation to sound and television broadcasts as they apply in relation to newspapers.

Powers of local authority to visit and assist persons formerly in their care

58. Where a person was at or after the time when he attained the age

---

[13] Words repealed by Children and Young Persons Act 1969 (c. 54), ss. 72 (4), 73 (4) (*d*), Sched. 6.

[14] Words repealed and added by Social Work (Scotland) Act 1968 (c. 49), ss. 95 (1), 97 (1), Sched. 8, para. 68.

[14a] Words substituted by Local Authority Social Services Act 1970 (c. 42), s. 14 (1), Sched. 2, para. 10.

[15] Subsection substituted by Children and Young Persons Act 1969 (c. 54), ss. 72 (3), 73 (4) (*c*), Sched. 5, para. 53.

of seventeen in the care of a local authority under the Children Act 1948, the principal Act or the principal Scottish Act, or by virtue of an order under the Matrimonial Proceedings (Children) Act 1958 or the Matrimonial Proceedings (Magistrates' Courts) Act 1960, but has ceased to be in their care, then, while he is under the age of twenty-one, the local authority, if so requested by him, may cause him to be visited, advised and befriended and, in exceptional circumstances, to be given financial assistance.

59. [*Repealed by Children and Young Persons Act* 1969 (*c.* 54), *ss.* 72 (4), 73 (4) (*d*), *Sched.* 6.]

Supplementary provisions

Expenses

60. There shall be paid out of moneys provided by Parliament any expenses incurred by the Secretary of State under this Act and any increase attributable to this Act in the moneys so payable under any other enactment.

61. [*Repealed by Children and Young Persons Act* 1969 (*c.* 54), *s.* 72 (4), *Sched.* 6.]

Effect of Act on general grants in Scotland

62.—(1) Any expenditure incurred by virtue of this Act by the council of a county or of a large burgh shall be relevant expenditure for the purposes of sections 2 and 3 of the Local Government and Miscellaneous Financial Provisions (Scotland) Act 1958 (which relate to general grants) whether or not it is expenditure specified in Schedule 1 to that Act.

(2) The Secretary of State shall have power, by an order made in the like manner and subject to the like provisions as a general grant order, to vary the provisions of any general grant order made before the commencement of this Act for a grant period ending after the commencement of this Act.

(3) Any order made by virtue of this section may be made for all or any of the years comprised in the said grant period, as may be specified in the order, and in respect of the year or years so specified shall increase the annual aggregate amount of the general grants to such extent as may appear to the Secretary of State to be appropriate having regard to any additional expenditure incurred or likely to be incurred by councils of counties or of large burghs in consequence of the passing of this Act.

(4) The provisions of this section shall have effect without prejudice to the exercise of any power conferred by section 2 (2) of the Local Government and Miscellaneous Financial Provisions (Scotland) Act 1958 (which confers power to vary general grant orders in consequence of unforeseen increases in the level of prices, costs or remuneration).

(5) In this section the expression " general grant order " and " grant period " have the meanings respectively assigned to them by subsection (5) and subsection (6) of section 1 of the Local Government and Miscellaneous Financial Provisions (Scotland) Act 1958.

(6) This section extends to Scotland only.

Interpretation

63.—(1) In this Act " the principal Act " means the Children and Young Persons Act 1933 and " the principal Scottish Act " means the Children and Young Persons (Scotland) Act 1937.

(2) References in this Act to any enactment are references thereto as amended and include references thereto as applied, by any other enactment including, except where the context otherwise requires, any enactment contained in this Act.

Amendments, transitional provisions, and repeals

64.—(1) The enactments mentioned in Schedule 3 to this Act shall have effect subject to the amendments specified therein.

(2) This Act shall have effect subject to the transitional provisions contained in Schedule 4 to this Act.

[*Subsection* (2) *repealed by Statute Law (Repeals) Act* 1974 (*c.* 22), *Sched., Pt. XI.*]

Citation, construction, commencement and extent

65.—(1) This Act may be cited as the Children and Young Persons Act 1963.

(2) This Act and the Children and Young Persons Acts 1933 to 1956 may be cited as the Children and Young Persons Acts 1933 to 1963, and this Act and the Children and Young Persons (Scotland) Acts 1937 and 1956 may be cited as the Children and Young Persons (Scotland) Acts 1937 to 1963.

(3) This Act, except in so far as it amends any Act not construed as one with the principal Act or the principal Scottish Act, shall be construed, in its application to England and Wales, as one with the principal Act and, in its application to Scotland, as one with the principal Scottish Act.

(4) The following provisions of this Act do not extend to Scotland, that is to say, Part I except sections 1, 10 and 32, sections 56 and 61, and Schedules 1 and 2 and Schedule 4 except paragraph 3.

(5) [. . .] [16] sections 42 [. . .] [16] of this Act, paragraphs 7, 8, [. . .] [16] and 50 of Schedule 3, and so much of Schedule 5 as relates to section 25 and section 26 of the principal Act, extend to Northern Ireland.

(6) This Act shall come into operation on such day as the Secretary of State may by order made by statutory instrument appoint, and different days may be so appointed for different purposes; and any reference in any provision of this Act to the commencement of this Act shall be construed as a reference to the time at which that provision comes into operation.

SCHEDULES

SCHEDULE 1

[*Repealed by Children and Young Persons Act* 1969 (*c.* 54), *s.* 72 (4), *Sched.* 6.]

SCHEDULE 2 [17]

CONSTITUTION OF JUVENILE COURTS

PART I

OUTSIDE METROPOLITAN AREA

Juvenile court panels

1. The following provisions of this Part of this Schedule shall have effect as respects any area outside the metropolitan stipendiary court area and the City of London.

[16] Words repealed by Children and Young Persons Act 1969 (c. 54), s. 72 (4), Sched. 6.
[17] Amended by Administration of Justice Act 1964 (c. 42), s. 12 (1) (2) (3).

2. A justice shall not be qualified to sit as a member of a juvenile court unless he is a member of a juvenile court panel, that is to say, a panel of justices specially qualified to deal with juvenile cases.

3. Subject to the following provisions of this Part of this Schedule, a juvenile court panel shall be formed for every petty sessions area.

Combined juvenile court panels

4. A magistrates' courts committee may make recommendations to the Secretary of State—

(a) for the formation of a combined juvenile court panel for two or more petty sessions areas, or

(b) for the dissolution of any such combined juvenile court panel,

if the committee's area comprises at least one of the petty sessions areas concerned.

5. It shall be the duty of the magistrates' courts committee for any area, if directed to do so by the Secretary of State, to review the functioning of juvenile courts in their area and on completion of the review to submit to the Secretary of State either a report making such recommendations as are mentioned in paragraph 4 of this Schedule or a report giving reasons for making no such recommendations.

6. Subject to the provisions of this Schedule—

(a) where a magistrates' courts committee make such recommendations to the Secretary of State, he may make an order giving effect to them subject to any modifications he thinks fit; and

(b) where a magistrates' courts committee fail to comply within six months with a direction of the Secretary of State under the preceding paragraph, or the Secretary of State is dissatisfied with the report submitted in pursuance of such a direction, he may make such order as he thinks fit for the purposes mentioned in paragraph 4 of this Schedule.

Effect of order establishing combined panel

7. Where a combined juvenile court panel is formed for any petty sessions areas any justice who is a member of the panel may exercise in relation to each of the areas any jurisdiction exercisable by him as a member of a juvenile court.

Restrictions on formation of combined panels

8. No order under this Schedule shall provide for the formation of a combined juvenile court panel for an area which includes—

(a) a county or part of a county and the whole or part of another county; or

(b) two county boroughs.

9. An order under this Schedule providing for the formation of a combined juvenile court panel for an area which comprises a borough having a separate magistrates' courts committee shall not be made except with the consent of every magistrates' courts committee the whole or part of whose area is included in the area for which the combined panel is formed.

Consultations and notices

10. A magistrates' courts committee, before submitting recommendations for an order under this Schedule, shall consult and, when submitting any such recommendations, shall give notice to—

(a) the justices acting for any petty sessions area concerned which is within the committee's area (except where the committee's area is a borough); and

(b) any other magistrates' courts committee the whole or part of whose area is concerned;

and shall also consult the said justices before commenting on any recommendations on which they are consulted under this paragraph by another magistrates' courts committee.

11. Where the Secretary of State proposes to make an order under this Schedule in a case where either no recommendations have been made to him or the proposed order departs from the recommendations made to him, he shall send a copy of the proposed order to the magistrates' courts committee for any area the whole or part of which is concerned and to the justices acting for any petty sessions area concerned.

12. Where notice of recommendations or a copy of a proposed order is required to be sent under the preceding paragraphs to any justices or committee, the Secre-

tary of State shall, before making an order, consider any representations made to him by the justices or committee, or by any juvenile court panel concerned, within one month from the time the notice was given or the copy of the proposed order was sent.

PART II

METROPOLITAN AREA

13. The following provisions of this Part of this Schedule shall have effect as respects the metropolitan stipendiary court area and the City of London (in this Part of this Schedule referred to as the metropolitan area).

14. Juvenile courts shall be constituted for the whole of the metropolitan area but shall sit for such divisions and in such places as the Secretary of State may by order specify, without prejudice, however, to their jurisdiction with respect to the whole area.

15. Subject to the following provisions of this Schedule—

(a) each juvenile court shall consist of a chairman and two other members and shall have both a man and a woman among its members;

(b) the chairman shall be a person nominated by the Secretary of State to act as chairman of juvenile courts for the metropolitan area and shall be either a metropolitan stipendiary magistrate or a justice of the peace for the county of London selected, in such manner as may be provided by an order of the Secretary of State, from a panel of such justices from time to time nominated by him; and

(c) the other members shall be justices so selected from that panel.

16. If at any time, by reason of illness or other emergency, no person nominated under paragraph 15 (b) of this Schedule is available to act as chairman of a juvenile court, any metropolitan stipendiary magistrate or, with the consent of the Secretary of State, any justice of the peace selected as aforesaid from the said panel, may act temporarily as chairman.

17. Where it appears to the chairman that a juvenile court cannot, without adjournment, be fully constituted, and that an adjournment would not be in the interests of justice, the chairman may sit with one other member (whether a man or a woman) or, if a metropolitan stipendiary magistrate, may sit alone.

18. The Secretary of State, in nominating any persons under this Part of this Schedule, shall have regard to the previous experience of the persons available and their special qualifications for dealing with juvenile cases; and every such nomination shall be for a specified period and shall be revocable by the Secretary of State.

[*Paragraph (19) repealed by Administration of Justice Act 1964 (c. 42), s. 41 (8), Sched. 5.*]

PART III

GENERAL

20. An order of the Secretary of State under this Schedule shall be made by statutory instrument and may be revoked or varied by a subsequent order thereunder.

21. Any such order may contain supplementary, incidental and consequential provisions.

. . . .

Married Women's Property Act 1964

(1964 c. 19)

An Act to amend the law relating to rights of property as between husband and wife. [25th March 1964]

Money and property derived from housekeeping allowance

1. If any question arises as to the right of a husband or wife to money derived from any allowance made by the husband for the expenses of the matrimonial home or for similar purposes, or to any property acquired out of such money, the money or property shall, in the absence of any agreement between them to the contrary, be treated as belonging to the husband and the wife in equal shares.

Short title and extent

2.—(1) This Act may be cited as the Married Women's Property Act 1964.

(2) This Act does not extend to Northern Ireland.

Adoption Act 1964

(1964 c. 57)

An Act to provide for effect to be given to certain adoption orders made outside Great Britain; to facilitate the proof of adoption orders in different parts of the United Kingdom; and for connected purposes. [16th July 1964]

Extension of enactments referring to adoption [1]

1. (1)–(2) [*Repealed by Children Act* 1975 (*c.* 72), *Sched.* 4.]

(3) An order authorising adoption made in the Isle of Man or in any of the Channel Islands shall have the same effect for the purposes of section 19 of the said Act of 1958 (citizenship) as an adoption order, if it is made after the commencement of this Act; and if such an order was made before the commencement of this Act in respect of a person who would have become a citizen of the United Kingdom and Colonies at the date of the order had this Act been then in force, he shall be a citizen of the United Kingdom and Colonies as from the commencement of this Act.

(4) [*Repealed by Children Act* 1975 (*c.* 72), *Sched.* 4.]

(5) Any such provision as is mentioned in subsection (1) of this section which, by virtue of subsection (4) of section 53 of the said Act of 1958, applies in relation to orders under that section shall, as respects anything done after the commencement of this Act, apply also in relation to similar orders made, whether before or after the commencement of this Act, in Northern Ireland, the Isle of Man or any of the Channel Islands, and shall be construed accordingly; and any such order made after the commencement of this Act shall also have the same effect as an adoption order for the purposes of the provisions mentioned in sub-section (2) of this section.

Evidence of adoptions etc.

2.—(1) Any document which under section 20 (2) or section 22 (2) of the Adoption Act 1958 or section 14 (9) of the Adoption of Children Act (Northern Ireland) 1950 or any corresponding enactment of the Parliament of Northern Ireland for the time being in force is receivable

[1] See Children Act 1975 (c. 72), Sched. 3, para. 44, *post.*

as evidence of any matter in any part of Great Britain or in Northern Ireland shall be so receivable also in the rest of Great Britain or, as the case may be, in Great Britain.

[*Subsection* (2) *repealed by Statute Law (Repeals) Act* 1974 (*c.* 22), *Sched.*, *Pt. XI.*]

Registration of adoptions outside Great Britain

3.[2]—(1) Where the Registrar General or the Registrar General for Scotland is notified by the authority maintaining a register of adoptions in Northern Ireland, the Isle of Man or any of the Channel Islands that an order has been made in that country authorising the adoption of an infant to whom an entry in the Registers of Births (or, as the case may be, the Register of Births) or the Adopted Children Register relates, he shall cause the entry to be marked with the word " Adopted " or " Re-adopted ", as the case may require, followed by the name, in brackets, of the country in which the order was made.

(2) Where, after an entry has been so marked, the Registrar General or the Registrar General for Scotland is notified as aforesaid that the order has been quashed, that an appeal against the order has been allowed or that the order has been revoked, he shall cause the marking to be cancelled; and a copy or extract of an entry in any register, being an entry the marking of which is cancelled under this subsection, shall be deemed to be an accurate copy if and only if both the marking and the cancellation are omitted therefrom.

(3) The preceding provisions of this section shall apply in relation to orders corresponding to orders under section 53 of the said Act of 1958 as they apply in relation to orders authorising the adoption of an infant; but any marking of an entry required by virtue of this subsection shall consist of the word " Provisionally " followed by the words mentioned in subsection (1) of this section.

(4) Without prejudice to subsections (2) and (3) of this section, where, after an entry in the Registers of Births or the Register of Births has been marked in accordance with this section, the birth is re-registered under section 14 of the Births and Deaths Registration Act 1953 or section 2 of the Registration of Births, Deaths and Marriages (Scotland) (Amendment) Act 1934 (re-registration of birth of legitimated persons), the entry made on the re-registration shall be marked in the like manner.

Short title, citation, construction and extent

4.—(1) This Act may be cited as the Adoption Act 1964.

(2) This Act, the Adoption Act 1958 and the Adoption Act 1960 may be cited together as the Adoption Acts 1958 to 1964.

(3) This Act shall be construed as one with the Adoption Act 1958.

(4) This Act, except so far as it extends the operation of section 19 of the Adoption Act 1958, does not extend to Northern Ireland.

---

[2] Amended by the Registration of Births, Deaths and Marriages (Scotland) Act 1965 (c. 49), s. 58 (1), Sched. 1, para. 10, and prospectively by Children Act 1975 (c. 72), Sched. 3, para. 45, *post*.

Administration of Estates (Small Payments) Act 1965

(1965 c. 32)

An Act to provide for increasing the limits in enactments and instruments which allow property to be disposed of on death without probate or other proof of title, or in pursuance of a nomination made by the deceased; to extend certain of the said enactments relating to an intestate's property to cases where the deceased leaves a will; and for connected purposes.

[5th August 1965]

Increase in amounts disposable on death without representation

1.—(1) In the enactments and instruments listed in Schedule 1 to this Act, of which—

(*a*) those listed in Part I are enactments authorising the disposal of property on death, without the necessity for probate or other proof of title, to persons appearing to be beneficially entitled thereto, to relatives or dependants of the deceased or to other persons described in the enactments, but subject to a limit which is in most cases £100 and which does not in any case exceed £100;

(*b*) those listed in Part II are enactments giving power to make rules or regulations containing corresponding provisions subject to a limit of £100; and

(*c*) those listed in Part III are such rules and regulations as aforesaid and instruments containing corresponding provisions made under other enactments and containing a limit which does not in any case exceed £200;

the said limit shall, subject to the provisions of that Schedule, in each case be £500 instead of the limit specified in the enactment or instrument; and for references to the said limits in those enactments and instruments there shall accordingly be substituted references to £500.

[*Subsection* (2) *repealed by National Debt Act* 1972 (*c.* 65), *s.* 17 (1), *Sched.*]

Increase in amounts disposable on death by nomination

2.—(1) In the enactments and instruments listed in Schedule 2 to this Act (which enable a person by nomination to dispose of property on his death up to a limit of £100 or, in some cases, £200) the said limit shall, subject to the provisions of that Schedule, in each case be £500 instead of the limit specified in the enactments or instrument; and for references to the said limits in the said enactments and instrument there shall accordingly be substituted references to £500.

(2) This section shall apply in relation to any nomination delivered at or sent to the appropriate office, or made in the appropriate book, after the expiration of a period of one month beginning with the date on which this Act is passed.

Extension of certain enactments relating to intestacies to cases where deceased leaves a will

3.—(1) The enactments mentioned in Schedule 3 to this Act (all of which are listed in Part I of Schedule 1 to this Act) shall have effect

F.L.S.—9

subject to the amendments in that Schedule, which are amendments extending the operation of those enactments to cases where the deceased leaves a will.

(2) This section shall not extend to Northern Ireland.

Estate duty

4.—(1) Section 25 (2) of the Local Government Superannuation Act 1953 (under which a certificate as to estate duty may be required before a payment without representation is made under that section), section 24 (4) of the Industrial and Provident Societies Act 1965 (under which a similar certificate is required before a payment is made on a nomination under that Act) and so much of section 61 (11) of the London Midland and Scottish Railway Act 1924, section 99 (12) of the Southern Railway Act 1924 and section 3 (12) of the London and North Eastern Railway Act 1944 (which relate to the railway savings banks) as contains corresponding provisions shall cease to have effect.

(2), (3) [*Repealed by Finance Act* 1975 (c. 7), *Sched.* 13.]

Power to amend or repeal corresponding or superseded enactments

5.—(1) If it appears to the Treasury that any provision in an Act (including a local Act) passed before this Act corresponds to any provision amended by section 1 or section 2 of this Act [or to section 28 (5) of the Trustee Savings Banks Act 1969] [1] [or to section 6 (1) of the National Debt Act 1972] [1a] [or to sections 66 (1) and (2), 67 or 68 of the Friendly Societies Act 1974] [1b] and contains a limit of less than £500, the Treasury may by order substitute a limit of £500 for the limit contained in that provision, but subject to such exceptions, if any, including exceptions as regards the operation of the order in Northern Ireland, the Isle of Man, the Channel Islands or any other place outside Great Britain, as may be specified in the order; and an order under this subsection may make such consequential amendments in the Act to which it relates as appear to the Treasury to be expedient.

(2) If it appears to the Treasury that any provision in a local Act passed before the Local Government Superannuation Act 1953 is wholly or mainly superseded by section 25 (1) of the said Act of 1953 as amended by section 1 of this Act, the Treasury may by order repeal that provision.

(3) An order under subsection (1) of this section amending a local Act may repeal any provision of that Act corresponding to any provision repealed by section 4 of this Act.

(4) No order shall be made under this section in respect of any provision in a local Act the Bill for which was promoted by a local authority except on the application of that authority or their successors.

(5) Any order under this section shall be made by statutory instrument subject to annulment in pursuance of a resolution of either House of Parliament.

---

[1] Words added by Trustee Savings Banks Act 1969 (c. 50), s. 96 (10).
[1a] Words added by National Debt Act 1972 (c. 65), s. 6 (3).
[1b] Words added by Friendly Societies Act 1974 (c. 46), Sched. 9.

Power to provide for further increases

6.—(1) [2] The Treasury may from time to time by order direct that—

(a) sections 1 and 2 of this Act, so far as they relate to any enactment; and

(b) section 8 of the Superannuation Act 1887, section 38 (2) of the Finance Act 1918, section 14 (2) of the Ministerial Salaries and Members' Pensions Act 1965 [section 24 of the Parliamentary and other Pensions Act 1972] [2a] and section 68 of the Friendly Societies Act 1974] [2b] (which contain provisions similar to the enactments to which section 1 of this Act relates but subject to a limit of £500); and

(c) section 66 (2) of the Merchant Shipping Act 1970) [2c] and

(d) section 6 (1) of the National Debt Act 1972) [1a]; and

(e) sections 66 and 67 of the said Act of 1974 (which contain provisions similar to the enactments to which section 2 of this Act relates but subject to a limit of £500)] [2b]

shall have effect as if for references to £500 there were substituted references to such higher amount as may be specified in the order.

(2) Any order under this section shall apply in relation to deaths occurring after the expiration of a period of one month beginning with the date on which the order comes into force, except that, so far as section 2 of this Act has effect by virtue of any such order, subsection (2) of that section shall apply as if for the reference to the date on which this Act is passed there were substituted a reference to the date on which the order come into force [and that any such order made by virtue of subsection (1) (e) of this section shall apply in relation to any nomination delivered at or sent to the appropriate office, or made in the appropriate book, after the expiration of a period of one month beginning with the date on which the order comes into force.] [2b]

(3) Where an order under this section [or section 29 of the Trustee Savings Banks Act 1969] [1] specifying any amount is in force, references in section 5 (1) of this Act to £500 shall be construed as references to the amount specified in the order.

(4) Any order under this section may be revoked by a subsequent order and shall be made by statutory instrument; and no such order shall be made unless a draft of the order has been laid before Parliament and approved by a resolution of each House of Parliament.

Short title, interpretation, extent, commencement and repeals

7.—(1) This Act may be cited as the Administration of Estates (Small Payments) Act 1965.

(2) Any reference in this Act to an enactment or instrument shall be construed as including a reference to that enactment or instrument as amended, extended or applied by any other enactment or instrument.

(3) The amendment of any instrument by this Act shall be without prejudice to any power of amending or revoking that instrument.

(4) Save as otherwise expressly provided, so far as this Act amends or gives power to amend, or repeals, any provision which extends to any place outside Great Britain it shall have the same extent.

(5) Subject to sections 2 (2) and 6 (2) of this Act, this Act shall apply

[2] Extended by National Savings Act 1971 (c. 29), s. 9 (2), and Local Government Act 1972 (c. 70), s. 119 (3), and amended by Superannuation (Miscellaneous Provisions) Act 1967 (c. 28), s. 6 (2).

[2a] Words added by Parliamentary and other Pensions Act 1972 (c. 48), s. 24 (4).

[2b] Words added by Friendly Societies Act 1973 (c. 46), Sched. 9.

[2c] Words added by Merchant Shipping Act 1970 (c. 36), Sched. 3, para. 11.

in relation to deaths occurring after the expiration of a period of one month beginning with the date on which it is passed.

(6) The enactments mentioned in Schedule 4 to this Act are hereby repealed to the extent specified in the third column of that Schedule, but this subsection shall not affect the operation of those enactments in relation to deaths occurring before the expiration of the said period.

SCHEDULES

SCHEDULE 1

STATUTORY PROVISIONS AUTHORISING DISPOSAL OF PROPERTY
ON DEATH WITHOUT REPRESENTATION

PART I

ENACTMENTS

Short title and chapter	Provision amended by section 1
The Friendly Societies Act 1829 (10 Geo. 4. c. 56).	Section 24.
The Army Pensions Act 1830 (11 Geo. 4 & 1 Will. 4. c. 41).	Section 5.
The Loan Societies Act 1840 (3 & 4 Vict. c. 110).	Section 11.
The Navy and Marines (Property of Deceased) Act 1865 (28 & 29 Vict. c. 111).	Sections 5, 6 and 8. [. . .] 2d
The Great Western Railway Act 1885 (48 & 49 Vict. c. cxlvii).	Section 45 (8).
The Regimental Debts Act 1893 (56 & 57 Vict. c. 5).	Sections 7 and 9 and, except in relation to liability to estate duty section 16. [. . .] 2e
The Taff Vale Railway Act 1895 (58 & 59 Vict. c. cxxii).	Section 18 (10). [. . .] 2f
The Superannuation (Ecclesiastical Commissioners and Queen Anne's Bounty) Act 1914 (4 & 5 Geo. 5. c. 5).	Section 7. [. . .] 3
The Constabulary (Ireland) Act 1922 (12 & 13 Geo. 5. c. 55).	Paragraph 15 (3) of Part II of the Schedule.
The London Midland and Scottish Railway Act 1924 (14 & 15 Geo. 5. c. liv).	Section 61 (11) except as it applies in Northern Ireland.
The Southern Railway Act 1924 (14 & 15 Geo. 5. c. lxvi).	Section 99 (12). [. . .] 3
The Government Annuities Act 1929 (19 & 20 Geo. 5. c. 29).	Sections 21 and 57.
The Superannuation (Various Services) Act 1938 (1 & 2 Geo. 6. c. 13).	Section 2.
The Greenwich Hospital Act 1942 (5 & 6 Geo. 6. c. 35).	Section 2.
The London and North Eastern Railway Act 1944 (7 & 8 Geo. 6. c. x).	Section 3 (12) (b).
The U.S.A. Veterans' Pensions (Administration) Act 1949 (12, 13 & 14 Geo. 6. c. 45).	Section 1 (3) (c).
The Local Government Superannuation Act 1953 (1 & 2 Eliz. 2. c. 25).	Section 25 (1).
The Building Societies Act 1962 (10 & 11 Eliz. 2. c. 37).	Section 46 (1), but not so as to affect paragraph 7 of Schedule 8.
The Industrial and Provident Societies Act 1965 (1965 c. 12).	Section 25.

2d Repealed by Industrial Relations Act 1971 (c. 723, s. 169, Sched. 9.
2e Repealed by Merchant Shipping Act 1970 (c. 36), s. 100 (3), Sched. 5.
2f Repealed by Friendly Societies Act 1974 (c. 46), Sched. 11.
3 Repealed by Teachers' Superannuation Act 1965 (c. 83), ss. 2 (1) (c), 8 (1) (b), Sched. 3, Pt. II.

PART II

ENABLING ENACTMENTS

Short title and chapter	Provision amended by section 1
The Pensions and Yeomanry Pay Act 1884 (47 & 48 Vict. c. 55).	Section 4.
The Elementary School Teachers (Superannuation) Act 1898 (61 & 62 Vict. c. 57).	Section 6 (1) (*d*).
	[. . .] ³ª
	[. . .] ⁴

PART III

INSTRUMENTS

Title and number	Provision amended by section 1
Rules of the Supreme Court	Rule 11 of Order 22.
Amended regulations dated 11th July 1907 and made by the Secretary of State for War under section 4 of the Pensions and Yeomanry Pay Act 1884.	Paragraph 1.
Regulations as to the suitors fund and fee fund accounts (S.R. & O. 1913/1332).	Regulation 13 (*b*) and (*c*) and Form 1 in the Appendix.
The Elementary School Teachers (Superannuation) Rules 1919 (S.R. & O. 1920/2298).	Rule 15.
Regulations dated 27th November 1920 and made by the Secretary of State for Air under section 4 of the Pensions and Yeomanry Pay Act 1884 as applied to the Royal Air Force by the Air Force (Application of Enactments) (No. 2) Order 1918.	Paragraph 1.
The Royal Irish Constabulary Pensions Order 1922 (S.R. & O. 1922/945).	Article 15 (3).
Supreme Court Fund Rules 1927 (S.R. & O. 1927/1184).	Rule 62 and Forms 63 and 64 in the Appendix.
The Trustee Savings Banks Regulations 1929 (S.R. & O. 1929/1048).	Regulation 28 (1).
The Savings Certificate Regulations 1933 (S.R. & O. 1933/1149).	Regulation 19 (1).
Rules of the Supreme Court (Northern Ireland) 1936 (S.R. & O. 1936/70).	Rule 12 of Order 22.
County Court Rules (S.R. & O. 1936/626)	Rule 22 of Order 48.
Treasury Order dated 8th April 1938 prescribing certain public departments for the purposes of section 8 of the Superannuation Act 1887 and making regulations with respect to the distribution without probate under the said section of sums due from a public department (S.R. & O. 1938/303).	Article 2 and the Schedule.
The Superannuation (Various Services) Regulations 1938 (S.R. & O. 1938/304).	Article 1 and the Schedule.
The Post Office Savings Bank Regulations 1938 (S.R. & O. 1938/556).	Regulation 39 (1).
The Compensation to Seamen (War Damage to Effects) Scheme 1945 (S.R. & O. 1945/1164).	Article 4.
The Navy and Marines (Property of Deceased) Order 1956 (S.I. 1956/1217).	Article 16.
The Premium Savings Bonds Regulations 1956 (S.I. 1956/1657).	Regulation 9.
The Teachers (Superannuation) (Scotland) Regulations 1957 (S.I. 1957/356).	Regulation 58 (1).
The Military Pensions (Commonwealth Relations Office) Regulations 1959 (S.I. 1959/735).	Regulation 2 and the Schedule.
The Court of Protection Rules 1960 (S.I. 1960/1146).	Rule 83 (2).
The Police Pensions Regulations 1962 (S.I. 1962/2756).	Regulation 57 (3).
The Firemen's Pension Scheme Order 1964 (S.I. 1964/1148).	Article 47 (3).

³ª Repealed by National Savings Bank Act 1971 (c. 29), s. 28 (1), Sched. 2.
⁴ Repealed by Trustee Savings Banks Act 1969 (c. 50), s. 96 (1), Sched. 3 Pt. I.

SCHEDULE 2

STATUTORY PROVISIONS AUTHORISING DISPOSAL OF
PROPERTY ON DEATH BY NOMINATION

Title and chapter or serial number	Provision amended by section 2
The Trade Union Act Amendment Act 1876 (39 & 40 Vict. c. 22).	Section 10 except as it applies in Northern Ireland.
The Great Western Railway Act 1885 (48 & 49 Vict. c. cxlvii).	Section 45 (7).
The Taff Vale Railway Act 1895 (58 & 59 Vict. c. cxxii).	Section 18 (9).
	[. . .] [2f]
The London Midland and Scottish Railway Act 1924 (14 & 15 Geo. 5. c. liv).	Section 61 (9).
The Southern Railway Act 1924 (14 & 15 Geo. 5. c. lxvi).	Section 99 (10).
The Trustee Savings Banks Regulations 1929 (S.R. & O. 1929/1048).	Regulations 11, 21 and 22.
The Industrial and Provident Societies Act 1965 (1965 c. 12).	Section 23 (3) (*c*).

SCHEDULE 3

EXTENSION OF ENACTMENTS RELATING TO INTESTACIES
THE LOAN SOCIETIES ACT 1840

(3 & 4 Vict. c. 110)

In section 11—

for the words "that no will was made and left by such deceased person" there shall be substituted the words "that no will of the deceased has been or will be proved";

[. . .] [5]

after the words "although no letters of administration shall have been taken out" there shall be inserted the words "and no probate of any will has been granted".

THE PROVIDENT NOMINATIONS AND SMALL
INTESTACIES ACT 1883

(46 & 47 Vict. c. 47)

[*Repealed by Industrial Relations Act* 1971 (*c.* 72), *s.* 169, *Sched.* 9.]

THE GREAT WESTERN RAILWAY ACT 1885

(48 & 49 Vict. c. cxlvii)

In section 45 (8) [. . .] [5] after the words "without letters of administration" there shall be inserted the words "or probate of any will".

THE TAFF VALE RAILWAY ACT 1895

(58 & 59 Vict. c. cxxii)

In section 18 (10) [. . .] [5] after the words "without letters of administration" there shall be inserted the words "or probate of any will".

THE FRIENDLY SOCIETIES ACT 1896

(59 & 60 Vict. c. 25)

[*Repealed by Friendly Societies Act* 1974 (*c.* 46), *Sched.* 11.]

[5] Words repealed by Statute Law (Repeals) Act 1974 (c. 22), Sched., Pt. XI.

1965 c. 32

THE LONDON MIDLAND AND SCOTTISH RAILWAY ACT 1924
(14 & 15 Geo. 5. c. liv)

In section 61 (11) [. . .]⁵ after the words "without letters of administration" there shall be inserted the words "or probate of any will".

THE SOUTHERN RAILWAY ACT 1924
(14 & 15 Geo. 5. c. lxvi)

In section 99 (12) [. . .]⁵ after the words "without letters of administration" there shall be inserted the words "or probate of any will".

THE BUILDING SOCIETIES ACT 1962
(10 & 11 Eliz. 2. c. 37)

In section 46—

[. . .]⁵

in subsection (2), after the words "without the grant of letters of administration" there shall be inserted the words "or probate of any will", [. . .]⁵

in subsection (3), for the words "died intestate" there shall be substituted the words "has died"; and

[. . .]⁵

THE INDUSTRIAL AND PROVIDENT SOCIETIES ACT 1965
(1965 c. 12)

In section 25 (1) [. . .]⁵ after the words "without letters of administration" there shall be inserted the words "or probate of any will".

SCHEDULE 4
[*Repealed by Statute Law (Repeals) Act* 1974 *(c. 22), Sched., Pt. XI.*]

Family Allowances Act 1965 [1]

(1965 c. 53)

Administrative provisions

Information as to, and proof of, age, marriage or death.

12. [Paragraphs 9 to 11 of Schedule 22 to the Social Security Act shall apply for the purposes of this Act as they apply for the purposes of that Act.] [1a]

Regulations

13.[1b]—(1) The Minister, in conjunction with the Treasury so far as relates to matters with respect to which the Treasury so direct, [. . .]²

---

[1] The whole of this Act is prospectively repealed by Sched. 5 to the Child Benefit Act 1975 (c. 61) with effect from a day or days to be appointed.

[1a] Words substituted by Social Security Act 1973 (c. 38), Sched. 27.

[1b] Amended by Family Allowances and National Insurance Act 1967 (c. 90), s. 2 (1) (2).

[2] Repealed by Post Office Act 1969 (c. 48), s. 141, Sched. 11, Pt. II.

263

may make regulations for prescribing anything which under this Act is to be prescribed and generally for carrying this Act into effect, and in particular, but without prejudice to the generality of this subsection—

(a) for prescribing the manner in which claims to allowances may be made;

(b) for specifying the circumstances in which a person is to be treated for the purposes of this Act as undergoing full-time instruction in a school or full-time training;

(c) for enabling a person to be appointed to exercise, on behalf of a claimant, or of a person to or by whom an allowance belongs or is receivable, who may be or become unable for the time being to act, any right or power which that claimant or person may be entitled to exercise under this Act, and for authorising a person so appointed to receive any sum on account of an allowance on behalf of that claimant or person;

(d) for imposing upon persons to whom allowances belong or by whom or on whose behalf sums on account of allowances are receivable the duty to furnish to the Minister information of facts affecting the right thereto;

(e) for making provision, in connection with the death of persons who had made claims for allowances or to whom allowances belonged or by whom sums on account of allowances were receivable, for enabling such claims to be proceeded with, [. . .] ³ for authorising payment or distribution of such sums to or amongst persons claiming as personal representatives, legatees, next of kin or creditors of such persons (or, in cases of illegitimacy of deceased persons, to or amongst others), and for dispensing with strict proof of the title of persons so claiming.

(2) Any regulations made under this Act by the Minister shall be made by statutory instrument and shall be subject to annulment in pursuance of a resolution of either House of Parliament.

(3) If any person contravenes or fails to comply with any requirement of regulations made under this Act, he shall be liable on summary conviction to a fine not exceeding ten pounds.

Interpretation

Provisions as to certain special circumstances affecting the operation of s. 3

17.—(1) A man and his wife shall not be deemed for the purposes of this Act to be living otherwise than together unless they are permanently living in separation either by agreement or under an order of a court, or one of them has deserted the other and the separation which is incident to the desertion has not come to an end.

(2) For the purposes of this Act, a child being legitimate issue of a deceased spouse of any person by an earlier marriage of the deceased spouse to another (including such a marriage which is void) shall be treated as issue of that person, and a child being illegitimate issue of a deceased spouse of any person shall be treated as issue of that person so far as regards any period during which the child is living with that person:

Provided that the foregoing provisions of this subsection shall not have effect in a case in which the marriage between the person in question and his or her deceased spouse was terminated otherwise than by the deceased spouse's death.

(3) Where a child born before the marriage of the child's parents has

³ Words repealed by National Insurance etc. Act 1969 (c. 4), s. 4 (4) (*b*).

been legitimated by virtue of the subsequent marriage of the parents, the child shall, for the purposes of this Act, be deemed to be issue of the marriage.

[*Subsection* (4) *repealed by Children Act* 1975 (*c.* 72), *Sched.* 4.]

(5) An illegitimate child shall not be treated for the purposes of this Act as being issue of the child's father.

(6) References in this Act to the parents, a parent, the father, or the mother of a child, or to an illegitimate child, shall be construed in accordance with the provisions of subsections (2) to (5) of this section.

(7) A child shall not be deemed for the purposes of this Act to have ceased to live with a person by reason of any temporary absence, and in particular by reason of absence at any school, and a person who has been contributing at any rate to the cost of providing for a child, or has been maintaining a child, shall not be treated as having ceased so to contribute, or to maintain the child, by reason of any temporary interruption or reduction of his contribution to the cost of providing for the child, and the question whether any such absence (other than at a school), interruption or reduction is or is not to be treated as temporary for the said purposes shall be determined by reference to such rules as may be prescribed.

[*Subsection* (8) *repealed by Social Security Act* 1973 (*c.* 38), *Sched.* 28.]

[*Subsection* (9) *repealed by National Insurance Act* 1971 (*c.* 50), *s.* 16 (3), *Sched.* 7.]

Definitions

19.—(1) In this Act, except where the context otherwise requires, the following expressions have the meanings hereby respectively assigned to them, that is to say—

" allowance " means an allowance under this Act;

" apprentice " means a person undergoing full-time training for any trade, business, profession, office, employment or vocation, and not in receipt of earnings exceeding two pounds a week (the weekly amount of a person's earnings being for this purpose calculated or estimated in such manner and on such basis as may be prescribed);

" the Insurance Act " means the National Insurance Act 1965;

" issue " means issue of the first generation;

" the Minister " means the Minister of Pensions and National Insurance.

[" The Social Security Act " means the Social Security Act 1973.] [4]

(2) Any reference in this Act to any other enactment shall, except so far as the context otherwise requires, be construed as a reference to that enactment as amended or applied by any other enactment, including any enactment contained in this Act.

Matrimonial Causes Act 1965 [1]

(1965 c. 72)

An Act to consolidate certain enactments relating to matrimonial causes, maintenance and declarations of legitimacy and British nationality, with corrections and improvements made under the Consolidation of Enactments (Procedure) Act 1949.

[8th November 1965]

PART I

DIVORCE, NULLITY AND OTHER MATRIMONIAL SUITS

Divorce

1–7. [*Repealed by Matrimonial Causes Act 1973 (c. 18), s. 54 (1) (b), Sched. 3.*]

Remarriage of divorced persons

8. [*Subsection (1) repealed by Matrimonial Causes Act 1973 (c. 18), s. 54 (1) (b), Sched. 3.*]

(2) No clergyman of the Church of England or the Church in Wales shall be compelled—

(a) to solemnise the marriage of any person whose former marriage has been dissolved and whose former spouse is still living; or

(b) to permit the marriage of such a person to be solemnised in the church or chapel of which he is the minister.

9–24. [*Repealed by Matrimonial Causes Act 1973 (c. 18), s. 54 (1) (b), Sched. 3.*]

Alteration of agreements by court after death of one party

25. [*Subsections (1) (2) and (3) repealed by Matrimonial Causes Act 1973 (c. 18), s. 54 (1) (b), Sched. 3. Subsection (4) and (5) repealed by Inheritance (Provision for Family and Dependants) Act 1975 (c. 63), Sched.*]

Maintenance from estate of deceased former spouse

26.–28A. [*These sections were repealed by Inheritance (Provision for Family and Dependants) Act 1975 (c. 63), Sched.*]

29–41. [*Repealed by Matrimonial Causes Act 1973 (c. 18), s. 51 (1) (b), Sched. 3.*]

PART IV

MISCELLANEOUS AND GENERAL

Miscellaneous

Condonation

42.[2]—(1.) [For the purpose of the Matrimonial Proceedings (Magistrates' Courts) Act 1960] [3] any presumption of condonation

---

[1] Explained by Matrimonial Causes Act 1967 (c. 56), ss. 7, 8.
[2] Subsections (1) (3) rtpealed, in so far as they apply to proceedings for divorce or judicial separation, by Divorce Reform Act 1969 (c. 55), s. 9 (2), Sched. 2.
[3] Words added by Matrimonial Causes Act 1973 (c. 18), s. 54 (1) (a), Sched. 2.

which arises from the continuance or resumption of marital intercourse may be rebutted by evidence sufficient to negative the necessary intent.

(2) For the purposes of [. . .] [4] the Matrimonial Proceedings (Magistrates' Courts) Act 1960, adultery or cruelty shall not be deemed to have been condoned by reason only of a continuation or resumption of cohabitation between the parties for one period not exceeding three months, or of anything done during such cohabitation, if it is proved that cohabitation was continued or resumed, as the case may be, with a view to effecting a reconciliation.

(3) [2] [For the purpose of the Matrimonial Proceedings (Magistrates' Courts Act 1960] [3] adultery which has been condoned shall not be capable of being revived.

Evidence

43.—(1) The evidence of a husband or wife shall be admissible in any proceedings to prove that marital intercourse did or did not take place between them during any period; [. . .] [5]

(2) The parties to any proceedings instituted in consequence of adultery and the husbands and wives of the parties shall be competent to give evidence in the proceedings; [. . .] [6]

(3) In any proceedings for nullity of marriage, evidence on the question of sexual capacity shall be heard in camera unless in any case the judge is satisfied that in the interests of justice any such evidence ought to be heard in open court.

44. [*Repealed by Matrimonial Causes Act 1973 (c. 18) s. 54 (1) (b), Sched. 3.*]

General

45. [*Repealed by Matrimonial Causes Act 1973 (c. 18), s. 54 (1) (b), Sched. 3.*]

Short title, interpretation, commencement and extent

46.[7]—(1) This Act may be cited as the Matrimonial Causes Act 1965.

[*Subsections (2) and (3) repealed by Matrimonial Causes Act 1973 (c. 18) s. 54 (1) (b), Sched. 3.*]

(4) [. . .], [8] this Act does not extend to Scotland or Northern Ireland.

---

[4] Words repealed by Divorce Reform Act 1969 (c. 55), s. 9 (2), Sched. 2.
[5] Words repealed by Matrimonial Causes Act 1973 (c. 18), s. 54 (1) (b), Sched. 3.
[6] Words repealed by Civil Evidence Act 1968 (c. 64), s. 16 (5).
[7] Extended by Adoption Act 1968 (c. 53), s. 10 (3).
[8] Words repealed by Matrimonial Causes Act 1973 (c. 18), s. 54 (1) (b), Sched. 3.

Supplementary Benefits Act 1966

(1966 c. 20)

PART III

RECOVERY OF EXPENSES

Liability to maintain

22.—(1) For the purposes of this Act—

(*a*) a man shall be liable to maintain his wife and his children, and

(*b*) a woman shall be liable to maintain her husband and her children;

and in this subsection the reference to a man's children includes a reference to children of whom he has been adjudged to be the putative father and the reference to a woman's children a reference to her illegitimate children.

(2) In the application of this section to Scotland, for the reference to children to whom a man has been adjudged to be the putative father there shall be substituted a reference to children his paternity of whom has been admitted or otherwise established.

Recovery of cost of benefit from persons liable for maintenance

23.—(1) The following provisions of this section shall apply where benefit is paid or claimed to meet requirements which are or include those of a person (in this section referred to as " the dependant ") whom another person is for the purposes of this Act liable to maintain, except where the dependant is an illegitimate child and the other person his father.

(2) The Commission may make a complaint against that other person to a magistrates' court and on such a complaint the court shall have regard to all the circumstances and, in particular, to the other person's resources and may order him to pay such sum, weekly or otherwise, as the court may consider appropriate.

(3) In determining whether to order any payments to be made in respect of benefit for any period before the complaint was made or the amount of any such payments the court shall disregard any excess of that other person's resources over what they were during that period.

(4) Any payments ordered to be made under this section shall be made—

(*a*) to the Minister in so far as they are attributable to any benefit (whether paid before or after the making of the order);

(*b*) to the person claiming benefit or (if different) the dependant; or

(*c*) to such other person as appears to the court expedient in the interests of the dependant;

and where the payments are ordered to be made to the Minister the Commission shall be a party to any proceedings with respect to the enforcement, revocation or variation of the order to which, but for this provision, the Minister would be a party.

(5) An order under this section shall be enforceable as an affiliation order, and any proceedings for such an order (but not proceedings for the enforcement, revocation or variation of such an order) shall be included among the proceedings which are domestic proceedings within the meaning of the Magistrates' Courts Act 1952; and section 56 of that Act (which defines " domestic proceedings ") shall have effect accordingly.

(6) The Maintenance Orders Act 1950 shall have effect as if an order under this section were included among the orders referred to in sub-sections (1) and (2) of section 4 and subsections (1) and (2) of section 9 and were a maintenance order within the meaning of Part II of that Act, that is to say, an order to which section 16 thereof applies; [. . .] [1]

(7) This section shall apply to Scotland subject to the following modifications—

(a) in subsection (1) the words from " except " to the end shall be omitted;

(b) for the reference to a complaint there shall be substituted a reference to an application;

(c) for any reference to a magistrates' court there shall be substituted a reference to the sheriff; and

(d) subsection (5), and, in subsection (6), the words from " and the Maintenance Orders Act 1958 " to the end, shall be omitted.

Affiliation orders

24.—(1) The following provisions of this section shall apply where benefit is paid to meet requirements which include those of an illegitimate child.

(2) If no affiliation order is in force the Commission may within three years from the time when any payment by way of benefit was made make application to a justice of the peace acting for the petty sessions area in which the mother of the child resides for a summons to be served under section 1 of the Affiliation Proceedings Act 1957.

(3) In any proceedings on an application under the preceding sub-section the court shall hear such evidence as the Commission may produce, [. . .] [2], and shall in all other respects, subject to the provisions of subsection (4) of this section, proceed as on an application made by the mother under the said section 1.

(4) An affiliation order made on an application under subsection (2) of this section may be made so as to provide that the payments, or a part of the payments, to be made thereunder shall, in lieu of being made to the mother or a person having the custody of the child, be made to the Minister or to such other person as the court may direct; and where the order provides for the payments to be made to the Minister the Commission shall be a party to any proceedings with respect to the enforcement, revocation or variation of the order to which, but for this provision, the Minister would be a party.

(5) On an application by the Commission in any proceedings under the said section 1 brought by the mother of the child an affiliation order may be made so as to provide as mentioned in subsection (4) of this section.

(6) Any affiliation order, whether made before or after the commencement of this Act, may on the application of the Commission be varied so as to provide as mentioned in subsection (4) of this section and any affiliation order which provides as mentioned in that subsection may on the application of the mother of the child be varied so as to provide that the payments thereunder shall be made to the mother or a person having the custody of the child.

(7) An application by the Commission under the preceding subsection may be made notwithstanding that the mother has died and no person has been appointed to have the custody of the child; and may, where the child is not in her care and she is not contributing to his maintenance, be made without making her a party to the proceedings.

[1] Words repealed by A.J.A. 1970 (c. 31), s. 54, Sched. 11.
[2] Words repealed by Affiliation Proceedings (Amendment) Act 1972 (c. 49), s. 1 (4) (b).

(8) Proceedings on an application under subsection (2) of this section shall be included among the proceedings which are domestic proceedings within the meaning of the Magistrates' Courts Act 1952; and section 56 of that Act (which defines " domestic proceedings ") shall have effect accordingly.

(9) The Maintenance Orders Act 1950 shall have effect as if this section were included in the enactments referred to in section 3 (1) of that Act and as if an order made on an application under subsection (2) of this section were a maintenance order within the meaning of Part II of that Act, that is to say, an order to which section 16 thereof applies; [. . .] [1]

(10) In the application of this section to Scotland, the following provisions shall have effect in substitution for subsections (2) to (9)—

(a) the Commission shall have the like right as the mother to raise an action of affiliation and aliment concluding for payment of aliment for the child;

(b) where in any action of affiliation and aliment in respect of the child, whether at the instance of the Commission under the foregoing paragraph or at the instance of the mother, the sheriff grants or has granted decree against any person for payment of aliment for the child, the sheriff may at the time of granting the decree or at any subsequent time on the application of the Commission, order that the sums due under the decree or any part thereof shall, in lieu of being paid to the mother of the child, be paid to the Minister or to such other person as the sheriff may direct;

(c) the Commission, if such an order is made in favour of the Minister or, if it is made in favour of another person, that person, shall have the like right to enforce the decree (so far as relating to the said sums) by diligence, including the right to take proceedings under the Civil Imprisonment (Scotland) Act 1882, as if the decree were a decree in favour of the Commission or other person;

(d) the Maintenance Orders Act 1950 shall have effect as if this subsection were included in the enactments referred to in section 8 (1) of that Act, and as if an order made on an application under paragraph (b) of this subsection were a maintenance order within the meaning of Part II of that Act, that is to say, an order to which section 16 thereof applies.

Orders under section 43 of National Assistance Act 1948

25.—(1) Any order made (whether before or after the commencement of this Act) under section 43 of the National Assistance Act 1948 shall be enforceable as an affiliation order, and accordingly section 56 (1) of that Act (recovery as civil debt) shall not apply to any sum due under such an order.

(2) Any proceedings for such an order (but not proceedings for the enforcement, revocation or variation of such an order) shall be included among the proceedings which are domestic proceedings within the meaning of the Magistrates' Courts Act 1952; and section 56 of that Act (which defines " domestic proceedings ") shall have effect accordingly.

(3) This section does not extend to Scotland.

Failure to maintain

30.—(1) Where a person persistently refuses or neglects to maintain himself or any person whom for the purposes of this Act he is liable to maintain, and in consequence of his refusal or neglect—

(a) benefit is awarded to meet requirements which are or include his or those of such a person; or

(b) free board and lodging are provided for him or such a person in a reception centre;

he shall be liable on summary conviction to imprisonment for a term not exceeding three months or to a fine not exceeding one hundred pounds or to both.

(2) For the purposes of this section a person shall not be deemed to refuse or neglect to maintain himself or any other person by reason only of anything done or omitted in furtherance of a trade dispute.

SCHEDULE 2

PROVISIONS FOR DETERMINING RIGHT TO AND AMOUNT OF BENEFIT

PART I

Aggregation of requirements and resources

3.—(1) Where a husband and wife are members of the same household their requirements and resources shall be aggregated and shall be treated as the husband's, and similarly, unless there are exceptional circumstances, as regards two persons cohabiting as man and wife.

(2) Where a person has to provide for the requirements of another person (not falling within the preceding sub-paragraph) who is a member of the same household, his requirements may be taken, and if that other person has not attained the age of sixteen shall be taken, to include the requirements of that other person, and in that case their resources also shall be aggregated.

Adjustment for exceptional circumstances

4.—(1) Where there are exceptional circumstances—

(a) benefit may be awarded at an amount exceeding that (if any) calculated in accordance with the preceding paragraphs;

(b) a supplementary allowance may be reduced below the amount so calculated or may be withheld;

as may be appropriate to take account of those circumstances.

(2) [...] [3]

PART II [4]

CALCULATION OF REQUIREMENTS

Application of paragraphs 9–13

8.—(1) Subject to sub-paragraph (2) of this paragraph, the amounts specified in paragraphs 9 to 13 of this Schedule are not applicable to persons falling within any of paragraphs 14 to 18 thereof.

(2) Where one only of the persons falling within paragraph 3 (1) of this Schedule falls within paragraph 16 or 18 thereof, sub-paragraph (1) of this paragraph shall not exclude the application of the said amounts to the other, but the amount applicable to him under the said paragraph 9 or the said paragraph 10 shall be [that applicable under] [4a] in sub-paragraph (b) or as the case may be (b) (i) thereof.

Amounts preceded by (a), (b) or(c) [4a]

8A.—(1) Where, in the following paragraphs, amounts are preceded by (a), (b) or (c)—

(a) the amount preceded by (a) is applicable if neither of the others is applicable;

(b) the amount preceded by (b) is applicable if either—

(i) the requirements are those of a person eligible for a supplementary

---

[3] Repealed by National Insurance and Supplementary Benefit Act 1973 (c. 42), Sched. 4.

[4] Amounts altered by S.I. 1974–854.

[4a] Substituted by 1973 (c. 42), Sched. 4.

pension and neither he nor a person whose requirements are aggregated with his under paragraph 3 of this Schedule is aged 80 years or more, or

(ii) requirements are those of a person who has been in receipt of a supplementary allowance for a continuous period of not less than two years and his right to the allowance is not, and was not at any time during the last two years of that period, subject to the condition of section 11 of this Act;

(c) the amount preceded by (c) is applicable if the requirements are those of a person eligible for a supplementary pension and either he or a person whose requirements are aggregated with his under paragraph 3 of this Schedule is aged 80 years or more.

(2) Where—

(a) an amount applicable under the following paragraphs to the requirements of any person is preceded by (b) or (c); and

(b) benefit is (or would but for this paragraph be) awarded in accordance with paragraph 4 of this Schedule at an increased amount so as to take account of exceptional expenses;

then, subject to sub-paragraph (3) below, the increase shall be made only to the extent that its weekly amount would (apart from this sub-paragraph) exceed—

(i) 50p where the amount applicable is preceded by (b), and

(ii) 75p where the amount applicable is preceded by (c).

(3) Sub-paragraph (2) above does not apply to an increase or part of an increase attributable to—

(a) heating expenses; or

(b) expenses taken into account, but not fully met, under paragraph 13 (1) (b) of this Schedule; or

(c) expenses of a person whose requirements are aggregated under paragraph 3 (2) of this Schedule with those of the persons entitled to the benefit.

Normal requirements 4

9. Requirements of persons other than blind persons—

(a) husband and wife or other persons falling within paragraph 3 (1) of this Schedule ... ...

    (a) 13·65
    (b) 16·35
    (c) 16·60

(b) person living alone or householder not falling within sub-paragraph (a) of this paragraph who is directly responsible for household necessities and rent (if any) ... ...

    (a) 8·40
    (b) 10·40
    (c) 10·65

(c) any other person aged—

  (i) not less than 18 years ... ...

    (a) 6·70
    (b) 8·40
    (c) 8·65

  (ii) less than 18 but not less than 16 years ... ...   5·15
  (iii) less than 16 but not less than 13 years ... ...   4·35
  (iv) less than 13 but not less than 11 years ... ...   3·55
  (v) less than 11 but not less than 5 years ... ...   2·90
  (vi) less than 5 years 2.40

Blind persons

10. Requirements of persons who are or include blind persons—

(a) husband and wife or other persons falling within paragraph 3 (1) of this Schedule—

  (i) if one of them blind ... ...

    (a) 14·90
    (b) 17·60
    (c) 17·85

  (ii) if both of them blind ... ...

    (a) 15·70
    (b) 18·40
    (c) 18·65

(b) any other blind person aged—

  (i) not less than 18 years ... ...

    (a) 9·65
    (b) 11·65
    (c) 11·90

(ii) less than 18 but not less than 16 years		6·05
(iii) less than 16 but not less than 13 years		4·35
(iv) less than 13 but not less than 11 years		3·55
(v) less than 11 but not less than 5 years		2.90
(vi) less than 5 years		2·40

[Persons disqualified for unemployment benefit

11—(1) If a person's right to a supplementary allowance is subject to the condition of section 11 of this Act, then, in relation to any period during which—

    (a) he is disqualified for receiving unemployment benefit by virtue of section [he is disqualified for receiving unemployment benefit under the Social Security Act 1975 by virtue of section 20 (1) of that Act] [4b] (disqualification by reference to conduct resulting in unemployment or conducing to its continuance) ; or

    (b) he is not so disqualified, but the circumstances are as mentioned in sub-paragraph (2) of this paragraph,

this Part of this Schedule shall have effect, as regards the determination of the amount of any supplementary allowance to which he is entitled, as if the amount specified in that entry in paragraph 9 or paragraph 10 of this Schedule which relates to his requirements (disregarding for this purpose the requirements of any other person which are to be or may be included in his by virtue only of paragraph 3 (2) of this Schedule) were reduced by a sum equal to 40 per cent. of the amount so specified or, if the amount so specified exceeds [the first of the amounts specified in paragraph 9 (b)] [4a] of this Schedule, 40 per cent. of the last mentioned amount (disregarding any amount by which that sum exceeds a multiple of 5p).

(2) The circumstances referred to in sub-paragraph (1) (b) of this paragraph are that the person concerned—

    (a) has not made a claim for unemployment benefit; or

    (b) has made such a claim, but the claim has not yet been determined; or

    (c) has had such a claim disallowed otherwise than by reason of his being disqualified as mentioned in sub-paragraph (1) (a) of this paragraph,

but in the opinion of the Commission he would be so disqualified if he were to make such a claim, or if his claim had been determined, or if it had not been disallowed for a different reason.

(3) [...] [5]

[Persons in receipt of supplementary pension

11. Additional requirements of person eligible for supplementary pension—

    (a) where he or a person whose requirements are aggregated with his under paragraph 3 of this Schedule is aged not less than 80 years ... ... £0·75

    (b) in any other case ... ... £0·50] [5b]

Persons in receipt of supplementary allowance for 2 years or more

12. Additional requirements of person in receipt of supplementary allowance where—

    (a) he has been in receipt thereof for a continuous period of not less than 2 years; and

    (b) his right to the allowance is not, and was not at any time during the last 2 years of that period, subject to the condition of section 11 of this Act ... ... [£0·50] [5a]

[Attendance requirements

12.—(1) The amounts applicable under the preceding paragraphs shall be increased by [£8·00] [4] in respect of the attendance requirements of a severely disabled person who either—

    (a) is entitled to attendance allowance in respect of his own disablement at the rate of [£8·00] [4] a week, or

---

[4b] Substituted by Social Security (Consequential Provisions) Act 1975 (c. 18), Sched. 2.
[5] Repealed by Social Security (Consequential Provisions) Act 1975 (c. 18), Sched. 1.
[5a] Amount substituted by S.I. 1970/1784.
[5b] Words substituted by S.I. 1971/1054, as amended by 1973 (c. 42), Sched. 4.

(*b*) is a child in respect of whose disablement some other person, being the person claiming or in receipt of benefit under this Act or a person whose requirements are aggregated with his under paragraph 3 of this Schedule, is entitled to attendance allowance at the rate of [£8·00] [4] a week.

(2) In this paragraph—

   (*a*) "attendance allowance" means an attendance allowance under Chapter II of Part II of the Social Security Act 1975;

   (*b*) "attendance requirements" in relation to a disabled person means that person's requirements, by reason of the severity of his physical or mental disablement, for such attention or supervision from another person as is referred to in section 35 (1) of the Social Security Act 1975 or, in relation to a disabled child, that subsection as modified by regulations made under subsection (5) of that section.

(3) For the purposes of this paragraph the provisions of regulations under Chapter VI of Part II of the Social Security Act 1975 relating to overlapping benefits shall not be treated as affecting the rate of attendance allowance to which a person is entitled.] [4b]

[(4) Where in respect of a severely disabled person (other than one to whom sub-paragraph (1) applies) there is entitlement to attendance allowance at the rate of [£5·35] [4] a week sub-paragraph (1) shall have effect as if for the references to [£8·00] [4] there were substituted references to [£5·35] [4] and for the reference to attendance requirements there were substituted a reference to such person's requirements for attendance by virtue of which that entitlement arises.[5c]

Rent

13.—(1) The amounts applicable under the preceding paragraphs shall be increased as follows—

   (*a*) where the person claiming or in receipt of benefit or a person whose requirements are aggregated with his under paragraph 3 (1) of this Schedule is a householder, by the amount of the net rent payable, reduced where appropriate under sub-paragraph (2) of this paragraph, or such part of that amount as is reasonable in the circumstances;

   (*b*) in any other case, by [£0·90].[4]

(2) Where a person other than one whose requirements are aggregated under paragraph 3 of this Schedule with the requirements of the householder resides, otherwise than as a sub-tenant, in the premises for which the rent is paid, then, unless the householder or a person whose requirements are aggregated with his under sub-paragraph (1) of that paragraph is blind, the amount mentioned in sub-paragraph (1) (*a*) of this paragraph may be reduced by an amount not exceeding such part of the net rent as is reasonably attributable to that other person.

(3) In this paragraph "net rent" means—

   (*a*) the rent payable for one week, and

   (*b*) so much of any outgoings borne by the householder as is attributable to one week, including, in particular, rates, a reasonable allowance towards any necessary expenditure on repairs or insurance, and such proportion as is for the time being attributable to interest of any sum payable in respect of a mortgage debt or heritable security charged on the house in which the householder resides, or on any interest therein;

less any proceeds of sub-letting any part of the premises in respect of which the rent is paid or the outgoings are incurred.

[(4) Where any amount of rent or rates is met by a rebate or allowance under Part II of the Housing Finance Act 1972, or by any rate rebate, the amount so met shall be deducted from the increase to be made under sub-paragraph (1) (*a*) of this paragraph.] [6]

[(4A) Where any amount of rent or rates is met by a rebate or allowance under Part II of the Housing (Financial Provisions) (Scotland) Act 1972, or by any rate rebate, the amount so met shall be deducted from the increase to be made under sub-paragraph (1) (*a*) of this paragraph.][7]

[5c] Words substituted by S.I. 1972/1145, as amended by S.I. 1973, c. 42, Sched. 4.

[6] Sub-paragraph added by Housing Finance Act 1972 (c. 47). s. 108 (3), Sched. 9, para. 5.

[7] Sub-paragraph added by Housing (Financial Provisions) (Scotland) Act 1972 (c. 46), s. 79 (1), Sched. 9, para. 5.

Trade disputes

14.—(1) Requirements of persons falling within paragraph 3 of this Schedule, where one or more is, but not both or all are, disqualified.

The amount which, if the persons were not persons falling within paragraph 3 of this Schedule, would be applicable under paragraph 9 (*c*) or 10 (*b*) thereof to the person or persons not disqualified, increased as under [paragraphs 12A and 13] [5b] of this Schedule in the case of the amounts mentioned therein.

(2) In this paragraph "disqualified" means, in relation to any person, that his own requirements are to be disregarded by virtue of section 10 of this Act.

Persons in local authority homes

15. Requirements of persons for whom accommodation is provided under Part III of the National Assistance Act 1948.

The aggregate of such of the sums prescribed for the purposes of subsections (3) and (4) of section 22 of that Act (minimum rate of payment for accommodation and personal requirements) as are applicable to his case.

Persons in hospital

16. Requirements of person residing as patient in any hospital.

Such amount, if any, as may be appropriate, having regard to all the circumstances.

Persons paying for board and lodging

17. Requirements of person paying inclusive charge for board and lodging.

Such amount as may be appropriate, not being less than the amount which would be applicable under paragraphs [9 to 12] [5c] of this Schedule.

Persons in legal custody

18. Requirements of person in prison or otherwise detained in legal custody.

Nil (except for any amount applicable by virtue of paragraph 3 of this Schedule).

PART III

CALCULATION OF RESOURCES

Disregard of capital value of dwellings

19. In taking into account the value to any person of an interest in the dwelling in which he resides, any sum which might be obtained by him by selling that interest or borrowing money upon the security thereof shall be disregarded.

Resources wholly disregarded

20. There shall be wholly disregarded—

   [(*a*) any maternity grant under section 21 of the Social Security Act 1975;
   (*b*) any death grant under section 32 of that Act] [4b];
   (*c*) any sums payable to any person as holder of the Victoria Cross or of the George Cross.

21. If the value of the capital resources taken into account would not exceed [£1,200] [8] they shall be wholly disregarded together with any income therefrom.

Calculation of income from capital resources

22. The capital resources taken into account, together with any income derived from them, shall be treated [as equivalent to a weekly income of 25p for each complete £50 of the excess of the value of the capital resources over £1,200] [8]

---

[8] Words substituted by Social Security Benefits Act 1975 (c. 11), Sched. 3.

Earnings

23. (1) Subject to [subparagraphs (1A) and (2)] of this paragraph, the weekly earnings of any person shall be taken to be his net weekly earnings reduced—

[(*a*) if he is the person claiming or in receipt of benefit and his right thereto is subject to the condition of section 11 of this Act by £2;

(*b*) in any other case by £4] [8]

[(1A) The weekly earnings of—

(*a*) a child; and

(*b*) a person disentitled to benefit by virtue of section 9 of this Act; where resources are aggregated by virtue of paragraph 3 (2) of this Schedule with those of the person having to provide for his requirements, shall be wholly disregarded] [8]

["(2) Where a person who by reason of a stoppage of work due to a trade dispute at his place of employment has been without employment for any period during the stoppage becomes engaged in remunerative full-time work again in consequence of the ending of the stoppage—

(*a*) any advance of earnings made or offered to him during so much of that engagement as falls within the period of fifteen days from the beginning thereof shall be taken into account in calculating or estimating his net weekly earnings; and

(*b*) for the purpose of any claim for benefit made by him during so much of that engagement as falls within that period, sub-paragraph (1) of this paragraph shall have effect as regards his weekly earnings (but not those of any other person) subject to the modification that the reduction provided for in paragraph (*b*) of that sub-paragraph shall be applied only to the amount, if any, by which his net weekly earnings exceed his net weekly earnings from his full-time work (instead of to the full amount of his net weekly earnings)."] [9]

Disregard of £4 a week of certain income [8]

24.—(1) Subject to the provisions of this paragraph and of paragraph 25 of this Schedule, there shall be disregarded £4 a week of the income taken into account except so far as it consists of earnings or of any sum taken account under paragraph 22 of this Schedule.

(2) This paragraph does not apply to income so far as it consists of—

(*a*) allowances under the Family Allowances Act 1965;

(*b*) any family income supplement under the Family Income Supplements Act 1970;

(*c*) any graduated retirement benefit under section 36 of the National Insurance Act 1965;

(*d*) any payment for the maintenance of a person whose requirements are taken into account in ascertaining the amount of benefit, being a payment made under the order of a court or a payment made by a person who for the purposes of this Act is liable to maintain the first-mentioned person.

[(*e*) any guaranteed minimum pension within the meaning of the Social Security Pensions Act 1975.] [10]

(3) This paragraph does not apply to income so far as it consists of any benefit under [Chapters I to III of Part II of the Social Security Act 1975] [11] [or Part II of the Social Security Pensions Act 1975] [10] except—

(*a*) £0·38 of—

(i) any increase of widow's allowance or widowed mother's allowance, being an increase in respect of an only, or the elder or eldest, qualifying child or a second qualifying child; or

(ii) any child's special allowance or any increase thereof in respect of a second qualifying child;

(*b*) £0·28 of—

(i) any increase of widow's allowance or widowed mother's allowance, being an increase in respect of any additional qualifying child beyond the first two; or

(ii) any increase of a child's special allowance in respect of any additional qualifying child beyond the second.

[9] Sub-paragraph (2) added by Social Security Act 1971 (c. 73), s. 1 (3) (*b*).
[10] Added by Social Security Provisions Act 1975 (c. 60), Sched. 4.
[11] Added by Social Security (Consequential Provisions) Act 1975 (c. 18), Sched. 2.

[(4) This paragraph does not apply to income so far as it consists of injury benefit under Part II of the Social Security Act 1975 or of industrial death benefit under that Part of that Act except—

(a) so much of—

    (i) any widow's pension payable at the higher permanent rate under section 68 of that Act, or

    (ii) any widower's pension under section 69 of that Act.

as exceeds [the sum specified in section 6 (1) (a) of the Social Security Pensions Act 1975] [10];

(b) £0·38 of any allowance under section 70 of that Act in respect of—

    (i) an only, or the elder or eldest qualifying child, or

    (ii) a second qualifying child;

(c) £0·28 of any allowance under that section in respect of any additional qualifying child beyond the first two;

(d) any parent's pension under section 71 of that Act;

(e) any relative's pension under section 72 of that Act.] [11]

(5) This paragraph does not apply to income so far as it consists of any pension or allowance for a widow or widower or in respect of children granted in respect of a death due to service or war injury under powers conferred by or under any of the Acts mentioned in paragraph (a) of sub-paragraph (6) of this paragraph or under any such scheme as is mentioned in paragraph (b) of that sub-paragraph except—

(a) so much of any pension or allowance for a widow or widower as exceeds [the sum specified in section 6 (1) (a) of the Social Security Pensions Act 1975] [10];

(b) £0·38 of any allowance in respect of an only, or the elder or eldest, child or a second child;

(c) £0·28 of any allowance in respect of any additional child beyond the first two.

(6) The Act and schemes mentioned in sub-paragraph (5) of this paragraph are—

(a) the Ministry of Pensions Act 1916, the Air Force (Constitution) Act 1917, the Personal Injuries (Emergency Provisions) Act 1939, the Pensions (Navy, Army, Air Force and Mercantile Marine) Act 1939, the Polish Resettlement Act 1947, the Home Guard Act 1951 and the Ulster Defence Regiment Act 1969;

(b) any scheme made under the Injuries in War (Compensation) Act 1914, or the Injuries in War Compensation Act 1914 (Session 2) and any War Risk Compensation Scheme for the Mercantile Marine;

and that sub-paragraph applies in relation to a pension or allowance for a woman who was living with a deceased person as his wife as it applies in relation to a pension or allowance for a widow.

(7) In this paragraph any reference to an allowance, pension, benefit or other payment of any description includes a reference to any analogous allowance, pension, benefit or payment.

Limited disregard of occupational pensions, etc.[8]

25.—(1) There shall not be disregarded under paragraph 24 of this Schedule more than £1 a week of any income so far as it consists of one or more payments of any kind to which this paragraph applies.

(2) This paragraph applies to—

(a) any pension or other periodical sum paid to, or to the widow of, a person by reason of any service or employment in which he was formerly engaged;

(b) any periodical sum paid to a person on account of his employment having terminated by reason of redundancy.

(3) Paragraphs (a) and (b) of sub-paragraph (2) above apply whether or not the payment is made by a former employer and whether or not there is any right to receive it; but paragraph (a) shall not be construed as applying to—

(a) any pension or allowance mentioned in paragraph 24 (4) or (5) of this Schedule or any other payment by way of compensation for injury, disease, disablement or death suffered by a person by reason of the service or employment in which he was engaged; or

(b) any payment out of a trust fund established for relieving hardship in particular cases and made at the discretion of the trustees of the fund.

Specific resources falling to be treated as income

[25A.—(1) In calculating a person's resources for purposes of this Schedule there shall be treated as income (and, subject to [paragraph 24 of this Schedule] [8] taken into account as such)—

    (*a*) any amount which, while he is employed in such circumstances as are mentioned in sub-paragraph (2) of this paragraph, becomes available to him (or would become available to him on application being duly made) by way of repayment of income tax deducted from his emoluments (whether in the same or any previous office or employment) in pursuance of section 204 of the Income and Corporation Taxes Act 1970 (pay as you earn), except so far as the repayment in question is attributable to any period of absence from work through sickness or other similar cause or to any period of unemployment; and

    (*b*) any payment which he receives or is entitled to obtain (whether from a trade union or any other source) by reason of being without employment for any period during a stoppage of work due to a trade dispute at his place of employment.

(2) The circumstances referred to in sub-paragraph (1) (*a*) of this paragraph are that the person concerned is employed in an office or employment and that his emoluments therefrom are assessable to income tax under Schedule E.] [12]

Further reduction of resources

26. Any resources not specified in the preceding provisions of this Schedule may be treated as reduced by such amount (if any) as may be reasonable in the circumstances of the case.

Resources deliberately abandoned

27. If a person has deprived himself of any resources for the purpose of securing benefit or increasing the amount thereof those resources may be taken into account as if they were still his.

Discretionary trusts

28. Any sum which is held on a discretionary trust for the benefit of a person may be treated as included in his resources.

Attribution of assets

29.—(1) Subject to the preceding paragraph and to the following provision of this paragraph, a person shall be deemed for the purposes of this Schedule to own an asset if he is absolutely entitled in possession to the whole beneficial interest therein and not otherwise.

(2) Where two or more persons are beneficially entitled in possession to any asset they shall be treated for the purposes of this Schedule as if each of them were entitled in possession to the whole beneficial interest in an equal share in the asset unless it appears that their respective beneficial interests are not equal; and in that case they shall be treated as respectively entitled in possession to the whole beneficial interest in such shares as appears to be just.

(3) In the application of this paragraph to Scotland the words "in possession" shall be omitted wherever they occur.

Family Provision Act 1966

(1966 c. 35)

An Act to amend the law of England and Wales in relation to the rights after a person's death of that person's spouse or former spouse and children, and to repeal section 47 (5) of the Administration of Estates Act 1925, as amended. [17th November 1966]

[12] Paragraph added by Social Security Act 1971 (c. 73), s. 1 (4).

Increase of net sum payable to surviving husband or wife on intestacy

1.—(1) In the case of a person dying after the coming into force of this section, section 46 (1) of the Administration of Estates Act 1925, as amended by section 1 of the Intestates' Estates Act 1952 and set out in Schedule 1 to that Act, shall apply as if the net sums charged by paragraph (i) on the residuary estate in favour of a surviving husband or wife were as follows, that is to say,—

    (*a*) under paragraph (2) of the Table (which charges a net sum of £5,000 where the intestate leaves issue) a sum of [£15,000] [1] or of such larger amount as may from time to time be fixed by order of the Lord Chancellor; and

    (*b*) under paragraph (3) of the Table (which charges a net sum of £20,000 where the intestate leaves certain close relatives but no issue) a sum of [£40,000] [1] or of such larger amount as may from time to time be so fixed.

(2) Accordingly in relation to the estate of a person dying after the coming into force of this section sections 46, 48 and 49 (as so amended and set out) of the Administration of Estates Act 1925 shall be further amended as follows:—

    (*a*) in the table in section 46 (1) (i) for the words " net sum of £5,000 " in paragraph (2), and for the words " net sum of £20,000 " in paragraph (3), there shall in each case be substituted the words " fixed net sum ", and at the end of the Table there shall be added—

        " The fixed net sums referred to in paragraphs (2) and (3) of this Table shall be of the amounts provided by or under section 1 of the Family Provision Act 1966 ";

    (*b*) in sections 46 (4) and 48 (2) (*a*) for the words " the net sum of £5,000 or, as the case may be, £20,000 ", and in section 49 (1) (*aa*) for the words " the net sum of £5,000 or £20,000 ", there shall in each case be substituted the words " the fixed net sum ";

and any reference in any other enactment to the said net sum of £5,000 or the said net sum of £20,000 shall have effect as a reference to the corresponding net sum of the amount fixed by or under this section.

(3) Any order of the Lord Chancellor under this section fixing the amount of either of the said net sums shall have effect (and, so far as relates to that sum, shall supersede any previous order) in relation to the estate of any person dying after the coming into force of the order.

(4) Any order of the Lord Chancellor under this section shall be made by statutory instrument, and a draft of the statutory instrument shall be laid before Parliament.

2–9. [*Repealed by Inheritance (Provision for Family and Dependants Act 1975 (c. 63), Sched.*]

Short title, repeal, etc.

10.—(1) This Act may be cited as the Family Provision Act 1966.

(2) [*Repealed by Inheritance (Provision for Family and Dependants) Act 1975 (c. 63), Sched.*]

(3) Nothing in this Act extends to Scotland or to Northern Ireland.

(4) [*Repealed by Inheritance (Provision for Family and Dependants) Act 1975 (c. 63), Sched.*]

SCHEDULES

[*Repealed by Inheritance (Provision for Family and Dependants) Act 1975 (c. 63), Sched.*]

---

[1] Sums replaced as from July 1, 1972, by Family Provision (Intestate Succession) Order 1972 (S.I. No. 916).

Matrimonial Causes Act 1967

(1967 c. 56)

An Act to confer jurisdiction on county courts in certain matrimonial proceedings; and for purposes connected therewith.

[21st July 1967]

Jurisdiction of county courts in undefended matrimonial causes

1.—(1) The Lord Chancellor may by order designate any county court as a divorce county court, and any court so designated shall have jurisdiction to hear and determine any undefended matrimonial cause, except that it shall have jurisdiction to try such a cause only if it is also designated in the order as a court of trial.

(2) The jurisdiction conferred by this Act on a divorce county court shall be exercisable throughout England and Wales, but rules of court may provide for a matrimonial cause pending in one such court to be heard and determined in another or partly in that and partly in another.

(3) Every matrimonial cause shall be commenced in a divorce county court, but rules of court—

(a) shall provide for the transfer to the High Court of any matrimonial cause which ceases to be undefended; and

(b) [1] may provide for the transfer to that court of matrimonial causes which remain undefended.

(4) Rules of court may provide for the transfer or retransfer from the High Court to a divorce county court of any matrimonial cause which is or again becomes undefended.

(5) Rules of court shall define the circumstances in which any matrimonial cause is to be treated for the purposes of this Act as undefended, and may make different provision with respect to matrimonial causes of different descriptions.

(6) The power to make an order under this section shall be exercisable by statutory instrument and includes power to vary or revoke such an order by a subsequent order.

Ancillary relief and protection of children

2.—(1) Subject to the following provisions of this section, a divorce county court shall have jurisdiction to exercise any power exercisable under [Part II or Part III of the Matrimonial Causes Act 1973] [2] in connection with any petition, decree or order pending in or made by such a court and to exercise any power under [section 27 or 35 of that Act.] [2]

(2) Any proceedings for the exercise of a power which a divorce county court has jurisdiction to exercise by virtue of this section shall be commenced in such divorce county court as may be prescribed by rules of court; but rules of court shall provide for the transfer to the High Court of any proceedings pending in a county court by virtue of this section in any case where the transfer appears to the county court to be desirable, [. . .] [2a]

[(3) A divorce county court shall not by virtue of this section have jurisdiction to exercise any power under section 32, 33, 36 or 38 of the

---

[1] Extended by Courts Act 1971 (c. 23), s. 45 (3).
[2] Words substituted by Matrimonial Causes Act 1973 (c. 18), s. 54 (1) (a), Sched. 2, para. 6.
[2a] Words repealed by Courts Act 1971 (c. 23), s. 56 (4), Sched. 11, Pt. IV.

Matrimonial Causes Act 1973; but nothing in this section shall prejudice the exercise by a county court of any jurisdiction conferred on county courts by any of those sections.] [2]

(4) Nothing in this section shall affect the jurisdiction of a magistrates' court under [section 35 of the Matrimonial Causes Act 1973.] [2]

Consideration of agreements or arrangements

3. Any provision to be made by rules of court for the purposes of [section 7 of the Matrimonial Causes Act 1973] [2] with respect to any power exercisable by the court on an application made before the presentation of a petition shall confer jurisdiction to exercise the power on divorce county courts.

County court proceedings in principal probate registry

4.[2b]—(1) Sections 1 to 3 of this Act shall not prevent the commencement of any proceedings in the [divorce registry],[3] except where rules of court under section 2 (2) of this Act otherwise provide; and the following provisions of this section shall have effect for the purpose of enabling proceedings to be dealt with in that registry as in a divorce county court.

(2) The jurisdiction conferred by this Act on divorce county courts shall be exercised in the [divorce registry] [3]—

(a) so far as it is exercisable by judges of such courts, at such sittings and in such places as the Lord Chancellor may direct; and

(b) so far as it is exercisable by registrars of such courts, by such registrars or by registrars and other officers of the [divorce registry],[3] according as rules of court may provide;

and rules of court may make provision for treating, for any purposes specified in the rules, proceedings pending in that registry with respect to which that jurisdiction is exercisable as pending in a divorce county court and for the application of [section 74 (3) of the Solicitors Act 1974] [3a] (amount of costs allowed on taxation in connection with proceedings in a county court) with respect to any proceedings so treated.

(3) The [divorce registry] [3] shall be treated as a divorce county court—

(a) for the purpose of any provision to be made by rules of court under section 1 (2) of this Act; and

(b) for the purpose of any provision to be made under section 2 (2) of this Act prescribing the county court in which any proceedings are to be commenced.

(4) Rules of court shall make provision for securing, with respect to proceedings dealt with under this section, that, as nearly as may be, the same consequences shall follow—

(a) as regards service of process, as if proceedings commenced in the [divorce registry] [3] had been commenced in a divorce county court; and

(b) as regards enforcement of orders, as if orders made in that registry in the exercise of the jurisdiction conferred by this Act on divorce county courts were orders made by such a court.

(5) The provision to be made by rules of court for the purposes of this Act for the transfer of proceedings between a divorce county court and the High Court shall, in the case of proceedings pending in the [divorce registry] [3] and dealt with or to be dealt with under this section, be provision for the proceedings to be treated, or as the case

---

[2b] Power to apply this section given in Courts Act 1971 (c. 23), s. 45 (5).

[3] Changed from " principal probate registry " by A.J.A. 1970 (c. 31), s. 1, Sched. 2, para. 26.

[3a] Words substituted by Solicitors Act 1974 (c. 47), Sched. 3.

may be no longer to be treated, for any purposes specified in the rules, as pending in a divorce county court; and any provision so made for the transfer of proceedings between divorce county courts shall include provision for the transfer to or from the [divorce registry] [3] of proceedings falling to be treated as pending in a divorce county court.

Assignment of county court judges to matrimonial proceedings

5. The jurisdiction conferred by this Act on divorce county courts, so far as it is exercisable by judges of such courts, shall be exercised by such county court judges as the Lord Chancellor may direct.

Appeals on questions of fact

6. Section 109 of the County Courts Act 1959 (appeals on questions of fact) shall have effect as if the proceedings mentioned in subsection (2) of that section included any proceedings with respect to which jurisdiction is conferred by this Act on divorce county courts.

7–8. [*Repealed by Matrimonial Causes Act 1973 (c. 18), s. 54 (1) (b), Sched. 3.*]

Remuneration of persons giving legal aid

9. Rules of court may provide that the sums payable under [section 10 (1) of the Legal Aid Act 1974] [3b] to a solicitor or counsel acting in an undefended matrimonial cause shall, at his election, be either—

(a) such fixed amount specified in the rules as may be applicable under the rules; or

(b) an amount ascertained on taxation or assessment of costs as provided by Schedule 3 to that Act;

and may provide for modifying the said Schedule in relation to any proceedings which by virtue of this Act are at any stage treated as pending in a divorce county court.

Interpretation

10.—(1) In this Act

" divorce county court " means a county court designated under section 1 of this Act;

[" Divorce registry ", means the principal registry of the Family Division of the High Court.] [4]

" matrimonial cause " has the same meaning as in the Supreme Court of Judicature (Consolidation) Act 1925, except that it includes an application under [section 3 of the Matrimonial Causes Act 1973] [5]

" undefended matrimonial cause " has the meaning assigned to it by section 1 (5) of this Act.

(2) References in this Act to a transfer to the High Court include references to a transfer to a district registry.

Short title, commencement and extent

11.—(1) This Act may be cited as the Matrimonial Causes Act 1967.

(2) This Act shall come into force on such day as the Lord Chancellor may by order made by statutory instrument appoint.[6]

(3) This Act does not extend to Scotland or to Northern Ireland.

[3b] Words substituted by Legal Aid Act 1974 (c. 4), Sched. 4.
[4] Added by A.J.A. 1970 (c. 31), Sched. 2, para. 28.
[5] Words substituted by Matrimonial Causes Act 1973 (c. 18), s. 54 (1) (a), Sched. 2, para. 6.
[6] Such an order (S.I. 1968 No. 228) was made with effect from April 11, 1968.

Matrimonial Homes Act 1967

(1967 c. 75)

An Act to amend the law of England and Wales as to the rights of a husband or wife to occupy a dwelling house which has been the matrimonial home; and for connected purposes.

[27th July 1967]

Protection against eviction, etc., from matrimonial home of spouse not entitled by virtue of estate, etc., to occupy it

1.—(1) Where one spouse is entitled to occupy a dwelling house by virtue of any estate or interest or contract or by virtue of any enactment giving him or her the right to remain in occupation, and the other spouse is not so entitled, then, subject to the provisions of this Act, the spouse not so entitled shall have the following rights (in this Act referred to as " rights of occupation ") : —

 (a) if in occupation, a right not to be evicted or excluded from the dwelling house or any part thereof by the other spouse except with the leave of the court given by an order under this section;

 (b) if not in occupation, a right with the leave of the court so given to enter into and occupy the dwelling house.

(2) So long as one spouse has rights of occupation, either of the spouses may apply to the court for an order declaring, enforcing, restricting or terminating those rights or regulating the exercise by either spouse of the right to occupy the dwelling house.

(3) On an application for an order under this section the court may make such order as it thinks just and reasonable having regard to the conduct of the spouses in relation to each other and otherwise, to their respective needs and financial resources, to the needs of any children and to all the circumstances of the case, and, without prejudice to the generality of the foregoing provision,—

 (a) may except part of the dwelling house from a spouse's rights of occupation (and in particular a part used wholly or mainly for or in connection with the trade, business or profession of the other spouse);

 (b) may order a spouse occupying the dwelling house or any part thereof by virtue of this section to make periodical payments to the other in respect of the occupation;

 (c) may impose on either spouse obligations as to the repair and maintenance of the dwelling house or the discharge of any liabilities in respect of the dwelling house.

(4) Orders under this section may, in so far as they have a continuing effect, be limited so as to have effect for a period specified in the order or until further order.

(5) Where a spouse is entitled under this section to occupy a dwelling house or any part thereof, any payment or tender made or other thing done by that spouse in or towards satisfaction of any liability of the other spouse in respect of rent, rates, mortgage payments or other outgoings affecting the dwelling house shall, whether or not it is made or done in pursuance of an order under this section, be as good as if made or done by the other spouse; and a spouse's occupation by virtue of this section shall for purposes of [the Rent Act 1968 (other than Part VI thereof)] [1] be treated as possession by the other spouse.

Where a spouse entitled under this section to occupy a dwelling house or any part thereof makes any payment in or towards satisfaction

[1] Substituted by the Rent Act 1968 (c. 23), Sched. 15.

of any liability of the other spouse in respect of mortgage payments affecting the dwelling house, the person to whom the payment is made may treat it as having been made by that other spouse, but the fact that that person has treated any such payment as having been so made shall not affect any claim of the first-mentioned spouse against the other to an interest in the dwelling house by virtue of the payment.

(6) The jurisdiction conferred on the court by this section shall be exercisable by the High Court or by a county court, and shall be exercisable by a county court notwithstanding that by reason of the amount of the net annual value for rating of the dwelling house or otherwise the jurisdiction would not but for this subsection be exercisable by a county court.

(7) In this Act "dwelling house" includes any building or part thereof which is occupied as a dwelling, and any yard, garden, garage or outhouse belonging to the dwelling house and occupied therewith.

(8) This Act shall not apply to a dwelling house which has at no time been a matrimonial home of the spouses in question; and a spouse's rights of occupation shall continue only so long as the marriage subsists and the other spouse is entitled as mentioned in subsection (1) above to occupy the dwelling house, except where provision is made by section 2 of this Act for those rights to be a charge on an estate or interest in the dwelling house.

[(9) It is hereby declared that a spouse who has an equitable interest in a dwelling house or in the proceeds of sale thereof, not being a spouse in whom is vested (whether solely or as a joint tenant) a legal estate in fee simple or a legal term of years absolute in the dwelling house, is to be treated for the purpose only of determining whether he or she has rights of occupation under this section as not being entitled to occupy the dwelling house by virtue of that interest.] [1a]

Effect of statutory rights of occupation as charge on dwelling house

2.—(1) Where, at any time during the subsistence of a marriage, one spouse is entitled to occupy a dwelling house by virtue of an estate or interest, then the other spouse's rights of occupation shall be a charge on that estate or interest, having the like priority as if it were an equitable interest created at whichever is the latest of the following dates, that is to say—

(a) the date when the spouse so entitled acquires the estate or interest;
(b) the date of the marriage; and
(c) the commencement of this Act.

(2) Notwithstanding that a spouse's rights of occupation are a charge on an estate or interest in the dwelling house, those rights shall be brought to an end by—

(a) the death of the other spouse, or
(b) the termination (otherwise than by death) of the marriage,

unless in the event of a matrimonial dispute or estrangement the court sees fit to direct otherwise by an order made under section 1 above during the subsistence of the marriage.

(3) Where a spouse's rights of occupation are a charge on the estate or interest of the other spouse—

(a) any order under section 1 above against the other spouse shall, except in so far as the contrary intention appears, have the like effect against persons deriving title under the other spouse and affected by the charge; and
(b) subsections (2) to (5) of section 1 above shall apply in relation

---

[1a] This subsection was added by the Matrimonial Proceedings and Property Act 1970 (c. 45), s. 38.

to any person deriving title under the other spouse and affected by the charge as they apply in relation to the other spouse.

(4) Where a spouse's rights of occupation are a charge on an estate or interest in the dwelling house, and that estate or interest is surrendered so as to merge in some other estate or interest expectant thereon in such circumstances that, but for the merger, the person taking the estate or interest of the other spouse would be bound by the charge, then the surrender shall have effect subject to the charge and the persons thereafter entitled to the other estate or interest shall, for so long as the estate or interest surrendered would have endured if not so surrendered be treated for all purposes of this Act as deriving title to the other estate or interest under the other spouse by virtue of the surrender.

(5) Where a spouse's rights of occupation are a charge on the estate or interest of the other spouse, and the other spouse—

(*a*) is adjudged bankrupt or makes a conveyance or assignment of his or her property (including that estate or interest) to trustees for the benefit of his or her creditors generally; or

(*b*) dies and his or her estate is insolvent;

then, notwithstanding that it is registered [under section 2 of the Land Charges Act 1972 or subsection 7 below],[1b] the charge shall be void against the trustee in bankruptcy, the trustees under the conveyance or assignment or the personal representatives of the deceased spouse, as the case may be.

[*Subsection 6 repealed by Land Charges Act 1972 (c. 61), s. 18, Sched. 5, except so far as it relates to paragraphs 1 and 4 of the Schedule.*]

[(6) At the end of section 10 (1) of the Land Charges Act 1925 (which lists the classes of charges on, or obligations affecting, land which may be registered as land charges) there shall be added the following paragraph:—

" Class F: A charge affecting any land by virtue of the Matrimonial Homes Act 1967 ";

and in the enactments mentioned in the Schedule to this Act there shall be made the consequential amendments provided for by that Schedule.]

(7) Where the title to the legal estate by virtue of which a spouse is entitled to occupy a dwelling house is registered under the Land Registration Act 1925 or any enactment replaced by that Act, registration of a land charge affecting the dwelling house by virtue of this Act shall be effected by registering a notice or caution under that Act, and a spouse's rights of occupation shall not be an overriding interest within the meaning of that Act affecting the dwelling house notwithstanding that the spouse is in actual occupation of the dwelling house.

(8) Where a spouse's rights of occupation are a charge on the estate or interest of the other spouse, and that estate or interest is the subject of a mortgage within the meaning of the Law of Property Act 1925, then if, after the date of creation of the mortgage, the charge is registered [under section 2 of the Land Charges Act 1972] [1b] the charge shall, for the purposes of section 94 of that Act (which regulates the rights of mortgagees to make further advances ranking in priority to subsequent mortgages), be deemed to be a mortgage subsequent in date to the first-mentioned mortgage.

Restriction on registration where spouse entitled to more than one charge

3. Where one spouse is entitled by virtue of section 2 above to a charge on the estate or interest of the other spouse in each of two or more dwelling houses, only one of the charges to which that spouse is so

---

[1b] Words substituted by Lands Charges Act 1972 (c. 61), s. 18 (1), Sched. 3, para. 8 (1) (2).

entitled shall be registered [under section 2 of the Land Charges Act 1972 or section 2 (7) above] [1c] at any one time, and if any of those charges is registered [under either of those provisions] [1c] the Chief Land Registrar, on being satisfied that any other of them is so registered, shall cancel the registration of the charge first registered.

Contract for sale of house affected by registered charge to include term requiring cancellation of registration before completion

4.—(1) Where one spouse is entitled by virtue of section 2 above to a charge on an estate or interest in a dwelling house and the charge is registered [under section 2 of the Land Charges Act 1972 or section 2 (7) above] [1d] it shall be a term of any contract for the sale of that estate or interest whereby the vendor agrees to give vacant possession of the dwelling house on completion of the contract that the vendor will before such completion procure the cancellation of the registration of the charge at his expense:

Provided that the foregoing provision shall not apply to any such contract made by a vendor who is entitled to sell the estate or interest in the dwelling house freed from any such charge.

(2) If, on the completion of such a contract as is referred to in subsection (1) above, there is delivered to the purchaser or his solicitor an application by the spouse entitled to the charge for the cancellation of the registration of that charge, the term of the contract for which subsection (1) above provides shall be deemed to have been performed.

(3) This section applies only if and so far as a contrary intention is not expressed in the contract.

(4) This section shall apply to a contract for exchange as it applies to a contract for sale.

(5) This section shall, with the necessary modifications, apply to a contract for the grant of a lease or underlease of a dwelling house as it applies to a contract for the sale of an estate or interest in a dwelling house.

Cancellation of registration after termination of marriage, etc.

5.—(1) Where a spouse's rights of occupation are a charge on the estate or interest of the other spouse in a dwelling house and the charge is registered [under section 2 of the Land Charges Act 1972 or section 2 (7) above] [1e] the Chief Land Registrar shall, subject to subsection (2) below, cancel the registration of the charge if he is satisfied—

(a) by the production of a certificate or other sufficient evidence, that either spouse is dead, or

(b) by the production of an official copy of a decree of a court, that the marriage in question has been terminated otherwise than by death, or

(c) by the production of an order of the court, that the spouse's rights of occupation constituting the charge have been terminated by the order.

(2) Where—

(a) the marriage in question has been terminated by the death of the spouse entitled to an estate or interest in the dwelling house or otherwise than by death, and

(b) an order affecting the charge of the spouse not so entitled had been made by virtue of section 2 (2) above,

then if, after the making of the order, registration of the charge was renewed or the charge registered in pursuance of subsection (3) below, the Chief Land Registrar shall not cancel the registration of the charge in

1c Words substituted by Land Charges Act 1972 (c. 61), s. 18 (1), Sched. 3, para. 9.
1d Words substituted by Land Charges Act 1972 (c. 61), s. 18 (1), Sched. 3, para. 10.
1e Words substituted by Land Charges Act 1972 (c. 61), s. 18 (1), Sched. 3, para. 11.

accordance with subsection (1) above unless he is also satisfied that the order has ceased to have effect.

(3) Where such an order has been made, then, for the purposes of subsection (2) above, the spouse entitled to the charge affected by the order may—

    (a) if before the date of the order the charge was registered [under section 2 of the Land Charges Act 1972 or section 2 (7) above] [1e] renew the registration of the charge, and

    (b) if before the said date the charge was not so registered, register the charge [under section 2 of the Land Charges Act 1972 or section 2 (7) of this Act;] [1e]

(4) Renewal of the registration of a charge in pursuance of subsection (3) above shall be effected in such manner as may be prescribed, and an application for such renewal or for registration of a charge in pursuance of that subsection shall contain such particulars of any order affecting the charge made by virtue of section 2 (2) above as may be prescribed.

(5) The renewal in pursuance of subsection (3) above of the registration of a charge shall not affect the priority of the charge.

(6) In this section " prescribed " means prescribed by rules made [under section 16 of the Land Charges Act 1972] [1e] or section 144 of the Land Registration Act 1925, as the circumstances of the case require.

Release of rights of occupation and postponement of priority of charge

6.—(1) A spouse entitled to rights of occupation may by a release in writing release those rights or release them as respects part only of the dwelling house affected by them.

(2) Where a contract is made for the sale of an estate or interest in a dwelling house, or for the grant of a lease or underlease of a dwelling house, being (in either case) a dwelling house affected by a charge registered [under section 2 of the Land Charges Act 1972 or section 2 (7) above] [1f] then, without prejudice to subsection (1) above, the rights of occupation constituting the charge shall be deemed to have been released on the happening of whichever of the following events first occurs, that is to say, the delivery to the purchaser or lessee, as the case may be, or his solicitor on completion of the contract of an application by the spouse entitled to the charge for the cancellation of the registration of the charge or the lodging of such an application at Her Majesty's Land Registry.

(3) A spouse entitled by virtue of section 2 above to a charge on an estate or interest of the other spouse may agree in writing that any other charge on, or interest in, that estate or interest shall rank in priority to the charge to which that spouse is so entitled.

Provision for case where Rent Acts apply and marriage is terminated by divorce, etc.

7.—(1) Where one spouse is entitled, either in his or her own right or jointly with the other spouse, to occupy a dwelling house by virtue of a [protected tenancy] [2] or of a statutory tenancy and the marriage is terminated by the grant of a decree of divorce or nullity of marriage, the court by which the decree is granted may make an order under subsection (2) or (3) below according to the circumstances.

(2) Where a spouse is entitled as aforesaid to occupy the dwelling house by virtue of a [protected tenancy],[2] the court may by order direct that, as from the date on which the decree is made absolute, there shall, by virtue of the order and without further assurance, be transferred to, and vested in, his or her former spouse—

    (a) the estate or interest which the spouse so entitled had in the

---

[1f] Words substituted by Land Charges Act 1972 (c. 61), s. 18 (1), Sched. 3, para. 12.
[2] Substituted by the Rent Act 1968 (c. 23), Sched. 15.

dwelling house immediately before that date by virtue of the lease or agreement creating the tenancy and any assignment of that lease or agreement, with all rights, privileges and appurtenances attaching to that estate or interest but subject to all covenants, obligations, liabilities and incumbrances to which it is subject; and

(b) where the said spouse is an assignee of such lease or agreement, the liability of the said spouse under any covenant of indemnity by the assignee expressed or implied in the assignment of the lease or agreement to that spouse;

and where such an order is made, any liability or obligation to which the said spouse is subject under any covenant having reference to the dwelling house in such lease or agreement, being a liability or obligation falling due to be discharged or performed on or after the date on which the decree is made absolute, shall not be enforceable against the said spouse.

(3) Where the spouse is entitled as aforesaid to occupy the dwelling house by virtue of a statutory tenancy, the court may by order direct that, as from the date on which the decree is made absolute, that spouse shall cease to be entitled to occupy the dwelling house and that his or her former spouse shall be deemed to be the tenant or, as the case may be, the sole tenant under that statutory tenancy; and the question whether the provisions of the [paragraphs 1 to 3 or, as the case may be, paragraphs 5 to 7 of Schedule 1 to the Rent Act 1968] [3] as to the succession by the widow of a deceased tenant or by a member of his family to the right to retain possession are capable of having effect in the event of the death of the person deemed by an order under this subsection to be the tenant or sole tenant under the statutory tenancy shall be determined according as those provisions have or have not already had effect in relation to the statutory tenancy.

(4) Where the court makes an order under this section it may by the order direct that both spouses shall be jointly and severally liable to discharge or perform any or all of the liabilities and obligations in respect of the dwelling house (whether arising under the tenancy or otherwise) which have at the date of the order fallen due to be discharged or performed by one only of the spouses or which, but for the direction, would before the date on which the decree is made absolute fall due to be discharged or performed by one only of them; and where the court gives such a direction it may further direct that either spouse shall be liable to indemnify the other in whole or in part against any payment made or expenses incurred by the other in discharging or performing any such liability or obligation.

(5) An order under this section may be made at any time after a decree nisi has been granted and before the decree is made absolute.

(6) Rules of court shall be made requiring the court before it makes an order under this section to give the landlord of the dwelling house to which the order will relate an opportunity of being heard.

(7) Where a spouse is entitled to occupy a dwelling house by virtue of a tenancy, this section shall not affect the operation of sections 1 and 2 above in relation to the other spouse's rights of occupation, and the court's power to make orders under this section shall be in addition to the powers conferred by those sections.

(8) [In this section the expressions " landlord," " protected tenancy," " statutory tenancy " and " tenancy " have the same meaning as in the Rent Act 1968.] [3]

Short title, commencement, extent and construction

8.—(1) This Act may be cited as the Matrimonial Homes Act 1967,

[3] Substituted by the Rent Act 1968 (c. 23), Sched. 15.

and shall come into operation on such date as the Lord Chancellor may by order made by statutory instrument appoint.

(2) This Act shall not extend to Scotland or Northern Ireland.

(3) [References in this Act to any enactment are references to that]⁴ enactment as amended, extended or applied by any other enactment, including this Act.

Section 2 (6)   **SCHEDULE**

CONSEQUENTIAL AMENDMENTS AS TO LAND CHARGES

[Paragraph (1) repealed by Law of Property Act 1969 (c. 59), ss. 16 (2), 17 (1), Sched. 2, Pt. II.]

[*Paragraphs* (2) *and* (3) *repealed by Land Charges Act* 1972 (c. 61), *s.* 18, *Sched.* 5.]

4. In Schedule 1 to the County Courts Act 1959 (which specifies the cases in which a county court has jurisdiction under certain enactments), at the end of the second column of the entry relating to section 10 (8) of the Land Charges Act 1925, there shall be added the following paragraph:—

"In a case where the land charge is within Class F, if the land affected by the charge is the subject of an order made by the court under section 1 of the Matrimonial Homes Act 1967 or an application for an order under the said section 1 relating to such land has been made to the court."

Abortion Act 1967

(1967 c. 87)

An Act to amend and clarify the law relating to termination of pregnancy by registered medical practitioners.

[27th October 1967]

Medical termination of pregnancy

1.—(1) Subject to the provisions of this section, a person shall not be guilty of an offence under the law relating to abortion when a pregnancy is terminated by a registered medical practitioner if two registered medical practitioners are of the opinion, formed in good faith—

(a) that the continuance of the pregnancy would involve risk to the life of the pregnant woman, or of injury to the physical or mental health of the pregnant woman or any existing children of her family, greater than if the pregnancy were terminated; or

(b) that there is a substantial risk that if the child were born it would suffer from such physical or mental abnormalities as to be seriously handicapped.

(2) In determining whether the continuance of a pregnancy would involve such risk of injury to health as is mentioned in paragraph (a) of subsection (1) of this section, account may be taken of the pregnant woman's actual or reasonably foreseeable environment.

(3) Except as provided by subsection (4) of this section, any treatment for the termination of pregnancy must be carried out in a hospital vested in the Minister of Health or the Secretary of State under the National Health Service Acts, or in a place for the time being approved for the purposes of this section by the said Minister or the Secretary of State.

(4) Subsection (3) of this section, and so much of subsection (1) as relates to the opinion of two registered medical practioners, shall not

---

⁴ Substituted by the Rent Act 1968 (c. 23), Sched. 15.

F.L.S.—10

apply to the termination of a pregnancy by a registered medical practitioner in a case where he is of the opinion, formed in good faith, that the termination is immediately necessary to save the life or to prevent grave permanent injury to the physical or mental health of the pregnant woman.

Notification

2.—(1) The Minister of Health in respect of England and Wales, and the Secretary of State in respect of Scotland, shall by statutory instrument make regulations to provide—

(*a*) for requiring any such opinion as is referred to in section 1 of this Act to be certified by the practitioners or practitioner concerned in such form and at such time as may be prescribed by the regulations, and for requiring the preservation and disposal of certificates made for the purposes of the regulations;

(*b*) for requiring any registered medical practitioner who terminates a pregnancy to give notice of the termination and such other information relating to the termination as may be so prescribed;

(*c*) for prohibiting the disclosure, except to such persons or for such purposes as may be so prescribed, of notices given or information furnished pursuant to the regulations.

(2) The information furnished in pursuance of regulations made by virtue of paragraph (*b*) of subsection (1) of this section shall be notified solely to the [Chief Medical Officer of the Department of Health and Social Security, or of the Welsh Office, or of the Scottish Home and Health Department] [1]

(3) Any person who wilfully contravenes or wilfully fails to comply with the requirements of regulations under subsection (1) of this section shall be liable on summary conviction to a fine not exceeding one hundred pounds.

(4) Any statutory instrument made by virtue of this section shall be subject to annulment in pursuance of a resolution of either House of Parliament.

Application of Act to visiting forces etc.

3.—(1) In relation to the termination of a pregnancy in a case where the following conditions are satisfied, that is to say—

(*a*) the treatment for termination of the pregnancy was carried out in a hospital controlled by the proper authorities of a body to which this section applies; and

(*b*) the pregnant woman had at the time of the treatment a relevant association with that body; and

(*c*) the treatment was carried out by a registered medical practitioner or a person who at the time of the treatment was a member of that body appointed as a medical practitioner for that body by the proper authorities of that body,

this Act shall have effect as if any reference in section 1 to a registered medical practitioner and to a hospital vested in a Minister under the National Health Service Acts included respectively a reference to such a person as is mentioned in paragraph (*c*) of this subsection and to a hospital controlled as aforesaid, and as if section 2 were omitted.

(2) The bodies to which this section applies are any force which is a visiting force within the meaning of any of the provisions of Part I of the Visiting Forces Act 1952 and any headquarters within the meaning of the Schedule to the International Headquarters and Defence Organisations Act 1964; and for the purposes of this section—

[1] Words substituted by 1969 S.I. No. 388.

(*a*) a woman shall be treated as having a relevant association at any time with a body to which this section applies if at that time—

(i) in the case of such a force as aforesaid, she had a relevant association within the meaning of the said Part I with the force; and

(ii) in the case of such a headquarters as aforesaid, she was a member of the headquarters or a dependant within the meaning of the Schedule aforesaid of such a member; and

(*b*) any reference to a member of a body to which this section applies shall be construed—

(i) in the case of such a force as aforesaid, as a reference to a member of or of a civilian component of that force within the meaning of the said Part I; and

(ii) in the case of such a headquarters as aforesaid as a reference to a member of that headquarters within the meaning of the Schedule aforesaid.

Conscientious objection to participation in treatment

4.—(1) Subject to subsection (2) of this section, no person shall be under any duty, whether by contract or by any statutory or other legal requirement, to participate in any treatment authorised by this Act to which he has a conscientious objection:

Provided that in any legal proceedings the burden of proof of conscientious objection shall rest on the person claiming to rely on it.

(2) Nothing in subsection (1) of this section shall affect any duty to participate in treatment which is necessary to save the life or to prevent grave permanent injury to the physical or mental health of a pregnant woman.

(3) In any proceedings before a court in Scotland, a statement on oath by any person to the effect that he has a conscientious objection to participating in any treatment authorised by this Act shall be sufficient evidence for the purpose of discharging the burden of proof imposed upon him by subsection (1) of this section.

Supplementary provisions

5.—(1) Nothing in this Act shall affect the provisions of the Infant Life (Preservation) Act 1929 (protecting the life of the viable foetus).

(2) For the purposes of the law relating to abortion, anything done with intent to procure the miscarriage of a woman is unlawfully done unless authorised by section 1 of this Act.

Interpretation

6. In this Act, the following expressions have meanings hereby assigned to them:—

"the law relating to abortion" means sections 58 and 59 of the Offences against the Person Act 1861, and any rule of law relating to the procurement of abortion;

"the National Health Service Acts" means the National Health Service Acts 1946 to 1966 or the National Health Service (Scotland) Acts 1947 to 1966.

Short title, commencement and extent

7.—(1) This Act may be cited as the Abortion Act 1967.

(2) This Act shall come into force on the expiration of the period of six months beginning with the date on which it is passed.

(3) This Act does not extend to Northern Ireland.

Maintenance Orders Act 1968

(1968 c. 36)

An Act to amend the enactments relating to matrimonial, guardianship and affiliation proceedings so far as they limit the weekly rate of the maintenance payments which may be ordered by magistrates' courts. [3rd July 1968]

Increase of maximum payments for children

1. The enactments described in the Schedule to this Act shall have effect subject to the amendments specified in the second column of that Schedule, being amendments removing the limits of fifty shillings and seven pounds ten shillings imposed by those enactments upon the weekly rate of the payments for the maintenance of a child, and for the maintenance of a party to a marriage, which may be required by order of a magistrates' court thereunder.

Supplementary

2. Any order made by a magistrates' court before the date of the commencement of this Act may be varied so as to include, from the date of the variation, provision for the payment of such increased sums as would have been lawful if the order had been made after the first mentioned date.

Short title, extent, commencement and repeal

3.—(1) This Act may be cited as the Maintenance Orders Act 1968.

(2) This Act does not extend to Scotland or Northern Ireland.

(3) This Act shall come into force at the expiration of the period of one month beginning with the day on which it is passed.

(4) Section 15 of the Matrimonial Proceedings (Magistrates' Courts) Act 1960 is hereby repealed.

Adoption Act 1968

(1968 c. 53)

An Act to make provision for extending the powers of courts in the United Kingdom with respect to the adoption of children; for enabling effect to be given in the United Kingdom to adoptions effected in other countries and to determinations of authorities in other countries with respect to adoptions; and for purposes connected with the matters aforesaid.

[26th July 1968]

Further provision for adoption in Great Britain

1–3. [*These sections were repealed by Children Act* 1975 (c. 72), Sched. 4.]

Recognition of adoptions and adoption proceedings taking place overseas

Extension of enactments to certain adoptions made overseas

4.—(1)–(2) [*Repealed by the Children Act 1975 (c. 72), Sched.* 4.]

(3) In this Act " overseas adoption " means an adoption of such a description as the Secretary of State may by order specify, being a description of adoptions of infants appearing to him to be effected under the law of any country outside Great Britain; and an order under this subsection may contain provision as to the manner in which evidence of an overseas adoption may be given.

Recognition of determinations made overseas in adoption proceedings

5.—(1) Where an authority of a convention country or a specified country having power under the law of that country—

   (a) to authorise or review the authorisation of a convention adoption or a specified order; or

   (b) to give or review a decision revoking or annulling a convention adoption, a specified order or an adoption order,

makes a determination in the exercise of that power, then, subject to section 6 of this Act and any subsequent determination having effect under this subsection, the determination shall have effect in Great Britain for the purpose of effecting, confirming or terminating the adoption in question or confirming its termination, as the case may be.

(2) In this Act " convention adoption " means an overseas adoption of a description designated by an order under section 4 (3) of this Act as that of an adoption regulated by the Convention.

Annulment etc. of certain adoptions and determinations made overseas

6.—(1) The court may, upon an application under this subsection, by order annul a convention adoption—

   (a) on the ground that at the relevant time the adoption was prohibited by a notified provision, if under the internal law then in force in the country of which the adopter was then a national or the adopters were then nationals the adoption could have been impugned on that ground;

   (b) on the ground that at the relevant time the adoption contravened provisions relating to consents of the internal law relating to adoption of the country of which the adopted person was then a national, if under that law the adoption could then have been impugned on that ground;

   (c) on any other ground on which the adoption can be impugned under the law for the time being in force in the country in which the adoption was effected.

(2) Where a person adopted by his father or mother alone by virtue of a convention adoption has subsequently become a legitimated person on the marriage of his father and mother, the court may, upon an application under this subsection by the parties concerned, by order revoke the adoption.

(3) The court may, upon an application under this subsection—

   (a) order that an overseas adoption or a determination shall cease to be valid in Great Britain on the ground that the adoption or determination is contrary to public policy or that the authority which purported to authorise the adoption or make the determination was not competent to entertain the case;

   (b) decide the extent, if any, to which a determination has been affected by a subsequent determination.

(4) Any court in Great Britain may, in any proceedings in that court,

decide that an overseas adoption or a determination shall, for the purposes of those proceedings, be treated as invalid in Great Britain on either of the grounds mentioned in subsection (3) of this section.

(5) Except as provided by this section, the validity of an overseas adoption or a determination shall not be impugned in proceedings in any court in Great Britain.

Provisions supplementary to section 6

7.—(1) Any application for an order under section 6 or a decision under section 6 (3) (*b*) of this Act shall be made in the prescribed manner and within such period, if any, as may be prescribed.

(2) No application shall be made under subsection (1) or subsection (2) of section 6 of this Act in respect of an adoption unless immediately before the application is made the person adopted or the adopter resides in Great Britain or, as the case may be, both adopters reside there.

(3) In deciding in pursuance of section 6 of this Act whether such an authority as is mentioned in section 5 (1) of this Act was competent to entertain a particular case, a court shall be bound by any finding of fact made by the authority and stated by the authority to be so made for the purpose of determining whether the authority was competent to entertain the case.

(4) In section 6 of this Act and this section—

" determination " means such a determination as is mentioned in section 5 (1) of this Act;

" notified provision " means a provision specified in an order of the Secretary of State as one in respect of which a notification to or by the Government of the United Kingdom was in force at the relevant time in pursuance of the provisions of the Convention relating to prohibitions contained in the national law of the adopter; and

" relevant time " means the time when the adoption in question purported to take effect under the law of the country in which it purports to have been effected.

Miscellaneous and general

Registration

8.—(1) The direction contained in an adoption order in pursuance of section 21 of the Act of 1958 (under which the Registrar General is required to register adoptions in the Adopted Children Register) shall include an instruction that the entry made in that register in consequence of the order shall be marked with the words " Convention order ".

(2) If the Registrar General is satisfied that an entry in the Registers of Births relates to a person adopted under an overseas adoption and that he has sufficient particulars relating to that person to enable an entry in the [form specified for the purposes of this subsection in regulations made by the Registrar General under Section 21 of the Act of 1958] [1] to be made in the Adopted Children Register in respect of that person, he shall—

(*a*) make such an entry in the Adopted Children Register; and

(*b*) if there is a previous entry in respect of that person in that register, mark the entry (or if there is more than one such entry the last of them) with the word " Re-adopted " followed by the name in brackets of the country in which the adoption was effected; and

---

[1] Words substituted by Children Act 1975 (c. 72), Sched. 3.

(*c*) unless the entry in the Registers of Births is already marked with the word " Adopted " (whether or not followed by other words), mark the entry with that word followed by the name in brackets of the country aforesaid;

[. . .]²

(3) If the Registrar General is satisfied—

(*a*) that an adoption order or an overseas adoption has ceased to have effect, whether on annulment or otherwise; or

(*b*) that any entry or mark was erroneously made in pursuance of subsection (2) of this section in any register mentioned in that subsection,

he may cause such alterations to be made in any such register as he considers are required in consequence of the cesser or to correct the error; and where an entry in such a register is amended in pursuance of this subsection, any copy or extract of the entry shall be deemed to be accurate if and only if it shows the entry as amended but without indicating that it has been amended.

(4) Without prejudice to subsection (3) of this section, where an entry in the Registers of Births is marked in pursuance of subsection (2) of this section and the birth in question is subsequently re-registered under section 14 of the Births and Deaths Registration Act 1953 (which provides for re-registration of the birth of a legitimated person) the entry made on re-registration shall be marked in the like manner.

(5) In the application of this section to Scotland—

(*a*) for any reference to the Registrar General or the Registers of Births there shall be substituted respectively a reference to the Registrar General of Births, Deaths and Marriages for Scotland and the register of births;

[(*b*) for the references to section 21 of the Act of 1958 there shall be substituted references to section 23 of that Act;]¹

[(*c*) in subsection (4), for the reference to section 14 of the Births and Deaths Registration Act 1953 there shall be substituted a reference to section 20 (1) of the Registration of Births, Deaths and Marriages (Scotland) Act 1965 (which provides for re-registration of births in certain cases).]¹

Nationality

9.—(1) If the Secretary of State by order declares that a description of persons specified in the order has, in pursuance of the Convention, been notified to the Government of the United Kingdom as the description of persons who are deemed to possess the nationality of a particular convention country, persons of that description shall, subject to the following provisions of this section, be treated for the purposes of this Act as nationals of that country.

(2) Subject to section 7 (3) of this Act and subsection (3) of this section, where it appears to the court in any proceedings under this Act, or to any court by which a decision in pursuance of section 6 (4) of this Act falls to be given, that a person is or was at a particular time a national of two or more countries, then—

(*a*) if it appears to the said court that he is or was then a United Kingdom national, he shall be treated for the purposes of those proceedings or that decision as if he were or had then been a United Kingdom national only;

(*b*) if, in a case not falling within paragraph (*a*) above, it appears to the said court that one only of those countries is or was then a

---

² Words repealed by *ibid*.

convention country, he shall be treated for those purposes as if he were or had then been a national of that country only;

(c) if, in a case not falling within paragraph (a) above, it appears to the said court that two or more of those countries are or were then convention countries, he shall be treated for those purposes as if he were or had then been a national of such one only of those convention countries as the said court considers is the country with which he is or was then most closely connected;

(d) in any other case, he shall be treated for those purposes as if he were or had then been a national of such one only of those countries as the said court considers is the country with which he is or was then most closely connected.

(3) A court in which proceedings are brought in pursuance of section 6 of this Act shall be entitled to disregard the provisions of subsection (2) of this section in so far as it appears to that court appropriate to do so for the purposes of those proceedings; but nothing in this subsection shall be construed as prejudicing the provisions of section 7 (3) of this Act.

(4) Where, after such inquiries as the court in question considers appropriate, it appears to the court in any proceedings under this Act, or to any court by which such a decision as aforesaid falls to be given, that a person has no nationality or no ascertainable nationality, he shall be treated for the purposes of those proceedings or that decision as a national of the country in which he resides or, where that country is one of two or more countries having the same law of nationality, as a national of those countries.

(5) Where an adoption order, [or a specified order] [1] ceases to have effect, either on annulment or otherwise, the cesser shall not affect the status as a citizen of the United Kingdom and Colonies of any person who, by virtue of section 19 (1) of the Act of 1958, became such a citizen in consequence of the order [. . .].[3]

Supplemental

10.—(1) In any case where the internal law of a country falls to be ascertained for the purposes of this Act by any court and there are in force in that country two or more systems of internal law, the relevant system shall be ascertained in accordance with any rule in force throughout that country indicating which of the systems is relevant in the case in question or, if there is no such rule, shall be the system appearing to that court to be most closely connected with the case.

(2)–(3) [*Repealed by Children Act* 1975 (c. 72), *Sched.* 4.]

Interpretation

11.[4]—(1) In this Act the following expressions have the following meanings unless the context otherwise requires, that is to say—

" the Act of 1958 " means the Adoption Act 1958;

" adoption order " has the meaning assigned to it by section 1 of this Act;

" the Convention " means the Convention mentioned in the preamble to this Act;

" convention adoption " has the meaning assigned to it by section 5 (2) of this Act;

" convention country " means any country (excluding Great Britain and a specified country) for the time being designated by an

---

[3] Words repealed by Children Act 1975 (c. 72), Sched. 4.
[4] See Children Act 1975 (c. 72), Sched. 3, para. 64, *post*.

order of the Secretary of State as a country in which, in his opinion, the Convention is in force;

" the court " means the High Court or the Court of Session;

" internal law ", in relation to any country, means the law applicable in a case where no question arises as to the law in force in any other country;

" overseas adoption " has the meaning assigned to it by section 4 (3) of this Act;

" prescribed " means prescribed by rules or, in Scotland, by act of sederunt;

[Definitions repealed by Children Act 1975 (c. 72), Sched. 4.]

" reside " means habitually reside and " resides " shall be construed accordingly;

" rules " means rules made under section 12 (1) of this Act;

" specified country " means, for the purposes of any provision of this Act, any of the following countries, that is to say, Northern Ireland, any of the Channel Islands, the Isle of Man and a colony, being a country designated for the purposes of that provision by order of the Secretary of State or, if no country is so designated, any of those countries;

" specified order " means an adoption order made under any enactment in force in a specified country and corresponding to section 1 of this Act; and

" United Kingdom national " means, for the purposes of any provision of this Act, a citizen of the United Kingdom and Colonies satisfying such conditions, if any, as the Secretary of State may by order specify for the purposes of that provision.

(2) Any reference in this Act to any enactment is a reference to it as amended, and includes a reference to it as applied, by or under any other enactment including this Act.

Rules and orders etc.

12.—(1) Provision in regard to any matter to be prescribed under this Act, [. . .] [3] and dealing generally with all matters of procedure and incidental matters arising out of this Act [. . .] [3] and for carrying this Act [. . .] [3] into effect shall be made, in England and Wales, by rules made by the Lord Chancellor and, in Scotland, by act of sederunt; [. . .] [3]—

(2) Any power to make orders or rules under this Act shall be exercisable by statutory instrument, and any statutory instrument [containing rules made by the Lord Chancellor under subsection (1) of this section] [1] shall be subject to annulment in pursuance of a resolution of either House of Parliament.

(3) An order made under any provision of this Act (except section 14 (2)) may be revoked or varied by a subsequent order under that provision.

(4) Any order or rules made under this Act may make different provision for different circumstances and may contain such incidental and transitional provisions as the authority making the order or rules considers expedient.

(5) References to an order in subsections (2) to (4) of this section do not include references to an order of a court.

13. [*Repealed by Northern Ireland Constitution Act* 1973 (*c.* 36), *Sched.* 6.]

Short title, commencement and extent

14.—(1) This Act may be cited as the Adoption Act 1968.

(2) This Act shall come into force on such date as the Secretary of State may by order appoint, and different dates may be appointed under this subsection for different purposes of this Act.

(3) This Act, [. . .] ³ except sections 9 (5) and this section, does not extend to Northern Ireland.

Theft Act 1968

(1968 c. 60)

General and consequential provisions

Husband and wife

30.—(1) This Act shall apply in relation to the parties to a marriage, and to property belonging to the wife or husband whether or not by reason of an interest derived from the marriage, as it would apply if they were not married and any such interest subsisted independently of the marriage.

(2) Subject to subsection (4) below, a person shall have the same right to bring proceedings against that person's wife or husband for any offence (whether under this Act or otherwise) as if they were not married, and a person bringing any such proceedings shall be competent to give evidence for the prosecution at every stage of the proceedings.

(3) Where a person is charged in proceedings not brought by that person's wife or husband with having committed any offence with reference to that person's wife or husband or to property belonging to the wife or husband, the wife or husband shall be competent to give evidence at every stage of the proceedings, whether for the defence or for the prosecution, and whether the accused is charged solely or jointly with any other person:

Provided that—

  (*a*) the wife or husband (unless compellable at common law) shall not be compellable either to give evidence or, in giving evidence, to disclose any communication made to her or him during the marriage by the accused; and

  (*b*) her or his failure to give evidence shall not be made the subject of any comment by the prosecution.

(4) Proceedings shall not be instituted against a person for any offence of stealing or doing unlawful damage to property which at the time of the offence belongs to that person's wife or husband, or for any attempt, incitement or conspiracy to commit such an offence, unless the proceedings are instituted by or with the consent of the Director of Public Prosecutions:

Provided that—

  (*a*) this subsection shall not apply to proceedings against a person for an offence—

    (i) if that person is charged with committing the offence jointly with the wife or husband; or

    (ii) if by virtue of any judicial decree or order (wherever made) that person and the wife or husband are at the time of the offence under no obligation to cohabit; and

  (*b*) this subsection shall not prevent the arrest, or the issue of a warrant for the arrest, of a person for an offence, or the remand in custody or on bail of a person charged with an offence, where the arrest (if without a warrant) is made, or the warrant of arrest issues on an information laid, by a person other than the wife or husband.

Effect on civil proceedings and rights

31.—(1) A person shall not be excused, by reason that to do so may incriminate that person or the wife or husband of that person of an offence under this Act—

(a) from answering any question put to that person in proceedings for the recovery or administration of any property, for the execution of any trust or for an account of any property or dealings with property; or

(b) from complying with any order made in any such proceedings;

but no statement or admission made by a person in answering a question put or complying with an order made as aforesaid shall, in proceedings for an offence under this Act, be admissible in evidence against that person or (unless they married after the making of the statement or admission) against the wife or husband of that person.

(2) Notwithstanding any enactment to the contrary, where property has been stolen or obtained by fraud or other wrongful means, the title to that or any other property shall not be affected by reason only of the conviction of the offender.

Civil Evidence Act 1968

(1968 c. 64)

Findings of adultery and paternity as evidence in civil proceedings

12.—(1) In any civil proceedings—

(a) the fact that a person has been found guilty of adultery in any matrimonial proceedings; and

(b) the fact that a person has been adjudged to be the father of a child in affiliation proceedings before any court in the United Kingdom,

shall (subject to subsection (3) below) be admissible in evidence for the purpose of proving, where to do so is relevant to any issue in those civil proceedings, that he committed the adultery to which the finding relates or, as the case may be, is (or was) the father of that child, whether or not he offered any defence to the allegation of adultery or paternity and whether or not he is a party to the civil proceedings; but no finding or adjudication other than a subsisting one shall be admissible in evidence by virtue of this section.

(2) In any civil proceedings in which by virtue of this section a person is proved to have been found guilty of adultery as mentioned in subsection (1) (a) above or to have been adjudged to be the father of a child as mentioned in subsection (1) (b) above—

(a) he shall be taken to have committed the adultery to which the finding relates or, as the case may be, to be (or have been) the father of that child, unless the contrary is proved; and

(b) without prejudice to the reception of any other admissible evidence for the purpose of identifying the facts on which the finding or adjudication was based, the contents of any document which was before the court, or which contains any pronouncement of the court, in the matrimonial or affiliation proceedings in question shall be admissible in evidence for that purpose.

(3) Nothing in this section shall prejudice the operation of any

enactment whereby a finding of fact in any matrimonial or affiliation proceedings is for the purposes of any other proceedings made conclusive evidence of any fact.

(4) Subsection (4) of section 11 of this Act shall apply for the purposes of this section as if the reference to subsection (2) were a reference to subsection (2) of this section.

(5) In this section—

" matrimonial proceedings " means any matrimonial cause in the High Court or a county court in England and Wales or in the High Court in Northern Ireland, any consistorial action in Scotland, or any appeal arising out of any such cause or action;

" affiliation proceedings " means, in relation to Scotland, any action of affiliation and aliment;

and in this subsection " consistorial action " does not include an action of aliment only between husband and wife raised in the Court of Session or an action of interim aliment raised in the sheriff court.

Privilege

Privilege against incrimination of self or spouse

14.—(1) The right of a person in any legal proceedings other than criminal proceedings to refuse to answer any question or produce any document or thing if to do so would tend to expose that person to proceedings for an offence or for the recovery of a penalty—

(a) shall apply only as regards criminal offences under the law of any part of the United Kingdom and penalties provided for by such law; and

(b) shall include a like right to refuse to answer any question or produce any document or thing if to do so would tend to expose the husband or wife of that person to proceedings for any such criminal offence or for the recovery of any such penalty.

(2) In so far as any existing enactment conferring (in whatever words) powers of inspection or investigation confers on a person (in whatever words) any right otherwise than in criminal proceedings to refuse to answer any question or give any evidence tending to incriminate that person, subsection (1) above shall apply to that right as it applies to the right described in that subsection; and every such existing enactment shall be construed accordingly.

(3) In so far as any existing enactment provides (in whatever words) that in any proceedings other than criminal proceedings a person shall not be excused from answering any question or giving any evidence on the ground that to do so may incriminate that person, that enactment shall be construed as providing also that in such proceedings a person shall not be excused from answering any question or giving any evidence on the ground that to do so may incriminate the husband or wife of that person.

(4) Where any existing enactment (however worded) that—

(a) confers powers of inspection or investigation; or

(b) provides as mentioned in subsection (3) above,

further provides (in whatever words) that any answer or evidence given by a person shall not be admissible in evidence against that person in any proceedings or class of proceedings (however described, and whether criminal or not), that enactment shall be construed as providing also that any answer or evidence given by that person shall not be admissible in evidence against the husband or wife of that person in the proceedings or class of proceedings in question.

(5) In this section " existing enactment " means any enactment

passed before this Act; and the references to giving evidence are references to giving evidence in any manner, whether by furnishing information, making discovery, producing documents or otherwise.

Abolition of certain privileges

16.—(1) The following rules of law are hereby abrogated except in relation to criminal proceedings, that is to say—

(a) the rule whereby, in any legal proceedings, a person cannot be compelled to answer any question or produce any document or thing if to do so would tend to expose him to a forfeiture; and

(b) the rule whereby, in any legal proceedings, a person other than a party to the proceedings cannot be compelled to produce any deed or other document relating to his title to any land.

(2) The rule of law whereby, in any civil proceedings, a party to the proceedings cannot be compelled to produce any document relating solely to his own case and in no way tending to impeach that case or support the case of any opposing party is hereby abrogated.

(3) Section 3 of the Evidence (Amendment) Act 1853 (which provides that a husband or wife shall not be compellable to disclose any communication made to him or her by his or her spouse during the marriage) shall cease to have effect except in relation to criminal proceedings.

(4) In section 43 (1) of the Matrimonial Causes Act 1965 (under which the evidence of a husband or wife is admissible in any proceedings to prove that marital intercourse did or did not take place between them during any period, but a husband or wife is not compellable in any proceedings to give evidence of the matters aforesaid), the words from " but a husband or wife " to the end of the subsection shall cease to have effect except in relation to criminal proceedings.

(5) A witness in any proceedings instituted in consequence of adultery, whether a party to the proceedings or not, shall not be excused from answering any question by reason that it tends to show that he or she has been guilty of adultery; and accordingly the proviso to section 3 of the Evidence Further Amendment Act 1869 and, in section 43 (2) of the Matrimonial Causes Act 1965, the words from " but " to the end of the subsection shall cease to have effect.

Family Law Reform Act 1969

(1969 c. 46)

An Act to amend the law relating to the age of majority, to persons who have not attained that age and to the time when a particular age is attained; to amend the law relating to the property rights of illegitimate children and of other persons whose relationship is traced through an illegitimate link; to make provision for the use of blood tests for the purpose of determining the paternity of any person in civil proceedings; to make provision with respect to the evidence required to rebut a presumption of legitimacy and illegitimacy; to make further provision, in connection with the registration of the birth of an illegitimate child, for entering the name of the father; and for connected purposes. [25th July 1969]

PART I [1]

REDUCTION OF AGE OF MAJORITY AND RELATED PROVISIONS

Reduction of age of majority from 21 to 18

1.[1a]—(1) As from the date on which this section comes into force a person shall attain full age on attaining the age of eighteen instead of on attaining the age of twenty-one; and a person shall attain full age on that date if he has then already attained the age of eighteen but not the age of twenty-one.

(2) The foregoing subsection applies for the purposes of any rule of law, and, in the absence of a definition or of any indication of a contrary intention, for the construction of " full age ", " infant ", " infancy ", " minor ", " minority " and similar expressions in—

    (a) any statutory provision, whether passed or made before, on or after the date on which this section comes into force; and

    (b) any deed, will or other instrument of whatever nature (not being a statutory provision) made on or after that date.

(3) In the statutory provisions specified in Schedule 1 to this Act for any reference to the age of twenty-one years there shall be substituted a reference to the age of eighteen years; but the amendment by this subsection of the provisions specified in Part II of that Schedule shall be without prejudice to any power of amending or revoking those provisions.

(4) This section does not affect the construction of any such expression as is referred to in subsection (2) of this section in any of the statutory provisions described in Schedule 2 to this Act, and the transitional provisions and savings contained in Schedule 3 to this Act shall have effect in relation to this section.

(5) The Lord Chancellor may by order made by statutory instrument amend any provision in any local enactment passed on or before the date on which this section comes into force (not being a provision described in paragraph 2 of Schedule 2 to this Act) by substituting a reference to the age of eighteen years for any reference therein to the age of twenty-one years; and any statutory instrument containing an order under this subsection shall be subject to annulment in pursuance of a resolution of either House of Parliament.

(6) In this section " statutory provision " means any enactment (including, except where the context otherwise requires, this Act) and any order, rule, regulation, byelaw or other instrument made in the exercise of a power conferred by any enactment.

(7) Notwithstanding any rule of law, a will or codicil executed before the date on which this section comes into force shall not be treated for the purposes of this section as made on or after that date by reason only that the will or codicil is confirmed by a codicil executed on or after that date.

Provisions relating to marriage

2.—(1) In the following enactments, that is to say—

    (a) section 7 (c) of the Foreign Marriage Act 1892 (persons under 21 intending to be married by a marriage officer to swear that necessary consents have been obtained);

    (b) paragraph 2 (c) of Part I of the Schedule to the Marriage with

---

[1] Parts I, II, and IV of this Act were brought into effect on January 1, 1970, by S.I. 1969/1140. Part III was brought into effect on March 1, 1972, by S.I. 1971/1857.
[1a] Applied by Finance Act 1969 (c. 32), s. 16.

Foreigners Act 1906 (persons under 21 seeking certificate to swear that necessary consents have been obtained);

(c) section 78 (1) of the Marriage Act 1949 (definition of " infant " as person under the age of 21),

for the words " twenty-one years " there shall be substituted the words " eighteen years ".

(2) In subsection (5) of section 3 of the said Act of 1949 (which defines the courts having jurisdiction to consent to the marriage of an infant)—

(a) for the words " the county court of the district in which any respondent resides " there shall be substituted the words " the county court of the district in which any applicant or respondent resides "; and

(b) after the words " or a court of summary jurisdiction " there shall be inserted the words " having jurisdiction in the place in which any applicant or respondent resides ".

(3) Where for the purpose of obtaining a certificate or licence for marriage under Part III of the said Act of 1949 a person declares that the consent of any person or persons whose consent to the marriage is required under the said section 3 has been obtained, the superintendent registrar may refuse to issue the certificate or licence for marriage unless satisfied by the production of written evidence that the consent of that person or of those persons has in fact been obtained.

(4) In this section any expression which is also used in the said Act of 1949 has the same meaning as in that Act.

Provisions relating to wills and intestacy

3.—(1) In the following enactments, that is to say—

(a) section 7 of the Wills Act 1837 (invalidity of wills made by persons under 21);

(b) sections 1 and 3 (1) of the Wills (Soldiers and Sailors) Act 1918 (soldier, etc., eligible to make will and dispose of real property although under 21),

in their application to wills made after the coming into force of this section, for the words " twenty-one years " there shall be substituted the words " eighteen years ".

(2) In section 47 (1) (i) of the Administration of Estates Act 1925 (statutory trusts on intestacy), in its application to the estate of an intestate dying after the coming into force of this section, for the words " twenty-one years " in both places where they occur there shall be substituted the words " eighteen years ".

(3) Any will which—

(a) has been made, whether before or after the coming into force of this section, by a person under the age of eighteen; and

(b) is valid by virtue of the provisions of section 11 of the said Act of 1837 and the said Act of 1918,

may be revoked by that person notwithstanding that he is still under that age whether or not the circumstances are then such that he would be entitled to make a valid will under those provisions.

(4) In this section " will " has the same meaning as in the said Act of 1837 and " intestate " has the same meaning as in the said Act of 1925.

4. [*Repealed by Guardianship of Minors Act 1971 (c. 3), s. 18 (2), Sched. 2, in relation to England and Wales.*]

Modification of other enactments relating to maintenance of children so as to preserve benefits up to age of 21

5.—[*Repealed by Inheritance (Provision of Family and Dependants) Act* 1975 (*c.* 63), *Sched.*]

(2) Where a child in respect of whom an affiliation order has been made under the Affiliation Proceedings Act 1957 has attained the age of eighteen and his mother is dead, of unsound mind or in prison—

> (*a*) any application for an order under subsection (2) or (3) of section 7 of that Act directing that payments shall be made under the affiliation order for any period after he has attained that age may be made by the child himself; and

> (*b*) the child himself shall be the person entitled to any payments directed by an order under that section to be so made for any such period as aforesaid.

(3) [*Repealed by Matrimonial Proceedings and Property Act* 1970 (*c.* 45), *s.* 42, *Sched.* 3.]

Maintenance for wards of court

6.—(1) In this section " the court " means any of the following courts in the exercise of its jurisdiction relating to the wardship of children, that is to say, the High Court, [. . .] [1b] and " ward of court " means a ward of the court in question.

(2) Subject to the provisions of this section, the court may make an order—

> (*a*) requiring either parent of a ward of court to pay to the other parent; or

> (*b*) requiring either parent or both parents of a ward of court to pay to any other person having the care and control of the ward,

such weekly or other periodical sums towards the maintenance and education of the ward as the court thinks reasonable having regard to the means of the person or persons on whom the requirement is imposed.

(3) An order under subsection (2) of this section may require such sums as are mentioned in that subsection to continue to be paid in respect of any period after the date on which the person for whose benefit the payments are to be made ceases to be a minor but not beyond the date on which he attains the age of twenty-one, and any order made as aforesaid may provide that any sum which is payable thereunder for the benefit of that person after he has ceased to be a minor shall be paid to that person himself.

(4) Subject to the provisions of this section, where a person who has ceased to be a minor but has not attained the age of twenty-one has at any time been the subject of an order making him a ward of court, the court may, on the application of either parent of that person or of that person himself, make an order requiring either parent to pay to the other parent, to anyone else for the benefit of that person or to that person himself, in respect of any period not extending beyond the date when he attains the said age, such weekly or other periodical sums towards his maintenance or education as the court thinks reasonable having regard to the means of the person on whom the requirement in question is imposed.

(5) No order shall be made under this section, and no liability under such an order shall accrue, at a time when the parents of the ward or

---

[1b] Words repealed by Courts Act 1971 (c. 23), Sched. 11.

former ward, as the case may be, are residing together, and if they so reside for a period of three months after such an order has been made it shall cease to have effect; but the foregoing provisions of this subsection shall not apply to any order made by virtue of subsection (2) (*b*) of this section.

(6) No order shall be made under this section requiring any person to pay any sum towards the maintenance or education of an illegitimate child of that person.

(7) Any order under this section, or under any corresponding enactment of the Parliament of Northern Ireland, shall be included among the orders to which section 16 of the Maintenance Orders Act 1950 applies; and any order under this section shall be included among the orders mentioned in section 2 (1) (*d*) of the Reserve and Auxiliary Forces (Protection of Civil Interests) Act 1951 [...] [1c]

(8) The court shall have power from time to time by an order under this section to vary or discharge any previous order thereunder.

Committal of wards of court to care of local authority and supervision of wards of court

7.—(1) In this section " the court " means any of the following courts in the exercise of its jurisdiction relating to the wardship of children, that is to say, the High Court, [...] [1b] and " ward of court " means a ward of the court in question.

(2) Where it appears to the court that there are exceptional circumstances making it impracticable or undesirable for a ward of court to be, or to continue to be, under the care of either of his parents or of any other individual the court may, if it thinks fit, make an order committing the care of the ward to a local authority; and thereupon Part II of the Children Act 1948 (which relates to the treatment of children in the care of a local authority) shall, subject to the next following subsection, apply as if the child had been received by the local authority into their care under section 1 of that Act.

(3) In subsection (2) of this section " local authority " means one of the local authorities referred to in subsection (1) of [section 43 of the Matrimonial Causes Act 1973] [2] (under which a child may be committed to the care of a local authority by a court having jurisdiction to make an order for its custody); and subsections (2) to (6) of that section (ancillary provisions) shall have effect as if any reference therein to that section included a reference to subsection (2) of this section.

(4) Where it appears to the court that there are exceptional circumstances making it desirable that a ward of court (not being a ward who in pursuance of an order under subsection (2) of this section is in the care of a local authority) should be under the supervision of an independent person, the court may, as respects such period as the court thinks fit, order that the ward be under the supervision of a welfare officer or of a local authority; and (section 44 (2) of the Matrimonial Causes Act 1973) [2] (ancillary provisions where a child is placed under supervision by a court having jurisdiction to make an order for its custody) shall have effect as if any reference therein to that section included a reference to this subsection.

(5) The court shall have power from time to time by an order under this section to vary or discharge any previous order thereunder.

[1c] Words repealed by A.J.A. 1970 (c. 31), s. 54, Sched. 11.
[2] Words substituted by Matrimonial Causes Act 1973 (c. 18), s. 54 (1) (*a*), Sched. 3.

Consent by persons over 16 to surgical, medical and dental treatment

8.—(1) The consent of a minor who has attained the age of sixteen years to any surgical, medical or dental treatment which, in the absence of consent, would constitute a trespass to his person, shall be as effective as it would be if he were of full age; and where a minor has by virtue of this section given an effective consent to any treatment it shall not be necessary to obtain any consent for it from his parent or guardian.

(2) In this section " surgical, medical or dental treatment " includes any procedure undertaken for the purposes of diagnosis, and this section applies to any procedure (including, in particular, the administration of an anaesthetic) which is ancillary to any treatment as it applies to that treatment.

(3) Nothing in this section shall be construed as making ineffective any consent which would have been effective if this section had not been enacted.

Time at which a person attains a particular age

9.[3]—(1) The time at which a person attains a particular age expressed in years shall be the commencement of the relevant anniversary of the date of his birth.

(2) This section applies only where the relevant anniversary falls on a date after that on which this section comes into force, and, in relation to any enactment, deed, will or other instrument, has effect subject to any provision therein.

Modification of enactments relating to Duke of Cornwall and other children of Her Majesty

10.—(1) Section 1 (1) of this Act shall apply for the construction of the expression " minor " in section 2 (2) of the Civil List Act 1952 (which relates to the amount payable for the Queen's Civil List while the Duke of Cornwall is for the time being a minor) and accordingly—

(*a*) section 2 (2) (*b*) of that Act (which relates to the three years during which the Duke is over 18 but under 21); and

(*b*) in section 2 (2) (*a*) of that Act the words " for each year whilst he is under the age of eighteen years ",

are hereby repealed except in relation to any period falling before section 1 of this Act comes into force.

(2) In section 4 (1) (*a*) of the said Act of 1952 (under which benefits are provided for the children of Her Majesty, other than the Duke of Cornwall, who attain the age of 21 or marry) for the words " twenty-one years " there shall be substituted the words " eighteen years " but no sum shall be payable by virtue of this subsection in respect of any period falling before section 1 of this Act comes into force.

(3) In section 38 of the Duchy of Cornwall Management Act 1863 (under which certain rights and powers of the Duke of Cornwall may, while he is under 21, be exercised on his behalf by the Sovereign or persons acting under Her authority) for the words " twenty-one years " wherever they occur there shall be substituted the words " eighteen years ".

---

[3] Excluded by Finance Act 1969 (c. 32), s. 11 (4).

Repeal of certain enactments relating to minors

11. The following enactments are hereby repealed—
   (a) the Infant Settlements Act 1855 (which enables a male infant over 20 and a female infant over 17 to make a marriage settlement), together with section 27 (3) of the Settled Land Act 1925, except in relation to anything done before the coming into force of this section;
   (b) in section 6 of the Employers and Workmen Act 1875 (powers of justices in respect of apprentices)—
      (i) the paragraph numbered (1) (power to direct apprentice to perform his duties), and
      (ii) the sentence following the paragraph numbered (2) (power to order imprisonment of an apprentice who fails to comply with direction);
   (c) in the Sexual Offences Act 1956, section 18 and paragraph 5 of Schedule 2 (fraudulent abduction of heiress).

Persons under full age may be described as minors instead of infants

12. A person who is not of full age may be described as a minor instead of as an infant, and accordingly in this Act " minor " means such a person as aforesaid.

13. [*Repealed by Northern Ireland Constitution Act* 1973 (*c*. 36), *Sched.* 6.]

PART II

PROPERTY RIGHTS OF ILLEGITIMATE CHILDREN

Right of illegitimate child to succeed on intestacy of parents, and of parents to succeed on intestacy of illegitimate child

14.—(1) Where either parent of an illegitimate child dies intestate as respects all or any of his or her real or personal property, the illegitimate child or, if he is dead, his issue, shall be entitled to take any interest therein to which he or such issue would have been entitled if he had been born legitimate.

(2) Where an illegitimate child dies intestate in respect of all or any of his real or personal property, each of his parents, if surviving, shall be entitled to take any interest therein to which that parent would have been entitled if the child had been born legitimate.

(3) In accordance with the foregoing provisions of this section, Part IV of the Administration of Estates Act 1925 (which deals with the distribution of the estate of an intestate) shall have effect as if—
   (a) any reference to the issue of the intestate included a reference to any illegitimate child of his and to the issue of any such child;
   (b) any reference to the child or children of the intestate included a reference to any illegitimate child or children of his; and
   (c) in relation to an intestate who is an illegitimate child, any reference to the parent, parents, father or mother of the intestate were a reference to his natural parent, parents, father or mother.

(4) For the purposes of subsection (2) of this section and of the provisions amended by subsection (3) (c) thereof, an illegitimate child

shall be presumed not to have been survived by his father unless the contrary is shown.

(5) This section does not apply to or affect the right of any person to take any entailed interest in real or personal property.

(6) The reference in section 50 (1) of the said Act of 1925 (which relates to the construction of documents) to Part IV of that Act, or to the foregoing provisions of that Part, shall in relation to an instrument inter vivos made, or a will or codicil coming into operation, after the coming into force of this section (but not in relation to instruments inter vivos made or wills or codicils coming into operation earlier) be construed as including references to this section.

(7) Section 9 of the Legitimacy Act 1926 (under which an illegitimate child and his issue are entitled to succeed on the intestacy of his mother if she leaves no legitimate issue, and the mother of an illegitimate child is entitled to succeed on his intestacy as if she were the only surviving parent) is hereby repealed.

(8) [*Repealed by Children Act* 1975 (*c*. 72), *Sched.* 4.]

(9) This section does not affect any rights under the intestacy of a person dying before the coming into force of this section.

Presumption that in dispositions of property references to children and other relatives include references to, and to persons related through, illegitimate children

15.—(1) In any disposition made after the coming into force of this section—

    (*a*) any reference (whether express or implied) to the child or children of any person shall, unless the contrary intention appears, be construed as, or as including, a reference to any illegitimate child of that person; and

    (*b*) any reference (whether express or implied) to a person or persons related in some other manner to any person shall, unless the contrary intention appears, be construed as, or as including, a reference to anyone who would be so related if he, or some other person through whom the relationship is deduced, had been born legitimate.

(2) The foregoing subsection applies only where the reference in question is to a person who is to benefit or to be capable of benefiting under the disposition or, for the purpose of designating such a person, to someone else to or through whom that person is related; but that subsection does not affect the construction of the word " heir " or " heirs " or of any expression which is used to create an entailed interest in real or personal property.

(3) In relation to any disposition made after the coming into force of this section, section 33 of the Trustee Act 1925 (which specifies the trusts implied by a direction that income is to be held on protective trusts for the benefit of any person) shall have effect as if—

    (*a*) the reference to the children or more remote issue of the principal beneficiary included a reference to any illegitimate child of the principal beneficiary and to anyone who would rank as such issue if he, or some other person through whom he is descended from the principal beneficiary, had been born legitimate; and

    (*b*) the reference to the issue of the principal beneficiary included a reference to anyone who would rank as such issue if he, or some other person through whom he is descended from the principal beneficiary, had been born legitimate.

(4) [*Repealed by Children Act* 1975 (*c*. 72), *Sched.* 4.]

(5) Where under any disposition any real or personal property or any interest in such property is limited (whether subject to any preceding limitation or charge or not) in such a way that it would, apart from this section, devolve (as nearly as the law permits) along with a dignity or title of honour, then, whether or not the disposition contains an express reference to the dignity or title of honour, and whether or not the property or some interest in the property may in some event become severed therefrom, nothing in this section shall operate to sever the property or any interest therein from the dignity or title, but the property or interest shall devolve in all respects as if this section had not been enacted.

(6) [*Repealed by Children Act* 1975 (*c.* 72), *Sched.* 4.]

(7) There is hereby abolished, as respects dispositions made after the coming into force of this section, any rule of law that a disposition in favour of illegitimate children not in being when the disposition takes effect is void as contrary to public policy.

(8) In this section " disposition " means a disposition, including an oral disposition, of real or personal property whether inter vivos or by will or codicil; and, notwithstanding any rule of law, a disposition made by will or codicil executed before the date on which this section comes into force shall not be treated for the purposes of this section as made on or after that date by reason only that the will or codicil is confirmed by a codicil executed on or after that date.

Meaning of " child " and " issue " in s. 33 of Wills Act 1837

16.—(1) In relation to a testator who dies after the coming into force of this section, section 33 of the Wills Act 1837 (gift to children or other issue of testator not to lapse if they predecease him but themselves leave issue) shall have effect as if—

(*a*) the reference to a child or other issue of the testator (that is, the intended beneficiary) included a reference to any illegitimate child of the testator and to anyone who would rank as such issue if he, or some other person through whom he is descended from the testator, had been born legitimate; and

(*b*) the reference to the issue of the intended beneficiary included a reference to anyone who would rank as such issue if he, or some other person through whom he is descended from the intended beneficiary, had been born legitimate.

(2) In this section " illegitimate child " includes an illegitimate child who is a legitimated person within the meaning of the Legitimacy Act 1926 or a person recognised by virtue of that Act or at common law as having been legitimated.

Protection of trustees and personal representatives

17. Notwithstanding the foregoing provisions of this Part of this Act, trustees or personal representatives may convey or distribute any real or personal property to or among the persons entitled thereto without having ascertained that there is no person who is or may be entitled to any interest therein by virtue of—

(*a*) section 14 of this Act so far as it confers any interest on illegitimate children or their issue or on the father of an illegitimate child; or

(*b*) section 15 or 16 of this Act,

and shall not be liable to any such person of whose claim they have not had notice at the time of the conveyance or distribution; but nothing in this section shall prejudice the right of any such person to follow the property, or any property representing it, into the hands of any person. other than a purchaser, who may have received it.

18.—[*Repealed by Inheritance (Provision for Family and Dependants) Act 1975 (c. 63), Sched.*]

Policies of assurance and property in industrial and provident societies

19.—(1) In section 11 of the Married Women's Property Act 1882 and section 2 of the Married Women's Policies of Assurance (Scotland) Act 1880 (policies of assurance effected for the benefit of children) the expression " children " shall include illegitimate children.

(2) In section 25 (2) of the Industrial and Provident Societies Act 1965 (application of property in registered society where member was illegitimate and is not survived by certain specified relatives) for the words " and leaves no widow, widower or issue, and his mother does not survive him " there shall be substituted the words " and leaves no widow, widower or issue (including any illegitimate child of the member) and neither of his parents survives him ".

(3) Subsection (1) of this section does not affect the operation of the said Acts of 1882 and 1880 in relation to a policy effected before the coming into force of that subsection; and subsection (2) of this section does not affect the operation of the said Act of 1965 in relation to a member of a registered society who dies before the coming into force of the said subsection (2).

PART III [32]

PROVISIONS FOR USE OF BLOOD TESTS IN DETERMINING PATERNITY

Power of court to require use of blood tests

20.—(1) In any civil proceedings in which the paternity of any person falls to be determined by the court hearing the proceedings, the court may, on an application by any party to the proceedings, give a direction for the use of blood tests to ascertain whether such tests show that a party to the proceedings is or is not thereby excluded from being the father of that person and for the taking, within a period to be specified in the direction, of blood samples from that person, the mother of that person and any party alleged to be the father of that person or from any, or any two, of those persons.

A court may at any time revoke or vary a direction previously given by it under this section.

(2) The person responsible for carrying out blood tests taken for the purpose of giving effect to a direction under this section shall make to the court by which the direction was given a report in which he shall state—

(*a*) the results of the tests;

(*b*) whether the party to whom the report relates is or is not excluded by the results from being the father of the person whose paternity is to be determined; and

(*c*) if that party is not so excluded, the value, if any, of the results in determining whether that party is that person's father;

and the report shall be received by the court as evidence in the proceedings of the matters stated therein.

[32] This Part was brought into force on March 1, 1972, by S.I. 1971/1857.

(3) A report under subsection (2) of this section shall be in the form prescribed by regulations made under section 22 of this Act.

(4) Where a report has been made to a court under subsection (2) of this section, any party may, with the leave of the court, or shall, if the court so directs, obtain from the person who made the report a written statement explaining or amplifying any statement made in the report, and that statement shall be deemed for the purposes of this section (except subsection (3) thereof) to form part of the report made to the court.

(5) Where a direction is given under this section in any proceedings, a party to the proceedings, unless the court otherwise directs, shall not be entitled to call as a witness the person responsible for carrying out the tests taken for the purpose of giving effect to the direction, or any person by whom any thing necessary for the purpose of enabling those tests to be carried out was done, unless within fourteen days after receiving a copy of the report he serves notice on the other parties to the proceedings, or on such of them as the court may direct, of his intention to call that person; and where any such person is called as a witness the party who called him shall be entitled to cross-examine him.

(6) Where a direction is given under this section the party on whose application the direction is given shall pay the cost of taking and testing blood samples for the purpose of giving effect to the direction (including any expenses reasonably incurred by any person in taking any steps required of him for the purpose), and of making a report to the court under this section, but the amount paid shall be treated as costs incurred by him in the proceedings.

Consents, etc., required for taking of blood samples

21.—(1) Subject to the provisions of subsections (3) and (4) of this section, a blood sample which is required to be taken from any person for the purpose of giving effect to a direction under section 20 of this Act shall not be taken from that person except with his consent.

(2) The consent of a minor who has attained the age of sixteen years to the taking from himself of a blood sample shall be as effective as it would be if he were of full age; and where a minor has by virtue of this subsection given an effective consent to the taking of a blood sample it shall not be necessary to obtain any consent for it from any other person.

(3) A blood sample may be taken from a person under the age of sixteen years, not being such a person as is referred to in subsection (4) of this section, if the person who has the care and control of him consents.

(4) A blood sample may be taken from a person who is suffering from mental disorder within the meaning of the Mental Health Act 1959 and is incapable of understanding the nature and purpose of blood tests if the person who has the care and control of him consents and the medical practitioner in whose care he is has certified that the taking of a blood sample from him will not be prejudicial to his proper care and treatment.

(5) The foregoing provisions of this section are without prejudice to the provisions of section 23 of this Act.

Power to provide for manner of giving effect to direction for use of blood tests

22.—(1) The Secretary of State may by regulations [3b] make provision as to the manner of giving effect to directions under section 20 of this Act and, in particular, any such regulations may—

[3b] See Blood Tests (Evidence of Paternity) (Amendment) Regs. 1975 (S.I. No. 896).

(a) provide that blood samples shall not be taken except by such medical practitioners as may be appointed by the Secretary of State;

(b) regulate the taking, identification and transport of blood samples;

(c) require the production at the time when a blood sample is to be taken of such evidence of the identity of the person from whom it is to be taken as may be prescribed by the regulations;

(d) require any person from whom a blood sample is to be taken, or, in such cases as may be prescribed by the regulations, such other person as may be so prescribed, to state in writing whether he or the person from whom the sample is to be taken, as the case may be, has during such period as may be specified in the regulations suffered from any such illness as may be so specified or received a transfusion of blood;

(e) provide that blood tests shall not be carried out except by such persons, and at such places, as may be appointed by the Secretary of State;

(f) prescribe the blood tests to be carried out and the manner in which they are to be carried out;

(g) regulate the charges that may be made for the taking and testing of blood samples and for the making of a report to a court under section 20 of this Act;

(h) make provision for securing that so far as practicable the blood samples to be tested for the purpose of giving effect to a direction under section 20 of this Act are tested by the same person;

(i) prescribe the form of the report to be made to a court under section 20 of this Act.

(2) The power to make regulations under this section shall be exercisable by statutory instrument which shall be subject to annulment in pursuance of a resolution of either House of Parliament.

Failure to comply with direction for taking blood tests

23.—(1) Where a court gives a direction under section 20 of this Act and any person fails to take any step required of him for the purpose of giving effect to the direction, the court may draw such inferences, if any, from that fact as appear proper in the circumstances.

(2) Where in any proceedings in which the paternity of any person falls to be determined by the court hearing the proceedings there is a presumption of law that that person is legitimate, then if—

(a) a direction is given under section 20 of this Act in those proceedings, and

(b) any party who is claiming any relief in the proceedings and who for the purpose of obtaining that relief is entitled to rely on the presumption fails to take any step required of him for the purpose of giving effect to the direction,

the court may adjourn the hearing for such period as it thinks fit to enable that party to take that step, and if at the end of that period he has failed without reasonable cause to take it the court may, without prejudice to subsection (1) of this section, dismiss his claim for relief notwithstanding the absence of evidence to rebut the presumption.

(3) Where any person named in a direction under section 20 of this Act fails to consent to the taking of a blood sample from himself or from any person named in the direction of whom he has the care and control, he shall be deemed for the purposes of this section to have failed to take a step required of him for the purpose of giving effect to the direction.

Penalty for personating another, etc., for purpose of providing blood sample

24. If for the purpose of providing a blood sample for a test required

to give effect to a direction under section 20 of this Act any person
personates another, or proffers a child knowing that it is not the child
named in the direction, he shall be liable—

(*a*) on conviction on indictment, to imprisonment for a term not
exceeding two years, or

(*b*) on summary conviction, to a fine not exceeding £400.

Interpretation of Part III

25. In this Part of this Act the following expressions have the
meanings hereby respectively assigned to them, that is to say—

" blood samples " means blood taken for the purpose of blood tests;

" blood tests " means blood tests carried out under this Part of this
Act and includes any test made with the object of ascertaining
the inheritable characteristics of blood;

" excluded " means excluded subject to the occurrence of mutation.

PART IV

MISCELLANEOUS AND GENERAL

Rebuttal of presumption as to legitimacy and illegitimacy

26. Any presumption of law as to the legitimacy or illegitimacy of
any person may in any civil proceedings be rebutted by evidence which
shows that it is more probable than not that that person is illegitimate
or legitimate, as the case may be, and it shall not be necessary to prove
that fact beyond reasonable doubt in order to rebut the presumption.

Entry of father's name on registration of birth of illegitimate child

27.—(1) In section 10 of the Births and Deaths Registration Act 1953
(which provides that the registrar shall not enter the name of any person
as the father of an illegitimate child except at the joint request of the
mother and the person acknowledging himself to be the father and
requires that person to sign the register together with the mother) for
the words from " except " onwards there shall be substituted the words
" except—

(*a*) at the joint request of the mother and the person acknowledging
himself to be the father of the child (in which case that person
shall sign the register together with the mother); or

(*b*) at the request of the mother on production of—

(i) a declaration in the prescribed form made by the mother
stating that the said person is the father of the child; and

(ii) a statutory declaration made by that person acknowledging himself to be the father of the child."

(2) If on the registration under Part I of the said Act of 1953 of the
birth of an illegitimate child no person has been entered in the register
as the father, the registrar may re-register the birth so as to show a
person as the father—

(*a*) at the joint request of the mother and of that person (in which
case the mother and that person shall both sign the register in
the presence of the registrar); or

(*b*) at the request of the mother on production of—

(i) a declaration in the prescribed form made by the mother
stating that the person in question is the father of the child;
and

(ii) a statutory declaration made by that person acknowledging himself to be the father of the child;

but no birth shall be re-registered as aforesaid except with the authority of the Registrar General and any such re-registration shall be effected in such manner as may be prescribed.

(3) A request under paragraph (*a*) or (*b*) of section 10 of the said Act of 1953 as amended by subsection (1) of this section may be included in a declaration under section 9 of that Act (registration of birth pursuant to a declaration made in another district) and, if a request under the said paragraph (*b*) is included in such a declaration, the documents mentioned in that paragraph shall be produced to the officer in whose presence the declaration is made and sent by him, together with the declaration, to the registrar.

(4) A request under paragraph (*a*) or (*b*) of subsection (2) of this section may, instead of being made to the registrar, be made by making and signing in the presence of and delivering to such officer as may be prescribed a written statement in the prescribed form and, in the case of a request under the said paragraph (*b*), producing to that officer the documents mentioned in that paragraph, and the officer shall send the statement together with the documents, if any, to the registrar; and thereupon that subsection shall have effect as if the request had been made to the registrar and, if the birth is re-registered pursuant to the request, the person or persons who signed the statement shall be treated as having signed the register as required by that subsection.

(5) This section shall be construed as one with the said Act of 1953; and in section 14 (1) (*a*) of that Act (re-registration of birth of legitimated person) the reference to section 10 of that Act shall include a reference to subsection (2) of this section.

Short title, interpretation, commencement and extent

28.—(1) This Act may be cited as the Family Law Reform Act 1969.

(2) Except where the context otherwise requires, any reference in this Act to any enactment shall be construed as a reference to that enactment as amended, extended or applied by or under any other enactment, including this Act.

(3) This Act shall come into force on such date as the Lord Chancellor may appoint by order made by statutory instrument, and different dates may be appointed for the coming into force of different provisions.[3c]

(4) In this Act—

> (*a*) section 1 and Schedule 1, so far as they amend the British Nationality Act 1948, have the same extent as that Act and are hereby declared for the purposes of section 3 (3) of the West Indies Act 1967 to extend to all the associated states;
>
> (*b*) section 2, so far as it amends any provision of the Foreign Marriage Act 1892 or the Marriage with Foreigners Act 1906, has the same extent as that provision;
>
> (*c*) [. . .][4] 6 (7), so far as they affect Part II of the Maintenance Orders Act 1950, extend to Scotland and Northern Ireland;
>
> (*d*) section 10, so far as it relates to the Civil List Act 1952, extends to Scotland and Northern Ireland;
>
> (*e*) section 11, so far as it relates to the Employers and Workmen Act 1875, extends to Scotland;
>
> (*f*) section 13 extends to Northern Ireland;
>
> (*g*) section 19 extends to Scotland;

but, save as aforesaid, this Act shall extend to England and Wales only.

3c Parts I, II and IV of the Act were brought into force on January 1, 1970, by S.I. 1969/1140. Part III was brought into force on March 1, 1972, by S.I. 1971/1857.
4 Words repealed by Guardianship of Minors Act 1971 (c. 3), s. 18 (1), Sched. 2.

SCHEDULES

SCHEDULE 1

STATUTORY PROVISIONS AMENDED BY SUBSTITUTING 18 FOR 21 YEARS

PART I

ENACTMENTS

Short title	*Section*	*Subject matter*
c. 24. The Tenures Abolition Act 1660.	Sections 8 and 9.	Custody of children under 21.
c. 22. The Trade Union Act Amendment Act 1876.	Section 9.	Persons under 21 but above 16 eligible as members of trade union but not of committee of management etc.
[...] [5a]		
c. 18. The Settled Land Act 1925.	Section 102 (5).	Management of land during minority.
c. 19. The Trustee Act 1925.	Section 31 (1) (ii), (2) (i) (*a*) and (*b*).	Power to apply income for maintenance and to accumulate surplus income during a minority.
c. 20. The Law of Property Act 1925.	Section 134 (1).	Restriction on executory limitations.
c. 49. The Supreme Court of Judicature (Consolidation) Act 1925.	Section 165 (1).	Probate not to be granted to infant if appointed sole executor until he attains the age of 21 years.
c. 56. The British Nationality Act 1948.	Section 32 (1) and (9).	Definition of "minor" and "full age" by reference to age of 21.
c. 44. The Customs and Excise Act 1952.	Section 244 (2) (*a*).	Entry invalid unless made by person over 21.
c. 46. The Hypnotism Act 1952.	Section 3.	Persons under 21 not to be hypnotised at public entertainment.
c. 63. The Trustee Savings Banks Act 1954.	Section 23.	Payments to persons under 21.
[...] [5]		
c. 5. The Adoption Act 1958.	Section 57 (1).	Definition of "infant" by reference to age of 21.
c. 22. The County Courts Act 1959.	Section 80.	Persons under 21 may sue for wages in same manner as if of full age.
[...] [5]		
c. 37. The Building Societies Act 1962.	Section 9.	Persons under 21 eligible as members of building society but cannot vote or hold office.
	Section 47.	Receipts given to building society by persons under 21 to be valid.
c. 2. The Betting, Gaming and Lotteries Act 1963.	Section 22 (1) and (3).	Offence of sending betting advertisements to persons under 21.
c. 12. The Industrial and Provident Societies Act 1965.	Section 20.	Persons under 21 but above 16 eligible as members of society but not of committee etc.

[5] Words repealed by Guardianship Act 1973 (c. 29), s. 9 (1), Sched. 3.
[5a] Words repealed by Friendly Societies Act 1974 (c. 46), Sched. 11.

PART II

RULES, REGULATIONS ETC.

	Title	Provision	Subject matter
1927 S.R. & O. 1184; 1953 S.I. 264.	The Supreme Court Funds Rules 1927 as amended by the Supreme Court Funds Rules 1953.	Rule 97 (1) (i).	Unclaimed moneys in court.
1929 S.R. & O. 1048.	The Trustee Savings Banks Regulations 1929.	Regulation 28 (2).	Payments to persons under 21.
1933 S.R. & O. 1149.	The Savings Certificates Regulations 1933.	Regulation 2 (1) (*a*).	Persons entitled to purchase and hold certificates.
		Regulation 21 (2).	Persons under disability.
1946 S.R. & O. 1156.	The North of Scotland Hydro-Electric Board (Borrowing and Stock) Regulations 1946.	Regulation 36 (1) and (2).	Stock held by persons under 21.
1949 S.I. 751.	The Gas (Stock) Regulations 1949.	Regulation 19 (1) and (2).	Stock held by persons under 21.
1954 S.I. 796.	The Non-Contentious Probate Rules 1954.	Rules 31 and 32.	Grants of probate on behalf of infant and where infant is co-executor.
1955 S.I. 1752.	The South of Scotland Electricity Board (Borrowing and Stock) Regulations 1955.	Regulation 30 (1) and (2).	Stock held by persons under 21.
1956 S.I. 1657.	The Premium Savings Bonds Regulations 1956.	Regulation 2 (1).	Persons entitled to purchase and hold bonds.
		Regulation 12 (2).	Persons under disability.
1957 S.I. 2228.	The Electricity (Stock) Regulations 1957.	Regulation 22 (1) and (2).	Stock held by persons under 21.
1963 S.I. 935.	The Exchange of Securities (General) Rules 1963.	Rule 1 (1).	Definition of "minor".
1965 S.I. 1420.	The Government Stock Regulations 1965.	Regulation 14 (1), (2), (3) and (5).	Stock held by persons under 21.
1965 S.I. 1500.	The County Court Funds Rules 1965.	Rule 36 (1) (*b*).	Unclaimed moneys in court.
1965 S.I. 1707.	The Mayor's and City of London Court Funds Rules 1965.	Rule 25 (1) (*b*).	Unclaimed moneys in court.
1968 S.I. 2049.	The Registration of Births, Deaths and Marriages Regulations 1968.	Regulation 63 and, in Schedule 1, Forms 15 to 18.	Forms of notice of marriage.

Section 1 (4)   SCHEDULE 2

STATUTORY PROVISIONS UNAFFECTED
BY SECTION 1

1. The Regency Acts 1937 to 1953.
2. The Representation of the People Acts (and any regulations, rules or other instruments thereunder), section 7 of the Parliamentary Elections Act 1695, section

57 of the Local Government Act 1933 and any statutory provision relating to municipal elections in the City of London within the meaning of section 167 (1) (*a*) of the Representation of the People Act 1949.

3. [*Repealed by Finance Act* 1969 (*c.* 32), *Sched.* 21.]

. . . .

Children and Young Persons Act 1969 [1]

(1969 C. 54)

An Act to amend the law relating to children and young persons; and for purposes connected therewith. [22nd October 1969]

PART I

CARE AND OTHER TREATMENT OF JUVENILES THROUGH COURT PROCEEDINGS

Care of children and young persons through juvenile courts

Care proceedings in juvenile courts

1.—(1) Any local authority, constable or authorised person who reasonably believes that there are grounds for making an order under this section in respect of a child or young person may, subject to section 2 (3) and (8) of this Act, bring him before a juvenile court.

(2) If the court before which a child or young person is brought under this section is of opinion that any of the following conditions is satisfied with respect to him, that is to say—

(*a*) his proper development is being avoidably prevented or neglected or his health is being avoidably impaired or neglected or he is being ill-treated; or

(*b*) it is probable that the condition set out in the preceding paragraph will be satisfied in his case, having regard to the fact that the court or another court has found that that condition is or was satisfied in the case of another child or young person who is or was a member of the household to which he belongs; or

(*bb*) it is probable that the conditions set out in paragraph (*a*) of this subsection will be satisfied in his case, having regard to the fact that a person who has been convicted of an offence mentioned in Schedule 1 to the Act of 1933 is, or may become, a member of the same household as the child;) [1a]

(*c*) he is exposed to moral danger; or

(*d*) he is beyond the control of his parent or guardian; or

(*e*) he is of compulsory school age within the meaning of the Education Act 1944 and is not receiving efficient full-time education suitable to his age, ability and aptitude; or

(*f*) he is guilty of an offence, excluding homicide,

and also that he is in need of care or control which he is unlikely to receive unless the court makes an order under this section in respect of him, then, subject to the following provisions of this section and sections 2 and 3 of this Act, the court may if it thinks fit make such an order.

---

[1] Parts of this Act are still not in force: for commencement provisions, and regulations made thereunder, see s. 73, *post.*
[1a] Words added by Children Act 1975 (c. 72), Sched. 3, para. 67.

(3) The order which a court may make under this section in respect of a child or young person is—

    (*a*) an order requiring his parent or guardian to enter into a recognisance to take proper care of him and exercise proper control over him; or

    (*b*) a supervision order; or

    (*c*) a care order (other than an interim order); or

    (*d*) a hospital order within the meaning of Part V of the Mental Health Act 1959; or

    (*e*) a guardianship order within the meaning of that Act.

(4) In any proceedings under this section the court may make orders in pursuance of paragraphs (*c*) and (*d*) of the preceding subsection but subject to that shall not make more than one of the orders mentioned in the preceding subsection, without prejudice to any power to make a further order in subsequent proceedings of any description; and if in proceedings under this section the court makes one of those orders and an order so mentioned is already in force in respect of the child or young person in question, the court may discharge the earlier order unless it is a hospital or guardianship order.

(5) An order under this section shall not be made in respect of a child or young person—

    (*a*) in pursuance of paragraph (*a*) of subsection (3) of this section unless the parent or guardian in question consents;

    (*b*) in pursuance of paragraph (*d*) or (*e*) of that subsection unless the conditions which, under section 60 of the said Act of 1959, are required to be satisfied for the making of a hospital or guardianship order in respect of a person convicted as mentioned in that section are satisfied in his case so far as they are applicable;

    (*c*) if he has attained the age of sixteen and is or has been married.

(6) In this section " authorised person " means a person authorised by order of the Secretary of State to bring proceedings in pursuance of this section and any officer of a society which is so authorised, and in sections 2 and 3 of this Act " care proceedings " means proceedings in pursuance of this section and " relevant infant " means the child or young person in respect of whom such proceedings are brought or proposed to be brought.

Provisions supplementary to s. 1

2.—(1) If a local authority receive information suggesting that there are grounds for bringing care proceedings in respect of a child or young person who resides or is found in their area, it shall be the duty of the authority to cause enquiries to be made into the case unless they are satisfied that such enquiries are unnecessary.

(2) If it appears to a local authority that there are grounds for bringing care proceedings in respect of a child or young person who resides or is found in their area, it shall be the duty of the authority to exercise their power under the preceding section to bring care proceedings in respect of him unless they are satisfied that it is neither in his interest nor the public interest to do so or that some other person is about to do so or to charge him with an offence.

(3) No care proceedings shall be begun by any person unless that person has given notice of the proceedings to the local authority for the area in which it appears to him that the relevant infant resides or, if it appears to him that the relevant infant does not reside in the area of a local authority, to the local authority for any area in which it appears to him that any circumstances giving rise to the proceedings arose; but

the preceding provisions of this subsection shall not apply where the person by whom the notice would fall to be given is the local authority in question.

(4) Without prejudice to any power to issue a summons or warrant apart from this subsection, a justice may issue a summons or warrant for the purpose of securing the attendance of the relevant infant before the court in which care proceedings are brought or proposed to be brought in respect of him; but subsections (3) and (4) of section 47 of the Magistrates' Courts Act 1952 (which among other things restrict the circumstances in which a warrant may be issued) shall apply with the necessary modifications to a warrant under this subsection as they apply to a warrant under that section and as if in subsection (3) after the word " summons " there were inserted the words " cannot be served or ".

(5) Where the relevant infant is arrested in pursuance of a warrant issued by virtue of the preceding subsection and cannot be brought immediately before the court aforesaid, the person in whose custody he is—

(*a*) may make arrangements for his detention in a place of safety for a period of not more than seventy-two hours from the time of the arrest (and it shall be lawful for him to be detained in pursuance of the arrangements); and

(*b*) shall within that period, unless within it the relevant infant is brought before the court aforesaid, bring him before a justice;

and the justice shall either make an interim order in respect of him or direct that he be released forthwith.

(6) Section 77 of the Magistrates' Courts Act 1952 (under which a summons or warrant may be issued to secure the attendance of a witness) shall apply to care proceedings as it applies to the hearing of a complaint.

(7) In determining whether the condition set out in subsection (2) (*b*) of the preceding section is satisfied in respect of the relevant infant, it shall be assumed that no order under that section is to be made in respect of him.

(8) In relation to the condition set out in subsection (2) (*e*) of the preceding section the references to a local authority in that section and subsections (1), (2) and (11) (*b*) of this section shall be construed as references to a local education authority; and in any care proceedings—

(*a*) the court shall not entertain an allegation that that condition is satisfied unless the proceedings are brought by a local education authority; and

(*b*) the said condition shall be deemed to be satisfied if the relevant infant is of the age mentioned in that condition and it is proved that he—

(i) is the subject of a school attendance order which is in force under section 37 of the Education Act 1944 and has not been complied with, or

(ii) is a registered pupil at a school which he is not attending regularly within the meaning of section 39 of that Act, or

(iii) is a person whom another person habitually wandering from place to place takes with him,

unless it is also proved that he is receiving the education mentioned in that condition;

but nothing in paragraph (*a*) of this subsection shall prevent any evidence from being considered in care proceedings for any purpose other than that of determining whether that condition is satisfied in respect of the relevant infant.

(9) If on application under this subsection to the court in which it is proposed to bring care proceedings in respect of a relevant infant who is not present before the court it appears to the court that he is under the age of five and either—

> (*a*) it is proved to the satisfaction of the court, on oath or in such other manner as may be prescribed by rules under section 15 of the Justices of the Peace Act 1949, that notice of the proposal to bring the proceedings at the time and place at which the application is made was served on the parent or guardian of the relevant infant at what appears to the court to be a reasonable time before the making of the application; or
>
> (*b*) it appears to the court that his parent or guardian is present before the court

the court may if it thinks fit, after giving the parent or guardian if he is present an opportunity to be heard, give a direction under this subsection in respect of the relevant infant; and a relevant infant in respect of whom such a direction is given by a court shall be deemed to have been brought before the court under section 1 of this Act at the time of the direction, and care proceedings in respect of him may be continued accordingly.

(10) If the court before which the relevant infant is brought in care proceedings is not in a position to decide what order, if any, ought to be made under the preceding section in respect of him, the court may make an interim order in respect of him.

(11) If it appears to the court before which the relevant infant is brought in care proceedings that he resides in a petty sessions area other than that for which the court acts, the court shall, unless it dismisses the case and subject to subsection (5) of the following section, direct that he be brought under the preceding section before a juvenile court acting for the petty sessions area in which he resides; and where the court so directs—

> (*a*) it may make an interim order in respect of him and, if it does so, shall cause the clerk of the court to which the direction relates to be informed of the case;
>
> (*b*) if the court does not make such an order it shall cause the local authority in whose area it appears to the court that the relevant infant resides to be informed of the case, and it shall be the duty of that authority to give effect to the direction within twenty-one days.

(12) The relevant infant may appeal to [the Crown Court] [1b] against any order made in respect of him under the preceding section except such an order as is mentioned in subsection (3) (*a*) of that section.

(13) Such an order as is mentioned in subsection (3) (*a*) of the preceding section shall not require the parent or guardian in question to enter into a recognisance for an amount exceeding fifty pounds or for a period exceeding three years or, where the relevant infant will attain the age of eighteen in a period shorter than three years, for a period exceeding that shorter period; and section 96 of the Magistrates' Courts Act 1952 (which relates to the forfeiture of recognisances) shall apply to a recognisance entered into in pursuance of such an order as it applies to a recognisance to keep the peace.

(14) For the purposes of this Act, care proceedings in respect of a relevant infant are begun when he is first brought before a juvenile court in pursuance of the preceding section in connection with the matter to which the proceedings relate.

[1b] Words substituted by Courts Act 1971 (c. 23), s. 56 (2), Sched. 9, Pt. I.

Further supplementary provisions relating to s. 1 (2) (f)

3.—(1) In any care proceedings, no account shall be taken for the purposes of the condition set out in paragraph (*f*) of subsection (2) of section 1 of this Act (hereafter in this section referred to as " the offence condition ") of an offence alleged to have been committed by the relevant infant if—

(*a*) in any previous care proceedings in respect of him it was alleged that the offence condition was satisfied in consequence of the offence; or

(*b*) the offence is a summary offence within the meaning of the Magistrates' Courts Act 1952 and, disregarding section 4 of this Act, the period for beginning summary proceedings in respect of it expired before the care proceedings were begun; or

(*c*) disregarding section 4 of this Act, he would if charged with the offence be entitled to be discharged under any rule of law relating to previous acquittal or conviction.

(2) In any care proceedings the court shall not entertain an allegation that the offence condition is satisfied in respect of the relevant infant unless the proceedings are brought by a local authority or a constable; but nothing in this or the preceding subsection shall prevent any evidence from being considered in care proceedings for any purpose other than that of determining whether the offence condition is satisfied in respect of the relevant infant.

(3) If in any care proceedings the relevant infant is alleged to have committed an offence in consequence of which the offence condition is satisfied with respect to him, the court shall not find the offence condition satisfied in consequence of the offence unless, disregarding section 4 of this Act, it would have found him guilty of the offence if the proceedings had been in pursuance of an information duly charging him with the offence and the court had had jurisdiction to try the information; and without prejudice to the preceding provisions of this subsection the same proof shall be required to substantiate or refute an allegation that the offence condition is satisfied in consequence of an offence as is required to warrant a finding of guilty or, as the case may be, of not guilty of the offence.

(4) A person shall not be charged with an offence if in care proceedings previously brought in respect of him it was alleged that the offence condition was satisfied in consequence of that offence.

(5) If in any care proceedings in which it is alleged that the offence condition is satisfied in respect of the relevant infant it appears to the court that the case falls to be remitted to another court in pursuance of subsection (11) of the preceding section but that it is appropriate to determine whether the condition is satisfied before remitting the case, the court may determine accordingly; and any determination under this subsection shall be binding on the court to which the case is remitted.

(6) Where in any care proceedings the court finds the offence condition satisfied with respect to the relevant infant in consequence of an indictable offence within the meaning of the Magistrates' Courts Act 1952 then, whether or not the court makes an order under section 1 of this Act—

[(*a*) [section 35 of the Powers of Criminal Courts Act 1973] [1c] (which relates to compensation for personal injury and loss or damage to property) shall apply as if the finding was a finding of guilty of the offence and as if the maximum amount which could be ordered

1c Words substituted by Powers of Criminal Courts Act 1973 (c. 62), Sched. 5.

to be paid under that section in respect of that offence were £100;][2]

(b) the court shall if the relevant infant is a child, and may if he is not, order any sum awarded by virtue of this subsection to be paid by his parent or guardian instead of by him unless it is satisfied that the parent or guardian cannot be found or has not conduced to the commission of the offence by neglecting to exercise due care or control of him, so however that an order shall not be made in pursuance of this paragraph unless the parent or guardian has been given an opportunity of being heard or has been required to attend the proceedings and failed to do so; [and

(c) any sum payable by a parent or guardian by virtue of the preceding paragraph may be recovered from him in like manner as if he had been convicted of the offence in question;][3] but where the finding in question is made in pursuance of the preceding subsection, the powers conferred by this subsection shall be exercisable by the court to which the case is remitted instead of by the court which made the finding.

[. . .][4]

(7) Where in any care proceedings the court finds the offence condition satisfied with respect to the relevant infant and he is a young person, the court may if it thinks fit and he consents, instead of making such an order as is mentioned in section 1 (3) of this Act, order him to enter into a recognisance for an amount not exceeding twenty-five pounds and for a period not exceeding one year to keep the peace or to be of good behaviour; and such an order shall be deemed to be an order under section 1 of this Act but no appeal to [the Crown Court][5] may be brought against an order under this subsection.

(8) Where in any care proceedings the court finds the offence condition satisfied with respect to the relevant infant in consequence of an offence which was not admitted by him before the court, then—

(a) if the finding is made in pursuance of subsection (5) of this section and the court to which the case is remitted decides not to make any order under section 1 of this Act in respect of the relevant infant; or

(b) if the finding is not made in pursuance of that subsection and the court decides as aforesaid,

the relevant infant may appeal to [the Crown Court][6] against the finding, and in a case falling within paragraph (a) of this subsection any notice of appeal shall be given within fourteen days after the date of the decision mentioned in that paragraph; and a person ordered to pay compensation by virtue of subsection (6) of this section may appeal to quarter sessions against the order.

[*Subsection* (9) *repealed by Courts Act* 1971 (*c*. 23), *s*. 56 (4), *Sched*. 11, *Pt. IV*.]

Consequential changes in criminal proceedings etc.

Prohibition of criminal proceedings for offences by children

4. A person shall not be charged with an offence, except homicide, by reason of anything done or omitted while he was a child.

[2] Paragraph (a) substituted by Criminal Justice Act 1972 (c. 71), s. 64 (1), Sched. 5.
[3] Paragraph (c) repealed by A.J.A. 1970 (c. 31), s. 54, Sched. 11.
[4] Words repealed by Criminal Damage Act 1971 (c. 48), s. 11 (8), Sched., Pt. I.
[5] Words substituted by Courts Act 1971 (c. 23), s. 56 (1) (2), Sched. 8, para. 59 (1).
[6] Words substituted by Courts Act 1971 (c. 23), s. 56 (2), Sched. 9, Pt. I.

Restrictions on criminal proceedings for offences by young persons

5.—(1) A person other than a qualified informant shall not lay an information in respect of an offence if the alleged offender is a young person.

(2) A qualified informant shall not lay an information in respect of an offence if the alleged offender is a young person unless the informant is of opinion that the case is of a description prescribed in pursuance of subsection (4) of this section and that it would not be adequate for the case to be dealt with by a parent, teacher or other person or by means of a caution from a constable or through an exercise of the powers of a local authority or other body not involving court proceedings or by means of proceedings under section 1 of this Act.

(3) A qualified informant shall not come to a decision in pursuance of the preceding subsection to lay an information unless—

(a) he has told the appropriate local authority that the laying of the information is being considered and has asked for any observations which the authority may wish to make on the case to the informant; and

(b) the authority either have notified the informant that they do not wish to make such observations or have not made any during the period or extended period indicated by the informant as that which in the circumstances he considers reasonable for the purpose or the informant has considered the observations made by the authority during that period;

but the informant shall be entitled to disregard the foregoing provisions of this subsection in any case in which it appears to him that the requirements of the preceding subsection are satisfied and will continue to be satisfied notwithstanding any observations which might be made in pursuance of this subsection.

(4) The Secretary of State may make regulations specifying, by reference to such considerations as he thinks fit, the descriptions of cases in which a qualified informant may lay an information in respect of an offence if the alleged offender is a young person; but no regulations shall be made under this subsection unless a draft of the regulations has been approved by a resolution of each House of Parliament.

(5) An information laid by a qualified informant in a case where the informant has reason to believe that the alleged offender is a young person shall be in writing and shall—

(a) state the alleged offender's age to the best of the informant's knowledge; and

(b) contain a certificate signed by the informant stating that the requirements of subsections (2) and (3) of this section are satisfied with respect to the case or that the case is one in which the requirements of the said subsection (2) are satisfied and the informant is entitled to disregard the requirements of the said subsection (3).

(6) If at the time when justices begin to inquire into a case, either as examining justices or on the trial of an information, they have reason to believe that the alleged offender is a young person and either—

(a) it appears to them that the person who laid the information in question was not a qualified informant when he laid it; or

(b) the information is not in writing or does not contain such a certificate as is mentioned in subsection (5) (b) of this section,

it shall be their duty to quash the information, without prejudice to the laying of a further information in respect of the matter in question; but no proceedings shall be invalidated by reason of a contravention of any provision of this section and no action shall lie, by reason only of such a contravention, in respect of proceedings in respect of which such a contravention has occurred.

(7) Nothing in the preceding provisions of this section applies to an information laid with the consent of the Attorney General or laid by or on behalf or with the consent of the Director of Public Prosecutions.

(8) It shall be the duty of a person who decides to lay an information in respect of an offence in a case where he has reason to believe that the alleged offender is a young person to give notice of the decision to the appropriate local authority unless he is himself that authority.

(9) In this section—

" the appropriate local authority ", in relation to a young person, means the local authority for the area in which it appears to the informant in question that the young person resides or, if the young person appears to the informant not to reside in the area of a local authority, the local authority in whose area it is alleged that the relevant offence or one of the relevant offences was committed; and

" qualified informant " means a servant of the Crown, a police officer and a member of a designated police force acting in his capacity as such a servant, officer or member, a local authority, the Greater London Council, the council of a county district and any body designated as a public body for the purposes of this section;

and in this subsection " designated " means designated by an order made by the Secretary of State; but nothing in this section shall be construed as preventing any council or other body from acting by an agent for the purposes of this section.

Summary trial of young persons

6.—(1) [7] Where a person under the age of seventeen appears or is brought before a magistrates' court on an information charging him with an offence, other than homicide, which is an indictable offence within the meaning of the Magistrates' Courts Act 1952, he shall be tried summarily unless—

(a) he is a young person and the offence is such as is mentioned in subsection (2) of section 53 of the Act of 1933 (under which young persons convicted on indictment of certain grave crimes may be sentenced to be detained for long periods) and the court considers that if he is found guilty of the offence it ought to be possible to sentence him in pursuance of that subsection; or

(b) he is charged jointly with a person who has attained the age of seventeen and the court considers it necessary in the interests of justice to commit them both for trial;

and accordingly in a case falling within paragraph (a) or paragraph (b) of this subsection [the court shall commit the accused for trial if either it is of the opinion that there is sufficient evidence to put him on trial or it has power under section 1 of the Criminal Justice Act 1967 so to commit him without consideration of the evidence] [8]

(2) In sections 18 (1) and 25 (1) of the said Act of 1952 (which provide for the trial on indictment of persons aged fourteen or over who are charged with certain summary offences within the meaning of that Act) for the word " fourteen " there shall be substituted the word " seventeen ".

[7] Subsection applied by Criminal Justice Act 1972 (c. 42), s. 44.
[8] Words substituted by Criminal Justice Act 1972 (c. 71), s. 64 (1), Sched. 5.

(3) If on trying a person summarily in pursuance of subsection (1) of this section the court finds him guilty, it may impose a fine of an amount not exceeding fifty pounds or may exercise the same powers as it could have exercised if he had been found guilty of an offence for which, but for [section 19 (1) of the Powers of Criminal Courts Act 1973],¹ᵃ it could have sentenced him to imprisonment for a term not exceeding three months.

Alterations in treatment of young offenders etc.

7.—(1) The minimum age at conviction which qualifies for a sentence of borstal training under section 20 of the Criminal Justice Act 1948 shall be seventeen instead of fifteen years; and accordingly in subsection (1) of that section and section 28 (1) of the Magistrates' Courts Act 1952 for the word " fifteen " there shall be substituted the word " seventeen ".

(2) In section 3 (1) of the said Act of 1948 (which authorises the court by or before which a person is convicted of an offence to make a probation order in respect of him) after the word " person " there shall be inserted the words " who has attained the age of seventeen ".

(3) If a court having power to order children or young persons of any class or description to be detained in a detention centre in pursuance of section 4 of the Criminal Justice Act 1961 or to attend at an attendance centre in pursuance of section 19 of the said Act of 1948 is notified in pursuance of this subsection by the Secretary of State that a detention centre or, as the case may be, an attendance centre will not be available for the reception from that court of children or young persons of that class or description after a date specified in the notification, the power in question shall not be exercisable by that court after that date; and the Secretary of State shall cause a copy of any notification under this subsection to be published in the London Gazette before the date specified in the notification.

(4) Section 5 of the said Act of 1961 (which provides for detention for defaults) shall cease to apply to young persons.

(5) An order sending a person to an approved school shall not be made after such day as the Secretary of State may by order specify for the purposes of this subsection.

(6) Sections 54 and 57 of the Act of 1933 (which among other things enable a child or young person found guilty of an offence to be sent to a remand home or committed to the care of a fit person) shall cease to have effect.

(7) Subject to the enactments requiring cases to be remitted to juvenile courts and to section 53 (1) of the Act of 1933 (which provides for detention for certain grave crimes), where a child is found guilty of homicide or a young person is found guilty of any offence by or before any court, that court or the court to which his case is remitted shall have power—

(a) if the offence is punishable in the case of an adult with imprisonment, to make a care order (other than an interim order) in respect of him; or

(b) to make a supervision order in respect of him; or

(c) with the consent of his parent or guardian, to order the parent or guardian to enter into a recognisance to take proper care of him and exercise proper control over him,

and if it makes such an order as is mentioned in this subsection while another such order made by any court is in force in respect of the child or young person, shall also have power to discharge the earlier order; and subsection (13) of section 2 of this Act shall apply to an order under paragraph (*c*) of this subsection as it applies to such an order as is mentioned in that subsection.

(8) Without prejudice to the power to remit any case to a juvenile court which is conferred on a magistrates' court other than a juvenile court by section 56 (1) of the Act of 1933, in a case where such a magistrates' court finds a person guilty of an offence and either he is a young person or was a young person when the proceedings in question were begun it shall be the duty of the court to exercise that power unless the court [is of the opinion that the case is one which can properly be dealt with by means of —

(*a*) an order discharging him absolutely or conditionally; or

(*b*) an order for the payment of a fine; or

(*c*) an order requiring his parent or guardian to enter into a recognisance to take proper care of him and exercise proper control over him, with or without any other order that the court has power to make when absolutely or conditionally discharging an offender.] [9]

Finger-printing of suspected young persons

8.—(1) If a police officer not below the rank of inspector makes an application on oath to a justice stating—

(*a*) that there is evidence sufficient to justify the laying of an information that a young person has or is suspected of having committed an offence punishable with imprisonment in the case of an adult; and

(*b*) that with a view to deciding, in accordance with section 5 of this Act, whether the information should be laid it is appropriate in the opinion of the officer for an order under subsection (2) of this section to be made in respect of the young person,

the justice may if he thinks fit issue a summons or warrant for the purpose of securing the attendance of the young person before a magistrates' court with a view to the making of such an order in respect of him.

(2) The court before which a young person appears in pursuance of a summons or warrant under the preceding subsection may if it thinks fit order his finger and palm prints to be taken by a constable.

(3) Subsections (2) and (4) of section 40 of the Magistrates' Courts Act 1952 (which respectively relate to the taking and destruction of finger and palm prints) shall have effect as if references to an order under that section included references to an order under the preceding subsection and, in relation to an order under the preceding subsection, as if for the words from " remanded " to " committed " in subsection (2) there were substituted the words " lawfully detained at any place, at that place " and as if the reference to acquittal in subsection (4) included a reference to a finding of a court that the condition set out in section 1 (2) (*f*) of this Act is not satisfied in consequence of the offence specified in the application mentioned in subsection (1) of this section.

Investigations by local authorities

9.—(1) Where a local authority or a local education authority brings proceedings under section 1 of this Act or proceedings for an offence alleged to have been committed by a young person or are notified that any such proceedings are being brought, it shall be the duty of the authority, unless they are of opinion that it is unnecessary to do so, to make such investigation and provide the court before which the proceedings are heard with such information relating to the home

[9] Words substituted by Criminal Justice Act 1972 (c. 71), s. 64 (1), Sched. 5.

surroundings, school record, health and character of the person in respect of whom the proceedings are brought as appear to the authority likely to assist the court.

(2) If the court mentioned in subsection (1) of this section requests the authority aforesaid to make investigations and provide information or to make further investigations and provide further information relating to the matters aforesaid, it shall be the duty of the authority to comply with the request.

Further limitations on publication of particulars of children and young persons etc.

10.—(1) In subsection (1) of section 49 of the Act of 1933 (which among other things imposes restrictions on reports of certain court proceedings concerning children or young persons but authorises the court or the Secretary of State, if satisfied that it is in the interests of justice to do so, to dispense with the requirements of that section)—

(a) the references to a young person concerned in the proceedings as the person in respect of whom they are taken shall be construed as including references to any person who has attained the age of seventeen but not eighteen and against or in respect of whom the proceedings are taken and, in the case of proceedings under Part I of this Act, any other person in respect of whom those proceedings are taken; and

(b) the references to a juvenile court shall, in relation to proceedings in pursuance of the provisions of sections 15 and 16 of this Act or on appeal from such proceedings, be construed as including a reference to any other magistrates' court or, as the case may be, the court in which the appeal is brought; and

(c) for the words " in the interests of justice so to do " there shall be substituted the words " appropriate to do so for the purpose of avoiding injustice to a child or young person " and after the word " section " there shall be inserted the words " in relation to him ".

(2) Where by virtue of paragraph (b) of the preceding subsection the said section 49 applies to any proceedings, it shall be the duty of the court in which the proceedings are taken to announce in the course of the proceedings that that section applies to them; and if the court fails to do so that section shall not apply to the proceedings in question.

(3) A notice displayed in pursuance of section 4 of the Criminal Justice Act 1967 (which requires the publication of a notice stating the result of proceedings before examining justices and containing particulars of the person to whom the proceedings related) shall not contain the name or address of any child or young person unless the justices in question have stated that in their opinion he would be mentioned in the notice apart from the foregoing provisions of this subsection and should be mentioned in it for the purpose of avoiding injustice to him.

Supervision

Supervision orders

11. Any provision of this Act authorising a court to make a supervision order in respect of any person shall be construed as authorising the court to make an order placing him under the supervision of a local authority designated by the order or of a probation officer; and in this Act " supervision order " shall be construed accordingly and " supervised person " and " supervisor ", in relation to a supervision order, mean respectively the person placed or to be placed under supervision by the order and the person under whose supervision he is placed or to be placed by the order.

Local authority functions under certain supervision orders

11A. The Secretary of State may make regulations with respect to the exercise by a local authority of their functions in a case where a person has been placed under their supervision by an order made under section 1 (3) (*b*) or 21 (2) of this Act.] [9a]

Power to include requirements in supervision orders

12.—(1) A supervision order may require the supervised person to reside with an individual named in the order who agrees to the requirement, but a requirement imposed by a supervision order in pursuance of this subsection shall be subject to any such requirement of the order as is authorised by the following provisions of this section.

(2) Subject to section 19 (6) of this Act, a supervision order may require the supervised person to comply with such directions of the supervisor as are mentioned in paragraph (*a*) or (*b*) or paragraphs (*a*) and (*b*) of this subsection, that is to say—

(*a*) directions requiring the supervised person to live for a single period specified in the directions at a place so specified;

(*b*) directions given from time to time requiring him to do all or any of the following things—

(i) to live at a place or places specified in the directions for a period or periods so specified,

(ii) to present himself to a person or persons specified in the directions at a place or places and on a day or days so specified,

(iii) to participate in activities specified in the directions on a day or days so specified;

but it shall be for the supervisor to decide whether and to what extent he exercises any power to give directions conferred on him by virtue of the preceding provisions of this subsection and to decide the form of any directions; and a requirement imposed by a supervision order in pursuance of this subsection shall be subject to any such requirement of the order as is authorised by subsection (4) of this section.

(3) The periods specified in directions given by virtue of subsection (2) of this section in pursuance of a supervision order shall be in accordance with the following provisions, that is to say—

(*a*) the aggregate of the periods specified in directions given by virtue of paragraph (*a*) and paragraph (*b*) of that subsection shall not exceed ninety days;

(*b*) the period specified in directions given by virtue of the said paragraph (*a*) shall not exceed ninety days and subject to paragraph (*e*) below shall not begin after the expiration of one year beginning with the date of the order or, if the directions are authorised solely by a variation of the order, with the date of the variation;

(*c*) the aggregate of the periods specified in directions given by virtue of the said paragraph (*b*) shall not exceed thirty days in the year beginning with the date aforesaid and thirty days in any year beginning with an anniversary of that date;

(*d*) if the order provides that any of the preceding paragraphs of this subsection is to have effect in relation to the order as if for a reference to ninety days or thirty days there were substituted a reference to a shorter period specified in the order, the paragraph in question shall have effect accordingly;

(*e*) for the purpose of calculating the period or periods in respect of which directions may be given in pursuance of the order—

[9a] Added by Children Act 1975 (c. 72), Sched. 3, para. 68.

(i) the supervisor shall be entitled to disregard any day in respect of which directions were previously given in pursuance of the order and on which the directions were not complied with;

(ii) a direction given in respect of one or more parts of a day shall be treated as given in respect of the whole of the day, and if during the year mentioned in paragraph (*b*) of this subsection the supervised person is given such directions as are there mentioned specifying a period beginning in that year but does not begin to comply with the directions during that year, the supervisor shall be entitled to disregard so much of that paragraph as prevents that period from beginning after the expiration of that year.

(4) Where a court which proposes to make a supervision order is satisfied, on the evidence of a medical practitioner approved for the purposes of section 28 of the Mental Health Act 1959, that the mental condition of a supervised person is such as requires and may be susceptible to treatment but is not such as to warrant his detention in pursuance of a hospital order under Part V of that Act, the court may include in the supervision order a requirement that the supervised person shall, for a period specified in the order, submit to treatment of one of the following descriptions so specified, that is to say—

(*a*) treatment by or under the direction of a fully registered medical practitioner specified in the order;

(*b*) treatment as a non-resident patient at a place specified in the order; or

(*c*) treatment as a resident patient in a hospital or mental nursing home within the meaning of the said Act of 1959, but not a special hospital within the meaning of that Act.

(5) A requirement shall not be included in a supervision order in pursuance of the preceding subsection—

(*a*) in any case, unless the court is satisfied that arrangements have been or can be made for the treatment in question and, in the case of treatment as a resident patient, for the reception of the patient;

(*b*) in the case of an order made or to be made in respect of a person who has attained the age of fourteen, unless he consents to its inclusion;

and a requirement so included shall not in any case continue in force after the supervised person becomes eighteen.

Selection of supervisor

13.—(1) A court shall not designate a local authority as the supervisor by a provision of a supervision order unless the authority agree or it appears to the court that the supervised person resides or will reside in the area of the authority.

(2) A court shall not insert in a supervision order a provision placing a child [9b] under the supervision of a probation officer unless the local authority of which the area is named or to be named in the order in pursuance of section 18 (2) (*a*) of this Act so request and a probation officer is already exercising or has exercised, in relation to another member of the household to which the child belongs, duties imposed [on probation officers by paragraph 8 of Schedule 3 to the Powers of Criminal Courts Act 1973 or by rules under paragraph 18 (1) (*b*)] [9c] of that Schedule.

(3) Where a provision of a supervision order places a person under the supervision of a probation officer, the supervisor shall be a probation

[9b] Under 12 years old: see 1970 S.I. No. 1882 and 1973 S.I. No. 485.
[9c] Words substituted by Powers of Criminal Courts Act 1973 (c. 62), Sched. 5.

officer appointed for or assigned to the petty sessions area named in the order in pursuance of section 18 (2) (*a*) of this Act and selected under arrangements made by the probation and after-care committee; but if the probation officer selected as aforesaid dies or is unable to carry out his duties or if the case committee dealing with the case think it desirable that another officer should take his place, another probation officer shall be selected as aforesaid for the purposes of the order.

Duty of supervisor

14. While a supervision order is in force it shall be the duty of the supervisor to advise, assist and befriend the supervised person.

Variation and discharge of supervision orders

15.—(1) If while a supervision order is in force in respect of a supervised person who has not attained the age of eighteen it appears to a juvenile court, on the application of the supervisor or the supervised person, that it is appropriate to make an order under this subsection, the court may make an order discharging the supervision order or varying it by—

(*a*) cancelling any requirement included in it in pursuance of section 12 or section 18 (2) (*b*) of this Act; or

(*b*) inserting in it (either in addition to or in substitution for any of its provisions) any provision which could have been included in the order if the court had then had power to make it and were exercising the power,

and may on discharging the supervision order make a care order (other than an interim order) in respect of the supervised person; but the powers of variation conferred by this subsection do not include power to insert in the supervision order, after the expiration of twelve months beginning with the date when the order was originally made, a requirement in pursuance of section 12 (2) (*a*) of this Act or, after the expiration of three months beginning with that date, a requirement in pursuance of section 12 (4) of this Act, unless in either case it is in substitution for such a requirement already included in the order.

(2) If on an application in pursuance of the preceding subsection, in a case where the supervised person has attained the age of seventeen and the supervision order was not made by virtue of section 1 of this Act or on the occasion of the discharge of a care order, it appears to the court appropriate to do so it may proceed as if the application were in pursuance of subsection (3) or, if it is made by the supervisor, in pursuance of subsections (3) and (4) of this section and as if in that subsection or those subsections, as the case may be, the word " seventeen " were substituted for the word " eighteen " and the words " a magistrates' court other than " were omitted.

(3) If while a supervision order is in force in respect of a supervised person who has attained the age of eighteen it appears to a magistrates' court other than a juvenile court, on the application of the supervisor or the supervised person, that it is appropriate to make an order under this subsection, the court may make an order discharging the supervision order or varying it by—

(*a*) inserting in it a provision specifying the duration of the order or altering or cancelling such a provision already included in it; or

(*b*) substituting for the provisions of the order by which the supervisor is designated or by virtue of which he is selected such other provisions in that behalf as could have been included in the order if the court had then had power to make it and were exercising the power; or (*c*) substituting for the name of an area included in the order in pursuance of section 18 (2) (*a*) of this Act the name of any other area of a local authority or petty sessions area, as the case may be, in which it appears to the court that the supervised person resides or will reside; or

(*d*) cancelling any provision included in the order by virtue of section 18 (2) (*b*) of this Act or inserting in it any provision prescribed for the purposes of that paragraph; or

(*e*) cancelling any requirement included in the order in pursuance of section 12 (1) or (2) of this Act.

(4) If while a supervision order is in force in respect of a supervised person who has attained the age of eighteen it is proved to the satisfaction of a magistrates' court other than a juvenile court, on the application of the supervisor, that the supervised person has failed to comply with any requirement included in the supervision order in pursuance of section 12 or section 18 (2) (*b*) of this Act, the court may—

(*a*) whether or not it also makes an order under subsection (3) of this section, order him to pay a fine of an amount not exceeding twenty pounds or, subject to subsection (10) of the following section, make an attendance centre order in respect of him;

(*b*) if it also discharges the supervision order, make an order imposing on him any punishment which it could have imposed on him if it had then had power to try him for the offence in consequence of which the supervision order was made and had convicted him in the exercise of that power;

and in a case where the offence in question is of a kind which the court has no power to try or has no power to try without appropriate consents, the punishment imposed by virtue of paragraph (*b*) of this subsection shall not exceed that which any court having power to try such an offence could have imposed in respect of it and shall not in any event exceed imprisonment for a term of six months and a fine of four hundred pounds.

(5) If a medical practitioner by whom or under whose direction a supervised person is being treated for his mental condition in pursuance of a requirement included in a supervision order by virtue of section 12 (4) of this Act is unwilling to continue to treat or direct the treatment of the supervised person or is of opinion—

(*a*) that the treatment should be continued beyond the period specified in that behalf in the order; or

(*b*) that the supervised person needs different treatment; or

(*c*) that he is not susceptible to treatment; or

(*d*) that he does not require further treatment,

the practitioner shall make a report in writing to that effect to the supervisor; and on receiving a report under this subsection the supervisor shall refer it to a juvenile court, and on such a reference the court may make an order cancelling or varying the requirement.

(6) The preceding provisions of this section shall have effect subject to the provisions of the following section.

Provisions supplementary to s. 15

16.—(1) Where the supervisor makes an application or reference under the preceding section to a court he may bring the supervised person before the court, and subject to subsection (5) of this section a court shall not make an order under that section unless the supervised person is present before the court.

(2) Without prejudice to any power to issue a summons or warrant apart from this subsection, a justice may issue a summons or warrant for the purpose of securing the attendance of a supervised person before the

court to which any application or reference in respect of him is made under the preceding section; but subsections (3) and (4) of section 47 of the Magistrates' Courts Act 1952 (which among other things restrict the circumstances in which a warrant may be issued) shall apply with the necessary modifications to a warrant under this subsection as they apply to a warrant under that section and as if in subsection (3) after the word " summons " there were inserted the words " cannot be served or ".

(3) Where the supervised person is arrested in pursuance of a warrant issued by virtue of the preceding subsection and cannot be brought immediately before the court referred to in that subsection, the person in whose custody he is—

(a) may make arrangements for his detention in a place of safety for a period of not more than seventy-two hours from the time of the arrest (and it shall be lawful for him to be detained in pursuance of the arrangements); and

(b) shall within that period, unless within it the relevant infant is brought before the court aforesaid, bring him before a justice;

and the justice shall either direct that he be released forthwith or—

(i) if he has not attained the age of eighteen, make an interim order in respect of him;

(ii) if he has attained that age, remand him.

(4) If on an application to a court under subsection (1) of the preceding section—

(a) the supervised person is brought before the court under a warrant issued or an interim order made by virtue of the preceding provisions of this section; or

(b) the court considers that it is likely to exercise its powers under that subsection to make an order in respect of the supervised person but, before deciding whether to do so, seeks information with respect to him which it considers is unlikely to be obtained unless the court makes an interim order in respect of him,

the court may make an interim order in respect of the supervised person.

(5) A court may make an order under the preceding section in the absence of the supervised person if the effect of the order is confined to one or more of the following, that is to say—

(a) discharging the supervision order;

(b) cancelling a provision included in the supervision order in pursuance of section 12 or section 18 (2) (b) of this Act;

(c) reducing the duration of the supervision order or any provision included in it in pursuance of the said section 12;

(d) altering in the supervision order the name of any area;

(e) changing the supervisor.

(6) A juvenile court shall not—

(a) exercise its powers under subsection (1) of the preceding section to make a care order or an order discharging a supervision order or inserting in it a requirement authorised by section 12 of this Act or varying or cancelling such a requirement except in a case where the court is satisfied that the supervised person either is unlikely to receive the care or control he needs unless the court makes the order or is likely to receive it notwithstanding the order;

(b) exercise its powers to make an order under subsection (5) of the preceding section except in such a case as is mentioned in paragraph (a) of this subsection;

(c) exercise its powers under the said subsection (1) to make an order inserting a requirement authorised by section 12 (4) of this Act in a supervision order which does not already contain such a requirement unless the court is satisfied as mentioned in the said section 12 (4) on such evidence as is there mentioned.

(7) Where the supervised person has attained the age of fourteen, then except with his consent a court shall not make an order under the preceding section containing provisions which insert in the supervision order a requirement authorised by section 12 (4) of this Act or which alter such a requirement already included in the supervision order otherwise than by removing it or reducing its duration.

(8) The supervised person may appeal to [the Crown Court] [10] against—

> (*a*) any order made under the preceding section, except an order made or which could have been made in the absence of the supervised person and an order containing only provisions to which he consented in pursuance of the preceding subsection;
>
> (*b*) the dismissal of an application under that section to discharge a supervision order.

(9) Where an application under the preceding section for the discharge of a supervision order is dismissed, no further application for its discharge shall be made under that section by any person during the period of three months beginning with the date of the dismissal except with the consent of a court having jurisdiction to entertain such an application.

(10) In paragraph (*a*) of subsection (4) of the preceding section " attendance centre order " means such an order to attend an attendance centre as is mentioned in subsection (1) of section 19 of the Criminal Justice Act 1948; and the provisions of that section shall accordingly apply for the purposes of that paragraph as if for the words from " has power " to " probation order " in subsection (1) there were substituted the words " considers it appropriate to make an attendance centre order in respect of any person in pursuance of section 15 (4) of the Children and Young Persons Act 1969 " and for references to an offender there were substituted references to the supervised person and as if subsection (5) were omitted.

(11) In this and the preceding section references to a juvenile court or any other magistrates' court, in relation to a supervision order, are references to such a court acting for the petty sessions area for the time being named in the order in pursuance of section 18 (2) (*a*) of this Act; and if while an application to a juvenile court in pursuance of the preceding section is pending the supervised person to whom it relates attains the age of seventeen or eighteen, the court shall deal with the application as if he had not attained the age in question.

Termination of supervision

17. A supervision order shall, unless it has previously been discharged, cease to have effect—

> (*a*) in any case, on the expiration of the period of three years, or such shorter period as may be specified in the order, beginning with the date on which the order was originally made;
>
> (*b*) if the order was made by virtue of section 1 of this Act or on the occasion of the discharge of a care order and the supervised person attains the age of eighteen on a day earlier than that on which the order would expire under paragraph (*a*) above, on that earlier day.

Supplementary provisions relating to supervision orders

18.—(1) A court shall not make a supervision order unless it is satis-

[10] Words substituted by Courts Act 1971 (c. 23), s. 56 (2), Sched. 9, Pt. I.

fied that the supervised person resides or will reside in the area of a local authority; and a court shall be entitled to be satisfied that the supervised person will so reside if he is to be required so to reside by a provision to be included in the order in pursuance of section 12 (1) of this Act.

(2) A supervision order—

> (*a*) shall name the area of the local authority and the petty sessions area in which it appears to the court making the order, or to the court varying any provision included in the order in pursuance of this paragraph, that the supervised person resides or will reside; and

> (*b*) may contain such prescribed provisions as the court aforesaid considers appropriate for facilitating the performance by the supervisor of his functions under section 14 of this Act, including any prescribed provisions for requiring visits to be made by the supervised person to the supervisor,

and in paragraph (*b*) of this subsection " prescribed " means prescribed by rules under section 15 of the Justices of the Peace Act 1949.

(3) A court which makes a supervision order or an order varying or discharging a supervised order shall forthwith send a copy of its order—

> (*a*) to the supervised person and, if the supervised person is a child, to his parent or guardian; and

> (*b*) to the supervisor and any person who has ceased to be the supervisor by virtue of the order; and

> (*c*) to any local authority who is not entitled by virtue of the preceding paragraph to such a copy and whose area is named in the supervision order in pursuance of the preceding subsection or has ceased to be so named by virtue of the court's order; and

> (*d*) where the supervised person is required by the order, or was required by the supervision order before it was varied or discharged, to reside with an individual or to undergo treatment by or under the direction of an individual or at any place, to the individual or the person in charge of that place; and

> (*e*) where a petty sessions area named in the order or discharged order in pursuance of subsection (2) of this section is not that for which the court acts, to the clerk to the justices for the petty sessions area so named;

and, in a case falling within paragraph (*e*) of this subsection, shall also send to the clerk to the justices in question such documents and information relating to the case as the court considers likely to be of assistance to them.

(4) Where a supervision order requires compliance with such directions as are mentioned in section 12 (2) of this Act, any expenditure incurred by the supervisor for the purposes of the directions shall be defrayed by the local authority of which the area is named in the order in pursuance of subsection (2) of this section.

Facilities for the carrying out of supervisors' directions

19.—(1) It shall be the duty of the children's regional planning committee for each planning area (hereafter in this section referred to as " the committee ") to make arrangements, with such persons as the committee thinks fit, for the provision by those persons of facilities for enabling directions given by virtue of section 12 (2) of this Act to persons resident in the area to be carried out effectively.

(2) The committee shall specify the arrangements made in pursuance of the preceding subsection in a scheme and shall submit the scheme to the Secretary of State for him to determine the date on which it is to come into force; and the Secretary of State shall, after consultation with

the committee and the relevant authorities, determine that date and notify his determination to the committee.

(3) On receiving a notification in pursuance of subsection (2) of this section in respect of a scheme, the committee shall send copies of the scheme and notification to each of the relevant authorities and to the clerk to the justices for each petty sessions area of which any part is included in the planning area in question; and each of the relevant authorities shall, as soon as practicable after receiving those documents, keep a copy of them available at their principal offices for inspection by members of the public at all reasonable hours and on demand by any person furnish him with a copy of them free of charge.

(4) If, after the scheme prepared by the committee under this section has come into force, any arrangements specified in it are cancelled or the committee makes arrangements for the purposes of this section other than arrangements so specified, the committee shall send notice of the cancellations or other arrangements, stating the date on which they are to come into force and the alterations in the scheme which they entail, to the Secretary of State and the authorities and clerks mentioned in subsection (3) of this section; and on and after that date the scheme shall have effect subject to those alterations and the relevant authorities shall have, in relation to the notice, the same duty as is imposed on them by that subsection in relation to the scheme.

(5) Arrangements in pursuance of this section shall not be made for any facilities unless the facilities are approved or are of a kind approved by the Secretary of State for the purposes of this section; but where arrangements in pursuance of this section are made by the committee with any of the relevant authorities for the provision of facilities by the authority it shall be the duty of the authority to provide those facilities while the scheme is in force and those arrangements are specified in it.

(6) A court shall not include in a supervision order any such requirements as are mentioned in section 12 (2) of this Act unless the court is satisfied that a scheme under this section is in force for the planning area in which the supervised person resides or will reside or that the date on which such a scheme is to come into force has been determined; and a supervisor authorised to give directions by virtue of any such requirements shall not, in pursuance of those requirements, give directions involving the use of facilities which are not for the time being specified in a scheme in force under this section for the planning area aforesaid.

Committal to care of local authorities

Orders for committal to care of local authorities

20.—(1) Any provision of this Act authorising the making of a care order in respect of any person shall be construed as authorising the making of an order committing him to the care of a local authority; and in this Act " care order " shall be construed accordingly and " interim order " means a care order containing provision for the order to expire with the expiration of twenty-eight days, or of a shorter period specified in the order, beginning—

(a) if the order is made by a court, with the date of the making of the order; and

(b) if it is made by a justice, with the date when the person to whom it relates was first in legal custody in connection with the matter in consequence of which the order is made.

(2) The local authority to whose care a person is committed by a care order shall be—

(a) except in the case of an interim order, the local authority in whose area it appears to the court making the order that that person resides or, if it does not appear to the court that he resides in the area of a local authority, any local authority in whose area it appears to the court that any offence was committed or any circumstances arose in consequence of which the order is made; and

(b) in the case of an interim order, such one of the local authorities mentioned in paragraph (a) of this subsection as the court or justice making the order thinks fit (whether or not the person in question appears to reside in their area).

(3) Subject to the provisions of the following section, a care order other than an interim order shall cease to have effect—

(a) if the person to whom it relates had attained the age of sixteen when the order was originally made, when he attains the age of nineteen; and

(b) in any other case, when that person attains the age of eighteen.

(4) A care order shall be sufficient authority for the detention by any local authority or constable of the person to whom the order relates until he is received into the care of the authority to whose care he is committed by the order.

Variation and discharge of care orders

21.—(1) If it appears to a juvenile court, on the application of a local authority to whose care a person is committed by a care order which would cease to have effect by virtue of subsection (3) (b) of the preceding section, that he is accommodated in a community home or a home provided by the Secretary of State and that by reason of his mental condition or behaviour it is in his interest or the public interest for him to continue to be so accommodated after he attains the age of eighteen, the court may order that the care order shall continue in force until he attains the age of nineteen; but the court shall not make an order under this subsection unless the person in question is present before the court.

(2) If it appears to a juvenile court, on the application of a local authority to whose care a person is committed by a care order or on the application of that person, that it is appropriate to discharge the order, the court may discharge it and on discharging it may, unless it was an interim order and unless the person to whom the discharged order related has attained the age of eighteen, make a supervision order in respect of him.

[(2A) A juvenile court shall not make an order under subsection (2) of this section in the case of a person who has not attained the age of 18 and appears to the court to be in need of care or control unless the court is satisfied that, whether through the making of a supervision order or otherwise, he will receive that care or control;] 10a

(3) Where an application under [subsection (2) of this section] 10a for the discharge of a care order is dismissed, then—

(a) in the case of an interim order, no further application for its discharge shall be made under that subsection except with the consent of a juvenile court (without prejudice to the power to make an application under subsection (4) of the following section); and

(b) in any other case, no further application for its discharge shall be made under this subsection by any person during the period of three months beginning with the date of the dismissal except with the consent of a juvenile court.

(4) The person to whom the relevant care order relates or related

10a Words added or substituted by Children Act 1975 (c. 72), Sched. 3, para. 69.

may appeal to [the Crown Court] [11] against an order under subsection (1) of this section or a supervision order made in pursuance of subsection (2) of this section or the dismissal of an application under the said subsection (2) for the discharge of the care order.

(5) The local authority to whose care a person is committed by a care order (other than an interim order) may, within the period of three months beginning with the date of the order, appeal to [the Crown Court] [11] against the provision of the order naming their area on the ground that at the time the order was made the person aforesaid resided in the area of another local authority named in the notice of appeal; but no appeal shall be brought by a local authority under this subsection unless they give notice in writing of the proposals to bring it to the other local authority in question before giving notice of appeal.

(6) References in this section to a juvenile court, in relation to a care order, are references to a juvenile court acting for any part of the area of the local authority to whose care a person is committed by the order or for the place where that person resides.

Termination of care order on adoption, etc.

21A. A care order relating to a child shall cease to have effect—
  (a) on the adoption of the child;
  (b) if an order under section 14 or section 25 of the Children Act 1975 is made in relation to the child;
  (c) if an order similar to an order under section 25 of the Children Act 1975 is made in Northern Ireland, the Isle of Man or any of the Channel Islands in relation to the child.] [10a]

Special provisions relating to interim orders

22.—(1) A juvenile court or a justice shall not make an interim order in respect of any person unless either—
  (a) that person is present before the court or justice; or
  (b) the court or justice is satisfied that he is under the age of five or cannot be present as aforesaid by reason of illness or accident.

(2) An interim order shall contain provision requiring the local authority to whose care a person is committed by the order to bring that person before a court specified in the order on the expiration of the order or at such earlier time as the specified court may require, so however that the said provision shall, if the court making the order considers it appropriate so to direct by reason of the fact that that person is under the age of five or by reason of illness or accident, require the local authority to bring him before the specified court on the expiration of the order only if the specified court so requires.

(3) A juvenile court acting for the same area as a juvenile court by which or a justice by whom an interim order has been made in respect of any person may, at any time before the expiration of the order, make a further interim order in respect of him; and the power to make an interim order conferred by this subsection is without prejudice to any other power to make such an order.

(4) The High Court may, on the application of a person to whom an interim order relates, discharge the order on such terms as the court thinks fit; but if on such an application the discharge of the order is refused, the local authority to whose care he is committed by the order shall not exercise in his case their powers under section 13 (2) of the Children Act 1948 (which enables them to allow a parent or other person to be in charge of him) except with the consent and in accordance with any directions of the High Court.

[11] Words substituted by Courts Act 1971 (c. 23), s. 56 (2), Sched. 9, Pt. I.

(5) If a court which has made or, apart from this subsection, would make an interim order in respect of a person who has attained the age of fourteen certifies that he is of so unruly a character that he cannot safely be committed to the care of a local authority and has been notified by the Secretary of State that a remand centre is available for the reception from the court of persons of his class or description, then, subject to the following provisions of this section, the court shall commit him to a remand centre for twenty-eight days or such shorter period as may be specified in the warrant; but in a case where an interim order is in force in respect of the person in question, a warrant under this subsection shall not be issued in respect of him except on the application of the local authority to whose care he is committed by the order and shall not be issued for a period extending beyond the date fixed for the expiration of the order, and on the issue of a warrant under this subsection in such a case the interim order shall cease to have effect.

In this subsection " court " includes a justice.

(6) Subsections (1), (3) and (4) of this section, so much of section 2 (11) (*a*) as requires the clerk to be informed and section 21 (2) to (4) of this Act shall apply to a warrant under subsection (5) of this section as they apply to an interim order but as if the words " is under the age of five or " in subsection (1) of this section were omitted.

Remand to care of local authorities etc.

23.—(1) Where a court—

    (*a*) remands or commits for trial a child charged with homicide or remands a child convicted of homicide; or

    (*b*) remands a young person charged with or convicted of one or more offences or commits him for trial or sentence,

and he is not released on bail, then, subject to the following provisions of this section, the court shall commit him to the care of a local authority in whose area it appears to the court that he resides or that the offence or one of the offences was committed.

(2) If the court aforesaid certifies that a young person is of so unruly a character that he cannot safely be committed to the care of a local authority under the preceding subsection, then if the court has been notified by the Secretary of State that a remand centre is available for the reception from the court of persons of his class or description, it shall commit him to a remand centre and, if it has not been so notified, it shall commit him to a prison.

(3) If, on the application of the local authority to whose care a young person is committed by a warrant under subsection (1) of this section, the court by which he was so committed or any magistrates' court having jurisdiction in the place where he is for the time being certifies as mentioned in subsection (2) of this section, the provisions of the said subsection (2) relating to committal shall apply in relation to him and he shall cease to be committed in pursuance of the said subsection (1).

(4) The preceding provisions of this section shall have effect subject to the provisions of section 28 of the Magistrates' Courts Act 1952 (which relates to committal to quarter sessions with a view to a borstal sentence).

(5) In this section " court " and " magistrates' court " include a justice; and notwithstanding anything in the preceding provisions of this section, section 105 (5) of the said Act of 1952 (which provides for remands to the custody of a constable for periods not exceeding three clear days) shall have effect in relation to a child or young person as if for the reference to three clear days there were substituted a reference to twenty-four hours.

Powers and duties of local authorities etc. with respect to persons committed to their care

24.—(1) It shall be the duty of a local authority to whose care a person is committed by a care order or by a warrant under subsection (1) of the preceding section to receive him into their care and, notwithstanding any claim by his parent or guardian, to keep him in their care while the order or warrant is in force.

(2) A local authority shall, subject to the following provisions of this section, have the same powers and duties with respect to a person in their care by virtue of a care order or such a warrant as his parent or guardian would have apart from the order or warrant and may (without prejudice to the preceding provisions of this subsection but subject to regulations made in pursuance of section 43 of this Act) restrict his liberty to such extent as the authority consider appropriate.

(3) A local authority shall not cause a person in their care by virtue of a care order to be brought up in any religious creed other than that in which he would have been brought up apart from the order.

(4) It shall be the duty of a local authority to comply with any provision included in an interim order in pursuance of section 22 (2) of this Act and, in the case of a person in their care by virtue of the preceding section, to permit him to be removed from their care in due course of law.

(5) If a person who is subject to a care order and has attained the age of five is accommodated in a community home or other establishment which he has not been allowed to leave during the preceding three months for the purpose of ordinary attendance at an educational institution or at work and it appears to the local authority to whose care he is committed by the order that—

    (a) communication between him and his parent or guardian has been so infrequent that it is appropriate to appoint a visitor for him; or

    (b) he has not lived with or visited or been visited by either of his parents or his guardian during the preceding twelve months,

it shall be the duty of the authority to appoint an independent person to be his visitor for the purposes of this subsection; and a person so appointed shall—

    (i) have the duty of visiting, advising and befriending the person to whom the care order relates; and

    (ii) be entitled to exercise on behalf of that person his powers under section 21 (2) of this Act; and

    (iii) be entitled to recover from the authority who appointed him any expenses reasonably incurred by him for the purposes of his functions under this subsection.

In this section " independent person " means a person satisfying such conditions as may be prescribed by regulations made by the Secretary of State with a view to securing that he is independent of the local authority in question and unconnected with any community home.

(6) A person's appointment as a visitor in pursuance of the preceding subsection shall be determined if the care order in question ceases to be in force or he gives notice in writing to the authority who appointed him that he resigns the appointment or the authority give him notice in writing that they terminate it; but the determination of such an appointment shall not prejudice any duty under the preceding subsection to make a further appointment.

(7) The functions conferred on a local authority by the preceding provisions of this section in respect of any person are in addition to the functions which, by virtue of section 27 of this Act, are conferred on the authority in respect of him by Part II of the Children Act 1948.

(8) While a care order other than an interim order is in force in respect of a person who has not attained the age of eighteen, it shall be the duty of his parent to keep the local authority to whose care he is committed by the order informed of the parent's address; and if the parent knows of the order and fails to perform his duty under this subsection, the parent shall be liable on summary conviction to a fine not exceeding ten pounds unless he shows that at the material time he was residing at the address of the other parent and had reasonable cause to believe that the other parent had kept the authority informed of their address.

Transfer

Transfers between England or Wales and Northern Ireland

25.—(1) If it appears to the Secretary of State, on the application of the welfare authority or the managers of the training school to whose care a person is committed by a fit person order or by virtue of a training school order, that his parent or guardian resides or will reside in the area of a local authority in England or Wales, the Secretary of State may make an order committing him to the care of that local authority; and while an order under this subsection is in force it shall have effect as if it were a care order and as if sections 20 (2) and (3) and 21 (1) and (5) of this Act were omitted and in section 31 (3) (*a*) of this Act for the reference to section 20 (3) there were substituted a reference to subsection (3) of this section.

(2) If it appears to the Minister of Home Affairs for Northern Ireland, on the application of the local authority to whose care a person is committed by a care order other than an interim order, that his parent or guardian resides or will reside in Northern Ireland, the said Minister may make an order committing him to the care of the managers of a training school or to the care of the welfare authority in whose area his parent or guardian resides or will reside; and the provisions of the Children and Young Persons Act (Northern Ireland) 1968 (except sections 83 (3) (*a*), 88 (3), 90 and 91 (3)) shall apply to an order under this subsection as if it were a training school order made on the date of the care order or, as the case may be, a fit person order.

If an order under this subsection commits a person to the care of the managers of a training school, the contributions to be made in respect of him under section 161 of the said Act of 1968 shall be made by such council as may be named in that order, being the council within whose district his parent proposes to reside or is residing at the time of the order.

(3) When a person is received into the care of a local authority or welfare authority or the managers of a training school in pursuance of an order under this section, the training school order, fit person order or care order in consequence of which the order under this section was made shall cease to have effect; and the order under this section shall, unless it is discharged earlier, cease to have effect—

(*a*) in the case of an order under subsection (1), on the earlier of the following dates, that is to say, the date when the person to whom the order relates attains the age of nineteen or the date when, by the effluxion of time, the fit person order aforesaid would have ceased to have effect or, as the case may be, the period of his detention under the training school order aforesaid would have expired;

(*b*) in the case of an order under subsection (2), on the date when the care order aforesaid would have ceased to have effect by the effluxion of time or—

(i) if the person to whom the order relates is committed by

it to the care of a welfare authority and will attain the age of eighteen before that date, when he attains that age;

(ii) if the order has effect by virtue of subsection (2) as a training school order and the period of supervision following the detention of the person in question in pursuance of the order expires before that date, when that period expires.

(4) An order under this section shall be sufficient authority for the detention in Northern Ireland, by any constable or by a person duly authorised by a local authority or welfare authority or the managers of a training school, of the person to whom the order relates until he is received into the care of the authority or managers to whose care he is committed by the order.

(5) In this section " training school ", " training school order " and " welfare authority " have the same meaning as in the said Act of 1968, and " fit person order " means an order under that Act committing a person to the care of a fit person.

Transfers between England or Wales and the Channel Islands or Isle of Man

26.—(1) The Secretary of State may by order designate for the purposes of this section an order of any description which—

(a) a court in the Isle of Man or any of the Channel Islands is authorised to make by the law for the time being in force in that country; and

(b) provides for the committal to the care of a public authority of a person who has not attained the age of eighteen; and

(c) appears to the Secretary of State to be of the same nature as a care order other than an interim order;

and in this section " relevant order " means an order of a description for the time being so designated and " the relevant authority ", in relation to a relevant order, means the authority in the Isle of Man or any of the Channel Islands to whose care the person to whom the order relates is, under the law of that country, committed by the order.

(2) The Secretary of State may authorise a local authority to receive into their care any person named in the authorisation who is the subject of a relevant order; and while such an authorisation is in force in respect of any person he shall, subject to the following subsection, be deemed to be the subject of a care order committing him to the care of the local authority.

(3) This Act shall have effect, in relation to a person in respect of whom an authorisation under this section is in force, as if sections 20 (2) and (3), 21 and 31 and in section 27 (4) the words from " and if " onwards were omitted; and it shall be the duty of a local authority who propose, in exercise of their powers under section 13 (2) of the Children Act 1948, to allow such a person to be under the charge and control of a person residing outside England and Wales to consult the relevant authority before exercising those powers.

(4) An authorisation given to a local authority under this section shall cease to have effect when—

(a) the local authority is informed by the Secretary of State that he has revoked it; or

(b) the relevant order to which the authorisation relates ceases to have effect by the effluxion of time under the law of the place where the order was made or the local authority is informed by the relevant authority that the order has been discharged under that law; or

(c) the person to whom the relevant order relates is again received into the care of the relevant authority;

and if a local authority having by virtue of this section the care of a person to whom a relevant order relates is requested by the relevant authority to make arrangements for him to be received again into the care of the relevant authority, it shall be the duty of the local authority to comply with the request.

Consequential modifications of ss. 11 and 12 of
Children Act 1948

Consequential modifications of 1948 c. 43 ss. 11 and 12

27.[11a]—(1) For section 11 of the Children Act 1948 (which specifies the children in respect of whom functions are conferred on local authorities by Part II of that Act) there shall be substituted the following section:—

Children to whom Part II applies

> 11. Except where the contrary intention appears, any reference in this Part of this Act to a child who is or was in the care of a local authority is a reference to a child who is or was in the care of the authority under section 1 of this Act or by virtue of a care order within the meaning of the Children and Young Persons Act 1969 or a warrant under section 23 (1) of that Act (which relates to remands in the care of local authorities).;

but nothing in the said section 11 as replaced by this subsection prejudices the application of any provision of the said Part II to any person by virtue of an enactment passed after that Act and before this Act.

(2) [*Repealed by Children Act 1975 (c. 72), Sched. 4.*]

(3) If the Secretary of State considers it necessary, for the purpose of protecting members of the public, to give directions to a local authority with respect to the exercise of their powers in relation to a particular child in their care, he may give such directions to the authority; and it shall be the duty of the authority, notwithstanding their general duty aforesaid, to comply with any such directions.

(4) Without prejudice to their general duty aforesaid, it shall be the duty of a local authority who have at any time had a child in their care throughout the preceding six months and have not during that period held a review of his case in pursuance of this subsection to review his case as soon as is practicable after the expiration of that period and, if a care order is in force with respect to him, to consider in the course of the review whether to make an application for the discharge of the order.

Detention

Detention of child or young person in place of safety

28.—(1) If, upon an application to a justice by any person for authority to detain a child or young person and take him to a place of safety, the justice is satisfied that the applicant has reasonable cause to believe that—

(*a*) any of the conditions set out in section 1 (2) (*a*) to (*e*) of this Act is satisfied in respect of the child or young person; or

(*b*) an appropriate court would find the condition set out in section 1 (2) (*b*) of this Act satisfied in respect of him; or

(*c*) the child or young person is about to leave the United Kingdom in contravention of section 25 of the Act of 1933 (which regulates the sending abroad of juvenile entertainers),

the justice may grant the application; and the child or young person in respect of whom an authorisation is issued under this subsection may be

11a See now Children Act 1975 (c. 72), Sched. 3, para. 11, *post.*

detained in a place of safety by virtue of the authorisation for twenty-eight days beginning with the date of authorisation, or for such shorter period beginning with that date as may be specified in the authorisation.

(2) Any constable may detain a child or young person as respects whom the constable has reasonable cause to believe that any of the conditions set out in section 1 (2) (a) to (d) of this Act is satisfied or that an appropriate court would find the condition set out in section 1 (2) (b) of this Act satisfied or that an offence is being committed under section 10 (1) of the Act of 1933 (which penalises a vagrant who takes a juvenile from place to place).

(3) A person who detains any person in pursuance of the preceding provisions of this section shall, as soon as practicable after doing so, inform him of the reason for his detention and take such steps as are practicable for informing his parent or guardian of his detention and of the reason for it.

(4) A constable who detains any person in pursuance of subsection (2) of this section or who arrests a child [11b] without a warrant otherwise than for homicide shall as soon as practicable after doing so secure that the case is enquired into by a police officer not below the rank of inspector or by the police officer in charge of a police station, and that officer shall on completing the enquiry either—

(a) release the person in question; or

(b) if the officer considers that he ought to be further detained in his own interests or, in the case of an arrested child, because of the nature of the alleged offence, make arrangements for his detention in a place of safety and inform him, and take such steps as are practicable for informing his parent or guardian, of his right to apply to a justice under subsection (5) of this section for his release;

and subject to the said subsection (5) it shall be lawful to detain the person in question in accordance with any such arrangements.

(5) It shall not be lawful for a child [11b] arrested without a warrant otherwise than for homicide to be detained in consequence of the arrest or such arrangements as aforesaid, or for any person to be detained by virtue of subsection (2) of this section or any such arrangements, after the expiration of the period of eight days beginning with the day on which he was arrested or, as the case may be, on which his detention in pursuance of the said subsection (2) began; and if during that period the person in question applies to a justice for his release, the justice shall direct that he be released forthwith unless the justice considers that he ought to be further detained in his own interests or, in the case of an arrested child, because of the nature of the alleged offence.

(6) If while a person is detained in pursuance of this section an application for an interim order in respect of him is made to a magistrates' court or a justice, the court or justice shall either make or refuse to make the order and, in the case of a refusal, may direct that he be released forthwith.

Release or further detention of arrested child or young person

29. [12]—(1) Where a person is arrested with or without a warrant and cannot be brought immediately before a magistrates' court, then if either—

(a) he appears to be a child and his arrest is for homicide; or

(b) he appears to be a young person and his arrest is for any offence,

---

[11b] Under 10 years old: see 1973 S.I. No. 485.
[12] Extended by Criminal Justice Act 1972 (c. 71), s. 43.

the police officer in charge of the police station to which he is brought or another police officer not below the rank of inspector shall forthwith enquire into the case and, subject to subsection (2) of this section, shall release him unless—

    (i) the officer considers that he ought in his own interests to be further detained; or

    (ii) the officer has reason to believe that he has committed homicide or another grave crime or that his release would defeat the ends of justice or that if he were released (in a case where he was arrested without a warrant) he would fail to appear to answer to any charge which might be made.

(2) A person arrested in pursuance of a warrant shall not be released in pursuance of subsection (1) of this section unless he or his parent or guardian (with or without sureties) enters into a recognisance for such amount as the officer aforesaid considers will secure his attendance at the hearing of the charge; and a recognisance entered into in pursuance of this subsection may, if the said officer thinks fit, be conditioned for the attendance of the parent or guardian at the hearing in addition to the person arrested.

(3) An officer who enquires into a case in pursuance of subsection (1) of this section and does not release the person to whom the enquiry relates shall, unless the officer certifies that it is impracticable to do so or that he is of so unruly a character as to make it inappropriate to do so, make arrangements for him to be taken into the care of a local authority and detained by the authority, and it shall be lawful to detain him in pursuance of the arrangements; and a certificate made under this subsection in respect of any person shall be produced to the court before which that person is first brought thereafter.

(4) Where an officer decides in pursuance of subsection (1) of this section not to release a person arrested without a warrant and it appears to the officer that a decision falls to be taken in pursuance of section 5 of this Act whether to lay an information in respect of an offence alleged to have been committed by that person, it shall be the duty of the officer to inform him that such a decision falls to be taken and to specify the offence.

(5) A person detained by virtue of subsection (3) of this section shall be brought before a magistrates' court within seventy-two hours from the time of his arrest unless within that period a police officer not below the rank of inspector certifies to a magistrates' court that by reason of illness or accident he cannot be brought before a magistrates' court within that period.

(6) Where in pursuance of the preceding subsection a person is brought before a court or a certificate in respect of any person is produced to a court and the court does not proceed forthwith to inquire into the case, then—

    (a) except in a case falling within paragraph (b) of this subsection, the court shall order his release; and

    (b) in a case where he was arrested in pursuance of a warrant or the court considers that he ought in his own interests to be further detained or the court has reason to believe as mentioned in subsection (1) (ii) of this section, the court shall remand him;

and where a court remands a person in pursuance of this subsection otherwise than on bail it shall, if he is not represented by counsel or a solicitor, inform him that he may apply to a judge of the High Court to be admitted to bail and shall, if he is not so represented or his counsel or solicitor so requests, give him a written notice stating the reason for so remanding him.

Detention of young offenders in community homes

30.—(1) The power to give directions under section 53 of the Act of 1933 (under which young offenders convicted on indictment of certain grave crimes may be detained in accordance with directions given by the Secretary of State) shall include power to direct detention by a local authority specified in the directions in a home so specified which is a community home provided by the authority or a controlled community home for the management, equipment and maintenance of which the authority are responsible; but a person shall not be liable to be detained in the manner provided by this section after he attains the age of nineteen.

(2) It shall be the duty of a local authority specified in directions given in pursuance of this section to detain the person to whom the directions relate in the home specified in the directions subject to and in accordance with such instructions relating to him as the Secretary of State may give to the authority from time to time; and the authority shall be entitled to recover from the Secretary of State any expenses reasonably incurred by them in discharging that duty.

Removal to borstal institutions of persons committed to care of local authorities

31.—(1) Where a person who has attained the age of fifteen is for the time being committed to the care of a local authority by a care order (other than an interim order) and accommodated in a community home and the authority consider that he ought to be removed to a borstal institution under this section, they may with the consent of the Secretary of State bring him before a juvenile court.

(2) If the court before which a person is brought in pursuance of this section is satisfied that his behaviour is such that it will be detrimental to the persons accommodated in any community home for him to be accommodated there, the court may order him to be removed to a borstal institution.

(3) Where an order is made under subsection (2) of this section with respect to any person, the care order aforesaid shall cease to have effect and he shall be treated as if he had been sentenced to borstal training on the date of the other order, except that—

> (a) where the day on which the care order would have ceased to have effect by virtue of section 20 (3) of this Act (disregarding section 21 (1)) is earlier than the end of the period of two years beginning with the date aforesaid he shall, subject to paragraph (b) of this subsection, not be liable to be detained by virtue of this subsection after that day; and

> (b) section 45 (4) of the Prison Act 1952 shall apply to him as if for the reference to two years from the date of his sentence there were substituted a reference to that day.

(4) If the court before which a person is brought in pursuance of this section is not in a position to decide whether to make an order under subsection (2) of this section in respect of him, it may make an order for his detention in a remand centre for a period not exceeding twenty-one days.

(5) An order under the preceding subsection may from time to time be varied or extended by the court which made the order or by any other magistrates' court acting for the same area as that court, but a court shall not exercise its powers under this subsection—

> (a) if the person to whom the order relates is not before the court, unless the court is satisfied that by reason of illness or accident he cannot be present;

> (b) so as to authorise the detention of that person after the ex-

piration of the period of eight weeks beginning with the date when the order was originally made.

(6) The provisions of the Magistrates' Courts Act 1952 and of any other enactment relating to summary proceedings (other than provisions relating to remand or legal aid) shall apply to proceedings for the removal of a person under this section as they apply to proceedings against a person charged with a summary offence.

(7) Where immediately before an order under paragraph (*f*) of section 34 (1) of this Act comes into force an order under this section is in force with respect to any person, the order under that paragraph shall not affect the other order or the application of this section to that person while the other order remains in force.

Detention of absentees

32.[12a]—(1) If any of the following persons, that is to say—

(*a*) a person committed to the care of a local authority by a care order or by a warrant under section 23 of this Act; or

(*b*) a person who, in pursuance of section 2 (5), 16 (3) or 28 of this Act, has been taken to a place of safety which is a community home provided by a local authority or a controlled community home; or

(*c*) a person in the care of a local authority in pursuance of arrangements under section 29 (3) of this Act; or

(*d*) a person sent to a remand home, special reception centre or training school or committed to the care of a fit person under the Children and Young Persons Act (Northern Ireland) 1968,

is absent from premises at which he is required by the local authority or the relevant Northern Ireland authority to live, or as the case may be is absent from the home, remand home, special reception centre or training school, at a time when he is not permitted by the local authority or the managers of the home or the relevant Northern Ireland authority to be absent from it, he may be arrested by a constable anywhere in the United Kingdom or the Channel Islands without a warrant and shall if so arrested be conducted, at the expense of the authority or managers, to the premises or other place aforesaid or such other premises as the authority or managers may direct.

(2) If a magistrates' court is satisfied by information on oath that there are reasonable grounds for believing that a person specified in the information can produce a person who is absent as mentioned in subsection (1) of this section, the court may issue a summons directed to the person so specified and requiring him to attend and produce the absent person before the court; and a person who without reasonable excuse fails to comply with any such requirement shall, without prejudice to any liability apart from this subsection, be guilty of an offence and liable on summary conviction to a fine of an amount not exceeding twenty pounds.

In the application of this subsection to Northern Ireland, " magistrates' court " means a magistrates' court within the meaning of the Magistrates' Courts Act (Northern Ireland) 1964.

(3) A person who knowingly compels, persuades, incites or assists another person to become or continue to be absent as mentioned in subsection (1) of this section shall be guilty of an offence and liable on summary conviction to imprisonment for a term not exceeding six months or a fine of an amount not exceeding one hundred pounds or both.

[12a] See now Children Act 1975 (c. 72), ss. 64 and 68, *post*, which insert new ss. 32A and 32B.

(4) The reference to a constable in subsection (1) of this section includes a reference to a person who is a constable under the law of any part of the United Kingdom, to a member of the police in Jersey and to an officer of police within the meaning of section 43 of the Larceny (Guernsey) Law 1958 or any corresponding law for the time being in force, and in that subsection "the relevant Northern Ireland authority" means in the case of a person committed to the care of a fit person, the fit person, and in the case of a person sent to a remand home, special reception centre or training school, the person in charge of that home or centre or the managers of that school.

(5) Nothing in this section authorises the arrest in Northern Ireland of, or the taking there of any proceedings in respect of, such a person as is mentioned in paragraph (*d*) of subsection (1) of this section.

33. [*Repealed by Legal Aid Act* 1974 (*c.* 4), *Sched.* 5.]

Transitional modifications of Part I for persons of specified ages

Transitional modifications of Part I for persons of specified ages

34.—(1) The Secretary of State may by order provide—

(*a*) that any reference to a child in section 4, 13 (2) or 28 (4) or (5) of this Act shall be construed as excluding a child who has attained such age as may be specified in the order;

(*b*) that any reference to a young person in section 5 of this Act (except subsection (8)) shall be construed as including a child, or excluding a young person, who has attained such age as may be so specified;

(*c*) that any reference to a young person in section 5 (8), 7 (7), 7 (8), 9 (1), 23 (1) or 29 (1) of this Act shall be construed as including a child who has attained such age as may be so specified;

(*d*) that section 7 (1) of this Act shall have effect as if for references to seventeen years there were substituted references to sixteen years;

(*e*) that section 23 (2) or (3) of this Act shall have effect as if the references to a young person excluded a young person who has not attained such age as may be so specified;

(*f*) that section 22 (5) of this Act shall have effect as if for the reference to the age of fourteen, or section 31 (1) of this Act shall have effect as if for the reference to the age of fifteen, there were substituted a reference to such greater age as may be so specified.

(2) In the case of a person who has not attained the age of seventeen but has attained such lower age as the Secretary of State may by order specify,[12b] no proceedings under section 1 of this Act or for an offence shall be begun in any court unless the person proposing to begin the proceedings has, in addition to any notice falling to be given by him to a local authority in pursuance of section 2 (3) or 5 (8) of this Act, given notice of the proceedings to a probation officer for the area for which the court acts; and accordingly in the case of such a person the reference in section 1 (1) of this Act to the said section 2 (3) shall be construed as including a reference to this subsection.

(3) In the case of a person who has attained such age as the Secretary of State may by order specify,[12b] an authority shall, without prejudice to subsection (2) of section 9 of this Act, not be required by virtue of

[12b] The age specified by 1973 S.I. No. 485 was 12 years.

subsection (1) of that section to make investigations or provide information which it does not already possess with respect to his home surroundings if, by direction of the justices or probation and after-care committee acting for any relevant area, arrangements are in force for information with respect to his home surroundings to be furnished to the court in question by a probation officer.

(4) Except in relation to section 13 (2) of this Act, references to a child in subsection (1) of this section do not include references to a person under the age of ten.

(5) In relation to a child tried summarily in pursuance of section 6 of this Act, for the words " fifty pounds " in subsection (3) of that section there shall be substituted the words " ten pounds ".

(6) Without prejudice to the generality of section 69 (4) of this Act, an order under this section may specify different ages for the purposes of different provisions of this Act specified in the order.

(7) A draft of any order proposed to be made under this section shall be laid before Parliament and, in the case of an order of which the effect is that the reference to a child in section 4 of this Act includes a child who has attained an age of more than twelve, shall not be made unless the draft has been approved by a resolution of each House of Parliament.

PART II

ACCOMMODATION ETC. FOR CHILDREN IN CARE, AND FOSTER CHILDREN

Community homes

Regional planning of accommodation for children in care

35.—(1) With a view to the preparation, in pursuance of the provisions of this Part of this Act, of regional plans for the provision of accommodation for children in the care of local authorities and for the equipment and maintenance of the accommodation, the Secretary of State may by order provide that any area specified in the order shall be a separate area (in this Act referred to as a " planning area ") for the purposes of those provisions.

(2) Before making an order under subsection (1) of this section, the Secretary of State shall consult each local authority whose area or any part of whose area is included in the planning area which he proposes should be specified in the order and such other local authorities, if any, as he thinks fit.

(3) [13] It shall be the duty of the local authorities whose areas are wholly or partly included in a planning area (in this Act referred to, in relation to such an area, as " the relevant authorities ") to establish for the area, within such period as may be provided by the order specifying the planning area or such longer period as the Secretary of State may allow, a body to be called the children's regional planning committee.

(4) The provisions of Schedule 2 to this Act shall have effect in relation to children's regional planning committees.

(5) In the case of an order under subsection (1) of this section which (by virtue of section 69 (3) of this Act) varies or revokes a previous order under that subsection—

(a) the reference in subsection (2) of this section to the planning area

---

[13] Exempted from s. 101 (8) of the Local Government Act 1972 (c. 70) by s. 101 (9) (*e*) of that Act.

which the Secretary of State proposes should be specified in the
order shall be construed as a reference to the planning area as
it would be if the variation were made or, as the case may be, to
the planning area as it is before the revocation; and

(b) the order may contain such transitional provisions (including
provisions as to the expenses and membership of any existing
or former children's regional planning committee for a planning area) as the Secretary of State thinks fit.

Regional plans for community homes

36.—(1) The children's regional planning committee for a planning
area (in this and the following section referred to as " the committee ")
shall prepare and submit to the Secretary of State, in accordance with
the following provisions of this section, a plan (in this Act referred to
as a " regional plan ") for the provision and maintenance of homes,
to be known as community homes, for the accommodation and maintenance of children in the care of the relevant authorities.

(2) The community homes for which provision may be made by a
regional plan shall be—

(a) community homes provided by the relevant authorities; and

(b) voluntary homes provided by voluntary organisations but in the
management of each of which the plan proposes that a relevant
authority should participate in accordance with an instrument
of management.

(3) Where a regional plan makes provision for any such voluntary
home as is referred to in paragraph (b) of subsection (2) of this section,
the plan shall designate the home as either a controlled community home
or an assisted community home, according as it is proposed in the plan
that the management, equipment and maintenance of the home should
be the responsibility of one of the relevant authorities or of the
voluntary organisation by which the home is provided.

(4) Every regional plan shall contain proposals—

(a) with regard to the nature and purpose of each of the community homes for which the plan makes provision; and

(b) for the provision of facilities for the observation of the
physical and mental condition of children in the care of the
relevant authorities and for the assessment of the most
suitable accommodation and treatment for those children.

(5) Before including provision in a regional plan that a community
home should be provided by any of the relevant authorities or that a
voluntary home provided by a voluntary organisation should be designated as a controlled or assisted community home, the committee shall
obtain the consent of the authority or voluntary organisation by which
the home is or is to be provided and, in the case of a home which is to
be designated as a controlled or assisted community home, the consent
of the local authority which it is proposed should be specified in the
instrument of management for the home.

(6) A regional plan shall be prepared in such form and shall contain such information as the Secretary of State may direct, either
generally or in relation to a particular planning area or particular
kinds of plans; and the Secretary of State may direct that the regional
plan for a particular planning area shall be submitted to him within
such period as may be specified in the direction or such longer period
as he may allow.

Approval and variation of regional plans

37.—(1) After considering any regional plan submitted to him under
section 36 of this Act and after making in the plan such modifications

349

(if any) as he may agree with the committee by which the plan was submitted and as he may consider appropriate for securing that the plan makes proper provision for the accommodation and maintenance of children in the care of the relevant authorities, the Secretary of State may approve the plan.

(2) Where the Secretary of State considers that, either with or without such modifications as are referred to in subsection (1) of this section, part but not the whole of a plan submitted to him under section 36 of this Act makes proper provision for the accommodation and maintenance of the children to whom that part of the plan relates, the Secretary of State may approve that part of the plan.

(3) Where the Secretary of State has approved part only of a regional plan, the committee for the planning area concerned shall prepare and submit to him under section 36 of this Act a further regional plan containing proposals to supplement that part of the previous plan which was approved by the Secretary of State.

(4) If, at any time after the approval of the whole or part of a regional plan by the Secretary of State, the committee for the planning area concerned consider that the plan, or such part of it as was approved, should be varied or replaced, they shall prepare and submit to the Secretary of State under section 36 of this Act a further regional plan for that purpose; and any such further regional plan may—

(a) take the form of a replacement for the regional plan or part thereof which was previously approved by the Secretary of State; or

(b) contain proposals for the amendment of that regional plan or part thereof.

(5) In relation to a further regional plan which contains proposals for supplementing or amending a regional plan or part of a regional plan which has been previously approved by the Secretary of State (in this subsection referred to as " the approved plan ")—

(a) section 36 (4) of this Act shall have effect as if references to a regional plan were references to the approved plan as it would have effect if supplemented or amended in accordance with the proposals contained in the further regional plan; and

(b) subsection (1) of this section shall have effect as if the reference therein to children in the care of the relevant authorities were a reference to the children to whom the proposals in the plan relate; and

(c) in so far as the further regional plan contains proposals under which a home would cease to be a community home, or would become a community home of a different description, or would be used for a purpose different from that provided for in the approved plan, the committee preparing the further plan shall, before submitting it to the Secretary of State, obtain the consent of the local authority or voluntary organisation by which the home is provided and, if the proposal is for a home to become or to cease to be a controlled or assisted community home, the consent of the local authority which it is proposed should be, or which is, specified in the instrument of management for the home.

(6) Where the Secretary of State approves a regional plan, in whole or in part, he shall give notice in writing of his approval to the committee for the planning area concerned specifying the date on which the plan is to come into operation, and the committee shall send a copy of the notice to each of the relevant authorities and to any voluntary organisation whose consent was required to any provision of the plan.

Provision of community homes by local authorities

38. Where a regional plan for a planning area includes provision for a community home to be provided by one of the relevant authorities, it shall be the duty of the local authority concerned to provide, manage, equip and maintain that home.

Instruments of management for assisted and controlled community homes

39.—(1) The Secretary of State may by order make an instrument of management providing for the constitution of a body of managers for any voluntary home which, in accordance with a regional plan approved by him, is designated as a controlled or assisted community home.

(2) Where in accordance with a regional plan approved by the Secretary of State, two or more voluntary homes are designated as controlled community homes or as assisted community homes, then if—

(*a*) those homes are, or are to be, provided by the same voluntary organisation; and

(*b*) the same local authority is to be represented on the body of managers for those homes,

a single instrument of management may be made by the Secretary of State under this section constituting one body of managers for those homes or for any two or more of them.

(3) The number of persons who, in accordance with an instrument of management under this section, constitute the body of managers for a voluntary home shall be such number, being a multiple of three, as may be specified in the instrument of management, but the instrument shall provide that a proportion of the managers shall be appointed by such local authority as may be so specified and—

(*a*) in the case of a voluntary home which is designated in a regional plan as a controlled community home, the proportion shall be two-thirds; and

(*b*) in the case of a voluntary home which is so designated as an assisted community home, the proportion shall be one-third.

(4) An instrument of management shall provide that the " foundation managers ", that is to say, those of the managers of the voluntary home to which the instrument relates who are not appointed by a local authority in accordance with subsection (3) of this section, shall be appointed, in such manner and by such persons as may be specified in the instrument,—

(*a*) so as to represent the interests of the voluntary organisation by which the home is, or is to be, provided; and

(*b*) for the purpose of securing that, as far as practicable, the character of the home as a voluntary home will be preserved and that, subject to section 40 (3) of this Act, the terms of any trust deed relating to the home are observed.

(5) An instrument of management under this section shall come into force on such date as may be specified in the instrument, and if such an instrument is in force in relation to a voluntary home the home shall be and be known as a controlled community home or an assisted community home, according to its designation in the regional plan.

Supplementary provisions as to instruments of management and trust deeds

40.—(1) An instrument of management for a controlled or assisted community home shall contain such provisions as the Secretary of State considers appropriate for giving effect to the provisions of regional plan by which the home is designated as a controlled or assisted community home, but nothing in the instrument of management for such a home shall affect the purposes for which the premises comprising the home are held.

(2) Without prejudice to the generality of subsection (1) of this section, an instrument of management may contain—

(a) provisions specifying the nature and purpose of the home or each of the homes to which it relates;

(b) provisions requiring a specified number or proportion of the places in that home or those homes to be made available to local authorities and to any other body specified in the instrument; and

(c) provisions relating to the management of that home or those homes and the charging of fees in respect of children placed therein or places made available to any local authority or other body.

(3) Subject to subsection (1) of this section, in the event of any inconsistency between the provisions of any trust deed and the instrument of management relating to a controlled or assisted community home, the instrument of management shall prevail over the provisions of the trust deed in so far as they relate to that home.

(4) After consultation with the voluntary organisation by which a controlled or assisted community home is provided and with the local authority specified in the instrument of management for the time being in force for that home, the Secretary of State may vary or revoke any provisions of that instrument of management by a further instrument of management.

(5) In this Act the expression " trust deed ", in relation to a voluntary home, means any instrument (other than an instrument of management) regulating the maintenance, management or conduct of the home or the constitution of a body of managers or trustees of the home.

Management of controlled community homes

41.—(1) The management, equipment and maintenance of a controlled community home shall be the responsibility of the local authority specified in the instrument of management for that home, and in the following provisions of this section " the responsible authority ", in relation to such a home, means the local authority responsible for its management, equipment and maintenance.

(2) Subject to the following provisions of this section, the responsible authority shall exercise their functions in relation to a controlled community home through the body of managers constituted by the instrument of management for the home, and any thing done, liability incurred or property acquired by the managers shall be done, incurred or acquired by the managers as agents of the responsible authority.

(3) In so far as any matter is reserved for the decision of the responsible authority, either by subsection (4) of this section or by the instrument of management for the controlled community home in question or by the service by the responsible authority on the managers or any of them of a notice reserving any matter, that matter shall be dealt with by the responsible authority themselves and not by the managers, but in dealing with any matter so reserved, the responsible authority shall have regard to any representations made to them by the managers.

(4) The employment of persons at a controlled community home shall be a matter reserved for the decision of the responsible authority, but where the instrument of management so provides the responsible authority may enter into arrangements with the voluntary organisation by which the home is provided whereby, in accordance with such terms as may be agreed between the responsible authority and the voluntary organisation, persons who are not in the employment of the responsible authority shall undertake duties at the home.

(5) The accounting year of the managers of a controlled community home shall be such as may be specified by the responsible authority and, before such date in each accounting year as may be so specified, the managers of a controlled community home shall submit to the responsible authority estimates, in such form as the authority may require, of expenditure and receipts in respect of the next accounting year; and any expenses incurred by the managers of a controlled community home with the approval of the responsible authority shall be defrayed by that authority.

(6) The managers of a controlled community home shall keep proper accounts in respect of that home and proper records in relation to the accounts, but where an instrument of management relates to more than one controlled community home, one set of accounts and records may be kept in respect of all the homes to which the instrument relates.

Management of assisted community homes

42.—(1) The management, equipment and maintenance of an assisted community home shall be the responsibility of the voluntary organisation by which the home is provided, and in the following provisions of this section " the responsible organisation ", in relation to such a home, means the voluntary organisation responsible for its management, equipment and maintenance.

(2) Subject to the following provisions of this section, the responsible organisation shall exercise its functions in relation to the home through the body of managers constituted by the instrument of management for the home, and any thing done, liability incurred or property acquired by the managers shall be done, incurred or acquired by the managers as agents of the responsible organisation.

(3) In so far as any matter is reserved for the decision of the responsible organisation, either by subsection (4) of this section or by the instrument of management for the assisted community home in question or by the service by the responsible organisation on the managers or any of them of a notice reserving any matter, that matter shall be dealt with by the responsible organisation itself and not by the managers, but in dealing with any matter so reserved the responsible organisation shall have regard to any representations made to the organisation by the managers.

(4) The employment of persons at an assisted community home shall be a matter reserved for the decision of the responsible organisation but, subject to subsection (5) of this section,—

(a) where the responsible organisation proposes to engage any person to work at the home or to terminate without notice the employment of any person at the home, the responsible organisation shall consult the local authority specified in the instrument of management and, if the local authority so directs, the responsible organisation shall not carry out its proposal without the consent of the local authority; and

(b) the local authority may, after consultation with the responsible organisation, require the organisation to terminate the employment of any person at the home.

(5) Paragraphs (a) and (b) of subsection (4) of this section shall not apply—

(a) in such cases or circumstances as may be specified by notice in writing given by the local authority to the responsible organisation; and

(b) in relation to the employment of any persons or class of persons specified in the instrument of management.

(6) The accounting year of the managers of an assisted community home shall be such as may be specified by the responsible organisation and, before such date in each accounting year as may be so specified, the managers of an assisted community home shall submit to the responsible organisation estimates, in such form as the organisation may require, of expenditure and receipts in respect of the next financial year; and all expenses incurred by the managers of an assisted community home with the approval of the responsible organisation shall be defrayed by the organisation.

(7) The managers of an assisted community home shall keep proper accounts in respect of that home and proper records in relation to those accounts, but where an instrument of management relates to more than one assisted community home, one set of accounts and records may be kept in respect of all the homes to which the instrument relates.

Control of premises used for, and conduct of, community homes

43.—(1) The Secretary of State may make regulations with respect to the conduct of community homes and for securing the welfare of the children in community homes.

(2) Without prejudice to the generality of subsection (1) of this section, regulations under this section may—

(a) impose requirements as to the accommodation and equipment to be provided in community homes and as to the medical arrangements to be made for protecting the health of the children in the homes;

(b) impose requirements as to the facilities which are to be provided for giving religious instruction to children in community homes;

(c) require the approval of the Secretary of State for the provision and use of accommodation for the purpose of restricting the liberty of children in community homes and impose other requirements as to the placing of a child in accommodation provided for that purpose, including a requirement to obtain the permission of the local authority or voluntary organisation in whose care the child is;

(d) authorise the Secretary of State to give and revoke directions requiring the local authority by whom a community home is provided or who are specified in the instrument of management for a controlled community home or the voluntary organisation by which an assisted community home is provided to accommodate in the home a child in the care of a local authority for whom no places are made available in that home or to take such action in relation to a child accommodated in the home as may be specified in the directions;

(e) require reviews of any permission given in pursuance of paragraph (c) above and provide for such a review to be conducted in a manner approved by the Secretary of State by a committee of persons representing the local authority or voluntary organisation in question but including at least one person satisfying such conditions as may be prescribed by the regulations with a view to securing that he is independent of the authority or organisation and unconnected with any community home containing such accommodation as is mentioned in the said paragraph (c);

(f) prescribe standards to which premises used for community homes are to conform;

(g) require the approval of the Secretary of State to the use of buildings for the purpose of community homes and to the doing of anything (whether by way of addition, diminution or alteration) which materially affects the buildings or grounds or other facilities or amenities available for children in community homes;

(*h*) provide that, to such extent as may be provided for in the regulations, the Secretary of State may direct that any provision of regulations under this section which is specified in the direction and makes any such provision as is referred to in paragraph (*a*), (*f*) or (*g*) above shall not apply in relation to a particular community home or the premises used for it, and may provide for the variation or revocation of any such direction by the Secretary of State.

(3) Without prejudice to the power to make regulations under this section conferring functions on the local authority or voluntary organisation by which a community home is provided or on the managers of a controlled or assisted community home, regulations under this section may confer functions in relation to a controlled or assisted community home on the local authority named in the instrument of management for the home.

(4) Where it appears to the Secretary of State that any premises used for the purposes of a community home are unsuitable for those purposes, or that the conduct of a community home is not in accordance with regulations made by him under this section or is otherwise unsatisfactory, he may by notice in writing served on the responsible body, direct that as from such date as may be specified in the notice the premises shall not be used for the purposes of a community home.

(5) Where the Secretary of State has given a direction in relation to a controlled or assisted community home under subsection (4) of this section and the direction has not been revoked, the Secretary of State may at any time by order revoke the instrument of management for that home.

(6) For the purposes of subsection (4) of this section the responsible body—

(*a*) in relation to a community home provided by a local authority, is that local authority;

(*b*) in relation to a controlled community home, is the local authority specified in the instrument of management for that home; and

(*c*) in relation to an assisted community home, is the voluntary organisation by which the home is provided.

Controlled and assisted community homes exempted from certain provisions as to voluntary homes

44. While a voluntary home is a controlled or assisted community home, the following enactments shall not apply in relation to it, that is to say,—

(*a*) sections 29 and 30 of the Children Act 1948 (compulsory registration of voluntary homes);

(*b*) section 31 of that Act (regulations as to conduct of voluntary homes); and

(*c*) section 93 of the Act of 1933 and section 32 of the Children Act 1948 (notification to Secretary of State of certain particulars relating to voluntary homes).

Determination of disputes relating to controlled and assisted community homes

45.—(1) Subject to subsection (5) of this section, where any dispute relating to a controlled community home arises between the local authority specified in the instrument of management and either the voluntary organisation by which the home is provided or any other local authority who have placed, or desire or are required to place, a child in their care in the home, the dispute may be referred by either party to the Secretary of State for his determination.

(2) Subject to subsection (5) of this section, where any dispute relating to an assisted community home arises between the voluntary organisation by which the home is provided and any local authority who have placed, or desire to place, a child in their care in the home, the dispute may be referred by either party to the Secretary of State for his determination.

(3) Where a dispute is referred to the Secretary of State under this section he may, in order to give effect to his determination of the dispute, give such directions as he thinks fit to the local authority or voluntary organisation concerned.

(4) The provisions of this section shall apply notwithstanding that the matter in dispute may be one which, under or by virtue of the preceding provisions of this Part of this Act, is reserved for the decision, or is the responsibility, of the local authority specified in the instrument of management or, as the case may be, the voluntary organisation by which the home is provided.

(5) Where any trust deed relating to a controlled or assisted community home contains provision whereby a bishop or any other ecclesiastical or denominational authority has power to decide questions relating to religious instruction given in the home, no dispute which is capable of being dealt with in accordance with that provision shall be referred to the Secretary of State under this section.

Discontinuance of approved schools etc. on establishment of community homes

46.—(1) If in the case of any approved school [or remand home within the meaning of the Criminal Justice Act 1948 or approved probation hostel or approved probation home within the meaning of the Powers of Criminal Courts Act 1973] [13a] (hereafter in this section referred to as an "approved institution") it appears to the Secretary of State that in consequence of the establishment of community homes for a planning area the institution as such is no longer required, he may by order provide that it shall cease to be an approved institution on a date specified in the order.

(2) The provisions of Schedule 3 to this Act shall have effect in relation to institutions which are, or by virtue of this section have ceased to be, approved institutions.

Discontinuance by voluntary organisation of controlled or assisted community home

47.—(1) The voluntary organisation by which a controlled or assisted community home is provided shall not cease to provide the home except after giving to the Secretary of State and the local authority specified in the instrument of management not less than two years' notice in writing of their intention to do so.

(2) A notice under subsection (1) of this section shall specify the date from which the voluntary organisation intends to cease to provide the home as a community home; and where such a notice is given and is not withdrawn before the date specified in it, then, subject to subsection (4) of this section the instrument of management for the home shall cease to have effect on that date and accordingly the home shall then cease to be a controlled or assisted community home.

(3) Where a notice is given under subsection (1) of this section, the local authority to whom the notice is given shall inform the children's regional planning committee responsible for the regional plan under

[13a] Words substituted by Powers of Criminal Courts Act 1973 (c. 62), Sched. 5.

which the voluntary home in question was designated as a controlled or assisted community home of the receipt and content of the notice.

(4) Where a notice is given under subsection (1) of this section and the body of managers for the home to which the notice relates give notice in writing to the Secretary of State that they are unable or unwilling to continue as managers of the home until the date specified in the first-mentioned notice, the Secretary of State may by order—

(a) revoke the instrument of management; and

(b) require the local authority who were specified in that instrument to conduct the home, until the date specified in the notice under subsection (1) of this section or such earlier date (if any) as may be specified for the purposes of this paragraph in the order, as if it were a community home provided by the local authority.

(5) Where the Secretary of State makes such a requirement as is specified in subsection (4) (b) of this section,—

(a) nothing in the trust deed for the home in question shall affect the conduct of the home by the local authority; and

(b) the Secretary of State may by order direct that for the purposes of any provision specified in the direction and made by or under any enactment relating to community homes (other than this section) the home shall, until the date or earlier date specified as mentioned in subsection (4) (b) of this section, be treated as an assisted community home or as a controlled community home, but except in so far as the Secretary of State so directs, the home shall until that date be treated for the purposes of any such enactment as a community home provided by the local authority; and

(c) on the date or earlier date specified as mentioned in subsection (4) (b) of this section the home shall cease to be a community home.

Financial provisions applicable on cessation of controlled or assisted community home

48.—(1) Where the instrument of management for a controlled or assisted community home ceases to have effect by virtue either of an order under section 43 (5) of this Act or of subsection (2) or subsection (4) (a) of section 47 of this Act, the voluntary organisation by which the home was provided or, if the premises used for the purposes of the home are not vested in that organisation, the persons in whom those premises are vested (in this section referred to as " the trustees of the home "), shall become liable, in accordance with the following provisions of this section, to make repayment in respect of any increase in the value of the premises and other property belonging to the voluntary organisation or the trustees of the home which is attributable to the expenditure of public money thereon.

(2) Where an instrument of management has ceased to have effect as mentioned in subsection (1) of this section and the instrument related—

(a) to a controlled community home; or

(b) to an assisted community home which, at any time before that instrument of management came into force, was a controlled community home,

then, on the home ceasing to be a community home, the voluntary organisation by which the home was provided or, as the case may be, the trustees of the home, shall pay to the local authority specified in that instrument of management a sum equal to that part of the value of any relevant premises which is attributable to expenditure by the local authority who at the time the expenditure was incurred had responsibility for the management, equipment and maintenance of the home by virtue of section 41 (1) of this Act.

(3) For the purposes of subsection (2) of this section, " relevant premises ", in relation to a controlled or assisted community home, means premises used for the purposes of the home and belonging to the voluntary organisation or the trustees of the home but erected, extended or improved, at any time while the home was a controlled community home, by the local authority having, at that time, such responsibility in relation to the home as is mentioned in subsection (2) of this section.

(4) Where an instrument of management has ceased to have effect as mentioned in subsection (1) of this section and the instrument related—

(a) to an assisted community home; or

(b) to a controlled community home which, at any time before that instrument of management came into force, was an assisted community home,

then, on the home ceasing to be a community home, the voluntary organisation by which the home was provided or, as the case may be, the trustees of the home, shall pay to the Secretary of State a sum equal to that part of the value of the premises and any other property used for the purposes of the home which is attributable to the expenditure of money provided by way of grant under section 65 of this Act.

(5) Where an instrument of management has ceased to have effect as mentioned in subsection (1) of this section and the controlled or assisted community home to which it related was conducted in premises which formerly were used as an approved school or were an approved probation hostel or home but which were designated as a community home in a regional plan approved by the Secretary of State, then, on the home ceasing to be a community home, the voluntary organisation by which the home was provided or, as the case may be, the trustees of the home, shall pay to the Secretary of State a sum equal to that part of the value of the premises concerned and of any other property used for the purposes of the home and belonging to the voluntary organisation or the trustees of the home which is attributable to the expenditure—

(a) of sums paid towards the expense of the managers of an approved school under section 104 of the Act of 1933; or

(b) of sums paid under [section 51 (3) (c) of the Powers of Criminal Courts Act 1973] [13a] in relation to expenditure on approved probation hostels or homes.

(6) The amount of any sum payable under this section by the voluntary organisation by which a controlled or assisted community home was provided or by the trustees of the home shall be determined in accordance with such arrangements—

(a) as may be agreed between the voluntary organisation by which the home was provided and the local authority concerned or, as the case may be, the Secretary of State; or

(b) in default of agreement, as may be determined by the Secretary of State;

and with the agreement of the local authority concerned or the Secretary of State, as the case may be, the liability to pay any sum under this section may be discharged, in whole or in part, by the transfer of any premises or other property used for the purposes of the home in question.

(7) The provisions of this section shall have effect notwithstanding anything in any trust deed for a controlled or assisted community home and notwithstanding the provisions of any enactment or instrument governing the disposition of the property of a voluntary organisation.

(8) Any sums received by the Secretary of State under this section shall be paid into the Consolidated Fund.

Consequential modifications of ss. 13 and 19 of Children Act 1948

Provision of accommodation and maintenance for children in care

49.[13b] For section 13 of the Children Act 1948 there shall be substituted the following section:—

Provision of accommodation and maintenance for children in care

13.—(1) A local authority shall discharge their duty to provide accommodation and maintenance for a child in their care in such one of the following ways as they think fit, namely,—

(*a*) by boarding him out on such terms as to payment by the authority and otherwise as the authority may, subject to the provisions of this Act and regulations thereunder, determine; or

(*b*) by maintaining him in a community home or in any such home as is referred to in section 64 of the Children and Young Persons Act 1969; or

(*c*) by maintaining him in a voluntary home (other than a community home) the managers of which are willing to receive him;

or by making such other arrangements as seem appropriate to the local authority.

(2) Without prejudice to the generality of subsection (1) of this section, a local authority may allow a child in their care, either for a fixed period or until the local authority otherwise determine, to be under the charge and control of a parent, guardian, relative or friend.

(3) The terms, as to payment and other matters, on which a child may be accommodated and maintained in any such home as is referred to in section 64 of that Act shall be such as the Secretary of State may from time to time determine.

Accommodation of persons over school age in convenient community home

50. For section 19 of the Children Act 1948 there shall be substituted the following section:—

Accommodation of persons over school age in convenient community home

19. A local authority may provide accommodation in a community home for any person who is over compulsory school age but has not attained the age of twenty-one if the community home is provided for children who are over compulsory school age and is near the place where that person is employed or seeking employment or receiving education or training.

Foster children

Modification of general duty of local authorities with respect to foster children

51. For section 1 of the Children Act 1958 (which imposes a duty on every local authority to secure that foster children are visited by officers of the authority) there shall be substituted the following section:—

Duty of local authorities to ensure well-being of foster children

1. It shall be the duty of every local authority to satisfy themselves as to the well-being of children within their area who are foster children within the meaning of this Part of this Act and, for that purpose, to secure that, so far as appears to the authority to be appropriate, the children are visited from time to time by officers of the authority and that such advice is given as to the care and maintenance of the children as appears to be needed.

[13b] See Children Act 1975 (c. 72), Sched. 3, para. 42, *post.*

Amendments of definitions of " foster child " and " protected child "

52.—(1) In subsection (1) of section 2 of the Children Act 1958 (which, subject to the following provisions of that section, defines a foster child for the purposes of Part I of that Act as a child below the upper limit of the compulsory school age whose care and maintenance are undertaken for reward for a period exceeding one month by a person who is not a relative or guardian of his) the words from " for reward " to " one month " shall be omitted.

(2) At the end of paragraph (*c*) of subsection (3) of the said section 2 (which provides that a child is not a foster child while he is in the care of any person in a school) there shall be added the words " in which he is receiving full time education ".

(3) After subsection (3) of the said section 2 there shall be inserted the following subsection:—

(3A) A child is not a foster child within the meaning of this Part of this Act at any time while his care and maintenance are undertaken by a person, other than a relative or guardian of his, if at that time—

(*a*) that person does not intend to, and does not in fact, undertake his care and maintenance for a continuous period of more than six days; or

(*b*) that person is not a regular foster parent and does not intend to, and does not in fact, undertake his care and maintenance for a continuous period of more than twenty-seven days;

and for the purposes of this subsection a person is a regular foster parent if, during the period of twelve months immediately preceding the date on which he begins to undertake the care and maintenance of the child in question, he had, otherwise than as a relative or guardian, the care and maintenance of one or more children either for a period of, or periods amounting in the aggregate to, not less than three months or for at least three continuous periods each of which was of more than six days.

(4) Section 37 of the Adoption Act 1958 (which defines " protected child " for the purposes of Part IV of that Act) shall have effect subject to the following modifications:—

(*a*) in paragraph (*a*) of subsection (1) (which refers to arrangements for placing a child in the care of a person who is not a parent, guardian or relative of his) after the words " relative of his " there shall be inserted the words " but who proposes to adopt him ";

(*b*) in subsection (1) (which among other matters excludes a foster child from the definition of " a protected child ") the words " but is not a foster child within the meaning of Part I of the Children Act 1958 " shall be omitted; and

(*c*) in subsection (2) (which excludes certain children from the definition of protected child, including children only temporarily in the care and possession of a person under such arrangements as are referred to in subsection (1) (*a*) of that section) the words from " by reason " to " that subsection, nor " shall be omitted.

(5) In consequence of the modifications of the definition of " protected child " specified in subsection (4) of this section, after subsection (4) of section 2 of the Children Act 1958 there shall be inserted the following subsection:—

" (4A) A child is not a foster child for the purposes of this Part of this Act while he is placed in the care and possession of a person who proposes to adopt him under arrangements made by such a local authority or registered adoption society as is referred to in Part II of the Adoption Act 1958 or while he is a protected child within the meaning of Part IV of that Act."

Modification of duty of persons maintaining foster children to notify local authority

53.—(1) Section 3 of the Children Act 1958 (which requires any person maintaining foster children to notify the local authority on each occasion on which he receives a foster child) shall have effect subject to the following provisions of this section.

(2) In subsection (1) of the section (which requires at least two weeks advance notice of, or, in an emergency, notice within one week after, the reception of a foster child) at the beginning there shall be inserted the words " Subject to the following provisions of this section ", after the words " two weeks " there shall be inserted the words " and not more than four weeks " and for the words " one week " there shall be substituted the words " forty-eight hours ".

(3) In subsection (2) of the section (which relates to the content of the notice) after the word " specify " there shall be inserted the words " the date on which it is intended that the child should be received or, as the case may be, on which the child was in fact received or became a foster child and ".

(4) After subsection (2) of the section there shall be inserted the following subsection :—

(2A) A person shall not be required to give notice under subsection (1) of this section in relation to a child if—

    (a) he has on a previous occasion given notice under that subsection in respect of that or any other child, specifying the premises at which he proposes to keep the child in question; and

    (b) he has not, at any time since that notice was given, ceased to maintain at least one foster child at those premises and been required by virtue of the following provisions of this section to give notice under subsection (5A) of this section in respect of those premises.

(5) In subsection (3) of the section (which relates to notification of changes of address of foster parents and requires similar periods of notice as under subsection (1))—

    (a) for the words " a foster child " there shall be substituted the words " one or more foster children ";

    (b) for the words " the child is kept " there shall be substituted the words " the child is, or the children are, kept ";

    (c) after the words " two weeks " there shall be inserted the words " and not more than four weeks "; and

    (d) for the words " one week " there shall be substituted the words " forty-eight hours ".

(6) So much of subsection (4) of the section as requires notification that a foster child has been removed or has removed himself from the care of the person maintaining him shall cease to have effect and, accordingly, in that subsection for the words " that person " there shall be substituted the words " the person who was maintaining him " and in subsection (5) of the section (which dispenses with the need for such a notice where a child ceases to be a foster child on his removal from a foster parent but empowers the local authority concerned to require certain particulars in such a case)—

    (a) for the words " ceases to be a foster child on his removal " there shall be substituted the words " is removed or removes himself ";

(*b*) the words " need not give notice under subsection (4) of this section but " shall be omitted; and

(*c*) for the words from " the same " onwards there shall be substituted the words " the name and address, if known, of the person (if any) into whose care the child has been removed ".

(7) After subsection (5) of the section there shall be inserted the following subsections:—

(5A) Subject to the provisions of the following subsection, where a person who has been maintaining one or more foster children at any premises ceases to maintain foster children at those premises and the circumstances are such that no notice is required to be given under subsection (3) or subsection (4) of this section, that person shall, within forty-eight hours after he ceases to maintain any foster child at those premises, give notice in writing thereof to the local authority.

(5B) A person need not give the notice required by the preceding subsection in consequence of his ceasing to maintain foster children at any premises if, at the time he so ceases, he intends within twenty-seven days again to maintain any of them as a foster child at those premises; but if he subsequently abandons that intention or the said period expires without his having given effect to it he shall give the said notice within forty-eight hours of that event.

Inspection of premises in which foster children are kept

54.—(1) In section 4 (1) of the Children Act 1958 (which empowers an officer of a local authority to inspect premises in the local authority's area in which foster children are being kept) after the word " in " in the second place where it occurs there shall be inserted the words " the whole or any part of ".

(2) After the said section 4 (1) there shall be inserted the following subsection:—

(1A) If it is shown to the satisfaction of a justice of the peace on sworn information in writing—

(*a*) that there is reasonable cause to believe that a foster child is being kept in any premises, or in any part thereof, and

(*b*) that admission to those premises or that part thereof has been refused to a duly authorised officer of the local authority or that such a refusal is apprehended or that the occupier is temporarily absent,

the justice may by warrant under his hand authorise an officer of the local authority to enter the premises, if need be by force, at any reasonable time within forty-eight hours of the issue of the warrant, for the purpose of inspecting the premises.

(3) At the end of paragraph (*b*) of section 14 (1) of the Children Act 1958 (which makes it an offence under that section to refuse to allow an inspection of any premises under section 4 (1) of that Act) there shall be added the words " or wilfully obstructs a person entitled to enter any premises by virtue of a warrant under subsection (1A) of that section ".

Imposition of requirements and prohibitions relating to the keeping of foster children

55.—(1) In section 4 (2) of the Children Act 1958 (which empowers a local authority to impose certain requirements on a person who keeps or proposes to keep foster children in premises used wholly or mainly for that purpose) for the word " mainly " there shall be substituted the word " partly ".

(2) After paragraph (*f*) of the said section 4 (2) there shall be inserted the following paragraphs:—

(g) the fire precautions to be taken in the premises;

(h) the giving of particulars of any foster child received in the premises and of any change in the number or identity of the foster children kept therein.

(3) In the words following the several paragraphs of the said section 4 (2), after the word " but " there shall be inserted the words " any such requirement may be limited to a particular class of foster children kept in the premises and " and for the words " (b) to (f) " there shall be substituted the words " (b) to (h) ".

(4) For subsection (3) of section 4 of the Children Act 1958 (which empowers a local authority to prohibit a person from keeping a particular foster child or any foster children at particular premises) there shall be substituted the following subsections:—

(3) Where a person proposes to keep a foster child in any premises and the local authority are of the opinion that—

(a) the premises are not suitable premises in which to keep foster children; or

(b) that person is not a suitable person to have the care and maintenance of foster children; or

(c) it would be detrimental to that child to be kept by that person in those premises;

the local authority may impose a prohibition on that person under subsection (3A) of this section.

(3A) A prohibition imposed on any person under this subsection may—

(a) prohibit him from keeping any foster child in premises specified in the prohibition; or

(b) prohibit him from keeping any foster child in any premises in the area of the local authority; or

(c) prohibit him from keeping a particular child specified in the prohibition in premises so specified.

(3B) Where a local authority have imposed a prohibition on any person under subsection (3A) of this section, the local authority may, if they think fit, cancel the prohibition, either of their own motion or on an application made by that person on the ground of a change in the circumstances in which a foster child would be kept by him.

(5) In section 5 (1) of the Children Act 1958 (which confers a right of appeal to a juvenile court within fourteen days of the imposition of a requirement or prohibition under section 4 of that Act) after the word " prohibition ", in the second place where it occurs, there shall be inserted the words " or, in the case of a prohibition imposed under subsection (3A) of that section, within fourteen days from the refusal by the local authority to accede to an application by him for the cancellation of the prohibition ".

Extension of disqualification for keeping foster children

56.—(1) In section 6 of the Children Act 1958 (which provides that a person shall not, without the consent of the local authority, maintain a foster child if one or more of a variety of orders has been made against him) there shall be made the following amendments, that is to say—

(a) in paragraph (b), after the word " 1933 ", there shall be inserted the words " the Children and Young Persons Act 1969 " and for the words from " in respect of " to " of which the " there shall be substituted the words " and by virtue of the order or requirement a ";

(b) at the end of paragraph (c) there shall be inserted the words " or has been placed on probation or discharged absolutely or conditionally for any such offence ";

(c) in paragraph (e), after the word " subsection " there shall be inserted the words " (3) or " and for the words from " refusing " onwards there shall be substituted the words " refusing, or an order under section five of that Act cancelling, the registration of any premises occupied by him or his registration "; and

(d) after paragraph (e) there shall be inserted the following paragraph: —

(f) an order has been made under section 43 of the Adoption Act 1958 for the removal of a protected child who was being kept or was about to be received by him.

(2) At the end of the said section 6 there shall be added the following subsection: —

(2) Where this section applies to any person, otherwise than by virtue of this subsection, it shall apply also to any other person who lives in the same premises as he does or who lives in premises at which he is employed;

and accordingly the said section 6 as amended by the preceding subsection shall be subsection (1) of that section.

Modifications of provisions as to offences

57.—(1) After subsection (1) of section 14 of the Children Act 1958 (which, among other matters, makes it an offence to maintain a foster child in contravention of section 6 of that Act) there shall be inserted the following subsection: —

(1A) Where section 6 of this Act applies to any person by virtue only of subsection (2) of that section, he shall not be guilty of an offence under paragraph (d) of subsection (1) of this section if he proves that he did not know, and had no reasonable ground for believing, that a person living or employed in the premises in which he lives was a person to whom that section applies.

(2) After subsection (2) of the said section 14 (which provides that offences under that section are punishable summarily) there shall be added the following subsection: —

(2A) If any person who is required, under any provision of this Part of this Act, to give a notice fails to give the notice within the time specified in that provision, then, notwithstanding anything in section 104 of the Magistrates' Courts Act 1952 (time limit for proceedings) proceedings for the offence may be brought at any time within six months from the date when evidence of the offence came to the knowledge of the local authority.

Inspection

Inspection of children's homes etc. by persons authorised by Secretary of State

58.[13c]—(1) Subject to subsection (2) of this section, the Secretary of State may cause to be inspected from time to time—

(a) any community home provided by a local authority under section 38 of this Act;

(b) any voluntary home (whether a community home or not);

(c) any other premises at which one or more children in the care of a local authority are being accommodated and maintained;

(d) any other premises at which one or more children are being boarded out by a voluntary organisation; and

(e) any other premises where a foster child within the meaning of Part I of the Children Act 1958 or a child to whom any of the provisions of that Part are extended by section 12 or section 13 of

[13c] See Children Act 1975 (c. 72), Sched. 3, para. 72, *post.*

that Act, or a protected child within the meaning of Part IV of the Adoption Act 1958 is being accommodated or maintained.

(2) Subsection (1) of this section does not apply to any home or other premises which is, as a whole, subject to inspection by or under the authority of a government department.

(3) An inspection under this section shall be conducted by a person authorised in that behalf by the Secretary of State, but an officer of a local authority shall not be so authorised except with the consent of that authority.

(4) Any person inspecting a home or other premises under this section may inspect the children therein and make such examination into the state and management of the home or other premises and the treatment of children therein as he thinks fit.

Powers of entry supplemental to s. 58

59.—(1) A person authorised to inspect any home or other premises under section 58 of this Act shall have a right to enter the home or other premises for that purpose and for any other purpose specified in subsection (4) of that section, but shall if so required produce some duly authenticated document showing his authority to exercise the power of entry conferred by this subsection.

(2) A person who obstructs the exercise by a person authorised as mentioned in subsection (1) of this section of a power of entry conferred thereby shall be liable on summary conviction to a fine not exceeding five pounds or, in the case of a second or subsequent conviction, to a fine not exceeding twenty pounds.

(3) A refusal to allow any such person as is mentioned in subsection (1) of this section to enter any such home or other premises as are mentioned in section 58 (1) of this Act shall be deemed, for the purposes of section 40 of the Act of 1933 (which relates to search warrants), to be a reasonable cause to suspect that a child or young person in the home or other premises is being neglected in a manner likely to cause him unnecessary suffering or injury to health.

PART III

MISCELLANEOUS AND GENERAL

Miscellaneous

Extradition offences

60.—(1) There shall be included—

(a) in the list of extradition crimes contained in Schedule 1 to the Extradition Act 1870; and

(b) among the descriptions of offences set out in Schedule 1 to the Fugitive Offenders Act 1967,

any offence of the kind described in section 1 of the Act of 1933 (which relates to cruelty to persons under sixteen) and any offence of the kind described in section 1 of the Indecency with Children Act 1960.

(2) Nothing in this Act shall be construed as derogating from the provisions of section 17 of the said Act of 1870 or section 16 (2) or 17 of the said Act of 1967 in their application to any provisions of those Acts respectively as amended by the preceding subsection.

Rules relating to juvenile court panels and composition of juvenile courts

61.—(1) Without prejudice to the generality of the power to make rules under section 15 of the Justices of the Peace Act 1949 relating to the procedure and practice to be followed by magistrates' courts, provision may be made by such rules with respect to any of the following matters, namely,—

    (*a*) the formation and revision of juvenile court panels, that is to say, panels of justices specially qualified to deal with juvenile cases and the eligibility of justices to be members of such panels;

    (*b*) the appointment of persons as chairmen of juvenile courts; and

    (*c*) the composition of juvenile courts.

(2) Rules making any such provisions as are referred to in subsection (1) of this section may confer powers on the Lord Chancellor with respect to any of the matters specified in the rules and may, in particular, provide for the appointment of juvenile court panels by him and for the removal from a juvenile court panel of any justice who, in his opinion, is unsuitable to serve on a juvenile court.

(3) Rules made by virtue of this section may make different provision in relation to different areas for which juvenile court panels are formed; and in the application of this section to the county palatine of Lancaster, for any reference in the preceding subsection to the Lord Chancellor there shall be substituted a reference to the Chancellor of the Duchy.

(4) Nothing in this section or in any rules made under section 15 of the said Act of 1949 shall affect—

    (*a*) the areas for which juvenile court panels are formed and juvenile courts are constituted;

    (*b*) the provisions of Part I of Schedule 2 to the Act of 1963 (and, as it has effect by virtue of section 17 (1) of that Act, Part I of Schedule 2 to the Act of 1933) with respect to the making of recommendations and orders relating to the formation of combined juvenile court panels; or

    (*c*) the provisions of paragraph 14 of that Schedule relating to the divisions of the metropolitan area for which juvenile courts sit;

but rules under the said section 15 may repeal, either generally or with respect to any part of the metropolitan area, any provision contained in paragraphs 15 to 18 of that Schedule (which contain provisions applicable in the metropolitan area with respect to certain of the matters referred to in subsection (1) of this section) and in subsections (2) and (3) of section 12 of the Administration of Justice Act 1964 (which amend those paragraphs).

(5) In this section " the metropolitan area " means the inner London area and the City of London.

Contributions in respect of children and young persons in care

62.—(1) The provisions of sections 86 to 88 of the Act of 1933 (which, as originally enacted, provided for contributions in respect of children and young persons committed to the care of a fit person or sent to an approved school) shall apply in relation to children and young persons committed to the care of a local authority by a care order which is not an interim order.

(2) Whether or not a contribution order has been made in respect of any child or young person in the care of a local authority, no contribution shall be payable in respect of him for any period during which he is allowed by the local authority to be under the charge and control of a parent, guardian, relative or friend, although remaining in the care of the local authority.

(3) Where a person (in this section referred to as a " contributory ") is liable under section 86 of the Act of 1933 to make a contribution in respect of a child or young person in the care of a local authority, then, subject to the following provisions of this section, the amount of his

contribution shall be such as may be proposed by the local authority and agreed by the contributory or, in default of agreement, as may be determined by a court in proceedings for, or for the variation of, a contribution order.

(4) The maximum contribution which may be proposed by a local authority in respect of a child or young person in their care shall be a weekly amount equal to the weekly amount which, in the opinion of the local authority, they would normally be prepared to pay if a child or young person of the same age were boarded out by them (whether or not the child or young person in respect of whom the contribution is proposed is in fact so boarded out and, if he is, whether or not the local authority are in fact paying that amount).

(5) No contribution order shall be made on a contributory in respect of a child or young person unless—

(a) the local authority in whose care he is have, by notice in writing given to the contributory, proposed an amount as the amount of his contribution; and

(b) either the contributory and the local authority have not, within the period of one month beginning with the day on which the notice was given to the contributory, agreed on the amount of his contribution or the contributory has defaulted in making one or more contributions of an amount which has been agreed.

(6) In proceedings for a contribution order, the court shall not order a contributory to pay a contribution greater than that proposed in the notice given to him under subsection (5) (a) of this section.

(7) In proceedings for the variation of a contribution order, the local authority concerned shall specify the weekly amount which, having regard to subsection (4) of this section, they propose should be the amount of the contribution and the court shall not vary the contribution order so as to require the contributory to pay a contribution greater than that proposed by the local authority.

(8) In this section—

" contribution " means a contribution under section 86 of the Act of 1933; and

" contribution order " means an order under section 87 of that Act.

Returns of information and presentation of reports etc. to Parliament

63.—(1) Every local authority shall, at such times and in such form as the Secretary of State may direct, transmit to the Secretary of State such particulars as he may require—

(a) with respect to the performance by the local authority of all or any of [their functions under the enactments mentioned in subsection (6) of this section] [14] and

(b) with respect to the children in relation to whom the authority have exercised those functions.

(2) Every voluntary organisation shall, at such times and in such form as the Secretary of State may direct, transmit to him such particulars as he may require with respect to the children who are accommodated and maintained in voluntary homes provided by the organisation or who have been boarded out by the organisation.

(3) The clerk of each juvenile court shall, at such times and in such form as the Secretary of State may direct, transmit to him such particulars as he may require with respect to the proceedings of the court.

(4) The Secretary of State shall in each year lay before Parliament a

---

[14] Words substituted by Local Authority Social Services Act 1970 (c. 42), s. 14 (1), Sched. 2, para. 11.

consolidated and classified abstract of the information transmitted to him under the preceding provisions of this section.

(5) The Secretary of State shall lay before Parliament in 1973 and in every third subsequent year a report with respect to the exercise by local authorities of [their functions under the enactments mentioned in sub-section (6) of this section] [14] the provision by voluntary organisations of facilities for children and such other matters relating to children as he thinks fit.

[(6) The enactments referred to in subsections (1) and (5) of this section are—

(a) Parts III and IV of the Children and Young Persons Act 1933;
(b) the Children Act 1948;
(c) the Children Act 1958;
(d) the Adoption Act 1958;
(e) section 9 of the Mental Health Act 1959 and section 10 of that Act so far as it relates to children and young persons in respect of whom the rights and powers of a parent are vested in a local authority as mentioned in subsection (1) (a) of that section;
(f) section 10 of the Mental Health (Scotland) Act 1960 so far as it relates to children and young persons in respect of whom the rights and powers of a parent are vested in a local authority as mentioned in subsection (1) (a) of that section;
(g) section (2) (1) (f) of the Matrimonial Proceedings (Magistrates' Courts) Act 1960, [section 44 of the Matrimonial Causes Act 1973] [15] and section 7 (4) of the Land Reform Act 1969;
(h) the Children and Young Persons Act 1963, except Part II and section 56;
(i) this Act.] [16]

Financial provisions

Expenses of Secretary of State in providing homes offering specialised facilities

64. There shall be defrayed out of moneys provided by Parliament any expenses incurred by the Secretary of State in providing, equipping and maintaining homes for the accommodation of children who are in the care of local authorities and are in need of particular facilities and services which are provided in those homes and are, in the opinion of the Secretary of State, unlikely to be readily available in community homes.

Grants in respect of secure accommodation

64A.—(1) The Secretary of State may make to local authorities out of moneys provided by Parliament grants of such amount and subject to such conditions as he may with the consent of the Treasury determine in respect of expenditure incurred by the authorities in providing secure accommodation in community homes other than assisted community homes.

(2) The Secretary of State may with the consent of the Treasury require the local authority to repay the grant, in whole or in part, if the secure accommodation in respect of which the grant was made (including such accommodation in a controlled community home) ceases to be used as such.

(3) In this section " secure accommodation " means accommodation provided for the purposes of restricting the liberty of children in a community home.] [16a]

---

[15] Words substituted by Matrimonial Causes Act 1973 (c. 18), s. 54 (1) (a), Sched. 2.
[16] Words added by Local Authority Social Services Act 1970 (c. 42), s. 14 (1), Sched. 2, para. 11.
[16a] Added by Children Act 1975 (c. 72), s. 71.

Grants to voluntary organisations etc.

65.—(1) The Secretary of State may make out of moneys provided by Parliament grants to voluntary organisations of such amounts and subject to such conditions as he may with the consent of the Treasury determine towards expenditure incurred by them in connection with the establishment, maintenance or improvement of voluntary homes which at the time the expenditure was incurred were assisted community homes or were designated as such in a regional plan which was then in operation, including expenses incurred by them in respect of the borrowing of money to defray any such expenditure.

(2) The power of the Secretary of State to make grants to voluntary organisations under section 46 of the Children Act 1948 (which relates to grants in respect of certain expenses incurred in connection with voluntary homes) shall not apply to expenditure incurred in connection with a voluntary home which, at the time the expenditure was incurred, was a controlled or assisted community home or was designated as such in a regional plan which was then in operation.

(3) Where an order has been made under section 46 of this Act in relation to an approved institution within the meaning of that section and no such provision as is referred to in paragraph 9 (1) of Schedule 3 to this Act is made by a regional plan in relation to any part of the premises of the institution, the Secretary of State may with the consent of the Treasury make out of moneys provided by Parliament grants towards the discharge by any person of any liability, other than an obligation to which paragraph 11 of that Schedule applies, which was incurred by that person in connection with the establishment, maintenance or improvement of the institution.

(4) No grant shall be made under subsection (3) of this section in respect of a liability relating to an institution unless it appears to the Secretary of State that, on or within a reasonable time after the date specified in the order referred to in that subsection, the premises of the institution are to be used for a purpose which is of benefit to children; and any grant made under that subsection shall be subject to such conditions as the Secretary of State may with the approval of the Treasury determine, including conditions with respect to the repayment in whole or in part of the grant, either by the person to whom the grant was made or by some other person who, before the grant was made, consented to accept the liability.

(5) Any sums received by the Secretary of State by virtue of any such condition as is referred to in subsection (4) of this section shall be paid into the Consolidated Fund.

Increase of rate support grants

66.—(1) The power to make an order under section 3 (1) of the Local Government Act 1966 increasing the amounts fixed by a rate support grant order for a particular year shall be exercisable, in accordance with subsection (2) of this section, in relation to any rate support grant order made before the date of the coming into operation of any provision of this Act (in this section referred to as " the relevant provision ") for a grant period ending after that date.

(2) Without prejudice to subsection (4) of the said section 3 (which empowers an order under subsection (1) of that section to vary the matters prescribed by a rate support grant order), an order under subsection (1) of that section made by virtue of this section may be made for such year or years comprised in the grant period concerned as may be specified in the order and in respect of the year or each of the years so specified shall increase the amounts fixed by the relevant rate support grant order as the aggregate amounts of the rate support grants and any

elements of the grants for that year to such extent and in such a manner as may appear to the Minister of Housing and Local Government to be appropriate, having regard to any additional expenditure incurred or likely to be incurred by local authorities in consequence of the coming into operation of the relevant provision.

(3) In this section " grant period " means the period for which a rate support grant order is made.

(4) There shall be defrayed out of moneys provided by Parliament any increase in rate support grants attributable to this Act.

Administrative expenses

67. Any administrative expenses of the Secretary of State under this Act shall be defrayed out of moneys provided by Parliament.

Supplemental

68. [*Repealed by Local Government Act* 1972 (*c.* 70), *s.* 272 (1), *Sched.* 30.]

Orders and regulations etc.

69.—(1) Any power conferred on the Secretary of State by this Act to make an order or regulations, except an order under section 25, 39 or 43 (5) or paragraph 23 or 24 of Schedule 4, shall be exercisable by statutory instrument; and any statutory instrument made in pursuance of this subsection, except an instrument containing only regulations under paragraph 8 (2) of Schedule 3 or an order under section 1 (6), 26, 46, 47, 72 (2) or 73 (2), or paragraph 11 (2) of Schedule 3, shall be subject to annulment in pursuance of a resolution of either House of Parliament.

(2) A statutory instrument containing regulations under subsection (4) of section 5 or an order under section 34 of this Act shall not be subject to annulment as aforesaid, but no such regulations or order shall be included in a statutory instrument containing provisions which do not require approval in pursuance of the said subsection (4) or, as the case may be, to which subsection (7) of the said section 34 does not apply.

(3) An order made or directions given by the Secretary of State under any provision of this Act, except an order under section 7 (5), may be revoked or varied by a subsequent order or subsequent directions under that provision.

(4) Any order or regulations made by the Secretary of State under this Act may—

(*a*) make different provision for different circumstances;

(*b*) provide for exemptions from any provisions of the order or regulations; and

(*c*) contain such incidental and supplemental provisions as the Secretary of State considers expedient for the purposes of the order or regulations.

Interpretation and ancillary provisions

70.—(1) In this Act, unless the contrary intention appears, the following expressions have the following meanings:—

" the Act of 1933 " means the Children and Young Persons Act 1933;

" the Act of 1963 " means the Children and Young Persons Act 1963;

" approved school order ", " guardian " and " place of safety " have the same meanings as in the Act of 1933;

" care order " has the meaning assigned to it by section 20 of this Act;

" child ", except in Part II (including Schedule 3) and sections 27, 63, 64 and 65 of this Act, means a person under the age of fourteen, and in that Part (including that Schedule) and those sections means a person under the age of eighteen and a person who has attained the age of eighteen and is the subject of a care order;

" instrument of management " means an instrument of management made under section 39 of this Act;

" interim order " has the meaning assigned to it by section 20 of this Act;

" local authority " [except in relation to proceedings under section 1 of this Act instituted by a local education authority, means the council of a non-metropolitan county or of a metropolitan district] [17] or London borough or the Common Council of the City of London;

" petty sessions area " has the same meaning as in the Magistrates' Courts Act 1952 except that, in relation to a juvenile court constituted for the metropolitan area within the meaning of Part II of Schedule 2 to the Act of 1963, it means such a division of that area as is mentioned in paragraph 14 of that Schedule;

" planning area " has the meaning assigned to it by section 35 (1) of this Act;

" police officer " means a member of a police force;

" regional plan " has the meaning assigned to it by section 36 (1) of this Act;

" the relevant authorities ", in relation to a planning area, has the meaning assigned to it by section 35 (3) of this Act;

" reside " means habitually reside, and cognate expressions shall be construed accordingly except in section 12 (4) and (5) of this Act;

" supervision order ", " supervised person " and " supervisor " have the meanings assigned to them by section 11 of this Act;

" trust deed ", in relation to a voluntary home, has the meaning assigned to it by section 40 (5) of this Act;

" voluntary home " has the same meaning as in Part V of the Act of 1933;

" voluntary organisation " has the same meaning as in the Children Act 1948; and

" young person " means a person who has attained the age of fourteen and is under the age of seventeen;

and it is hereby declared that, in the expression " care or control ", " care " includes protection and guidance and " control " includes discipline.

(2) Without prejudice to any power apart from this subsection to bring proceedings on behalf of another person, any power to make an application which is exercisable by a child or young person by virtue of section 15 (1), 21 (2), 22 (4) or (6) or 28 (5) of this Act shall also be exercisable on his behalf by his parent or guardian; and in this subsection " guardian " includes any person who was a guardian of the child or young person in question at the time when any supervision order, care order or warrant to which the application relates was originally made.

(3) In section 99 (1) of the Act of 1933 (under which the age which a court presumes or declares to be the age of a person brought before it is deemed to be his true age for the purposes of that Act) the references to that Act shall be construed as including references to this Act.

[17] Words substituted by Local Government Act 1972 (c. 70), s. 195 (6), Sched. 23, para. 16.

(4) Subject to the following subsection, any reference in this Act to any enactment is a reference to it as amended, and includes a reference to it as applied, by or under any other enactment including this Act.

(5) Any reference in this Act to an enactment of the Parliament of Northern Ireland shall be construed as a reference to that enactment as amended by any Act of that Parliament, whether passed before or after this Act, and to any enactment of that Parliament for the time being in force which re-enacts the said enactment with or without modifications.

Application to Isles of Scilly

71. This Act shall have effect, in its application to the Isles of Scilly, with such modifications as the Secretary of State may by order specify.

Transitional provisions, minor amendments and repeals etc.

72.—(1) The transitional provisions and savings set out in Part I of Schedule 4 to this Act shall have effect.

(2) The transitional provisions set out in Part II of Schedule 4 to this Act shall have effect until such day as the Secretary of State may by order specify for the purposes of this subsection (being the day on and after which those provisions will in his opinion be unnecessary in consequence of the coming into force of provisions of the Social Work (Scotland) Act 1968) and shall be deemed to have been repealed on that day by an Act of Parliament passed after this Act.

(3) The enactments mentioned in Schedule 5 to this Act shall have effect subject to the amendments specified in that Schedule (which are minor amendments and amendments consequential on the provisions of this Act).

(4) Subject to subsection (1) of this section, the enactments mentioned in the first and second columns of Schedule 6 to this Act are hereby repealed to the extent specified in the third column of that Schedule.

(5) In accordance with Part II of this Act and the said Schedules 5 and 6, sections 1 to 6 and 14 of the Children Act 1958 are to have effect, after the coming into force of so much of that Part and those Schedules as relates to those sections, as set out in Schedule 7 to this Act, but without prejudice to any other enactment affecting the operation of those sections.

Citation, commencement and extent

73.—(1) This Act may be cited as the Children and Young Persons Act 1969, and this Act and the Children and Young Persons Acts 1933 to 1963 may be cited together as the Children and Young Persons Acts 1933 to 1969.

(2) This Act shall come into force on such day as the Secretary of State may by order appoint, and different days may be appointed under this subsection for different provisions of this Act or for different provisions of this Act so far as they apply to such cases only as may be specified in the order.[17a]

(3) Without prejudice to the generality of section 69 (4) of this Act, an order under the preceding subsection may make such transitional provision as the Secretary of State considers appropriate in connection with the provisions brought into force by the order, including such adaptations of those provisions and of any other provisions of this Act

[17a] The following sections were brought into force by 1970 S.I. No. 1498 on the dates shown:

On January 1, 1971: ss. 1–3, 5 (8)–(9) (part), 7 (2), (4)–(8), 9–23, 24 (1)–(4), (7)–(8) 25–28, 29 (1)–(3), (5)–(6), 30–34, 46 (2) (part), 56 (1) (*a*), 61, 62 (1), (3)–(8), 72 (1) (part), (3)–(5) (part), Scheds. 1 (part), 3–7 (part).

On April 1, 1971: s. 24 (5)–(6).

then in force as appear to him appropriate for the purposes or in consequence of the operation of any provision of this Act before the coming into force of any other provision of this Act or of a provision of the Social Work (Scotland) Act 1968.

(4) This section and the following provisions only of this Act extend to Scotland, that is to say—

(*a*) sections 10 (1) and (2), 32 (1), (3) and (4), 56 and 57 (1);

(*b*) section 72 (2) and Part II of Schedule 4;

(*c*) paragraphs 25, 26, 33, 35, 38, 42, 43, 53, 54 and 57 to 83 of Schedule 5 and section 72 (3) so far as it relates to those paragraphs;

(*d*) section 72 (4) and Schedule 6 so far as they relate to the Merchant Shipping Act 1894, the Superannuation (Miscellaneous Provisions) Act 1948, sections 10, 53, 55 and 59 of the Act of 1963, the Family Allowances Act 1965 and the Social Work (Scotland) Act 1968.

(5) This section and the following provisions only of this Act extend to Northern Ireland, that is to say—

(*a*) sections 25 and 32;

(*b*) section 72 (3) and Schedule 5 so far as they relate to section 29 of the Criminal Justice Act 1961 and provisions of the Social Work (Scotland) Act 1968 which extend to Northern Ireland; and

(*c*) section 72 (4) and Schedule 6 so far as they relate to section 83 of the Act of 1933, paragraph 13 of Schedule 2 to the Children and Young Persons (Scotland) Act 1937, section 29 of the Criminal Justice Act 1961, sections 10 (1) and (2), 53 (1) and 65 (5) of, and paragraphs 27, 34 and 50 of Schedule 3 to, the Act of 1963 and sections 73 (2), 76 (1) and (2) and 77 (1) (*b*) of the Social Work (Scotland) Act 1968;

and section 32 (2) and (3) of this Act shall be treated for the purposes of section 6 of the Government of Ireland Act 1920 as if it had been passed before the day appointed for the said section 6 to come into operation.

(6) Section 26 of this Act and this section, and section 72 (4) of this Act and Schedule 6 to this Act so far as they relate to paragraph 13 of Schedule 2 to the Children and Young Persons (Scotland) Act 1937 and section 53 (1) of, and paragraph 34 of Schedule 3 to, the Act of 1963, extend to the Channel Islands and the Isle of Man, and section 32 (1) and (4) of this Act and this section extend to the Channel Islands.

(7) It is hereby declared that the provisions of sections 69 and 70 of this Act extend to each of the countries aforesaid so far as is appropriate for the purposes of any other provisions of this Act extending to the country in question.

SCHEDULES

SCHEDULE 1

[*Repealed by Legal Aid Act 1974 (c. 4), Sched. 5.*]

Section 35 (4)   SCHEDULE 2

CHILDREN'S REGIONAL PLANNING COMMITTEES

1.—(1) Subject to the following provisions of this Schedule, the children's regional planning committee for a planning area (in this Schedule referred to as "the committee") shall consist of such number of persons selected and appointed in such manner and holding office on such terms as the relevant authorities may from time to time approve.

(2) No person who is disqualified by virtue of section 59 of the Local Government Act 1933 from being a member of any local authority which is one of the relevant authorities for a planning area may be a member of the committee for that area.

2.—(1) Subject to sub-paragraph (2) of this paragraph, the relevant authorities for a planning area shall so exercise their powers under paragraph 1 (1) of this Schedule as to secure that each authority nominates as a member of the committee for the area at least one person who is not so nominated by any other of the relevant authorities.

(2) If the Secretary of State considers that owing to special circumstances the requirement imposed by sub-paragraph (1) of this paragraph could be dispensed with in the case of a particular authority he may direct accordingly.

(3) The members of the committee for a planning area who are nominated by the relevant authorities are in the following provisions of this Schedule referred to as " the nominated members ".

3.—(1) Without prejudice to any power of co-option conferred on the committee for a planning area under paragraph 1 (1) of this Schedule, but subject to paragraph 4 of this Schedule, the nominated members of the committee may co-opt other persons to serve as members of the committee, either generally or in relation only to such matters as may be specified by the nominated members.

(2) Where any persons are co-opted to serve as members of the committee for a planning area in relation only to such matters as are specified by the nominated members then, subject to any directions given by the relevant authorities, the extent to which those persons shall be entitled to attend, speak and vote at meetings of the committee shall be such as may be determined by the nominated members.

4. The relevant authorities for a planning area shall so exercise their powers under paragraph 1 (1) of this Schedule, and the nominated members of the committee for a planning area shall so limit any exercise of their power under paragraph 3 of this Schedule, as to secure that at all times a majority of the members of the committee for the planning area are members of the relevant authorities.

5. Subject to any directions given by the relevant authorities, the procedure and quorum of the committee for a planning area shall be such as may be determined by the nominated members.

6. Section 93 (1) of the Local Government Act 1933 (which relates to the expenses of joint committees of local authorities) shall apply to the committee for a planning area as it applies to such a joint committee as is mentioned in that section, but as if—

(a) for references to the local authorities by whom the committee is appointed there were substituted references to the relevant authorities; and

(b) for paragraphs (a) and (b) of subsection (1) of that section there were substituted the words " by the Secretary of State ";

and [Part VIII of the Local Government Act 1972] [18] (which relates to accounts and audit) shall apply to the accounts of the committee for a planning area as it applies to the accounts of such a joint committee as is mentioned in [section 154 (1)] [18] of that Act.

Section 46 (2) SCHEDULE 3

APPROVED SCHOOLS AND OTHER INSTITUTIONS

Provisions as to staff

1.—(1) This paragraph applies where it appears to the Secretary of State that on the date specified in an order under section 46 of this Act (in the following provisions of this Schedule referred to as a " section 46 order ") all or any of the premises used for the purposes of the institution to which the order relates are to be used for the purposes—

(a) of a community home, or

(b) of a school of any of the following descriptions, namely, a county school, a voluntary school which is a controlled or aided school, or a special school;

and in this Schedule " the specified date ", in relation to an institution to which a section 46 order relates, means the date specified in that order.

(2) Where this paragraph applies the Secretary of State may, by the section 46 order, make such provision as he considers appropriate with respect to—

(a) the transfer of existing staff to the employment of the authority, voluntary

[18] Words substituted by Local Government Act 1972 (c. 70), s. 251 (2), Sched. 29, para. 16.

organisation or other body of persons responsible for the employment of persons at the community home or school, as the case may be; and

(*b*) the transfer to a local authority or voluntary organisation specified in the order of any liabilities (including contingent and future liabilities) with respect to the payment of superannuation and other benefits to or in respect of existing staff and retired staff.

[(3) In respect of any such superannuation or other benefits as are referred to in sub-paragraph (2) (*b*) of this paragraph, being benefits to which a person became entitled before the specified date and to which the Pensions (Increase) Act 1971 does not apply, the section 46 order may contain such provisions for securing the payment of additional amounts (calculated by reference to increases under that Act or under any enactment repealed by it) as the Secretary of State considers appropriate having regard to any arrangements obtaining with respect to those benefits before the specified date.] [19]

(4) Where this paragraph applies the section 46 order—

(*a*) shall contain provisions for the protection of the interests of any existing staff whose employment is transferred as mentioned in sub-paragraph (2) (*a*) of this paragraph;

(*b*) may contain provisions for the protection of the interests of existing staff whose employment is not so transferred; and

(*c*) may contain provisions applying, amending or repealing any provision made by or under any enactment and relating to the conditions of service of existing staff or the payment of superannuation and other benefits to or in respect of existing or retired staff;

and in a case falling within sub-paragraph (1) (*b*) of this paragraph any provisions made under paragraph (*a*) of this sub-paragraph shall have effect notwithstanding any provision made by or under any enactment and relating to the remuneration of teachers.

(5) In this paragraph " existing staff " in relation to a section 46 order means persons who, immediately before the specified date, were employed for the purposes of the institution to which the order relates, and " retired staff " in relation to such an order means persons who, at some time before the specified date, were employed for those purposes but ceased to be so employed before the specified date.

2. [*Sub-paragraph* (1) *repealed by Local Government Act* 1972 (*c.* 70), *s.* 272 (1), Sched. 30.]

(2) In accordance with sub-paragraph (1) of this paragraph, subsection (2) of the said section 60 shall be amended as follows :

(*a*) after the words " under the regulations " there shall be inserted the words " or, in a case to which paragraph 2 of Schedule 3 to the Children and Young Persons Act 1969 applies, by the Secretary of State "; and

(*b*) after the words " order under Part I of the Police Act 1964 " there shall be inserted the words " or of an order under section 46 of the Children and Young Persons Act 1969 ".

(3) Where a section 46 order is made in relation to an approved institution but paragraph 1 of this Schedule does not apply in relation to that institution, the section 46 order may make such provision as the Secretary of State considers appropriate with respect to the transfer to him of any such liabilities as are referred to in sub-paragraph (2) (*b*) of that paragraph and the payment by him of any such additional amount as is referred to in sub-paragraph (3) of that paragraph.

Use of premises as homes for children in care

3.—(1) If on the day specified for the purposes of section 7 (5) of this Act premises are used for the purposes of an approved school, then during the period (in this Schedule referred to, in relation to an approved school, as " the interim period ") beginning immediately after that day and ending on the day on which the school ceases to be an approved school (whether by virtue of a section 46 order or otherwise) those premises may be used for the accommodation and maintenance of children in the care of local authorities.

(2) If during the interim period the premises of an approved school are used for the accommodation and maintenance of children in the care of a local authority then, during that period,

---

[19] Sub-paragraph (3) substituted by Pensions Increase Act 1971 (c. 56), s. 7 (2), Sched. 3, para. 5.

Children and Young Persons Act 1969

(*a*) any reference in section 21 (1) or section 31 of this Act to a community home includes a reference to those premises; and

(*b*) for the reference in section 18 (1) (*c*) of the Criminal Justice Act 1961 (directions of Secretary of State as to management of approved schools) to persons under the care of the managers there shall be substituted a reference to the children in the care of local authorities who are accommodated and maintained in those premises.

(3) At the request of the managers of an approved school the Secretary of State may, at any time during the interim period, give a direction—

(*a*) that so much as may be specified in the direction of any rules made under paragraph 1 (1) of Schedule 4 to the Act of 1933 (approved school rules) and of any rules made by the managers and approved by him under paragraph 1 (2) of that Schedule shall no longer apply in relation to that school; and

(*b*) that, in place of those rules, so much as may be specified in the direction of any regulations made under section 43 of this Act shall apply, subject to such adaptations and modifications as may be so specified, in relation to the approved school as if it were a community home.

(4) If the effect of the application, by a direction under sub-paragraph (3) above, of any provision of regulations made under section 43 of this Act in relation to an approved school would be to impose any duty or confer any power on a local authority in relation to that school, the Secretary of State shall not give a direction applying that provision except with the consent of the local authority concerned.

4.—(1) If on the day specified for the purposes of section 7 (5) of this Act a remand home was designated under section 11 of the Act of 1963 as a classifying centre then, during the period beginning immediately after that day and ending on the date specified in a section 46 order relating to that home, the home may be used for the accommodation and maintenance of children in the care of local authorities.

(2) In this Schedule "classifying centre" means a remand home designated as mentioned in sub-paragraph (1) of this paragraph and, in relation to a classifying centre, the period specified in that sub-paragraph is referred to as "the interim period".

(3) During the interim period—

(*a*) the expenses of a local authority in providing and maintaining a classifying centre in relation to the whole or part of the expenses of which a direction has been given by the Secretary of State under section 11 (3) of the Act of 1963 shall be treated for the purposes of section 104 of the Act of 1933 as if they were expenses incurred by the authority as managers of an approved school;

(*b*) subsections (4) and (5) of section 106 of the Act of 1933 shall apply in relation to a classifying centre as they apply in relation to an approved school the managers of which are a local authority; and

(*c*) any reference in section 21 (1) or section 31 of this Act to a community home includes a reference to a classifying centre.

5.—(1) Where a section 46 order is made in relation to an approved school or approved probation hostel or home and, in a regional plan approved by the Secretary of State, the whole or any part of the premises of the institution is designated as a controlled or assisted community home, the premises so designated may, after the specified date, be used for the purpose specified in the regional plan.

(2) Without prejudice to any power to vary the provisions of a trust deed relating to a community home consisting of premises designated as mentioned in sub-paragraph (1) of this paragraph, the purpose referred to in that sub-paragraph shall be deemed to be included among the purposes for which the premises are held in accordance with a trust deed relating to that home.

6.—(1) Where a section 46 order is made in relation to an approved institution (other than an institution provided by a local authority) and, in a regional plan approved by the Secretary of State, the whole or any part of the premises of the institution is designated as a community home to be provided by a local authority, then if the Secretary of State is satisfied that the premises so designated were to a substantial extent provided with the assistance of grants under section 104 of the

376

Act of 1933 or [section 51 of the Powers of Criminal Courts Act 1973] [19a], he may, by an authorisation in writing under this paragraph, authorise the transfer of the premises so designated to that local authority.

(2) The transfer of any premises in pursuance of an authorisation under this paragraph—

(a) shall be on such terms, as to payment and other matters, as may be agreed between the local authority concerned and the trustees or other persons in whom the premises are vested and, if the authorisation so provides, as may be approved by the Secretary of State;

(b) shall not take effect before the specified date; and

(c) shall operate to vest the premises transferred in the local authority free from any charitable trust and from any other obligation requiring the use of the premises for the purposes of an approved institution.

(3) Before giving an authorisation under this paragraph authorising the transfer of any premises belonging to a charity or otherwise held on charitable trusts, the Secretary of State shall consult the Charity Commissioners.

7. The provisions of paragraphs 3 to 6 of this Schedule shall have effect notwithstanding anything in the law relating to charities or in any deed or other instrument regulating the purposes for which any premises may be used.

Financial provisions

8.—(1) During the period which is the interim period in relation to an approved school or to a classifying centre falling within paragraph 4 (3) (a) of this Schedule contributions shall be payable by local authorities to the managers of that school or, as the case may be, the local authority providing the classifying centre in respect of children in the care of the authorities who are accommodated and maintained in the school premises or the classifying centre in accordance with paragraph 3 (1) or paragraph 4 (1) of this Schedule.

(2) The contributions payable by a local authority under sub-paragraph (1) above in respect of a child in their care shall be payable throughout the time during which the child is accommodated and maintained in the approved school or classifying centre concerned and shall be such as may be prescribed by regulations made by the Secretary of State.

9.—(1) Where a section 46 order is made in relation to an approved institution, other than an institution provided by a local authority, and in a regional plan approved by the Secretary of State the whole or any part of the premises of the approved institution is designated as a community home, then,—

(a) on the coming into force of an instrument of management for a voluntary home which consists of or includes the premises so designated; or

(b) on the transfer of the premises so designated to a local authority in pursuance of an authorisation under paragraph 6 of this Schedule,

any such obligation relating to that institution as is referred to in sub-paragraph (2) of this paragraph shall cease.

(2) Sub-paragraph (1) of this paragraph applies to any obligation arising by virtue of a condition imposed under either of the following enactments, namely,—

(a) section 104 of the Act of 1933 (expenses of managers of an approved school); or

(b) [section 51 of the Powers of Criminal Courts Act 1973] [19a] (expenditure in connection with approved probation hostels or homes).

(3) In a case falling within sub-paragraph (1) of this paragraph, the section 46 order may contain provisions requiring the responsible authority or organisation or, as the case may be, the local authority to whom the premises are transferred, to pay to the Secretary of State such sum as he may determine in accordance with sub-paragraph (4) of this paragraph by way of repayment of a proportion of any grants made in relation to the former approved institution under either of the enactments referred to in sub-paragraph (2) of this paragraph, but where the community home concerned is an assisted community home, the section 46 order may provide that, with the consent of the Treasury, the Secretary of State may reduce the sum to be paid to him in accordance with the preceding provisions of this sub-paragraph to such sum as he thinks fit.

(4) For the purpose of determining any such sum as is mentioned in sub-paragraph (3) of this paragraph, the Secretary of State shall assess—

[19a] Words substituted by Powers of Criminal Courts Act 1973 (c. 62), Sched. 5.

(*a*) the amount which in his opinion represents the proportion of the total amount of the grants paid in respect of expenditure in connection with the former approved institution which was attributable to expenditure of a capital nature; and

(*b*) the amount which in his opinion represents the proportion of the contributions paid by local authorities under section 90 of the Act of 1933 or, as the case may be, the proportion of the sums paid by probation committees under rules made under [Schedule 3 to the Powers of Criminal Courts Act 1973] [19a] which (in either case) should be treated as having been paid on account of expenditure of a capital nature in connection with the former approved institution;

and the sum determined by the Secretary of State for the purpose of sub-paragraph (3) of this paragraph shall be equal to the amount by which the amount assessed under paragraph (*a*) above exceeds twice the amount assessed under paragraph (*b*) above.

(5) If the instrument of management for an assisted community home ceases to have effect as mentioned in subsection (1) of section 48 of this Act there shall be deducted from any sum which is payable to the Secretary of State under subsection (5) of that section any sums paid to him by the responsible organisation in respect of the assisted community home in pursuance of any such provisions of a section 46 order relating to the former approved institution as are referred to in sub-paragraph (3) of this paragraph.

(6) In this paragraph "the former approved institution", in relation to a community home, means the approved institution the whole or part of the premises of which are comprised in that home.

10.—(1) The provisions of this paragraph apply where in a regional plan approved by the Secretary of State, the whole or any part of the premises of an approved institution to which a section 46 order relates is designated as a controlled or assisted community home and an instrument of management for a community home which consists of or includes the premises so designated has come into force; and in this paragraph "the former approved institution", in relation to such a community home, means the approved institution the whole or part of the premises of which are comprised in that home.

(2) Where this paragraph applies and the community home concerned is a controlled community home, then—

(*a*) the Secretary of State may, by the section 46 order, make such provision as he considers appropriate for the transfer to the responsible authority of any rights, liabilities and obligations which, immediately before the specified date, were rights, liabilities and obligations of the managers of, or the society or person carrying on, the former approved institution; and

(*b*) except in so far as the section 46 order otherwise provides, any legal proceedings pending immediately before the specified date by or against those managers or that society or person shall be continued on and after that date, with the substitution of the responsible authority for those managers or that society or person as a party to the proceedings.

(3) Where this paragraph applies and the community home concerned is an assisted community home but the responsible organisation does not consist of the persons who were the managers of or, as the case may be, is not the society or person who carried on, the former approved institution, paragraphs (*a*) and (*b*) of sub-paragraph (2) of this paragraph shall apply with the substitution for any reference to the responsible authority of a reference to the responsible organisation.

(4) If any liabilities of a voluntary organisation which is the responsible organisation in relation to an assisted community home falling within sub-paragraph (1) of this paragraph were incurred by the organisation before the specified date or were transferred to the organisation by the section 46 order (by virtue of sub-paragraph (3) of this paragraph) and, in either case, had the former approved institution continued to be an approved institution, any expenditure incurred in meeting those liabilities would have been eligible for a grant out of moneys provided by Parliament—

(*a*) under section 104 (1) (*a*) of the Act of 1933 as the expenses of the managers of an approved school, or

(b) under section 77 (3) (*b*) of the Criminal Justice Act 1948 [or under section 51 (3) (*c*) of the Powers of Criminal Courts Act 1973] [19a], as expenditure

378

falling within that section and relating to an approved probation hostel or home,
then any expenditure incurred after the specified date by the responsible organisation in meeting those liabilities shall be deemed for the purposes of section 65 (1) of this Act to be expenditure incurred by the responsible organisation in connection with the assisted community home in question.

11.—(1) Where a section 46 order is made in relation to an approved institution and no such provision as is referred to in sub-paragraph (1) of paragraph 9 of this Schedule is made by a regional plan in relation to any part of the premises of the institution, the person or persons on whom falls any such obligation (in this paragraph referred to as a "repayment obligation") relating to the institution as is referred to in sub-paragraph (2) of that paragraph may apply to the Secretary of State for an order under this paragraph.

(2) If, on an application under sub-paragraph (1) of this paragraph, it appears to the Secretary of State that on or within a reasonable time after the specified date the premises of the institution concerned or the proceeds of sale of the whole or any part of those premises are to be used for a purpose which is of benefit to children, he may with the consent of the Treasury make an order—

(*a*) substituting for the conditions under which the repayment obligation arose such different conditions as he considers appropriate with respect to the repayment of any sum to which the repayment obligation relates; and

(*b*) if the person or persons on whom the repayment obligation falls so request, imposing any liability to repay a sum in pursuance of the substituted conditions referred to in paragraph (*a*) above on such other person or persons as consent to accept the liability and as, in the opinion of the Secretary of State, will be able to discharge that liability.

Interpretation

12. In this Schedule—

"approved institution" has the same meaning as in section 46 of this Act;

"the responsible authority", in relation to a controlled community home, has the same meaning as in section 41 of this Act;

"the responsible organisation", in relation to an assisted community home, has the same meaning as in section 42 of this Act; and

"section 46 order" and, in relation to an institution to which such an order relates, "specified date" have the meanings assigned to them by paragraph 1 (1) of this Schedule.

Section 72 (1) (2) SCHEDULE 4

TRANSITIONAL PROVISIONS AND SAVINGS

PART I

GENERAL

1. For the purposes of subsection (4) of section 1 and subsection (7) of section 7 of this Act, any order under the Act of 1933 committing a child or young person to the care of a fit person other than a local authority, any supervision order under that Act and any order to enter into recognisances in pursuance of section 62 (1) (*c*) of that Act shall be deemed to be such an earlier order as is mentioned in those subsections.

2.—(1) Nothing in section 4 of this Act affects any proceedings against a person for an offence with which by virtue of that section he has ceased to be chargeable since the proceedings were begun; but where a person is found guilty of an offence and by reason of that section could not have been charged with it on the date of finding, then, subject to sections 1 (5) and 2 (13) of this Act, the court may make an order under section 1 of this Act in respect of the offender or an order discharging him absolutely but shall not have power to make any other order in consequence of the finding.

(2) Nothing in section 4 of this Act shall be construed as preventing any act or omission which occurred outside the United Kingdom from being a civil offence for the purposes of the Army Act 1955, the Air Force Act 1955, or the Naval Discipline Act 1957, or from being dealt with under any of those Acts.

3. Nothing in section 5 of this Act affects any information laid in respect of a person before the date on which apart from this paragraph the information would have been required by virtue of that section to contain a statement of his age.

4. Where a person is committed for trial by a jury before subsection (1) of section 6 of this Act comes into force, or claims to be tried by a jury before subsection (2) of that section comes into force, proceedings in respect of the offence in question shall not be affected by the coming into force of that subsection.

5.—(1) The coming into force of section 7 (1) or of an order under section 34 (1) (d) of this Act shall not affect any sentence of borstal training passed before the date when the said section 7 (1) or the order came into force or any committal for sentence before that date under section 28 (1) of the Magistrates' Courts Act 1952; but a sentence of borstal training shall not be passed on any person (including a person to whom such a committal relates) if on the date of the relevant conviction he had not attained the minimum age which is for the time being specified in section 20 (1) of the Criminal Justice Act 1948.

(2) Nothing in section 7 (2) of this Act affects a probation order made before the coming into force of the said section 7 (2).

6. No order shall be made under section 19 (1) of the Criminal Justice Act 1948, at any time after the coming into force of this paragraph and before the coming into force of paragraph 23 of Schedule 5 to this Act, in respect of a person under the age of seventeen in consequence of a default within the meaning of the Criminal Justice Act 1961.

7.—(1) Every approved school order in force on the specified day shall cease to have effect at the end of that day; and after that day—

    (a) no person shall be detained by virtue of section 73 or section 82 of the Act of 1933 or an order under paragraph 2 of Schedule 2 to the said Act of 1961 or be subject to supervision in pursuance of that Schedule; and

    (b) no person who has attained the age of nineteen shall be detained by virtue of a warrant under section 15 of the said Act of 1961.

(2) A person who has not attained the age of nineteen on the specified day and who, but for sub-paragraph (1) of this paragraph, would after that day have been the subject of an approved school order or liable to b_ detained or subject to supervision as mentioned in that sub-paragraph shall be deemed from the end of that day—

    (a) to be the subject of a care order made by the court which made the approved school order in question on the same day as that order and committing him to the care of the local authority named in the approved school order in pursuance of section 70 (2) of the Act of 1933 or, if no authority is so named, of a local authority nominated in relation to him by the Secretary of State; and

    (b) in the case where he would have been subject to supervision as aforesaid, to have been allowed by the said local authority to be under the charge and control of the person last nominated in relation to him in pursuance of paragraph 1 (1) of Schedule 2 to the said Act of 1961;

but nothing in this paragraph shall be construed as affecting the validity of a warrant under the said section 15 in relation to a person who has not attained the age of nineteen.

In relation to a person in respect of whom two or more approved school orders would have been in force after the specified day but for sub-paragraph (1) of this paragraph, references to such an order in paragraph (a) of this sub-paragraph are to the later or latest of the orders.

(3) The Secretary of State may from time to time nominate another local authority in the place of a local authority nominated by him in pursuance of the preceding sub-paragraph or this sub-paragraph.

(4) A person who is the subject of a care order by virtue of sub-paragraph (2) of this paragraph and who was unlawfully absent on the specified day from an approved school in which he was then required to be shall, until the local authority to whose care he is committed by the order direct otherwise, be deemed for the purposes of section 32 of this Act to be duly required by the authority to live after that day in the premises which on that day constituted the school.

(5) A person who on the specified day is the subject of an approved school order or subject to supervision in pursuance of the said Schedule 2 or eligible for assistance under paragraph 7 of that Schedule and is not the subject of a care order from the end of that day by virtue of sub-paragraph (2) of this paragraph shall be deemed

for the purposes of section 20 of the Children Act 1948 and section 58 of the Act of 1963 (which authorise local authorities to provide assistance for persons formerly in care) to have been in the care of a local authority under the Children Act 1948 on that day, notwithstanding that he may then have attained the age of eighteen; and in relation to such a person the reference in the said section 58 to the local authority shall be construed as a reference to any local authority.

(6) If an order under section 88 of the Act of 1933 is in force at the end of the specified day in respect of payments under an affiliation order made for the maintenance of a person who is deemed by virtue of this paragraph to be subject to a care order after that day, the order under that section shall after that day be deemed to have been made by virtue of the care order, under that section as modified by this Act.

(7) A direction restricting discharge which was given under section 74 of the Mental Health Act 1959 in respect of a person detained by virtue of an approved school order and which is in force at the end of the specified day shall cease to have effect at the end of that day.

(8) References to an approved school order in this paragraph, except in sub-paragraph (2) (*a*), include references to an order of the competent authority under subsection (1) of section 83 of the Act of 1933 and such an order as is mentioned in subsection (3) of that section; and in relation to those orders this paragraph shall have effect as if for sub-paragraph (2) (*a*) there were substituted the following—

" (*a*) to be the subject of a care order made by a court in England on the date when the order for his detention in a school was made under the relevant law mentioned in section 83 of the Act of 1933 and committing him to the care of a local authority nominated in relation to him by the Secretary of State; and "

(9) In this paragraph " the specified day " means the day specified for the purposes of section 7 (5) of this Act.

8.—(1) An order under the Act of 1933 committing a child or young person to the care of a local authority as a fit person and in force on the date when section 7 (6) of this Act comes into force shall be deemed on and after that date to be a care order committing him to the care of that authority.

(2) Sub-paragraph (6) of the preceding paragraph shall have effect for the purposes of this paragraph as if for references to that paragraph and the specified day there were substituted respectively references to this paragraph and the day preceding the date mentioned in the preceding sub-paragraph.

9. Except as provided by paragraph 1 of this Schedule and this paragraph, nothing in this Act affects—

(*a*) an order under the Act of 1933 committing a child or young person to the care of a fit person other than a local authority and in force on the date when section 7 (6) of this Act comes into force; or

(*b*) the operation of any enactment in relation to such an order;

but where an application for the variation or revocation of the order is considered on or after that date by a juvenile court in pursuance of section 84 (6) of the Act of 1933, the court shall have power (to the exclusion of its powers under the said section 84 (6)) to refuse the application or to revoke the order and, where it revokes the order, to make a care order in respect of the child or young person in question.

10. Without prejudice to the preceding paragraph, a person who is subject to such an order as is mentioned in sub-paragraph (*a*) of that paragraph is not a foster-child within the meaning of Part I of the Children Act 1958.

11. Notwithstanding anything in section 20 (3) or 21 (1) of this Act, an order which is a care order by virtue of paragraph 8 of this Schedule and a care order made by virtue of paragraph 9 of this Schedule shall, unless previously revoked, cease to have effect when the child or young person in question attains the age of eighteen.

12.—(1) Where a supervision order under the Children and Young Persons Acts 1933 to 1963 is in force on the date when this paragraph comes into force or where an order under section 52 of the Act of 1963 (whether made before, on or after that date) falls to be treated by virtue of subsection (3) of that section as a supervision order under the Act of 1933, the order and, in relation to the order, any enactment amended or repealed by this Act shall, subject to the following provisions of this paragraph, have effect as if this Act had not been passed; and the order may be altered or revoked accordingly.

(2) A juvenile court before which the person to whom such a supervision order relates is brought after the date aforesaid in pursuance of subsection (1) of section 66 of the Act of 1933 shall not have power to make such an order as is mentioned in that subsection in respect of him but shall instead have power to revoke the supervision order and make a care order in respect of him on being satisfied that he is unlikely to receive the care or control he needs unless the court makes a care order; and section 6 (1) of the Act of 1963 shall not apply in a case where the court exercises its power under this sub-paragraph.

(3) Where such a supervision order contains a provision requiring residence in an institution which has become a community home, the provision shall be construed as requiring residence in the home; and in such a case any reference to an institution of the kind in question in rules under the [Powers of Criminal Courts Act 1973] [19a] providing for the making of payments to the body or person by whom the institution is managed shall be construed as a reference to the home.

(4) References to a supervision order in sub-paragraphs (2) and (3) of this paragraph include references to an order under the said section 52.

13.—(1) During the period beginning with the coming into force of section 35 of this Act and ending with the coming into operation of a regional plan for a particular planning area—

(a) sections 15 and 16 of the Children Act 1948 shall continue to apply in relation to each of the relevant authorities; and

(b) each of the relevant authorities may continue to exercise the power conferred by subsection (2) of section 19 of that Act, as it had effect immediately before the passing of this Act, to accommodate persons in hostels provided under that section; and

(c) section 77 (1) of the Act of 1933 shall continue to apply in relation to each of the relevant authorities as if for the words "the duty of" there were substituted the words "lawful for".

(2) Where different parts of the area of a local authority are comprised in different planning areas then, in relation to that local authority, the period specified in sub-paragraph (1) of this paragraph shall not expire until a regional plan has come into operation for each of those planning areas.

(3) If on the submission of a regional plan for a planning area to the Secretary of State part only of the plan is approved by him, any reference in the preceding provisions of this paragraph to the coming into operation of a regional plan for that area shall be construed as a reference to the coming into operation of a further regional plan containing all necessary supplementary proposals for that area.

14. If immediately before the coming into force of section 49 of this Act any person has, under section 3 (3) of the Children Act 1948, the care and control of a child (within the meaning of that Act) with respect to whom a resolution under section 2 of that Act is in force, then after the coming into force of that section the child shall again be in the care of the local authority by whom the resolution was passed but shall be deemed to have been allowed by that authority, under section 13 (2) of that Act (as substituted by the said section 49), to be under the charge and control of that person, on the same terms as were applicable under the said section 3 (3).

15. It shall be lawful for a person detained in any place in pursuance of section 27 of the Criminal Justice Act 1948 at the time when paragraph 24 of Schedule 5 to this Act comes into force to be detained there thereafter, until he is next delivered thence in due course of law, as if that paragraph had not come into force.

16. Nothing in paragraph 29 of Schedule 5 to this Act affects the operation of section 2 (4) of the Children Act 1958 in relation to a supervision order made under the Children and Young Persons (Scotland) Act 1937.

17. Nothing in Schedule 6 to this Act affects the operation of section 15 (3) of the Adoption Act 1958 in relation to a fit person order made under the Children and Young Persons (Scotland) Act 1937.

18. Nothing in any provision of Schedule 6 to this Act affects any order which, immediately before the coming into force of that provision, is in force by virtue of any enactment repealed by that provision.

Part II

Interim provisions pending commencement of provisions of Social Work (Scotland) Act 1968

19. Where a court in England or Wales by which a child or young person is found guilty of an offence is satisfied that he resides or will reside in Scotland, the court shall have power, without prejudice to its other powers and notwithstanding anything in section 7 (2) of this Act, to make a probation order in respect of him in accordance with sections 3 and 9 of the Criminal Justice Act 1948.

20. In section 51 (1) of the Act of 1963, for the words " principal Act " there shall be substituted the words " Children and Young Persons Act 1969 in proceedings under section 1 of that Act."

21. In section 51 (2) of the Act of 1963, for the words from " proposes " to " this Act " there shall be substituted ", or a supervision order under the Children and Young Persons Act 1969 has been made in proceedings under section 1 of that Act, proposes to reside or is residing in Scotland " and for the words " specified in the supervision order " there shall be substituted the words " for which the supervision order would have continued in force if it had been allowed to continue in force until it ceased to have effect by the effluxion of time."

22. Where a juvenile court in England or Wales is satisfied that a person who has not attained the age of eighteen and in respect of whom a supervision order made by virtue of section 7 (7) (*b*) of this Act or section 7A (4) of the Criminal Justice (Scotland) Act 1949 is in force resides or will reside in Scotland, the court may discharge the order and exercise the like powers to make a probation order in accordance with sections 3 and 9 of the Criminal Justice Act 1948 in respect of him as if in the proceedings it had duly found him guilty of the offence in consequence of which the supervision order was made and section 7 (2) of this Act had not been passed; but a probation order made by virtue of this paragraph shall not continue in force after the date on which the discharged supervision order would have ceased to have effect by the effluxion of time.

23.—(1) Where it appears to the local authority to whose care a person is committed by a care order that his parent or guardian resides or will reside in Scotland and that it is appropriate to transfer him to the care of the managers of an approved school in Scotland, the authority shall make a report on the case to the Secretary of State; and thereupon the Secretary of State may, if he thinks fit, make an order transferring the person in question to the care of the managers of such a school.

(2) The provisions of the Children and Young Persons (Scotland) Acts 1937 to 1963 shall apply to an order made under this paragraph as if it were an approved school order made by a juvenile court in Scotland on the date on which the care order in question was originally made; but notwithstanding anything in section 75 of the said Act of 1937 such an order shall cease to have effect on the date when the care order in question would have ceased to have effect by the effluxion of time and the contributions to be made under section 94 of the said Act of 1937 in respect of the person to whom the order under this paragraph relates shall be made by the authority nominated for the purpose in the order under this paragraph, being the education authority within whose area it appears to the Secretary of State at the time that order is made that his parent or guardian resides or will reside.

(3) When a person is received into the care of the managers of an approved school in pursuance of an order under this paragraph, the care order in question shall cease to have effect.

24. If it appears to the Secretary of State that the parent or guardian of a person who has not attained the age of nineteen and is the subject of an approved school order in force under the Children and Young Persons (Scotland) Act 1937, or such other order as is mentioned in subsection (1) or subsection (3) of section 87 of that Act, resides or will reside in the area of a local authority in England or Wales, the Secretary of State may make an order committing that person to the care of that authority; and an order under this paragraph shall have effect as if it were a care order made on the date on which the approved school or other order was made, but as if sections 20 (2) and 21 (5) of this Act were omitted.

MINOR AND CONSEQUENTIAL AMENDMENTS OF ENACTMENTS

The Police (Property) Act 1897

[*Paragraph* (1) *repealed by Criminal Justice Act* 1972 (*c.* 71), *s.* 64 (2), *Sched.* 6, *Pt. II.*]

The Act of 1933

2. In section 10 of the Act of 1933, after subsection (1) there shall be inserted the following subsection :—

(1A) Proceedings for an offence under this section shall not be instituted except by a local education authority; and before instituting such proceedings the authority shall consider whether it would be appropriate, instead of or as well as instituting the proceedings, to bring the child or young person in question before a juvenile court under section 1 of the Children and Young Persons Act 1969.

3. In section 34 (2) of the Act of 1933, after the words "be taken" there shall be inserted the words "by the person who arrested him".

4. In section 46 of the Act of 1933, after subsection (1) there shall be inserted the following subsection :—

(1A) If a notification that the accused desires to plead guilty without appearing before the court is received by the clerk of a court in pursuance of section 1 of the Magistrates' Courts Act 1957 and the court has no reason to believe that the accused is a child or young person, then, if he is a child or young person he shall be deemed to have attained the age of seventeen for the purposes of subsection (1) of this section in its application to the proceedings in question.

5. In section 55 (1) of the Act of 1933, for the words "charged with" there shall be substituted the words "found guilty of" and after the word "care" there shall be inserted the words "or control".

6. In section 56 (1) of the Act of 1933, for the word "resides" there shall be substituted the words "habitually resides".

7. Section 63 of the Act of 1933 shall cease to have effect.

8. In section 86 (1) of the Act of 1933 for the words from "an order" to "approved school" there shall be substituted the words "a care order which is not an interim order has been made in respect of a child or young person".

9.—(1) In subsection (1) of section 87 of the Act of 1933, for the words from "an order has" to "same time, and" there shall be substituted the words "a care order which is not an interim order has been made in respect of a child or young person then, subject to section 62 of the Children and Young Persons Act 1969".

(2) For subsection (2) of that section, there shall be substituted the following subsection :—

(2) A contribution order in respect of a child or young person may be made on the application of the local authority entitled to receive contributions in respect of him.

(3) In subsection (3) of that section for the words from "in the case", in the first place where they occur, onwards there shall be substituted the words "as long as the child or young person to whom it relates is in the care of the local authority concerned".

10.—(1) In subsection (1) of section 88 of the Act of 1933 for the words from "ordered" to "approved school" there shall be substituted the words "the subject of a care order (other than an interim order)"; for the words "that court" there shall be substituted the words "the court which makes the order"; for the words "the person who is" there shall be substituted the words "the local authority who are", and for the words "the persons by whom, and in the circumstances in which" there shall be substituted the words "the local authorities by whom".

(2) In subsection (2) (*c*) of that section, for the words "person who was" there shall be substituted the words "local authority who were".

(3) In subsection (4) of that section, for paragraphs (*a*) and (*b*) there shall be substituted the words "after the child or young person to whom that order relates has ceased to be the subject of the care order by virtue of which the order under this section was made or, where this section applies by virtue of section 23 of the Children Act 1948, after he has ceased to be in the care of a local authority under

section 1 of that Act or, in either case, if he is allowed by the local authority to be under the charge and control of a parent, guardian, relative or friend, although remaining in the care of the local authority ".

11. In section 106 (2) (*a*) of the Act of 1933, for the words from " fifty-seven " to " Schedule to " there shall be substituted the words " eighty-seven and eighty-eight of ".

12.—(1) In section 107 (1) of the Act of 1933, after the words " that is to say " there shall be inserted the following words :—

" care order " and " interim order " have the same meanings as in the Children and Young Persons Act 1969.

(2) In the said section 107 (1), in the definition of " place of safety ", for the words " any home provided by a local authority under Part II of the Children Act 1948 any remand home or " there shall be substituted the words " a community home provided by a local authority or a controlled community home, any ".

(3) Section 107 (2) of the Act of 1933 shall cease to have effect.

The Education Act 1944

13. For subsections (2) to (5) of section 40 of the Education Act 1944 there shall be substituted the following subsections :—

(2) Proceedings for such offences as aforesaid shall not be instituted except by a local education authority; and before instituting such proceedings the authority shall consider whether it would be appropriate, instead of or as well as instituting the proceedings, to bring the child in question before a juvenile court under section 1 of the Children and Young Persons Act 1969.

(3) The court by which a person is convicted of an offence against section 37 of this Act or before which a person is charged with an offence against section 39 of this Act may if it thinks fit direct the authority who instituted the proceedings to bring the child to whom the proceedings relate before a juvenile court under the said section 1; and it shall be the duty of the authority to comply with the direction.

(4) Where a child in respect of whom a school attendance order is in force is brought before a juvenile court by a local education authority under the said section 1 and the court finds that the condition set out in subsection (2) (*e*) of that section is not satisfied with respect to him, the court may direct that the order shall cease to be in force.

The Children Act 1948

14. In section 4 (3) of the Children Act 1948, the proviso shall cease to have effect.

15. In section 20 (1) of the said Act of 1948, for the words " any such person as is mentioned in subsection (1) of the last foregoing section " there shall be substituted the words " any person over compulsory school age but under the age of twenty one who is, or has at any time after ceasing to be of compulsory school age been, in the care of a local authority ".

16. In section 23 (1) of the said Act of 1948 for the words from " committed " in the second place where it occurs to the end of the subsection there shall be substituted the words " in the care of a local authority by virtue of such an order as is mentioned in subsection (1) of the said section 86 ".

17.—(1) In section 26 (1) of the said Act of 1948 for paragraph (*b*) there shall be substituted the following paragraph :—

(*b*) an illegitimate child is in the care of a local authority by virtue of such an order as is mentioned in section 86 (1) of the Children and Young Persons Act 1933, or.

(2) In subsections (3) and (4) (*b*) of the said section 26, for the words " person who is " there shall be substituted the words " local authority who are ", and in subsection (4) of that section for the words " (*b*) or (*c*) " there shall be substituted the words " or (*b*) ".

[18. In section 39 (1) of the said Act of 1938 after paragraph (*h*) there shall be inserted the following paragraph :—

(*i*) the Children and Young Persons Act 1969.] [20]

19. In section 43 (1) of the said Act of 1948 for the words from " Parts IV and

[20] Words repealed by Local Authority (Social Services) Act 1970 (c. 42), s. 14, Sched. 3.

V." onwards there shall be substituted the words "the Children and Young Persons Act 1933 to 1969, the Adoption Act 1958 and the Adoption Act 1968".

20.—(1) In subsection (1) of section 51 of the said Act of 1948, for the words from "homes" to "this Act" there shall be substituted the words "community homes provided by them or in controlled community homes" and at the end of that subsection there shall be added the words "or sections 2 (5), 16 (3) or 28 of the Children and Young Persons Act 1969 and of children detained by them in pursuance of arrangements under section 29 (3) of that Act".

(2) In subsection (3) of the said section 51, for the words from "home" to "this Act" there shall be substituted the words "community home provided by a local authority or a controlled community home".

21.—(1) In subsection (3) of section 54 of the said Act of 1948, after the word "area" in the first place where it occurs there shall be inserted the words "other than community homes" and after the word "any" in the last place where it occurs, there shall be inserted the word "such".

(2) In subsection (4) of that section, for the words from "as a fit person" to the end of the subsection there shall be substituted the words "by a care order within the meaning of the Children and Young Persons Act 1969 or by a warrant under section 23 (1) of that Act."

(3) In subsection (5) of that section, for the words from "ninety-four" to "1933" there shall be substituted the words "section 58 of the Children and Young Persons Act 1969".

22. In section 59 (1) of the said Act of 1948, at the end of the definition of "child" there shall be added the words "and any person who has attained that age and is the subject of a care order within the meaning of the Children and Young Persons Act 1969".

The Criminal Justice Act 1948

23. In section 19 (1) of the Criminal Justice Act 1948, after the words "who is" there shall be inserted the words "not less than seventeen but".

24. For section 27 of the said Act of 1948 there shall be substituted the following section:—

Remand of persons aged 17 to 20

27.—(1) Where a court remands a person charged with or convicted of an offence or commits him for trial or sentence and he is not less than seventeen but under twenty-one years old and is not released on bail, then, if the court has been notified by the Secretary of State that a remand centre is available for the reception from the court of persons of his class or description, it shall commit him to a remand centre and, if it has not been so notified, it shall commit him to a prison.

(2) Where a person is committed to a remand centre in pursuance of this section, the centre shall be specified in the warrant and he shall be detained there for the period for which he is remanded or until he is delivered thence in due course of law.

(3) In this section "court" includes a justice; and nothing in this section affects the provisions of section 105 (5) of the Magistrates' Courts Act 1952 (which provides for remands to the custody of a constable).

The Criminal Justice (Scotland) Act 1949

25. In section 7 of the Criminal Justice (Scotland) Act 1949, after the words "that the offender" in subsection (1) and "that the probationer" in subsection (2) there shall be inserted the words "has attained the age of seventeen and".

26. After section 7 of the said Act of 1949 there shall be inserted the following section:—

Further provisions as to probation orders relating to persons residing or formerly residing in England

7A.—(1) Where the court by which a probation order is made under section 2 of this Act or subsection (6) of this section is satisfied that the person to whom the order relates is under the age of seventeen and resides or will reside in England, subsection (2) of the said section 2 shall not apply to the order but the order shall name the petty sessions area in which that person resides or will reside and the court shall send notification of the order to the clerk to the justices for that area.

(2) Where a probation order has been made under section 2 of this Act or subsection (6) of this section and the court which made the order or the appropriate court is satisfied that the person to whom the

order relates is under the age of seventeen and proposes to reside or is residing in England, the power of that court to amend the order under Schedule 2 to this Act shall include power, without summoning him and without his consent, to insert in the order the name of the petty sessions area aforesaid; and where the court exercises the power conferred on it by virtue of this subsection it shall send notification of the order to the clerk aforesaid.

(3) A court which sends a notification to a clerk in pursuance of the foregoing provisions of this section shall send to him with it three copies of the probation order in question and such other documents and information relating to the case as it considers likely to be of assistance to the juvenile court mentioned in the following subsection.

(4) It shall be the duty of the clerk to whom a notification is sent in pursuance of the foregoing provisions of this section to refer the notification to a juvenile court acting for the petty sessions area named in the order, and on such a reference the court—

 (a) may make a supervision order under the Children and Young Persons Act 1969 in respect of a person to whom the notification relates; and

 (b) if it does not make such an order, shall dismiss the case.

(5) A supervision order made by virtue of the foregoing subsection shall not include a requirement authorised by section 12 of the said Act of 1969 unless the supervised person is before the court when the supervision order is made, and in relation to a supervision order made by virtue of that subsection—

 (a) section 15 of that Act shall have effect as if in subsection (4) paragraph (b) and the words following it were omitted; and

 (b) section 17 (a) of that Act shall have effect as if the second reference to the supervision order were a reference to the probation order in consequence of which the supervision order is made;

and when a juvenile court disposes of a case referred to it in pursuance of the foregoing subsection, the probation order in consequence of which the reference was made shall cease to have effect.

(6) The court which, in pursuance of subsection (1) of section 73 of the Social Work (Scotland) Act 1968, considers a case referred to it in consequence of a notification under paragraph (i) of that subsection (which relates to a case in which a person subject to a supervision order made by virtue of this section moves to Scotland)—

 (a) may, if it is of opinion that the person to whom the notification relates should continue to be under supervision, make a probation order in respect of him for a period specified in the order; and

 (b) if it does not make such an order, shall dismiss the case;

and when the court disposes of a case in pursuance of this subsection the supervision order aforesaid shall cease to have effect.

(7) Notwithstanding any provision to the contrary in section 2 of this Act, a probation order made by virtue of the foregoing subsection which includes only requirements having the like effect as any requirement or provision of the supervision order to which the notification relates may be made without summoning the person to whom the notification relates and without his consent, and shall specify a period of supervision which shall expire not later than the date on which that supervision order would have ceased to have effect by the effluxion of time; and, except as aforesaid, Part I of this Act shall apply to that probation order.

(8) In this section "petty sessions area" has the same meaning as in the said Act of 1969.

The Sexual Offences Act 1956

27. In section 37 (7) of the Sexual Offences Act 1956, for the words "section twenty or twenty-one of the Magistrates' Courts Act 1952 (which relate" in paragraph (a) there shall be substituted the words "section 6 of the Children and Young Persons Act 1969 (which relates" and for the words "that Act" in paragraph (b) there shall be substituted the words "the Magistrates' Courts Act 1952".

Children and Young Persons Act 1969

2

The Affiliation Proceedings Act 1957

28.—(1) In section 5 (2) (*a*) of the Affiliation Proceedings Act 1957, for the words from "fit person" to "school" there shall be substituted the words "local authority".

(2) In section 7 (4) of that Act, for paragraph (*a*) there shall be substituted the following paragraph:—

(*a*) subject to the next following subsection, so as to require payments thereunder to be made in respect of any period when the child is in the care of a local authority under section 1 of the Children Act 1948 or by virtue of a care order (other than an interim order) within the meaning of the Children and Young Persons Act 1969;

(3) In section 7 (6) of that Act, for the words from "a person" onwards there shall be substituted the words "by virtue of such a care order as aforesaid".

The Children Act 1958

29. In section 2 (4) of the Children Act 1958, for the words "supervision order or" there shall be substituted the words "supervision order within the meaning of the Children and Young Persons Act 1969 or a".

30. In section 9 of the said Act of 1958, after the words "foster child" there shall be inserted the words "for reward".

31. In section 12 (1) of the said Act of 1958, for the words "one month" there shall be substituted the words "two weeks".

32. In section 17 of the said Act of 1958, after the words "that is to say" there shall be inserted the words "" approved school" has the same meaning as in the Children and Young Persons (Scotland) Act 1937;" and, in the definition of "place of safety", for the word "home" in the first place where it occurs there shall be substituted the words "community home" and for the words "under Part II of the Children Act 1948, remand" there shall be substituted the words "a controlled community".

The Adoption Act 1958

33.—(1) In section 4 (3) of the Adoption Act 1958, for paragraph (*a*) there shall be substituted the following paragraph:—

(*a*) section 24 of the Children and Young Persons Act 1969 (which relates to the powers and duties of local authorities with respect to persons committed to their care in pursuance of that Act).

34. In section 15 (3) of the said Act of 1958, for the words "the last mentioned order" there shall be substituted the words "or to the care of a local authority by a care order (other than an interim order) in force under the Children and Young Persons Act 1969, the fit person order or care order as the case may be".

35. In section 37 (2) of the said Act of 1958, for the words " (4) or (5) " there shall be substituted the words "or (4) ".

36. In section 57 (1) of the said Act of 1958, in the definition of "place of safety", for the word "home" in the first place where it occurs there shall be substituted the words "community home" and for the words "under Part II of the Children Act 1948, remand" there shall be substituted the words "a controlled community".

The Mental Health Act 1959

37.—(1) In subsection (1) of section 9 of the Mental Health Act 1959 for the words from "or other accommodation" to "section fifteen of that Act" there shall be substituted the words "provided under section 38 of the Children and Young Persons Act 1969" and for the words "that Act" there shall be substituted the words "the Children Act 1948".

(2) In subsection (2) of the said section 9, for the words "or other accommodation provided under the said section fifteen" there shall be substituted the words "provided under the said section 38".

38. In section 10 (1) (*a*) of the said Act of 1959 for sub-paragraph (i) there shall be substituted the following sub-paragraph:—

(i) section 24 of the Children and Young Persons Act 1969 (which relates to the powers and duties of local authorities with respect to persons committed to their care in pursuance of that Act).

39. In section 50 of the said Act of 1959, for paragraph (*a*) there shall be substituted the following paragraph:—

(a) section 24 of the Children and Young Persons Act 1969 (which relates to the powers and duties of local authorities with respect to persons committed to their care in pursuance of that Act).

40. In section 60 (6) of the said Act of 1959, after the word "offence" there shall be inserted the words "or make any such order as is mentioned in paragraphs (b) or (c) of section 7 (7) of the Children and Young Persons Act 1969 in respect of the offender".

41. In section 62 (4) of the said Act of 1959 for the words "section 62 of the Children and Young Persons Act 1933" there shall be substituted the words "section 1 of the Children and Young Persons Act 1969".

The Mental Health (Scotland) Act 1960

42. In section 10 (1) (a) of the Mental Health (Scotland) Act 1960, for sub-paragraph (ii) there shall be substituted the following sub-paragraph:—
(ii) section 24 of the Children and Young Persons Act 1969 (which relates to the powers and duties of local authorities in England and Wales with respect to persons committed to their care).

43. In section 46 of the said Act of 1960, for paragraph (b) there shall be substituted the following paragraph:—
(b) section 24 of the Children and Young Persons Act 1969 (which relates to the powers and duties of local authorities in England and Wales with respect to persons committed to their care).

The Criminal Justice Act 1961

44. For section 5 (1) of the Criminal Justice Act 1961 there shall be substituted the following:—

Defaulters already detained in detention centre

5.—(1) Where a court has power to commit a person to prison for any term for a default and that person has attained the age of seventeen and is detained in a detention centre under a previous sentence or warrant, the court may, subject to the provisions of this section, commit him to a detention centre for a term not exceeding the term aforesaid or six months, whichever is the shorter.

and subsection (3) of section 6 of that Act shall be subsection (6) of section 5 of that Act.

45. In section 9 of the said Act of 1961, for the words from the beginning to "that Act", where they first occur, there shall be substituted the words "Where an order for conditional discharge under section seven of the Criminal Justice Act 1948".

46. In section 29 (3) (a) of the said Act of 1961, for the words "that Act" there shall be substituted the words "the Children and Young Persons Act 1933".

The Act of 1963

47. In section 3 (1) of the Act of 1963, for the words "section 62 of the principal Act" there shall be substituted the words "section 1 of the Children and Young Persons Act 1969".

48. In section 23 of the Act of 1963, in subsection (1) (b), for the words "that Act" there shall be substituted the words "the principal Act" and, in subsection (5), for the words from "for his detention" onwards there shall be substituted the words "within the meaning of the Children and Young Persons Act 1969".

49. In section 29 (1) of the Act of 1963, for the words "before a juvenile court under section 62 or section 65 of the principal Act" there shall be substituted the words "under section 1 of the Children and Young Persons Act 1969 or for an offence"; and section 29 (2) of the Act of 1963 shall cease to have effect.

50.—(1) In subsection (1) of section 30 of the Act of 1963, for the words "the person who" there shall be substituted the words "the local authority who".

(2) In subsection (3) of that section, for the words "subsections (3) and (4)" there shall be substituted "subsection (3)" and at the end of that subsection there shall be added the words "section 62 of the Children and Young Persons Act 1969".

(3) In subsection (4) of that section for the words from "a magistrates' court", in the first place where they occur, to the end of the subsection there shall be substituted the words "a magistrates' court acting for the area or part of the area of the local authority which is the applicant."

(4) In subsection (5) of that section for the words "14 (1) of this Act keep the

person" there shall be substituted the words " 24 (8) of the Children and Young Persons Act 1969 keep the local authority ".

51. In section 45 (1) of the Act of 1963, after the words " the Children Act 1958 " there shall be inserted the words " the Children and Young Persons Act 1969 ".

52. In section 49 (1) of the Act of 1963, for the words " section 3 (3) ", there shall be substituted the words " section 13 (2) " and for the words " over the care " in both places there shall be substituted the word " charge ".

53. For subsection (3) of section 57 of the Act of 1963 there shall be substituted the following subsection :—

> (3) The said sections 39 and 49 shall extend to Scotland and the said sections 46 and 54 shall extend to England and Wales, but—
>> (*a*) references to a court in the said sections 39 and 49 shall not include a court in Scotland; and
>> (*b*) references to a court in the said sections 46 and 54 shall not include a court in England or Wales.

The Family Allowances Act 1965

54.[21]—(1) In subsection (1) (*b*) of section 11 of the Family Allowances Act 1965, for the words " said Act of " there shall be substituted the words " Children and Young Persons Act ".

(2) In subsection (2) of that section for the words " said Act of 1933 " there shall be substituted the words " Children and Young Persons Act 1969 (other than an interim order) " and for the words from " 5 (1) " to " 1956 " there shall be substituted the words " 13 (2) of the Children Act 1948 ".

(3) In subsection (3) of that section, for the words " 3 or 4 " there shall be substituted the words " 4 or 13 (2) ".

The Criminal Justice Act 1967

55. In sections 2 and 9 of the Criminal Justice Act 1967, after subsection (3) of each section there shall be inserted the following subsection :—

> (3A) In the case of a statement which indicates in pursuance of subsection (3) (*a*) of this section that the person making it has not attained the age of fourteen, subsection (2) (*b*) of this section shall have effect as if for the words from " made " onwards there were substituted the words " understands the importance of telling the truth in it."

56. In section 3 (3) of the Criminal Justice Act 1967, for the words " 19 or 20 of the Magistrates' Courts Act 1952 " there shall be substituted the words " or 19 of the Magistrates' Courts Act 1952 or section 6 of the Children and Young Persons Act 1969 ".

The Social Work (Scotland) Act 1968

57. After section 44 (1) of the Social Work (Scotland) Act 1968, there shall be inserted the following subsection :—

> (1A) A supervision requirement imposing a condition as to the place where a child is to reside in England or Wales shall be a like authority as in Scotland for the person in charge of the place to restrict the child's liberty to such an extent as that person may consider appropriate having regard to the terms of the supervision requirement.

58.—(1) In section 72 of the said Act of 1968, after subsection (1) there shall be inserted the following subsection :—

> (1A) The juvenile court in England or Wales to which notification of a supervision requirement is sent under this section may make a supervision order in respect of the person to whom the notification relates but, notwithstanding anything in section 76 (1) of this Act, shall not include in the order a requirement authorised by section 12 of the Children and Young Persons Act 1969 unless that person is before the court when the supervision order is made; and in relation to a supervision order made by virtue of this subsection—
>> (*a*) section 15 of that Act shall have effect as if subsection (2) were omitted; and
>> (*b*) section 17 of that Act shall have effect as if in paragraph (*a*) the references to three years and the date on which the order was originally

[21] Prospectively repealed by Child Benefit Act 1975 (c. 61), Sched. 5.

made were respectively references to one year and the date on which the said notification was sent and as if in paragraph (*b*) the words from "the order was" to "and" were omitted.

(2) In subsection (2) of that section, after the word "court" there shall be inserted the words "in Northern Ireland".

(3) In subsection (4) of that section for the words from "includes" to "1963" there shall be substituted the words ", in relation to England and Wales, has the same meaning as in the said Act of 1969".

59.—(1) In section 73 of the said Act of 1968, in subsection (1), after the word "reporter", in the second place where it occurs, there shall be inserted the following words:—

(i) in the case of a supervision order made by virtue of section 7A (4) of the Criminal Justice (Scotland) Act 1949, to notify the appropriate court and to transmit to that court all documents and certified copies of documents relating to the case which the reporter has received by virtue of section 76 of this Act;

(ii) in any other case.

and at the end of that subsection there shall be inserted the following paragraph:—

In this subsection "the appropriate court" means the sheriff having jurisdiction in the area in which the child proposes to reside or is residing or, where the original probation order was imposed by the High Court of Justiciary, that Court.

(2) After subsection (1) of that section there shall be inserted the following subsection:—

(1A) Where a court in England or Wales is satisfied that a child in respect of whom the court proposes to make a supervision order is residing or proposes to reside in Scotland, the court may make the order notwithstanding anything in subsection (1) of section 18 of the Children and Young Persons Act 1969 (which relates to residence of the supervised person in England or Wales); and where the court makes a supervision order by virtue of this subsection—

(a) the areas to be named in the order in pursuance of subsection (2) (a) of the said section 18 shall be those in which the court is sitting;

(b) the order may require the supervised person to comply with directions of the supervisor with respect to his departure to Scotland, and any such requirement shall, for the purposes of sections 15 and 16 of that Act (which relate to the variation and discharge of supervision orders), be deemed to be included in the order in pursuance of section 12 (2) of that Act; and

(c) the court shall send notification of the order as mentioned in paragraph (b) of the foregoing subsection and the provisions of that subsection relating to the duty of the reporter shall apply accordingly.

(3) In subsection (2) of that section for the word "subsection" there shall be substituted the words "provisions of this section."

60. In section 74 of the said Act of 1968, after subsection (5) there shall be inserted the following subsection:—

(6) An order under this section committing a child to the care of a local authority shall have effect as if it were a care order under the Children and Young Persons Act 1969, but as if sections 20 (2) and 21 (5) of that Act and in section 20 (3) of that Act paragraph (a) and the words 'in any other case' in paragraph (b) were omitted.

61.—(1) In section 75 of the said Act of 1968, in subsection (1) after the word "order" there shall be inserted the words "or an order under section 74 (3) of this Act relating to a training school".

(2) In subsection (2) of that section, for the words from "under", where it first occurs, to "1944" there shall be substituted the words "by a care order (other than an interim order) within the meaning of the Children and Young Persons Act 1969 or an order under section 74 (3) of this Act" and after the word "1947" there shall be inserted the words "or the said section 74 (3)".

(3) In subsection (3) of that section, after the words "training school order" there shall be inserted the words "or order under the said section 74 (3) relating to a training school".

(4) In subsection (4) of that section after the word "order" there shall be inserted the words "under the said section 74 (3) or".

62. In section 76 (4) of the said Act of 1968, after the word "order" there shall

be inserted the words "or order under section 74 (3) of this Act relating to a training school".

63. In section 90 (1) of the said Act of 1968, the words "or to prescribe any matter," shall be omitted.

64. In section 94 (1) of the said Act of 1968—

(1) after the definition of "place of safety" there shall be inserted the words—

"prescribed" means—

    (*a*) in section 3, prescribed by regulations,

    (*b*) in section 44, prescribed by rules, and

    (*c*) in sections 62 (2), 66 (1) and (2), 94, paragraphs 2 (2) and (3), 4 (3) and (4) of Schedule 7, prescribed by order,

(2) in the definition of "supervision order" after the word "1963" there shall be inserted the words "and includes a supervision order within the meaning of the Children and Young Persons Act 1969".

65. In section 97 (1) of the said Act of 1968—

(1) after the words "that is to say—" there shall be inserted the words "section 44 (1) (except head (*b*)) and (1A)",

(2) after the words "Part V" there shall be inserted the words "section 98 (3)" and "Schedule 2, paragraphs 7 and 13".

66. In section 98 of the said Act of 1968, after subsection (2) there shall be inserted the following subsection:—

(3) An order under this section may make such transitional provisions as appear to the Secretary of State to be necessary or expedient in connection with the provisions thereby brought into force, including such adaptations of those provisions or of any provision of this Act then in force as appear to the Secretary of State necessary or expedient for the purposes or in consequence of the operation of any provision of this Act before the coming into force of any other provision of this Act or of the Children and Young Persons Act 1969.

67. In Schedule 2 to the said Act of 1968, in paragraph 10, to section 50 of the Children and Young Persons (Scotland) Act 1937 as substituted by that paragraph, there shall be added the following subsection:—

(2) The provisions of the foregoing subsection so far as they relate to section 54 of this Act shall extend to England and Wales.

68. In Schedule 2 to the said Act of 1968, in paragraph 19, after the word "'children'" there shall be inserted the words ", for the word 'offenders' there shall be substituted the word 'children', and for the word 'offender' in the three places where that word occurs there shall be substituted the word 'child'".

69. In Schedule 7 to the said Act of 1968, in paragraph 1 (1) (*a*), for the words "section 63" there shall be substituted the words "section 62".

70. In Schedule 8 to the said Act of 1968, in paragraph 7—

(*a*) for sub-paragraph (1) of that paragraph there shall be substituted the following sub-paragraph:—

(1) In section 87, for subsection (1), there shall be substituted the following subsection—

(1) Any person detained in a training school under the law in force in Northern Ireland may, with the consent of the Secretary of State, be transferred by order of the competent authority in Northern Ireland to such place in Scotland as the Secretary of State may direct for the purposes of undergoing residential training, and shall be subject to the provisions of this Act and of the Criminal Justice (Scotland) Act 1963 as if the order sending him to the school in Northern Ireland were an order for committal for residential training made under section 58A of this Act made upon the same date, and as if the order were an authority for his detention for a period not exceeding the period for which he might be detained under the training school order made in respect of him.;

(*b*) in sub-paragraph (2) of that paragraph at the end there shall be inserted the words "; and in section 87 (2) and (4) the words "England or", wherever they occur, shall be omitted";

(*c*) in sub-paragraph (3) of that paragraph the words "to such" shall be omitted;

(*d*) after sub-paragraph (3) of that paragraph there shall be inserted the following sub-paragraphs—

> (4) In section 87 (5) the words "in relation to England, the Secretary of State, and," shall be omitted.
>
> (5) In section 87 subsection (6) shall be omitted.

71. In Schedule 8 to the said Act of 1968, in paragraph 9 (2), for the word "for" there shall be substituted the word "of".

72. In Schedule 8 to the said Act of 1968, in paragraph 10, at the end there shall be inserted the following words—

> "after the definition of "Street" there shall be inserted the following definition—
>> 'Training school order' has the same meaning as in the Social Work (Scotland) Act 1968'".

73. In Schedule 8 to the said Act of 1968, in paragraph 17 (1), for the words "in Scotland" there shall be substituted the words ", within the meaning of the Social Work (Scotland) Act 1968".

74. In Schedule 8 to the said Act of 1968, in paragraph 38, for the words "In section 15 (4)" there shall be substituted the words—

> "(1) In section 15 (3), for the words "the last mentioned order" there shall be substituted the words "or to the care of a local authority by a care order (other than an interim order) in force under the Children and Young Persons Act 1969, the fit person order or care order as the case may be".
>
> (2) In subsection (4)".

75. In Schedule 8 to the said Act of 1968, in sub-paragraph (1) of paragraph 51, for the words from "include" where it secondly occurs to the end of the sub-paragraph there shall be substituted the words "include"; and paragraph (*e*) shall be omitted."

76. In Schedule 8 to the said Act of 1968, in paragraph 54, for the word "and" where that word first occurs there shall be substituted the word "or" and after the words ""by virtue of"" there shall be inserted the words "where those words secondly occur".

77. In Schedule 8 to the said Act of 1968, after paragraph 59, there shall be inserted the following paragraph:—

Criminal Justice Act 1961

59A. In section 32 (2), after paragraph (*g*), there shall be inserted the following paragraph—

> (*h*) section 58A of the Children and Young Persons (Scotland) Act 1937.

78.[22] In Schedule 8 to the said Act of 1968, for paragraph 74 (1), there shall be substituted the following sub-paragraph—

> 74.—(1) For section 11 (1) (*a*) there shall be substituted the following paragraph—
>> (*a*) during which his or her residence in a residential establishment is required by a supervision requirement made under section 44 of the Social Work (Scotland) Act 1968, and the child is not absent from the residential establishment under supervision;
>
> in paragraph (*b*), for the words "the said Act of 1937", there shall be substituted the words "the Children and Young Persons (Scotland) Act 1937", after paragraph (*b*) there shall be inserted the following paragraph:—
>> (*bb*) during which the child is liable to undergo residential training under committal by virtue of section 58A of the said Act of 1937, and is not released under that section;
>
> and for paragraph (*c*) there shall be substituted the following paragraph:—
>> (*c*) during which the child is accommodated by virtue of rules made by the Secretary of State under section 45 of the Social Work (Scotland) Act 1968".

79. In Part I of Schedule 9 to the said Act of 1968, in the entry relating to the Children and Young Persons (Scotland) Act 1937, in the third column, after the words "Sections 68 to 86" there shall be inserted the following words:—

[22] Prospectively repealed by Child Benefit Act 1975 (c. 61), Sched. 5.

"In section 87 (2) and (4) the words "England or" wherever they occur, in subsection (5) the words "in relation to England, the Secretary of State, and" and subsection (6)."

80. In Part I of Schedule 9 to the said Act of 1968, in the entry relating to the Children Act 1958, in the third column, for the words "Section 2 (6) and (7)" there shall be substituted the words—

In section 2, in subsection (4) the words from "or by virtue of" to "of an approved school", and subsections (6) and (7).

81. In Part I of Schedule 9 to the said Act of 1968, in the entry relating to section 15 (3) of the Adoption Act 1958, in the third column, for the words "'or the Children' to '1937'" there shall be substituted the following words "'fit person by' to 'care of a' and the words 'fit person order or' and 'as the case may be'".

82. In Part II of Schedule 9 to the said Act of 1968, in the entry relating to the Children Act 1958, in the third column, the entry relating to section 17 shall be omitted.

83. In Part II of Schedule 9 to the said Act of 1968, in the entry relating to the Family Allowances Act 1965, in the third column, for the words from "11," to "(2)," there shall be substituted the word "11 (2),".

$$\cdot\quad\cdot\quad\cdot\quad\cdot\quad\cdot\quad\cdot\quad\cdot$$

Administration of Justice Act 1970

(1970 c. 31)

Redistribution of business among divisions of the High Court

1.—(1) The Probate, Divorce and Admiralty Division of the High Court shall be re-named the Family Division; and the principal probate registry shall be re-named the principal registry of the Family Division.

(2) There shall be assigned to the Family Division all causes and matters involving the exercise of the High Court's jurisdiction in proceedings specified in Schedule 1 to this Act.

(3) Causes and matters involving the exercise of the High Court's Admiralty jurisdiction, or its jurisdiction as a prize court, shall be assigned to the Queen's Bench Division.

(4) As respects the exercise of the High Court's probate jurisdiction—

(a) non-contentious or common form probate business shall continue to be assigned to the Family Division; and

(b) all other probate business shall be assigned to the Chancery Division.

(5) In section 5 of the Supreme Court of Judicature (Consolidation) Act 1925 (which enables Her Majesty, on the recommendation of the judges, by Order in Council to alter the number of divisions of the High Court or of puisne judges to be attached to any division) for the reference to a report or recommendation of the council of judges there shall be substituted a reference to a recommendation of the Lord Chancellor, the Lord Chief Justice, the Master of the Rolls, the President of the Family Division and the Vice-Chancellor.

(6) In accordance with the foregoing subsections—

(a) the enactments specified in Schedule 2 to this Act (that is to say, the said Act of 1925 and other enactments relative to the High Court, its jurisdiction, judges, divisions and business) shall be amended as shown in that Schedule; and

(b) references in any other enactment or document to the Probate, Divorce and Admiralty Division, the President of that division, the principal probate registry, the principal (or senior) probate registrar and a probate registrar shall, so far as may be necessary to preserve the effect of the enactment or document, be construed respectively as references to the Family Division and to the President, principal registry, principal registrar and a registrar of that division.

(7) This section is not to be taken as affecting any of the following provisions of the said Act of 1925—

    (a) section 55 (which provides for the distribution of business in the High Court to be regulated by rules);

    (b) section 57 (which enables the Lord Chancellor to assign or re-assign the jurisdiction of the court among divisions and judges);

    (c) section 58 (which provides for the assignment of causes and matters);

    (d) section 59 (which enables an action to be transferred at any stage from one division to another).

(8) Notwithstanding anything in section 114 (3) of the said Act of 1925 (appointment of officers attached to a division), the right of filling any vacancy in the office of the Admiralty registrar or assistant Admiralty registrar shall be vested in the Lord Chancellor; and any other officer of the Supreme Court who is to be employed in the Admiralty registry shall be appointed by the Lord Chancellor.

SCHEDULES

SCHEDULE 1 [1]

HIGH COURT BUSINESS ASSIGNED TO FAMILY DIVISION

Business at first instance

Proceedings consisting of a matrimonial cause, or any matter arising out of or connected with such a cause; proceedings for a degree of presumption of death and dissolution of marriage; and any other proceedings with respect to which rules of court may be made by virtue of [section 50 (1) of the Matrimonial Causes Act 1973].[1a]

Proceedings for a declaration—

    (a) under section 39 of the Matrimonial Causes Act 1965, as to a person's legitimacy, or the validity of a marriage, or a person's right to be deemed a British subject; or

    (b) with respect to a person's matrimonial status.

Proceedings in relation to the wardship of minors.

Proceedings under the Adoption Acts 1958 and 1968.

Proceedings under [the Guardianship of Minors Acts 1971 and 1973] [2] and otherwise in relation to the guardianship of minors, except proceedings for the appointment of a guardian of a minor's estate alone.

Proceedings under section 3 of the Marriage Act 1949 for obtaining the court's consent to the marriage of a minor.

[. . .].[3]

Proceedings in which a parent or guardian of a minor applies for a writ of habeas corpus ad subjiciendum relative to the custody, care or control of the minor.

Proceedings under the following enactments:—

    (a) the Maintenance Orders (Facilities for Enforcement) Act 1920 (enforcement in England and Wales of orders made overseas for periodical payments to a man's wife or dependant);

    (b) Part II of the Maintenance Orders Act 1950 (enforcement in England and Wales of certain maintenance and other orders made in Scotland or Northern Ireland);

    (c) the Maintenance Orders Act 1958 (registration and enforcement of certain maintenance and other orders);

    (d) Part II of this Act.

[. . .].[3]

---

[1] See Children Act 1975 (c. 72), Sched. 3, para. 73, *post*.
[1a] Words substituted by Matrimonial Causes Act 1973 (c. 18), s. 54 (1) (a), Sched. 2.
[2] Words substituted by Guardianship Act 1973 (c. 29), s. 9 (2).
[3] Words repealed by Matrimonial Causes Act 1973 (c. 18), s. 54 (1) (a), Sched. 2

Appellate business

Proceedings on appeal under—

(a) [section 16 (2) of the Guardianship of Minors Act 1971] [4] (appeal to High Court from order of county court under that Act);

(b) [section 16 (3) of the said Act of 1971] [4] (corresponding appeal from a magistrates' court);

(c) section 11 of the Matrimonial Proceedings (Magistrates' Courts) Act 1960 (appeal from certain decisions of a magistrates' court under that Act).

Proceedings on appeal from a magistrates' court under section 10 of the Adoption Act 1958 against the making of, or refusal to make, an adoption order.

Proceedings on appeal from a magistrates' court under section 4 (7) of the Maintenance Orders Act 1958 against the variation of, or refusal to vary, an order registered in accordance with the provisions of that Act.

Proceedings on appeal under section 13 of the Administration of Justice Act 1960 (appeal in cases of contempt of court) from an order or decision of a magistrates' court under section 54 (3) of the Magistrates' Courts Act 1952 where the order or decision was made to enforce an order of such a court under [the Guardianship of Minors Acts 1971 and 1973] [2] or the Matrimonial Proceedings (Magistrates' Court) Act 1960.

Proceedings on appeal by case stated against an order or determination of a court of quarter sessions, or a magistrates' court, made or given in affiliation proceedings.

Proceedings on appeal by case stated against an order or determination of a magistrates' court with regard to the enforcement of—

(a) an order for the payment of money made by virtue of the Matrimonial Proceedings (Magistrates' Courts) Act 1960;

(b) an order for the payment of money registered in a magistrates' court under the Maintenance Orders Act 1958 or registered in a court in England and Wales under Part II of the Maintenance Orders Act 1950 or the Maintenance Orders (Facilities for Enforcement) Act 1920 or confirmed by a magistrates' court under the last-mentioned Act.

Proceedings on appeal by case stated against an order or determination of a magistrates' court under [section 35 of the Matrimonial Causes Act 1973] [1] (alteration of maintenance agreement between spouses).

. . . .

SCHEDULE 4

Taxes, Social Insurance Contributions, etc. subject to Special Enforcement Provisions in Part II

1. Income tax or any other tax or liability recoverable under section 65, 66 or 68 of the Taxes Management Act 1970.

2. Selective employment tax under section 44 of the Finance Act 1966.

3. Contributions under—

section 3 (flat-rate) or section 4 (graduated) of the National Insurance Act 1965;

section 1 of the National Health Service Contributions Act 1965; or

section 2 of the National Insurance (Industrial Injuries) Act 1965.

4. Redundancy Fund contributions under section 27 of the Redundancy Payments Act 1965.

SCHEDULE 6

[*Schedule 6 repealed by Attachment of Earnings Act* 1971 (*c.* 32), *s.* 29 (2), *Sched.* 6.]

SCHEDULE 7

Schedule 7 repealed by Attachment of Earnings Act 1971 (*c.* 32), *s.* 29 (2), *Sched.* 6.]

---

[4] Words substituted by Guardianship of Minors Act 1971 (c. 3), s. 18 (1), Sched. 1.

Law Reform (Miscellaneous Provisions) Act 1970

(1970 c. 33)

ARRANGEMENT OF SECTIONS

Legal consequences of termination of contract to marry

SECT.
1. Engagements to marry not enforceable at law.
2. Property of engaged couples.
3. Gifts between engaged couples.

Damages for adultery

4. Abolition of right to claim damages for adultery.

Enticement of spouse, etc.

5. Abolition of actions for enticement, seduction and harbouring of spouse or child.

Maintenance for survivor of void marriage

6. Orders for maintenance of surviving party to void marriage from estate of other party.

Supplemental

7. Citation, repeal, commencement and extent.

SCHEDULE—Enactments repealed.

An Act to abolish actions for breach of promise of marriage and make provision with respect to the property of, and gifts between, persons who have been engaged to marry; to abolish the right of a husband to claim damages for adultery with his wife; to abolish actions for the enticement or harbouring of a spouse, or for the enticement, seduction or harbouring of a child; to make provision with respect to the maintenance of survivors of void marriages; and for purposes connected with the matters aforesaid. [29th May 1970]

Legal consequences of termination of contract to marry

Engagements to marry not enforceable at law

1.—(1) An agreement between two persons to marry one another shall not under the law of England and Wales have effect as a contract giving rise to legal rights and no action shall lie in England and Wales for breach of such an agreement, whatever the law applicable to the agreement.

(2) This section shall have effect in relation to agreements entered into before it comes into force, except that it shall not affect any action commenced before it comes into force.

Property of engaged couples

2.—(1) Where an agreement to marry is terminated, any rule of law relating to the rights of husbands and wives in relation to property in which either or both has or have a beneficial interest, including any such rule as explained by section 37 of the Matrimonial Proceedings and Property Act 1970, shall apply, in relation to any property in which either or both of the parties to the agreement had a beneficial interest while the agreement was in force, as it applies in relation to property in which a husband or wife has a beneficial interest.

(2) Where an agreement to marry is terminated, section 17 of the Married Women's Property Act 1882 and section 7 of the Matrimonial

Law Reform (Miscellaneous Provisions) Act 1970

Causes (Property and Maintenance) Act 1958 (which sections confer power on a judge of the High Court or a county court to settle disputes between husband and wife about property) shall apply, as if the parties were married, to any dispute between, or claim by, one of them in relation to property in which either or both had a beneficial interest while the agreement was in force; but an application made by virtue of this section to the judge under the said section 17, as originally enacted or as extended by the said section 7, shall be made within three years of the termination of the agreement.

Gifts between engaged couples

3.—(1) A party to an agreement to marry who makes a gift of property to the other party to the agreement on the condition (express or implied) that it shall be returned if the agreement is terminated shall not be prevented from recovering the property by reason only of his having terminated the agreement.

(2) The gift of an engagement ring shall be presumed to be an absolute gift; this presumption may be rebutted by proving that the ring was given on the condition, express or implied, that it should be returned if the marriage did not take place for any reason.

Damages for adultery

4. [*Repealed by Matrimonial Causes Act 1973 (c. 18), s. 54(1) (b), Sched. 3.*]

Enticement of spouse, etc.

Abolition of actions for enticement, seduction and harbouring of spouse or child

5. No person shall be liable in tort under the law of England and Wales—

(a) to any other person on the ground only of his having induced the wife or husband of that other person to leave or remain apart from the other spouse;

(b) to a parent (or person standing in the place of a parent) on the ground only of his having deprived the parent (or other person) of the services of his or her child by raping, seducing or enticing that child; or

(c) to any other person for harbouring the wife or child of that other person,

except in the case of a cause of action accruing before this Act comes into force if an action in respect thereof has been begun before this Act comes into force.

6. [*Repealed by Inheritance (Provision for Family and Dependants) Act 1975 (c. 63), Sched.*]

Supplemental

Citation, repeal, commencement and extent

7.—(1) This Act may be cited as the Law Reform (Miscellaneous Provisions) Act 1970.

(2) The enactments specified in the Schedule to this Act are hereby repealed to the extent specified in the third column of that Schedule, but the repeal of those enactments shall not affect any action commenced or petition presented before this Act comes into force or any claim made in any such action or on any such petition.

(3) This Act shall come into force on 1st January 1971.

(4) This Act does not extend to Scotland or Northern Ireland.

Marriage (Registrar General's Licence) Act 1970

(1970 c. 34)

An Act to permit marriages on unregistered premises; and for purposes connected therewith. [29th May 1970]

Marriages which may be solemnised by Registrar General's licence

1.—(1) Subject to the provisions of subsection (2) below, any marriage which may be solemnised on the authority of a certificate of a superintendent registrar may be solemnised on the authority of the Registrar General's licence elsewhere than at a registered building or the office of a superintendent registrar;

Provided that any such marriage shall not be solemnised according to the rites of the Church of England or the Church in Wales.

(2) The Registrar General shall not issue any licence for the solemnising of a marriage as is mentioned in subsection (1) above unless he is satisfied that one of the persons to be married is seriously ill and is not expected to recover and cannot be moved to a place at which under the provisions of the Marriage Act 1949 (hereinafter called the " principal Act ") the marriage could be solemnised.

Notice of marriage

2.—(1) Where a marriage is intended to be solemnised on the authority of the Registrar General's licence, notice shall be given in the prescribed form by either of the persons to be married to the superintendent registrar of the registration district in which it is intended that the marriage shall be solemnised, and the notice shall state by or before whom it is intended that the marriage shall be solemnised.

(2) The provisions of section 27 (4) of the principal Act (which relate to entries in the marriage notice book) shall apply to notices of marriage on the authority of the Registrar General's licence.

(3) The provisions of section 28 of the principal Act (declaration to accompany notice of marriage) shall apply to the giving of notice under this Act with the exception of paragraph (b) of subsection (1) of that section and with the modification that in section 28 (2) references to the

registrar of births and deaths or of marriages and deputy registrar shall be omitted.

Evidence of capacity, consent etc., to be produced

3. The person giving notice to the superintendent registrar under the provisions of the foregoing section shall produce to the superintendent registrar such evidence as the Registrar General may require to satisfy him—

(*a*) that there is no lawful impediment to the marriage;

(*b*) that the consent of any person whose consent to the marriage is required under section 3 of the principal Act, as amended by the Family Law Reform Act 1969, has been duly given; and

(*c*) that there is sufficient reason why a licence should be granted;

(*d*) that the conditions contained in section 1 (2) of this Act are satisfied and that the person in respect of whom such conditions are satisfied is able to and does understand the nature and purport of the marriage ceremony:

Provided that the certificate of a registered medical practitioner shall be sufficient evidence of any or all of the matters in subsection (1) (*d*) of this section referred to.

Application to be reported to Registrar General

4. Upon receipt of any notice and evidence as mentioned in sections 2 and 3 above respectively the superintendent registrar shall inform the Registrar General and shall comply with any directions he may give for verifying the evidence given.

Caveat against issue of Registrar General's licence

5. The provisions of section 29 of the principal Act (caveat against issue of certificate or licence) shall apply to the issue of a licence by the Registrar General with the modification that a caveat may be entered with either the superintendent registrar or the Registrar General and in either case it shall be for the Registrar General to examine into the matter of the caveat and to decide whether or not the licence should be granted and his decision shall be final, and with a further modification that the references to the superintendent registrar in that section shall refer to the superintendent registrar of the registration district in which the marriage is intended to be solemnised.

Marriage of persons under eighteen

6. The provisions of section 3 of the principal Act (marriage of persons under 18) shall apply for the purposes of this Act to a marriage intended to be solemnised by Registrar General's licence as they apply to a marriage intended to be solemnised on the authority of a certificate of a superintendent registrar under Part III of the principal Act with the modification that if the consent of any person whose consent is required under that Act cannot be obtained by reason of absence or inaccessibility or by reason of his being under any disability, the superintendent registrar shall not be required to dispense with the necessity for the consent of that person and the Registrar General may dispense with the necessity of obtaining the consent of that person, whether or not there is any other person whose consent is also required.

Issue of licence by Registrar General

7. Where the marriage is intended to be solemnised on the authority of the Registrar General and he is satisfied that sufficient grounds exist why a licence should be granted he shall issue a licence in the prescribed form unless—

(a) any lawful impediment to the issue of the licence has been shown to his satisfaction to exist; or

(b) the issue of the licence has been forbidden under section 30 of the principal Act.

Period of validity of licence

8.—(1) A marriage may be solemnised on the authority of the Registrar General's licence at any time within one month from the day on which the notice of marriage was entered in the marriage notice book.

(2) If the marriage is not solemnised within the said period of one month, the notice of marriage and the licence shall be void, and no person shall solemnise the marriage on the authority thereof.

Place of solemnisation

9. A marriage on the authority of the Registrar General's licence shall be solemnised in the place stated in the notice of marriage.

Manner of solemnisation

10.—(1) Any marriage to be solemnised on the authority of the Registrar General's licence shall be solemnised at the wish of the persons to be married either—

(a) according to such form or ceremony, not being the rites or ceremonies of the Church of England or the Church in Wales, as the persons to be married shall see fit to adopt, or

(b) by civil ceremony.

(2) Except where the marriage is solemnised according to the usages of the Society of Friends or is a marriage between two persons professing the Jewish religion according to the usages of the Jews, it shall be solemnised in the presence of a registrar:

Provided that where the marriage is to be by civil ceremony it shall be solemnised in the presence of the superintendent registrar as well as the registrar.

(3) Except where the marriage is solemnised according to the usages of the Society of Friends or is a marriage between two persons professing the Jewish religion according to the usages of the Jews, the persons to be married shall in some part of the ceremony in the presence of two or more witnesses and the registrar and, where appropriate, the superintendent registrar, make the declaration and say to one another the words prescribed by section 44 (3) of the principal Act.

(4) No person who is a clergyman within the meaning of section 78 of the principal Act shall solemnise any marriage which is solemnised on the authority of the Registrar General.

Civil marriage followed by religious ceremony

11.—(1) If the parties to a marriage solemnised on the authority of the Registrar General's licence before a superintendent registrar desire to add the religious ceremony ordained or used by the church or persuasion of which they are members and have given notice of their desire so to do a clergyman or minister of that church or persuasion upon the production of a certificate of their marriage before the superintendent registrar and upon the payment of the customary fees (if any), may, if he sees fit, read or celebrate in the presence of the parties to the marriage the marriage service of the church or persuasion to which he belongs or nominate some other minister to do so.

(2) The provisions of section 46 (2) and (3) of the principal Act shall

apply to such a reading or celebration as they apply to the reading or celebration of a marriage service following a marriage solemnised in the office of a superintendent registrar.

Proof of certain matters not necessary to validity of marriages

12. The provisions of section 48 of the principal Act (proof of certain matters not necessary to validity of marriages) shall apply with the appropriate modifications to a marriage solemnised under the authority of the Registrar General's licence as they apply to a marriage solemnised under the authority of a certificate of a superintendent registrar.

Void marriages

13. The provisions of section 49 of the principal Act (void marriages) shall apply to a marriage under the authority of the Registrar General's licence:—

(a) with the substitution in paragraph (b) for the words from " certificate for marriage " onwards of the words " Registrar General's licence ";

(b) with the omission of paragraph (c);

(c) with the substitution for paragraph (d) of the words " on the authority of a licence which is void by virtue of section 8 (2) of the Marriage (Registrar General's Licence) Act 1970 ";

(d) with the substitution for paragraph (e) of the words " in any place other than the place specified in the notice of marriage and the Registrar General's licence ";

(e) with the substitution for paragraphs (f) and (g) of the words " in the absence of a registrar or, where the marriage is by civil ceremony, of a superintendent registrar, except where the marriage is solemnised according to the usages of the Society of Friends or is a marriage between two persons professing the Jewish religion according to the usages of the Jews ".

Documentary authority for marriage

14. Where a marriage is to be solemnised on the authority of the Registrar General's licence a document issued by the superintendent registrar stating that the Registrar General's licence has been granted and that authority for the marriage to be solemnised has been given shall be delivered before the marriage to the following person, that is to say—

(a) if the marriage is to be solemnised according to the usages of the Society of Friends, the registering officer of that Society for the place where the marriage is to be solemnised;

(b) if the marriage is to be solemnised according to the usages of persons professing the Jewish religion, the officer of the synagogue by whom the marriage is required to be registered under Part IV of the principal Act;

(c) in any other case, the registrar in whose presence the marriage is to be solemnised.

Registration of marriages

15. A marriage solemnised on the authority of the Registrar General's licence shall be registered in accordance with the provisions of the principal Act which apply to the registration of marriages solemnised in the presence of a registrar or according to the usages of the Society of Friends or of persons professing the Jewish religion.

Offences

16.—(1) It shall be an offence knowingly and wilfully—

    (a) to solemnise a marriage by Registrar General's licence in any place other than the place specified in the licence;

    (b) to solemnise a marriage by Registrar General's licence without the presence of a registrar except in the case of a marriage according to the usages of the Society of Friends or a marriage between two persons professing the Jewish religion according to the usages of the Jews;

    (c) to solemnise a marriage by Registrar General's licence after the expiration of one month from the date of entry of the notice of marriage in the marriage notice book;

    (d) to give false information by way of evidence as required by section 3 of this Act;

    (e) to give a false certificate as provided for in section 3 (1) (d) of this Act;

and any person found guilty of any of the above-mentioned offences shall be liable on summary conviction to a fine not exceeding £100 or on indictment to a fine not exceeding £500 or to imprisonment not exceeding three years or to both such fine and such imprisonment.

(2) A superintendent registrar who knowingly and wilfully solemnises or permits to be solemnised in his presence, or a registrar who knowingly and wilfully registers a marriage by Registrar General's licence which is void by virtue of Part III of the principal Act as amended by this Act shall be guilty of an offence and shall be liable on summary conviction to a fine not exceeding £100 or on indictment to a fine not exceeding £500 or to imprisonment not exceeding three years or to both such fine and such imprisonment.

(3) No prosecution under this section shall be commenced after the expiration of three years from the commission of the offence.

(4) The provisions of sections 75 (1) (a) and 75 (2) (a) of the principal Act shall not apply to a marriage solemnised on the authority of the Registrar General's licence.

Fees

17.—(1) A fee of £15 shall be payable to the Registrar General in respect of the issue of his licence and he shall have power to remit the fee in whole or in part in any case where it appears to him that the payment of the fee would cause hardship to the parties to the intended marriage.

(2) The Registrar General shall pay to the superintendent registrar a fee of £3 for the entry of the notice of marriage and a fee of £2 to a superintendent registrar and £2 to a registrar for attending a marriage by Registrar General's licence and these fees shall be retained by those officers.

Regulations

18.—(1) The Registrar General, with the approval of the Secretary of State may by statutory instrument make regulations prescribing anything which is required in this Act to be prescribed.

(2) Any power to make regulations shall include power to vary or revoke those regulations.

Saving

19. Nothing in this Act shall affect the right of the Archbishop of Canterbury or of any other person by virtue of the Ecclesiastical Licences

Act of 1533 to grant special licences to marry at any convenient time or place, or affect the validity of any marriage solemnised on the authority of such a licence.

Short title, construction, citation, extent and commencement

20.—(1) This Act may be cited as the Marriage (Registrar General's Licence) Act 1970.

(2) This Act shall be construed as one with the Marriage Acts 1949 to 1960, and this Act and the Marriage Acts 1949 to 1960 may be cited together as the Marriages Acts 1949 to 1970.

(3) This Act shall not extend to Scotland or Northern Ireland.

(4) This Act shall come into force on 1st January 1971.

Family Income Supplements Act 1970

(1970 c. 55)

An Act to provide for the payment of a new benefit for certain families with small incomes; and for purposes connected therewith.   [17th December 1970]

Family Income Supplement

1.—(1) For the purpose of this Act a family shall consist of the following members of a household—

(*a*) one man or single woman engaged, and normally engaged, in remunerative full-time work; and

(*b*) if the person mentioned in paragraph (*a*) above is a man and the household includes a woman to whom he is married or who lives with him as his wife, that woman; and

(*c*) the child or children whose requirements are provided for, in whole or in part, by the person or either of the persons mentioned in the preceding paragraphs.

(2) A benefit, to be known as a family income supplement, shall be paid (on a claim duly made thereto) for any family in Great Britain if the weekly amount of its resources, so far as taken into account for the purposes of this Act, falls short of the prescribed amount.

Prescribed amount

2.—(1) The prescribed amount for any family shall be—

(*a*) if the family includes one child, [£31·50] [1]; and

(*b*) if the family includes more than one child, [£31·50] [1] plus [£3·50] [1] for each additional child.

(2) Regulations may substitute higher amounts for those for the time being specified in this section.

Amount of family income supplement

3.—(1) Subject to the following provisions of this section, the weekly rate of a family income supplement shall be one half of the difference between the amounts mentioned in section 1 (2) of this Act but shall not in any case exceed [£7·00].[2]

[1] Amounts substituted by Family Income Supplements (Computation) Regulations (1975 S.I. No. 879).
[2] Amount substituted by Family Income Supplements (Computation) Regulations (1975 S.I. No. 879). In the case of a family which includes three or more children, there is now substituted a reference to £7.00 increased by £0.50 for each additional child.

(2) Where the weekly rate would be £0·10 or less the family income supplement shall not be payable.

(3) Where the weekly rate exceeds £0·10 but would not be a multiple of £0·10 it shall be increased to the nearest multiple.

(4) Regulations may vary the proportion and increase the amounts for the time being specified in this section.

Resources taken into account

4.—(1) The resources of a family taken into account for the purposes of this Act shall be the aggregate of the normal gross income of its members, excluding, except where regulations otherwise provide, the income of any child.

(2) For the purposes of this Act a person's normal gross income and the weekly amount thereof shall be calculated or estimated in such manner as regulations may provide; and regulations may, in particular, provide—

   (a) for making deductions in ascertaining the amount of any income;

   (b) for disregarding the whole or part of the income from any source specified in the regulation; and

   (c) for treating capital resources, other than such as may be specified in the regulations, and any income not consisting of money, as equivalent to gross income of such amount as may be so specified.

Claim to and payment of family income supplement

5.—(1) Any claim to a family income supplement shall be made to the Secretary of State and any family income supplement shall be paid by him.

(2) Where a family includes both a man and a woman the claim shall, except where regulations otherwise provide, be made by them jointly and any sums payable by way of the supplement shall be receivable by either of them; in any other case the claim shall be made and the sums shall be receivable by the man or woman included in the family.

Determination of right to, and amount of, family income supplement

6.—(1) Any question as to the right to or the amount of a family income supplement shall be referred to and determined by the Supplementary Benefits Commission, whose decision shall be final, subject to the provisions of this Act as to appeals.

[(2) Unless regulations otherwise provide, any such question shall be determined as at the date when the claim to the family income supplement is made.

(3) Any family income supplement determined by the Commission to be payable shall be payable for a period of fifty-two weeks, or such other period as may be prescribed by regulations, beginning with the said date or some other date so prescribed and, subject to any provision of regulations, the rate at which it is payable shall not be affected by any change of circumstances during that period.] [2a]

Appeals

7.—(1) A person claiming or in receipt of a family income supple-

---

[2a] Substituted by Pensioners and Family Income Supplement Payments Act 1972 (c. 75), 3. By s. 3 (2) of that Act, regulations made under the unamended section 6 must be read " as if for any reference to 26 weeks there were substituted a reference to 52 weeks."

ment may appeal to the Appeal Tribunal against any determination of the Supplementary Benefits Commission under this Act or a refusal by the Commission to review such a determination (in a case where regulations provide for a review).

(2) On an appeal under this section the Appeal Tribunal may confirm the determination appealed against (or, if the appeal is against a refusal to review a determination, confirm the refusal) or substitute therefor any determination which the Commission could have made, and any determination of the Tribunal shall be final.

(3) The Appeal Tribunal for the purposes of this Act shall be such of the Tribunals constituted in accordance with the provisions of Schedule 3 to the Ministry of Social Security Act 1966 (constitution and proceedings of Appeal Tribunals) as under that Schedule has jurisdiction in the case in question.

Prevention of double payments and recovery of overpayments

8.—(1) Notwithstanding any change of circumstances during a period for which a family income supplement is payable for any family, no person who was included in that family at the time the claim to the supplement was made shall be treated during that period as included in any other family, except where regulations otherwise provide.

(2) Regulations may make provision for securing that no family income supplement is paid for any family during any period during which the requirements of any person included in the family are taken into account for the purposes of any benefit under the Ministry of Social Security Act 1966.

(3) Regulations may provide for the recovery of sums paid by way of family income supplement where it is found that the sums were not due and the persons by whom the sums were receivable cannot satisfy the Supplementary Benefits Commission or the Appeal Tribunal that they had disclosed all material facts.

(4) Where any amount is recoverable under regulations made by virtue of the preceding subsection it may, without prejudice to any other method of recovery, be recovered by deduction from any family income supplement or from any [benefit under the Social Security Acts 1975] [3] or the Family Allowances Acts 1965 to 1969.

Family income supplement to be inalienable

9. Every assignment of, or charge on, a family income supplement, and every agreement to assign or charge a family income supplement, shall be void; and on the bankruptcy or, in Scotland, on the sequestration of the estate, of a person entitled to a family income supplement the supplement shall not pass to any trustee or other person acting on behalf of his creditors.

Regulations

10.—(1) Any power conferred by this Act to make regulations shall be exercisable by the Secretary of State.

(2) Regulations may make such provision, in addition to any authorised by any other provision of this Act, as appears to the Secretary of State to be necessary or expedient for carrying this Act into effect, and, in particular, but without prejudice to the generality of the power conferred by this section,—

  (a) for determining the circumstances in which a person is to be treated as being, or as not being, engaged or normally engaged in remunerative full-time work;

---

[3] Words substituted by Social Security (Consequential Provisions) Act 1975 (c. 18) Sched. 2, as amended by Social Security Pensions Act 1975 (c. 60), Sched. 4.

(b) for determining the circumstances in which a person is to be treated as providing or as not providing, in whole or in part, for the requirements of a child;

(c) for determining the circumstances in which a family is to be treated as being, or as not being, in Great Britain;

(d) for treating, in such circumstances as may be prescribed by the regulations, a person of or over the age of sixteen as being a child (within the meaning of this Act);

(e) for the manner in which claims to family income supplement are to be made and dealt with;

(f) for treating claims to family income supplement made in such circumstances as may be prescribed by the regulations as having been made at such date earlier than that at which they are made as may be so prescribed and for requiring references in this Act to the date of such a claim to be construed accordingly;

(g) for prescribing the evidence which is to be provided in support of claims to family income supplement;

(h) for the review by the Supplementary Benefits Commission of determinations under this Act made by the Commission or the Appeals Tribunal;

(i) for suspending payment of family income supplement pending the determination of questions;

(j) for extinguishing the right to the payment of any sum by way of family income supplement if payment is not obtained within such period, not being less than twelve months, as may be prescribed by the regulations from the date on which the right is treated under the regulations as having arisen.

(3) Regulations may make different provision for different classes of case and otherwise for different circumstances.

(4) The power to make regulations shall be exercisable by statutory instrument which, except in the case of regulations under section 2 or section 3 of this Act, shall be subject to annulment in pursuance of a resolution of either House of Parliament.

(5) No regulations shall be made under section 2 or section 3 of this Act unless a draft thereof has been laid before Parliament and approved by each House of Parliament.

False statements

11. If any person, for the purpose of obtaining any payment of family income supplement, whether for himself or for some other person, or for any other purpose connected with this Act,

(a) makes any statement or representation which he knows to be false; or

(b) produces or furnishes, or causes or knowingly allows to be produced or furnished any document or information which he knows to be false in a material particular,

he shall be liable on summary conviction to a fine not exceeding £100, or to imprisonment for a term not exceeding three months, or to both.

Legal proceedings

12.—(1) Any person authorised by the Secretary of State in that behalf may conduct any proceedings under this Act before a magistrates' court although not a barrister or solicitor.

(2) Notwithstanding anything in any Act, proceedings for an offence under this Act may be begun at any time within the period of three months from the date on which evidence, sufficient in the opinion of the Secretary of State to justify a prosecution for the offence, comes

to his knowledge, or within the period of twelve months from the commission of the offence, whichever period last expires.

(3) For the purposes of subsection (2) of this section, a certificate purporting to be signed by or on behalf of the Secretary of State as to the date on which such evidence as is mentioned in that subsection came to his knowledge shall be conclusive evidence thereof.

(4) The preceding subsections shall not apply to Scotland, but proceedings in Scotland for an offence under this Act may, notwithstanding anything in section 23 of the Summary Jurisdiction (Scotland) Act 1954, be commenced at any time within the period of three months from the date on which evidence sufficient in the opinion of the appropriate authority to justify proceedings comes to his knowledge, or within the period of twelve months from the commission of the offence, whichever period last expires; and for the purposes of this subsection—

　　(a) " the appropriate authority " means the Secretary of State or, in the case of proceedings which are not preceded by a report of the facts made by the Secretary of State to the Lord Advocate, means the Lord Advocate;

　　(b) a certificate of the appropriate authority as to the date on which such evidence as is mentioned above comes to his knowledge shall be conclusive evidence; and

　　(c) subsection (2) of the said section 23 (date of commencement of proceedings) shall have effect as it has effect for the purposes of that section.

(5) In any proceedings for an offence under this Act, the wife or husband of the accused shall be competent to give evidence, whether for or against the accused, but shall not be compellable either to give evidence or, in giving evidence, to disclose any communication made to her or to him by the accused during the marriage.

Amendments of Ministry of Social Security Act 1966

13.—(1) In section 16 (1) of the Ministry of Social Security Act 1966 (prevention of duplication of payments) the following shall be added after paragraph (d):—

　　" or

　　(e) a family income supplement under the Family Income Supplements Act 1970 ".

(2) For the purposes of sub-paragraph (2) of paragraph 5 of Schedule 2 to that Act (adjustment of benefit under that Act to normal earnings) the amount that would be a person's net weekly earnings if he were engaged in full-time work in his normal occupation shall be taken to include the weekly amount of any family income supplement which, if he were so engaged, would be payable for the family of which he is a member; and the weekly amount of any family income supplement actually receivable by him shall be included among the amounts mentioned in sub-paragraph (3) of that paragraph.

(3) [*Repealed by Social Security Benefits Act* 1975 (*c.* 11), *Sched.* 6.]

Amendment of Administration of Justice Act 1970

14. [*Repealed by Attachment of Earnings Act* 1971 (*c.* 32), *s.* 29 (2), *Sched.* 6.]

Expenses

15. There shall be paid out of moneys provided by Parliament—

　　(a) any sums payable by way of family income supplement;

　　(b) any expenses of the Secretary of State attributable to this Act; and

(c) any increase attributable to this Act in the sums payable under any other Act out of moneys provided by Parliament.

Commencement of family income supplement

16.—(1) No family income supplement shall be paid for any period preceding such day as the Secretary of State may by order made by statutory instrument appoint.[4]

(2) An order under this section may (before the day appointed by it) be varied or revoked by a subsequent order thereunder.

(3) A statutory instrument made by virtue of this section shall be laid before Parliament after being made.

Interpretation, short title and extent

17.—(1) In this Act—

" child ", except where regulations otherwise provide, means a person under the age of sixteen;

" family " has the meaning assigned to it by section 1 (1) of this Act;

" regulations " means regulations under this Act; and

" single woman " means any woman other than one who is a member of the same household as a man to whom she is married or with whom she is living as his wife.

(2) This Act may be cited as the Family Income Supplements Act 1970.

(3) This Act does not extend to Northern Ireland.

Guardianship of Minors Act 1971
(1971 c. 3)

An Act to consolidate certain enactments relating to the guardianship and custody of minors.　　　　　[17th February 1971]

General principles
Principle on which questions relating to custody, upbringing etc. of minors are to be decided

1. Where in any proceedings before any court (whether or not a court as defined in section 15 of this Act)—

(a) the custody or upbringing of a minor; or

(b) the administration of any property belonging to or held on trust for a minor, or the application of the income thereof,

is in question, the court, in deciding that question, shall regard the welfare of the minor as the first and paramount consideration, and shall not take into consideration whether from any other point of view the claim of the father, [. . .] [1] in respect of such custody, upbringing, administration or application is superior to that of the mother, or the claim of the mother is superior to that of the father.

Equal right of mother to apply to court

2. [*Repealed by Guardianship Act* 1973 (*c.* 29), *s.* 9 (1), *Sched.* 3.]

Appointment, removal and powers of guardians
Rights of surviving parent as to guardianship

3.—(1) On the death of the father of a minor, the mother, if

---

[4] The Act was brought into operation on May 3, 1971, by 1971 S.I. No. 225. See also 1971 S.I.'s No. 226, 227, 622 and 702; 1972 No. 14, 135 and 1282; 1973 No. 177 and 1362; 1974 No. 59 and 905.

[1] Words repealed by Guardianship Act 1973 (c. 29), s. 9 (1), Sched. 3.

surviving, shall, subject to the provisions of this Act, be guardian of the minor either alone or jointly with any guardian appointed by the father; and—

(a) where no guardian has been appointed by the father; or

(b) in the event of the death or refusal to act of the guardian or guardians appointed by the father,

the court may, if it thinks fit, appoint a guardian to act jointly with the mother.

(2) On the death of the mother of a minor, the father, if surviving, shall, subject to the provisions of this Act, be guardian of the minor either alone or jointly with any guardian appointed by the mother; and—

(a) where no guardian has been appointed by the mother; or

(b) in the event of the death or refusal to act of the guardian or guardians appointed by the mother,

the court may, if it thinks fit, appoint a guardian to act jointly with the father.

Power of father and mother to appoint testamentary guardians

4.—(1) The father of a minor may by deed or will appoint any person to be guardian of the minor after his death.

(2) The mother of a minor may by deed or will appoint any person to be guardian of the minor after her death.

(3) Any guardian so appointed shall act jointly with the mother or father, as the case may be, of the minor so long as the mother or father remains alive unless the mother or father objects to his so acting.

(4) If the mother or father so objects, or if the guardian so appointed considers that the mother or father is unfit to have the custody of the minor, the guardian may apply to the court, and the court may either—

(a) refuse to make any order (in which case the mother or father shall remain sole guardian); or

(b) make an order that the guardian so appointed—

    (i) shall act jointly with the mother or father; or

    (ii) shall be the sole guardian of the minor.

(5) Where guardians are appointed by both parents, the guardians so appointed shall, after the death of the surviving parent, act jointly.

(6) If under section 3 of this Act a guardian has been appointed by the court to act jointly with a surviving parent, he shall continue to act as guardian after the death of the surviving parent; but, if the surviving parent has appointed a guardian, the guardian appointed by the court shall act jointly with the guardian appointed by the surviving parent.

Power of court to appoint guardian for minor having no parent etc.

5.—(1) Where a minor has no parent, no guardian of the person, and no other person having parental rights with respect to him, the court, on the application of any person, may, if it thinks fit, appoint the applicant to be the guardian of the minor.

(2) A court may entertain an application under this section to appoint a guardian of a minor notwithstanding that, by virtue of a resolution under section 2 of the Children Act 1948, a local authority have parental rights with respect to him; but where on such an application the court appoints a guardian the resolution shall cease to have effect.

Power of High Court to remove or replace guardian

6. The High Court may, in its discretion, on being satisfied that it is for the welfare of the minor, remove from his office any testamentary guardian or any guardian appointed or acting by virtue of this Act, and may also, if it deems it to be for the welfare of the minor, appoint another guardian in place of the guardian so removed.

Disputes between joint guardians

7. Where two or more persons act as joint guardians of a minor and they are unable to agree on any question affecting the welfare of the minor, any of them may apply to the court for its direction, and the court may make such order regarding the matters in difference as it may think proper.

Continuation of certain powers of guardians

8. [*Repealed by Guardianship Act 1973 (c. 29), s. 9 (1), Sched. 3.*]

Orders for custody and maintenance

Orders for custody and maintenance on application of mother or father

9.[1a]—(1) The court may, on the application of the mother or father of a minor (who may apply without next friend), make such order regarding—

  (a) the custody of the minor; and

  (b) the right of access to the minor of his mother or father,

as the court thinks fit having regard to the welfare of the minor and to the conduct and wishes of the mother and father.

(2) Where the court makes an order under subsection (1) of this section giving the custody of the minor to [any person, whether or not one of the parents],[2] the court may make a further order requiring [payment to that person by the parent or either of the parents excluded from having that custody of][2] such weekly or other periodical sum towards the maintenance of the minor as the court thinks reasonable having regard to the means of [that parent].[2]

(3) An order may be made under subsection (1) or (2) of this section notwithstanding that the parents of the minor are then residing together, but—

  (a) no such order shall be enforceable, and no liability thereunder shall accrue, while they are residing together; and

  (b) any such order shall cease to have effect if for a period of three months after it is made they continue to reside together.

[Provided that, unless the court in making the order directs otherwise, paragraphs (a) and (b) above shall not apply to any provision of the order giving the custody of the minor to a person other than one of the parents or made with respect to a minor of whom custody is so given.][3]

(4) An order under subsection (1) or (2) of this section may be varied or discharged by a subsequent order made on the application of either parent or [(before or after the death of either parent) on the application of any other person having the custody of the minor by virtue of an order under subsection (1) of this section][3] after the death of either parent on the application of any guardian under this Act.

[1a] Prospectively amended by Children Act 1975 (c. 72), Sched. 3, para. 75, *post.*
[2] Words substituted by Guardianship Act 1973 (c. 29), s. 2 (1), Sched. 2.
[3] Words added by Guardianship Act 1973 (c. 29), s. 2 (1), Sched. 2.

Orders for custody and maintenance where person is guardian to exclusion of surviving parent

10.—(1) Where the court makes an order under section 4 (4) of this Act that a person shall be the sole guardian of a minor to the exclusion of his mother or father, the court may—

    (*a*) make such order regarding—

        (i) the custody of the minor; and

        (ii) the right of access to the minor of his mother or father,

    as the court thinks fit having regard to the welfare of the minor; and

    (*b*) make a further order requiring the mother or father to pay to the guardian such weekly or other periodical sum towards the maintenance of the minor as the court thinks reasonable having regard to the means of the mother or father.

(2) The powers conferred by subsection (1) of this section may be exercised at any time and include power to vary or discharge any order previously made under those powers.

Orders for custody and maintenance where joint guardians disagree

11. The powers of the court under section 7 of this Act shall, where one of the joint guardians is the mother or father of the minor, include power—

    (*a*) to make such order regarding—

        (i) the custody of the minor; and

        (ii) the right of access to the minor of his mother or father,

    as the court thinks fit having regard to the welfare of the minor;

    (*b*) to make an order requiring the mother or father to pay such weekly or other periodical sum towards the maintenance of the minor as the court thinks reasonable having regard to the means of the mother or father;

    (*c*) to vary or discharge any order previously made under that section.

Orders for maintenance of persons between 18 and 21

12.—(1) An order under section 9, 10 or 11 of this Act for the payment of sums towards the maintenance of a minor may require such sums to continue to be paid in respect of any period after the date on which he ceases to be a minor but not extending beyond the date on which he attains the age of twenty-one; and any order which is made as aforesaid may provide that any sum which is payable thereunder for the benefit of a person who has ceased to be a minor shall be paid to that person himself.

(2) Subject to subsection (3) of this section and to section 14 (4) of this Act, where a person who has ceased to be a minor but has not attained the age of twenty-one has, while a minor, been the subject of an order under this Act or under any enactment repealed by this Act, the court may, on the application of either parent of that person or of that person himself, make an order requiring either parent to pay—

    (*a*) to the other parent;

    (*b*) to anyone else for the benefit of that person; or

    (*c*) to that person himself,

in respect of any period not extending beyond the date when he attains the said age, such weekly or other periodical sum towards his maintenance as the court thinks reasonable having regard to the means of the person on whom the requirement is imposed.

(3) No order shall be made under subsection (2) of this section, and

no liability under such an order shall accrue, at a time when the parents of the person in question are residing together, and if they so reside for a period of three months after such an order has been made it shall cease to have effect.

(4) An order under subsection (2) of this section may be varied or discharged by a subsequent order made on the application of any person by or to whom payments were required to be made under the previous order.

Enforcement of order for custody and maintenance

13.[3a]—(1) Where an order made by a magistrates' court under this Act contains a provision committing to [any person] [4] the legal custody of any minor, a copy of the order may be served on any person in whose actual custody the minor may for the time being be, and thereupon the provision may, without prejudice to any other remedy open to [the person given custody],[4] be enforced under section 54 (3) of the Magistrates' Courts Act 1952 as if it were an order of the court requiring [the person so served] [4] to give up the minor to [the person given custody].[4]

(2) Any person for the time being under an obligation to make payments in pursuance of any order for the payment of money under this Act shall give notice of any change of address to such person (if any) as may be specified in the order, and any person failing without reasonable excuse to give such a notice shall be liable on summary conviction to a fine not exceeding £10.

(3) An order of a magistrates' court for the payment of money under this Act may be enforced in like manner as an affiliation order, and the enactments relating to affiliation orders shall apply accordingly with the necessary modifications.

Illegitimate children

Application of Act to illegitimate children

14.—(1) Subject to the provisions of this section, subsection (1) of section 9 of this Act shall apply in relation to a minor who is illegitimate as it applies in relation to a minor who is legitimate, and references in that subsection, and in any other provision of this Act so far as it relates to proceedings under that subsection, to the father or mother or parent of a minor shall be construed accordingly.

(2) No order shall be made by virtue of subsection (1) of this section under subsection (2) of the said section 9.

(3) For the purposes of sections 3, 4, 5 and 10 of this Act, a person being the natural father of an illegitimate child and being entitled to his custody by virtue of an order in force under section 9 of this Act, as applied by this section, shall be treated as if he were the lawful father of the minor; but any appointment of a guardian made by virtue of this subsection under section 4 (1) of this Act shall be of no effect unless the appointor is entitled to the custody of the minor as aforesaid immediately before his death.

(4) No order shall be made under section 12 (2) of this Act requiring any person to pay any sum towards the maintenance of an illegitimate child of that person.

Jurisdiction and procedure

Courts having jurisdiction under this Act

15.—(1) Subject to the provisions of this section, " the court " for the purposes of this Act means—

3a Prospectively amended by Children Act 1975 (c. 72), Sched. 3, para. 75, *post.*
4 Words substituted by Guardianship Act 1973 (c. 29), s. 2 (1), Sched. 2.

    (*a*) the High Court;

    (*b*) the county court of the district in which the respondent (or any of the respondents) or the applicant or the minor to whom the application relates resides; or

    (*c*) a magistrates' court having jurisdiction in the place in which any of the said persons resides.

(2) A magistrates' court shall not be competent to entertain—

    (*a*) any application (other than an application for the variation or discharge of an existing order under this Act) relating to a minor who has attained the age of sixteen unless the minor is physically or mentally incapable of self-support; or

    (*b*) any application involving the administration or application of any property belonging to or held in trust for a minor, or the income thereof.

(3) A county court or magistrates' court shall not have jurisdiction under this Act in any case where the respondent or any of the respondents resides in Scotland or Northern Ireland—

    (*a*) except in so far as such jurisdiction may be exercisable by virtue of the following provisions of this section; or

    (*b*) unless a summons or other originating process can be served and is served on the respondent or, as the case may be, on the respondents in England or Wales.

(4) An order under this Act giving the custody of a minor to [to a person resident in England or Wales] [4] whether with or without an order [requiring payments to be made] [4] towards the minor's maintenance, may be made, if [one parent] [4] resides in Scotland or Northern Ireland and [the other parent] [4] and the minor in England or Wales, by a magistrates' court having jurisdiction in the place in which [the other parent] [4] resides.

(5) It is hereby declared that a magistrates' court has jurisdiction—

    (*a*) in proceedings under this Act by a person residing in Scotland or Northern Ireland against a person residing in England or Wales for an order relating to the custody of a minor (including, [. . .],[5] an order [requiring payments to be made] [4] towards the minor's maintenance);

    (*b*) in proceeding by or against a person residing in Scotland or Northern Ireland for the revocation, revival or variation of any such order.

(6) Where proceedings for an order under subsection (1) of section 9 of this Act relating to the custody of a minor are brought in a magistrates court by [a person] [4] residing in Scotland or Northern Ireland, the court shall have jurisdiction to make any order in respect of the minor under [that section] [4] on the application of the respondent in the proceedings.

Appeals and procedure

16.—(1) Where any application has been made under this Act to a county court, [the High Court may] [5a] at the instance of any party to the application, order the application to be removed to the High Court and there proceeded with on such terms as to costs as it thinks proper.

(2) An appeal shall lie to the High Court from any order [made on an application under this Act by a county court].[6]

(3) Subject to subsection (4) of this section, where on an application

---

[5] Words repealed by Guardianship Act 1973 (c. 29), s. 2 (1), Sched. 2.

[5a] Words substituted by Children Act 1975 (c. 72), Sched. 3, para. 75.

[6] Words substituted by Guardianship Act 1973 (c. 29), s. 2 (7).

to a magistrates' court under this Act the court makes or refuses to make an order, an appeal shall lie to the High Court.

(4) Where an application is made to a magistrates' court under this Act, and the court considers that the matter is one which would more conveniently be dealt with by the High Court [the magistrate's court shall] [5a] refuse to make an order, and in that case no appeal shall lie to the High Court.

[" (5) In relation to applications made to a magistrates' court under [section 3 (3) or 4 (3A) of the Guardianship Act 1973 for the discharge or variation of a supervision order or, as the case may be, an order giving the care of a minor to a local authority or an order requiring payments to be made to an authority to whom care of a minor is so given] [5a] rules made under section 15 of the Justices of the Peace Act 1949 may make provision as to the persons who are to be made defendants on the application; and if on any such application there are two or more defendants, the power of the court under section 55 (1) of the Magistrates' Courts Act 1952 shall be deemed to include power, whatever adjudication the court makes on the complaint, to order any of the parties to pay the whole or part of the costs of all or any of the other parties."] [4]

Saving for powers of High Court and other courts

17.—(1) Nothing in this Act shall restrict or affect the jurisdiction of the High Court to appoint or remove guardians or otherwise in respect of minors.

(2) Nothing in section 15 (4), (5) or (6) of this Act shall be construed as derogating from any jurisdiction exercisable, apart from those provisions, by any court in England or Wales; and it is hereby declared that any jurisdiction conferred by those provisions is exercisable notwithstanding that any party to the proceedings is not domiciled in England and Wales.

Supplementary

Consequential amendments, repeals and savings

18.—(1) The enactments specified in Schedule 1 to this Act shall have effect subject to the amendments there specified, being amendments consequential on this Act.

(2) The enactments specified in Schedule 2 to this Act are hereby repealed to the extent specified in the third column of that Schedule.

(3) Any application, order or other thing made, done or having effect under or for the purposes of an enactment repealed by this Act and pending or in force immediately before the commencement of this Act shall be deemed to have been made or done under or for the purposes of the corresponding enactment in this Act; and any proceeding or other thing begun under any enactment so repealed may be continued under this Act as if begun thereunder.

(4) So much of any document as refers expressly or by implication to any enactment repealed by this Act shall, if and so far as the nature of the subject-matter of the document permits, be construed as referring to this Act or the corresponding enactment therein, as the case may require.

(5) Nothing in this section shall be taken as prejudicing the general application of section 38 of the Interpretation Act 1889 with regard to the effect of repeals.

Transitory provisions pending coming into force of s. 1 (2) of Administration of Justice Act 1970

19. Until the coming into force of section 1 (2) of the Administration of Justice Act 1970 this Act shall have effect subject to the following modifications, that is to say—

(a) in section 6 after the words " High Court " there shall be inserted the words " in any division thereof ";

(b) after section 15 (1) there shall be inserted the words " Any application under this Act to the High Court shall be made to the Chancery Division in such manner as may be prescribed by rules of court ";

(c) in subsection (1) of section 16 after the words " proceeded with " there shall be inserted the words " before a judge of the Chancery Division ", at the end of subsection (2) of that section there shall be added the words " and subject to rules of court any such appeal shall be heard by a judge of the Chancery Division in chambers or in court as he shall direct " and in subsection (3) of that section after the word " shall " there shall be inserted the words " in accordance with rules of court ";

(d) in section 17 (1) after the words " High Court " there shall be inserted the words " or of any division thereof ".

Short title, interpretation, extent and commencement

20.—(1) This Act may be cited as the Guardianship of Minors Act 1971.

(2) In this Act " maintenance " includes education.

(3) References in this Act to any enactment are references thereto as amended, and include references thereto as applied, by any other enactment.

(4) This Act—

(a) so far as it amends the Maintenance Orders Act 1950, extends to Scotland and Northern Ireland;

(b) so far as it amends the Army Act 1955 and the Air Force Act 1955, extends to Northern Ireland,

but, save as aforesaid, extends to England and Wales only.

(5) This Act shall come into force at the expiration of the period of one month beginning with the day on which it is passed.

. . . . . .

Attachment of Earnings Act 1971

(1971 c. 32)

An Act to consolidate the enactments relating to the attachment of earnings as a means of enforcing the discharge of monetary obligations.   [12th May 1971]

Cases in which attachment is available

Courts with power to attach earnings

1.—(1) The High Court may make an attachment of earnings order to secure payments under a High Court maintenance order.

(2) A county court may make an attachment of earnings order to secure—

(a) payments under a High Court or a county court maintenance order;

(b) the payment of a judgment debt, other than a debt of less than

£5 or such other sum as may be prescribed by county court rules; or

(c) payments under an administration order.

(3) A magistrates' court may make an attachment of earnings order to secure—

(a) payments under a magistrates' court maintenance order;

(b) the payment of any sum adjudged to be paid by a conviction or treated (by any enactment relating to the collection and enforcement of fines, costs, compensation or forfeited recognisances) as so adjudged to be paid; or

(c) the payment of any sum required to be paid by a legal aid contribution order.

(4) The following provisions of this Act apply, except where otherwise stated, to attachment of earnings orders made, or to be made, by any court.

(5) Any power conferred by this Act to make an attachment of earnings order includes a power to make such an order to secure the discharge of liabilities arising before the coming into force of this Act.

Principal definitions

2. In this Act—

(a) " maintenance order " means any order specified in Schedule 1 to this Act and includes such an order which has been discharged if any arrears are recoverable thereunder;

(b) " High Court maintenance order ", " county court maintenance order " and " magistrates' court maintenance order " mean respectively a maintenance order enforceable by the High Court, a county court and a magistrates' court;

(c) " judgment debt " means a sum payable under—

(i) a judgment or order enforceable by a court in England and Wales (not being a magistrates' court);

(ii) an order of a magistrates' court for the payment of money recoverable summarily as a civil debt; or

(iii) an order of any court which is enforceable as if it were for the payment of money so recoverable,

but does not include any sum payable under a maintenance order or an administration order;

(d) " the relevant adjudication ", in relation to any payment secured or to be secured by an attachment of earnings order, means the conviction, judgment, order or other adjudication from which there arises the liability to make the payment; and

(e) " the debtor ", in relation to an attachment of earnings order, or to proceedings in which a court has power to make an attachment of earnings order, or to proceedings arising out of such an order, means the person by whom payment is required by the relevant adjudication to be made.

Application for order and conditions of court's power to make it

3.—(1) The following persons may apply for an attachment of earnings order:—

(a) the person to whom payment under the relevant adjudication is required to be made (whether directly or through an officer of any court);

(b) where the relevant adjudication is an administration order, any one of the creditors scheduled to the order;

(c) without prejudice to paragraph (a) above, where the application is to a magistrates' court for an order to secure maintenance payments, and there is in force an order under section 52 (1) of the Magistrates' Courts Act 1952, or section 19 (2) of the Maintenance Orders Act 1950, that those payments be made to the clerk of a magistrates' court, the clerk of that court;

(*d*) in the following cases the debtor—

(i) where the application is to a magistrates' court; or

(ii) where the application is to the High Court or a county court for an order to secure maintenance payments.

(2) An application for an attachment of earnings order to secure maintenance payments shall not be made, except by the debtor, unless at least fifteen days have elapsed since the making of the related maintenance order.

(3) For an attachment of earnings order to be made on the application of any person other than the debtor it must appear to the court that the debtor has failed to make one or more payments required by the relevant adjudication.

(4) Where proceedings are brought—

(*a*) in the High Court or a county court for the enforcement of a maintenance order by committal under section 5 of the Debtors Act 1869; or

(*b*) in a magistrates' court for the enforcement of a maintenance order under section 64 of the Magistrates' Courts Act 1952 (distress or committal),

then, subject to subsection (5) below, the court may make an attachment of earnings order to secure payments under the maintenance order, instead of dealing with the case under section 5 of the said Act of 1869 or, as the case may be, section 64 of the said Act of 1952.

(5) The court shall not, except on the application of the debtor, make an attachment of earnings order to secure payments under a maintenance order if it appears to it that the debtor's failure to make payments in accordance with the maintenance order is not due to his wilful refusal or culpable neglect.

(6) Where proceedings are brought in a county court for an order of committal under section 5 of the Debtors Act 1869 in respect of a judgment debt for any of the taxes, contributions [premiums] or liabilities specified in Schedule 2 to this Act, the court may, in any circumstances in which it has power to make such an order, make instead an attachment of earnings order to secure the payment of the judgment debt.

(7) A county court shall not make an attachment of earnings order to secure the payment of a judgment debt if there is in force an order or warrant for the debtor's committal, under section 5 of the Debtors Act 1869, in respect of that debt; but in any such case the court may discharge the order or warrant with a view to making an attachment of earnings order instead.

Administration orders in the county court

Extension of power to make administration order

4.—(1) Where, on an application to a county court for an attachment of earnings order to secure the payment of a judgment debt, it appears to the court that the debtor also has other debts, the court—

(*a*) shall consider whether the case may be one in which all the debtor's liabilities should be dealt with together and that for that purpose an order should be made for the administration of his estate; and

(*b*) if of opinion that it may be such a case, shall have power (whether or not it makes the attachment of earnings order applied for), with a view to making an administration order, to order the

¹ Word added by Social Security Act 1973 (c. 38), Sched. 27.

debtor to furnish to the court a list of all his creditors and the amounts which he owes to them respectively.

(2) If, on receipt of the list referred to in subsection (1) (*b*) above, it appears to the court that the debtor's whole indebtedness amounts to not more than the amount for the time being specified in section 148 (1) (*b*) of the County Courts Act 1959 (limit of total indebtedness governing county court's power to make administration order on application of debtor), the court may make such an order in respect of the debtor's estate.

This subsection is subject to section 20 (3) of the Administration of Justice Act 1965 (which requires that, before an administration order is made, notice is to be given to all the creditors and thereafter restricts the right of any creditor to institute bankruptcy proceedings).

(3) Where under subsection (1) above a county court orders a person to furnish to it a list of all his creditors, the making of the order shall, for the purposes of the Bankruptcy Act 1914, be an act of bankruptcy by him.

(4) Nothing in this section is to be taken as prejudicing any right of a debtor to apply, under section 148 of the County Courts Act 1959, for an administration order.

Attachment of earnings to secure payments under administration order

5.—(1) Where a county court makes an administration order in respect of a debtor's estate, it may also make an attachment of earnings order to secure the payments required by the administration order.

(2) At any time when an administration order is in force a county court may (with or without an application) make an attachment of earnings order to secure the payments required by the administration order, if it appears to the court that the debtor has failed to make any such payment.

(3) The power of a county court under this section to make an attachment of earnings order to secure the payments required by an administration order shall, where the debtor is already subject to an attachment of earnings order to secure the payment of a judgment debt, include power to direct that the last-mentioned order shall take effect (with or without variation under section 9 of this Act) as an order to secure the payments required by the administration order.

Consequences of attachment order

Effect and contents of order

6.—(1) An attachment of earnings order shall be an order directed to a person who appears to the court to have the debtor in his employment and shall operate as an instruction to that person—

(*a*) to make periodical deductions from the debtor's earnings in accordance with Part I of Schedule 3 to this Act; and

(*b*) at such times as the order may require, or as the court may allow, to pay the amounts deducted to the collecting officer of the court, as specified in the order

(2) For the purposes of this Act, the relationship of employer and employee shall be treated as subsisting between two persons if one of them as a principal and not as a servant or agent, pays to the other any sums defined as earnings by section 24 of this Act.

(3) An attachment of earnings order shall contain prescribed particulars enabling the debtor to be identified by the employer.

(4) Except where it is made to secure maintenance payments, the order shall specify the whole amount payable under the relevant adjudication (or so much of that amount as remains unpaid), including any relevant costs.

419

(5) The order shall specify—

    (*a*) the normal deduction rate, that is to say, the rate (expressed as a sum of money per week, month or other period) at which the court thinks it reasonable for the debtor's earnings to be applied to meeting his liability under the relevant adjudication; and

    (*b*) the protected earnings rate, that is to say the rate (so expressed) below which, having regard to the debtor's resources and needs, the court thinks it reasonable that the earnings actually paid to him should not be reduced.

(6) In the case of an order made to secure payments under a maintenance order (not being an order for the payment of a lump sum), the normal deduction rate—

    (*a*) shall be determined after taking account of any right or liability of the debtor to deduct income tax when making the payments; and

    (*b*) shall not exceed the rate which appears to the court necessary for the purpose of—

        (i) securing payment of the sums falling due from time to time under the maintenance order, and

        (ii) securing payment within a reasonable period of any sums already due and unpaid under the maintenance order.

(7) For the purposes of an attachment of earnings order, the collecting officer of the court shall be (subject to later variation of the order under section 9 of this Act)—

    (*a*) in the case of an order made by the High Court, either—

        (i) the proper officer of the High Court, or

        (ii) the registrar of such county court as the order may specify;

    (*b*) in the case of an order made by a county court, the registrar of that court; and

    (*c*) in the case of an order made by a magistrates' court, the clerk either of that court or of another magistrates' court specified in the order.

Compliance with order by employer

7.—(1) Where an attachment of earnings order has been made, the employer shall, if he has been served with the order, comply with it; but he shall be under no liability for non-compliance before seven days have elapsed since the service.

(2) Where a person is served with an attachment of earnings order directed to him and he has not the debtor in his employment, or the debtor subsequently ceases to be in his employment, he shall (in either case), within ten days from the date of service or, as the case may be, the cesser, give notice of that fact to the court.

(3) Part II of Schedule 3 to this Act shall have effect with respect to the priority to be accorded as between two or more attachment of earnings orders directed to a person in respect of the same debtor.

(4) On any occasion when the employer makes, in compliance with the order, a deduction from the debtor's earnings—

    (*a*) he shall be entitled to deduct, in addition, five new pence, or such other sum as may be prescribed by order made by the Lord Chancellor, towards his clerical and administrative costs; and

    (*b*) he shall give to the debtor a statement in writing of the total amount of the deduction.

(5) An order of the Lord Chancellor under subsection (4) (*a*) above—

(a) may prescribe different sums in relation to different classes of cases;

(b) may be varied or revoked by a subsequent order made under that paragraph; and

(c) shall be made by statutory instrument subject to annulment by resolution of either House of Parliament.

Interrelation with alternative remedies open to creditor

8.—(1) Where an attachment of earnings order has been made to secure maintenance payments, no order or warrant of commitment shall be issued in consequence of any proceedings for the enforcement of the related maintenance order begun before the making of the attachment of earnings order.

(2) Where a county court has made an attachment of earnings order to secure the payment of a judgment debt—

(a) no order or warrant of commitmemnt shall be issued in consequence of any proceedings for the enforcement of the debt begun before the making of the attachment of earnings order; and

(b) so long as the order is in force, no execution for the recovery of the debt shall issue against any property of the debtor without the leave of the county court.

(3) An attachment of earnings order made to secure maintenance payments shall cease to have effect upon the making of an order of commitment or the issue of a warrant of commitment for the enforcement of the related maintenance order, or upon the exercise for that purpose of the power conferred on a magistrates' court by section 65 (2) of the Magistrates' Courts Act 1952 to postpone the issue of such a warrant.

(4) An attachment of earnings order made to secure the payment of a judgment debt shall cease to have effect on the making of an order of commitment or the issue of a warrant of commitment for the enforcement of the debt.

(5) An attachment of earnings order made to secure any payment specified in section 1 (3) (b) or (c) of this Act shall cease to have effect on the issue of a warrant committing the debtor to prison for default in making that payment.

Subsequent proceedings

Variation, lapse and discharge of orders

9.—(1) The court may make an order discharging or varying an attachment of earnings order.

(2) Where an order is varied, the employer shall, if he has been served with notice of the variation, comply with the order as varied; but he shall be under no liability for non-compliance before seven days have elapsed since the service.

(3) Rules of court may make provision—

(a) as to the circumstances in which an attachment of earnings order may be varied or discharged by the court of its own motion;

(b) in the case of an attachment of earnings order made by a magistrates' court, for enabling a single justice, on an application made by the debtor on the ground of a material change in his resources and needs since the order was made or last varied, to vary the order for a period of not more than four weeks by an increase of the protected earnings rate.

(4) Where an attachment of earnings order has been made and the person to whom it is directed ceases to have the debtor in his employment, the order shall lapse (except as respects deduction from earnings

paid after the cesser and payment to the collecting officer of amounts
deducted at any time) and be of no effect unless and until the court
again directs it to a person (whether the same as before or another)
who appears to the court to have the debtor in his employment.

(5) The lapse of an order under subsection (4) above shall not prevent its being treated as remaining in force for other purposes.

Normal deduction rate to be reduced in certain cases

10.—(1) The following provisions shall have effect, in the case of an
attachment of earnings order made to secure maintenance payments,
where it appears to the collecting officer of the court that—

(*a*) the aggregate of the payments made for the purposes of the
related maintenance order by the debtor (whether under the
attachment of earnings order or otherwise) exceeds the aggregate
of the payments required up to that time by the maintenance
order; and

(*b*) the normal deduction rate specified by the attachment of earnings order (or, where two or more such orders are in force in
relation to the maintenance order, the aggregate of the normal
deduction rates specified by those orders) exceeds the rate of
payments required by the maintenance order; and

(*c*) no proceedings for the variation or discharge of the attachment
of earnings order are pending.

(2) In the case of an order made by the High Court or a county
court, the collecting officer shall give the prescribed notice to the person
to whom he is required to pay sums received under the attachment of
earnings order, and to the debtor; and the court shall make the appropriate variation order, unless the debtor requests it to discharge the
attachment of earnings order, or to vary it in some other way, and the
court thinks fit to comply with the request.

(3) In the case of an order made by a magistrates' court, the
collecting officer shall apply to the court for the appropriate variation
order; and the court shall grant the application unless the debtor
appears at the hearing and requests the court to discharge the attachment
of earnings order, or to vary it in some other way, and the court thinks
fit to comply with the request.

(4) In this section, " the appropriate variation order " means an
order varying the attachment of earnings order in question by reducing
the normal deduction rate specified thereby so as to secure that that
rate (or, in the case mentioned in subsection (1) (*b*) above, the aggregate of the rates therein mentioned)—

(*a*) is the same as the rate of payments required by the maintenance
order; or

(*b*) is such lower rate as the court thinks fit having regard to the
amount of the excess mentioned in subsection (1) (*a*).

Attachment order in respect of maintenance payments to cease to have effect on occurrence of certain events

11.—(1) An attachment of earnings order made to secure maintenance payments shall cease to have effect—

(*a*) upon the grant of an application for registration of the related
maintenance order under section 2 of the Maintenance Orders
Act 1958 (which provides for the registration in a magistrates'
court of a High Court or county court maintenance order, and
for registration in the High Court of a magistrates' court maintenance order);

(*b*) where the related maintenance order is registered under Part I of the said Act of 1958, upon the giving of notice with respect thereto under section 5 of that Act (notice with view to cancellation of registration);

(c) subject to subsection (3) below, upon the discharge of the related maintenance order while it is not registered under Part I of the said Act of 1958;

(d) upon the related maintenance order ceasing to be registered in a court in England or Wales, or becoming registered in a court in Scotland or Northern Ireland, under Part II of the Maintenance Orders Act 1950.

(2) Subsection (1) (a) above shall have effect, in the case of an application for registration under section 2 (1) of the said Act of 1958, notwithstanding that the grant of the application may subsequently become void under subsection (2) of that section.

(3) Where the related maintenance order is discharged as mentioned in subsection (1) (c) above and it appears to the court discharging the order that arrears thereunder will remain to be recovered after the discharge, that court may, if it thinks fit, direct that subsection (1) shall not apply.

Termination of employer's liability to make deductions

12.—(1) Where an attachment of earnings order ceases to have effect under section 8 or 11 of this Act, the proper officer of the prescribed court shall give notice of the cesser to the person to whom the order was directed.

(2) Where, in the case of an attachment of earnings order made otherwise to secure maintenance payments, the whole amount payable under the relevant adjudication has been paid, and also any relevant costs, the court shall give notice to the employer that no further compliance with the order is required.

(3) Where an attachment of earnings order—

(a) ceases to have effect under section 8 or 11 of this Act; or

(b) is discharged under section 9.

the person to whom the order has been directed shall be under no liability in consequence of his treating the order as still in force at any time before the expiration of seven days from the date on which the notice required by subsection (1) above or, as the case may be, a copy of the discharging order is served on him.

Administrative provisions

Application of sums received by collecting officer

13.—(1) Subject to subsection (3) below, the collecting officer to whom a person makes payments in compliance with an attachment of earnings order shall, after deducting such court fees, if any, in respect of proceedings for or arising out of the order, as are deductible from those payments, deal with the sums paid in the same way as he would if they had been paid by the debtor to satisfy the relevant adjudication.

(2) Any sums paid to the collecting officer under an attachment of earnings order made to secure maintenance payments shall, when paid to the person entitled to receive those payments, be deemed to be payments made by the debtor (with such deductions, if any, in respect of income tax as the debtor is entitled or required to make) so as to discharge—

(a) first, any sums for the time being due and unpaid under the related maintenance order (a sum due at an earlier date being discharged before a sum due at a later date); and (*b*) secondly, any costs incurred in proceedings relating to the related maintenance order which were payable by the debtor when the attachment of earnings order was made or last varied.

(3) Where a county court makes an attachment of earnings order to secure the payment of a judgment debt and also, under section 4 (1) of this Act, orders the debtor to furnish to the court a list of all his creditors, sums paid to the collecting officer in compliance with the attachment of earnings order shall not be dealt with by him as mentioned in subsection (1) above, but shall be retained by him pending the decision of the court whether or not to make an administration order and shall then be dealt with by him as the court may direct.

Power of court to obtain statements of earnings etc.

14.—(1) Where in any proceedings a court has power to make an attachment of earnings order, it may—

(*a*) order the debtor to give to the court, within a specified period, a statement signed by him of—

(i) the name and address of any person by whom earnings are paid to him:

(ii) specified particulars as to his earnings and anticipated earnings, and as to his resources and needs; and

(iii) specified particulars for the purpose of enabling the debtor to be identified by any employer of his;

(*b*) order any person appearing to the court to have the debtor in his employment to give to the court, within a specified period, a statement signed by him or on his behalf of specified particulars of the debtor's earnings and anticipated earnings.

(2) Where an attachment of earnings order has been made, the court may at any time thereafter while the order is in force make such an order as is described in subsection (1) (*a*) or (*b*) above.

(3) In the case of an application to a magistrates' court for an attachment of earnings order, or for the variation or discharge of such an order, the power to make an order under subsection (1) or (2) above shall be exercisable also, before the hearing of the application, by a single justice.

(4) Without prejudice to subsections (1) to (3) above, rules of court may provide that where notice of an application for an attachment of earnings order is served on the debtor, it shall include a requirement that he shall give to the court, within such period and in such manner as may be prescribed, a statement in writing of the matters specified in subsection (1) (*a*) above and of any other prescribed matters which are, or may be, relevant under section 6 of this Act to the determination of the normal deduction rate and the protected earnings rate to be specified in any order made on the application.

(5) In any proceedings in which a court has power to make an attachment of earnings order, and in any proceedings for the making, variation or discharge of such an order, a document purporting to be a statement given to the court in compliance with an order under subsection (1) (*a*) or (*b*) above, or with any such requirement of a notice of application for an attachment of earnings order as is mentioned in subsection (4) above, shall, in the absence of proof to the contrary, be deemed to be a statement so given and shall be evidence of the facts stated therein.

Obligation of debtor and his employers to notify changes of employment and earnings

15. While an attachment of earnings order is in force—

(*a*) the debtor shall from time to time notify the court in writing of every occasion on which he leaves any employment, or becomes employed or re-employed, not later (in each case) than seven days from the date on which he did so;

(b) the debtor shall, on any occasion when he becomes employed or re-employed, include in his notification under paragraph (a) above particulars of his earnings and anticipated earnings from the relevant employment; and

(c) any person who becomes the debtor's employer and knows that the order is in force and by what court it was made shall, within seven days of his becoming the debtor's employer or of acquiring that knowledge (whichever is the later) notify that court in writing that he is the debtor's employer, and include in his notification a statement of the debtor's earnings and anticipated earnings.

Power of court to determine whether particular payments are earnings

16.—(1) Where an attachment of earnings order is in force, the court shall, on the application of a person specified in subsection (2) below, determine whether payments to the debtor of a particular class or description specified by the application are earnings for the purposes of the order; and the employer shall be entitled to give effect to any determination for the time being in force under this section.

(2) The persons referred to in subsection (1) above are—

(a) the employer;

(b) the debtor;

(c) the person to whom payment under the relevant adjudication is required to be made (whether directly or through an officer of any court); and

(d) without prejudice to paragraph (c) above, where the application is in respect of an attachment of earnings order made to secure payments under a magistrates' court maintenance order, the collecting officer.

(3) Where an application under this section is made by the employer, he shall not incur any liability for non-compliance with the order as respects any payments of the class or description specified by the application which are made by him to the debtor while the application, or any appeal in consequence thereof, is pending; but this subsection shall not, unless the court otherwise orders, apply as respects such payments if the employer subsequently withdraws the application or, as the case may be, abandons the appeal.

Consolidated attachment orders

17.—(1) The powers of a county court under sections 1 and 3 of this Act shall include power to make an attachment of earnings order to secure the payment of any number of judgment debt; and the powers of a magistrates' court under those sections shall include power to make an attachment of earnings order to secure the discharge of any number of such liabilities as are specified in section 1 (3).

(2) An attachment of earnings order made by virtue of this section shall be known as a consolidated attachment order.

(3) The power to make a consolidated attachment order shall be exercised subject to and in accordance with rules of court; and rules made for the purposes of this section may provide—

(a) for the transfer from one court to another—

(i) of an attachment of earnings order, or any proceedings for or arising out of such an order; and

(ii) of functions relating to the enforcement of any liability
capable of being secured by attachment of earnings;

(*b*) for enabling a court to which any order, proceedings or functions
have been transferred under the rules to vary or discharge an
attachment of earnings order made by another court and to
replace it (if the court thinks fit) with a consolidated attachment
order;

(*c*) for the cases in which any power exercisable under this section or
the rules may be exercised by a court of its own motion or on
the application of a prescribed person;

(*d*) for requiring the clerk or registrar of a court who receives payments made to him in compliance with an attachment of earnings
order, instead of complying with section 13 of this Act, to deal
with them as directed by the court or the rules; and

(*e*) for modifying or excluding provisions of this Act or Part III of
the Magistrates' Courts Act 1952, but only so far as may be
necessary or expedient for securing conformity with the operation of rules made by virtue of paragraphs (*a*) to (*d*) of this subsection.

Special provisions with respect to magistrates' courts

Certain action not to be taken by collecting officer except on request

18.—(1) The clerk of a magistrates' court who is entitled to receive
payments under a maintenance order for transmission to another person
shall not—

(*a*) apply for an attachment of earnings order to secure payments
under the maintenance order; or

(*b*) except as provided by section 10 (3) of this Act, apply for an
order discharging or varying such an attachment of earnings
order; or

(*c*) apply for a determination under section 16 of this Act,

unless he is requested in writing to do so by a person entitled to receive
the payments through him.

(2) Where the clerk is so requested—

(*a*) he shall comply with the request unless it appears to him
unreasonable in the circumstances to do so; and

(*b*) the person by whom the request was made shall have the
same liabilities for all the costs properly incurred in or about
any proceedings taken in pursuance of the request as if the
proceedings had been taken by that person.

(3) For the purposes of subsection (2) (*b*) above, any application
made by the clerk as required by section 10 (3) of this Act shall be
deemed to be made on the request of the person in whose favour the
attachment of earnings order in question was made.

Procedure on applications

19.—(1) Subject to rules of court made by virtue of the following
subsection, an application to a magistrates' court for an attachment of
earnings order, or an order discharging or varying an attachment of
earnings order, shall be made by complaint.

(2) Rules of court may make provision excluding subsection (1) in
the case of such an application as is referred to in section 9 (3) (*b*) of
this Act.

(3) An application to a magistrates' court for a determination under
section 16 of this Act shall be made by complaint.

(4) For the purposes of section 43 of the Magistrates' Courts Act

1952 (which provides for the issue of a summons directed to the person against whom an order may be made in pursuance of a complaint)—

(*a*) the power to make an order in pursuance of a complaint by the debtor for an attachment of earnings order, or the discharge or variation of such an order, shall be deemed to be a power to make an order against the person to whom payment under the relevant adjudication is required to be made (whether directly or through an officer of any court); and

(*b*) the power to make an attachment of earnings order, or an order discharging or varying an attachment of earnings order, in pursuance of a complaint by any other person (including a complaint in proceedings to which section 3 (4) (*b*) of this Act applies) shall be deemed to be a power to make an order against the debtor.

(5) A complaint for an attachment of earnings order may be heard notwithstanding that it was not made within the six months allowed by section 104 of the Magistrates' Courts Act 1952.

Jurisdiction in respect of persons residing outside England and Wales

20.—(1) It is hereby declared that a magistrates' court has jurisdiction to hear a complaint by or against a person residing outside England and Wales for the discharge or variation of an attachment of earnings order made by a magistrates' court to secure maintenance payments; and where such a complaint is made, the following provisions shall have effect.

(2) If the person resides in Scotland or Northern Ireland, section 15 of the Maintenance Orders Act 1950 (which relates to the service of process on persons residing in those countries) shall have effect in relation to the complaint as it has effect in relation to the proceedings therein mentioned.

(3) Subject to the following subsection, if the person resides outside the United Kingdom and does not appear at the time and place appointed for the hearing of the complaint, the court may, if it thinks it reasonable in all the circumstances to do so, proceed to hear and determine the complaint at the time and place appointed for the hearing, or for any adjourned hearing, in like manner as if the person had then appeared.

(4) Subsection (3) above shall apply only if it is proved to the satisfaction of the court, on oath or in such other manner as may be prescribed, that the complainant has taken such steps as may be prescribed to give to the said person notice of the complaint and of the time and place appointed for the hearing of it.

Costs on application under s. 16

21.—(1) On making a determination under section 16 of this Act, a magistrates' court may in its discretion make such order as it thinks just and reasonable for payment by any of the persons mentioned in subsection (2) of that section of the whole or any part of the costs of the determination (but subject to section 18 (2) (*b*) of this Act).

(2) Costs ordered to be paid under this section shall—

(*a*) in the case of costs to be paid by the debtor to the person in whose favour the attachment of earnings order in question was made, be deemed—

(i) if the attachment of earnings order was made to secure maintenance payments, to be a sum due under the related maintenance order, and

(ii) otherwise, to be a sum due to the clerk of the court; and

(*b*) in any other case, be enforceable as a civil debt.

Miscellaneous provisions

Persons employed under the Crown

22.—(1) The fact that an attachment of earnings order is made at the suit of the Crown shall not prevent its operation at any time when the debtor is in the employment of the Crown.

(2) Where a debtor is in the employment of the Crown and an attachment of earnings order is made in respect of him, then for the purposes of this Act—

    (*a*) the chief officer for the time being of the department, office or other body in which the debtor is employed shall be treated as having the debtor in his employment (any transfer of the debtor from one department, office or body to another being treated as a change of employment); and

    (*b*) any earnings paid by the Crown or a Minister of the Crown, or out of the public revenue of the United Kingdom, shall be treated as paid by the said chief officer.

(3) If any question arises, in proceedings for or arising out of an attachment of earnings order, as to what department, office or other body is concerned for the purposes of this section, or as to who for those purposes is the chief officer thereof, the question shall be referred to and determined by the Minister for the Civil Service; but that Minister shall not be under any obligation to consider a reference under this subsection unless it is made by the court.

(4) A document purporting to set out a determination of the said Minister under subsection (3) above and to be signed by an official of the Civil Service Department shall, in any such proceedings as are mentioned in that subsection, be admissible in evidence and be deemed to contain an accurate statement of such a determination unless the contrary is shown.

(5) This Act shall have effect notwithstanding any enactment passed before 29th May 1970 and preventing or avoiding the attachment or diversion of sums due to a person in respect of service under the Crown, whether by way of remuneration, pension or otherwise.

Enforcement provisions

23.—(1) If, after being served with notice of an application to a county court for an attachment of earnings order or for the variation of such an order, the debtor fails to attend on the day and at the time specified for any hearing of the application, the court may adjourn the hearing and order him to attend at a specified time on another day; and if the debtor—

    (*a*) fails to attend at that time on that day; or

    (*b*) attends, but refuses to be sworn or give evidence,

he may be ordered by the judge to be imprisoned for not more than fourteen days.

(2) Subject to this section, a person commits an offence if—

    (*a*) being required by section 7 (1) or 9 (2) of this Act to comply with an attachment of earnings order, he fails to do so; or

    (*b*) being required by section 7 (2) of this Act to give a notice for the purposes of that subsection, he fails to give it, or fails to give it within the time required by that subsection; or

    (*c*) he fails to comply with an order under section 14 (1) of this Act or with any such requirement of a notice of application for an attachment of earnings order as is mentioned in section 14 (4), or fails (in either case) to comply within the time required by the order or notice; or

    (*d*) he fails to comply with section 15 of this Act; or

428

(e) he gives a notice for the purposes of section 7 (2) of this Act, or a notification for the purposes of section 15, which he knows to be false in a material particular, or recklessly gives such a notice or notification which is false in a material particular; or

(f) in purported compliance with section 7 (2) or 15 of this Act, or with an order under section 14 (1), or with any such requirement of a notice of application for an attachment of earnings order as is mentioned in section 14 (4), he makes any statement which he knows to be false in a material particular, or recklessly makes any statement which is false in a material particular.

(3) Where a person commits an offence under subsection (2) above in relation to proceedings in, or to an attachment of earnings order made by, the High Court or a county court, he shall be liable on summary conviction to a fine of not more than £25 or he may be ordered by a judge of the High Court or the county court judge (as the case may be) to pay a fine of not more than £25 or, in the case of an offence specified in subsection (4) below, to be imprisoned for not more than fourteen days; and where a person commits an offence under subsection (2) otherwise than as mentioned above in this subsection, he shall be liable on summary conviction to a fine of not more than £25.

(4) The offences referred to above in the case of which a judge may impose imprisonment are—

(a) an offence under subsection (2) (c) or (d), if committed by the debtor; and

(b) an offence under subsection (2) (e) or (f), whether committed by the debtor or any other person.

(5) It shall be a defence—

(a) for a person charged with an offence under subsection (2) (a) above to prove that he took all reasonable steps to comply with the attachment of earnings order in question;

(b) for a person charged with an offence under subsection (2) (b) to prove that he did not know, and could not reasonably be expected to know, that the debtor was not in his employment, or (as the case may be) had ceased to be so, and that he gave the required notice as soon as reasonably practicable after the fact came to his knowledge.

(6) Where a person is convicted or dealt with for an offence under subsection (2) (a), the court may order him to pay, to whoever is the collecting officer of the court for the purposes of the attachment of earnings order in question, any sums deducted by that person from the debtor's earnings and not already paid to the collecting officer.

(7) Where under this section a person is ordered by a judge of the High Court or a county court judge to be imprisoned, the judge may at any time revoke the order and, if the person is already in custody, order his discharge.

(8) Any fine imposed by a judge of the High Court under subsection (3) above and any sums ordered by the High Court to be paid under subsection (6) above shall be recoverable in the same way as a fine imposed by that court in the exercise of its jurisdiction to punish for contempt of court; section 179 of the County Courts Act 1959 (enforcement of fines) shall apply to payment of a fine imposed by a county court judge under subsection (3) and of any sums ordered by a county court judge to be paid under subsection (6); and any sum ordered by a magistrates' court to be paid under subsection (6) shall be recoverable as a sum adjudged to be paid on a conviction by that court.

(9) For the purposes of section 13 of the Administration of Justice

Act 1960 (appeal in cases of contempt of court), subsection (3) above shall be treated as an enactment enabling the High Court or a county court to deal with an offence under subsection (2) above as if it were contempt of court.

(10) In this section references to proceedings in a court are to proceedings in which that court has power to make an attachment of earnings order or has made such an order.

Meaning of " earnings "

24.—(1) For the purposes of this Act, but subject to the following subsection, " earnings " are any sums payable to a person—

(*a*) by way of wages or salary (including any fees, bonus, commission, overtime pay or other emoluments payable in addition to wages or salary or payable under a contract of service);

(*b*) by way of pension (including an annuity in respect of past services, whether or not rendered to the person paying the annuity, and including periodical payments by way of compensation for the loss, abolition or relinquishment, or diminution in the emoluments, of any office or employment).

(2) The following shall not be treated as earnings:—

(*a*) sums payable by any public department of the Government of Northern Ireland or of a territory outside the United Kingdom;

(*b*) pay or allowances payable to the debtor as a member of Her Majesty's forces;

(*c*) pension, allowances or benefit payable under any of the enactments specified in Schedule 4 to this Act (being enactments relating to social security);

(*d*) pension or allowances payable in respect of disablement or disability;

(*e*) wages payable to a person as a seaman, other than wages payable to him as a seaman of a fishing boat.

(3) In subsection (2) (*e*) above, expressions used in the Merchant Shipping Act 1894 have the same meanings as in that Act.

General interpretation

25.—(1) In this Act, except where the context otherwise requires—

" administration order " means an order made under, and so referred to in Part VII of the County Courts Act 1959;

" the court ", in relation to an attachment of earnings order, means the court which made the order, subject to rules of court as to the venue for, and the transfer of, proceedings in county courts and magistrates' courts;

" debtor " and " relevant adjudication " have the meanings given by section 2 of this Act;

" the employer ", in relation to an attachment of earnings order, means the person who is required by the order to make deductions from earnings paid by him to the debtor;

" judgment debt " has the meaning given by section 2 of this Act;

" legal aid contribution order " means an order under [section 32 of the Legal Aid Act 1974] [1a];

" maintenance order " has the meaning given by section 2 of this Act;

" maintenance payments " means payments required under a maintenance order;

" prescribed " means prescribed by rules of court; and

" rules of court ", in relation to a magistrates' court, means rules under section 15 of the Justices of the Peace Act 1949;

[1a] Words substituted by Legal Aid Act 1974 (c. 4), Sched. 4.

and, in relation to a magistrates' court, references to a single justice are to a justice of the peace acting for the same petty sessions area as the court.

(2) Any reference in this Act to sums payable under a judgment or order, or to the payment of such sums, includes a reference to costs and the payment of them; and the references in sections 6 (4) and 12 (2) to relevant costs are to any costs of the proceedings in which the attachment of earnings order in question was made, being costs which the debtor is liable to pay.

(3) References in sections 6 (5) (*b*), 9 (3) (*b*) and 14 (1) (*a*) of this Act to the debtor's needs include references to the needs of any person for whom he must, or reasonably may, provide.

(4) Earnings which, in pursuance of a scheme under the Dock Workers (Regulation of Employment) Act 1946, are paid to a debtor by a body responsible for the local administration of the scheme acting as agent for the debtor's employer or as delegate of the body responsible for the general administration of the scheme shall be treated for the purposes of this Act as paid to the debtor by the last-mentioned body acting as principal.

(5) Any power to make rules which is conferred by this Act is without prejudice to any other power to make rules of court.

(6) This Act, so far as it relates to magistrates' courts, and Part III of the Magistrates' Courts Act 1952 shall be construed as if this Act were contained in that Part.

(7) References in this Act to any enactment include references to that enactment as amended by or under any other enactment, including this Act.

General

Transitional provision

26.—(1) As from the appointed day, an attachment of earnings order made before that day under Part II of the Maintenance Orders Act 1958 (including an order made under that Part of that Act as applied by section 46 or 79 of the Criminal Justice Act 1967) shall take effect as an attachment of earnings order made under the corresponding power in this Act, and the provisions of this Act shall apply to it accordingly, so far as they are capable of doing so.

(2) Rules of court may make such provision as the rule-making authority considers requisite—

(*a*) for enabling an attachment of earnings order to which subsection (1) above applies to be varied so as to bring it into conformity, as from the appointed day, with the provisions of this Act, or to be replaced by an attachment of earnings order having effect as if made under the corresponding power in this Act;

(*b*) to secure that anything required or authorised by this Act to be done in relation to an attachment of earnings order made thereunder is required or, as the case may be, authorised to be done in relation to an attachment of earnings order to which the said subsection (1) applies.

(3) In this section " the appointed day " means the day appointed under section 54 of the Administration of Justice Act 1970 for the coming into force of Part II of that Act.

Consequential amendment of enactments

27.—(1) In consequence of the repeals effected by this Act, section 20 of the Maintenance Orders Act 1958 (which contains certain provisions about magistrates' courts and their procedure), except subsection

(6) of that section (which amends section 52 (3) of the Magistrates' Courts Act 1952), shall have effect as set out in Schedule 5 to this Act.

(2) In section 156 (1) of the County Courts Act 1959 (which confers power to make rules of court with respect to administration orders), for the words " section 29 of the Administration of Justice Act 1970 " there shall be substituted the words " section 4 of the Attachment of Earnings Act 1971."

(3) In section 95 (4) of the Merchant Shipping Act 1970 (saving, in relation to fishermen's wages, of provisions in Part II of the Administration of Justice Act 1970) for the words " Part II of the Administration of Justice Act 1970 " there shall be substituted the words " the Attachment of Earnings Act 1971."

28. [*Repealed by Northern Ireland Constitution Act* 1973 (*c.* 36), *Sched.* 6.]

Citation, repeal, extent and commencement

29.—(1) This Act may be cited as the Attachment of Earnings Act 1971.

(2) The enactments specified in Schedule 6 of this Act are hereby repealed to the extent specified in the third column of that Schedule.

(3) This Act, except section 20 (2), does not extend to Scotland and, except sections 20 (2) [. . .],[1b] does not extend to Northern Ireland.

(4) This Act shall come into force on the day appointed under section 54 of the Administration of Justice Act 1970 for the coming into force of Part II of that Act.

SCHEDULES

Section 2

SCHEDULE 1 [1c]

MAINTENANCE ORDERS TO WHICH THIS ACT APPLIES

1. An order for alimony, maintenance or other payments made, or having effect as if made, under Part II of the Matrimonial Causes Act 1965 (ancillary relief in actions for divorce etc.).

2. An order for payments to or in respect of a child, being an order made, or having effect as if made, under Part III of the said Act of 1965 (maintenance of children following divorce, etc.).

3. [An order for periodical or other payments made, or having effect as if made, under Part II of the Matrimonial Causes Act 1973.] [1d]

4. An order for maintenance or other payments to or in respect of a spouse or child, being an order made, or having effect as if made, under the Matrimonial Proceedings (Magistrates' Courts) Act 1960.

5. An order under—
   (a) section 9 (2), 10 (1), 11 or 12 (2) of the Guardianship of Minors Act 1971 [or section 2 (3) or 2 (4) (a) of the Guardianship Act 1973] [2] (payments for maintenance of persons who are, or have been, in guardianship); or
   (b) section 6 of the Family Law Reform Act 1969 (payments for maintenance of ward of court).

6. An affiliation order (that is to say an order under section 4 of the Affiliation Proceedings Act 1957, section 44 of the National Assistance Act 1948, section 26 of the Children Act 1948 or section 24 of the Ministry of Social Security Act 1966).

7. An order under section 87 of the Children and Young Persons Act 1933,

[1b] Words repealed by Northern Ireland Constitution Act 1973 (c. 36), Sched. 6.
[1c] Prospectively amended by Children Act 1975 (c. 72), Sched. 3, para. 76, *post.*
[1d] Words substituted by Matrimonial Causes Act 1973 (c. 18), s. 54 (1) (a), Sched. 2.
[2] Words added by Guardianship Act 1973 (c. 29), s. 9 (3).

section 30 of the Children and Young Persons Act 1963 or section 23 of the Ministry of Social Security Act 1966 (various provisions for obtaining contributions from a person whose dependants are assisted or maintained out of public funds).

8. An order under section 43 of the National Assistance Act 1948 (recovery of costs of maintaining assisted person).

9. An order to which section 16 of the Maintenance Orders Act 1950 applies by virtue of subsection (2) (*b*) or (*c*) of that section (that is to say an order made by a court in Scotland or Northern Ireland and corresponding to one of those specified in the foregoing paragraphs) and which has been registered in a court in England and Wales under Part II of that Act.

10. A maintenance order within the meaning of the Maintenance Orders (Facilities for Enforcement) Act 1920 (Commonwealth orders enforceable in the United Kingdom) registered in, or confirmed by, a court in England and Wales under that Act.

Section 3

SCHEDULE 2

TAXES, SOCIAL SECURITY CONTRIBUTIONS ETC. RELEVANT FOR PURPOSES OF SECTION 3 (6)

1. Income tax or any other tax or liability recoverable under section 65, 66 or 68 of the Taxes Management Act 1970.

2. Selective employment tax under section 44 of the Finance Act 1966.

3. Contributions under—
    section 3 (flat-rate) or section 4 (graduated) of the National Insurance Act 1965;
    section 1 of the National Health Service Contributions Act 1965; or
    section 2 of the National Insurance (Industrial Injuries) Act 1965.

4. Redundancy Fund contributions under section 27 of the Redundancy Payments Act 1965.

Sections 6 and 7

SCHEDULE 3

DEDUCTIONS BY EMPLOYER UNDER ATTACHMENT OF EARNINGS ORDER

PART I

SCHEME OF DEDUCTIONS

Preliminary definitions

1. The following three paragraphs have effect for defining and explaining, for purposes of this Schedule, expressions used therein.

2. " Pay-day ", in relation to earnings paid to a debtor, means an occasion on which they are paid.

3. " Attachable earnings ", in relation to a pay-day, are the earnings which remain payable to the debtor on that day after deduction by the employer of—
    (*a*) income tax;
    (*b*) contributions under any of the following enactments—
        the National Insurance Act 1965,
        the National Insurance (Industrial Injuries) Act 1965, or
        the National Health Service Contributions Act 1965;
    (*c*) amounts deductible under any enactment, or in pursuance of a request in writing by the debtor, for the purposes of a superannuation scheme within the meaning of the Wages Councils Act 1959.

4. On any pay-day—
    (*a*) " the normal deduction " is arrived at by applying the normal deduction rate (as specified in the relevant attachment of earnings order) with respect to the period since the last pay-day or, if it is the first pay-day of the debtor's employment with the employer, since the employment began; and

(*b*) "the protected earnings" are arrived at by applying the protected earnings rate ((as so specified) with respect to the said period.

Employer's deduction (judgment debts and administration orders)

5. In the case of an attachment of earnings order made to secure the payment of a judgment debt or payments under an administration order, the employer shall on any pay-day—
   (*a*) if the attachable earnings exceed the protected earnings, deduct from the attachable earnings the amount of the excess or the normal deduction, whichever is the less;
   (*b*) make no deduction if the attachable earnings are equal to, or less than, the protected earnings.

Employer's deduction (other cases)

6.—(1) The following provision shall have effect in the case of an attachment of earnings order to which paragraph 5 above does not apply.
   (2) If on a pay-day the attachable earnings exceed the sum of—
      (*a*) the protected earnings; and
      (*b*) so much of any amount by which the attachable earnings on any previous pay-day fell short of the protected earnings as has not been made good by virtue of this sub-paragraph on another previous pay-day,
then, in so far as the excess allows, the employer shall deduct from the attachable earnings the amount specified in the following sub-paragraph.
   (3) The said amount is the sum of—
      (*a*) the normal deduction; and
      (*b*) so much of the normal deduction on any previous pay-day as was not deducted on that day and has not been paid by virtue of this sub-paragraph on any other previous pay-day.
   (4) No deduction shall be made on any pay-day when the attachable earnings are equal to, or less than, the protected earnings.

PART II
PRIORITY AS BETWEEN ORDERS

7. Where the employer is required to comply with two or more attachment of earnings orders in respect of the same debtor, all or none of which orders are made to secure either the payment of judgment debts or payments under an administration order, then on any pay-day the employer shall, for the purpose of complying with Part I of this Schedule,—
   (*a*) deal with the orders according to the respective dates on which they were made, disregarding any later order until an earlier one has been dealt with;
   (*b*) deal with any later order as if the earnings to which it relates were the residue of the debtor's earnings after the making of any deduction to comply with any earlier order.

8. Where the employer is required to comply with two or more attachment of earnings orders, and one or more (but not all) of those orders are made to secure either the payment of judgment debts or payments under an administration order, then on any pay-day the employer shall, for the purpose of complying with Part I of this Schedule—
   (*a*) deal first with any order which is not made to secure the payment of a judgment debt or payments under an administration order (complying with paragraph 7 above if there are two or more such orders); and
   (*b*) deal thereafter with any order which is made to secure the payment of a judgment debt or payments under an administration order as if the earnings to which it relates were the residue of the debtor's earnings after the making of any deduction to comply with an order having priority by virtue of sub-paragraph (*a*) above; and
   (*c*) if there are two or more orders to which sub-paragraph (*b*) above applies, comply with paragraph 7 above in respect of those orders.

SCHEDULE 4

ENACTMENTS PROVIDING BENEFITS WHICH ARE NOT TO BE TREATED AS
DEBTOR'S EARNINGS

The National Insurance Act 1965.
The National Insurance (Industrial Injuries) Act 1965.
The Family Allowances Act 1965.
The Ministry of Social Security Act 1966.
The Industrial Injuries and Diseases (Old Cases) Act 1967.
The Family Income Supplements Act 1970.

Section 27   SCHEDULE 5

SECTION 20 OF MAINTENANCE ORDERS ACT 1958 AS HAVING EFFECT
IN CONSEQUENCE OF THIS ACT

Special provisions as to magistrates' courts

20.—(1) Notwithstanding anything in this Act, the clerk of a magistrates' court
who is entitled to receive payments under a maintenance order for transmission to
another person shall not apply for the registration of the maintenance order under
Part I of this Act or give notice in relation to the order in pursuance of subsection (1) of section five thereof unless he is requested in writing to do so by a
person entitled to receive the payments through him; and where the clerk is
requested as aforesaid—

(i) he shall comply with the request unless it appears to him unreasonable in
the circumstances to do so;

(ii) the person by whom the request was made shall have the same liabilities for
all the costs properly incurred in or about any proceedings taken in pursuance of the request as if the proceedings had been taken by that person.

(2) An application to a magistrates' court by virtue of subsection (2) of section
four of this Act for the variation of a maintenance order shall be made by
complaint.

· · · · · ·

(8) For the avoidance of doubt it is hereby declared that a complaint may be
made to enforce payment of a sum due and unpaid under a maintenance order
notwithstanding that a previous complaint has been made in respect of that sum
or a part thereof and whether or not an order was made in pursuance of the
previous complaint.

Section 29   SCHEDULE 6

ENACTMENTS REPEALED

Chapter	Short Title	Extent of Repeal
6 & 7 Eliz. 2. c. 39.	The Maintenance Orders Act 1958.	Section 9. In section 20, in subsection (1) the words " or Part II of the Administration of Justice Act 1970 ", the word " or " at the end of paragraph (*a*), paragraphs (*b*) and (*c*) and the words from " and for the purposes " onwards; in subsection (2), the words " Subject to rules of court made by virtue of section 18 (3) (*c*) of the Administration of Justice Act 1970 ", and the words " and an application to a magistrates' court for an attachment of earnings order, or an order discharging or varying an attachment of earnings order "; and subsections (3), (4), (5) and (7).

SCHEDULE 6—*cont.*

Chapter	Short Title	Extent of Repeal
1970 c. 31.	The Administration of Justice Act 1970.	In section 23 (2), the words " except paragraph (*a*) of subsection (3) of section 20 ". Sections 13 to 26. Section 27 (1) and (2). In section 28— in subsection (1), the definitions of " Act of 1958 ", " administration order ", " the court ", " debtor ", " judgment debt ", " relevant adjudication ", " the employer ", " legal aid contribution order ", and the words from " ' maintenance payments ' " onwards; and subsections (2) to (5). Section 29 (1) to (4). Section 30 (3) and (4). In section 53, the words " 24 or ". In section 54 (6), the words " and 27 " and " and 7 ". Schedules 5, 6 and 7.
1970 c. 55.	The Family Income Supplements Act 1970.	Section 14.

Recognition of Divorces and Legal Separations Act 1971

(1971 c. 53)

An Act to amend the law relating to the recognition of divorces and legal separations. [27th July 1971]

Decrees of divorce and judicial separation granted in British Isles

Recognition in Great IBritain of divorces and judicial separations granted in the IBritish Isles

1. Subject to section 8 of this Act, the validity of a decree of divorce or judicial separation granted after the commencement of this section shall, [if it was granted under the law of any part of the British Isles, be recognised throughout the United Kingdom].[1]

Overseas divorces and legal separations

Recognition in Great Britain of overseas divorces and legal separations

2. Sections 3 to 5 of this Act shall have effect, subject to section 8 of this Act, as respects the recognition in [the United Kingdom][1] of the validity of overseas divorces and legal separations, that is to say, divorces and legal separations which—

---

[1] Words substituted by Domicile and Matrimonial Proceedings Act 1973 (c. 45), s. 15 (2).

(*a*) have been obtained by means of judicial or other proceedings in any country outside the British Isles; and

(*b*) are effective under the law of that country.

Grounds for recognition

3.—(1) The validity of an overseas divorce or legal separation shall be recognised if, at the date of the institution of the proceedings in the country in which it was obtained—

(*a*) either spouse was habitually resident in that country; or

(*b*) either spouse was a national of that country.

(2) In relation to a country the law of which uses the concept of domicile as a ground of jurisdiction in matters of divorce or legal separation, subsection (1) (*a*) of this section shall have effect as if the reference to habitual residence included a reference to domicile within the meaning of that law.

(3) In relation to a country comprising territories in which different systems of law are in force in matters of divorce or legal separation, the foregoing provisions of this section (except those relating to nationality) shall have effect as if each territory were a separate country.

Cross-proceedings and divorces following legal separations

4.—(1) Where there have been cross-proceedings, the validity of an overseas divorce or legal separation obtained either in the original proceedings or in the cross-proceedings shall be recognised if the requirements of paragraph (*a*) or (*b*) of section 3 (1) of this Act are satisfied in relation to the date of the institution either of the original proceedings or of the cross-proceedings.

(2) Where a legal separation the validity of which is entitled to recognition by virtue of the provisions of section 3 of this Act or of subsection (1) of this section is converted, in the country in which it was obtained, into a divorce, the validity of the divorce shall be recognised whether or not it would itself be entitled to recognition by virtue of those provisions.

Proof of facts relevant to recognition

5.—(1) For the purpose of deciding whether an overseas divorce or legal separation is entitled to recognition by virtue of the foregoing provisions of this Act, any finding of fact made (whether expressly or by implication) in the proceedings by means of which the divorce or legal separation was obtained and on the basis of which jurisdiction was assumed in those proceedings shall—

(*a*) if both spouses took part in the proceedings, be conclusive evidence of the fact found; and

(*b*) in any other case, be sufficient proof of that fact unless the contrary is shown.

(2) In this section " finding of fact " includes a finding that either spouse was habitually resident or domiciled in, or a national of, the country in which the divorce or legal separation was obtained; and for the purposes of subsection (1) (*a*) of this section, a spouse who has appeared in judicial proceedings shall be treated as having taken part in them.

General provisions

Certain existing rules of recognition to continue in force

[6.—(1) In this section " the common law rules " means the rules of law relating to the recognition of divorces or legal separations obtained in the country of the spouses' domicile or obtained elsewhere and recognised as valid in that country.

(2) In any circumstances in which the validity of a divorce or a legal separation obtained in a country outside the British Isles would be recognised only by virtue only of the common law rules if either—

    (*a*) the spouses had at the material time both been domiciled in that country; or

    (*b*) the divorce or separation were recognised as valid under the law of the spouses' domicile,

its validity shall also be recognised if subsection (3) below is satisfied in relation to it.

(3) This subsection is satisfied in relation to a divorce or legal separation obtained in a country outside the British Isles if either—

    (*a*) one of the spouses was at the material time domiciled in that country and the divorce or separation was recognised as valid under the law of domicile of the other spouse; or

    (*b*) neither of the spouses having been domiciled in that country at the material time, the divorce or separation was recognised as valid under the law of the domicile of each of the spouses respectively.

(4) For any purpose of subsection (2) or (3) above " the material time", in relation to a divorce or a legal separation, means the time of the institution of proceedings in the country in which it was obtained.

(5) Section 2 to 5 of this Act are without prejudice to the recognition of the validity of divorces and legal separations obtained outside the British Isles by virtue of the common law rules (as extended by this section), or of any enactment other than this Act; but, subject to this section, no divorce or legal separation so obtained shall be recognised as valid in the United Kingdom except as provided by those sections.] [1a]

Non-recognition of divorce by third country no bar to re-marriage

7. Where the validity of a divorce obtained in any country is entitled to recognition by virtue of [sections 1 to 5 or section 6 (2)] [2] of this Act or by virtue of any rule or enactment preserved by [section 6 (5)] [2] of this Act, neither spouse shall be precluded from re-marrying in [the United Kingdom] [1] on the ground that the validity of the divorce would not be recognised in any other country.

Exemptions from recognition

8.—(1) The validity of—

    (*a*) a decree of divorce or judical separation granted under the law of any part of the British Isles; or

    (*b*) a divorce or legal separation obtained outside the British Isles,

shall not be recognised in any part of [the United Kingdom] [1] if it was granted or obtained at a time when, according to the law of that part of [the United Kingdom] [1] (including its rules of private international law and the provisions of this Act), there was no subsisting marriage between the parties.

(2) Subject to subsection (1) of this section, recognition by virtue of [sections 1 to 5 or section 6 (2)] [3] this Act or of any rule preserved by [section 6 (5)] [3] thereof of the validity of a divorce or legal separation obtained outside the British Isles may be refused if, and only if—

    (*a*) it was obtained by one spouse—

[1a] Substituted by Domicile and Matrimonial Proceedings Act 1973 (c. 45), s. 2 (2) with saving for common law rules, and previous enactments, as to recognition.
[2] Words substituted by Domicile and Matrimonial Proceedings Act 1973 (c. 45), s. 2 (3).
[3] Words substituted by Domicile and Matrimonial Proceedings Act 1973 (c. 45), s. 2 (4).

(i) without such steps having been taken for giving notice of the proceedings to the other spouse as, having regard to the nature of the proceedings and all the circumstances, should reasonably have been taken; or

(ii) without the other spouse having been given (for any reason other than lack of notice) such opportunity to take part in the proceedings as, having regard to the matters aforesaid, he should reasonably have been given; or

(b) its recognition would manifestly be contrary to public policy.

(3) Nothing in this Act shall be contrued as requiring the recognition of any findings of fault made in any proceedings for divorce or separation or of any maintenance, custody or other ancillary order made in any such proceedings.

Powers of Parliament of Northern Ireland

9. Notwithstanding anything in the Government of Ireland Act 1920, the Parliament of Northern Ireland shall have power to make laws for purposes similar to the purposes of this Act.

Short title, interpretation, transitional provisions and commencement

10.—(1) This Act may be cited as the Recognition of Divorces and Legal Separations Act 1971.

(2) In this Act " the British Isles " means the United Kingdom, the Channel Islands and the Isle of Man.

(3) In this Act " country " includes a colony or other dependent territory of the United Kingdom but for the purposes of this Act a person shall be treated as a national of such a territory only if it has a law of citizenship or nationality separate from that of the United Kingdom and he is a citizen or national of that territory under that law.

(4) The provisions of this Act relating to overseas divorces and legal separations and other divorces and legal separations obtained outside the British Isles apply to a divorce or legal separation obtained before the date of the commencement of those provisions as well as to one obtained on or after that date and, in the case of a divorce or legal separation obtained before that date—

(a) require, or, as the case may be, preclude, the recognition of its validity in relation to any time before that date as well as in relation to any subsequent time; but

(b) do not affect any property rights to which any person became entitled before that date or apply where the question of the validity of the divorce or legal separation has been decided by any competent court in the British Isles before that date.

(5) Section 9 of this Act shall come into operation on the passing of this Act and the remainder on 1st January 1972.

Matrimonial Proceedings (Polygamous Marriages) Act 1972

(1972 c. 38)

An Act to enable matrimonial relief to be granted, and declarations concerning the validity of a marriage to be made, notwithstanding that the marriage in question was entered into under a law which permits polygamy, and to make a consequential amendment in the Nullity of Marriage Act 1971

[29th June 1972]

Matrimonial relief and declarations of validity in respect of polygamous marriages: England and Wales

1. [*Repealed by Matrimonial Causes Act* 1973 (*c.* 18), *s.* 54 (1) (*b*), *Sched.* 3.]

Matrimonial relief and declarations as to validity in respect of polygamous marriages: Scotland

2.—(1) A court in Scotland shall not be precluded from entertaining proceedings for, or granting, any such decree as is mentioned in subsection (2) below by reason only that the marriage to which the proceedings relate was entered into under a law which permits polygamy.

(2) The decrees referred to in subsection (1) above are—

    (*a*) a decree of divorce;

    (*b*) a decree of nullity of marriage;

    (*c*) a decree of dissolution of marriage under section 5 of the Divorce (Scotland) Act 1938 (presumption of death and dissolution of marriage);

    (*d*) a decree of judicial separation;

    (*e*) a decree of separation and aliment, adherence and aliment, or interim aliment;

    (*f*) a decree of declarator that a marriage is valid or invalid;

    (*g*) any other decree involving a determination as to the validity of a marriage;

and the reference in subsection (1) above to granting such a decree as aforesaid includes a reference to making any ancillary order which the court has power to make in proceedings for such a decree.

(3) This section has effect whether or not either party to the marriage in question has for the time being any spouse additional to the other party; and provision may be made by rules of court—

    (*a*) for requiring notice of proceedings brought by virtue of this section to be served on any such other spouse; and

    (*b*) for conferring on any such other spouse the right to be heard in any such proceedings,

in such cases as may be specified in the rules.

Matrimonial relief and declarations of validity in respect of polygamous marriages: Northern Ireland

3.—(1) A court in Northern Ireland shall not be precluded from granting matrimonial relief or making a declaration concerning the validity of a marriage by reason only that the marriage in question was entered into under a law which permits polygamy.

(2) In this section " matrimonial relief " means—

    (*a*) a decree of divorce, nullity of marriage or judicial separation;

    (*b*) a decree under section 12 of the Matrimonial Causes Act (Northern Ireland) 1939 (dissolution of marriage on presumption of death);

    (*c*) an order under section 4 of the Law Reform (Miscellaneous Provisions) Act (Northern Ireland) 1951 (wilful neglect to maintain);

    (*d*) an order made under any provision of the said Act of 1939, or under section 4 of the said Act of 1951, which confers a power exercisable in connection with, or in connection with any proceedings for, any such decree or order as is mentioned in the foregoing paragraphs;

    (*e*) an order under the Summary Jurisdiction (Separation and Maintenance) Act (Northern Ireland) 1945.

(3) In this section " a declaration concerning the validity of a marriage " means—

(a) a declaration that a marriage is valid or invalid; and

(b) any other declaration involving a determination as to the validity of a marriage,

being a declaration in a decree granted under the Legitimacy Declaration Act (Ireland) 1868 or a declaration made in proceedings brought by virtue of rules of court relating to declaratory judgments.

(4) This section has effect whether or not either party to the marriage in question has for the time being any spouse additional to the other party; and provision may be made by rules of court—

(a) for requiring notice of proceedings brought by virtue of this section to be served on any such other spouse; and

(b) for conferring on any such other spouse the right to be heard in any such proceedings,

in such cases as may be specified in the rules.

Amendment of s. 1 of Nullity of Marriage Act 1971

4. [*Repealed by Matrimonial Causes Act* 1973 (*c.* 18), *s.* 54 (1) (*b*), *Sched.* 3.]

Short title, interpretations and powers of Northern Ireland Parliament

5.—(1) This Act may be cited as the Matrimonial Proceedings (Polygamous Marriages) Act 1972.

(2) References in this Act to any enactment shall be construed as references to that enactment as amended, and as including references thereto as extended or applied, by any subsequent enactment.

(3) In subsection (2) of this section " enactment " includes an enactment of the Parliament of Northern Ireland; [. . .] [1]

Children Act 1972

(1972 c. 44)

An Act to secure that the minimum age at which children may be employed is not affected by any further change in the school-leaving age.　　　　　　　　　　　　　　　　[27th July 1972]

Minimum age of employment

1.—(1) Notwithstanding any change in the age governing the time when children may leave school, the minimum age at which, under section 18 (1) of the Children and Young Persons Act 1933 or section 28 (1) of the Children and Young Persons (Scotland) Act 1937, it is lawful for a child to be employed shall remain the age of 13 years.

(2) Accordingly in each of those sections for subsection (1) (*a*) there shall be substituted the paragraph—

" (*a*) so long as he is under the age of thirteen years ";

and in subsection (2) (which allows the general rules in subsection (1) to be modified by local authority bye-laws) for paragraph (*a*) (i) there shall be substituted the sub-paragraph—

---

[1] Words repealed by Northern Ireland Constitution Act 1973 (c. 36), Sched. 6.

" (i) the employment of children under the age of thirteen years (notwithstanding anything in paragraph (*a*) of the last foregoing subsections) by their parents or guardians in light agricultural or horticultural work."

Short title, repeal and extent

2.—(1) This Act may be cited as the Children Act 1972.

(2) The enactments mentioned in the Schedule to this Act are hereby repealed to the extent specified in column 3 of the Schedule.

(3) Nothing in this Act extends to Northern Ireland.

SCHEDULE

ENACTMENTS REPEALED

Chapter	Short Title	Extent of Repeal
7 & 8 Geo. 6, c. 31.	The Education Act 1944.	In Schedule 8, the entry relating to the Children and Young Persons Act 1933, section 18.
8 & 9 Geo. 6, c. 37.	The Education (Scotland) Act 1945.	In Schedule 4, so much of the entry for the Children and Young Persons (Scotland) Act 1937 as relates to section 28 of that Act.
11 & 12 Geo. 6, c. 40.	The Education (Miscellaneous Provisions) Act 1948.	In Part II of Schedule 1 the entry relating to the Children and Young Persons Act 1933 section 18 (1) (*a*).
1963 c. 37.	The Children and Young Persons Act 1963.	In Schedule 3, paragraph 29 (1).

. . . .

Matrimonial Causes Act 1973

(1973 c. 18)

An Act to consolidate certain enactments relating to matrimonial proceedings, maintenance agreements, and declarations of legitimacy, validity of marriage and British nationality, with amendments to give effect to recommendations of the Law Commission. [23rd May 1973]

PART I

DIVORCE, NULLITY AND OTHER MATRIMONIAL SUITS

Divorce

Divorce or breakdown of marriage

1.—(1) Subject to section 3 below, a petition for divorce may be presented to the court by either party to a marriage on the ground that the marriage has broken down irretrievably.

(2) The court hearing a petition for divorce shall not hold the marriage to have broken down irretrievably unless the petitioner satisfies the court of one or more of the following facts, that is to say—

(a) that the respondent has committed adultery and the petitioner finds it intolerable to live with the respondent;

(b) that the respondent has behaved in such a way that the petitioner cannot reasonably be expected to live with the respondent;

(c) that the respondent has deserted the petitioner for a continuous period of at least two years immediately preceding the presentation of the petition;

(d) that the parties to the marriage have lived apart for a continuous period of at least two years immediately preceding the presentation of the petition (hereafter in this Act referred to as " two years' separation ") and the respondent consents to a decree being granted;

(e) that the parties to the marriage have lived apart for a continuous period of a least five years immediately preceding the presentation of the petition (hereafter in this Act referred to as " five years' separation ").

(3) On a petition for divorce it shall be the duty of the court to inquire, so far as it reasonably can, into the facts alleged by the petitioner and into any facts alleged by the respondent.

(4) If the court is satisfied on the evidence of any such fact as is mentioned in subsection (2) above, then, unless it is satisfied on all the evidence that the marriage has not broken down irretrievably, it shall, subject to sections 3 (3) and 5 below, grant a decree of divorce.

(5) Every decree of divorce shall in the first instance be a decree nisi and shall not be made absolute before the expiration of six months from its grant unless the High Court by general order from time to time fixes a shorter period, or unless in any particular case the court in which the proceedings are for the time being pending from time to time by special order fixes a shorter period than the period otherwise applicable for the time being by virtue of this subsection.

Supplemental provisions as to facts raising presumption of breakdown

2.—(1) One party to a marriage shall not be entitled to rely for the purposes of section 1 (2) (a) above on adultery committed by the other if, after it became known to him that the other had committed that adultery, the parties have lived with each other for a period exceeding, or periods together exceeding, six months.

(2) Where the parties to a marriage have lived with each other after it became known to one party that the other had committed adultery, but subsection (1) above does not apply, in any proceedings for divorce in which the petitioner relies on that adultery the fact that the parties have lived with each other after that time shall be disregarded in determining for the purposes of section 1 (2) (a) above whether the petitioner finds it intolerable to live with the respondent.

(3) Where in any proceedings for divorce the petitioner alleges that the respondent has behaved in such a way that the petitioner cannot reasonably be expected to live with him, but the parties to the marriage have lived with each other for a period or periods after the date of the occurrence of the final incident relied on by the petitioner and held by the court to support his allegation, that fact shall be disregarded in determining for the purposes of section 1 (2) (b) above whether the petitioner cannot reasonably be expected to live with the respondent if the length of that period or of those periods together was six months or less.

(4) For the purposes of section 1 (2) (c) above the court may treat a period of desertion as having continued at a time when the deserting party was incapable of continuing the necessary intention if the evidence before the court is such that, had that party not been so incapable, the court would have inferred that his desertion continued at that time.

(5) In considering for the purposes of section 1 (2) above whether the period for which the respondent has deserted the petitioner or the period for which the parties to a marriage have lived apart has been continuous, no account shall be taken of any one period (not exceeding six months) or of any two or more periods (not exceeding six months in all) during which the parties resumed living with each other, but no period during which the parties lived with each other shall count as part of the period of desertion or of the period for which the parties to the marriage lived apart, as the case may be.

(6) For the purposes of section 1 (2) (d) and (e) above and this section a husband and wife shall be treated as living apart unless they are living with each other in the same household, and references in this section to the parties to a marriage living with each other shall be construed as references to their living with each other in the same household.

(7) Provision shall be made by rules of court for the purpose of ensuring that where in pursuance of section 1 (2) (d) above the petitioner alleges that the respondent consents to a decree being granted the respondent has been given such information as will enable him to understand the consequences to him of his consenting to a decree being granted and the steps which he must take to indicate that he consents to the grant of a decree.

Restrictions on petitions for divorce within three years of marriage

3.—(1) Subject to subsection (2) below, no petition for divorce shall be presented to the court before the expiration of the period of three years from the date of the marriage (hereafter in this section referred to as " the specified period ").

(2) A judge of the court may, on an application made to him, allow the presentation of a petition for divorce within the specified period on the ground that the case is one of exceptional hardship suffered by the petitioner or of exceptional depravity on the part of the respondent; but in determining the application the judge shall have regard to the interests of any child of the family and to the question whether there is reasonable probability of a reconciliation between the parties during the specified period.

(3) If it appears to the court, at the hearing of a petition for divorce presented in pursuance of leave granted under subsection (2) above, that the leave was obtained by the petitioner by any misrepresentation or concealment of the nature of the case, the court may—

(a) dismiss the petition, without prejudice to any petition which may be brought after the expiration of the specified period upon the same facts, or substantially the same facts, as those proved in support of the dismissed petition; or

(b) if it grants a decree, direct that no application to make the decree abolute shall be made during the specified period.

(4) Nothing in this section shall be deemed to prohibit the presentation of a petition based upon matters which occurred before the expiration of the specified period.

Divorce not precluded by previous judicial separation

4.—(1) A person shall not be prevented from presenting a petition for divorce, or the court from granting a decree of divorce, by reason only that the petitioner or respondent has at any time, on the same facts or substantially the same facts as those proved in support of the petition, been granted a decree of judicial separation or an order under, or having effect as if made under, the Matrimonial Proceedings (Magistrates' Courts)

Act 1960 or any corresponding enactments in force in Northern Ireland, the Isle of Man or any of the Channel Islands.

(2) On a petition for divorce in such a case as is mentioned in sub-section (1) above, the court may treat the decree or order as sufficient proof of any adultery, desertion or other fact by reference to which it was granted, but shall not grant a decree of divorce without receiving evidence from the petitioner.

(3) Where a petition for divorce in such a case follows a decree of judicial separation or an order containing a provision exempting one party to the marriage from the obligation to cohabit with the other, for the purposes of that petition a period of desertion immediately preceding the institution of the proceedings for the decree or order shall, if the parties have not resumed cohabitation and the decree or order has been continuously in force since it was granted, be deemed immediately to precede the presentation of the petition.

Refusal of decree in five year separation cases on ground of grave hardship to respondent

5.—(1) The respondent to a petition for divorce in which the petitioner alleges five years' separation may oppose the grant of a decree on the ground that the dissolution of the marriage will result in grave financial or other hardship to him and that it would in all the circumstances be wrong to dissolve the marriage.

(2) Where the grant of a decree is opposed by virtue of this section, then—

(*a*) if the court finds that the petitioner is entitled to rely in support of his petition on the fact of five years' separation and makes no such finding as to any other fact mentioned in section 1 (2) above, and

(*b*) if apart from this section the court would grant a decree on the petition,

the court shall consider all the circumstances, including the conduct of the parties to the marriage and the interests of those parties and of any children or other persons concerned, and if of opinion that the dissolution of the marriage will result in grave financial or other hardship to the respondent and that it would in all the circumstances be wrong to dissolve the marriage it shall dismiss the petition.

(3) For the purposes of this section hardship shall include the loss of the chance of acquiring any benefit which the respondent might acquire if the marriage were not dissolved.

Attempts at reconciliation of parties to marriage

6.—(1) Provision shall be made by rules of court for requiring the solicitor acting for a petitioner for divorce to certify whether he has discussed with the petitioner the possibility of a reconciliation and given him the names and addresses of persons qualified to help effect a reconciliation between parties to a marriage who have become estranged.

(2) If at any stage of proceedings for divorce it appears to the court that there is a reasonable possibility of a reconciliation between the parties to the marriage, the court may adjourn the proceedings for such period as it thinks fit to enable attempts to be made to effect such a reconciliation.

The power conferred by the foregoing provision is additional to any other power of the court to adjourn proceedings.

Consideration by the court of certain agreements or arrangements

7. Provision may be made by rules of court for enabling the parties to a marriage, or either of them, on application made either before or after the presentation of a petition for divorce, to refer to the court any agreement or arrangement made or proposed to be made between them, being an agreement or arrangement which relates to, arises out of, or is connected with, the proceedings for divorce which are contemplated or, as the case may be, have begun, and for enabling the court to express an opinion, should it think it desirable to do so, as to the reasonableness of the agreement or arrangement and to give such directions, if any, in the matter as it thinks fit.

Intervention of Queen's Proctor

8.—(1) In the case of a petition for divorce—

    (*a*) the court may, if it thinks fit, direct all necessary papers in the matter to be sent to the Queen's Proctor, who shall under the directions of the Attorney-General instruct counsel to argue before the court any question in relation to the matter which the court considers it necessary or expedient to have fully argued;

    (*b*) any person may at any time during the progress of the proceedings or before the decree nisi is made absolute give information to the Queen's Proctor on any matter material to the due decision of the case, and the Queen's Proctor may thereupon take such steps as the Attorney-General considers necessary or expedient.

(2) Where the Queen's Proctor intervenes or shows cause against a decree nisi in any proceedings for divorce, the court may make such order as may be just as to the payment by other parties to the proceedings of the costs incurred by him in so doing or as to the payment by him of any costs incurred by any of those parties by reason of his so doing.

(3) The Queen's Proctor shall be entitled to charge as part of the expenses of his office—

    (*a*) the costs of any proceedings under subsection (1) (*a*) above;

    (*b*) where his reasonable costs of intervening or showing cause as mentioned in subsection (2) above are not fully satisfied by any order under that subsection, the amount of the difference;

    (*c*) if the Treasury so directs, any costs which he pays to any parties under an order made under subsection (2).

Proceedings after decree nisi: general powers of court

9.—(1) Where a decree of divorce has been granted but not made absolute, then, without prejudice to section 8 above, any person (excluding a party to the proceedings other than the Queen's Proctor) may show cause why the decree should not be made absolute by reason of material facts not having been brought before the court; and in such a case the court may—

    (*a*) notwithstanding anything in section 1 (5) above (but subject to sections 10 (2) to (4) and 41 below) make the decree absolute; or

    (*b*) rescind the decree; or

    (*c*) require further inquiry; or

    (*d*) otherwise deal with the case as it thinks fit.

(2) Where a decree of divorce has been granted and no application for it to be made absolute has been made by the party to whom it was granted, then, at any time after the expiration of three months from the earliest date on which that party could have made such an application, the party against whom it was granted may make an application to the court, and on that application the court may exercise any of the powers mentioned in paragraphs (*a*) to (*d*) of subsection (1) above.

Proceedings after decree nisi: special protection for respondent in separation cases

10.—(1) Where in any case the court has granted a decree of divorce on the basis of a finding that the petitioner was entitled to rely in support of his petition on the fact of two years' separation coupled with the respondent's consent to a decree being granted and has made no such finding as to any other fact mentioned in section 1 (2) above, the court may, on an application made by the respondent at any time before the decree is made absolute, rescind the decree if it is satisfied that the petitioner misled the respondent (whether intentionally or unintentionally) about any matter which the respondent took into account in deciding to give his consent.

(2) The following provisions of this section apply where—

   (a) the respondent to a petition for divorce in which the petitioner alleged two years' or five years' separation coupled, in the former case, with the respondent's consent to a decree being granted, has applied to the court for consideration under subsection (3) below of his financial position after the divorce; and

   (b) the court has granted a decree on the petition on the basis of a finding that the petitioner was entitled to rely in support of his petition on the fact of two years' or five years' separation (as the case may be) and has made no such finding as to any other fact mentioned in section 1 (2) above.

(3) The court hearing an application by the respondent under subsection (2) above shall consider all the circumstances, including the age, health, conduct, earning capacity, financial resources and financial obligations of each of the parties, and the financial position of the respondent as, having regard to the divorce, it is likely to be after the death of the petitioner should the petitioner die first; and, subject to subsection (4) below, the court shall not make the decree absolute unless it is satisfied—

   (a) that the petitioner should not be required to make any financial provision for the respondent, or

   (b) that the financial provision made by the petitioner for the respondent is reasonable and fair or the best that can be made in the circumstances.

(4) The court may if it thinks fit make the decree absolute notwithstanding the requirements of subsection (3) above if—

   (a) it appears that there are circumstances making it desirable that the decree should be made absolute without delay, and

   (b) the court has obtained a satisfactory undertaking from the petitioner that he will make such financial provision for the respondent as the court may approve.

Nullity

Grounds on which a marriage is void

11. A marriage celebrated after 31st July 1971 shall be void on the following grounds only, that is to say—

   (a) that it is not a valid marriage under the provisions of the Marriages Acts 1949 to 1970 (that is to say where—

     (i) the parties are within the prohibited degrees of relationship;

     (ii) either party is under the age of sixteen; or

     (iii) the parties have intermarried in disregard of certain requirements as to the formation of marriage);

   (b) that at the time of the marriage either party was already lawfully married;

(c) that the parties are not respectively male and female;

(d) in the case of a polygamous marriage entered into outside England and Wales, that either party was at the time of the marriage domiciled in England and Wales.

For the purposes of paragraph (d) of this subsection a marriage may be polygamous although at its inception neither party has any spouse additional to the other.

Grounds on which a marriage is voidable

12. A marriage celebrated after 31st July 1971 shall be voidable on the following grounds only, that is to say—

(a) that the marriage has not been consummated owing to the incapacity of either party to consummate it;

(b) that the marriage has not been consummated owing to the wilful refusal of the respondent to consummate it;

(c) that either party to the marriage did not validly consent to it, whether in consequence of duress, mistake, unsoundness of mind or otherwise;

(d) that at the time of the marriage either party, though capable of giving a valid consent, was suffering (whether continuously or intermittently) from mental disorder within the meaning of the Mental Health Act 1959 of such a kind or to such an extent as to be unfitted for marriage;

(e) that at the time of the marriage the respondent was suffering from veneral disease in a communicable form;

(f) that at the time of the marriage the respondent was pregnant by some person other than the petitioner.

Bars to relief where marriage is voidable

13.—(1) The court shall not, in proceedings instituted after 31st July 1971, grant a decree of nullity on the ground that a marriage is voidable if the respondent satisfies the court—

(a) that the petitioner, with knowledge that it was open to him to have the marriage avoided, so conducted himself in relation to the respondent as to lead the respondent reasonably to believe that he would not seek to do so; and

(b) that it would be unjust to the respondent to grant the decree.

(2) Without prejudice to subsection (1) above, the court shall not grant a decree of nullity by virtue of section 12 above on the grounds mentioned in paragraph (c), (d), (e) or (f) of that section unless it is satisfied that proceedings were instituted within three years from the date of the marriage.

(3) Without prejudice to subsections (1) and (2) above, the court shall not grant a decree of nullity by virtue of section 12 above on the grounds mentioned in paragraph (e) or (f) of that section unless it is satisfied that the petitioner was at the time of the marriage ignorant of the facts alleged.

Marriages governed by foreign law or celebrated abroad under English law

14.—(1) Where, apart from this Act, any matter affecting the validity of a marriage would fall to be determined (in accordance with the rules of private international law) by reference to the law of a country outside England and Wales, nothing in section 11, 12 or 13 (1) above shall—

(a) preclude the determination of that matter as aforesaid; or

(b) require the application to the marriage of the grounds or bar there mentioned except so far as applicable in accordance with those rules.

(2) In the case of a marriage which purports to have been celebrated under the Foreign Marriage Acts 1892 to 1947 or has taken place outside England and Wales and purports to be a marriage under common law, section 11 above is without prejudice to any ground on which the marriage may be void under those Acts or, as the case may be, by virtue of the rules governing the celebration of marriages outside England and Wales under common law.

Application of ss. 1 (5), 8 and 9 to nullity proceedings

15. Sections 1 (5), 8 and 9 above shall apply in relation to proceedings for nullity of marriage as if for any reference in those provisions to divorce there were substituted a reference to nullity of marriage.

Effect of degree of nullity in case of voidable marriage

16. A decree of nullity granted after 31st July 1971 in respect of a voidable marriage shall operate to annul the marriage only as respects any time after the decree has been made absolute, and the marriage shall, notwithstanding the decree, be treated as if it had existed up to that time.

Other matrimonial suits

Judicial separation

17.—(1) A petition for judicial separation may be presented to the court by either party to a marriage on the ground that any such fact as is mentioned in section 1 (2) above exists, and the provisions of section 2 above shall apply accordingly for the purposes of a petition for judicial separation alleging any such fact, as they apply in relation to a petition for divorce alleging that fact.

(2) On a petition for judicial separation it shall be the duty of the court to inquire, so far as it reasonably can, into the facts alleged by the petitioner and into any facts alleged by the respondent, but the court shall not be concerned to consider whether the marriage has broken down irretrievably, and if it is satisfied on the evidence of any such fact as is mentioned in section 1 (2) above it shall, subject to section 41 below, grant a decree of judicial separation.

(3) Sections 6 and 7 above shall apply for the purpose of encouraging the reconciliation of parties to proceedings for judicial separation and of enabling the parties to a marriage to refer to the court for its opinion an agreement or arrangement relevant to actual or contemplated proceedings for judicial separation, as they apply in relation to proceedings for divorce.

Effects of judicial separation

18.—(1) Where the court grants a decree of judicial separation it shall no longer be obligatory for the petitioner to cohabit with the respondent.

(2) If while a decree of judicial separation is in force and the separation is continuing either of the parties to the marriage dies intestate as respects all or any of his or her real or personal property, the property as respects which he or she died intestate shall devolve as if the other party to the marriage had then been dead.

(3) Notwithstanding anything in section 2 (1) (a) of the Matrimonial Proceedings (Magistrates' Courts) Act 1960, a provision in force under an order made, or having effect as if made, under that section exempting one party to a marriage from the obligation to cohabit with the other shall not have effect as a decree of judicial separation for the purposes of subsection (2) above.

Presumption of death and dissolution of marriage

19.—(1) Any married person who alleges that reasonable grounds exist for supposing that the other party to the marriage is dead may, [. . .]¹ present a petition to the court to have it presumed that the other party is dead and to have the marriage dissolved, and the court may, if satisfied that such reasonable grounds exist, grant a decree of presumption of death and dissolution of the marriage.

(2) [*Subsection (2) repealed by Domicile and Matrimonial Proceedings Act 1973 (c. 45), s. 17 (2), Sched. 6.*]

(3) In any proceedings under this section the fact that for a period of seven years or more the other party to the marriage has been continually absent from the petitioner and the petitioner has no reason to believe that the other party has been living within that time shall be evidence that the other party is dead until the contrary is proved.

(4) Sections 1 (5), 8 and 9 above shall apply to a petition and a decree under this section as they apply to a petition for divorce and a decree of divorce respectively.

[*Subsection (5) repealed by Domicile and Matrimonial Proceedings Act 1973 (c. 45), s. 17 (2), Sched. 6.*]

(6) It is hereby declared that neither collusion nor any other conduct on the part of the petitioner which has at any time been a bar to relief in matrimonial proceedings constitutes a bar to the grant of a decree under this section.

General

Relief for correspondent in divorce proceedings

20. If in any proceedings for divorce the respondent alleges and proves any such fact as is mentioned in subsection (2) of section 1 above (treating the respondent as the petitioner and the petitioner as the respondent for the purposes of that subsection) the court may give to the respondent the relief to which he would have been entitled if he had presented a petition seeking that relief.

PART II

FINANCIAL RELIEF FOR PARTIES TO MARRIAGE AND CHILDREN OF FAMILY

Financial provision and property adjustment orders

Financial provision and property adjustment orders

21.—(1) The financial provision orders for the purposes of this Act are the orders for periodical or lump sum provision available (subject to the provisions of this Act) under section 23 below for the purpose of adjusting the financial position of the parties to a marriage and any children of the family in connection with proceedings for divorce, nullity of marriage or judicial separation and under section 27 (6) below on proof of neglect by one party to a marriage to provide, or to make a proper contribution towards, reasonable maintenance for the other or a child of the family, that is to say—

(a) any order for periodical payments in favour of a party to a marriage under section 23 (1) (a) or 27 (6) (a) or in favour of a child of the family under section 23 (1) (d), (2) or (4) or 27 (6) (d);

(b) any order for secured periodical payments in favour of a party to a marriage under section 23 (1) (b) or 27 (6) (b) or in favour of a child of the family under section 23 (1) (e), (2) or (4) or 27 (6) (e); and

¹ Words repealed by Domicile and Matrimonial Proceedings Act 1973 (c. 45), s. 17 (2), Sched. 6.

(c) any order for lump sum provision in favour of a party to a marriage under section 23 (1) (c) or 27 (6) (c) or in favour of a child of the family under section 23 (1) (f), (2) or (4) or 27 (6) (f);

and references in this Act (except in paragraphs 17 (1) and 23 of Schedule 1 below) to periodical payments orders, secured periodical payments orders, and orders for the payment of a lump sum are references to all or some of the financial provision orders requiring the sort of financial provision in question according as the context of each reference may require.

(2) The property adjustment orders for the purposes of this Act are the orders dealing with property rights available (subject to the provisions of this Act) under section 24 below for the purpose of adjusting the financial position of the parties to a marriage and any children of the family on or after the grant of a decree of divorce, nullity of marriage or judicial separation, that is to say—

(a) any order under subsection (1) (a) of that section for a transfer of property;

(b) any order under subsection (1) (b) of that section for a settlement of property; and

(c) any order under subsection (1) (c) or (d) of that section for a variation of settlement.

Ancillary relief in connection with divorce proceedings, etc.

Maintenance pending suit

22. On a petition for divorce, nullity of marriage or judicial separation, the court may make an order for maintenance pending suit, that is to say, an order requiring either party to the marriage to make to the other such periodical payments for his or her maintenance and for such term, being a term beginning not earlier than the date of the presentation of the petition and ending with the date of the determination of the suit, as the court thinks reasonable.

Financial provision orders in connection with divorce proceedings, etc.

23.—(1) On granting a decree of divorce, a decree of nullity of marriage or a decree of judicial separation or at any time thereafter (whether, in the case of a decree of divorce or of nullity of marriage, before or after the decree is made absolute), the court may make any one or more of the following orders, that is to say—

(a) an order that either party to the marriage shall make to the other such periodical payments, for such term, as may be specified in the order;

(b) an order that either party to the marriage shall secure to the other to the satisfaction of the court such periodical payments, for such term, as may be so specified;

(c) an order that either party to the marriage shall pay to the other such lump sum or sums as may be so specified;

(d) an order that a party to the marriage shall make to such person as may be specified in the order for the benefit of a child of the family, or to such a child, such periodical payments, for such term, as may be so specified;

(e) an order that a party to the marriage shall secure to such person as may be so specified for the benefit of such a child, or to such a child, to the satisfaction of the court, such periodical payments, for such term, as may be so specified;

(f) an order that a party to the marriage shall pay to such person as may be so specified for the benefit of such a child, or to such a child, such lump sum as may be so specified;

451

subject, however, in the case of an order under paragraph (*d*), (*e*) or (*f*) above, to the restrictions imposed by section 29 (1) and (3) below on the making of financial provision orders in favour of children who have attained the age of eighteen.

(2) The court may also, subject to those restrictions, make any one or more of the orders mentioned in subsection (1) (*d*), (*e*) and (*f*) above—

(*a*) in any proceedings for divorce, nullity of marriage or judicial separation, before granting a decree; and

(*b*) where any such proceedings are dismissed after the beginning of the trial, either forthwith or within a reasonable period after the dismissal.

(3) Without prejudice to the generality of subsection (1) (*c*) or (*f*) above—

(*a*) an order under this section that a party to a marriage shall pay a lump sum to the other party may be made for the purpose of enabling that other party to meet any liabilities or expenses reasonably incurred by him or her in maintaining himself or herself or any child of the family before making an application for an order under this section in his or her favour;

(*b*) an order under this section for the payment of a lump sum to or for the benefit of a child of the family may be made for the purpose of enabling any liabilities or expenses reasonably incurred by or for the benefit of that child before the making of an application for an order under this section in his favour to be met; and

(*c*) an order under this section for the payment of a lump sum may provide for the payment of that sum by instalments of such amount as may be specified in the order and may require the payment of the instalments to be secured to the satisfaction of the court.

(4) The power of the court under subsection (1) or (2) (*a*) above to make an order in favour of a child of the family shall be exercisable from time to time; and where the court makes an order in favour of a child under subsection (2) (*b*) above, it may from time to time, subject to the restrictions mentioned in subsection (1) above, make a further order in his favour of any of the kinds mentioned in subsection (1) (*d*), (*e*) or (*f*) above.

(5) Without prejudice to the power to give a direction under section 30 below for the settlement of an instrument by conveyancing counsel, where an order is made under subsection (1) (*a*), (*b*) or (*c*) above on or after granting a decree of divorce or nullity of marriage, neither the order nor any settlement made in pursuance of the order shall take effect unless the decree has been made absolute.

Property adjustment orders in connection with divorce proceedings, etc.

24. On granting a decree of divorce, a decree of nullity of marriage or a decree of judicial separation or at any time thereafter (whether, in the case of a decree of divorce or of nullity of marriage, before or after the decree is made absolute), the court may make any one or more of the following orders, that is to say—

(*a*) an order that a party to the marriage shall transfer to the other party, to any child of the family or to such person as may be specified in the order for the benefit of such a child such property as may be so specified, being property to which the first-mentioned party is entitled, either in possession or reversion;

(*b*) an order that a settlement of such property as may be so specified, being property to which a party to the marriage is so

452

entitled, be made to the satisfaction of the court for the benefit of the other party to the marriage and of the children of the family or either or any of them;

(c) an order varying for the benefit of the parties to the marriage and of the children of the family or either or any of them any ante-nuptial or post-nuptial settlement (including such a settlement made by will or codicil) made on the parties to the marriage;

(d) an order extinguishing or reducing the interest of either of the parties to the marriage under any such settlement;

subject, however, in the case of an order under paragraph (a) above, to the restrictions imposed by section 29 (1) and (3) below on the making of orders for a transfer of property in favour of children who have attained the age of eighteen.

(2) The court may make an order under subsection (1) (c) above notwithstanding that there are no children of the family.

(3) Without prejudice to the power to give a direction under section 30 below for the settlement of an instrument by conveyancing counsel, where an order is made under this section on or after granting a decree of divorce or nullity of marriage, neither the order nor any settlement made in pursuance of the order shall take effect unless the decree has been made absolute.

Matters to which court is to have regard in deciding how to exercise its powers under sections 23 and 24

25.—(1) It shall be the duty of the court in deciding whether to exercise its powers under section 23 (1) (a), (b) or (c) or 24 above in relation to a party to the marriage and, if so, in what manner, to have regard to all the circumstances of the case including the following matters, that is to say—

(a) the income, earning capacity, property and other financial resources which each of the parties to the marriage has or is likely to have in the foreseeable future;

(b) the financial needs, obligations and responsibilities which each of the parties to the marriage has or is likely to have in the fore-seeable future;

(c) the standard of living enjoyed by the family before the breakdown of the marriage;

(d) the age of each party to the marriage and the duration of the marriage;

(e) any physical or mental disability of either of the parties to the marriage;

(f) the contributions made by each of the parties to the welfare of the family, including any contribution made by looking after the home or caring for the family;

(g) in the case of proceedings for divorce or nullity of marriage, the value to either of the parties to the marriage of any benefit (for example, a pension) which, by reason of the dissolution or annulment of the marriage, that party will lose the chance of acquiring;

and so to exercise those powers as to place the parties, so far as it is practicable and, having regard to their conduct, just to do so, in the financial position in which they would have been if the marriage had not broken down and each had properly discharged his or her financial obligations and responsibilities towards the other.

(2) Without prejudice to subsection (3) below, it shall be the duty of the court in deciding whether to exercise its powers under section 23 (1) (d), (e) or (f), (2) or (4) or 24 above in relation to a child of the

family and, if so, in what manner, to have regard to all the circumstances of the case including the following matters, that is to say—
  (a) the financial needs of the child;
  (b) the income, earning capacity (if any), property and other financial resources of the child;
  (c) any physical or mental disability of the child;
  (d) the standard of living enjoyed by the family before the breakdown of the marriage;
  (e) the manner in which he was being and in which the parties to the marriage expected him to be educated or trained;
and so to exercise those powers as to place the child, so far as it is practicable and, having regard to the considerations mentioned in relation to the parties to the marriage in paragraph (a) and (b) of subsection (1) above, just to do so, in the financial position in which the child would have been if the marriage had not broken down and each of those parties had properly discharged his or her financial obligations and responsibilities towards him.

(3) It shall be the duty of the court in deciding whether to exercise its powers under section 23 (1) (d), (e) or (f), (2) or (4) or 24 above against a party to a marriage in favour of a child of the family who is not the child of that party and, if so, in what manner, to have regard (among the circumstances of the case)—
  (a) to whether that party had assumed any responsibility for the child's maintenance and, if so, to the extent to which, and the basis upon which, that party assumed such responsibility and to the length of time for which that party discharged such responsibility;
  (b) to whether in assuming and discharging such responsibility that party did so knowing that the child was not his or her own;
  (c) to the liability of any other person to maintain the child.

Commencement of proceedings for ancillary relief, etc.

26.—(1) Where a petition for divorce, nullity of marriage or judicial separation has been presented, then, subject to subsection (2) below, proceedings for maintenance pending suit under section 22 above, for a financial provision order under section 23 above, or for a property adjustment order may be begun, subject to and in accordance with rules of court, at any time after the presentation of the petition.

(2) Rules of court may provide, in such cases as may be prescribed by the rules—
  (a) that applications for any such relief as is mentioned in subsection (1) above shall be made in the petition or answer; and
  (b) that applications for any such relief which are not so made, or are not made until after the expiration of such period following the presentation of the petition or filing of the answer as may be so prescribed, shall be made only with the leave of the court.

Financial provision in case of neglect to maintain

Financial provision orders, etc., in case of neglect by party to marriage to maintain other party or child of the family

27.—(1) Either party to a marriage may apply to the court for an order under this section on the ground that the other party to the marriage (in this section referred to as the respondent)—
  (a) being the husband, has wilfully neglected—
      (i) to provide reasonable maintenance for the applicant, or
      (ii) to provide, or to make a proper contribution towards, reasonable maintenance for any child of the family to whom this section applies;

(*b*) being the wife, has wilfully neglected to provide, or to make a proper contribution towards, reasonable maintenance—

  (i) for the applicant in a case where, by reason of the impairment of the applicant's earning capacity through age, illness or disability of mind or body, and having regard to any resources of the applicant and the respondent respectively which are, or should properly be made, available for the purpose, it is reasonable in all the circumstances to expect the respondent so to provide or contribute, or

  (ii) for any child of the family to whom this section applies.

(2) [1a] The court shall not entertain an application under this section unless it would have jurisdiction to entertain proceedings by the applicant for judicial separation.

(3) This section applies to any child of the family for whose maintenance it is reasonable in all the circumstances to expect the respondent to provide or towards whose maintenance it is reasonable in all the circumstances to expect the respondent to make a proper contribution.

(4) Where the child of the family to whom the application under this section relates is not the child of the respondent, then, in deciding—

(*a*) whether the respondent has been guilty of wilful neglect to provide, or to make a proper contribution towards, reasonable maintenance for the child, and

(*b*) what order, if any, to make under this section in favour of the child,

the court shall have regard to the matters mentioned in section 25 (3) above.

(5) Where on an application under this section it appears to the court that the applicant or any child of the family to whom the application relates is in immediate need of financial assistance, but it is not yet possible to determine what order, if any, should be made on the application, the court may make an interim order for maintenance, that is to say, an order requiring the respondent to make to the applicant until the determination of the application such periodical payments as the court thinks reasonable.

(6) Where on an application under this section the applicant satisfies the court of any ground mentioned in subsection (1) above, the court may make such one or more of the following orders as it thinks just, that is to say—

(*a*) an order that the respondent shall make to the applicant such periodical payments, for such term, as may be specified in the order;

(*b*) an order that the respondent shall secure to the applicant, to the satisfaction of the court, such periodical payments, for such term, as may be so specified;

(*c*) an order that the respondent shall pay to the applicant such lump sum as may be so specified;

(*d*) an order that the respondent shall make to such person as may be specified in the order for the benefit of the child to whom the application relates, or to that child, such periodical payments, for such term, as may be so specified;

(*e*) an order that the respondent shall secure to such person as may be so specified for the benefit of that child, or to that child, to the satisfaction of the court, such periodical payments, for such term, as may be so specified;

(*f*) an order that the respondent shall pay to such person as may be so specified for the benefit of that child, or to that child, such lump sum as may be so specified;

subject, however, in the case of an order under paragraph (*d*), (*e*) or (*f*)

[1a] Amended by 1973 (c. 45), s. 6 (1), *post.*

above, to the restrictions imposed by section 29 (1) and (3) below on the making of financial provision orders in favour of children who have attained the age of eighteen.

(7) Without prejudice to the generality of subsection (6) (*c*) or (*f*) above, an order under this section for the payment of a lump sum—

(*a*) may be made for the purpose of enabling any liabilities or expenses reasonably incurred in maintaining the applicant or any child of the family to whom the application relates before the making of the application to be met;

(*b*) may provide for the payment of that sum by instalments of such amount as may be specified in the order and may require the payment of the instalments to be secured to the satisfaction of the court.

(8) For the purpose of proceedings on an application under this section adultery which has been condoned shall not be capable of being revived, and any presumption of condonation which arises from the continuance or resumption of marital intercourse may be rebutted by evidence sufficient to negative the necessary intent.

Additional provisions with respect to financial provision and property adjustment orders

Duration of continuing financial provision orders in favour of party to marriage, and effect of remarriage

28.—(1) The term to be specified in a periodical payments or secured periodical payments order in favour of a party to a marriage shall be such term as the court thinks fit, subject to the following limits, that is to say—

(*a*) in the case of a periodical payments order, the term shall begin not earlier than the date of the making of an application for the order, and shall be so defined as not to extend beyond the death of either of the parties to the marriage or, where the order is made on or after the grant of a decree of divorce or nullity of marriage, the remarriage of the party in whose favour the order is made; and

(*b*) in the case of a secured periodical payments order, the term shall begin not earlier than the date of the making of an application for the order, and shall be so defined as not to extend beyond the death or, where the order is made on or after the grant of such a decree, the remarriage of the party in whose favour the order is made.

(2) Where a periodical payments or secured periodical payments order in favour of a party to a marriage is made otherwise than on or after a grant of a decree of divorce or nullity of marriage, and the marriage in question is subsequently dissolved or annulled but the order continues in force, the order shall, notwithstanding anything in it, cease to have effect on the remarriage of that party, except in relation to any arrears due under it on the date of the remarriage.

(3) If after the grant of a decree dissolving or annulling a marriage either party to that marriage remarries, that party shall not be entitled to apply, by reference to the grant of that decree, for a financial provision order in his or her favour, or for a property adjustment order, against the other party to that marriage.

Duration of continuing financial provision orders in favour of children, and age limit on making certain orders in their favour

29.—(1) Subject to subsection (3) below, no financial provision order and no order for a transfer of property under section 24 (1) (*a*) above shall be made in favour of a child who has attained the age of eighteen.

(2) The term to be specified in a periodical payments or secured periodical payments order in favour of a child may begin with the date of the making of an application for the order in question or any later date but—

(a) shall not in the first instance extend beyond the date of the birthday of the child next following his attaining the upper limit of the compulsory school age (that is to say, the age that is for the time being that limit by virtue of section 35 of the Education Act 1944 together with any Order in Council made under that section) unless the court thinks it right in the circumstances of the case to specify a later date; and

(b) shall not in any event, subject to subsection (3) below, extend beyond the date of the child's eighteenth birthday.

(3) Subsection (1) above, and paragraph (b) of subsection (2), shall not apply in the case of a child, if it appears to the court that—

(a) the child is, or will be, or if an order were made without complying with either or both of those provisions would be, receiving instruction at an educational establishment or undergoing training for a trade, profession or vocation, whether or not he is also, or will also be, in gainful employment; or

(b) there are special circumstances which justify the making of an order without complying with either or both of those provisions.

(4) Any periodical payments order in favour of a child shall, notwithstanding anything in the order, cease to have effect on the death of the person liable to make payments under the order, except in relation to any arrears due under the order on the date of the death.

Direction for settlement of instrument for securing payments or effecting property adjustment

30. Where the court decides to make a financial provision order requiring any payments to be secured or a property adjustment order—

(a) it may direct that the matter be referred to one of the conveyancing counsel of the court for him to settle a proper instrument to be executed by all necessary parties; and

(b) where the order is to be made in proceedings for divorce, nullity of marriage or judicial separation it may, if it thinks fit, defer the grant of the decree in question until the instrument has been duly executed.

Variation, discharge and enforcement of certain orders, etc.

Variation, discharge, etc., of certain orders for financial relief

31.—(1) Where the court has made an order to which this section applies, then, subject to the provisions of this section, the court shall have power to vary or discharge the order or to suspend any provision thereof temporarily and to revive the operation of any provision so suspended.

(2) This section applies to the following orders, that is to say—

(a) any order for maintenance pending suit and any interim order for maintenance;

(b) any periodical payments order;

(c) any secured periodical payments order;

(d) any order made by virtue of section 23 (3) (c) or 27 (7) (b) above (provision for payment of a lump sum by instalments);

(e) any order for a settlement of property under section 24 (1) (b) or for a variation of settlement under section 24 (1) (c) or (d) above, being an order made on or after the grant of a decree of judicial separation.

(3) The powers exercisable by the court under this section in relation to an order shall be exercisable also in relation to any instrument executed in pursuance of the order.

(4) The court shall not exercise the powers conferred by this section in relation to an order for a settlement under section 24 (1) (*b*) or for a variation of settlement under section 24 (1) (*c*) or (*d*) above except on an application made in proceedings—

(*a*) for the rescission of the decree of judicial separation by reference to which the order was made, or

(*b*) for the dissolution of the marriage in question.

(5) No property adjustment order shall be made on an application for the variation of a periodical payments or secured periodical payments order made (whether in favour of a party to a marriage or in favour of a child of the family) under section 23 above, and no order for the payment of a lump sum shall be made on an application for the variation of a periodical payments or secured periodical payments order in favour of a party to a marriage (whether made under section 23 or under section 27 above).

(6) Where the person liable to make payments under a secured periodical payments order has died, an application under this section relating to that order may be made by the person entitled to payments under the order or by the personal representatives of the deceased person, but no such application shall, except with the permission of the court, be made after the end of the period of six months from the date on which representation in regard to the estate of that person is first taken out.

(7) In exercising the powers conferred by this section the court shall have regard to all the circumstances of the case, including any change in any of the matters to which the court was required to have regard when making the order to which the application relates and, where the party against whom that order was made has died, the changed circumstances resulting from his or her death.

(8) The personal representatives of a deceased person against whom a secured periodical payments order was made shall not be liable for having distributed any part of the estate of the deceased after the expiration of the period of six months referred to in subsection (6) above on the ground that they ought to have taken into account the possibility that the court might permit an application under this section to be made after that period by the person entitled to payments under the order; but this subsection shall not prejudice any power to recover any part of the estate so distributed arising by virtue of the making of an order in pursuance of this section.

(9) In considering for the purposes of subsection (6) above the question when representation was first taken out, a grant limited to settled land or to trust property shall be left out of account and a grant limited to real estate or to personal estate shall be left out of account unless a grant limited to the remainder of the estate has previously been made or is made at the same time.

Payment of certain arrears unenforceable without the leave of the court

32.—(1) A person shall not be entitled to enforce through the High Court or any county court the payment of any arrears due under an order for maintenance pending suit, an interim order for maintenance or any financial provision order without the leave of that court if those arrears became due more than twelve months before proceedings to enforce the payment of them are begun.

(2) The court hearing an application for the grant of leave under this section may refuse leave, or may grant leave subject to such restrictions and conditions (including conditions as to the allowing of time for

payment or the making of payment by instalments) as that court thinks proper, or may remit the payment of the arrears or of any part thereof.

(3) An application for the grant of leave under this section shall be made in such manner as may be prescribed by rules of court.

Orders for repayment in certain cases of sums paid under certain orders

33.—(1) Where on an application made under this section in relation to an order to which this section applies it appears to the court that by reason of—

(*a*) a change in the circumstances of the person entitled to, or liable to make, payments under the order since the order was made, or

(*b*) the changed circumstances resulting from the death of the person so liable,

the amount received by the person entitled to payments under the order in respect of a period after those circumstances changed or after the death of the person liable to make payments under the order, as the case may be, exceeds the amount which the person so liable or his or her personal representatives should have been required to pay, the court may order the respondent to the application to pay to the applicant such sum, not exceeding the amount of the excess, as the court thinks just.

(2) This section applies to the following orders, that is to say—

(*a*) any order for maintenance pending suit and any interim order for maintenance;

(*b*) any periodical payments order; and

(*c*) any secured periodical payments order.

(3) An application under this section may be made by the person liable to make payments under an order to which this section applies or his or her personal representatives and may be made against the person entitled to payments under the order or her or his personal representatives.

(4) An application under this section may be made in proceedings in the High Court or a county court for—

(*a*) the variation or discharge of the order to which this section applies, or

(*b*) leave to enforce, or the enforcement of, the payment of arrears under that order;

but when not made in such proceedings shall be made to a county court, and accordingly references in this section to the court are references to the High Court or a county court, as the circumstances require.

(5) The jurisdiction conferred on a county court by this section shall be exercisable notwithstanding that by reason of the amount claimed in the application the jurisdiction would not but for this subsection be exercisable by a county court.

(6) An order under this section for the payment of any sum may provide for the payment of that sum by instalments of such amount as may be specified in the order.

Maintenance agreements

Validity of maintenance agreements

34.—(1) If a maintenance agreement includes a provision purporting to restrict any right to apply to a court for an order containing financial arrangements, then—

(*a*) that provision shall be void; but

(*b*) any other financial arrangements contained in the agreement shall not thereby be rendered void or unenforceable and shall, unless they are void or unenforceable for any other reason (and subject to sections 35 and 36 below), be binding on the parties to the agreement.

(2) In this section and in section 35 below—

" maintenance agreement " means any agreement in writing made, whether before or after the commencement of this Act, between the parties to a marriage, being—

(a) an agreement containing financial arrangements, whether made during the continuance or after the dissolution or annulment of the marriage; or

(b) a separation agreement which contains no financial arrangements in a case where no other agreement in writing between the same parties contains such arrangements;

" financial arrangements " means provisions governing the rights and liabilities towards one another when living separately of the parties to a marriage (including a marriage which has been dissolved or annulled) in respect of the making or securing of payments or the disposition or use of any property, including such rights and liabilities with respect to the maintenance or education of any child, whether or not a child of the family.

Alteration of agreements by court during lives of parties

35.—(1) Where a maintenance agreement is for the time being subsisting and each of the parties to the agreement is for the time being either domiciled or resident in England and Wales, then, subject to subsection (3) below, either party may apply to the court or to a magistrates' court for an order under this section.

(2) If the court to which the application is made is satisfied either—

(a) that by reason of a change in the circumstances in the light of which any financial arrangements contained in the agreement were made or, as the case may be, financial arrangements were omitted from it (including a change foreseen by the parties when making the agreement), the agreement should be altered so as to make different, or, as the case may be, so as to contain, financial arrangements, or

(b) that the agreement does not contain proper financial arrangements with respect to any child of the family,

then subject to subsections (3), (4) and (5) below, that court may by order make such alterations in the agreement—

(i) by varying or revoking any financial arrangements contained in it, or

(ii) by inserting in it financial arrangements for the benefit of one of the parties to the agreement or of a child of the family,

as may appear to that court to be just having regard to all the circumstances, including, if relevant, the matters mentioned in section 25 (3) above; and the agreement shall have effect thereafter as if any alteration made by the order had been made by agreement between the parties and for valuable consideration.

(3) A magistrates' court shall not entertain an application under subsection (1) above unless both the parties to the agreement are resident in England and Wales and at least one of the parties is resident in the petty sessions area (within the meaning of the Magistrates' Courts Act 1952) for which the court acts, and shall not have power to make any order on such an application except—

(a) in a case where the agreement includes no provision for periodical payments by either of the parties, an order inserting provision for the making by one of the parties of periodical payments for the maintenance of the other party or for the maintenance of any child of the family;

(b) in a case where the agreement includes provision for the making by one of the parties of periodical payments, an order increasing or reducing the rate of, or terminating, any of those payments.

(4) Where a court decides to alter, by order under this section, an agreement by inserting provision for the making or securing by one of the parties to the agreement of periodical payments for the maintenance of the other party or by increasing the rate of the periodical payments which the agreement provides shall be made by one of the parties for the maintenance of the other, the term for which the payments or, as the case may be, the additional payments attributable to the increase are to be made under the agreement as altered by the order shall be such term as the court may specify, subject to the following limits, that is to say—

(a) where the payments will not be secured, the term shall be so defined as not to extend beyond the death of either of the parties to the agreement or the remarriage of the party to whom the payments are to be made;

(b) where the payments will be secured, the term shall be so defined as not to extend beyond the death or remarriage of that party.

(5) Where a court decides to alter, by order under this section, an agreement by inserting provision for the making or securing by one of the parties to the agreement of periodical payments for the maintenance of a child of the family or by increasing the rate of the periodical payments which the agreement provides shall be made or secured by one of the parties for the maintenance of such a child, then, in deciding the term for which under the agreement as altered by the order the payments, or as the case may be, the additional payments attributable to the increase are to be made or secured for the benefit of the child, the court shall apply the provisions of section 29 (2) and (3) above as to age limits as if the order in question were a periodical payments or secured periodical payments order in favour of the child.

(6) For the avoidance of doubt it is hereby declared that nothing in this section or in section 34 above affects any power of a court before which any proceedings between the parties to a maintenance agreement are brought under any other enactment (including a provision of this Act) to make an order containing financial arrangements or any right of either party to apply for such an order in such proceedings.

Alteration of agreements by court after death of one party

36.—(1) Where a maintenance agreement within the meaning of section 34 above provides for the continuation of payment under the agreement after the death of one of the parties and that party dies domiciled in England and Wales, the surviving party or the personal representatives of the deceased party may, subject to subsections (2) and (3) below, apply to the High Court or a county court for an order under section 35 above.

(2) An application under this section shall not, except with the permission of the High Court or a county court, be made after the end of the period of six months from the date on which representation in regard to the estate of the deceased is first taken out.

(3) A county court shall not entertain an application under this section, or an application for permission to make an application under this section, unless it would have jurisdiction by virtue of [section 22 of the Inheritance (Provision for Family and Dependents) Act 1975] [2]

---

[2] Substituted by Inheritance (Provision for Family Dependants) Act 1975 (c. 63), s. 26.

(which confers jurisdiction on county courts in proceedings under [that Act if the value of the property mentioned in that section] ² does not exceed £5,000 or such larger sum as may be fixed by order of the Lord Chancellor) to hear and determine proceedings for an order under [section 2 of that Act] ² in relation to the deceased's estate.

(4) If a maintenance agreement is altered by a court on an application made in pursuance of subsection (1) above, the like consequences shall ensue as if the alteration had been made immediately before the death by agreement between the parties and for valuable consideration.

(5) The provisions of this section shall not render the personal representatives of the deceased liable for having distributed any part of the estate of the deceased after the expiration of the period of six months referred to in subsection (2) above on the ground that they ought to have taken into account the possibility that a court might permit an application by virtue of this section to be made by the surviving party after that period; but this subsection shall not prejudice any power to recover any part of the estate so distributed arising by virtue of the making of an order in pursuance of this section.

(6) Section 31 (9) above shall apply for the purposes of subsection (2) above as it applies for the purposes of subsection (6) of section 31.

(7) Subsection (3) of [section 22 of the Inheritance (Provision for Family and Dependants) Act 1975 (which enables rules of court to provide for the transfer from a county court to the High Court or from the High Court to a county court of proceedings for an order under section 2 of that Act) and paragraphs (*a*) and (*b*) of subsection (4)] ² of that section (provisions relating to proceedings commenced in county court before coming into force of order of the Lord Chancellor under that section) shall apply in relation to proceedings consisting of any such application as is referred to in subsection (3) above as they apply in relation to [proceedings for an order under section 2 of that Act].²

Miscellaneous and supplemental

Avoidance of transactions intended to prevent or reduce financial relief

37.—(1) For the purposes of this section " financial relief " means relief under any of the provisions of sections 22, 23, 24, 27, 31 (except subsection (6)) and 35 above, and any reference in this section to defeating a person's claim for financial relief is a reference to preventing financial relief from being granted to that person, or to that person for the benefit of a child of the family, or reducing the amount of any financial relief which might be so granted, or frustrating or impeding the enforcement of any order which might be or has been made at his instance under any of those provisions.

(2) Where proceedings for financial relief are brought by one person against another, the court may, on the application of the first-mentioned person—

    (*a*) if it is satisfied that the other party to the proceedings is, with the intention of defeating the claim for financial relief, about to make any disposition or to transfer out of the jurisdiction or otherwise deal with any property, make such order as it thinks fit for restraining the other party from so doing or otherwise for protecting the claim;

    (*b*) if it is satisfied that the other party has, with that intention, made a reviewable disposition and that if the disposition were set aside financial relief or different financial relief would be granted to the applicant, make an order setting aside the disposition;

    (*c*) if it is satisfied, in a case where an order has been obtained under any of the provisions mentioned in subsection (1) above by the applicant against the other party, that the other party has, with that intention, made a reviewable disposition, make an order setting aside the disposition;

and an application for the purposes of paragraph (b) above shall be made in the proceedings for the financial relief in question.

(3) Where the court makes an order under subsection (2) (b) or (c) above setting aside a disposition it shall give such consequential directions as it thinks fit for giving effect to the order (including directions requiring the making of any payments or the disposal of any property).

(4) Any disposition made by the other party to the proceedings for financial relief in question (whether before or after the commencement of those proceedings) is a reviewable disposition for the purposes of subsection (2) (b) and (c) above unless it was made for valuable consideration (other than marriage) to a person who, at the time of the disposition, acted in relation to it in good faith and without notice of any intention on the part of the other party to defeat the applicant's claim for financial relief.

(5) Where an application is made under this section with respect to a disposition which took place less than three years before the date of the application or with respect to a disposition or other dealing with property which is about to take place and the court is satisfied—

(a) in a case falling within subsection (2) (a) or (b) above, that the disposition or other dealing would (apart from this section) have the consequence, or

(b) in a case falling within subsection (2) (c) above, that the disposition has had the consequence,

of defeating the applicant's claim for financial relief, it shall be presumed, unless the contrary is shown, that the person who disposed of or is about to dispose of or deal with the property did so or, as the case may be, is about to do so, with the intention of defeating the applicant's claim for financial relief.

(6) In this section " disposition " does not include any provision contained in a will or codicil but, with that exception, includes any conveyance, assurance or gift of property of any description, whether made by an instrument or otherwise.

(7) This section does not apply to a disposition made before 1st January 1968.

Order for repayment in certain cases of sums paid after cessation of order by reason of remarriage

38.—(1) Where—

(a) a periodical payments or secured periodical payments order in favour of a party to a marriage (hereafter in this section referred to as " a payments order ") has ceased to have effect by reason of the remarriage of that party, and

(b) the person liable to make payments under the order or his or her personal representatives made payments in accordance with it in respect of a period after the date of the remarriage in the mistaken belief that the order was still subsisting,

the person so liable or his or her personal representatives shall not be entitled to bring proceedings in respect of a cause of action arising out of the circumstances mentioned in paragraphs (a) and (b) above against the person entitled to payments under the order or her or his personal representatives, but may instead make an application against that person or her or his personal representatives under this section.

(2) On an application under this section the court may order the respondent to pay to the applicant a sum equal to the amount of the payments made in respect of the period mentioned in subsection (1) (b)

above or, if it appears to the court that it would be unjust to make that order, it may either order the respondent to pay to the applicant such lesser sum as it thinks fit or dismiss the application.

(3) An application under this section may be made in proceedings in the High Court or a county court for leave to enforce, or the enforcement of, payment of arrears under the order in question, but when not made in such proceedings shall be made to a county court; and accordingly references in this section to the court are references to the High Court or a county court, as the circumstances require.

(4) The jurisdiction conferred on a county court by this section shall be exercisable notwithstanding that by reason of the amount claimed in the application the jurisdiction would not but for this subsection be exercisable by a county court.

(5) An order under this section for the payment of any sum may provide for the payment of that sum by instalments of such amount as may be specified in the order.

(6) The clerk of a magistrates' court to whom any payments under a payments order are required to be made, and the collecting officer under an attachment of earnings order made to secure payments under a payments order, shall not be liable—

(*a*) in the case of the clerk, for any act done by him in pursuance of the payments order after the date on which that order ceased to have effect by reason of the remarriage of the person entitled to payments under it, and

(*b*) in the case of the collecting officer, for any act done by him after that date in accordance with any enactment or rule of court specifying how payments made to him in compliance with the attachment of earnings order are to be dealt with.

if, but only if, the act was one which he would have been under a duty to do had the payments order not so ceased to have effect and the act was done before notice in writing of the fact that the person so entitled had remarried was given to him by or on behalf of that person, the person liable to make payments under the payments order or the personal representatives of either of those persons.

(7) In this section " collecting officer," in relation to an attachment of earnings order, means the officer of the High Court, the registrar of a county court or the clerk of a magistrates' court to whom a person makes payments in compliance with the order.

Settlement, etc., made in compliance with a property adjustment order may be avoided on bankruptcy of settlor

39. The fact that a settlement or transfer of property had to be made in order to comply with a property adjustment order shall not prevent that settlement or transfer from being a settlement of property to which section 42 (1) of the Bankruptcy Act 1914 (avoidance of certain settlements) applies.

Payments, etc., under order made in favour of person suffering from mental disorder

40. Where the court makes an order under this Part of this Act requiring payments (including a lump sum payment) to be made, or property to be transferred, to a party to a marriage and the court is satisfied that the person in whose favour the order is made is incapable, by reason of mental disorder within the meaning of the Mental Health Act 1959, of managing and administering his or her property and affairs then, subject to any order, direction or authority made or given in relation to that person under Part VIII of that Act, the court may order the payments to be made, or as the case may be, the property to be transferred, to such persons having charge of that person as the court may direct.

PART III

PROTECTION, CUSTODY, ETC., OF CHILDREN

Restrictions on decrees for dissolution, annulment or separation affecting children

41.—(1) The Court shall not make absolute a decree of divorce or of nullity of marriage, or grant a decree of judicial separation, unless the court, by order, has declared that it is satisfied—

(*a*) that for the purposes of this section there are no children of the family to whom this section applies; or

(*b*) that the only children who are or may be children of the family to whom this section applies are the children named in the order and that—

    (i) arrangements for the welfare of every child so named have been made and are satisfactory or are the best that can be devised in the circumstances; or

    (ii) it is impracticable for the party or parties appearing before the court to make any such arrangements; or

(*c*) that there are circumstances making it desirable that the decree should be made absolute or should be granted, as the case may be, without delay notwithstanding that there are or may be children of the family to whom this section applies and that the court is unable to make a declaration in accordance with paragraph (*b*) above.

(2) The court shall not make an order declaring that it is satisfied as mentioned in subsection (1) (*c*) above unless it has obtained a satisfactory undertaking from either or both of the parties to bring the question of the arrangements for the children named in the order before the court within a specified time.

(3) If the court makes absolute a decree of divorce or of nullity of marriage, or grants a decree of judicial separation, without having made an order under subsection (1) above the decree shall be void but, if such an order was made, no person shall be entitled to challenge the validity of the decree on the ground that the conditions prescribed by subsections (1) and (2) above were not fulfilled.

(4) If the court refuses to make an order under subsection (1) above in any proceedings for divorce, nullity of marriage or judicial separation, it shall, on an application by either party to the proceedings, make an order declaring that it is not satisfied as mentioned in that subsection.

(5) This section applies to the following children of the family, that is to say—

(*a*) any minor child of the family who at the date of the order under subsection (1) above is—

    (i) under the age of sixteen, or

    (ii) receiving instruction at an educational establishment or undergoing training for a trade, profession or vocation, whether or not he is also in gainful employment; and

(*b*) any other child of the family to whom the court by an order under that subsection directs that this section shall apply;

and the court may give such a direction if it is of opinion that there are special circumstances which make it desirable in the interest of the child that this section should apply to him.

(6) In this section " welfare," in relation to a child, includes the custody and education of the child and financial provision for him.

Orders for custody and education of children in cases of divorce, etc., and for custody in cases of neglect

42.—(1) The court may make such order as it thinks fit for the custody and education of any child of the family who is under the age of eighteen—

> (*a*) in any proceedings for divorce, nullity of marriage or judicial separation, before or on granting a decree or at any time thereafter (whether, in the case of a decree of divorce or nullity of marriage, before or after the decree is made absolute);
>
> (*b*) where any such proceedings are dismissed after the beginning of the trial, either forthwith or within a reasonable period after the dismissal;

and in any case in which the court has power by virtue of this subsection to make an order in respect of a child it may instead, if it thinks fit, direct that proper proceedings be taken for making the child a ward of court.

(2) Where the court makes an order under section 27 above, the court shall also have power to make such order as it thinks fit with respect to the custody of any child of the family who is for the time being under the age of eighteen; but the power conferred by this subsection and any order made in exercise of that power shall have effect only as respects any period when an order is in force under that section and the child is under that age.

(3) Where the court grants or makes absolute a decree of divorce or grants a decree of judicial separation, it may include in the decree a declaration that either party to the marriage in question is unfit to have the custody of the children of the family.

(4) Where a decree of divorce or of judicial separation contains such a declaration as is mentioned in subsection (3) above, then, if the party to whom the declaration relates is a parent of any child of the family, that party shall not, on the death of the other parent, be entitled as of right to the custody or the guardianship of that child.

(5) Where an order in respect of a child is made under this section, the order shall not affect the rights over or with respect to the child of any person, other than a party to the marriage in question, unless the child is the child of one or both of the parties to that marriage and that person was a party to the proceedings on the application for an order under this section.

(6) The power of the court under subsection (1) (*a*) or (2) above to make an order with respect to a child shall be exercisable from time to time; and where the court makes an order under subsection (1) (*b*) above with respect to a child it may from time to time until that child attains the age of eighteen make a further order with respect to his custody and education.

(7) The court shall have power to vary or discharge an order made under this section or to suspend any provision thereof temporarily and to revive the operation of any provision so suspended.

Power to commit children to care of local authority

43.—(1) Where the court has jurisdiction by virtue of this Part of this Act to make an order for the custody of a child and it appears to the court that there are exceptional circumstances making it impracticable or undesirable for the child to be entrusted to either of the parties to the marriage or to any other individual, the court may if it thinks fit make an order committing the care of the child to the council of a county other than a metropolitan county, or of a metropolitan district or London borough or the Common Council of the City of London (hereafter in this section referred to as " the local authority "); and thereupon

Part II of the Children Act 1948 (which relates to the treatment of children in the care of a local authority) shall, subject to the provisions of this section, apply as if the child had been received by the local authority into their care under section 1 of that Act.

(2) The authority specified in an order under this section shall be the local authority for the area in which the child was, in the opinion of the court, resident before the order was made to commit the child to the care of a local authority, and the court shall before making an order under this section hear any representations from the local authority, including any representations as to the making of a financial provision order in favour of the child.

(3) While an order made by virtue of this section is in force with respect to a child, the child shall continue in the care of the local authority notwithstanding any claim by a parent or other person.

(4) An order made by virtue of this section shall cease to have effect as respects any child when he becomes eighteen, and the court shall not make an order committing a child to the care of a local authority under this section after he has become seventeen.

(5) In the application of Part II of the Children Act 1948 by virtue of this section—

    (a) the exercise by the local authority of their powers under sections 12 to 14 of that Act (which among other things relate to the accommodation and welfare of a child in the care of a local authority) shall be subject to any directions given by the court; and

    (b) section 17 of that Act (which relates to arrangements for the emigration of such a child) shall not apply.

(6) It shall be the duty of any parent or guardian of a child committed to the care of a local authority under this section to secure that the local authority are informed of his address for the time being, and a person who knowingly fails to comply with this subsection shall be liable on summary conviction to a fine not exceeding ten pounds.

(7) The court shall have power from time to time by an order under this section to vary or discharge any provision made in pursuance of this section.

(8) So long as by virtue of paragraph 13 of Schedule 4 to the Children and Young Persons Act 1969 sections 15 and 16 of the Children Act 1948 continue to apply in relation to a local authority, subsection (5) (a) above shall have effect in relation to that authority as if for the reference to sections 12 to 14 of the last-mentioned Act there were substituted a reference to sections 12 to 16 of that Act.

(9) Subject to the following provisions of this subsection, until 1st April 1974 subsection (1) above shall have effect as if for the words " other than a metropolitan county, or of a metropolitan district " there were substituted the words " county borough ".

An order (or orders) made under section 273 (2) of the Local Government Act 1972 (orders bringing provisions of that Act into force before 1st April 1974) may appoint an earlier date (or, as the case may be, different dates for different purposes or areas) on which subsection (1) above shall cease to have effect as mentioned above.

Power to provide for supervision of children

44.—(1) Where the court has jurisdiction by virtue of this Part of this Act to make an order for the custody of a child and it appears to the court that there are exceptional circumstances making it desirable that the child should be under the supervision of an independent person, the court may, as respects any period during which the child is, in exercise of that jurisdiction, committed to the [care of any person] [2a] order that the child be under the supervision of an officer appointed under this section as a welfare officer or under the supervision of a local authority.

(2) Where the court makes an order under this section for supervision by a welfare officer, the officer responsible for carrying out the order shall be such probation officer as may be selected under arrangements made by the Secretary of State; and where the order is for supervision by a local authority, that authority shall be the council of a county other than a metropolitan county, or of a metropolitan district or London borough selected by the court and specified in the order or, if the Common Council of the City of London is so selected and specified, that Council.

(3) The court shall not have power to make an order under this section as respects a child who in pursuance of an order under section 43 above is in the care of a local authority.

(4) Where a child is under the supervision of any person in pursuance of this section the jurisdiction possessed by a court to vary any financial provision order in the child's favour or any order made with respect to his custody or education under this Part of this Act shall, subject to any rules of court, be exercisable at the instance of that court itself.

(5) The court shall have power from time to time by an order under this section to vary or discharge any provision made in pursuance of this section.

(6) Subject to the following provisions of this subsection, until 1st April 1974 subsection (2) above shall have effect as if for the words " other than a metropolitan county, or of a metropolitan district " there were substituted the words " county borough ".

An order (or orders) made under section 273 (2) of the Local Government Act 1972 may appoint an earlier date (or, as the case may be, different dates for different purposes or areas) on which subsection (2) above shall cease to have effect as mentioned above.

PART IV

MISCELLANEOUS AND SUPPLEMENTAL

Declarations of legitimacy, etc.

45.—(1) Any person who is a British subject, or whose right to be deemed a British subject depends wholly or in part on his legitimacy or on the validity of any marriage, may, if he is domiciled in England and Wales or in Northern Ireland or claims any real or personal estate situate in England and Wales, apply by petition to the High Court for a decree declaring that he is the legitimate child of his parents, or that the marriage of his father and mother or of his grandfather and grandmother was a valid marriage or that his own marriage was a valid marriage.

(2) Any person claiming that he or his parent or any remoter ancestor became or has become a legitimated person may apply by petition to the High Court, or may apply to a county court in the manner prescribed by county court rules, for a decree declaring that he or his parent or remoter ancestor, as the case may be, became or has become a legitimated person.

In this subsection " legitimated person " means a person legitimated by the Legitimacy Act 1926, and includes a person recognised under section 8 of that Act as legitimated.

[2a] Words substituted by Children Act 1975 (c. 72), Sched. 3, para. 78.

(3) Where an application under subsection (2) above is made to a county court, the county court, if it considers that the case is one which owing to the value of the property involved or otherwise ought to be dealt with by the High Court, may, and if so ordered by the High Court shall, transfer the matter to the High Court; and on such a transfer the proceeding shall be continued in the High Court as if it had been originally commenced by petition to the court.

(4) Any person who is domiciled in England and Wales or in Northern Ireland or claims any real or personal estate situate in England and Wales may apply to the High Court for a decree declaring his right to be deemed a British subject.

(5) Applications to the High Court under the preceding provisions of this section may be included in the same petition, and on any application under the preceding provisions of this section the High Court or, as the case may be, the county court shall make such decree as it thinks just, and the decree shall be binding on Her Majesty and all other persons whatsoever, so however that the decree shall not prejudice any person—

(*a*) if it is subsequently proved to have been obtained by fraud or collusion; or

(*b*) unless that person has been given notice of the application in the manner prescribed by rules of court or made a party to the proceedings or claims through a person so given notice or made a party.

(6) A copy of every application under this section and of any affidavit accompanying it shall be delivered to the Attorney-General at least one month before the application is made, and the Attorney-General shall be a respondent on the hearing of the application and on any subsequent proceedings relating thereto.

(7) Where any application is made under this section, such persons as the court hearing the application thinks fit shall, subject to rules of court, be given notice of the application in the manner prescribed by rules of court, and any such persons may be permitted to become parties to the proceedings and to oppose the application.

(8) No proceedings under this section shall affect any final judgment or decree already pronounced or made by any court of competent jurisdiction.

(9) The court hearing an application under this section may direct that the whole or any part of the proceedings shall be heard in camera, and an application for a direction under this subsection shall be heard in camera unless the court otherwise directs.

Additional jurisdiction in proceedings by a wife

46. [*Repealed by Domicile and Matrimonial Proceedings Act, 1973, (c. 45), s. 17 (2), Sched. 6.*]

Matrimonial relief and declarations of validity in respect of polygamous marriages

47.—(1) A court in England and Wales shall not be precluded from granting matrimonial relief or making a declaration concerning the validity of a marriage by reason only that the marriage in question was entered into under a law which permits polygamy.

(2) In this section " matrimonial relief " means—

(*a*) any decree under Part 1 of this Act;

(*b*) a financial provision order under section 27 above;

(*c*) an order under section 35 above altering a maintenance agreement;

(*d*) an order under any provision of this Act which confers a power exercisable in connection with, or in connection with

proceedings for, any such decree or order as is mentioned in
paragraphs (*a*) to (*c*) above;

(*e*) an order under the Matrimonial Proceedings (Magistrates'
Courts) Act 1960.

(3) In this section " a declaration concerning the validity of a marriage " means—

(*a*) a declaration that a marriage is valid or invalid; and

(*b*) any other declaration involving a determination as to the validity
of a marriage;

being a declaration in a decree granted under section 45 above or a
declaration made in the exercise by the High Court of its jurisdiction to
grant declaratory relief in any proceedings notwithstanding that a
declaration is the only substantive relief sought in those proceedings.

(4) This section has effect whether or not either party to the marriage
in question has for the time being any spouse additional to the other
party; and provision may be made by rules of court—

(*a*) for requiring notice of proceedings brought by virtue of this section to be served on any such other spouse; and

(*b*) for conferring on any such other spouse the right to be heard in
any such proceedings,

in such cases as may be prescribed by the rules.

Evidence

48.—(1) The evidence of a husband or wife shall be admissible in
any proceedings to prove that marital intercourse did or did not take
place between them during any period.

(2) In any proceedings for nullity of marriage, evidence on the question of sexual capacity shall be heard in camera unless in any case the
judge is satisfied that in the interests of justice any such evidence ought
to be heard in open court.

Parties to proceedings under this Act

49.—(1) Where in a petition for divorce or judicial separation, or
in any other pleading praying for either form of relief, one party to a
marriage alleges that the other has committed adultery, he or she shall
make the person alleged to have committed adultery with the other party
to the marriage a party to the proceedings unless excused by the court
on special grounds from doing so.

(2) Rules of court may, either generally or in such cases as may be
prescribed by the rules, exclude the application of subsection (1) above
where the person alleged to have committed adultery with the other
party to the marriage is not named in the petition or other pleading.

(3) Where in pursuance of subsection (1) above a person is made a
party to proceedings for divorce or judicial separation, the court may,
if after the close of the evidence on the part of the person making the
allegation of adultery it is of opinion that there is not sufficient evidence
against the person so made a party, dismiss him or her from the suit.

(4) Rules of court may make provision, in cases not falling within
subsection (1) above, with respect to the joinder as parties to proceedings
under this Act of persons involved in allegations of adultery or other
improper conduct made in those proceedings, and with respect to the
dismissal from such proceedings of any parties so joined; and rules of
court made by virtue of this subsection may make different provision for
different cases.

(5) In every case in which adultery with any party to a suit is
alleged against any person not made a party to the suit or in which the
court considers, in the interest of any person not already a party to the
suit, that that person should be made a party to the suit, the court may

if it thinks fit allow that person to intervene upon such terms, if any, as the court thinks just.

Matrimonial causes rules

50.[2b]—(1) [2c] The authority having power to make rules of court for the purposes of—

(a) this Act, the Matrimonial Causes Act 1967 (which confers jurisdiction on county courts in certain matrimonial proceedings), section 45 of the Courts Act 1971 (transfer of matrimonial proceedings between High Court and county court, etc.) [. . .][3];

(b) proceedings in the High Court or a divorce county court for an order under section 7 of the Matrimonial Homes Act 1967 (transfer of protected or statutory tenancy under Rent Act 1968 on dissolution or annulment of marriage);

(c) certain other proceedings in the High Court, that is to say—

    (i) proceedings in the High Court under section 17 of the Married Women's Property Act 1882, not being proceedings in the divorce registry treated by virtue of rules made under this section for the purposes of section 45 of the Courts Act 1971 as pending in a county court;

    (ii) proceedings in the High Court under section 1 of the Matrimonial Homes Act 1967 (rights of occupation of matrimonial home for spouse not otherwise entitled);

    (iii) proceedings in which the only substantive relief sought is a declaration with respect to a person's matrimonial status; or

(d) any enactment passed after this Act which relates to any matter dealt with in this Act, the Matrimonial Causes Act 1967 [. . .][3];

shall, subject to the exceptions listed in subsection (2) below, be the Lord Chancellor together with any four or more of the following persons, namely, the President of the Family Division, one puisne judge attached to that division, one registrar of the divorce registry, two Circuit judges, one registrar appointed under the County Courts Act 1959, two practising barristers being members of the General Council of the Bar and two practising solicitors of whom one shall be a member of the Council of the Law Society and the other a member of the Law Society and also of a local law society.

All the members of the authority, other than the Lord Chancellor himself and the President of the Family Division, shall be appointed by the Lord Chancellor for such time as he may think fit.

(2) The following shall be excepted from the purposes mentioned in subsection (1) above—

(a) proceedings in a county court in the exercise of a jurisdiction exercisable by any county court whether or not it is a divorce county court, that is to say, proceedings in a county court under section 32, 33, 36, 38 or 45 above [. . .][3];

(b) section 47 above, in so far as it relates to proceedings in a county court under section 45 above or to proceedings for an order under the Matrimonial Proceedings (Magistrates' Courts) Act 1960;

(c) any enactment passed after this Act in so far as it relates to proceedings in a county court in the exercise of any such jurisdiction as is mentioned in paragraph (a) above or to any aspect of section 47 above which is excepted by paragraph (b) above.

[2b] Prospectively amended by Children Act 1975 (c. 72), Sched. 3, para. 79, *post.*

[2c] Amended, and sub-para. (c) added, by 1973 (c. 45), s. 6 (2), *post.*

[3] Words deleted by Inheritance (Provision for Family and Dependants) Act 1975 (c. 63), Sched.

(3) Rules of court made under this section may apply, with or without modification, any rules of court made under the Supreme Court of Judicature (Consolidation) Act 1925, the County Courts Act 1959 or any other enactment and—

(*a*) may modify or exclude the application of any such rules or of any provision of the County Courts Act 1959;

(*b*) may provide for the enforcement in the High Court of orders made in a divorce county court;

and, without prejudice to the generality of the preceding provisions, may make with respect to proceedings in a divorce county court any provision regarding the Official Solicitor or any solicitor of the Supreme Court which could be made by rules of court with respect to proceedings in the High Court.

(4) The power to make rules of court by virtue of subsection (1) above shall be exercisable by statutory instrument, which shall be subject to annulment in pursuance of a resolution of either House of Parliament.

(5) In this section " divorce county court " means a county court designated under section 1 of the Matrimonial Causes Act 1967 and " divorce registry " means the principal registry of the Family Division of the High Court.

Fees in matrimonial proceedings

51. The fees to be taken in any proceedings to which rules under section 50 above apply shall be such as the Lord Chancellor with the concurrence of the Treasury may from time to time by order made by statutory instrument prescribe.

Interpretation

52.—(1) In this Act—

[Definition repealed by Children Act 1975 (c. 72), Sched. 4.]

" child ", in relation to one or both of the parties to a marriage, includes an illegitimate [. . .] [4] child of that party or, as the case may be, of both parties;

" child of the family ", in relation to the parties to a marriage, means—

(*a*) a child of both of those parties; and

(*b*) any other child, not being a child who has been boarded-out with those parties by a local authority or voluntary organisation, who has been treated by both of those parties as a child of their family;

" the court " (except where the context otherwise requires) means the High Court or, where a county court has jurisdiction by virtue of the Matrimonial Causes Act 1967, a county court;

" custody ", in relation to a child, includes access to the child;

" education " includes training.

(2) In this Act—

(*a*) references to financial provision orders, periodical payments and secured periodical payments orders and orders for the payment of a lump sum, and references to property adjustment orders, shall be construed in accordance with section 21 above; and

(*b*) references to orders for maintenance pending suit and to interim orders for maintenance shall be construed respectively in accordance with section 22 and section 27 (5) above.

(3) For the avoidance of doubt it is hereby declared that references

4 Words repealed by Children Act 1975 (c. 72), Sched. 4.

in this Act to remarriage include references to a marriage which is by law void or voidable.

(4) Except where the contrary intention is indicated, references in this Act to any enactment include references to that enactment as amended, extended or applied by or under any subsequent enactment, including this Act.

Transitional provisions and savings

53. Schedule 1 to this Act shall have effect for the purpose of—
- (a) the transition to the provisions of this Act from the law in force before the commencement of this Act;
- (b) the preservation for limited purposes of certain provisions superseded by provisions of this Act or by enactments repealed and replaced by this Act; and
- (c) the assimilation in certain respects to orders under this Act of orders made, or deemed to have been made, under the Matrimonial Causes Act 1965.

Consequential amendments and repeals

54.—(1) Subject to the provisions of Schedule 1 to this Act—
- (a) the enactments specified in Schedule 2 to this Act shall have effect subject to the amendments specified in that Schedule, being amendments consequential on the provisions of this Act or on enactments repealed by this Act; and
- (b) the enactments specified in Schedule 3 to this Act are hereby repealed to the extent specified in the third column of that Schedule.

(2) The amendment of any enactment by Schedule 2 to this Act shall not be taken as prejudicing the operation of section 38 of the Interpretation Act 1889 (which relates to the effect of repeals).

Citation, commencement and extent

55.—(1) This Act may be cited as the Matrimonial Causes Act 1973.

(2) This Act shall come into force on such day as the Lord Chancellor may appoint by order made by statutory instrument.[5]

(3) Subject to the provisions of paragraphs 3 (2) and 7 (3) of Schedule 2 below, this Act does not extend to Scotland or Northern Ireland.

SCHEDULES

SCHEDULE 1

TRANSITIONAL PROVISIONS AND SAVINGS

PART I

MISCELLANEOUS AND GENERAL

General transitional provisions and savings

1. Without prejudice to the provisions of section 38 of the Interpretation Act 1889 (which relates to the effect of repeals)—
- (a) nothing in any repeal made by this Act shall affect any order or rule made, direction given or thing done, or deemed to have been made, given or done, under any enactment repealed by this Act, and every such order, rule, direction or thing shall, if in force at the commencement of this Act, continue in force and, so far as it could have been made, given or done

[5] The Act was brought into force on January 1, 1974, by 1973 S.I. No. 1972.

under this Act, be deemed to have been made, given or done under the corresponding provisions of this Act; and

(*b*) any reference in any document (including an enactment) to any enactment repealed by this Act, whether a specific reference or a reference to provisions of a description which includes, or apart from any repeal made by this Act includes, the enactment so repealed, shall be construed as a reference to the corresponding enactment in this Act.

2. Without prejudice to paragraph 1 above, but subject to paragraph 3 below, any application made or proceeding begun, or deemed to have been made or begun, under any enactment repealed by this Act, being an application or proceeding which is pending at the commencement of this Act, shall be deemed to have been made or begun under the corresponding provision of this Act.

3. Nothing in Part I of this Act shall apply in relation to any petition for divorce or judicial separation presented before 1st January 1971 and notwithstanding any repeal or amendment made by this Act the Matrimonial Causes Act 1965 (hereafter in this Schedule referred to as the Act of 1965) and any rules of court made for the purposes of that Act shall continue to have effect in relation to proceedings on any such petition which are pending at the commencement of this Act as they had effect immediately before the commencement of this Act.

4. Notwithstanding any repeal or amendment made by this Act, the Act of 1965 and any rules of court made for the purposes of that Act shall continue to have effect in relation to—

(*a*) any proceedings on a petition for damages for adultery or for restitution of conjugal rights presented before 1st January 1971 which are pending at the commencement of this Act, and

(*b*) any proceedings for relief under section 21 or 34 (1) (*c*) of the Act of 1965 brought in connection with proceedings on a petition for restitution of conjugal rights so presented, being proceedings for relief which are themselves pending at the commencement of this Act,

as they had effect immediately before the commencement of this Act; and nothing in Schedule 2 below shall affect the operation of any other enactment in relation to any such proceedings.

5. Nothing in any repeal made by this Act shall affect any order made, or deemed to have been made, under the Act of 1965 which was continued in force by paragraph 1 of Schedule 1 to the Matrimonial Proceedings and Property Act 1970 notwithstanding the repeal by the last-mentioned Act of the provision of the Act of 1965 under which the order had effect, and every such order shall, if in force at the commencement of this Act, continue in force subject to the provisions of this Act.

6. Nothing in sections 11 to 14 or 16 of this Act affects any law or custom relating to the marriage of members of the Royal Family.

7. Nothing in section 50 (1) (*a*) or (*c*) above affects—

(*a*) any rules of court made under the Supreme Court of Judicature (Consolidation) Act 1925 for the purposes of proceedings under section 39 of the Act of 1965 and having effect by virtue of paragraph 1 (*b*) above in relation to proceedings under section 45 above;

(*b*) any rules of court so made for the purposes of proceedings under section 17 of the Married Women's Property Act 1882 or under section 1 of the Matrimonial Homes Act 1967; or

(*c*) any rules of court so made for the purposes of the exercise by the High Court of its jurisdiction to grant declaratory relief in proceedings in which the only substantive relief sought is a declaration with respect to a person's matrimonial status;

but rules of court made under section 50 may revoke any rules of court made under the said Act of 1925 in so far as they apply for any such purposes.

Transitional provisions derived from the Act of 1965

8. Any agreement between the petitioner and the respondent to live separate and apart, whether or not made in writing, shall be disregarded for the purposes of section 1 (2) (*c*) above (including that paragraph as it applies, by virtue of section 17 above, to proceedings for judicial separation) if the agreement was entered into before 1st January 1938 and either—

(*a*) at the time when the agreement was made the respondent had deserted the petitioner without cause; or

(b) the court is satisfied that the circumstances in which the agreement was made and the parties proceeded to live separate and apart were such as, but for the agreement, to amount to desertion of the petitioner by the respondent.

9. Where the party chargeable under a maintenance agreement within the meaning of section 34 above died before 17th August 1957, then—

(a) subsection (1) of that section shall not apply to the agreement unless there remained undistributed on that date assets of that party's estate (apart from any property in which he had only a life interest) representing not less than four-fifths of the value of that estate for probate after providing for the discharge of the funeral, testamentary and administrative expenses, debts and liabilities payable thereout (other than any liability arising by virtue of that subsection); and

(b) nothing in that subsection shall render liable to recovery, or impose any liability upon the personal representatives of that party in respect of, any part of that party's estate which had been distributed before that date.

10. No right or liability shall attach by virtue of section 34 (1) above in respect of any sum payable under a maintenance agreement within the meaning of that section in respect of a period before 17th August 1957.

Part II

PRESERVATION FOR LIMITED PURPOSES OF CERTAIN PROVISIONS OF PREVIOUS ENACTMENTS

Nullity

11.—(1) Subject to sub-paragraphs (2) and (3) below, a marriage celebrated before 1st August 1971 shall (without prejudice to any other grounds on which a marriage celebrated before that date is by law void or voidable) be voidable on the ground—

(a) that the marriage has not been consummated owing to the wilful refusal of the respondent to consummate it; or

(b) that at the time of the marriage either party to the marriage—

(i) was of unsound mind, or

(ii) was suffering from mental disorder within the meaning of the Mental Health Act 1959 of such a kind or to such an extent as to be unfitted for marriage and the procreation of children, or

(iii) was subject to recurrent attacks of insanity or epilepsy; or

(c) that the respondent was at the time of the marriage suffering from venereal disease in a communicable form; or

(d) that the respondent was at the time of the marriage pregnant by some person other than the petitioner.

(2) In relation to a marriage celebrated before 1st November 1960, for heads (ii) and (iii) of sub-paragraph (1) (b) above there shall be substituted the following heads—

" (ii) was a mental defective within the meaning of the Mental Deficiency Acts 1913 to 1938, or

(iii) was subject to recurrent fits of insanity or epilepsy; or ".

(3) The court shall not grant a decree of nullity in a case falling within sub-paragraph (1) (b), (c) or (d) above unless it is satisfied that—

(a) the petitioner was at the time of the marriage ignorant of the facts alleged; and

(b) proceedings were instituted within a year from the date of the marriage; and

(c) marital intercourse with the consent of the petitioner has not taken place since the petitioner discovered the existence of the grounds for a decree;

and where the proceedings with respect to the marriage are instituted after 31st July 1971 the application of section 13 (1) above in relation to the marriage shall be without prejudice to the preceding provisions of this sub-paragraph.

(4) Nothing in this paragraph shall be construed as validating a marriage which is by law void but with respect to which a decree of nullity has not been granted.

12. Where a decree of nullity was granted on or before 31st July 1971 in respect of a voidable marriage, any child who would have been the legitimate child of the

parties to the marriage if at the date of the decree it had been dissolved instead of being annulled shall be deemed to be their legitimate child.

Succession on intestacy in case of judicial separation

13. Section 18 (2) above shall not apply in a case where the death occurred before 1st August 1970, but section 20 (3) of the Act of 1965 (which provides that certain property of a wife judicially separated from her husband shall devolve, on her death intestate, as if her husband had then been dead) shall continue to apply in any such case.

Validation of certain void or voidable decrees

14. Any decree of divorce, nullity of marriage or judicial separation which, apart from this paragraph, would be void or voidable on the ground only that the provisions of section 33 of the Act of 1965 (restriction on the making of decrees of dissolution or separation where children are affected) or of section 2 of the Matrimonial Proceedings (Children) Act 1958 (corresponding provision replaced by section 33) had not been complied with when the decree was made absolute or granted, as the case may be, shall be deemed always to have been valid unless—

   (*a*) the court declared the decree to be void before 1st January 1971, or

   (*b*) in proceedings for the annulment of the decree pending at that date the court has before the commencement of this Act declared or after that commencement declares the decree to be void.

Part III

Assimilation in certain respects to Orders under this Act of Orders made, etc., under the Act of 1965, etc.

Cesser on remarriage of orders made, etc., under the Act of 1965 and recovery of sums mistakenly paid thereafter

15.—(1) An order made, or deemed to have been made, under section 16 (1) (*a*) or (*b*) of the Act of 1965 (including either of those paragraphs as applied by section 16 (3) or by section 19) shall, notwithstanding anything in the order, cease to have effect on the remarriage after the commencement of this Act of the person in whose favour the order was made, except in relation to any arrears due under it on the date of the remarriage.

(2) An order for the payment of alimony made, or deemed to have been made, under section 20 of the Act of 1965, and an order made, or deemed to have been made, under section 21 or 22 of that Act shall, if the marriage of the parties to the proceedings in which the order was made was or is subsequently dissolved or annulled but the order continues in force, cease to have effect on the remarriage after the commencement of this Act of the party in whose favour the order was made, except in relation to any arrears due under it on the date of the remarriage.

16. Section 38 above shall apply in relation to an order made or deemed to have been made under section 16 (1) (including that subsection as applied by section 16 (3) and by section 19), 20 (1), 21 or 22 of the Act of 1965 as it applies in relation to a periodical payments or secured periodical payments order in favour of a party to a marriage.

Variation, etc., of certain orders made, etc., under the Act of 1965

17.—(1) Subject to the provisions of this paragraph, section 31 above shall apply, as it applies to the orders mentioned in subsection (2) thereof, to an order (other than an order for the payment of a lump sum) made or deemed to have been made under any of the following provisions of the Act of 1965, that is to say—

   (*a*) section 15 (except in its application to proceedings for restitution of conjugal rights);

   (*b*) section 16 (1) (including that subsection as applied by section 16 (3) and by section 19);

476

(*c*) section 20 (1) and section 17 (2) as applied by section 20 (2);

(*d*) section 22;

(*e*) section 34 (1) (*a*) or (*b*), in so far as it relates to the maintenance of a child, and section 34 (3).

(2) Subject to the provisions of this paragraph, the court hearing an application for the variation of an order made or deemed to have been made under any of the provisions of the Act of 1965 mentioned in sub-paragraph (1) above shall have power to vary that order in any way in which it would have power to vary it had the order been made under the corresponding provision of Part II of this Act.

(3) Section 31, as it applies by virtue of sub-paragraph (1) above, shall have effect as if for subsections (4), (5) and (6) there were substituted the following subsections—

" (4) The court shall not exercise the powers conferred by this section in relation to an order made or deemed to have been made under section 17 (2) of the Act of 1965, as applied by section 20 (2) of that Act, in connection with the grant of a decree of judicial separation except on an application made in proceedings—

(*a*) for the rescission of that decree, or

(*b*) for the dissolution of the marriage in question.

(5) No order for the payment of a lump sum and no property adjustment order shall be made on an application for the variation of any order made or deemed to have been made under section 16 (1) (including that subsection as applied by section 16 (3) or by section 19), 20 (1), 22, 34 (1) (*a*) or (*b*) or 34 (3) of the Act of 1965.

(6) In the case of an order made or deemed to have been made under section 16 (1) (including that subsection as applied by section 16 (3) or by section 19), 22 or 34 (3) of the Act of 1965 and requiring a party to a marriage to secure an annual sum or periodical payments to any other person, an application under this section relating to that order may be made after the death of the person liable to make payments under the order by the person entitled to the payments or by the personal representatives of the deceased person, but no such application shall, except with the permission of the court, be made after the end of the period of six months from the date on which representation in regard to the estate of that person is first taken out";

and in that section, as it so applies, the reference in subsection (8) to a secured periodical payments order shall be construed as a reference to any such order as is mentioned in subsection (6).

(4) In relation to an order made before 16th December 1949 on or after granting a decree of divorce or nullity of marriage and deemed, by virtue of paragraph 1 of Schedule 1 to the Act of 1965, to have been made under section 16 (1) (*a*) of that Act (secured provision), the powers conferred by this paragraph shall not be exercised unless the court is satisfied that the case is one of exceptional hardship which cannot be met by discharge, variation or suspension of any other order made by reference to that decree, being an order made, or deemed by virtue of that paragraph to have been made, under section 16 (1) (*b*) of that Act (unsecured periodical payments).

18.—(1) Subsections (1) and (3) of section 31 above shall apply to an order made or deemed to have been made under section 15 of the Act of 1965 in its application to proceedings for restitution of conjugal rights, or under section 21 or 34 (1) (*c*) of that Act, as they apply to the orders mentioned in subsection (2) of section 31.

(2) In exercising the powers conferred by virtue of this paragraph the court shall have regard to all the circumstances of the case, including any change in any of the matters to which the court was required to have regard when making the order to which the application relates.

19. Section 42 (7) above shall apply in relation to an order for the custody or education of a child made or deemed to have been made under section 34 of the Act of 1965, and in relation to an order for the custody of a child made or deemed to have been made under section 35 of that Act, as it applies in relation to an order made under section 42.

*Orders made under the Act of 1965 to count as orders under
this Act for certain purposes*

20. The power of the court under section 23 (1) or (2) (*a*) or 42 (1) (*a*) above
to make from time to time a financial provision order or, as the case may be, an order
for custody or education in relation to a child of the family shall be exercisable notwithstanding the making of a previous order or orders in relation to the child under
section 34 (1) (*a*) of the Act of 1965; and where the court has made an order in
relation to a child under section 34 (1) (*b*) of that Act sections 23 (4) and 42 (6)
above shall apply respectively in relation to that child as if the order were an order
made under section 23 (2) (*b*) or section 42 (1) (*b*), as the case may be.

21. Where the court has made an order under section 22 of the Act of 1965 the
court shall have the like power to make orders under section 42 above with respect
to the custody of any child of the family as it has where it makes an order under
section 27 above.

*Application of provisions of this Act with respect to enforcement of arrears and
recovery of excessive payments to certain orders made, etc., under the Act of 1965*

22. Section 32 above shall apply in relation to the enforcement, by proceedings
begun after 1st January 1971 (whether before or after the commencement of this
Act), of the payment of arrears due under an order made, or deemed to have been
made, under any of the following provisions of the Act of 1965, that is to say—

(*a*) section 15;
(*b*) section 16 (1) (including that subsection as applied by section 16 (3) and by
section 19);
(*c*) section 20 (1);
(*d*) section 21;
(*e*) section 22;
(*f*) section 34 (1), in so far as it relates to the maintenance of a child, and section
34 (3);

as it applies in relation to the enforcement of the payment of arrears due under any
such order as is mentioned in that section.

23. Section 33 above shall apply to an order (other than an order for the payment of a lump sum) made or deemed to have been made under any of the provisions of the Act of 1965 mentioned in paragraph 22 above as it applies to the
orders mentioned in section 33 (2).

*Avoidance under this Act of transactions intended to defeat claims for relief
and relief granted under the Act of 1965*

24.—(1) Section 37 above shall apply in relation to proceedings for relief under
section 21 or 34 (1) (*c*) of the Act of 1965 continuing by virtue of paragraph 4 (*b*)
above as it applies in relation to proceedings for relief under any of the provisions
of this Act specified in section 37 (1).

(2) Without prejudice to sub-paragraph (1) above, section 37 shall also apply
where an order has been obtained under any of the following provisions of the Act
of 1965, that is to say—

(*a*) section 16 (1) (including that subsection as applied by section 16 (3) and by
section 19);
(*b*) section 17 (2) (including that subsection as applied by section 20 (2));
(*c*) section 20 (1);
(*d*) section 21;
(*e*) section 22;
(*f*) section 24;
(*g*) section 31;
(*h*) section 34 (1), in so far as it relates to the maintenance of a child, and
section 34 (3);
(*i*) section 35;

as it applies where an order has been obtained under any of the provisions of this
Act specified in section 37 (1).

Care and supervision of children

25.—(1) Sections 43 and 44 above shall apply where the court has jurisdiction by virtue of paragraph 4 (b) above to make an order for the custody of a child under section 34 (1) (c) of the Act of 1965 as they apply where the court has jurisdiction to make an order for custody under Part III of this Act, but as if the reference in section 43 (2) to a financial provision order in favour of the child were a reference to an order for payments for the maintenance and education of the child.

(2) Without prejudice to the effect of paragraph 1 (a) of this Schedule in relation to an order made under section 36 or 37 of the Act of 1965 which could have been made under section 43 or, as the case may be, section 44 above, any order made under section 36 or 37 of that Act by virtue of the jurisdiction of the court to make an order for the custody of a child under section 34 (1) (c) of that Act shall be deemed to have been made under section 43 or 44 above, as the case may require.

26. Section 44 (4) above shall apply in relation to the jurisdiction possessed by a court to vary an order made or deemed to have been made with respect to a child's custody, maintenance or education under Part III of the Act of 1965 as it applies in relation to the jurisdiction possessed by a court to vary any financial provision order in a child's favour and any order made with respect to a child's custody or education under Part III of this Act.

SCHEDULE 2

CONSEQUENTIAL AMENDMENTS

1. In section 225 of the Supreme Court of Judicature (Consolidation) Act 1925 (interpretation), in the definition of "matrimonial cause", for the words from "jactitation" to "rights" there shall be substituted the words "or jactitation of marriage".

2. In section 2 (1) of the Limitation (Enemies and War Prisoners) Act 1945, in the definition of "statute of limitation" for the words "subsection (1) of section seven of the Matrimonial Causes Act 1937" there shall be substituted the words "section 13 (2) of the Matrimonial Causes Act 1973 and paragraph 11 (3) of Schedule 1 to that Act".

3.—(1) In section 16 of the Maintenance Orders Act 1950 (orders enforceable under Part II of that Act)—

(a) in subsection (2) (a), for sub-paragraph (i) there shall be substituted the following sub-paragraph:—

"(i) sections 15 to 17, 19 to 22, 30, 34 and 35 of the Matrimonial Causes Act 1965 and sections 22, 23 (1), (2) and (4) and 27 of the Matrimonial Causes Act 1973"; and

(b) in subsection (2) (c), for sub-paragraph (v) there shall be substituted the following sub-paragraph:—

"(v) any enactment of the Parliament of Northern Ireland containing provisions corresponding with section 22 (1), 34 or 35 of the Matrimonial Causes Act 1965, with section 22, 23 (1), (2) or (4) or 27 of the Matrimonial Causes Act 1973, or with section 12 (2) of the Guardianship of Minors Act 1971".

(2) Sub-paragraph (1) above extends to Scotland and Northern Ireland, and the references to section 16 (2) (c) of the Maintenance Orders Act 1950 in paragraph 8 of Schedule 8 to the Administration of Justice Act 1970 and paragraph 9 of Schedule 1 to the Attachment of Earnings Act 1971 shall be construed as references to section 16 (2) (c) as amended by sub-paragraph (1) (b) above.

4. In section 109 (2) of the County Courts Act 1959 (proceedings in which appeals on questions of fact are to lie) the following paragraph shall be inserted after paragraph (f) (in place of the paragraph inserted by section 34 (2) of the Matrimonial Proceedings and Property Act 1970):—

"(g) any proceedings on an application under section 13A of the Matrimonial Proceedings (Magistrates' Courts) Act 1960 or under section 33, 36 or 38 of the Matrimonial Causes Act 1973".

5.—(1) [Repealed by Inheritance (Provision for Family and Dependants) Act 1975 (c. 63), Sched.]

(2) In section 42 of [the Matrimonial Causes Act 1965] [5] (provisions as to condonation), at the beginning of subsections (1) and (3) there shall be inserted the words " For the purposes of the Matrimonial Proceedings (Magistrates' Courts) Act 1960 ".

6.—(1) In section 2 of the Matrimonial Causes Act 1967 (jurisdiction of divorce county court with respect to ancillary relief and the protection of children)—

(*a*) in subsection (1), for the words " Part II or Part III of the Matrimonial Causes Act 1965 " there shall be substituted the words " Part II or Part III of the Matrimonial Causes Act 1973 ", and for the words " section 22 or section 24 of that Act " in the subsection as originally enacted there shall be substituted the words " section 27 or 35 of that Act " (in place of the words substituted for the words originally enacted by paragraph 2 (1) (*a*) of Schedule 2 to the Matrimonial Proceedings and Property Act 1970);

(*b*) for subsection (3) as originally enacted there shall be substituted the following subsection (in place of that substituted by paragraph 2 (1) (*b*) of Schedule 2 to the Matrimonial Proceedings and Property Act 1970) :—

" (3) A divorce county court shall not by virtue of this section have jurisdiction to exercise any power under section 32, 33, 36 or 38 of the Matrimonial Causes Act 1973; but nothing in this section shall prejudice the exercise by a county court of any jurisdiction conferred on county courts by any of those sections "; and

(*c*) in subsection (4) as originally enacted, for the words from " section 24 " to the end of the subsection there shall be substituted the words " section 35 of the Matrimonial Causes Act 1973 " (in place of the words substituted for the words originally enacted by paragraph 2 (1) (*c*) of Schedule 2 to the Matrimonial Proceedings and Property Act 1970).

(2) In section 3 of that Act (consideration of agreements or arrangements by divorce county courts) for the words " section 5 (2) of the Matrimonial Causes Act 1965 " there shall be substituted the words " section 7 of the Matrimonial Causes Act 1973 ".

(3) In section 10 of that Act (interpretation), in the definition of " matrimonial cause " in subsection (1), for the words from " section 2 of the Matrimonial Causes Act 1965 " to " that Act " there shall be substituted the words " section 3 of the Matrimonial Causes Act 1973 ".

7.—(1) In subsection (1) of section 2 of the Domestic and Appellate Proceedings (Restriction of Publicity) Act 1968 (restriction of publicity for certain proceedings) for the words in paragraph (*a*) " section 39 of the Matrimonial Causes Act 1965 " there shall be substituted the words " section 45 of the Matrimonial Causes Act 1973 ", the following paragraph shall be substituted for the paragraph (*c*) inserted in the subsection by paragraph 3 of Schedule 2 to the Matrimonial Proceedings and Property Act 1970 :—

" (*c*) proceedings under section 27 of the Matrimonial Causes Act 1973 (which relates to proceedings by a wife against her husband, or by a husband against his wife, for financial provision) and any proceedings for the discharge or variation of an order made under that section or for the temporary suspension of any provision of any such order or the revival of the operation of any provision so suspended ";

subsection (2) of that section shall be omitted, and the references in subsection (3) of that section to subsection (1) and to subsection (1) (*a*) thereof shall be construed as references to subsection (1) and to subsection (1) (*a*) as they respectively have effect by virtue of this sub-paragraph.

(2) In section 4 (3) of that Act, for the words " or 2 (2) of this Act " there shall be substituted the words " of this Act or to section 45 (9) of the Matrimonial Causes Act 1973 ".

(3) Sub-paragraph (2) above extends to Northern Ireland.

8. In section 7 of the Family Law Reform Act 1969 (committal of wards of court to care of local authority and supervision of wards of court)—

(*a*) in subsection (3), for the words " section 36 of the Matrimonial Causes Act

---

[5] Substituted by Inheritance (Provision for Family and Dependants) Act 1975 (c. 63), s. 26.

1965 " there shall be substituted the words " section 43 of the Matrimonial Causes Act 1973 ";

(*b*) in subsection (4), for the words from " subsections (2) " to " 1965 " there shall be substituted the words " section 44 (2) of the Matrimonial Causes Act 1973 ".

9. In section 63 (6) of the Children and Young Persons Act 1969 (local authority functions to be the subject of reports to Parliament by the Secretary of State), in paragraph (*g*), for the words " section 37 of the Matrimonial Causes Act 1965 " there shall be substituted the words " section 44 of the Matrimonial Causes Act 1973 ".

10.—(1) In Schedule 1 to the Administration of Justice Act 1970 (High Court business assigned to the Family Division)—

(*a*) for the words (in the first paragraph) " section 7 (1) of the Matrimonial Causes Act 1967 " there shall be substituted the words " section 50 (1) of the Matrimonial Causes Act 1973 ";

(*b*) the paragraphs relating respectively to proceedings for a declaration, to proceedings under section 17 of the Married Women's Property Act 1882, and to proceedings under section 1 of the Matrimonial Homes Act 1967 shall be omitted; and

(*c*) for the words (in the last paragraph) " section 24 of the Matrimonial Causes Act 1965 " there shall be substituted the words " section 35 of the Matrimonial Causes Act 1973 ".

(2) In Schedule 8 to that Act (as it applies to define maintenance orders both for the purposes of Part II of that Act and for the purposes of the Maintenance Orders Act 1958) the following paragraph shall be inserted after paragraph 2 :—

" 2A. An order for periodical or other payments made, or having effect as if made, under Part II of the Matrimonial Causes Act 1973 ".

11. In Schedule 1 to the Local Authority Social Services Act 1970 the entry relating to section 37 of the Matrimonial Causes Act 1965 shall be omitted, and the following entry shall be added at the end of the Schedule—

" Matrimonial Causes Act 1973 Section 44 | Supervision of child subject to court order in matrimonial proceedings ".

12. In section 45 of the Courts Act 1971 (transfer of matrimonial proceedings between High Court and county court, etc.)—

(*a*) in subsection (1), for paragraphs (*a*) and (*b*) there shall be substituted the following paragraphs :—

[...][6]

(*b*) Part II or Part III of the Matrimonial Causes Act 1973 ";

(*b*) in subsection (6), after the word " under " there shall be inserted the words " section 50 of the Matrimonial Causes Act 1973 for the purposes of "; and

(*c*) subsection (7) shall be omitted.

13. In Schedule 1 to the Attachment of Earnings Act 1971 (maintenance orders to which the Act applies) for paragraph 3 there shall be substituted the following paragraph—

" 3. An order for periodical or other payments made, or having effect as if made, under Part II of the Matrimonial Causes Act 1973 ".

[6] Words repealed by Inheritance (Provision for Family and Dependants) Act 1975 (c. 63), Sched.

Education (Work Experience) Act 1973

(1973 c. 23)

An Act to enable education authorities to arrange for children under school-leaving age to have work experience, as part of their education. [23rd May 1973]

Work experience in last year of compulsory schooling

1.—(1) Subject to subsection (2) below, the enactments relating to the prohibition or regulation of the employment of children shall not apply to the employment of a child in his last year of compulsory schooling where the employment is in pursuance of arrangements made or approved by the local education authority or, in Scotland, the education authority with a view to providing him with work experience as part of his education.

(2) Subsection (1) above shall not be taken to permit the employment of any person in any way contrary to—

(*a*) an enactment which in terms applies to persons of less than, or not over, a specified age expressed as a number of years; or

(*b*) section 1 (2) of the Employment of Women, Young Persons and Children Act 1920 or (when it comes into force) section 51 (1) of the Merchant Shipping Act 1970 (prohibition of employment of children in ships);

(3) No arrangements shall be made under subsection (1) above for a child to be employed in any way which would be contrary to an enactment prohibiting or regulating the employment of young persons if he were a young person (within the meaning of that enactment) and not a child; and where a child is employed in pursuance of arrangements so made, then so much of any enactment as regulates the employment of young persons (whether by excluding them from any description of work, or prescribing the conditions under which they may be permitted to do it, or otherwise howsoever) and would apply in relation to him if he were of an age to be treated as a young person for the purposes of that enactment shall apply in relation to him, in and in respect of the employment arranged for him, in all respects as if he were of an age to be so treated.

(4) In this Act—

" enactment " includes any byelaw, regulation or other provision having effect under an enactment;

other expressions which are also used in the Education Acts shall have the same meaning in this section as in those Acts; and

" the Education Acts " means in England and Wales the Education Acts 1944 to 1973 and, in Scotland, the Education (Scotland) Acts 1939 to 1971;

and for the purposes of subsection (1) above a child is in his last year of compulsory schooling at any time during the period of twelve months before he attains the upper limit of compulsory school age or, in Scotland, school age.

Citation and extent

2.—(1) This Act may be cited as the Education (Work Experience) Act 1973; and—

(*a*) in relation to England and Wales, this Act shall be included among the Acts which may be cited together as the Education Acts 1944 to 1973; and (*b*) in relation to Scotland the Education Acts and this Act may be cited together as the Education (Scotland) Acts 1939 to 1973.

(2) Nothing in this Act extends to Northern Ireland.

Employment of Children Act 1973

(1973 c. 24)

An Act to make further provision with respect to restrictions on the employment of persons under the upper limit of school age and to the means of imposing and enforcing such restrictions; and for connected purposes. [23rd May 1973]

Regulation of children's employment

1.—(1) In this Act, "the Act of 1933" means the Children and Young Persons Act 1933 and "the Act of 1937" means the Children and Young Persons (Scotland) Act 1937.

(2) In section 18 (2) of the Act of 1933 and section 28 (2) of the Act of 1937, the power of local authorities and, in Scotland, education authorities to make byelaws with respect to the employment of children shall be replaced by a power for the Secretary of State to make regulations for the purposes mentioned in those subsections respectively, any such regulations to be contained in a statutory instrument subject to annulment in pursuance of a resolution of either House of Parliament.

(3) In accordance with subsection (2) above and with a view—

(*a*) to making the consequential changes in Part II of the Act of 1933 and Part III of the Act of 1937 which follow from that subsection;

(*b*) to extending the powers exercisable under section 18 of the Act of 1933 and section 28 of the Act of 1937 for regulating the employment of children; and

(*c*) to increasing the penalties for contraventions of those Acts in relation to employment,

the Acts of 1933 and 1937 shall have effect with the amendments shown in Part I of Schedule 1 to this Act.

(4) As amended by subsection (3) above, section 18 of the Act of 1933 is as set out in Part II of Schedule 1 to this Act; and (as so amended) section 28 of the Act of 1937 is also as there set out, but with the differences specified in the note at the end of the Schedule.

(5) Section 19 of the Act of 1933 and section 29 of the Act of 1937 (power of local authorities to make byelaws with respect to the employment of persons under the age of eighteen) shall cease to have effect.

(6) If it appears to the Secretary of State in the case of a local Act that—

(*a*) it contains provisions relating to, or authorising the making of byelaws in respect of, the employment of children; and

(*b*) those provisions are no longer required having regard to cognate provisions of any public general Act for the time being in force (and in particular the provision made by subsection (2) above),

he may by order amend or repeal those provisions of the local Act; and an order under this subsection shall be made by statutory instrument subject to annulment in pursuance of a resolution of either House of Parliament.

Supervision by education authorities

2.—(1) The following powers shall be exercisable in England and Wales by a local education authority and, in Scotland, by an education authority in cases where the authority have reason to suppose that a child is, or is to become, employed (whether or not in the authority's area).

(2) The authority may by a notice served—

(*a*) on the child's parent or guardian or a person who has actual custody of the child; or

(*b*) on a person appearing to have the child in his employment or to be about to employ him,

require the person served to furnish to the authority, within such period as may be specified in the notice, particulars of how the child is, or is to be, employed and at what times and for what periods.

(3) If it appears to the authority that a child is for the time being, or is to become, employed in ways, or at times or for periods, which are not unlawful apart from this section but are unsuitable for the child, by reference to his age or state of health, or otherwise prejudicial to his education, they may, by a notice served on any such person as is mentioned in paragraph (*a*) or (*b*) of subsection (2) above as one on whom a notice may be served, either—

(*a*) prohibit the child's employment in any manner specified in the notice; or

(*b*) require his employment in any manner so specified to be subject to such conditions (specified in the notice and to be complied with by the person served with it) as the authority think fit to impose in the interests of the child.

(4) Any person who—

(*a*) being served with a notice under subsection (2) above—

(i) fails to furnish the particulars required by the notice within the period specified thereby, or

(ii) in purported compliance with the notice, makes any statement which he knows to be false in a material particular, or recklessly makes any statement which is false in a material particular; or

(*b*) being served with a notice under subsection (3) prohibiting a child's employment in any manner specified in the notice, employs or causes or permits the child to be employed in that manner contrary to the prohibition; or

(*c*) being served with such a notice requiring compliance by him with any conditions, wilfully fails to comply with them,

shall be guilty of an offence.

(5) A person guilty of an offence under subsection (4) above shall be liable on summary conviction—

(*a*) in the case of an offence under paragraph (*a*) of the subsection, to a fine of not more than £20 or, if he has previously been convicted of an offence under that paragraph, to a fine of not more than £50;

(*b*) in the case of an offence under paragraph (*b*) or (*c*) of the subsection, to a fine of not more than £50, or if he has previously been convicted of an offence under either paragraph, to a fine of not more than £100.

(6) For purposes of this section, a person who assists in a trade or occupation carried on for profit shall be deemed to be employed notwithstanding that he receives no reward for his labour.

3.—(1) This Act may be cited as the Employment of Children Act 1973.

(2) In this Act—

(*a*) " child " means a person who is not for the purposes of the Education Acts over compulsory school age, or in Scotland school age;

(*b*) " the Education Acts " means in England and Wales the Education Acts 1944 to 1971 and, in Scotland, the Education (Scotland) Acts 1939 to 1971;

and any reference in this Act to an enactment shall, except in so far as the context otherwise requires, be construed as a reference to that enactment as amended by or under any other enactment, including an enactment contained in this Act.

(3) The enactments specified in Schedule 2 to this Act are hereby repealed to the extent specified in column 3 of the Schedule.

(4) This Act shall come into force on such day as the Secretary of State may appoint by order made by statutory instrument and—

(*a*) different days may be so appointed for different purposes of any one or more provisions of this Act; and

(*b*) an order under this subsection bringing section 1 (2) or (3) of this Act into force may include such transitional provisions or savings as appear to the Secretary of State to be necessary or expedient for temporarily preserving the power to make, and the effect of, byelaws notwithstanding the coming into force of regulations.

(5) Nothing in this Act extends to Northern Ireland.

SCHEDULES

SCHEDULE 1

AMENDMENTS OF ACTS OF 1933 AND 1937: AMENDED TEXT OF 1933 s. 18 AND 1937 s. 28

PART I

AMENDMENTS OF THE TWO ACTS

The Children and Young Persons Act 1933 (*c.* 12)

1.—(1) In section 18 of the Act of 1933—

(*a*) in subsection (2) for " A local authority may make byelaws." substitute " The Secretary of State may make regulations "; and

(*b*) in subsections (1), (2) and (3) for " byelaw " and " byelaws " substitute respectively " regulation " and " regulations ".

(2) In section 18 (2) of the Act of 1933, after paragraph (*c*) insert—

" (*d*) prohibiting the employment of children otherwise than under and in accordance with a permit to be issued by the local education authority on application made in accordance with the regulations, and imposing on children and others requirements in connection with permits;

(*e*) requiring employers to furnish particulars with respect to children employed, or proposed to be employed, by them and to keep and produce records."

(3) At the end of section 18 of the Act of 1933, insert—

" (4) Regulations of the Secretary of State under this section shall be made by statutory instrument subject to annulment in pursuance of a resolution of either House of Parliament.".

2. In section 21 (1) of the Act of 1933—

(*a*) after " byelaw " insert " or regulation "; and

(b) for "twenty pounds" and "fifty pounds" substitute respectively "£50" and "£100".

3. In section 28 (1) of the Act of 1933 after "byelaw" insert "or regulation".
4. In section 30 of the Act of 1933, after "byelaws" insert "or regulations".

The Children and Young Persons (Scotland) Act 1937 (c. 37)

5.—(1) In section 28 of the Act of 1937—

(a) in subsection (2), for "An education authority may make byelaws" substitute "The Secretary of State may make regulations"; and

(b) in subsections (1), (2) and (3), for "byelaw" and "byelaws" substitute respectively "regulation" and "regulations".

(2) In section 28 (2) of the Act of 1937, after paragraph (c) insert—

" (d) prohibiting the employment of children otherwise than under and in accordance with a permit to be issued by the education authority on application made in accordance with the regulations, and imposing on children and others requirements in connection with permits;

(e) requiring employers to furnish particulars with respect to children employed, or proposed to be employed, by them and to keep and produce records."

(3) At the end of section 28 of the Act of 1937, insert—

" (4) Regulations of the Secretary of State under this section shall be made by statutory instrument subject to annulment in pursuance of a resolution of either House of Parliament.".

6. In section 31 (1) of the Act of 1937—

(a) after "byelaw" insert "or regulation"; and

(b) for "twenty pounds" and "fifty pounds" substitute respectively "£50" and "£100".

7. In section 36 (1) of the Act of 1937, after "byelaw" insert "or regulation".
8. In section 37 of the Act of 1937, after "byelaws", insert "or regulations".

PART II

1933 s. 18 AND 1937 s. 28 AS AMENDED

.—(1) Subject to the provisions of this section and of any regulations made thereunder no child shall be employed—

(a) so long as he is under the age of thirteen years; or

(b) before the close of school hours on any day on which he is required to attend school; or

(c) before seven o'clock in the morning or after seven o'clock in the evening on any day; or

(d) for more than two hours on any day on which he is required to attend school; or

(e) for more than two hours on any Sunday; or

(f) to lift, carry or move anything so heavy as to be likely to cause injury to him.

(2) The Secretary of State may make regulations with respect to the employment of children, and any such regulations may distinguish between children of different ages and sexes and between different localities, trades, occupations and circumstances, and may contain provisions—

(a) authorising—

(i) the employment of children under the age of thirteen years (notwithstanding anything in paragraph (a) of the last foregoing subsection) by their parents or guardians in light agricultural or horticultural work;

(ii) the employment of children (notwithstanding anything in paragraph (b) of the last foregoing subsection) for not more than one hour before the commencement of school hours on any day on which they are required to attend school;

(b) prohibiting absolutely the employment of children in any specified occupation;

(c) prescribing—

(i) the age below which children are not to be employed;

(ii) the number of hours in each day or in each week, for which, and the times of day at which, they may be employed;

(iii) the intervals to be allowed to them for meals and rest;

(iv) the holidays or half-holidays to be allowed to them;

(v) any other conditions to be observed in relation to their employment;

(d) prohibiting the employment of children otherwise than under and in accordance with a permit to be issued by the local education authority on application made in accordance with the regulations, and imposing on children and others requirements in connection with permits;

(e) requiring employers to furnish particulars with respect to children employed, or proposed to be employed, by them and to keep and produce records;

so, however, that no such regulations shall modify the restrictions contained in the last foregoing subsection save in so far as is expressly permitted by paragraph (a) of this subsection, and any restriction contained in any such regulations shall have effect in addition to the said restrictions.

(3) Nothing in this section, or in any regulation made under this section, shall prevent a child from taking part in a performance—

(a) under the authority of a licence granted under this Part of this Act; or

(b) in a case where by virtue of section 37 (3) of the Children and Young Persons Act 1963 no licence under that section is required for him to take part in the performance.

(4) Regulations of the Secretary of State under this section shall be made by statutory instrument subject to annulment in pursuance of a resolution of either House of Parliament.

NOTE: Section 28 of the Act of 1937 is to be read as above set out, except that, in subsection (1) (b) and (d) and in subsection (2) (a) (ii), for " required " there shall be substituted " under obligation "; and in subsection (2) (d), " local " should be omitted.

Section 3 (3)   SCHEDULE 2

REPEALS

Chapter	Short Title	Extent of Repeal
1933 c. 12.	The Children and Young Persons Act 1933.	Section 19.
1937 c. 37.	The Children and Young Persons (Scotland) Act 1937.	Section 29.
1944 c. 31.	The Education Act 1944.	Section 59.
1962 c. 47.	The Education (Scotland) Act 1962.	Section 137.
1969 c. 49.	The Education (Scotland) Act 1969.	Section 22.

Guardianship Act 1973

(1973 c. 29)

An Act to amend the law of England and Wales as to the guardianship of minors so as to make the rights of a mother equal with those of a father, and so as to make further provision with respect to applications and orders under section 9 of the Guardianship of Minors Act 1971 and with respect to the powers of a guardian under that Act in relation to the minor's property, and to amend section 4 (2) of the Matrimonial Proceedings (Magistrates' Courts) Act 1960; to make provision in relation to like matters for Scotland; and for purposes connected therewith.   [5th July 1973]

PART I
ENGLAND AND WALES

Equality of parental rights

1.—(1) In relation to the custody or upbringing of a minor, and in relation to the administration of any property belonging to or held in trust for a minor or the application of income of any such property, a mother shall have the same rights and authority as the law allows to a father, and the rights and authority of mother and father shall be equal and be exercisable by either without the other.

(2) An agreement for a man or woman to give up in whole or in part, in relation to any child of his or hers, the rights and authority referred to in subsection (1) above shall be unenforceable, except that an agreement made between husband and wife which is to operate only during their separation while married may, in relation to a child of theirs, provide for either of them to do so; but no such agreement between husband and wife shall be enforced by any court if the court is of opinion that it will not be for the benefit of the child to give effect to it.

(3) Where a minor's father and mother disagree on any question affecting his welfare, either of them may apply to the court for its direction, and (subject to subsection (4) below) the court may make such order regarding the matters in difference as it may think proper.

(4) Subsection (3) above shall not authorise the court to make any order regarding the custody of a minor or the right of access to him of his father or mother.

(5) An order under subsection (3) above may be varied or discharged by a subsequent order made on the application of either parent or, after the death of either parent, on the application of any guardian under the Guardianship of Minors Act 1971, or (before or after the death of either parent) on the application of any other person having the custody of the minor.

(6) Section 15 (1) to (3) and section 16 of the Guardianship of Minors Act 1971 (jurisdiction and procedure) shall apply for the purposes of subsections (3) to (5) above as if they were contained in section 9 of that Act, except that section 15 (3) shall not exclude any jurisdiction of a county court or a magistrates' court in proceedings against a person residing in Scotland or Northern Ireland for the revocation, revival or variation of any order under subsection (3) above.

(7) Nothing in the foregoing provisions of this section shall affect the operation of any enactment requiring the consent of both parents in a matter affecting a minor, or be taken as applying in relation to a minor who is illegitimate.

(8) In the Sexual Offences Act 1956 there shall be substituted for section 38 the provisions set out in Schedule 1 to this Act, and in the Mental Health Act 1959 in section 49 (4) (*d*) (under which for purposes of that Act a man deprived under the said section 38 of authority over a patient is not to be treated as the patient's nearest relative) for the word " man " there shall be substituted the word " person "; but, save as aforesaid, nothing in this section shall be taken to affect the provisions of the Mental Health Act 1959 as to the person who is " the nearest relative " for purposes of the Act.

Jurisdiction and orders on applications under s. 9 of Guardianship of Minors Act 1971

2.—(1) In sections 9, 13, 15 and 16 of the Guardianship of Minors Act 1971 there shall be made the amendments provided for by Part I of Schedule 2 to this Act (being amendments providing for mother and father to be treated alike in relation to applications under section 9 of that Act, and amendments relating to cases in which custody is given to an individual other than one of the parents); and accordingly section 9 and section 15 (3) to (6) shall have effect as they are set out in Part II of that Schedule with the amendments required by this subsection.

(2) Where an application made under section 9 of the Guardianship of Minors Act 1971 relates to the custody of a minor under the age of sixteen, then subject to sections 3 and 4 below—

(a) if by an order made on that application any person is given the custody of the minor, but it appears to the court that there are exceptional circumstances making it desirable that the minor should be under the supervision of an independent person, the court may order that the minor shall be under the supervision of a specified local authority or under the supervision of a probation officer;

(b) if it appears to the court that there are exceptional circumstances making it impracticable or undesirable for the minor to be entrusted to either of the parents or to any other individual, the court may commit the care of the minor to a specified local authority.

(3) Where the court makes an order under subsection (2) (b) above committing the care of a minor to a local authority, the court may make a further order requiring the payment by either parent to that authority while it has the care of the minor of such weekly or other periodical sum towards the maintenance of the minor as the court thinks reasonable having regard to the means of that parent.

(4) On an application under section 9 of the Guardianship of Minors Act 1971 the court may, in any case where it adjourns the hearing of the application for more than seven days, make an interim order, to have effect until such date as may be specified in the order and containing—

(a) provision for payment by either parent to the other, or to any person given the custody of the minor, of such weekly or other periodical sum towards the maintenance of the minor as the court thinks reasonable having regard to the means of the parent on whom the requirement is imposed; and

(b) where by reason of special circumstances the court thinks it proper, any provision regarding the custody of the minor or the right of access to the minor of the mother or father;

but an interim order under this subsection shall not be made to have effect after the end of the three months beginning with the date of the order or of any previous interim order made under this subsection with respect to the application, and shall cease to have effect on the making of a final order or on the dismissal of the application.

(5) A magistrates' court may also make such an interim order where under section 16 (4) of the Guardianship of Minors Act 1971 it refuses to make an order on an application under section 9 on the ground that the matter is one that would more conveniently be dealt with by the High Court; but an interim order under this subsection shall not be made so as to have effect after the end of the three months beginning with the date of the order.

(6) Where an application under section 9 of the Guardianship of Minors Act 1971 relates to a minor who is illegitimate, references in subsections (2) and (4) (b) above and in sections 3 and 4 below to the father or mother or parent of the minor shall be construed accordingly (but subsections (3) and (4) (a) above shall not apply).

(7) In section 16 (2) of the Guardianship of Minors Act 1971 (which provides for appeals from orders made by a county court under that Act)

for the words " made by a county court under this Act " there shall be substituted the words " made on an application under this Act by a county court ".

(8) For purposes of this section " local authority " means the council of a non-metropolitan county or a metropolitan district or London borough, or the Common Council of the City of London, and, until the coming into force of the Local Government Act 1972, includes the council of any county or county borough; and the matters which under section 2 of the Local Authority Social Services Act 1970 are to stand referred to an authority's social services committee shall include all matters relating to the discharge by the authority of functions under this section.

Additional provisions as to supervision orders

3.—(1) Where the court makes an order under section 2 (2) (a) above (in this section referred to as a " supervision order "), and the order provides for supervision by a probation officer, then—

(a) if it is an order of the High Court, the officer responsible for carrying out the order shall be such probation officer as may be selected under arrangements made by the Secretary of State; and

(b) in any other case the order shall be for supervision by a probation officer appointed for or assigned to the petty sessions area in which, in the opinion of the court, the minor is or will be resident, and the officer responsible for carrying out the order shall be selected in like manner as if the order were a probation order.

(2) A supervision order shall cease to have effect when the minor attains the age of 16; and where a supervision order is made at a time when the parents of the minor are residing together—

(a) the order may direct that it is to cease to have effect if for a period of three months after it is made they continue to reside together; and

(b) the order (whether or not it includes a direction under paragraph (a) above) may direct that it is not to operate while they are residing together.

(3) A supervision order may be varied or discharged by a subsequent order made on the application of either parent or after the death of either parent, on the application of any guardian under the Guardianship of Minors Act 1971, or (before or after the death of either parent) on the application of any other person having the custody of the minor by virtue of an order under section 9 (1) of that Act or on that of the probation officer or local authority having the supervision of the minor by virtue of the order; and section 16 of that Act shall have effect in relation to applications under this subsection as it has effect in relation to applications under that Act, and section 16 (5) shall apply as it applies in relation to the applications there mentioned.

(4) Without prejudice to subsection (3) above, in relation to supervision orders of magistrates' courts the rules made under section 15 of the Justices of the Peace Act 1949 may make provision for substituting from time to time a probation officer appointed for or assigned to a different petty sessions area or, as the case may be, a different local authority, if in the opinion of the court the minor is or will be resident in that petty sessions area or, as the case may be, in the area of that authority.

(5) [*Repealed by Children Act 1975 (c. 72), Sched. 4.*]

Additional provisions as to order committing care of minor to local authority

4.[1]—(1) An order under section 2 (2) (*b*) above committing the care of a minor to a local authority shall commit him to the care (while a minor) of the authority in whose area he is, in the opinion of the court, resident immediately before being so committed.

(2) Before making an order under section 2 (2) (*b*) above the court shall inform the local authority of the court's proposal to make the order, and shall hear any representations from the authority, including any representations as to the making also of an order under section 2 (3) above for payments to the authority.

(3) In relation to an order under section 2 (2) (*b*) above committing the care of a minor to a local authority, or to an order under section 2 (3) requiring payments to be made to an authority to whom the care of a minor is so committed, the following provisions of the Guardianship of Minors Act 1971, that is to say, sections 9 (3) and (4), 12 (2), 13, 15 (4) to (6) and 16 (5), shall apply as if the order under section 2 (2) (*b*) above were an order under section 9 of that Act giving custody of the minor to a person other than one of the parents (and the local authority were lawfully given that custody by the order), and any order for payment to the local authority were an order under section 9 (2) requiring payment to be made to them as a person so given that custody.

(4) On the making of an order under section 2 (2) (*b*) above with respect to a minor, Parts II and III of the Children Act 1948 together with sections 30, 47 and 58 of the Children and Young Persons Act 1963 (which relate to the treatment of children in the care of a local authority and to contributions towards their maintenance) shall apply as if the minor had been received by the local authority into their care under section 1 of the Children Act 1948, except that—

> (*a*) the exercise by the local authority of their powers under sections 12 and 13 of that Act shall, where the order is made by the High Court, be subject to any directions given by the court; and
>
> (*b*) section 17 of that Act (which relates to arrangements for emigration) shall not apply; and
>
> (*c*) section 24 (2) of that Act (which provides for a child's father and mother to be liable to make contributions in respect of him) shall not apply, but so that references to the local authority who are entitled to receive contributions shall be construed as if section 24 (2) did apply.

(5) While an order under section 2 (2) (*b*) above remains in force with respect to a minor, the minor shall continue in the care of the local authority notwithstanding any claim by a parent or other person.

(6) Each parent or guardian of a child for the time being in the care of a local authority by virtue of an order under section 2 (2) (*b*) above shall give notice to the authority of any change of address of that parent or guardian, and any person who without reasonable excuse fails to comply with this subsection shall be liable on summary conviction to a fine not exceeding £10.

Additional provisions as to interim orders

5.—(1) There shall be no appeal under section 16 of the Guardianship of Minors Act 1971 from an interim order under section 2 (4) or (5) above if the appeal relates only to a provision requiring payments to be made towards the maintenance of a minor.

(2) Section 9 (3) and (4) and section 13 of the Guardianship of Minors Act 1971 shall apply to any such interim order as they apply to an order under section 9 (1) or (2).

(3) Where in the case of an application under section 9 of the

---

[1] Prospectively amended by Children Act 1975 (c. 72), Sched. 3, para. 80, *post.*

Guardianship of Minors Act 1971 the applicant or the respondent (or any of the respondents) resides in Scotland or Northern Ireland, then—

(a) a county court or magistrates' court may exercise the jurisdiction to make, vary or discharge interim orders requiring payments to be made towards the maintenance of the minor or interim orders relating to the custody of the minor in any case in which, in accordance with section 15 (4) or (5) of the Guardianship of Minors Act 1971, the court could make an order under section 9 of that Act relating to the custody of the minor or, as the case may be, could vary or discharge such an order; and

(b) a magistrates' court shall have jurisdiction to make an interim order on the application of the respondent in any case in which, in accordance with section 15 (6) of that Act, the court could make an order under section 9 of that Act.

Evidence on applications under s. 9 of Guardianship of Minors Act 1971

6.—(1) If the court dealing with an application under [section 5 or 9 of the Guardianship of Minors Act 1971 or section 1 (3) or]² 3 (3) of this Act requests a local authority to arrange for an officer of the authority to make to the court a report, orally or in writing, with respect to any specified matter (being a matter appearing to the court to be relevant to the application), or requests a probation officer to make such a report to the court, it shall be the duty of the local authority or probation officer to comply with the request.

[(2) A report made in pursuance of subsection (1) above to a magistrates' court shall be made to the court at a hearing of the application unless it is in writing in which case—

(a) a copy of the report shall be given to each party to the proceedings or to his counsel or solicitor either before or during a hearing of the application; and

(b) if the court thinks fit, the report, or such part of the report as the court requires, shall be read aloud at a hearing of the application.

(3) A magistrates' court may and, if requested to do so at the hearing by a party to the proceedings or his counsel or solicitor, shall, require the officer by whom the report was made to give evidence of or with respect to the matters referred to in the report and if the officer gives such evidence, any party to the proceedings may give or call evidence with respect to any such matter or any matter referred to in the officer's evidence.

(3A) A magistrates' court may take account of—

(a) any statement contained in a report made at a hearing of the application or of which copies have been given to the parties or their representatives in accordance with subsection (2) (a) above; and

(b) any evidence given by the officer under subsection (3) above,

in so far as the statement or evidence is, in the opinion of the court, relevant to the application, notwithstanding any enactment or rule of law to the contrary.] ¹ᵃ

(4) Where for the purpose of subsection (1) above a magistrates' court adjourns the hearing of an application, then, subject to section 46 (2) of the Magistrates' Courts Act 1952 (which provides for the notice required of a resumed hearing), the court may resume the hearing at the time and place appointed notwithstanding the absence of both or all of the parties.

¹ᵃ Subs. (2) and (3) substituted, and subs. (5) added, by Children Act 1975 (c. 72), s. 90.
² Substituted by *ibid.*, Sched. 3, para. 81.

(5) Section 2 (8) above shall apply in relation to this section as it applies in relation to section 2.

[(6) A single justice may request a report under subsection (1) of this section before the hearing of the application, but in such a case the report shall be made to the court which hears the application, and the foregoing provisions of this section shall apply accordingly.] [1a]

Power of Guardians

7.—(1) Subject to subsection (2) below, a guardian under the Guardianship of Minors Act 1971, besides being guardian of the person of the minor, shall have all the rights, powers and duties of a guardian of the minor's estate, including in particular the right to receive and recover in his own name for the benefit of the minor property of whatever description and wherever situated which the minor is entitled to receive or recover.

(2) Nothing in subsection (1) above shall restrict or affect the power of the High Court to appoint a person to be, or to act as, the guardian of a minor's estate either generally or for a particular purpose; and subsection (1) above shall not apply to a guardian under the Guardianship of Minors Act 1971 so long as there is a guardian of the minor's estate alone.

Amendment of Matrimonial Proceedings (Magistrates' Courts) Act 1960 s. 4 (2)

8. Section 4 (2) of the Matrimonial Proceedings (Magistrates' Courts) Act 1960 (under which a magistrates' court has power in certain proceedings under that Act to call for a report by a probation officer or by an officer of a local authority employed in connection with functions specified in the now repealed section 39 (1) of the Children Act 1948) shall be amended by omitting the words " or by such an officer of a local authority as is mentioned in subsection (7) of section 3 of this Act," and by adding at the end the words " or for such a report by an officer of a local authority employed in connection with functions of the authority under the Children and Young Persons Acts 1933 to 1969 ".

Consequential amendments, and repeals

9.—(1) In the enactments mentioned in the following subsections there shall be made the amendments there provided for (being amendments consequential on the foregoing provisions of this Act); and the enactments mentioned in Schedule 3 to this Act are hereby repealed to the extent specified in column 3 of that Schedule.

(2) The words " the Guardianship of Minors Acts 1971 and 1973 " shall be substituted for the words " the Guardianship of Infants Acts 1886 and 1925 " wherever they occurred in any of the following enactments as originally enacted, that is to say—

(a) in the Legal Aid and Advice Act 1949, in Schedule 1, in paragraph 3 (b) of Part I (the proceedings for which legal aid may be given in magistrates' courts);

(b) in the Magistrates' Courts Act 1952, in sections 52 (2), 56 (1) and 57 (4) (periodical payments through justices' clerk, and definition of " domestic proceedings ");

(c) in the Administration of Justice Act 1970, in Schedule 1 (High Court business assigned to Family Division).

(3) The following enactments, as amended by the Guardianship of Minors Act 1971 (which as so amended relate to the enforcement of orders under that Act for the payment of money) shall be further amended as follows—

> (*a*) in the Reserve and Auxiliary Forces (Protection of Civil Interests) Act 1951, in section 2 (1) (*d*), after the words " the Guardianship of Minors Act 1971 " there shall be inserted the words " or under section 2 (4) (*a*) of the Guardianship Act 1973 ";
>
> (*b*) in the Maintenance Orders Act 1950, in section 16 (2) (*a*) (iii), and in the Administration of Justice Act 1970, in Schedule 8, in paragraph 4 (*a*), and in the Attachment of Earnings Act 1971, in Schedule 1, in paragraph 5 (*a*), after the words " the Guardianship of Minors Act 1971 " there shall in each case be inserted the words " or section 2 (3) or 2 (4) (*a*) of the Guardianship Act 1973 ";

PART II

SCOTLAND

Equality of parental rights

10.—(1) In relation to a pupil or minor, and to the administration of any property belonging to or held in trust for a pupil or minor or the application of income of any such property, a mother shall have the same rights and authority as the law allows to a father (and shall accordingly hold the office of tutor to a pupil or, as the case may be, curator to a minor) and the rights and authority of mother and father shall be equal and be exercisable by either without the other.

(2) An agreement for a man or woman to give up in whole or in part, in relation to any child of his or hers, the rights and authority referred to in subsection (1) above shall be unenforceable, except that an agreement made between husband and wife which is to operate only during their separation while married may, in relation to a child of theirs, provide for either of them to do so; but no such agreement between husband and wife shall be enforced by any court if the court is of the opinion that it will not be for the benefit of the child to give effect to it.

(3) Where a father and mother of a pupil or minor disagree on any question affecting his welfare, either of them may apply to the Court of Session or to any sheriff court, having jurisdiction under the Guardianship of Infants Act 1886, for the court's direction, and (subject to subsection (4) below) the court may make such order regarding the matters in difference as it may think proper.

(4) Subsection (3) above shall not authorise the court to make any order regarding the custody of a pupil or minor or the right of access to him of his father or mother.

(5) An order under subsection (3) above may be varied or discharged by a subsequent order made on the application of either parent or, after the death of either parent, on the application of any guardian under the Guardianship of Infants Acts 1886 and 1925, or (before or after the death of either parent) on the application of any person having the custody of the pupil or minor; and the power conferred on the court by this subsection may be exercised in proceedings by or against a person residing in England or Wales or Northern Ireland.

(6) Nothing in the foregoing provisions of this section shall affect the operation of any enactment requiring the consent of both parents in a matter affecting a pupil or minor or be taken as applying in relation to a pupil or minor who is illegitimate.

(7) Nothing in the said provisions shall be taken to affect the provisions of the Mental Health (Scotland) Act 1960 as to the person who is " the nearest relative " for the purposes of that Act.

(8) In the Guardianship of Infants Act 1925 in section 1 the words

" or any right at common law possessed by the father " and section 2 are hereby repealed.

Jurisdiction and orders relating to care and custody of children

11.[3]—(1) Where an application made under section 5 of the Guardianship of Infants Act 1886, as read with section 3 of the Guardianship of Infants Act 1925, section 16 of the Administration of Justice Act 1928 and section 1 of the Custody of Children (Scotland) Act 1939, or under section 2 (1) of the Illegitimate Children (Scotland) Act 1930 relates to the custody of a child—

(a) if it appears to the court that there are exceptional circumstances making it impracticable or undesirable for the child to be entrusted to either of the parents or to any other individual, the court may commit the care of the child to a specified local authority;

(b) if by order made on that application either parent or any other person (other than a local authority) is given the custody of the child, but it appears to the court that there are exceptional circumstances making it desirable that the child should be under the supervision of a local authority, the court may order that the child shall be under the supervision of a specified local authority, subject to any directions given by the court;

but any order made by virtue of the above paragraphs shall cease to have effect when the child attains the age of sixteen.

(2) While an order made by virtue of this section committing the care of a child to a local authority is in force with respect to any child the child shall continue in the care of the local authority notwithstanding any claim by a parent or other person.

(3) Where the court makes an order by virtue of subsection (1) (a) above committing the care of a child to a local authority, the court may make a further order requiring the payment by either parent to that authority while it has the care of the child of such weekly or other periodical sum towards the maintenance of the child as the court thinks reasonable having regard to the means of that parent.

(4) Before making an order by virtue of subsection (1) (a) above, the court shall hear any representations from the local authority, including any representations as to the making of an order under subsection (3) above for payments to the authority.

(5) On the making of an order by virtue of this section committing the care of a child to a local authority Part II of the Social Work (Scotland) Act 1968 (which relates to the treatment of children in care of local authorities) shall, subject to the provisions of this section, apply as if the child had been received by the local authority into their care under section 15 of that Act, so however that—

(a) the exercise by the local authority of their powers under or by virtue of sections 20 to 22 of that Act shall be subject to any directions given by the court; and

(b) section 23 of that Act (which relates to arrangements for the emigration of a child under the care of a local authority) shall not apply.

(6) In section 3 of the Guardianship of Infants Act 1925 and in section 7 of the Maintenance Orders Act 1950 there shall be made the amendments provided for in Part I of Schedule 4 to this Act (being amendments providing for mother and father to be treated alike for the purposes of the said section 3 and amendments relating to cases in which custody is given to an individual other than one of the parents); and

---

[3] Prospectively amended by Children Act 1975 (c. 72), s. 48, *post*.

accordingly section 3 and 7 shall have effect as they are set out in Part II of the Schedule with the amendments required by this subsection.

Provisions supplementary to section 11

12.[3]—(1) Any order made by virtue of section 11 above may from time to time be varied or may be discharged by a subsequent order on the application of—

(a) either parent, or

(b) (after the death of either parent) any guardian under the Guardianship of Infants Act 1886, or

(c) any other person having custody of the child, or

(d) the specified local authority having the care or supervision of the child.

(2) (a) Where an application is made under section 5 of the Guardianship of Infants Act 1886 or under section 2 (1) of the Illegitimate Children (Scotland) Act 1930 or for the variation or discharge of any order made under the said Acts or by virtue of section 11 of this Act, the court shall have power to appoint a specified local authority or an individual not being an officer of the local authority to investigate and report to the court on all the circumstances of the child and on the proposed arrangements for the care and upbringing of the child.

(b) If on consideration of a report furnished in pursuance of this subsection the court, either ex proprio motu or on the application of any person concerned, thinks it expedient to do so, it may require the person who furnished the report to appear and be examined on oath regarding any matter dealt with in the report, and such person may be examined or cross-examined accordingly.

(c) Any expenses incurred in connection with the preparation of a report by a local authority or other person appointed under this subsection shall form part of the expenses of the action and be defrayed by such party to the action as the court may direct, and the court may certify the amount of the expenses so incurred.

(3) Each parent or guardian of a child for the time being in the care of a local authority by virtue of an order under section 11 (1) (a) above shall give notice to the authority of any change of address of that parent or guardian and any person who without reasonable excuse fails to comply with this subsection shall be liable on summary conviction to a fine not exceeding £10.

Interpretation of Part II

13.—(1) In this Part of this Act—

" child " means a child under sixteen years of age;

" specified local authority " means a local authority within the meaning of the Social Work (Scotland) Act 1968.

Consequential amendments

14. The enactments specified in Schedule 5 to this Act shall have effect subject to the amendments set out in the Schedule, being amendments consequential on the foregoing provisions of this Part of this Act.

PART III

GENERAL

Short title, citation, extent and commencement

15.—(1) This Act may be cited as the Guardianship Act 1973; and—

(a) Part I of this Act and the Guardianship of Minors Act 1971 may be cited together as the Guardianship of Minors Acts 1971 and 1973; and

(b) Part II of this Act and the Guardianship of Infants Acts 1886 and 1925 may be cited together as the Guardianship of Children (Scotland) Acts 1886 to 1973.

(2) Part I of this Act shall not extend to Scotland or to Northern Ireland, and Part II shall not extend to England and Wales or to Northern Ireland, except that each Part shall extend throughout the United Kingdom in so far as it amends section 16 of the Maintenance Orders Act 1950.

(3) This Act shall come into force on such day as the Secretary of State may appoint by order made by statutory instrument, and different days may be appointed for the coming into force of different provisions.

SCHEDULES

Section 1

SCHEDULE 1

Provisions Substituted for Sexual Offences Act 1956 s. 38

(1) On a person's conviction of an offence under section 10 of this Act against a girl under the age of eighteen, or of an offence under section 11 of this Act against a boy under that age, or of attempting to commit such an offence, the court may by order divest that person of all authority over the girl or boy.

(2) An order divesting a person of authority over a girl or boy under the foregoing subsection may, if that person is the guardian of the girl or boy, remove that person from the guardianship.

(3) An order under this section may appoint a person to be the guardian of the girl or boy during his or her minority or any less period.

(4) An order under this section may be varied from time to time or rescinded by the High Court and, if made on conviction of an offence against a girl or boy who is a defective, may, so far as it has effect for any of the purposes of the Mental Health Act 1959, be rescinded either before or after the girl or boy has attained the age of eighteen.

Section 2

SCHEDULE 2

Amendments of Guardianship of Minors Act 1971 ss. 9, 13, and 16, and Amended Text of s. 9 and s. 15 (3)—(6)

Part I

Amendments

1.—(1) Section 9 of the Guardianship of Minors Act 1971 is to be amended in accordance with sub-paragraphs (2) to (4) below.

(2) In section 9 (2) there shall be substituted—

(a) for the words " the mother ", where they first occur, the words " any person (whether or not one of the parents) "; and

(b) for the words " the father to pay to the mother " the words " payment to that person by the parent or either of the parents excluded from having that custody of "; and

(c) for the words " the father ", where they last occur, the words " that parent ".

(3) At the end of section 9 (3) there shall be added—

" Provided that, unless the court in making the order directs otherwise, paragraphs (a) and (b) above shall not apply to any provision of the order giving the custody of the minor to a person other than one of the parents or made with respect to a minor of whom custody is so given ".

(4) In section 9 (4) the words " (in the case of an order under subsection (1)) " shall be omitted, and at the end of section 9 (4) there shall be added the words " or (before or after the death of either parent) on the application of any other person

having the custody of the minor by virtue of an order under subsection (1) of
this section ".

2. In section 13 (1) of the Guardianship of Minors Act 1971 (which provides for
the enforcement of orders of a magistrates' court committing to the applicant the
legal custody of a minor) for the words " the applicant " there shall be substituted
the words " any person "; at the first place where the applicant is mentioned, and
the words " the person given the custody " at the other two places; and for the
words " that person " there shall be substituted the words " the person so served.

3.—(1) Section 15 of the Guardianship of Minors Act 1971 is to be amended
in accordance with sub-paragraphs (2) to (4) below.

(2) In section 15 (4) there shall be substituted—

    (*a*) for the words " to the mother " where they first occur, the words " to a
person resident in England or Wales "; and

    (*b*) for the words " requiring the father to make payments to the mother "
the words " requiring payments to be made "; and

    (*c*) for the words " the father ", where they last occur, the words " one
parent " and for the words " the mother ", in the last two places where
they occur, the words " the other parent ".

(3) In section 15 (5) the words " in the case of proceedings by the mother " shall
be omitted, and for the words " requiring the father to make payments to the
mother " there shall be substituted the words " requiring payments to be made ".

(4) In section 15 (6) for the words " a woman " there shall be substituted the
words " a person ", and for the words " that subsection " there shall be substituted
the words " that section ".

4. At the end of section 16 of the Guardianship of Minors Act 1971 there shall
be added as subsection (5)—

    " (5) In relation to applications made to a magistrates' court under section 9
of this Act for the discharge or variation of an order giving the custody of a
minor to a person other than one of the parents or made with respect to a
minor of whom custody is so given, rules made under section 15 of the Justices
of the Peace Act 1949 may make provision as to the persons who are to be
made defendants on the application; and if on any such application there are
two or more defendants, the power of the court under section 55 (1) of the
Magistrates' Courts Act 1952 shall be deemed to include power, whatever
adjudication the court makes on the complaint, to order any of the parties to
pay the whole or part of the costs of all or any of the other parties."

PART II

TEXT OF S. 9 AND S. 15 (3) TO (6), AS AMENDED

Section 9, as amended

9.—(1) The court may, on the application of the mother or father of a minor
(who may apply without next friend), make such order regarding—

    (*a*) the custody of the minor; and

    (*b*) the right of access to the minor of his mother or father,

as the court thinks fit having regard to the welfare of the minor and to the conduct
and wishes of the mother and father.

(2) Where the court makes an order under subsection (1) of this section giving
the custody of the minor to any person (whether or not one of the parents), the
court may make a further order requiring payment to that person by the parent or
either of the parents excluded from having that custody of such weekly or other
periodical sum towards the maintenance of the minor as the court thinks reasonable
having regard to the means of that parent.

(3) An order may be made under subsection (1) or (2) of this section notwithstanding that the parents of the minor are then residing together, but—

    (*a*) no such order shall be enforceable, and no liability thereunder shall accrue,
while they are residing together; and

    (*b*) any such order shall cease to have effect if for a period of three months after
it is made they continue to reside together:

Provided that, unless the court in making the order directs otherwise, paragraphs
(*a*) and (*b*) above shall not apply to any provision of the order giving the custody
of the minor to a person other than one of the parents or made with respect to a
minor of whom custody is so given.

(4) An order under subsection (1) or (2) of this section may be varied or discharged by a subsequent order made on the application of either parent or after the death of either parent on the application of any guardian under this Act, or (before or after the death of either parent) on the application of any other person having the custody of the minor by virtue of an order under subsection (1) of this section.

Section 15 (3) *to* (6) *as amended*

(3) A county court or magistrates' court shall not have jurisdiction under this Act in any case where the respondent or any of the respondents resides in Scotland or Northern Ireland—

- (*a*) except in so far as such jurisdiction may be exercisable by virtue of the following provisions of this section; or
- (*b*) unless a summons or other originating process can be served and is served on the respondent or, as the case may be, on the respondents in England or Wales.

(4) An order under this Act giving the custody of a minor to a person resident in England or Wales, whether with or without an order requiring payments to be made towards the minor's maintenance, may be made, if one parent resides in Scotland or Northern Ireland and the other parent and the minor in England or Wales, by a magistrates' court having jurisdiction in the place in which the other parent resides.

(5) It is hereby declared that a magistrates' court has jurisdiction—

- (*a*) in proceedings under this Act by a person residing in Scotland or Northern Ireland against a person residing in England or Wales for an order relating to the custody of a minor (including an order requiring payments to be made towards the minor's maintenance);
- (*b*) in proceedings by or against a person residing in Scotland or Northern Ireland for the revocation, revival or variation of any such order.

(6) Where proceedings for an order under subsection (1) of section 9 of this Act relating to the custody of a minor are brought in a magistrates' court by a person residing in Scotland or Northern Ireland, the court shall have jurisdiction to make any order in respect of the minor under that section on the application of the respondent in the proceedings.

Section 9   SCHEDULE 3

REPEALS UNDER PART I OF THIS ACT

Chapter	Short Title	Extent of Repeal
12 Chas. 2, c. 24.	The Tenures Abolition Act 1660.	Section 9.
36 & 37 Vict. c. 12.	The Custody of Infants Act 1873.	The preamble, and section 2.
7 & 8 Eliz. 2, c. 72.	The Mental Health Act 1959.	Section 127 (2).
1969 c. 46.	The Family Law Reform Act 1969.	In Part I of Schedule 1 the entry relating to the Sexual Offences Act 1956 and that relating to the Mental Health Act 1959.
1971 c. 3.	The Guardianship of Minors Act 1971.	In section 1 the words " or any right at common law possessed by the father ". Section 2. Section 8. In Schedule 1 the entry relating to the Legal Aid and Advice Act 1949 and that relating to the Magistrates' Courts Act 1952, and in the entry relating to the Administration of Justice Act 1970 the words from " for " where first occurring to " 1971 " where next occurring.

Guardianship Act 1973

SCHEDULE 4

AMENDMENTS OF GUARDIANSHIP OF INFANTS ACT 1925 s. 3, AND OF MAINTENANCE
ORDERS ACT 1950 s. 7, AND TEXTS AS AMENDED

PART I

Guardianship of Infants Act 1925, s. 3

1.—(1) Section 3 of the Guardianship of Infants Act 1925 is to be amended in accordance with sub-paragraphs (2) to (6) below.

(2) In section 3 (1) for the words "mother of the infant is then residing with the father of the infant", there shall be substituted the words "parents are then residing together".

(3) In section 3 (2) there shall be substituted—

(a) for the words "the mother", where they first occur, the words "any person (whether or not one of the parents)"; and

(b) for the words "the mother is then residing with the father", the words "the parents are residing together"; and

(c) for the words "the father shall pay to the mother" the words "the parent or either of the parents excluded from having that custody shall pay to that person"; and

(d) for the words "the father", where they last occur, the words "that parent".

(4) In section 3 (3) there shall be substituted—

(a) for the words "mother resides with the father", the words "parents are residing together"; and

(b) for the words "the mother of the infant continues to reside with the father", the words "they continue to reside together".

(5) At the end of section 3 (3) there shall be added—

"Provided that unless the court in making the order directs otherwise, this subsection shall not apply to any provisions of the order giving the custody of the child to a person other than one of the parents or made with respect to a child of whom custody is so given."

(6) In section 3 (4), for the words "either of the father or the mother of the infant" there shall be substituted the words "of either parent or of any other person having the custody of the child by virtue of an order made under section 5 of the Guardianship of Infants Act 1886.".

Maintenance Orders Act 1950, s. 7

2. In section 7 of the Maintenance Orders Act 1950 there shall be substituted—

(a) for the words "to the mother", where they first occur, the words "to a person resident in Scotland"; and

(b) for the words "requiring the father to make payments to the mother" the words "requiring payments to be made"; and

(c) for the words "the father", where they last occur, the words "one parent" and for the words "the mother", in the last two places where they occur, the words "the other parent".

PART II

TEXTS OF s. 3 AND s. 7 AS AMENDED

Guardianship of Infants Act 1925, s. 3, as amended

3.—(1) The power of the court under section five of the Guardianship of Infants Act 1886 to make an order as to the custody of an infant and the right of access thereto may be exercised notwithstanding that the parents are then residing together.

(2) Where the court under the said section as so amended makes an order giving the custody of the infant to any person (whether or not one of the parents), then, whether or not the parents are residing together, the court may further order that the parent or either of the parents excluded from having that custody shall pay to that person towards the maintenance of the infant such weekly or other periodical sum as the court, having regard to the means of that parent, may think reasonable.

(3) No such order, whether for custody or maintenance, shall be enforceable

500

and no liability thereunder shall accrue while the parents are residing together, and any such order shall cease to have effect if for a period of three months after it is made they continue to reside together:

Provided that unless the court in making the order directs otherwise, this subsection shall not apply to any provisions of the order giving the custody of the child to a person other than one of the parents or made with respect to a child of whom custody is so given.

(4) Any order so made may, on the application of either parent or of any other person having the custody of the child by virtue of an order made under section five of the Guardianship of Infants Act 1886, be varied or discharged by a subsequent order.

Maintenance Orders Act 1950, s. 7, as amended

7. An order under the Guardianship of Infants Acts 1886 and 1925, giving the custody of a pupil child to a person resident in Scotland, whether with or without an order requiring payments to be made towards the maintenance of the pupil child, may be made, if one parent resides in England or Northern Ireland and the other parent and the pupil child in Scotland, by the sheriff within whose jurisdiction the other parent resides.

Section 14

SCHEDULE 5

CONSEQUENTIAL AMENDMENTS RELATING TO SCOTLAND

1. In section 5 of the Guardianship of Infants Act 1886, at the end there shall be added—

"or (whether before or after the death of either parent) of any other person having the custody of the child by virtue of an order made under this section".

2. In section 8 of the Guardianship of Infants Act 1925, for the words "as amended by this Act" there shall be substituted the words "by virtue of section 3 of this Act or under section 11 (3) of the Guardianship Act 1973".

3. In section 2 (1) of the Illegitimate Children (Scotland) Act 1930, after the words "either parent", where they last occur, there shall be inserted the words "or of any other person having the custody of the child by virtue of an order made under this section".

4. In section 16 (2) (b) of the Maintenance Orders Act 1950, after sub-paragraph (vi) there shall be inserted the following sub-paragraph—

"(vii) an order for the payment of weekly or other periodical sums under subsection (3) of section 11 of the Guardianship Act 1973;".

5. In section 8 (1) (d) of the Reserve and Auxiliary Forces (Protection of Civil Interests) Act 1951, after "1925" there shall be inserted the words "or under subsection (3) of section 11 of the Guardianship Act 1973".

6. In section 8 (1) (d) of the Law Reform (Miscellaneous Provisions) (Scotland) Act 1966, after "1958" there shall be inserted the words "or by virtue of Part II of the Guardianship Act 1973".

7. In section 2 (2) of the Social Work (Scotland) Act 1968, in sub-paragraph (c), at the end there shall be added "and sections 11 and 12 of the Guardianship Act 1973".

Domicile and Matrimonial Proceedings Act 1973

(1973 c. 45)

An Act to amend the law relating to the domicile of married women and persons not of full age, to matters connected with domicile and to jurisdiction in matrimonial proceedings including actions for reduction of consistorial decrees; to make further provision about the recognition of divorces and legal separations; and for purposes connected therewith. **[25th July 1973]**

PART I

DOMICILE

Husband and wife

Abolition of wife's dependent domicile

1.—(1) Subject to subsection (2) below, the domicile of a married woman as at any time after the coming into force of this section shall, instead of being the same as her husband's by virtue only of marriage, be ascertained by reference to the same factors as in the case of any other individual capable of having an independent domicile.

(2) Where immediately before this section came into force a woman was married and then had her husband's domicile by dependence, she is to be treated as retaining that domicile (as a domicile of choice, if it is not also her domicile of origin) unless and until it is changed by acquisition or revival of another domicile either on or after the coming into force of this section.

(3) This section extends to England and Wales, Scotland and Northern Ireland.

Amendments of Recognition Act consequent on s. 1

2.—(1) The Recognition of Divorces and Legal Separations Act 1971 shall be amended in accordance with this section.

(2) For section 6 of the Act (saving for common law rules, and previous enactments, as to recognition) there shall be substituted—

" Existing common law and statutory rules

6.—(1) In this section " the common law rules " means the rules of law relating to the recognition of divorces or legal separations obtained in the country of the spouses' domicile or obtained elsewhere and recognised as valid in that country.

(2) In any circumstances in which the validity of a divorce or legal separation obtained in a country outside the British Isles would be recognised by virtue only of the common law rules if either—

(*a*) the spouses had at the material time both been domiciled in that country; or

(*b*) the divorce or separation were recognised as valid under the law of the spouses' domicile,

its validity shall also be recognised if subsection (3) below is satisfied in relation to it.

(3) This subsection is satisfied in relation to a divorce or legal separation obtained in a country outside the British Isles if either—

(*a*) one of the spouses was at the material time domiciled in that country and the divorce or separation was recognised as valid under the law of the domicile of the other spouse; or

(*b*) neither of the spouses having been domiciled in that country at the material time, the divorce or separation was recognised as valid under the law of the domicile of each of the spouses respectively.

(4) For any purpose of subsection (2) or (3) above " the material time," in relation to a divorce or legal separation, means the time of the institution of proceedings in the country in which it was obtained.

(5) Sections 2 to 5 of this Act are without prejudice to the recognition of the validity of divorces and legal separations obtained outside the British Isles by virtue of the common law rules (as extended by this section), or of any enactment other than this Act; but, subject to this section, no divorce or legal separation so obtained shall be recognised as valid in the United Kingdom except as provided by those sections."

(3) In section 7 of the Act (non-recognition of divorce by third country no bar to re-marriage)—

(a) for " the foregoing provisions " there shall be substituted " sections 1 to 5 or section 6 (2) "; and

(b) for " section 6 " there shall be substituted " section 6 (5) ".

(4) In section 8 (2) of the Act (particular circumstances in which recognition may be refused)—

(a) after " by virtue of " there shall be inserted " sections 2 to 5 or section 6 (2) of "; and

(b) for " section 6 " there shall be substituted " section 6 (5) ".

(5) This section extends to England and Wales, Scotland and Northern Ireland.

Minors and pupils

Age at which independent domicile can be advised

3.—(1) The time at which a person first becomes capable of having an independent domicile shall be when he attains the age of sixteen or marries under that age; and in the case of a person who immediately before 1st January 1974 was incapable of having an independent domicile, but had then attained the age of sixteen or been married, it shall be that date.

(2) This section extends to England and Wales and Northern Ireland (but not to Scotland).

Dependent domicile of child not living with his father

4.—(1) Subsection (2) of this section shall have effect with respect to the dependent domicile of a child as at any time after the coming into force of this section when his father and mother are alive but living apart.

(2) The child's domicile as at that time shall be that of his mother if—

(a) he then has his home with her and has no home with his father; or

(b) he has at any time had her domicile by virtue of paragraph (a) above and has not since had a home with his father.

(3) As at any time after the coming into force of this section, the domicile of a child whose mother is dead shall be that which she last had before she died if at her death he had her domicile by virtue of subsection (2) above and he has not since had a home with his father.

(4) Nothing in this section prejudices any existing rule of law as to the cases in which a child's domicile is regarded as being, by dependence, that of his mother.

(5) In this section, " child " means a person incapable of having an independent domicile; [. . .].[1]

(6) This section extends to England and Wales, Scotland and Northern Ireland.

PART II

JURISDICTION IN MATRIMONIAL PROCEEDINGS (ENGLAND AND WALES)

Jurisdiction of High Court and county courts

5.—(1) Subsections (2) to (5) below shall have effect, subject to section 6 (3) and (4) of this Act, with respect to the jurisdiction of the court to entertain—

[1] Words repealed by Children Act 1975 (c. 72), Sched. 4.

(a) proceedings for divorce, judicial separation or nullity of marriage; and

(b) proceedings for death to be presumed and a marriage to be dissolved in pursuance of section 19 of the Matrimonial Causes Act 1973;

and in this Part of this Act " the court " means the High Court and a divorce county court within the meaning of the Matrimonial Causes Act 1967.

(2) The court shall have jurisdiction to entertain proceedings for divorce or judicial separation if (and only if) either of the parties to the marriage—

(a) is domiciled in England and Wales on the date when the proceedings are begun; or

(b) was habitually resident in England and Wales throughout the period of one year ending with that date.

(3) The court shall have jurisdiction to entertain proceedings for nullity of marriage if (and only if) either of the parties to the marriage—

(a) is domiciled in England and Wales on the date when the proceedings are begun; or

(b) was habitually resident in England and Wales throughout the period of one year ending with that date; or

(c) died before that date and either—

(i) was at death domiciled in England and Wales, or

(ii) had been habitually resident in England and Wales throughout the period of one year ending with the date of death.

(4) The court shall have jurisdiction to entertain proceedings for death to be presumed and a marriage to be dissolved if (and only if) the petitioner—

(a) is domiciled in England and Wales on the date when the proceedings are begun; or

(b) was habitually resident in England and Wales throughout the period of one year ending with that date.

(5) The court shall, at any time when proceedings are pending in respect of which it has jurisdiction by virtue of subsection (2) or (3) above (or of this subsection), also have jurisdiction to entertain other proceedings, in respect of the same marriage, for divorce, judicial separation or nullity of marriage, notwithstanding that jurisdiction would not be exercisable under subsection (2) or (3).

(6) Schedule 1 to this Act shall have effect as to the cases in which matrimonial proceedings in England and Wales are to be, or may be, stayed by the court where there are concurrent proceedings elsewhere in respect of the same marriage, and as to the other matters dealt with in that Schedule; but nothing in the Schedule—

(a) requires or authorises a stay of proceedings which are pending when this section comes into force; or

(b) prejudices any power to stay proceedings which is exercisable by the court apart from the Schedule.

Miscellaneous amendments, transitional provision and savings

6.—(1) In section 27 (2) of the Matrimonial Causes Act 1973 (which excludes the court's jurisdiction on a maintenance application unless it would have jurisdiction to decree judicial separation), for the words from " unless " onwards there shall be substituted the words " unless—

(a) the applicant or the respondent is domiciled in England and Wales on the date of the application; or

(b) the applicant has been habitually resident there throughout the period of one year ending with that date; or

(c) the respondent is resident there on that date.".

(2) In subsection (1) of section 50 of the Matrimonial Causes Act 1973 (scope of the Matrimonial Causes Rules), the word " or " at the end of paragraph (c) shall be omitted and after paragraph (d) there shall be inserted the following words

" or

(e) any enactment contained in Part II of or Schedule 1 to the Domicile and Matrimonial Proceedings Act 1973 which does not fall within paragraph (d) above ".

(3) No proceedings for divorce shall be entertained by the court by virtue of section 5 (2) or (5) of this Act while proceedings for divorce or nullity of marriage, begun before the commencement of this Act, are pending (in respect of the same marriage) in Scotland, Northern Ireland, the Channel Islands or the Isle of Man; and provision may be made by rules of court as to when for the purposes of this subsection proceedings are to be treated as begun or pending in any of those places.

(4) Nothing in this Part of this Act—

(a) shall be construed to remove any limitation imposed on the jurisdiction of a county court by section 1 of the Matrimonial Causes Act 1967;

(b) affects the court's jurisdiction to entertain any proceedings begun before the commencement of this Act.

PART III

JURISDICTION IN CONSISTORIAL CAUSES (SCOTLAND)

Jurisdiction of Court of Session

7.—(1) Subsections (2) to (8) below shall have effect, subject to section 12 (6) of this Act, with respect to the jurisdiction of the Court of Session to entertain—

(a) an action for divorce, separation, declarator of nullity of marriage, declarator of marriage, declarator of freedom and putting to silence; and

(b) proceedings for presumption of death and dissolution of marriage under section 5 of the Divorce (Scotland) Act 1938.

(2) The Court shall have jurisdiction to entertain an action for divorce, separation or declarator of freedom and putting to silence if (and only if) either of the parties to the marriage in question—

(a) is domiciled in Scotland on the date when the action is begun; or

(b) was habitually resident in Scotland throughout the period of one year ending with that date.

(3) The Court shall have jurisdiction to entertain an action for declarator of marriage or declarator of nullity of marriage if (and only if) either of the parties to the marriage—

(a) is domiciled in Scotland on the date when the action is begun; or

(b) was habitually resident in Scotland throughout the period of one year ending with that date; or

(c) died before that date and either—

(i) was at death domiciled in Scotland, or

(ii) had been habitually resident in Scotland throughout the period of one year ending with the date of death.

(4) The Court shall have jurisdiction to entertain proceedings for

decree of presumption of death and dissolution of marriage if (and only if)—

    (*a*) the petitioner is domiciled in Scotland on the date when the proceedings are begun or was habitually resident there through-the period of one year ending with that date; or

    (*b*) the person whose death is sought to be presumed was domiciled in Scotland on the date on which he was last known to be alive, or had been habitually resident there throughout the period of one year ending with that date.

(5) The Court shall, at any time when proceedings are pending in respect of which it has jurisdiction by virtue of subsection (2) or (3) above (or of this subsection), also have jurisdiction to entertain other proceedings, in respect of the same marriage, for divorce, separation or declarator of marriage, declarator of nullity of marriage or declarator of freedom and putting to silence, notwithstanding that jurisdiction would not be exercisable under subsection (2) or (3).

(6) Nothing in this section affects the rules governing the jurisdiction of the Court of Session to entertain, in an action for divorce, an application for payment by a co-defender of damages or expenses.

(7) The foregoing provisions of this section are without prejudice to any rule of law whereby the Court of Session has jurisdiction in certain circumstances to entertain actions for separation as a matter of necessity and urgency.

(8) No action for divorce in respect of a marriage shall be entertained by the Court of Session by virtue of subsection (2) or (5) above while proceedings for divorce or nullity of marriage, begun before the commencement of this Act, are pending (in respect of the same marriage) in England and Wales, Northern Ireland, the Channel Islands or the Isle of Man; and provision may be made by rules of court as to when, for the purposes of this subsection, proceedings are to be treated as begun or pending in any of those places.

Jurisdiction of sheriff court in respect of actions for separation

8.—(1) Subsections (2) to (4) below shall have effect, subject to section 12 (6) of this Act, with respect to the jurisdiction of the sheriff court to entertain an action for separation.

(2) The court shall have jurisdiction to entertain an action for separation if (and only if)—

    (*a*) either party to the marriage in question—

        (i) is domiciled in Scotland at the date when the action is begun, or

        (ii) was habitually resident there throughout the period of one year ending with that date; and

    (*b*) either party to the marriage—

        (i) was resident in the sheriffdom for a period of forty days ending with that date, or

        (ii) had been resident in the sheriffdom for a period of not less than forty days ending not more than forty days before the said date, and has no known residence in Scotland at that date.

(3) In respect of any marriage, the court shall have jurisdiction to entertain an action for separation (notwithstanding that jurisdiction would not be exercisable under subsection (2) above) if it is begun at a time when an original action is pending in respect of the marriage; and for this purpose " original action " means an action in respect of which the court has jurisdiction by virtue of subsection (2), or of this subsection.

(4) The foregoing provisions of this section are without prejudice

to any jurisdiction of a sheriff court to entertain an action of separation remitted to it in pursuance of any enactment or rule of court.

Jurisdiction in respect of actions for reduction of consistorial decrees

9. Subject to section 12 (6) of this Act, the Court of Session shall have jurisdiction to entertain an action for reduction of a decree granted (whether before or after the commencement of this Act) by a Scottish court in any consistorial proceedings whether or not the Court would have jurisdiction to do so apart from this section.

Ancillary and collateral orders

10.—(1) Where after the commencement of this Act—

(a) an application is made to the Court of Session or to a sheriff court for—
　(i) the making as respects any person or property of an order under any of the enactments or rules of law specified in Part I or Part II of Schedule 2 to this Act, or
　(ii) the variation or recall as respects any person or property of an order made (whether before or after the commencement of this Act) under any of those enactments or rules of law; and

(b) the application is competently made in connection with an action for any of the following remedies, namely, divorce, separation, declarator of marriage and declarator of nullity of marriage (whether the application is made in the same proceedings or in other proceedings and whether it is made before or after the pronouncement of a final decree in the action),

then, if the court has or, as the case may be, had by virtue of this Act or of any enactment or rule of law in force before the commencement of this Act jurisdiction to entertain the action, it shall have jurisdiction to entertain the application as respects the person or property in question whether or not it would have jurisdiction to do so apart from this subsection.

(2) It is hereby declared that where—

(a) the Court of Session has jurisdiction by virtue of this section to entertain an application for the variation or recall as respects any person of an order made by it, and

(b) the order is one to which section 8 (variation and recall by the sheriff of certain orders made by the Court of Session) of the Law Reform (Miscellaneous Provisions) (Scotland) Act 1966 applies,

then, for the purposes of any application under the said section 8 for the variation or recall of the order in so far as it relates to that person, the sheriff, as defined in that section, has jurisdiction as respects that person to exercise the power conferred on him by that section.

Sisting of certain actions

11. The provisions of Schedule 3 to this Act shall have effect with respect to the sisting of actions for any of the following remedies, namely, divorce, separation, declarator of marriage or declarator of nullity of marriage, and with respect to the other matters mentioned in that Schedule; but nothing in that Schedule—

(a) requires or authorises a sist of an action which is pending when this Act comes into force; or

(b) prejudices any power to sist an action which is exercisable by any court apart from the Schedule.

Supplementary

12.—(1) In relation to any action for any of the following three remedies, namely, declarator of marriage, declarator of nullity of marriage, and declarator of freedom and putting to silence, references in this Part of this Act to the marriage shall be construed as including references to the alleged, or, as the case may be, the purported, marriage.

(2) References in this Part of this Act to an action for a particular remedy shall be construed, in relation to a case where the remedy is sought along with other remedies in one action, as references to so much of the proceedings in the action as relates to the particular remedy.

(3) References in this Part of this Act to the remedy of separation shall be construed, in relation to an action in a sheriff court, as references to the remedy of separation and aliment.

(4) For the purposes of this Act the period during which an action in the Court of Session or a sheriff court is pending shall be regarded as including any period while the taking of an appeal is competent and the period while any proceedings on appeal are pending; and in this subsection references to an appeal include references to a reclaiming motion.

(5) In this Part of this Act any reference to an enactment shall, unless the contrary intention appears, be construed as a reference to that enactment as amended or extended, and as including a reference thereto as applied, by or under any other enactment (including this Act).

(6) Nothing in this Part of this Act affects any court's jurisdiction to entertain any proceedings begun before the commencement of this Act.

(7) Subject to subsection (6) above, the enactments described in Schedule 4 to this Act shall have effect subject to the amendments therein specified, being amendments consequential on the provisions of this Part of this Act.

PART IV

JURISDICTION IN MATRIMONIAL PROCEEDINGS
(NORTHERN IRELAND)

Jurisdiction of High Court in Northern Ireland

13.—(1) Subsections (2) to (5) below shall have effect, subject to section 14 of this Act, with respect to the jurisdiction of the court to entertain—

(a) proceedings for divorce, judicial separation or nullity of marriage; and

(b) proceedings for death to be presumed and a marriage to be dissolved in pursuance of section 12 of the Matrimonial Causes Act (Northern Ireland) 1939;

and in this Part of this Act " the court " means the High Court in Northern Ireland.

(2) The court shall have jurisdiction to entertain proceedings for divorce or judicial separation if (and only if) either of the parties to the marriage—

(a) is domiciled in Northern Ireland on the date when the proceedings are begun; or

(b) was habitually resident in Northern Ireland throughout the period of one year ending with that date.

(3) The court shall have jurisdiction to entertain proceedings for nullity of marriage if (and only if) either of the parties to the marriage—

(*a*) is domiciled in Northern Ireland on the date when the proceedings are begun; or

(*b*) was habitually resident in Northern Ireland throughout the period of one year ending with that date; or

(*c*) died before that date and either—

    (i) was at death domiciled in Northern Ireland, or

    (ii) had been habitually resident in Northern Ireland throughout the period of one year ending with the date of death.

(4) The court shall have jurisdiction to entertain proceedings for death to be presumed and a marriage to be dissolved if (and only if) the petitioner—

(*a*) is domiciled in Northern Ireland on the date when the proceedings are begun; or

(*b*) was habitually resident in Northern Ireland throughout the period of one year ending with that date.

(5) The court shall, at any time when proceedings are pending in respect of which it has jurisdiction by virtue of subsection (2) or (3) above (or of this subsection), also have jurisdiction to entertain other proceedings, in respect of the same marriage, for divorce, judicial separation or nullity of marriage, notwithstanding that jurisdiction would not be exercisable under subsection (2) or (3).

(6) Schedule 5 to this Act shall have effect for applying in Northern Ireland, in relation to the High Court in Northern Ireland, Schedule 1 to this Act with the necessary modifications.

Transitional provision and saving

14.—(1) No proceedings for divorce shall be entertained by the court by virtue of section 13 (2) or (5) of this Act while proceedings for divorce or nullity of marriage begun before the commencement of this Act are pending (in respect of the same marriage) in England and Wales, Scotland, the Channel Islands or the Isle of Man; and provision may be made by rules under section 7 of the Northern Ireland Act 1962 as to when for the purposes of this subsection proceedings are to be treated as begun or pending in any of those places.

(2) In section 4 (1) of the Law Reform (Miscellaneous Provisions) Act (Northern Ireland) 1951 (which confers on the court jurisdiction to entertain an application for maintenance by a wife where it would have jurisdiction to entertain proceedings for judicial separation) for the words from " if it would " to " separation " the following shall be substituted—

" if—

(*a*) the wife or the husband is domiciled in Northern Ireland; or

(*b*) the wife has been habitually resident there throughout the period of one year ending with that date or;

(*c*) the husband is resident there on that date.".

(3) Nothing in this Part of this Act affects the court's jurisdiction to entertain any proceedings begun before the commencement of this Act.

PART V

MISCELLANEOUS AND GENERAL

Extension of Recognition Act to Northern Ireland

15.—(1) The Recognition of Divorces and Legal Separations Act 1971 (as amended by this Act) shall extend to Northern Ireland.

(2) In section 1 of that Act (recognition of divorces etc. as between territories forming part of the British Isles) the following shall be substituted for paragraphs (*a*) and (*b*)—

" if it was granted under the law of any part of the British Isles, be recognised throughout the United Kingdom ";
and in each of sections 2, 7 and 8 of that Act for " Great Britain " there shall be substituted " the United Kingdom ".

(3) In so far as section 1 of that Act operates as part of the law of Northern Ireland, it shall do so only in relation to a decree of divorce or judicial separation granted after the coming into force of this section; and as respects the recognition in Northern Ireland of any such divorce or separation as is referred to in section 10 (4) of the Act (transitional provisions) that subsection shall have effect as if any reference in it to the date of the commencement of the provisions of the Act there referred to were a reference to the date of the coming into force of this section.

(4) This section shall be deemed for the purposes of section 6 of the Government of Ireland Act 1920 to have been passed before the day referred to in that section as the appointed day.

Non-judicial divorces

16.—(1) No proceeding in the United Kingdom, the Channel Islands or the Isle of Man shall be regarded as validly dissolving a marriage unless instituted in the courts of law of one of those countries.

(2) Notwithstanding anything in section 6 of the Recognition of Divorces and Legal Separations Act 1971 (as substituted by section 2 of this Act), a divorce which—

    (a) has been obtained elsewhere than in the United Kingdom, the Channel Islands and the Isle of Man; and

    (b) has been so obtained by means of a proceeding other than a proceeding instituted in a court of law; and

    (c) is not required by any of the provisions of sections 2 to 5 of that Act to be recognised as valid,

shall not be regarded as validly dissolving a marriage if both parties to the marriage have throughout the period of one year immediately preceding the institution of the proceeding been habitually resident in the United Kingdom.

(3) This section does not affect the validity of any divorce obtained before its coming into force and recognised as valid under rules of law formerly applicable.

Citation, etc.

17.—(1) This Act may be cited as the Domicile and Matrimonial Proceedings Act 1973.

(2) Subject to sections 6 (4), 12 (6) and 14 (3) of this Act, the enactments specified in Schedule 6 to this Act (including certain enactments of the Parliament of Northern Ireland) are hereby repealed to the extent specified in the third column of that Schedule.

(3) So long as section 2 of the Southern Rhodesia Act 1965 remains in force, this Act shall have effect subject to such provision as may (before or after this Act comes into force) be made by Order in Council under and for the purposes of that section.

(4) Part II of this Act extends to England and Wales only; Part III extends to Scotland only; Part IV extends to Northern Ireland only; and this Part extends to the whole of the United Kingdom.

(5) This Act shall come into force on 1st January 1974.

SCHEDULES

SCHEDULE 1

STAYING OF MATRIMONIAL PROCEEDINGS (ENGLAND AND WALES)

Interpretation

1. The following five paragraphs have effect for the interpretation of this Schedule.

2. " Matrimonial proceedings " means any proceedings so far as they are one or more of the five following kinds, namely, proceedings for—

> divorce,
> judicial separation,
> nullity of marriage,
> a declaration as to the validity of a marriage of the petitioner, and
> a declaration as to the subsistence of such a marriage.

3.—(1) " Another jurisdiction " means any country outside England and Wales.

(2) " Related jurisdiction " means any of the following countries, namely, Scotland, Northern Ireland, Jersey, Guernsey and the Isle of Man (the reference to Guernsey being treated as including Alderney and Sark).

4.—(1) References to the trial or first trial in any proceedings do not include references to the separate trial of an issue as to jurisdiction only.

(2) For purposes of this Schedule, proceedings in the court are continuing if they are pending and not stayed.

5. Any reference in this Schedule to proceedings in another jurisdiction is to proceedings in a court of that jurisdiction, and to any other proceedings in that jurisdiction, which are of a description prescribed for the purposes of this paragraph; and provision may be made by rules of court as to when proceedings of any description in another jurisdiction are continuing for the purposes of this Schedule.

6. " Prescribed " means prescribed by rules of court.

Duty to furnish particulars of concurrent proceedings in another jurisdiction

7. While matrimonial proceedings are pending in the court in respect of a marriage and the trial or first trial in those proceedings has not begun, it shall be the duty of any person who is a petitioner in the proceedings, or is a respondent and has in his answer included a prayer for relief, to furnish, in such manner and to such persons and on such occasions as may be prescribed, such particulars as may be prescribed of any proceedings which—

> (*a*) he knows to be continuing in another jurisdiction; and
> (*b*) are in respect of that marriage or capable of affecting its validity or subsistence.

Obligatory stays

8.—(1) Where before the beginning of the trial or first trial in any proceedings for divorce which are continuing in the court it appears to the court on the application of a party to the marriage—

> (*a*) that in respect of the same marriage proceedings for divorce or nullity of marriage are continuing in a related jurisdiction; and
> (*b*) that the parties to the marriage have resided together after its celebration; and
> (*c*) that the place where they resided together when the proceedings in the court were begun or, if they did not then reside together, where they last resided together before those proceedings were begun, is in that jurisdiction; and
> (*d*) that either of the said parties was habitually resident in that jurisdiction throughout the year ending with the date on which they last resided together before the date on which the proceedings in the court were begun,

it shall be the duty of the court, subject to paragraph 10 (2) below, to order that the proceedings in the court be stayed.

(2) References in sub-paragraph (1) above to the proceedings in the court are, in the case of proceedings which are not only proceedings for divorce, to the proceedings so far as they are proceedings for divorce.

Discretionary stays

9.—(1) Where before the beginning of the trial or first trial in any matrimonial proceedings which are continuing in the court it appears to the court—

(a) that any proceedings in respect of the marriage in question, or capable of affecting its validity or subsistence, are continuing in another jurisdiction; and

(b) that the balance of fairness (including convenience) as between the parties to the marriage is such that it is appropriate for the proceedings in that jurisdiction to be disposed of before further steps are taken in the proceedings in the court or in those proceedings so far as they consist of a particular kind of matrimonial proceedings,

the court may then, if it thinks fit, order that the proceedings in the court be stayed or, as the case may be, that those proceedings be stayed so far as they consist of proceedings of that kind.

(2) In considering the balance of fairness and convenience for the purposes of sub-paragraph (1) (b) above, the court shall have regard to all factors appearing to be relevant, including the convenience of witnesses and any delay or expense which may result from the proceedings being stayed, or not being stayed.

(3) In the case of any proceedings so far as they are proceedings for divorce, the court shall not exercise the power conferred on it by sub-paragraph (1) above while an application under paragraph 8 above in respect of the proceedings is pending.

(4) If, at any time after the beginning of the trial or first trial in any matrimonial proceedings which are pending in the court, the court declares by order that it is satisfied that a person has failed to perform the duty imposed on him in respect of the proceedings by paragraph 7 above, sub-paragraph (1) above shall have effect in relation to those proceedings and, to the other proceedings by reference to which the declaration is made, as if the words "before the beginning of the trial or first trial" were omitted; but no action shall lie in respect of the failure of a person to perform such a duty.

Supplementary

10.—(1) Where an order staying any proceedings is in force in pursuance of paragraph 8 or 9 above, the court may, if it thinks fit, on the application of a party to the proceedings, discharge the order if it appears to the court that the other proceedings by reference to which the order was made are stayed or concluded, or that a party to those other proceedings has delayed unreasonably in prosecuting them.

(2) If the court discharges an order staying any proceedings and made in pursuance of paragraph 8 above, the court shall not again stay those proceedings in pursuance of that paragraph.

11.—(1) The provisions of sub-paragraphs (2) and (3) below shall apply (subject to sub-paragraph (4)) where proceedings for divorce, judicial separation or nullity of marriage are stayed by reference to proceedings in a related jurisdiction for divorce, judicial separation or nullity of marriage; and in this paragraph—

"custody" includes access to the child in question;

"education" includes training;

"lump sum order" means such an order as is mentioned in paragraph (f) of section 23 (1) of the Matrimonial Causes Act 1973 (lump sum payment for children), being an order made under section 23 (1) or (2) (a);

"the other proceedings", in relation to any stayed proceedings, means the proceedings in another jurisdiction by reference to which the stay was imposed;

"relevant order" means—

(a) an order under section 22 of the Matrimonial Causes Act 1973 (maintenance for spouse pending suit),

(b) such an order as is mentioned in paragraph (d) or (e) of section 23 (1) of that Act (periodical payments for children) being an order made under section 23 (1) or (2) (a),

(c) an order under section 42 (1) (a) of that Act (orders for the custody and education of children), and

(d) except for the purposes of sub-paragraph (3) below, any order restraining a person from removing a child out of England and Wales or out of the custody, care or control of another person; and

"stayed" means stayed in pursuance of this Schedule.

(2) Where any proceedings are stayed, then, without prejudice to the effect of the stay apart from this paragraph—

(a) the court shall not have power to make a relevant order or a lump sum order in connection with the stayed proceedings except in pursuance of paragraph (*c*) below; and

(*b*) subject to paragraph (*c*) below, any relevant order made in connection with the stayed proceedings shall, unless the stay is previously removed or the order previously discharged, cease to have effect on the expiration of the period of three months beginning with the date on which the stay was imposed; but

(*c*) if the court considers that, for the purpose of dealing with circumstances needing to be dealt with urgently, it is necessary during or after that period to make a relevant order or a lump sum order in connection with the stayed proceedings or to extend or further extend the duration of a relevant order made in connection with the stayed proceedings, the court may do so and the order shall not cease to have effect by virtue of paragraph (*b*) above.

(3) Where any proceedings are stayed and at the time when the stay is imposed an order is in force, or at a subsequent time an order comes into force, which was made in connection with the other proceedings and provides for any of the four following matters, namely, periodical payments for a spouse of the marriage in question, periodical payments for a child, the custody of a child and the education of a child then, on the imposition of the stay in a case where the order is in force when the stay is imposed and on the coming into force of the order in any other case—

(*a*) any relevant order made in connection with the stayed proceedings shall cease to have effect in so far as it makes for a spouse or child any provision for any of those matters as respects which the same or different provision for that spouse or child is made by the other order;

(*b*) the court shall not have power in connection with the stayed proceedings to make a relevant order containing for a spouse or child provision for any of those matters as respects which any provision for that spouse or child is made by the other order; and

(*c*) if the other order contains provision for periodical payments for a child, the court shall not have power in connection with the stayed proceedings to make a lump sum order for that child.

(4) If any proceedings are stayed so far as they consist of matrimonial proceedings of a particular kind but are not stayed so far as they consist of matrimonial proceedings of a different kind, sub-paragraphs (2) and (3) above shall not apply to the proceedings but, without prejudice to the effect of the stay apart from this paragraph, the court shall not have power to make a relevant order or a lump sum order in connection with the proceedings so far as they are stayed; and in this sub-paragraph references to matrimonial proceedings do not include proceedings for a declaration.

(5) Nothing in this paragraph affects any power of the court—

(*a*) to vary or discharge a relevant order so far as the order is for the time being in force; or

(*b*) to enforce a relevant order as respects any period when it is or was in force; or

(*c*) to make a relevant order or a lump sum order in connection with proceedings which were but are no longer stayed.

SCHEDULE 2

ANCILLARY AND COLLATERAL ORDERS (SCOTLAND)

PART I

Enactments and rules of law referred to in section 10 (1) and in Schedule 3 paragraph 11 (1)

1. Any rule of law empowering a court to make an order for payment of interim aliment *pendente lite* by one party to the marriage in question for the benefit of the other, including any such rule as extended by section 4 of the Married Women's Property (Scotland) Act 1920.

2. Any rule of law empowering the Court of Session to make an order for payment of aliment (other than interim aliment *pendente lite*) by one party to the marriage in question for the benefit of the other, in connection with an action for

separation, including any such rule, as extended by section 4 of the Married Women's Property (Scotland) Act 1920.

3. Paragraph (2) of section 5 of the Sheriff Courts (Scotland) Act 1907 so far as relating to orders for aliment or for regulating the custody of a child.

4. Section 9 (orders with respect to children) of the Conjugal Rights (Scotland) Amendment Act 1861 as extended by section 1 of the Custody of Children (Scotland) Act 1939 and by sections 7 and 14 of the Matrimonial Proceedings (Children) Act 1958.

5. Section 10 of the Matrimonial Proceedings (Children) Act 1958 so far as relating to orders committing the care of a child to an individual.

6. Section 13 (power to prohibit in certain cases removal of child furth of Scotland or out of control of person having custody of him) of the Matrimonial Proceedings (Children) Act 1958.

7. Any enactment or rule of law empowering a court to vary or recall an order the power to make which is conferred by any enactment mentioned in this Part of this Schedule or by any rule of law so mentioned.

PART II

Further enactments and rules of law referred to in section 10 (1)

8. Section 7 (guardianship in case of divorce or judicial separation) of the Guardianship of Infants Act 1886.

9. Section 2 (effect of divorce on property rights) of the Divorce (Scotland) Act 1938, both as originally enacted and as substituted by section 7 of the Divorce (Scotland) Act 1964.

10. Section 10 of the Matrimonial Proceedings (Children) Act 1958, as far as relating to orders committing the care of a child to a local authority.

11. Section 12 (power of court to provide for supervision of child) of the Matrimonial Proceedings (Children) Act 1958.

12. Section 26 (orders for financial provision on divorce) and section 27 (orders relating to settlements and other dealings) of the Succession (Scotland) Act 1964.

13. Any rule of law empowering a court, in connection with an action for declarator of nullity of marriage, to make an order for restitution of property as between the parties to the marriage or for the payment of damages by either of those parties.

14. Any rule of law empowering a court to make an order for the payment of expenses of the action in question by either party to the marriage.

15. Any enactment or rule of law empowering a court to vary or recall an order the power to make which is conferred by any enactment mentioned in this Part of this Schedule or by any rule of law so mentioned.

Section 11   SCHEDULE 3

SISTING OF CONSISTORIAL ACTIONS (SCOTLAND)

Interpretation

1. The following six paragraphs have effect for the interpretation of this Schedule.

2. "Consistorial action" means any action so far as it is one or more of the following, namely, actions for—

 divorce,
 separation,
 declarator of marriage,
 declarator of nullity of marriage.

3.—(1) "Another jurisdiction" means any country outside Scotland.

(2) "Related jurisdiction" means any of the following countries, namely, England and Wales, Northern Ireland, Jersey, Guernsey and the Isle of Man (the reference to Guernsey being treated as including Alderney and Sark).

4. For the purposes of this Schedule—

 (a) in any action in the Court of Session or a sheriff court neither the taking of evidence on commission nor a separate proof relating to any preliminary plea shall be regarded as part of the proof in the action; and

 (b) any such action is continuing if it is pending and not sisted.

5. Any reference in this Schedule to proceedings in another jurisdiction is to proceedings in a court of that jurisdiction and to any other proceedings in that jurisdiction which are of a description prescribed for the purposes of this paragraph; and provision may be made by rules of court as to when proceedings of any description in another jurisdiction are continuing for the purposes of this Schedule.

6. " Prescribed " means prescribed by rules of court.

Duty to furnish particulars of concurrent proceedings in another jurisdiction

7. While any consistorial action is pending in the Court of Session or a sheriff court and proof in that action has not begun, it shall be the duty of the pursuer, and of any other person who has entered appearance in the action, to furnish, in such manner and to such persons and on such occasions as may be prescribed, such particulars as may be so prescribed of any proceedings which—

(*a*) he knows to be continuing in another jurisdiction; and

(*b*) are in respect of that marriage or capable of affecting its validity.

Mandatory sists

8. Where before the beginning of the proof in any action for divorce which is continuing in the Court of Session it appears to the Court on the application of a party to the marriage—

(*a*) that in respect of the same marriage proceedings for divorce or nullity of marriage are continuing in a related jurisdiction; and

(*b*) that the parties to the marriage have resided together after the marriage was contracted; and

(*c*) that the place where they resided together when the action in the Court was begun or, if they did not then reside together, where they last resided together before the date on which that action was begun is in that jurisdiction; and

(*d*) that either of the said parties was habitually resident in that jurisdiction throughout the year ending with the date on which they last resided together before the date on which that action was begun;

it shall be the duty of the Court, subject to paragraph 10 (2) below, to sist the action before it.

Discretionary sists

9.—(1) Where before the beginning of the proof in any consistorial action which is continuing in the Court of Session or in a sheriff court, it appears to the court concerned—

(*a*) that any other proceedings in respect of the marriage in question or capable of affecting its validity are continuing in another jurisdiction, and

(*b*) that the balance of fairness (including convenience) as between the parties to the marriage is such that it is appropriate for those other proceedings to be disposed of before further steps are taken in the action in the said court,

the court may then if it thinks fit sist that action.

(2) In considering the balance of fairness and convenience for the purposes of sub-paragraph (1) (*b*) above, the court shall have regard to all factors appearing to be relevant, including the convenience of witnesses and any delay or expense which may result from the proceedings being sisted, or not being sisted.

(3) Sub-paragraph (1) above is without prejudice to the duty imposed on the Court of Session by paragraph 8 above.

(4) If, at any time after the beginning of the proof in any consistorial action which is pending in the Court of Session or a sheriff court, the court concerned is satisfied that a person has failed to perform the duty imposed on him in respect of the action and any such other proceedings as aforesaid by paragraph 7 above, sub-paragraph (1) of this paragraph shall have effect in relation to that action and to the other proceedings as if the words "before the beginning of the proof" were omitted; but no action in respect of the failure of a person to perform such a duty shall be competent.

Supplementary

10.—(1) Where an action is sisted in pursuance of paragraph 8 or 9 above, the court may if it thinks fit, on the application of a party to the action, recall the sist if it appears to the court that the other proceedings by reference to which the action was sisted are sisted or concluded or that a party to those other proceedings has delayed unreasonably in prosecuting those other proceedings.

(2) Where an action has been sisted in pursuance of paragraph 8 above by reference to some other proceedings, and the court recalls the sist in pursuance of the preceding sub-paragraph, the court shall not again sist the action in pursuance of the said paragraph 8.

11.—(1) The provisions of sub-paragraphs (2) and (3) below shall apply where an action for any of the following remedies, namely, divorce, separation and declarator of nullity of marriage, is sisted by reference to proceedings in a related jurisdiction for any of those remedies; and in this paragraph—

"custody" includes access to the child in question;

"the other proceedings", in relation to any sisted action, means the proceedings in another jurisdiction by reference to which the action was sisted;

"relevant order" means an interim order made by virtue of any of the enactments or rules of law specified in Part I of Schedule 2 to this Act; and

"sisted" means sisted in pursuance of this Schedule.

(2) Where an action such as is mentioned in sub-paragraph (1) above is sisted, then, without prejudice to the effect of the sist apart from this paragraph—

    (*a*) the court shall not have power to make a relevant order in connection with the sisted action except in pursuance of paragraph (*c*) below; and

    (*b*) subject to the said paragraph (*c*), any relevant order made in connection with the sisted action shall (unless the sist or the relevant order has been previously recalled) cease to have effect on the expiration of the period of three months beginning with the date on which the sist comes into operation; but

    (*c*) if the court considers that as a matter of necessity and urgency it is necessary during or after that period to make a relevant order in connection with the sisted action or to extend or further extend the duration of a relevant order made in connection with the sisted action, the court may do so, and the order shall not cease to have effect by virtue of paragraph (*b*) above.

(3) Where any action such as is mentioned in sub-paragraph (1) above is sisted and at the time when the sist comes into operation, an order is in force, or at a subsequent time an order comes into force, being an order made in connection with the other proceedings and providing for any of the following four matters, namely periodical payments for a spouse of the marriage in question, periodical payments for a child, the custody of a child, and the education of a child, then, as from the time when the sist comes into operation (in a case where the order is in force at that time) or (in any other case) on the coming into force of the order,—

    (*a*) any relevant order made in connection with the sisted action shall cease to have effect in so far as it makes for a spouse or child any provision for any of the said matters as respects which the same or different provision for that spouse or child is made by the other order; and

    (*b*) the court shall not have power in connection with the sisted action to make a relevant order containing for a spouse or child provision for any of the matters aforesaid as respects which any provision for that spouse or child is made by the other order.

(4) Nothing in this paragraph affects any power of a court—

    (*a*) to vary or recall a relevant order in so far as the order is for the time being in force; or

    (*b*) to enforce a relevant order as respects any period when it is or was in force; or

    (*c*) to make a relevant order in connection with an action which was, but is no longer, sisted.

Section 12   SCHEDULE 4

Consequential Amendments of Scottish Enactments

1. In section 6 of the Sheriff Courts (Scotland) Act 1907, at the beginning, there shall be inserted the words "Subject to section 8 of the Domicile and Matrimonial Proceedings Act 1973".

2. In section 5 of the Divorce (Scotland) Act 1938, in subsection (1), after the words "death of the other party, and" there shall be inserted the words "subject to subsection (3) of this section"; and at the end of the said section 5 there shall be inserted the following subsection:

"(3) In proceedings on any such petition the court shall have jurisdiction to entertain the petition if, and only if,—

(*a*) the petitioner is domiciled in Scotland on the date when the proceedings are begun, or was habitually resident there throughout the period of one year ending with that date; or

(*b*) the person whose death is sought to be presumed was domiciled in Scotland on the date on which he was last known to be alive, or had been habitually resident there throughout the period of one year ending with that date".

Section 13   SCHEDULE 5

STAYING OF MATRIMONIAL PROCEEDINGS (NORTHERN IRELAND)

1. Schedule 1 to this Act shall extend to Northern Ireland with the modifications specified below.

2. For paragraph 3, substitute the following—

"3.—(1) "Another jurisdiction" means any country outside Northern Ireland.

(2) "Related jurisdiction" means any of the following countries, namely, England and Wales, Scotland, Jersey, Guernsey and the Isle of Man (the reference to Guernsey being treated as including Alderney and Sark)."

3. In paragraph 6, for "rules of court" substitute "rules made under section 7 of the Northern Ireland Act 1962".

4.—(1) In paragraph 11 (1), omit the definition of "lump sum order", and—

(*a*) for sub-paragraphs (*a*) to (*c*) of the definition of "relevant order" substitute—

"(*a*) any order under section 19 or 22 of the Matrimonial Causes Act (Northern Ireland) 1939"; and

(*b*) in paragraph (*d*) of that definition, for "England and Wales" substitute "Northern Ireland".

(2) in paragraph 11 (2) (*a*) and (*c*), omit "or a lump sum order"; and omit paragraph 11 (3) (*c*).

Section 17   SCHEDULE 6

REPEALS

Chapter	Short Title	Extent of Repeal
2 & 3 Geo. 6. c. 13 (N.I.)	The Matrimonial Causes Act (Northern Ireland) 1939.	Section 26.
7 & 8 Geo. 6. c. 43.	The Matrimonial Causes (War Marriages) Act 1944.	Section 3.
1946 c. 16 (N.I.)	The Marriage and Matrimonial Causes Act (Northern Ireland) 1946.	Section 3.
12, 13 & 14 Geo. 6. c. 100.	The Law Reform (Miscellaneous Provisions) Act 1949.	In section 2, subsections (1), (2) and (3).
14 Geo. 6. c. 37.	The Maintenance Orders Act 1950.	In section 6 (2), the words "an action of separation and aliment".
1951 c. 7 (N.I.)	The Law Reform (Miscellaneous Provisions) Act (Northern Ireland) 1951.	Section 1.
10 & 11 Eliz. 2. c. 21.	The Commonwealth Immigrants Act 1962.	Section 20.
1973 c. 18	The Matrimonial Causes Act 1973.	In section 19, in subsection (1) the words "subject to subsection (2) below", subsections (2) and (5). Section 46.

Inheritance (Provision for Family and Dependants) Act 1975

(1975 c. 63)

ARRANGEMENT OF SECTIONS

An Act to make fresh provision for empowering the court to make orders for the making out of the estate of a deceased person of provision for the spouse, former spouse, child, child of the family or dependant of that person; and for matters connected therewith. **[12th November 1975]**

Application for financial provision from deceased's estate

1.—(1) Where after the commencement of this Act a person dies domiciled in England and Wales and is survived by any of the following persons:—

(*a*) the wife or husband of the deceased;

(*b*) a former wife or former husband of the deceased who has not remarried;

(*c*) a child of the deceased;

(*d*) any person (not being a child of the deceased) who, in the case of any marriage to which the deceased was at any time a party, was treated by the deceased as a child of the family in relation to that marriage;

(*e*) any person (not being a person included in the foregoing paragraphs of this subsection) who immediately before the death of the deceased was being maintained, either wholly or partly, by the deceased;

that person may apply to the court for an order under section 2 of this Act on the ground that the disposition of the deceased's estate effected by his will or the law relating to intestacy, or the combination of his will and that law, is not such as to make reasonable financial provision for the applicant.

(2) In this Act " reasonable financial provision "—

(*a*) in the case of an application made by virtue of subsection (1) (*a*) above by the husband or wife of the deceased (except where the marriage with the deceased was the subject of a decree of judicial separation and at the date of death the decree was in force and the separation was continuing), means such financial provision as it would be reasonable in all the circumstances of the case for a husband or wife to receive, whether or not that provision is required for his or her maintenance;

(*b*) in the case of any other application made by virtue of subsection (1) above, means such financial provision as it would be reasonable in all the circumstances of the case for the applicant to receive for his maintenance.

(3) For the purposes of subsection (1) (*e*) above, a person shall be treated as being maintained by the deceased, either wholly or partly, as the case may be, if the deceased, otherwise than for full valuable consideration, was making a substantial contribution in money or money's worth towards the reasonable needs of that person.

Powers of court to make orders

2.—(1) Subject to the provisions of this Act, where an application is made for an order under this section, the court may, if it is satisfied that the disposition of the deceased's estate effected by his will or the law relating to intestacy, or the combination of his will and that law, is not such as to make reasonable financial provision for the applicant, make any one or more of the following orders: —

(*a*) an order for the making to the applicant out of the net estate of the deceased of such periodical payments and for such term as may be specified in the order;

(*b*) an order for the payment to the applicant out of that estate of a lump sum of such amount as may be so specified;

(*c*) an order for the transfer to the applicant of such property comprised in that estate as may be so specified;

(*d*) an order for the settlement for the benefit of the applicant of such property comprised in that estate as may be so specified;

(*e*) an order for the acquisition out of property comprised in that estate of such property as may be so specified and for the transfer of the property so acquired to the applicant or for the settlement thereof for his benefit;

(*f*) an order varying any ante-nuptial or post-nuptial settlement (including such a settlement made by will) made on the parties to a marriage to which the deceased was one of the parties, the variation being for the benefit of the surviving party to that marriage, or any child of that marriage, or any person who was treated by the deceased as a child of the family in relation to that marriage.

(2) An order under subsection (1) (*a*) above providing for the making out of the net estate of the deceased of periodical payments may provide for—

(*a*) payments of such amount as may be specified in the order,

(*b*) payments equal to the whole of the income of the net estate or of such portion thereof as may be so specified,

(*c*) payments equal to the whole of the income of such part of the net estate as the court may direct to be set aside or appropriated for the making out of the income thereof of payments under this section,

or may provide for the amount of the payments or any of them to be determined in any other way the court thinks fit.

(3) Where an order under subsection (1) (*a*) above provides for the making of payments of an amount specified in the order, the order may direct that such part of the net estate as may be so specified shall be set aside or appropriated for the making out of the income thereof of those payments; but no larger part of the net estate shall be so set aside or appropriated than is sufficient, at the date of the order, to produce by the income thereof the amount required for the making of those payments.

(4) An order under this section may contain such consequential and supplemental provisions as the court thinks necessary or expedient for the purpose of giving effect to the order or for the purpose of securing that the order operates fairly as between one beneficiary of the estate of the deceased and another and may, in particular, but without prejudice to the generality of this subsection—

(*a*) order any person who holds any property which forms part of the net estate of the deceased to make such payment or transfer such property as may be specified in the order;

(*b*) vary the disposition of the deceased's estate effected by the will or the law relating to intestacy, or by both the will and the law relating to intestacy, in such manner as the court thinks fair and reasonable having regard to the provisions of the order and all the circumstances of the case;

(*c*) confer on the trustees of any property which is the subject of an order under this section such powers as appear to the court to be necessary or expedient.

Matters to which court is to have regard in exercising powers under s. 2

3.—(1) Where an application is made for an order under section 2 of this Act, the court shall, in determining whether the disposition of the deceased's estate effected by his will or the law relating to intestacy, or the combination of his will and that law, is such as to make reasonable financial provision for the applicant and, if the court considers that reasonable financial provision has not been made, in determining whether and in what manner it shall exercise its powers under that section, have regard to the following matters, that is to say—

(*a*) the financial resources and financial needs which the applicant has or is likely to have in the foreseeable future;

(*b*) the financial resources and financial needs which any other applicant for an order under section 2 of this Act has or is likely to have in the foreseeable future;

(*c*) the financial resources and financial needs which any beneficiary of the estate of the deceased has or is likely to have in the foreseeable future;

    (*d*) any obligations and responsibilities which the deceased had towards any applicant for an order under the said section 2 or towards any beneficiary of the estate of the deceased;

    (*e*) the size and nature of the net estate of the deceased;

    (*f*) any physical or mental disability of any applicant for an order under the said section 2 or any beneficiary of the estate of the deceased;

    (*g*) any other matter, including the conduct of the applicant or any other person, which in the circumstances of the case the court may consider relevant.

    (2) Without prejudice to the generality of paragraph (*g*) of subsection (1) above, where an application for an order under section 2 of this Act is made by virtue of section 1 (1) (*a*) or 1 (1) (*b*) of this Act, the court shall, in addition to the matters specifically mentioned in paragraphs (*a*) to (*f*) of that subsection, have regard to—

    (*a*) the age of the applicant and the duration of the marriage;

    (*b*) the contribution made by the applicant to the welfare of the family of the deceased, including any contribution made by looking after the home or caring for the family;

and, in the case of an application by the wife or husband of the deceased, the court shall also, unless at the date of death a decree of judicial separation was in force and the separation was continuing, have regard to the provision which the applicant might reasonably have expected to receive if on the day on which the deceased died the marriage, instead of being terminated by death, had been terminated by a decree of divorce.

    (3) Without prejudice to the generality of paragraph (*g*) of subsection (1) above, where an application for an order under section 2 of this Act is made by virtue of section 1 (1) (*c*) or 1 (1) (*d*) of this Act, the court shall, in addition to the matters specifically mentioned in paragraphs (*a*) to (*f*) of that subsection, have regard to the manner in which the applicant was being or in which he might expect to be educated or trained, and where the application is made by virtue of section 1 (1) (*d*) the court shall also have regard—

    (*a*) to whether the deceased had assumed any responsibility for the applicant's maintenance and, if so, to the extent to which and the basis upon which the deceased assumed that responsibility and to the length of time for which the deceased discharged that responsibility;

    (*b*) to whether in assuming and discharging that responsibility the deceased did so knowing that the applicant was not his own child;

    (*c*) to the liability of any other person to maintain the applicant.

    (4) Without prejudice to the generality of paragraph (*g*) of subsection (1) above, where an application for an order under section 2 of this Act is made by virtue of section 1 (1) (*e*) of this Act, the court shall, in addition to the matters specifically mentioned in paragraphs (*a*) to (*f*) of that subsection, have regard to the extent to which and the basis upon which the deceased assumed responsibility for the maintenance of the applicant and to the length of time for which the deceased discharged that responsibility.

    (5) In considering the matters to which the court is required to have regard under this section, the court shall take into account the facts as known to the court at the date of the hearing.

    (6) In considering the financial resources of any person for the purposes of this section the court shall take into account his earning capacity and in considering the financial needs of any person for the purposes of this section the court shall take into account his financial obligations and responsibilities.

Time-limit for applications

4. An application for an order under section 2 of this Act shall not, except with the permission of the court, be made after the end of the period of six months from the date on which representation with respect to the estate of the deceased is first taken out.

Interim orders

5.—(1) Where on an application for an order under section 2 of this Act it appears to the court—

(a) that the applicant is in immediate need of financial assistance, but it is not yet possible to determine what order (if any) should be made under that section; and

(b) that property forming part of the net estate of the deceased is or can be made available to meet the need of the applicant;

the court may order that, subject to such conditions or restrictions, if any, as the court may impose and to any further order of the court, there shall be paid to the applicant out of the net estate of the deceased such sum or sums and (if more than one) at such intervals as the court thinks reasonable; and the court may order that, subject to the provisions of this Act, such payments are to be made until such date as the court either makes an order under the said section 2 or decides not to exercise its powers under that section.

(2) Subsections (2), (3) and (4) of section 2 of this Act shall apply in relation to an order under this section as they apply in relation to an order under that section.

(3) In determining what order, if any, should be made under this section the court shall, so far as the urgency of the case admits, have regard to the same matters as those to which the court is required to have regard under section 3 of this Act.

(4) An order made under section 2 of this Act may provide that any sum paid to the applicant by virtue of this section shall be treated to such an extent and in such manner as may be provided by that order as having been paid on account of any payment provided for by that order.

Variation, discharge etc. of orders for periodical payments

6.—(1) Subject to the provisions of this Act, where the court has made an order under section 2 (1) (a) of this Act (in this section referred to as " the original order ") for the making of periodical payments to any person (in this section referred to as " the original recipient "), the court, on an application under this section, shall have power by order to vary or discharge the original order or to suspend any provision of it temporarily and to revive the operation of any provision so suspended.

(2) Without prejudice to the generality of subsection (1) above, an order made on an application for the variation of the original order may—

(a) provide for the making out of any relevant property of such periodical payments and for such term as may be specified in the order to any person who has applied, or would but for section 4 of this Act be entitled to apply, for an order under section 2 of this Act (whether or not, in the case of any application, an order was made in favour of the applicant);

(b) provide for the payment out of any relevant property of a lump sum of such amount as may be so specified to the original recipient or to any such person as is mentioned in paragraph (a) above;

(c) provide for the transfer of the relevant property, or such part thereof as may be so specified, to the original recipient or to any such person as is so mentioned.

(3) Where the original order provides that any periodical payments payable thereunder to the original recipient are to cease on the occurrence of an event specified in the order (other than the remarriage of a former wife or former husband) or on the expiration of a period so specified, then, if, before the end of the period of six months from the date of the occurrence of that event or of the expiration of that period, an application is made for an order under this section, the court shall have power to make any order which it would have had power to make if the application had been made before that date (whether in favour of the original recipient or any such person as is mentioned in subsection (2) (a) above and whether having effect from that date or from such later date as the court may specify).

(4) Any reference in this section to the original order shall include a reference to an order made under this section and any reference in this section to the original recipient shall include a reference to any person to whom periodical payments are required to be made by virtue of an order under this section.

(5) An application under this section may be made by any of the following persons, that is to say—

(a) any person who by virtue of section 1 (1) of this Act has applied, or would but for section 4 of this Act be entitled to apply, for an order under section 2 of this Act,

(b) the personal representatives of the deceased,

(c) the trustees of any relevant property, and

(d) any beneficiary of the estate of the deceased.

(6) An order under this section may only affect—

(a) property the income of which is at the date of the order applicable wholly or in part for the making of periodical payments to any person who has applied for an order under this Act, or

(b) in the case of an application under subsection (3) above in respect of payments which have ceased to be payable on the occurrence of an event or the expiration of a period, property the income of which was so applicable immediately before the occurrence of that event or the expiration of that period, as the case may be,

and any such property as is mentioned in paragraph (a) or (b) above is in subsections (2) and (5) above referred to as " relevant property ".

(7) In exercising the powers conferred by this section the court shall have regard to all the circumstances of the case, including any change in any of the matters to which the court was required to have regard when making the order to which the application relates.

(8) Where the court makes an order under this section, it may give such consequential directions as it thinks necessary or expedient having regard to the provisions of the order.

(9) No such order as is mentioned in sections 2 (1) (d), (e) or (f), 9, 10 or 11 of this Act shall be made on an application under this section.

(10) For the avoidance of doubt it is hereby declared that, in relation to an order which provides for the making of periodical payments which are to cease on the occurrence of an event specified in the order (other than the remarriage of a former wife or former husband) or on the expiration of a period so specified, the power to vary an order includes power to provide for the making of periodical payments after the expiration of that period or the occurrence of that event.

Payment of lump sums by instalments

7.—(1) An order under section 2 (1) (b) or 6 (2) (b) of this Act for the payment of a lump sum may provide for the payment of that sum by instalments of such amount as may be specified in the order.

(2) Where an order is made by virtue of subsection (1) above the court shall have power, on an application made by the person to whom the lump sum is payable, by the personal representatives of the deceased or by the trustees of the property out of which the lump sum is payable, to vary that order by varying the number of instalments payable, the amount of any instalment and the date on which any instalment becomes payable.

Property available for financial provision

Property treated as part of " net estate "

8.—(1) Where a deceased person has in accordance with the provisions of any enactment nominated any person to receive any sum of money or other property on his death and that nomination is in force at the time of his death, that sum of money, after deducting therefrom any capital transfer tax payable in respect thereof, or that other property, to the extent of the value thereof at the date of the death of the deceased after deducting therefrom any capital transfer tax so payable, shall be treated for the purposes of this Act as part of the net estate of the deceased; but this subsection shall not render any person liable for having paid that sum or transferred that other property to the person named in the nomination in accordance with the directions given in the nomination.

(2) Where any sum of money or other property is received by any person as a donatio mortis causa made by a deceased person, that sum of money, after deducting therefrom any capital transfer tax payable thereon, or that other property, to the extent of the value thereof at the date of the death of the deceased after deducting therefrom any capital transfer tax so payable, shall be treated for the purposes of this Act as part of the net estate of the deceased; but this subsection shall not render any person liable for having paid that sum or transferred that other property in order to give effect to that donatio mortis causa.

(3) The amount of capital transfer tax to be deducted for the purposes of this section shall not exceed the amount of that tax which has been borne by the person nominated by the deceased or, as the case may be, the person who has received a sum of money or other property as a donatio mortis causa.

Property held on a joint tenancy

9.—(1) Where a deceased person was immediately before his death beneficially entitled to a joint tenancy of any property, then, if, before the end of the period of six months from the date on which representation with respect to the estate of the deceased was first taken out, an application is made for an order under section 2 of this Act, the court for the purpose of facilitating the making of financial provision for the applicant under this Act may order that the deceased's severable share of that property, at the value thereof immediately before his death, shall, to such extent as appears to the court to be just in all the circumstances of the case, be treated for the purposes of this Act as part of the net estate of the deceased.

(2) In determining the extent to which any severable share is to be treated as part of the net estate of the deceased by virtue of an order under subsection (1) above, the court shall have regard to any capital transfer tax payable in respect of that severable share.

(3) Where an order is made under subsection (1) above, the provisions

of this section shall not render any person liable for anything done by him before the order was made.

(4) For the avoidance of doubt it is hereby declared that for the purposes of this section there may be a joint tenancy of a chose in action.

Powers of court in relation to transactions intended to defeat applications for financial provision

Dispositions intended to defeat applications for financial provision

10.—(1) Where an application is made to the court for an order under section 2 of this Act, the applicant may, in the proceedings on that application, apply to the court for an order under subsection (2) below.

(2) Where on an application under subsection (1) above the court is satisfied—

(a) that, less than six years before the date of the death of the deceased, the deceased with the intention of defeating an application for financial provision under this Act made a disposition, and

(b) that full valuable consideration for that disposition was not given by the person to whom or for the benefit of whom the disposition was made (in this section referred to as " the donee ") or by any other person, and

(c) that the exercise of the powers conferred by this section would facilitate the making of financial provision for the applicant under this Act,

then, subject to the provisions of this section and of sections 12 and 13 of this Act, the court may order the donee (whether or not at the date of the order he holds any interest in the property disposed of to him or for his benefit by the deceased) to provide, for the purpose of the making of that financial provision, such sum of money or other property as may be specified in the order.

(3) Where an order is made under subsection (2) above as respects any disposition made by the deceased which consisted of the payment of money to or for the benefit of the donee, the amount of any sum of money or the value of any property ordered to be provided under that subsection shall not exceed the amount of the payment made by the deceased after deducting therefrom any capital transfer tax borne by the donee in respect of that payment.

(4) Where an order is made under subsection (2) above as respects any disposition made by the deceased which consisted of the transfer of property (other than a sum of money) to or for the benefit of the donee, the amount of any sum of money or the value of any property ordered to be provided under that subsection shall not exceed the value at the date of the death of the deceased of the property disposed of by him to or for the benefit of the donee (or if that property has been disposed of by the person to whom it was transferred by the deceased, the value at the date of that disposal thereof) after deducting therefrom any capital transfer tax borne by the donee in respect of the transfer of that property by the deceased.

(5) Where an application (in this subsection referred to as " the original application ") is made for an order under subsection (2) above in relation to any disposition, then, if, on an application under this subsection by the donee or by any applicant for an order under section 2 of this Act the court is satisfied—

(a) that, less than six years before the date of the death of the deceased, the deceased with the intention of defeating an application for financial provision under this Act made a disposition other than the disposition which is the subject of the original application, and

(*b*) that full valuable consideration for that other disposition was not given by the person to whom or for the benefit of whom that other disposition was made or by any other person,

the court may exercise in relation to the person to whom or for the benefit of whom that other disposition was made the powers which the court would have had under subsection (2) above if the original application had been made in respect of that other disposition and the court had been satisfied as to the matters set out in paragraphs (*a*), (*b*) and (*c*) of that subsection; and where any application is made under this subsection, any reference in this section (except in subsection (2) (*b*)) to the donee shall include a reference to the person to whom or for the benefit of whom that other disposition was made.

(6) In determining whether and in what manner to exercise its powers under this section, the court shall have regard to the circumstances in which any disposition was made and any valuable consideration which was given therefor, the relationship, if any, of the donee to the deceased, the conduct and financial resources of the donee and all the other circumstances of the case.

(7) In this section " disposition " does not include—

(*a*) any provision in a will, any such nomination as is mentioned in section 8 (1) of this Act or any donatio mortis causa, or

(*b*) any appointment of property made, otherwise than by will, in the exercise of a special power of appointment,

but, subject to these exceptions, includes any payment of money (including the payment of a premium under a policy of assurance) and any conveyance, assurance, appointment or gift of property of any description, whether made by an instrument or otherwise.

(8) The provisions of this section do not apply to any disposition made before the commencement of this Act.

Contracts to leave property by will

11.—(1) Where an application is made to court for an order under section 2 of this Act, the applicant may, in the proceedings on that application, apply to the court for an order under this section.

(2) Where on an application under subsection (1) above the court is satisfied—

(*a*) that the deceased made a contract by which he agreed to leave by his will a sum of money or other property to any person or by which he agreed that a sum of money or other property would be paid or transferred to any person out of his estate, and

(*b*) that the deceased made that contract with the intention of defeating an application for financial provision under this Act, and

(*c*) that when the contract was made full valuable consideration for that contract was not given or promised by the person with whom or for the benefit of whom the contract was made (in this section referred to as " the donee ") or by any other person, and

(*d*) that the exercise of the powers conferred by this section would facilitate the making of financial provision for the applicant under this Act,

then, subject to the provisions of this section and of sections 12 and 13 of this Act, the court may make any one or more of the following orders, that is to say—

(i) if any money has been paid or any other property has been transferred to or for the benefit of the donee in accordance with the contract, an order directing the donee to provide, for the purpose of the making of that financial provision, such sum of money or other property as may be specified in the order;

(ii) if the money or all the money has not been paid or the property or all the property has not been transferred in accordance with the contract, an order directing the personal representatives not to make any payment or transfer any property, or not to make any further payment or transfer any further property, as the case may be, in accordance therewith or directing the personal representatives only to make such payment or transfer such property as may be specified in the order.

(3) Notwithstanding anything in subsection (2) above, the court may exercise its powers thereunder in relation to any contract made by the deceased only to the extent that the court considers that the amount of any sum of money paid or to be paid or the value of any property transferred or to be transferred in accordance with the contract exceeds the value of any valuable consideration given or to be given for that contract, and for this purpose the court shall have regard to the value of property at the date of the hearing.

(4) In determining whether and in what manner to exercise its powers under this section, the court shall have regard to the circumstances in which the contract was made, the relationship, if any, of the donee to the deceased, the conduct and financial resources of the donee and all the other circumstances of the case.

(5) Where an order has been made under subsection (2) above in relation to any contract, the rights of any person to enforce that contract or to recover damages or to obtain other relief for the breach thereof shall be subject to any adjustment made by the court under section 12 (3) of this Act and shall survive to such extent only as is consistent with giving effect to the terms of that order.

(6) The provisions of this section do not apply to a contract made before the commencement of this Act.

Provisions supplementary to ss. 10 and 11

12.—(1) Where the exercise of any of the powers conferred by section 10 or 11 of this Act is conditional on the court being satisfied that a disposition or contract was made by a deceased person with the intention of defeating an application for financial provision under this Act, that condition shall be fulfilled if the court is of the opinion that, on a balance of probabilities, the intention of the deceased (though not necessarily his sole intention) in making the disposition or contract was to prevent an order for financial provision being made under this Act or to reduce the amount of the provision which might otherwise be granted by an order thereunder.

(2) Where an application is made under section 11 of this Act with respect to any contract made by the deceased and no valuable consideration was given or promised by any person for that contract then, notwithstanding anything in subsection (1) above, it shall be presumed, unless the contrary is shown, that the deceased made that contract with the intention of defeating an application for financial provision under this Act.

(3) Where the court makes an order under section 10 or 11 of this Act it may give such consequential directions as it thinks fit (including directions requiring the making of any payment or the transfer of any property) for giving effect to the order or for securing a fair adjustment of the rights of the persons affected thereby.

(4) Any power conferred on the court by the said section 10 or 11 to order the donee, in relation to any disposition or contract, to provide any

sum of money or other property shall be exercisable in like manner in relation to the personal representative of the donee, and—

(a) any reference in section 10 (4) to the disposal of property by the donee shall include a reference to disposal by the personal representative of the donee, and

(b) any reference in section 10 (5) to an application by the donee under that subsection shall include a reference to an application by the personal representative of the donee;

but the court shall not have power under the said section 10 or 11 to make an order in respect of any property forming part of the estate of the donee which has been distributed by the personal representative; and the personal representative shall not be liable for having distributed any such property before he has notice of the making of an application under the said section 10 or 11 on the ground that he ought to have taken into account the possibility that such an application would be made.

Provisions as to trustees in relation to ss. 10 and 11

13.—(1) Where an application is made for—

(a) an order under section 10 of this Act in respect of a disposition made by the deceased to any person as a trustee, or

(b) an order under section 11 of this Act in respect of any payment made or property transferred, in accordance with a contract made by the deceased, to any person as a trustee,

the powers of the court under the said section 10 or 11 to order that trustee to provide a sum of money or other property shall be subject to the following limitation (in addition, in a case of an application under section 10, to any provision regarding the deduction of capital transfer tax) namely, that the amount of any sum of money or the value of any property ordered to be provided—

(i) in the case of an application in respect of a disposition which consisted of the payment of money or an application in respect of the payment of money in accordance with a contract, shall not exceed the aggregate of so much of that money as is at the date of the order in the hands of the trustee and the value at that date of any property which represents that money or is derived therefrom and is at that date in the hands of the trustee;

(ii) in the case of an application in respect of a disposition which consisted of the transfer of property (other than a sum of money) or an application in respect of the transfer of property (other than a sum of money) in accordance with a contract, shall not exceed the aggregate of the value at the date of the order of so much of that property as is at that date in the hands of the trustee and the value at that date of any property which represents the first-mentioned property or is derived therefrom and is at that date in the hands of the trustee.

(2) Where any such application is made in respect of a disposition made to any person as a trustee or in respect of any payment made or property transferred in pursuance of a contract to any person as a trustee, the trustee shall not be liable for having distributed any money or other property on the ground that he ought to have taken into account the possibility that such an application would be made.

(3) Where any such application is made in respect of a disposition made to any person as a trustee or in respect of any payment made or property transferred in accordance with a contract to any person as a trustee, any reference in the said section 10 or 11 to the donee shall be construed as including a reference to the trustee or trustees for the time

being of the trust in question and any reference in subsection (1) or (2) above to a trustee shall be construed in the same way.

Special provisions relating to cases of divorce, separation etc.

Provision as to cases where no financial relief was granted in divorce proceedings etc.

14.—(1) Where, within twelve months from the date on which a decree of divorce or nullity of marriage has been made absolute or a decree of judicial separation has been granted, a party to the marriage dies and—

(a) an application for a financial provision order under section 23 of the Matrimonial Causes Act 1973 or a property adjustment order under section 24 of that Act has not been made by the other party to that marriage, or

(b) such an application has been made but the proceedings thereon have not been determined at the time of the death of the deceased,

then, if an application for an order under section 2 of this Act is made by that other party, the court shall, notwithstanding anything in section 1 or section 3 of this Act, have power, if it thinks it just to do so, to treat that party for the purposes of that application as if the decree of divorce or nullity of marriage had not been made absolute or the decree of judicial separation had not been granted, as the case may be.

(2) This section shall not apply in relation to a decree of judicial separation unless at the date of the death of the deceased the decree was in force and the separation was continuing.

Restriction imposed in divorce proceedings etc. on application under this Act

15.—(1) On granting a decree of divorce, a decree of nullity of marriage or a decree of judicial separation or at any time thereafter, the court may, if the court considers it just to do so and the parties to the marriage agree, order that either party to the marriage shall not be entitled on the death of the other party to apply for an order under section 2 of this Act.

(2) In the case of a decree of divorce or nullity of marriage an order may be made under subsection (1) above before or after the decree is made absolute, but if it is made before the decree is made absolute it shall not take effect unless the decree is made absolute.

(3) Where an order made under subsection (1) above on the grant of a decree of divorce or nullity of marriage has come into force with respect to a party to a marriage, then, on the death of the other party to that marriage, the court shall not entertain any application for an order under section 2 of this Act made by the first-mentioned party.

(4) Where an order made under subsection (1) above on the grant of a decree of judicial separation has come into force with respect to any party to a marriage, then, if the other party to that marriage dies while the decree is in force and the separation is continuing, the court shall not entertain any application for an order under section 2 of this Act made by the first-mentioned party.

Variation and discharge of secured periodical payments orders made under Matrimonial Causes Act 1973

16.—(1) Where an application for an order under section 2 of this Act is made to the court by any person who was at the time of the death of the deceased entitled to payments from the deceased under a secured periodical payments order made under the Matrimonial Causes Act 1973, then, in the proceedings on that application, the court shall have power, if an application is made under this section by that person or by the personal representative of the deceased, to vary or discharge that periodical payments order or to revive the operation of any provision thereof which has been suspended under section 31 of that Act.

(2) In exercising the powers conferred by this section the court shall have regard to all the circumstances of the case, including any order which the court proposes to make under section 2 or section 5 of this Act and any change (whether resulting from the death of the deceased or otherwise) in any of the matters to which the court was required to have regard when making the secured periodical payments order.

(3) The powers exercisable by the court under this section in relation to an order shall be exercisable also in relation to any instrument executed in pursuance of the order.

Variation and revocation of maintenance agreements

17.—(1) Where an application for an order under section 2 of this Act is made to the court by any person who was at the time of the death of the deceased entitled to payments from the deceased under a maintenance agreement which provided for the continuation of payments under the agreement after the death of the deceased, then, in the proceedings on that application, the court shall have power, if an application is made under this section by that person or by the personal representative of the deceased, to vary or revoke that agreement.

(2) In exercising the powers conferred by this section the court shall have regard to all the circumstances of the case, including any order which the court proposes to make under section 2 or section 5 of this Act and any change (whether resulting from the death of the deceased or otherwise) in any of the circumstances in the light of which the agreement was made.

(3) If a maintenance agreement is varied by the court under this section the like consequences shall ensue as if the variation had been made immediately before the death of the deceased by agreement between the parties and for valuable consideration.

(4) In this section " maintenance agreement ", in relation to a deceased person, means any agreement made, whether in writing or not and whether before or after the commencement of this Act, by the deceased with any person with whom he entered into a marriage, being an agreement which contained provisions governing the rights and liabilities towards one another when living separately of the parties to that marriage (whether or not the marriage has been dissolved or annulled) in respect of the making or securing of payments or the disposition or use of any property, including such rights and liabilities with respect to the maintenance or education of any child, whether or not a child of the deceased or a person who was treated by the deceased as a child of the family in relation to that marriage.

Availability of court's powers under this Act in applications under ss. 31 and 36 of the Matrimonial Causes Act 1973

18.—(1) Where—

    (*a*) a person against whom a secured periodical payments order was made under the Matrimonial Causes Act 1973 has died and an application is made under section 31 (6) of that Act for the variation or discharge of that order or for the revival of the operation of any provision thereof which has been suspended, or

    (*b*) a party to a maintenance agreement within the meaning of section 34 of that Act has died, the agreement being one which provides for the continuation of payments thereunder after the death of one of the parties, and an application is made under section 36 (1) of that Act for the alteration of the agreement under section 35 thereof,

the court shall have power to direct that the application made under the said section 31 (6) or 36 (1) shall be deemed to have been accompanied by an application for an order under section 2 of this Act.

(2) Where the court gives a direction under subsection (1) above it shall have power, in the proceedings on the application under the said section 31 (6) or 36 (1), to make any order which the court would have had power to make under the provisions of this Act if the application under the said section 31 (6) or 36 (1), as the case may be, had been made jointly with an application for an order under the said section 2; and the court shall have power to give such consequential directions as may be necessary for enabling the court to exercise any of the powers available to the court under this Act in the case of an application for an order under section 2.

(3) Where an order made under section 15 (1) of this Act is in force with respect to a party to a marriage, the court shall not give a direction under subsection (1) above with respect to any application made under the said section 31 (6) or 36 (1) by that party on the death of the other party.

Miscellaneous and supplementary provisions

Effect, duration and form of orders

19.—(1) Where an order is made under section 2 of this Act then for all purposes, including the purposes of the enactments relating to capital transfer tax, the will or the law relating to intestacy, or both the will and the law relating to intestacy, as the case may be, shall have effect and be deemed to have had effect as from the deceased's death subject to the provisions of the order.

(2) Any order made under section 2 or 5 of this Act in favour of—
  (a) an applicant who was the former husband or former wife of the deceased, or
  (b) an applicant who was the husband or wife of the deceased in a case where the marriage with the deceased was the subject of a decree of judicial separation and at the date of death the decree was in force and the separation was continuing,

shall, in so far as it provides for the making of periodical payments, cease to have effect on the remarriage of the applicant, except in relation to any arrears due under the order on the date of the remarriage.

(3) A copy of every order made under this Act shall be sent to the principal registry of the Family Division for entry and filing, and a memorandum of the order shall be endorsed on, or permanently annexed to, the probate or letters of administration under which the estate is being administered.

Provisions as to personal representatives

20.—(1) The provisions of this Act shall not render the personal representative of a deceased person liable for having distributed any part of the estate of the deceased, after the end of the period of six months from the date on which representation with respect to the estate of the deceased is first taken out, on the ground that he ought to have taken into account the possibility—
  (a) that the court might permit the making of an application for an order under section 2 of this Act after the end of that period, or

(*b*) that, where an order has been made under the said section 2, the court might exercise in relation thereto the powers conferred on it by section 6 of this Act,

but this subsection shall not prejudice any power to recover, by reason of the making of an order under this Act, any part of the estate so distributed.

(2) Where the personal representative of a deceased person pays any sum directed by an order under section 5 of this Act to be paid out of the deceased's net estate, he shall not be under any liability by reason of that estate not being sufficient to make the payment, unless at the time of making the payment he has reasonable cause to believe that the estate is not sufficient.

(3) Where a deceased person entered into a contract by which he agreed to leave by his will any sum of money or other property to any person or by which he agreed that a sum of money or other property would be paid or transferred to any person out of his estate, then, if the personal representative of the deceased has reason to believe that the deceased entered into the contract with the intention of defeating an application for financial provision under this Act, he may, notwithstanding anything in that contract, postpone the payment of that sum of money or the transfer of that property until the expiration of the period of six months from the date on which representation with respect to the estate of the deceased is first taken out or, if during that period an application is made for an order under section 2 of this Act, until the determination of the proceedings on that application.

Admissibility as evidence of statements made by deceased

21. In any proceedings under this Act a statement made by the deceased, whether orally or in a document or otherwise, shall be admissible under section 2 of the Civil Evidence Act 1968 as evidence of any fact stated therein in like manner as if the statement were a statement falling within section 2 (1) of that Act; and any reference in that Act to a statement admissible, or given or proposed to be given, in evidence under section 2 thereof or to the admissibility or the giving in evidence of a statement by virtue of that section or to any statement falling within section 2 (1) of that Act shall be construed accordingly.

Jurisdiction of county courts

22.—(1) A county court shall have jurisdiction to hear and determine any application for an order under section 2 of this Act (including any application for permission to apply for such an order and any application made, in the proceedings on an application for an order under the said section 2, for an order under any other provision of this Act) where it is shown to the satisfaction of the court that the value at the date of the death of the deceased of all property included in his net estate for the purposes of this Act by virtue of paragraph (a) of the definition thereof in section 25 (1) of this Act does not exceed the sum of £5,000 or such larger sum as may from time to time be fixed for this purpose by order of the Lord Chancellor.

(2) Where a county court makes an order under section 2 of this Act, the court shall have all the jurisdiction of the High Court for the purpose of any further proceedings in relation thereto under section 6 of this Act.

(3) Rules of court may provide for the transfer from a county court to the High Court, or from the High Court to a county court, of any proceedings for an order under section 2 of this Act.

(4) Any order of the Lord Chancellor under subsection (1) above

shall be made by statutory instrument, and a draft of the statutory instrument shall be laid before Parliament; and—

(a) in relation to proceedings commenced in a county court after the making but before the coming into force of any such order the court may, if it thinks fit, refuse to make an order under section 66 of the County Courts Act 1959 (transfer to High Court of proceedings outside jurisdiction of county court) if the proceedings are within the jurisdiction of the county court as extended by the order of the Lord Chancellor; but

(b) the coming into force of any such order of the Lord Chancellor shall not be taken to affect any order previously made under the said section 66.

Determination of date on which representation was first taken out

23. In considering for the purposes of this Act when representation with respect to the estate of a deceased person was first taken out, a grant limited to settled land or to trust property shall be left out of account, and a grant limited to real estate or to personal estate shall be left out of account unless a grant limited to the remainder of the estate has previously been made or is made at the same time.

Effect of this Act on s. 46 (1) (vi) of Administration of Estates Act 1925

24. Section 46 (1) (vi) of the Administration of Estates Act 1925, in so far as it provides for the devolution of property on the Crown, the Duchy of Lancaster or the Duke of Cornwall as bona vacantia, shall have effect subject to the provisions of this Act.

Interpretation

25.—(1) In this Act—

" beneficiary " in relation to the estate of a deceased person, means—

(a) a person who under the will of the deceased or under the law relating to intestacy is beneficially interested in the estate or would be so interested if an order had not been made under this Act, and

(b) a person who has received any sum of money or other property which by virtue of section 8 (1) or 8 (2) of this Act is treated as part of the net estate of the deceased or would have received that sum or other property if an order had not been made under this Act;

" child " includes an illegitimate child and a child en ventre sa mere at the death of the deceased;

" the court " means the High Court, or where a county court has jurisdiction by virtue of section 22 of this Act, a county court;

" former wife " or " former husband " means a person whose marriage with the deceased was during the deceased's lifetime dissolved or annulled by a decree of divorce or of nullity of marriage made under the Matrimonial Causes Act 1973;

" net estate " in relation to a deceased person, means: —

(a) all property of which the deceased had power to dispose by his will (otherwise than by virtue of a special power of appointment) less than the amount of his funeral, testamentary and administration expenses, debts and liabilities, including any capital transfer tax payable out of his estate on his death;

(b) any property in respect of which the deceased held a general power of appointment (not being a power exercisable by will) which has not been exercised;

> > > (*c*) any sum of money or other property which is treated
> > > for the purposes of this Act as part of the net estate of
> > > the deceased by virtue of section 8 (1) or (2) of this Act;
> > > (*d*) any property which is treated for the purposes of
> > > this Act as part of the net estate of the deceased by virtue
> > > of an order made under section 9 of the Act;
> > > (*e*) any sum of money or other property which is, by
> > > reason of a disposition or contract made by the deceased,
> > > ordered under section 10 or 11 of this Act to be provided
> > > for the purpose of the making of financial provision under
> > > this Act;
> > " property " includes any chose in action;
> > " reasonable financial provision " has the meaning assigned to it
> > by section 1 of this Act;
> > " valuable consideration " does not include marriage or a promise
> > of marriage;
> > " will " includes codicil.

(2) For the purposes of paragraph (*a*) of the definition of " net
estate " in subsection (1) above a person who is not of full age and
capacity shall be treated as having power to dispose by will of all property
of which he would have had power to dispose by will if he had been of
full age and capacity.

(3) Any reference in this Act to provision out of the net estate of a
deceased person includes a reference to provision extending to the whole
of that estate.

(4) For the purposes of this Act any reference to a wife or husband
shall be treated as including a reference to a person who in good faith
entered into a void marriage with the deceased unless either—

> (*a*) the marriage of the deceased and that person was dissolved or
> annulled during the lifetime of the deceased and the dissolution
> or annulment is recognised by the law of England and Wales, or
> (*b*) that person has during the lifetime of the deceased entered into a
> later marriage.

(5) Any reference in this Act to remarriage or to a person who has
remarried includes a reference to a marriage which is by law void
or voidable or to a person who has entered into such a marriage, as the
case may be, and a marriage shall be treated for the purposes of this Act
as a remarriage, in relation to any party thereto, notwithstanding that
the previous marriage of that party was void or voidable.

(6) Any reference in this Act to an order or decree made under the
Matrimonial Causes Act 1973 or under any section of that Act shall be
construed as including a reference to an order or decree which is deemed
to have been made under that Act or under that section thereof, as the
case may be.

(7) Any reference in this Act to any enactment is a reference to that
enactment as amended by or under any subsequent enactment.

Consequential amendments, repeals and transitional provisions

26. [*The amendments and repeals under this section and under
the Schedule to the Act have been noted in the appropriate places in the
legislation concerned.*]

Short title, commencement and extent

27.—(1) This Act may be cited as the Inheritance (Provision for
Family and Dependants) Act 1975.

(2) This Act does not extend to Scotland or Northern Ireland.

(3) This Act shall come into force on 1st April 1976.

Children Act 1975 [1]

(1975 C. 72)

ARRANGEMENT OF SECTIONS

[1] Much of this Act is still not in force. For commencement and transitional provisions, see s. 108, *post*.

PART III

CARE

Children in care of local authorities

Children in care of voluntary organisations in England and Wales

Conflict of interest between parent and child

Absence from care and children in need of secure accommodation

Further amendments of Social Work (Scotland) Act 1968

PART IV

FURTHER AMENDMENTS OF LAW OF ENGLAND AND WALES

Explanation of concepts

PART V

MISCELLANEOUS AND SUPPLEMENTAL

Foster children

An Act to make further provision for children.

[12th November 1975]

PART I

ADOPTION

The Adoption Services

Establishment of Adoption Services

1.—(1) It is the duty of every local authority to establish and maintain within their area a service designed to meet the needs, in relation to adoption, of—

    (*a*) children who have been or may be adopted,

    (*b*) parents and guardians of such children, and

    (*c*) persons who have adopted or may adopt a child,

and for that purpose to provide the requisite facilities, or secure that they are provided by approved adoption societies.

(2) The facilities to be provided as part of the service maintained under subsection (1) include—

    (*a*) temporary board and lodging where needed by pregnant women, mothers or children;

    (*b*) arrangements for assessing children and prospective adopters, and placing children for adoption;

    (*c*) counselling for persons with problems relating to adoption.

(3) The facilities of the service maintained under subsection (1) shall be provided in conjunction with the local authority's other social services and with approved adoption societies in their area, so that help may be given in a co-ordinated manner without duplication, omission or avoidable delay.

(4) The services maintained under subsection (1) by local authorities in England and Wales may be collectively referred to as " the Adoption Service " and those maintained by local authorities in Scotland, as " the Scottish Adoption Service ", and a local authority or approved adoption society may be referred to as an adoption agency.

Local authorities' social services

2. The social services referred to in section 1 (3) are the functions of a local authority which stand referred to the authority's social services committee or, in Scotland, social work committee, including, in particular but without prejudice to the generality of the foregoing, a local authority's functions relating to—

    (*a*) the promotion of the welfare of children by diminishing the need to receive children into care or keep them in care, including (in exceptional circumstances) the giving of assistance in cash;

    (*b*) the welfare of children in the care of a local authority;

    (*c*) the welfare of children who are foster children within the meaning of the Children Act 1958;

    (*d*) children who are subject to supervision orders made in matrimonial proceedings;

    (*e*) the provision of residential accommodation for expectant mothers and young children and of day-care facilities;

    (*f*) the regulation and inspection of nurseries and child minders;

    (*g*) care and other treatment of children through court proceedings and children's hearings.

Duty to promote welfare of child

3. In reaching any decision relating to the adoption of a child, a court or adoption agency shall have regard to all the circumstances, first consideration being given to the need to safeguard and promote the welfare of the child throughout his childhood; and shall so far as practicable ascertain the wishes and feelings of the child regarding the decision and give due consideration to them, having regard to his age and understanding.

Approval of adoption societies

4.—(1) A body desiring to act as an adoption society or, if it is already an adoption society, desiring to continue to act as such in

England and Wales or in Scotland may, in the manner specified by regulations made by the Secretary of State, apply to the Secretary of State for his approval to its doing so.

(2) On an application under subsection (1), the Secretary of State shall take into account the matters relating to the applicant specified in subsections (3) to (5) and any other relevant considerations, and if, but only if, he is satisfied that the applicant is likely to make, or, if the applicant is an approved adoption society, is making, an effective contribution to the Adoption Service or, as the case may be, to the Scottish Adoption Service, he shall by notice to the applicant give his approval, which shall be operative from a date specified in the notice or, in the case of a renewal of approval, from the date of the notice.

(3) In considering the application, the Secretary of State shall have regard, in relation to the period for which approval is sought, to the following—

    (*a*) the applicant's adoption programme, including, in particular, its ability to make provision for children who are free for adoption,

    (*b*) the number and qualifications of its staff,

    (*c*) its financial resources, and

    (*d*) the organisation and control of its operations.

(4) Where it appears to the Secretary of State that the applicant is likely to operate extensively within the area of a particular local authority he shall ask the authority whether they support the application, and shall take account of any views about it put to him by the authority.

(5) Where the applicant is already an approved adoption society or, whether before or after the passing of this Act, previously acted as an adoption society, the Secretary of State, in considering the application, shall also have regard to the record and reputation of the applicant in the adoption field, and the areas within which and the scale on which it is currently operating or has operated in the past.

(6) If after considering the application the Secretary of State is not satisfied that the applicant is likely to make or, as the case may be, is making an effective contribution to the Adoption Service or, as the case may be, to the Scottish Adoption Service, the Secretary of State shall, subject to section 6 (1) and (2), by notice inform the applicant that his application is refused.

(7) If not withdrawn earlier under section 5, approval given under this section shall last for a period of three years from the date on which it becomes operative, and shall then expire or, in the case of an approved adoption society whose further application for approval is pending at that time, shall expire on the date that application is granted or, as the case may be, refused.

Withdrawal of approval

5.—(1) If, while approval of a body under section 4 is operative, it appears to the Secretary of State that the body is not making an effective contribution to the Adoption Service or, as the case may be, to the Scottish Adoption Service, he shall subject to section 6 (3) and (4) by notice to the body withdraw the approval from a date specified in the notice.

(2) If an approved adoption society fails to provide the Secretary of State with information required by him for the purpose of carrying out his functions under subsection (1), or fails to verify such information in the manner required by him, he may by notice to the society withdraw the approval from a date specified in the notice.

Children Act 1975

(3) Where approval is withdrawn under subsection (1) or (2) or expires the Secretary of State may direct the body concerned to make such arrangements as to children who are in its care and other transitional matters as seem to him expedient.

Procedure on refusal to approve, or withdrawal of approval from, societies

6.—(1) Before notifying a body which has applied for approval that the application is refused in accordance with section 4 (6) the Secretary of State shall serve on the applicant a notice—

(a) setting out the reasons why he proposes to refuse the application;

(b) informing the applicant that he may make representations in writing to the Secretary of State within 28 days of the date of service of the notice.

(2) If any representations are made by the applicant in accordance with subsection (1), the Secretary of State shall give further consideration to the application taking into account those representations.

(3) The Secretary of State shall, before withdrawing approval of an adoption society in accordance with section 5 (1), serve on the society a notice—

(a) setting out the reasons why he proposes to withdraw the approval; and

(b) informing the society that they may make representations in writing to the Secretary of State within 28 days of the date of service of the notice.

(4) If any representations are made by the society in accordance with subsection (3), the Secretary of State shall give further consideration to the withdrawal of approval under section 5 (1) taking into account those representations.

(5) This section does not apply where the Secretary of State, after having considered any representations made by the applicant in accordance with this section, proposes to refuse approval or, as the case may be, to withdraw approval for reasons which have already been communicated to the applicant in a notice under this section.

Inactive or defunct adoption societies

7.—(1) If it appears to the Secretary of State that an approved adoption society, or one in relation to which approval has been withdrawn under section 5 or has expired, is inactive or defunct he may, in relation to any child who is or was in the care of the society, direct what appears to him to be the appropriate local authority to take any such action as might have been taken by the society or by the society jointly with the authority; and if apart from this section the authority would not be entitled to take that action, or would not be entitled to take it without joining the society in the action, it shall be entitled to do so.

(2) Before giving a direction under subsection (1) the Secretary of State shall, if practicable, consult both the society and the authority.

Adoption orders

Adoption orders

8.—(1) An adoption order is an order vesting the parental rights and duties relating to a child in the adopters, made on their application by an authorised court.

(2) The order does not affect the parental rights and duties so far as they relate to any period before the making of the order.

(3) The making of the order operates to extinguish—

(a) any parental right or duty relating to the child which—

540

           (i) is vested in a person (not being one of the adopters) who was the parent or guardian of the child immediately before the making of the order, or

           (ii) is vested in any other person by virtue of the order of any court; and

    (b) any duty arising by virtue of an agreement or the order of a court to make payments, so far as the payments are in respect of the child's maintenance for any period after the making of the order or any other matter comprised in the parental duties and relating to such a period.

(4) Subsection (3) (b) does not apply to a duty arising by virtue of an agreement—

    (a) which constitutes a trust, or

    (b) which expressly provides that the duty is not to be extinguished by the making of an adoption order.

(5) An adoption order may not be made in relation to a child who is or has been married.

(6) An adoption order shall not be made in Scotland in relation to a child who is a minor unless with the consent of the minor; except that where the court is satisfied that the minor is incapable of giving his consent to the making of the order, it may dispense with that consent.

(7) An adoption order may contain such terms and conditions as the court thinks fit.

(8) An adoption order may be made notwithstanding that the child is an adopted child.

(9) Schedule 1 contains for England and Wales further provisions about the effect of adoption and related or comparable provisions about legitimation.

(10) Schedule 2 has effect as respects the status conferred in Scotland by adoption and related matters.

Child to live with adopters before order made

9.—(1) Where—

    (a) the applicant, or one of the applicants, is a parent, step-parent or relative of the child, or

    (b) the child was placed with the applicants by an adoption agency or in pursuance of an order of the High Court,

an adoption order shall not be made unless the child is at least 19 weeks old and at all times during the preceding 13 weeks had his home with the applicants or one of them.

(2) Where subsection (1) does not apply, an adoption order shall not be made unless the child is at least twelve months old and at all times during the preceding twelve months had his home with the applicants or one of them.

(3) An adoption order shall not be made unless the court is satisfied that sufficient opportunities to see the child with the applicant or, in the case of an application by a married couple, both applicants together in the home environment have been afforded—

    (a) where the child was placed with the applicant by an adoption agency, to that agency, or

    (b) in any other case, to the local authority within whose area the home is.

Adoption by married couple

10.—(1) Subject to sections 37 (1) and 53 (1), an adoption order may be made on the application of a married couple where each has

541

attained the age of 21 but an adoption order shall not otherwise be made on the application of more than one person.

(2) An adoption order shall not be made on the application of a married couple unless—

    (*a*) at least one of them is domiciled in a part of the United Kingdom, or in the Channel Islands or the Isle of Man, or

    (*b*) the application is for a Convention adoption order and section 24 is complied with.

(3) Where the application is made to a court in England or Wales and the married couple consist of a parent and step-parent of the child, the court shall dismiss the application if it considers the matter would be better dealt with under section 42 (orders for custody etc.) of the Matrimonial Causes Act 1973.

Adoption by one person

11.—(1) Subject to sections 37 (1) and 53 (1), an adoption order may be made on the application of one person where he has attained the age of 21 and—

    (*a*) is not married, or

    (*b*) is married and the court is satisfied that—

        (i) his spouse cannot be found, or

        (ii) the spouses have separated and are living apart, and the separation is likely to be permanent, or

        (iii) his spouse is by reason of ill health, whether physical or mental, incapable of making an application for an adoption order.

(2) An adoption order shall not be made on the application of one person unless—

    (*a*) he is domiciled in a part of the United Kingdom, or in the Channel Islands or the Isle of Man, or

    (*b*) the application is for a Convention adoption order and section 24 is complied with.

(3) An adoption order shall not be made on the application of the mother or father of the child alone unless the court is satisfied that—

    (*a*) the other natural parent is dead or cannot be found, or

    (*b*) there is some other reason justifying the exclusion of the other natural parent,

and where such an order is made the reason justifying the exclusion of the other natural parent shall be recorded by the court.

(4) Where the application is made to a court in England or Wales and the applicant is a step-parent of the child the court shall dismiss the application if it considers the matter would be better dealt with under section 42 (orders for custody etc.) of the Matrimonial Causes Act 1973.

Parental agreement

12.—(1) An adoption order shall not be made unless—

    (*a*) the child is free for adoption; or

    (*b*) in the case of each parent or guardian of the child the court is satisfied that—

        (i) he freely, and with full understanding of what is involved, agrees unconditionally to the making of the adoption order (whether or not he knows the identity of the applicants), or

        (ii) his agreement to the making of the adoption order should be dispensed with on a ground specified in subsection (2).

(2) The grounds mentioned in subsection (1) (*b*) (ii) are that the parent or guardian—

(*a*) cannot be found or is incapable of giving agreement;

(*b*) is withholding his agreement unreasonably;

(*c*) has persistently failed without reasonable cause to discharge the parental duties in relation to the child;

(*d*) has abandoned or neglected the child;

(*e*) has persistently ill-treated the child;

(*f*) has seriously ill-treated the child (subject to subsection (5)).

(3) Subsection (1) does not apply in any case where the child is not a United Kingdom national and the application for the adoption order is for a Convention adoption order.

(4) Agreement is ineffective for the purposes of subsection (1) (*b*) (i) if given by the mother less than six weeks after the child's birth.

(5) Subsection (2) (*f*) does not apply unless (because of the ill-treatment or for other reasons) the rehabilitation of the child within the household of the parent or guardian is unlikely.

(6) A child is free for adoption if he is the subject of an order under section 14 and the order has not been revoked under section 16.

Religious upbringing of adopted child

13. An adoption agency shall in placing a child for adoption have regard (so far as is practicable) to any wishes of the child's parents and guardians as to the religious upbringing of the child.

Freeing child for adoption

14.—(1) Where, on an application by an adoption agency, an authorised court is satisfied in the case of each parent or guardian of the child that—

(*a*) he freely, and with full understanding of what is involved, agrees generally and unconditionally to the making of an adoption order, or

(*b*) his agreement to the making of an adoption order should be dispensed with on a ground specified in section 12 (2),

the court shall, subject to subsection (5), make an order declaring the child free for adoption.

(2) No application shall be made under subsection (1) unless—

(*a*) it is made with the consent of a parent or guardian of the child, or

(*b*) the adoption agency is applying for dispensation under subsection (1) (*b*) of the agreement of each parent or guardian of the child, and the child is in the care of the adoption agency.

(3) No agreement required under subsection (1) (*a*) shall be dispensed with under subsection (1) (*b*) unless the child is already placed for adoption or the court is satisfied that it is likely that the child will be placed for adoption.

(4) An agreement by the mother of the child is ineffective for the purposes of this section if given less than six weeks after the child's birth.

(5) An order under this section shall not be made in Scotland in relation to a child who is a minor unless with the consent of the child; except that where the court is satisfied that the minor is incapable of giving his consent to the making of the order, it may dispense with that consent.

(6) On the making of an order under this section, the parental rights

and duties relating to the child vest in the adoption agency, and subsections (2) and (3) of section 8 apply as if the order were an adoption order and the agency were the adopters.

(7) Before making an order under this section the court shall satisfy itself that each parent or guardian who can be found has been given an opportunity of making, if he so wishes, a declaration that he prefers not to be involved in future questions concerning the adoption of the child; and any such declaration shall be recorded by the court.

(8) Before making an order under this section in the case of an illegitimate child whose father is not its guardian, the court shall satisfy itself in relation to any person claiming to be the father that either—

(a) he has no intention of applying for custody of the child under section 9 of the Guardianship of Minors Act 1971 or under section 2 of the Illegitimate Children (Scotland) Act 1930, or

(b) if he did apply for custody under either of those sections the application would be likely to be refused.

Progress reports to former parent

15.—(1) This section and section 16 apply to any person (" the former parent ") who was required to be given an opportunity of making a declaration under section 14 (7) but did not do so.

(2) Within the 14 days following the date twelve months after the making of the order under section 14, the adoption agency in which the parental rights and duties were vested on the making of the order, unless it has previously by notice to the former parent informed him that an adoption order has been made in respect of the child, shall by notice to the former parent inform him—

(a) whether an adoption order has been made in respect of the child, and, (if not)

(b) whether the child has his home with a person with whom he has been placed for adoption.

(3) If at the time when the former parent is given notice under subsection (2) an adoption order has not been made in respect of the child, it is thereafter the duty of the adoption agency to give notice to the former parent of the making of an adoption order (if and when made), and meanwhile to give the former parent notice whenever the child is placed for adoption or ceases to have his home with a person with whom he has been placed for adoption.

(4) If at any time the former parent by notice makes a declaration to the adoption agency that he prefers not to be involved in future questions concerning the adoption of the child—

(a) the agency shall secure that the declaration is recorded by the court which made the order under section 14, and

(b) the agency is released from the duty of complying further with subsection (3) as respects that former parent.

Revocation of section 14 order

16.—(1) The former parent, at any time more than twelve months after the making of the order under section 14 when—

(a) no adoption order has been made in respect of the child, and

(b) the child does not have his home with a person with whom he has been placed for adoption,

may apply to the court which made the order for a further order revoking it on the ground that he wishes to resume the parental rights and duties.

(2) While the application is pending the adoption agency having the parental rights and duties shall not place the child for adoption without the leave of the court.

(3) Where an order freeing a child for adoption is revoked under this section—

(a) the parental rights and duties relating to the child are vested in the individual or, as the case may be, the individuals in whom they vested immediately before that order was made;

(b) if the parental rights and duties, or any of them, vested in a local authority or voluntary organisation immediately before the order freeing the child for adoption was made, those rights and duties are vested in the individual, or as the case may be, the individuals in whom they vested immediately before they were vested in the authority or organisation; and

(c) any duty extinguished by virtue of section 8 (3) (b) is forthwith revived,

but the revocation does not affect any right or duty so far as it relates to any period before the date of the revocation.

(4) Subject to subsection (5) if the application is dismissed on the ground that to allow it would contravene the principle embodied in section 3—

(a) the former parent who made the application shall not be entitled to make any further application under subsection (1) in respect of the child, and

(b) the adoption agency is released from the duty of complying further with section 15 (3) as respects that parent.

(5) Subsection (4) (a) shall not apply where the court which dismissed the application gives leave to the former parent to make a further application under subsection (1), but such leave shall not be given unless it appears to the court that because of a change in circumstances or for any other reason it is proper to allow the application to be made.

Care etc. of child on refusal of adoption order

17.—(1) Where on an application for an adoption order in relation to a child under the age of 16 the court refuses to make the adoption order then—

(a) if it appears to the court that there are exceptional circumstances making it desirable that the child should be under the supervision of an independent person, the court may order that the child shall be under the supervision of a specified local authority or under the supervision of a probation officer;

(b) if it appears to the court that there are exceptional circumstances making it impracticable or undesirable for the child to be entrusted to either of the parents or to any other individual, the court may by order commit the child to the care of a specified local authority.

(2) Where the court makes an order under subsection (1) (b) the order may require the payment by either parent to the local authority, while it has the care of the child, of such weekly or other periodical sum towards the maintenance of the child as the court thinks reasonable.

(3) Sections 3 and 4 of the Guardianship Act 1973 (which contain supplementary provisions relating to children who are subject to supervision, or in the care of local authorities, by virtue of orders made under section 2 of that Act) apply in relation to an order under this section as they apply in relation to an order under section 2 of that Act.

(4) In the application of this section to Scotland—

(a) the words " or under the supervision of a probation officer " in subsection (1) (a) do not apply;

(b) subsection (3) does not apply; and

(c) subsections (2), (4) and (5) of section 11 of the Guardianship

Act 1973 apply in relation to an order under this section as they apply in relation to an order under that section.

Need to notify local authority of adoption application

18.—(1) An adoption order shall not be made in respect of a child who was not placed with the applicant by an adoption agency unless the applicant has, at least three months before the date of the order, given notice to the local authority within whose area he has his home of his intention to apply for the adoption order.

(2) On receipt of such a notice the local authority shall investigate the matter and submit to the court a report of their investigation.

(3) Under subsection (2), the local authority shall in particular investigate—

(a) so far as is practicable, the suitability of the applicant, and any other matters relevant to the operation of section 3 in relation to the application; and

(b) whether the child was placed with the applicant in contravention of section 29 of the 1958 Act.

Interim orders

19.—(1) Where on an application for an adoption order the requirements of sections 12 (1) and 18 (1) are complied with the court may postpone the determination of the application and make an order vesting the legal custody of the child in the applicants for a probationary period not exceeding two years upon such terms for the maintenance of the child and otherwise as the court thinks fit.

(2) Where the probationary period specified in an order under subsection (1) is less than two years, the court may by a further order extend the period to a duration not exceeding two years in all.

Guardian ad litem and reporting officer

20.—(1) For the purpose of any application for an adoption order or an order under section 14, 16 or 25, rules shall provide for the appointment, in such cases as are prescribed,—

(a) of a person to act as guardian ad litem of the child upon the hearing of the application, with the duty of safeguarding the interests of the child in the prescribed manner;

(b) of a person to act as reporting officer for the purpose of witnessing agreements to adoption and performing such other duties as the rules may prescribe.

(2) A person who is employed—

(a) in the case of an application for an adoption order, by the adoption agency by whom the child was placed; or

(b) in the case of an application under section 14 by the adoption agency by whom the application was made; or

(c) in the case of an application under section 16 by the adoption agency with the parental rights and duties relating to the child,

shall not be appointed to act as guardian ad litem or reporting officer for the purposes of the application but, subject to that, the same person may if the court thinks fit be both guardian ad litem and reporting officer.

(3) Rules may provide for the reporting officer to be appointed before the application is made.

(4) In relation to Scotland, references in this section to a guardian ad litem shall be construed as references to a curator ad litem.

Hearings of applications etc. in private

21.—(1) Proceedings in the High Court under this Part may be disposed of in chambers.

(2) All proceedings in the county court under this Part shall be heard and determined in camera.

(3) Proceedings in the magistrates' court under this Part shall be domestic proceedings for the purposes of the Magistrates' Courts Act 1952 but section 57 (2) (d) of that Act shall not apply in relation to any proceedings under this Part.

(4) In relation to Scotland, all proceedings before the court under this Part shall be heard and determined in camera unless the court otherwise directs.

Making of order

22.—(1) In the case of—

(a) an application for an adoption order in relation to a child who is not free for adoption;

(b) an application for an order under section 14,

rules shall require every person who can be found and whose agreement or consent to the making of the order is required to be given or dispensed with under this Act to be notified of a date and place where he may be heard on the application and of the fact that, unless he wishes or the court requires, he need not attend.

(2) In the case of an application under section 25 rules shall require every person who can be found, and whose agreement to the making of the order would be required if the application were for an adoption order (other than a Convention adoption order), to be notified as aforesaid.

(3) Where an application for an adoption order relates to a child placed by an adoption agency, the agency shall submit to the court a report on the suitability of the applicants and any other matters relevant to the operation of section 3, and shall assist the court in any manner the court may direct.

(4) The court shall not proceed to hear an application for an adoption order in relation to a child where a previous application for a British adoption order made in relation to the child by the same persons was refused by any court unless—

(a) in refusing the previous application the court directed that this subsection should not apply, or

(b) it appears to the court that because of a change in circumstances or for any other reason it is proper to proceed with the application.

(5) The court shall not make an adoption order in relation to a child unless it is satisfied that the applicants have not, as respects the child, contravened section 50 of the 1958 Act (prohibition of certain payments in relation to adoption).

(6) In the application of this section to Scotland for the reference to hearing an application in subsection (4) there shall be substituted a reference to determining an application.

Transfer of parental rights and duties between adoption agencies

23. On the joint application of an adoption agency in which the parental rights and duties relating to a child who is in Great Britain are vested under section 14 (6) or this section and any other adoption agency, an authorised court may if it thinks fit by order transfer the parental rights and duties to the latter agency.

Convention adoption orders

24.—(1) An adoption order shall be made as a Convention adoption order if the application is for a Convention adoption order and the following conditions are satisfied both at the time of the application and when the order is made.

(2) The child—

    (*a*) must be a United Kingdom national or a national of a Convention country, and

    (*b*) must habitually reside in British territory or a Convention country, and

    (*c*) must not be, or have been, married.

(3) The applicant or applicants and the child must not all be United Kingdom nationals living in British territory.

(4) If the application is by a married couple, either—

    (*a*) each must be a United Kingdom national or a national of a Convention country, and both must habitually reside in Great Britain, or

    (*b*) both must be United Kingdom nationals, and each must habitually reside in British territory or a Convention country.

and if the applicants are nationals of the same Convention country the adoption must not be prohibited by a specified provision (as defined in subsection (8)) of the internal law of that country.

(5) If the application is by one person, either—

    (*a*) he must be a United Kingdom national or a national of a Convention country, and must habitually reside in Great Britain, or

    (*b*) he must be a United Kingdom national, and must habitually reside in British territory or a Convention country,

and if he is a national of a Convention country the adoption must not be prohibited by a specified provision (as defined in subsection (8)) of the internal law of that country.

(6) If the child is not a United Kingdom national the order shall not be made—

    (*a*) except in accordance with the provisions, if any, relating to consents and consultations of the internal law relating to adoption of the Convention country of which the child is a national, and

    (*b*) unless the court is satisfied that each person who consents to the order in accordance with that internal law does so with the full understanding of what is involved.

(7) The reference to consents and consultations in subsection (6) does not include a reference to consent by and consultation with the applicant and members of the applicant's family (including his or her spouse), and for the purposes of subsection (6) consents may be proved in the manner prescribed by rules and the court shall be treated as the authority by whom, under the law mentioned in subsection (6), consents may be dispensed with and the adoption in question may be effected; and where the provisions there mentioned require the attendance before that authority of any person who does not reside in Great Britain, that requirement shall be treated as satisfied for the purposes of subsection (6) if—

    (*a*) that person has been given a reasonable opportunity of communicating his opinion on the adoption in question to the proper officer or clerk of the court, or to an appropriate authority of the country in question, for transmission to the court; and

    (*b*) where he has availed himself of that opportunity, his opinion has been transmitted to the court.

(8) In subsections (4) and (5) "specified provision" means a provision specified in an order of the Secretary of State as one notified

to the Government of the United Kingdom in pursuance of the provisions of the Convention which relate to prohibitions on an adoption contained in the national law of the Convention country in question.

(9) Sections 9 and 10 (1) (ascertainment of nationality, and internal law of foreign country) of the Adoption Act 1968 shall apply with any necessary modifications for the purposes of this section as they apply for the purposes of that Act.

Adoption of children abroad

25.—(1) Where on an application made in relation to a child by a person who is domiciled in England and Wales or Scotland an authorised court is satisfied that he intends to adopt the child under the law of or within the country in which the applicant is domiciled, the court may, subject to the following provisions of this section, make an order vesting in him the parental rights and duties relating to the child.

(2) The provisions of this Part relating to adoption orders, except sections 8 (1), (9) and (10), 10 (2), 11 (2), 14 to 16, 19, 22 (1), 23 and 24, shall apply in relation to orders under this section as they apply in relation to adoption orders subject to the modification that in section 9 (1) for " 19 " and " 13 " there are substituted " 32 " and " 26 " respectively.

(3) Sections 20 to 23 and 24 (4) and (5) of the 1958 Act shall apply in relation to an order under this section as they apply in relation to an adoption order except that any entry in the Registers of Births, the Register of Births or the Adopted Children Register which is required to be marked in consequence of the making of an order under this section, in lieu of being marked with the word " Adopted " or " Re-adopted " (with or without the addition of the word " (Scotland) " or " (England) ") be marked with the words " Proposed Foreign Adoption " or " Proposed Foreign Re-adoption ", as the case may require.

(4) References in Parts III and IV of the 1958 Act to an adoption order include references to an order under this section, and references in this Act and in the 1958 Act to the placing of children for adoption or to the making of arrangements for adoption include references to the placing of children for adoption abroad or the making of arrangements for adoption abroad.

Amendments of Adoption Act 1958

Obtaining of birth certificate by adopted person

26.—(1) In section 20 of the 1958 Act, in subsection (5), after the word " except " there are inserted the words " in accordance with section 20A of this Act or ".

(2) The following section is inserted in the 1958 Act after section 20:—

Disclosure of birth records of adopted persons

20A.—(1) Subject to subsections (4) and (6) of this section the Registrar General shall on an application made in the prescribed manner by an adopted person a record of whose birth is kept by the Registrar General and who has attained the age of 18 years supply to that person on payment of the prescribed fee (if any) such information as is necessary to enable that person to obtain a certified copy of the record of his birth.

(2) On an application made in the prescribed manner by an

adopted person under the age of 18 years a record of whose birth is kept by the Registrar General and who is intending to be married in England or Wales, and on payment of the prescribed fee (if any), the Registrar General shall inform the applicant whether or not it appears from information contained in the registers of live births or other records that the applicant and the person whom he intends to marry may be within the prohibited degrees of relationship for the purposes of the Marriage Act 1949.

(3) It shall be the duty of the Registrar General and each local authority and approved adoption society to provide counselling for adopted persons who apply for information under subsection (1) of this section.

(4) Before supplying any information to an applicant under subsection (1) of this section, the Registrar General shall inform the applicant that counselling services are available to him—

(a) at the General Register Office; or

(b) from the local authority for the area where the applicant is at the time the application is made; or

(c) from the local authority for the area where the court sat which made the adoption order relating to the applicant; or

(d) if the applicant's adoption was arranged by an adoption society which is approved under section 4 of the Children Act 1975, from that society.

(5) If the applicant chooses to receive counselling from a local authority or an adoption society under subsection (4) the Registrar General shall send to the authority or society of the applicant's choice the information to which the applicant is entitled under subsection (1).

(6) The Registrar General shall not supply a person who was adopted before the date on which the Children Act 1975 was passed with any information under subsection (1) of this section unless that person has attended an interview with a counsellor either at the General Register Office or in pursuance of arrangements made by the local authority or adoption society from whom the applicant is entitled to receive counselling in accordance with subsection (4).

(7) In this section " prescribed " means prescribed by regulations made by the Registrar General.".

Counselling in Scotland for adopted person seeking information about his birth

27. In section 22 of the 1958 Act—

(a) the following words are added at the end of subsection (4)—

" or a local authority or an approved adoption society which is providing counselling, under subsection (4A) of this section, for that adopted person.";

(b) the following subsections are inserted after subsection (4)—

" (4A) Where the Registrar General for Scotland furnishes an adopted person with information under subsection (4) of this section, he shall advise that person that counselling services are available—

(a) from the local authority for the area where the adopted person lives; or

(b) if the adopted person's adoption was arranged by an adoption society which is approved under section 4 of the Children Act 1975, from that society,

and it shall be the duty of such local authority and approved adoption society to provide counselling for adopted persons who have been furnished with information under subsection

(4) and who apply to them for counselling in respect of that information.

(4B) Where an adopted person has arranged to receive counselling under subsection (4A), the Registrar General for Scotland shall, on receipt of a request from the local authority or adoption society which is providing that counselling, and on payment of the appropriate fee, send to the authority or society an extract of the entry relating to the adopted person in the Register of Births.".

Restriction on arranging adoption and placing of children

28. In section 29 of the 1958 Act—

(a) the following subsection is substituted for subsections (1) and (2)—

" (1) A person other than an adoption agency shall not make arrangements for the adoption of a child, or place a child for adoption, unless—

(a) the proposed adopter is a relative of the child, or

(b) he is acting in pursuance of an order of the High Court ";

(b) the following subsections are inserted after subsection (1)—

" (2) An adoption society approved under the Children Act 1975 only as respects England and Wales shall not act as an adoption society in Scotland, except to the extent that it considers it necessary to do so in the interests of a person mentioned in section 1 (1) of that Act.

(2A) An adoption society approved under the Children Act 1975 only as respects Scotland shall not act as an adoption society in England or Wales, except to the extent that it considers it necessary to do so in the interests of a person mentioned in section 1 (1) of that Act.";

(c) in subsection (3)—

(i) the following is inserted after paragraph (b)—

" or

(c) receives a child placed with him in contravention of subsection (1) of this section ";

(ii) for the words " six months " there are substituted the words " three months " and for the words " one hundred pounds " there are substituted the words " £400 ";

(d) the following subsection is substituted for subsection (5)—

" (5) Section 17 of the Children Act 1975 shall apply where a person is convicted of a contravention of subsection (1) of this section as it applies where an application for an adoption order is refused.".

Restrictions on removal of child pending adoption

29. The following sections are substituted for section 34 of the 1958 Act—

" Restrictions on removal where adoption agreed or application made under section 14 of Children Act 1975

34.—(1) While an application for an adoption order is pending in a case where a parent or guardian of the child has agreed to the making of the adoption order (whether or not he knows the identity of the applicant), the parent or guardian is not entitled, against the will of the person with whom the child has his home, to remove the child from the custody of that person except with the leave of the court.

(2) While an application is pending for an order under section 14 of the Children Act 1975 and—

(a) the child is in the care of the adoption agency making the application, and

(b) the application was not made with the consent of each parent or guardian of the child,

no parent or guardian of the child who did not consent to the application is entitled, against the will of the person with whom the child has his home, to remove the child from the custody of that person except with the leave of the court.

(3) Any person who contravenes subsection (1) or (2) of this section commits an offence and shall be liable on summary conviction to imprisonment for a term not exceeding three months or a fine not exceeding £400 or both.

Restrictions on removal where applicant has provided home for five years

34A.—(1) While an application for an adoption order in respect of a child made by the person with whom the child has had his home for the five years preceding the application is pending, no person is entitled, against the will of the applicant, to remove the child from the applicant's custody except with the leave of the court or under authority conferred by any enactment or on the arrest of the child.

(2) Where a person (" the prospective adopter ") gives notice in writing to the local authority within whose area he has his home that he intends to apply for an adoption order in respect of a child who for the preceding five years has had his home with the prospective adopter, no person is entitled, against the will of the prospective adopter, to remove the child from the prospective adopter's custody, except with the leave of a court or under authority conferred by any enactment or on the arrest of the child, before—

(a) the prospective adopter applies for the adoption order, or

(b) the period of three months from the receipt of the notice by the local authority expires,

whichever occurs first.

(3) In any case where subsection (1) or (2) of this section applies, and—

(a) the child was in the care of a local authority before he began to have his home with the applicant or, as the case may be, the prospective adopter, and

(b) the child remains in the care of the authority,

the authority shall not remove the child from the actual custody of the applicant or of the prospective adopter except in accordance with sections 35 and 36 of this Act or with the leave of the court.

(4) A local authority which receives such notice as aforesaid in respect of a child whom the authority know to be in the care of another local authority or of a voluntary organisation shall, not more than seven days after the receipt of the notice, inform that other authority or the organisation in writing that they have received the notice.

(5) Subsection (2) of this section does not apply to any further notice served by the prospective adopter on any local authority in respect of the same child during the period referred to in paragraph (b) of that subsection or within 28 days after its expiry.

(6) Any person who contravenes subsection (1) or (2) of this section commits an offence and shall be liable on summary conviction to imprisonment for a term not exceeding three months or a fine not exceeding £400 or both.

(7) The Secretary of State may by order made by statutory instrument a draft of which has been approved by each House of Parliament amend subsection (1) or (2) of this section to substitute a different period for the period of five years mentioned in that sub-section (or the period which, by a previous order under this subsection, was substituted for that period).

(8) In relation to Scotland, subsection (3) of this section does not apply where the removal of the child is authorised, in terms of Part III of the Social Work (Scotland) Act 1968, by a justice of the peace or a children's hearing.".

Return of child taken away in breach of section 34 or 34A of 1958 Act

30.—(1) An authorised court may on the application of a person from whose custody a child has been removed in breach of section 34 or 34A of the 1958 Act order the person who has so removed the child to return the child to the applicant.

(2) An authorised court may on the application of a person who has reasonable grounds for believing that another person is intending to remove a child from the applicant's custody in breach of section 34 or 34A of the 1958 Act by order direct that other person not to remove the child from the applicant's custody in breach of the said section 34 or 34A.

(3) If, in the case of an order made by the High Court under sub-section (1), the High Court or, in the case of an order made by a county court under subsection (1), a county court is satisfied that the child has not been returned to the applicant, the court may make an order authorising an officer of the court to search such premises as may be specified in the order for the child and, if the officer finds the child, to return the child to the applicant.

(4) If a justice of the peace is satisfied by information on oath that there are reasonable grounds for believing that a child to whom an order under subsection (1) relates is in premises specified in the information, he may issue a search warrant authorising a constable to search the premises for the child; and if a constable acting in pursuance of a warrant under this section finds the child, he shall return the child to the person on whose application the order under subsection (1) was made.

(5) An order under subsection (3) may be enforced in like manner as a warrant for committal.

(6) Subsections (3), (4) and (5) do not apply to Scotland.

Return of child on refusal of adoption order

31. In section 35 of the 1958 Act, the following subsection is inserted after subsection (5)—

" (5A) Where an application for an adoption order is refused the court may, if it thinks fit, at any time before the expiry of the period of seven days mentioned in subsection (3) of this section order that period to be extended to a duration, not exceeding six weeks, specified in the order.".

Payment of allowances to adopters

32. In section 50 (prohibition of certain payments in relation to adoption) of the 1958 Act, the following subsections are inserted at the end—

" (4) If an adoption agency submits to the Secretary of State a scheme for the payment by the agency of allowances to persons who have adopted or intend to adopt a child where arrangements for the adoption were made, or are to be made, by that agency, and the Secretary of State approves the scheme, this section shall not apply to any payment made in accordance with the scheme.

(5) The Secretary of State, in the case of a scheme approved by him under subsection (4) of this section, may at any time—

(a) make, or approve the making by the agency of, alterations to the scheme;

(b) revoke the scheme.

(6) The Secretary of State shall, within seven years of the date on which section 32 of the Children Act 1975 comes into force and, thereafter, every five years, publish a report on the operation of the schemes since that date or since the publication of the last report.

(7) Subject to the following subsection, subsection (4) of this section shall expire on the seventh anniversary of the date on which it comes into force.

(8) The Secretary of State may by order made by statutory instrument at any time before the said anniversary, repeal subsection (7) of this section.

(9) An order under subsection (8) of this section shall not be made unless—

(a) a report has been published under subsection (6) of this section, and

(b) a draft of the order has been laid before Parliament and approved by resolution of each House.

(10) Notwithstanding the expiry of subsection (4) of this section or the revocation of a scheme approved under this section, subsection (1) of this section shall not apply in relation to any payment made, whether before or after the expiry of subsection (4) or the revocation of the scheme, in accordance with a scheme which was approved under this section to a person to whom such payments were made, where the scheme was not revoked, before the expiry of subsection (4) or, if the scheme was revoked, before the date of its revocation.".

PART II

CUSTODY

Custodianship orders

Custodianship orders

33.—(1) An authorised court may on the application of one or more persons qualified under subsection (3) make an order vesting the legal custody of a child in the applicant or, as the case may be, in one or more of the applicants if the child is in England or Wales at the time the application is made.

(2) An order under subsection (1) may be referred to as a custodianship order, and the person in whom legal custody of the child is vested under the order may be referred to as the custodian of the child.

(3) The persons qualified to apply for a custodianship order are—

(a) a relative or step-parent of the child—

(i) who applies with the consent of a person having legal custody of the child, and

(ii) with whom the child has had his home for the three months preceding the making of the application;

(b) any person—
> (i) who applies with the consent of a person having legal custody of the child, and
>
> (ii) with whom the child has had his home for a period or periods before the making of the application which amount to at least twelve months and include the three months preceding the making of the application;

(c) any person with whom the child has had his home for a period or periods before the making of the application which amount to at least three years and include the three months preceding the making of the application.

(4) The mother or father of the child is not qualified under any paragraph of subsection (3).

(5) A step-parent of the child is not qualified under any paragraph of subsection (3) if in proceedings for divorce or nullity of marriage the child was named in an order made under paragraph (b) or (c) of section 41 (1) (arrangements for welfare of children of family) of the Matrimonial Causes Act 1973.

(6) If no person has legal custody of the child, or the applicant himself has legal custody or the person with legal custody cannot be found, paragraphs (a) and (b) of subsection (3) apply with the omission of sub-paragraph (i).

(7) The Secretary of State may by order a draft of which has been approved by each House of Parliament amend subsection (3) (c) to substitute a different period for the period of three years mentioned in that paragraph (or the period which, by a previous order under this subsection, was substituted for that period).

(8) Subsection (5) does not apply—
(a) if the parent other than the one the step-parent married is dead or cannot be found, or
(b) if the order referred to in subsection (5) was made under subsection (1) (c) of section 41 of the Matrimonial Causes Act 1973 and it has since been determined that the child was not a child of the family to whom that section applied.

(9) For the avoidance of doubt, it is hereby declared that the provisions of section 1 of the Guardianship of Minors Act 1971 apply to applications made under this Part of this Act.

(10) This section and sections 34 to 46 do not apply to Scotland.

Access and maintenance

34.—(1) An authorised court may, on making a custodianship order or while a custodianship order is in force, by order—
(a) on the application of the child's mother or father, make such provision as it thinks fit requiring access to the child to be given to the applicant;
(b) on the application of the custodian, require the child's mother or father (or both) to make to the applicant such periodical payments towards the maintenance of the child as it thinks reasonable;
(c) on the application of the child's mother or father, revoke an order requiring the applicant to contribute towards the child's maintenance made (otherwise than under this section) by any court;
(d) on the application of the child's mother or father or the custodian, vary an order made (otherwise than under this section) by any court requiring the mother or father to contribute towards the child's maintenance—

       (i) by altering the amount of the contributions;

       (ii) by substituting the custodian for the person to whom the contributions were ordered to be made.

(2) References in subsection (1) to the child's mother or father include any person in relation to whom the child was treated as a child of the family (as defined in section 52 (1) of the Matrimonial Causes Act 1973) but the court in deciding whether to make an order under subsection (1) (*b*) against a person who is not the child's mother or father shall have regard (among the circumstances of the case)—

    (*a*) to whether that person had assumed any responsibility for the child's maintenance and, if he did, to the extent to which and the basis on which he did so, and to the length of time during which he discharged that responsibility;

    (*b*) to the liability of any other person to maintain that child.

(3) No order shall be made under subsection (1) (*b*) requiring the father of an illegitimate child to make any payments to the child's custodian.

(4) Subsections (2), (3), (4) and (6) (orders as to supervision, local authority care, maintenance etc. of children) of section 2 of the Guardianship Act 1973 and sections 3 and 4 of that Act (supplementary provisions) shall apply to an application for a custodianship order as they apply to an application under section 9 of the Guardianship of Minors Act 1971, subject to the following modifications, that is to say—

    (*a*) in section 2 (2) (*b*) and (4) (*a*) of the Guardianship Act 1973 any reference to a parent of the minor to whom the order relates shall be construed as including a reference to any other individual;

    (*b*) section 3 (3) of that Act shall have effect as if the words " or the custodian " were inserted after the words " application of either parent ".

(5) A local authority may make contributions to a custodian towards the cost of the accommodation and maintenance of the child, except where the custodian is the husband or wife of a parent of the child.

Revocation and variation of orders

35.—(1) An authorised court may by order revoke a custodianship order on the application of—

    (*a*) the custodian, or

    (*b*) the mother or father, or a guardian, of the child, or

    (*c*) any local authority in England or Wales.

(2) The court shall not proceed to hear an application made by any person for the revocation of a custodianship order where a previous such application made by the same person was refused by that or any other court unless—

    (*a*) in refusing the previous application the court directed that this subsection should not apply, or

    (*b*) it appears to the court that because of a change in circumstances or for any other reason it is proper to proceed with the application.

(3) The custodian of a child may apply to an authorised court for the revocation or variation of any order made under section 34 in respect of that child.

(4) Any other person on whose application an order under section 34 was made, or who was required by such an order to contribute towards the maintenance of the child, may apply to an authorised court for the revocation or variation of that order.

(5) Any order made under section 34 in respect of a child who is the

subject of a custodianship order shall cease to have effect on the revocation of the custodianship order.

(6) A custodianship order made in respect of a child, and any order made under section 34 in respect of the child, shall cease to have effect when the child attains the age of 18 years.

Care etc. of child on revocation of custodianship order

36.—(1) Before revoking a custodianship order the court shall ascertain who would have legal custody of the child, if, on the revocation of the custodianship order, no further order were made under this section.

(2) If the child would not be in the legal custody of any person, the court shall, if it revokes the custodianship order, commit the care of the child to a specified local authority.

(3) If there is a person who would have legal custody of the child on the revocation of the custodianship order, the court shall consider whether it is desirable in the interests of the welfare of the child for the child to be in the legal custody of that person and—

(a) if the court is of the opinion that it would not be so desirable, it shall on revoking the custodianship order commit the care of the child to a specified local authority;

(b) if it is of the opinion that while it is desirable for the child to be in the legal custody of that person, it is also desirable in the interests of the welfare of the child for him to be under the supervision of an independent person, the court shall, on revoking the custodianship order, order that the child shall be under the supervision of a specified local authority or of a probation officer.

(4) Before exercising its functions under this section the court shall, unless it has sufficient information before it for the purpose, request—

(a) a local authority to arrange for an officer of the authority, or

(b) a probation officer,

to make to the court a report, orally or in writing, on the desirability of the child returning to the legal custody of any individual, and it shall be the duty of the local authority or probation officer to comply with the request.

(5) Where the court makes an order under subsection (3) (a) the order may require the payment by either parent to the local authority, while it has the care of the child, of such weekly or other periodical sum towards the maintenance of the child as the court thinks reasonable.

(6) Sections 3 and 4 of the Guardianship Act 1973 (which contain supplementary provisions relating to children who are subject to supervision, or in the care of local authority, by virtue of orders made under section 2 of that Act) apply in relation to an order under this section as they apply in relation to an order under section 2 of that Act.

(7) Subsections (2) to (6) of section 6 of the Guardianship Act 1973 shall apply in relation to reports which are requested by magistrates' courts under this section as they apply to reports under subsection (1) of that section.

Custodianship order on application for adoption or guardianship

37.—(1) Where on an application for an adoption order by a relative of the child or by the husband or wife of the mother or father of the child, whether alone or jointly with his or her spouse, the requirements of section 12 or, where the application is for a Convention adoption order, section 24 (6) are satisfied, but the court is satisfied—

(a) that the child's welfare would not be better safeguarded and

557

promoted by the making of adoption order in favour of the applicant, than it would be by the making of a custodianship order in his favour, and

(b) that it would be appropriate to make a custodianship order in the applicant's favour,

the court shall direct the application to be treated as if it had been made by the applicant under section 33, but if the application was made jointly by the father or mother of the child and his or her spouse, the court shall direct the application to be treated as if made by the father's wife or the mother's husband alone.

(2) Where on an application for an adoption order made—

(a) by a person who is neither a relative of the child nor the husband or wife of the mother or father of the child; or

(b) by a married couple neither of whom falls within paragraph (a),

the said requirements are satisfied but the court is of opinion that it would be more appropriate to make a custodianship order in favour of the applicant, it may direct the application to be treated as if it had been made by the applicant under section 33.

(3) Where on an application under section 9 (orders for custody and maintenance on application of mother or father) of the Guardianship of Minors Act 1971 the court is of opinion that legal custody should be given to a person other than the mother or father, it may direct the application to be treated as if it had been made by that person under section 33.

(4) Where a direction is given under this section the applicant shall be treated (if such is not the case) as if he were qualified to apply for a custodianship order and this Part, except section 40, shall have effect accordingly.

(5) Subsection (1) does not apply to an application made by a step-parent whether alone or jointly with another person in any case where the step-parent is prevented by section 33 (5) from being qualified to apply for a custodianship order in respect of the child.

(6) Subsections (1) and (2) do not apply to an application for an adoption order made by the child's mother or father alone.

Disputes between joint custodians

38. If two persons have a parental right or duty vested in them jointly by a custodianship order or by virtue of section 44 (2) but cannot agree on its exercise or performance, either of them may apply to an authorised court, and the court may make such order regarding the exercise of the right or performance of the duty as it thinks fit.

Reports by local authorities and probation officers

39.—(1) A court dealing with an application made under this Part, or an application which is treated as if made under section 33, may request—

(a) a local authority to arrange for an officer of the authority, or

(b) a probation officer,

to make to the court a report, orally or in writing, with respect to any specified matter which appears to the court to be relevant to the application, and it shall be the duty of the local authority or probation officer to comply with the request.

(2) Subsections (2) to (6) of section 6 of the Guardianship Act 1973 shall apply in relation to reports which are requested by magistrates' courts under this section as they apply to reports under subsection (1) of that section.

Notice of application to be given to local authority

40.—(1) A custodianship order shall not be made unless the applicant has given notice of the application for the order to the local authority in whose area the child resides within the seven days following the making of the application, or such extended period as the court or local authority may allow.

(2) On receipt of a notice given by the applicant under subsection (1) the local authority shall arrange for an officer of the authority to make a report to the court (so far as is practicable) on the matters prescribed under subsection (3) and on any other matter which he considers to be relevant to the application.

(3) The Secretary of State shall by regulations prescribe matters which are to be included in a report under subsection (2) and, in particular, but without prejudice to the generality of the foregoing, the prescribed matters shall include—

   (a) the wishes and feelings of the child having regard to his age and understanding and all other matters relevant to the operation of section 1 (principle on which questions relating to custody are to be decided) of the Guardianship of Minors Act 1971 in relation to the application;

   (b) the means and suitability of the applicant;

   (c) information of a kind specified in the regulations relating to members of the applicant's household;

   (d) the wishes regarding the application, and the means, of the mother and father of the child.

(4) Subsections (2), (3) and (3A) of section 6 of the Guardianship Act 1973 shall apply to a report under this section which is submitted to a magistrates' court.

Restriction on removal of child where applicant has provided home for three years

41.—(1) While an application for a custodianship order in respect of a child made by the person with whom the child has at the time the application is made had his home for a period (whether continuous or not) amounting to at least three years is pending, another person is not entitled, against the will of the applicant, to remove the child from the applicant's custody except with the leave of a court or under authority conferred by any enactment or on the arrest of the child.

(2) In any case where subsection (1) applies, and

   (a) the child was in the care of a local authority before he began to have his home with the applicant, and

   (b) the child remains in the care of a local authority,

the authority in whose care the child is shall not remove the child from the applicant's custody except with the applicant's consent or the leave of a court.

(3) Any person who contravenes subsection (1) commits an offence and shall be liable on summary conviction to imprisonment for a term not exceeding three months or a fine not exceeding £400 or both.

(4) The Secretary of State may by order a draft of which has been approved by each House of Parliament amend subsection (1) to substitute a different period for the period mentioned in that subsection (or the period which, by a previous order under this subsection, was substituted for that period).

Return of child taken away in breach of section 41

42.—(1) An authorised court may on the application of a person from whose custody a child has been removed in breach of section 41 order the person who has so removed the child to return the child to the applicant.

(2) An authorised court may on the application of a person who has reasonable grounds for believing that another person is intending to remove a child from the applicant's custody in breach of section 41 by order direct that other person not to remove the child from the applicant's custody in breach of that section.

(3) If, in the case of an order made by the High Court under subsection (1), the High Court or, in the case of an order made by a county court under subsection (1), a county court is satisfied that the child has not been returned to the applicant, the court may make an order authorising an officer of the court to search such premises as may be specified in the order for the child and, if the officer finds the child, to return the child to the applicant.

(4) If a justice of the peace is satisfied by information on oath that there are reasonable grounds for believing that a child to whom an order under subsection (1) relates is in premises specified in the information, he may issue a search warrant authorising a constable to search the premises for the child; and if a constable acting in pursuance of a warrant under this section finds the child, he shall return the child to the person on whose application the order under subsection (1) was made.

(5) An order under subsection (3) may be enforced in like manner as a warrant for committal.

Enforcement of orders made by magistrates' courts

43.—(1) If at a time when the custodian is entitled to actual custody of the child by virtue of a custodianship order made by a magistrates' court any other person has actual custody of him, a copy of the custodianship order may be served on that person and thereupon the order may, without prejudice to any other remedy open to the custodian, be enforced under section 54 (3) of the Magistrates' Courts Act 1952 as if it were an order of a magistrates' court requiring that person to give up the child to the custodian.

(2) Any person for the time being under an obligation to make payments in pursuance of any order for the payment of money made by a magistrates' court under section 34 shall give notice of any change of address to such person (if any) as may be specified in the order; and if he fails without reasonable excuse to give such a notice he commits an offence and shall be liable on summary conviction to a fine not exceeding £10.

(3) An order for the payment of money made by a magistrates' court under section 34 may be enforced in like manner as an affiliation order, and the enactments relating to affiliation orders shall apply accordingly with the necessary modifications.

Effect of custodianship order on existing custody

44.—(1) While a custodianship order has effect in relation to a child the right of any person other than the custodian to legal custody of the child is suspended, but, subject to any further order made by any court, revives on the revocation of the custodianship order.

(2) Subsection (1) does not apply where the person already having custody is a parent of the child and the person who becomes custodian under the order is the husband or wife of the parent; and in such a case the spouses have the legal custody jointly.

Affiliation order on application by custodian

45.—(1) Where a custodianship order subsists in respect of an illegitimate child, and no affiliation order relating to the child has been made under the Affiliation Proceedings Act 1957, the custodian of the child may apply to a justice of the peace acting for the petty sessions area in which the child or the child's mother resides for a summons to be served under section 1 of that Act.

(2) The court shall proceed on the application as on a complaint under that section, but the person entitled to any payments under an affiliation order made on the application shall be the custodian.

(3) An application may not be made under subsection (1)—

    (a) if the custodian is married to the child's mother, or

    (b) more than three years after the custodianship order was made.

Procedure in magistrates' courts

46.—(1) It is hereby declared that any jurisdiction conferred on a magistrates' court by virtue of this Part is exercisable notwithstanding that the proceedings are brought by or against a person residing outside England and Wales.

(2) A magistrates' court may, subject to subsection (3), proceed on an application for an order under this Part notwithstanding that the defendant has not been served with the summons, and rules may prescribe matters as to which the court is to be satisfied before proceeding in such a case.

(3) A magistrates' court shall not—

    (a) make an order under this Part requiring a person to make payments towards the maintenance of a child, or

    (b) vary an order under this Part so as to increase a person's liability to make payments towards the maintenance of a child,

unless the person has been served with the summons.

(4) Rules may make provision as to the persons who are to be made defendants to a complaint for an order under this Part, and where there are two or more defendants to such a complaint the power of the court under section 55 (1) of the Magistrates' Courts Act 1952 (power to award costs etc.) shall be deemed to include power, whatever adjudication the court makes, to order any of the parties to pay the whole or part of the costs of all or any of the parties.

(5) In this section, " rules " means rules made under section 15 of the Justices of the Peace Act 1949.

Custody in Scotland

Granting of custody

47.—(1) Without prejudice to any existing enactment or rule of law conferring a—

    (a) right to apply for custody of a child;

    (b) power to grant custody of a child;

any relative, step-parent or foster parent of the child is qualified to apply for, and subject to subsection (2) may be granted, such custody in the same manner as any person so qualified before the commencement of this Act.

(2) Except in the case of an application under section 2 of the Illegitimate Children (Scotland) Act 1930, custody of a child shall not be granted in any proceedings to a person other than a parent or guardian of the child unless that person—

    (a) being a relative or step-parent of the child, has the consent of a parent or guardian of the child and has had care and possession of the child for the three months preceding the making of the application for custody; or

    (b) has the consent of a parent or guardian of the child and has had care and possession of the child for a period or periods, before such application, which amounted to at least twelve months and included the three months preceding such application; or

(*c*) has had care and possession of the child for a period or periods before such application which amounted to at least three years and included the three months preceding such application; or

(*d*) while not falling within paragraph (*a*), (*b*) or (*c*), can show cause, having regard to section 1 of the Guardianship of Infants Act 1925 (the principle on which questions relating to custody, upbringing etc. of children are to be decided) why an order should be made awarding him custody of the child.

(3) Nothing in this section shall prejudice any ancillary power of the court in any proceedings relative to custody.

(4) The Secretary of State may by order a draft of which has been approved by each House of Parliament amend subsection (2) (*c*) to substitute a different period for the period of three years mentioned in that paragraph (or the period which by a previous order under this subsection was substituted for that period).

(5) In relation to a grant of custody to which this section applies,

(*a*) " guardian " has the same meaning as in the 1958 Act;

(*b*) " foster parent " means a person who, at the commencement of the proceedings in which the grant is made, has had care and possession of the child for a period or periods amounting to at least twelve months, whether or not that person continues to have care and possession of the child;

(*c*) " relative " has the same meaning as in the 1958 Act, except that, where the child is illegitimate, " relative " does not include the father of the child.

(6) The form and manner of any consent required in terms of subsection (2) (*a*) or (*b*) may be prescribed by act of sederunt.

Miscellaneous provisions relative to custody

48.—(1) A person making an application relating to the custody of a child shall, so far as practicable and in such manner as may be prescribed by act of sederunt, give notice of that application to each known parent of the child, and for this purpose the father of an illegitimate child shall be regarded as a parent of the child.

(2) Any order made by virtue of this Part of this Act may be varied or discharged by a subsequent order, either by the Court *ex proprio motu* or on the application of any person concerned.

(3) In section 11 (1) of the Guardianship Act 1973, for the words from " Where an application " to " relates to the custody of a child " there is substituted " Where an application relating to the custody of a child, other than an application to which Part II of the Matrimonial Proceedings (Children) Act 1958 applies, is made to a court ".

(4) In section 12 (2) (*a*) of the Guardianship Act 1973, for the words from " Where an application " to " by virtue of section 11 of this Act " there is substituted " Where any application, other than one to which Part II of the Matrimonial Proceedings (Children) Act 1958 applies, is made to a court for custody of a child or for the variation or discharge of any order (including an order made by virtue of section 11 above) relating to the custody of a child ".

Notice to local authority of certain custody applications

49.—(1) Where an applicant for custody of a child is a relative, step-parent or foster parent of the child, an order awarding custody to that applicant shall not except on cause shown be made unless the applicant—

(a) in any case where at the time of the application he resided in Scotland, has, within the seven days following the making of the application, given notice thereof to the local authority within whose area he resided at that time;

(b) in any other case, has within such time as the court may direct given, to such local authority in Scotland as the court may specify, notice of the making of the application.

(2) On receipt of a notice under subsection (1) the local authority shall investigate and report to the court on all the circumstances of the child and on the proposed arrangements for the care and upbringing of the child.

(3) Paragraphs (b) and (c) of subsection (2) of section 12 of the Guardianship Act 1973 shall apply in relation to an investigation and report in terms of this section as they apply in relation to an investigation and report in terms of paragraph (a) of subsection (2) of that section.

Payments towards maintenance of children

50. Without prejudice to any existing powers and duties to make payments in respect of the maintenance of children, where custody of a child has been awarded to a person other than a parent of the child any local authority may make to that person payments for or towards the maintenance of the child.

Restriction on removal of child where applicant has provided home for three years

51.—(1) Where a person has applied for custody of a child, it shall be an offence, except with the authority of a court or under authority conferred by any enactment or on the arrest of the child, to remove the child from the custody of the applicant against the will of the applicant if—

(a) the child has been in the care and possession of that person for a period or periods before the making of the application which amount to at least three years; and

(b) the application is pending in any court.

(2) In any case where subsection (1) applies, and

(a) the child was in the care of a local authority before he began to have his home with the applicant, and

(b) the child remains in the care of a local authority,

the authority in whose care the child is shall not remove the child from the applicant's custody except—

(i) with the applicant's consent;

(ii) with the leave of a court; or

(iii) with the authority, in terms of Part III of the Social Work (Scotland) Act 1968, of a justice of the peace or a children's hearing.

(3) Any person who contravenes the provisions of subsection (1) commits an offence and shall be liable on summary conviction to imprisonment for a term not exceeding three months or a fine not exceeding £400 or both.

(4) The Secretary of State may by order, a draft of which has been approved by each House of Parliament, amend subsection (1) to substitute a different period for the period mentioned in that subsection (or for the period which, by a previous order under this subsection, was substituted for that period).

Return of child taken away in breach of section 51

52. A court in which an application for custody of a child is pending may—

(*a*) on the application of a person from whose custody the child has been removed in breach of section 51, order the person who has so removed the child to return the child to the applicant;

(*b*) on the application of a person who has reasonable grounds for believing that another person is intending to remove the child from the applicant's custody in breach of section 51, by order direct that other person not to remove the child from the applicant's custody in breach of that section.

Custody order on application for adoption in Scotland

53.—(1) Without prejudice to the provisions of section 19 (power to make an interim order giving custody), where on an application for an adoption order in respect of a child the applicant is a person qualified to apply for custody of the child, and the court is of opinion—

(*a*) in the case of an applicant who is a relative of the child or a husband or wife of the mother or father of the child (whether applying alone or jointly with his or her spouse)—

(i) that the child's welfare would not be better safeguarded and promoted by the making of an adoption order in favour of the applicant than it would be by the making of a custody order in his favour; and

(ii) that it would be appropriate to make a custody order in favour of the applicant; or

(*b*) in any other case, that the making of a custody order in favour of the applicant would be more appropriate than the making of an adoption order in his favour,

the court shall direct that the application is to be treated as if it had been made for custody of the child; but where such a direction is made the court shall not cease to have jurisdiction by reason only that it would not have had jurisdiction to hear an application by the applicant for custody of the child.

(2) In the application of this Part of this Act to any case where a direction under subsection (1) has been made—

(*a*) for references in section 47 (2) to the making of an application for custody there shall be substituted references to the making of an application for an adoption order;

(*b*) for the references in section 49 and paragraph (*a*) of subsection (1) of section 51 to the making of an application there shall be substituted references to the making of a direction in terms of subsection (1) of this section;

(*c*) in section 51 (1) for the words " for custody of " there shall be substituted the words " for an adoption order in respect of ".

(3) For the purposes of section 11 of the Guardianship Act 1973, any application in respect of which a direction has been made under subsection (1) of this section, is an application for custody of a child.

Jurisdiction of Scottish courts in certain applications for custody

54.—(1) Without prejudice to any existing grounds of jurisdiction, the court shall have jurisdiction in proceedings for custody of a child if at the time of application for such custody—

(*a*) the child resides in Scotland; and

(*b*) the child is domiciled in England and Wales; and

(*c*) the person applying for custody is a person qualified, in terms of subsections (3) to (8) of section 33 of this Act, to apply in England or Wales for a custodianship order in respect of the child.

(2) For the purposes of this section, " the court " means—
    (a) the Court of Session; or
    (b) the sheriff court of the sheriffdom within which the child resides.

Interpretation and extent of sections 47 to 55

55.—(1) In sections 47 to 54 " child " means a person under the age of sixteen.

(2) Sections 47 to 54 and this section apply to Scotland only.

PART III

CARE

Children in care of local authorities

Restriction on removal of child from care

56.—(1) In section 1 of the Children Act 1948, the following subsections are inserted after subsection (3)—

" (3A) Except in relation to an act done—
    (a) with the consent of the local authority, or
    (b) by a parent or guardian of the child who has given the local authority not less than 28 days' notice of his intention to do it,

subsection (8) (penalty for taking away a child in care) of section 3 of this Act shall apply to a child in the care of a local authority under this section (notwithstanding that no resolution is in force under section 2 of this Act with respect to the child) if he has been in the care of that local authority throughout the preceding six months; and for the purposes of the application of paragraph (b) of that subsection in such a case a parent or guardian of the child shall not be taken to have lawful authority to take him away.

(3B) The Secretary of State may by order a draft of which has been approved by each House of Parliament amend subsection (3A) of this section by substituting a different period for the period of 28 days or of six months mentioned in that subsection (or the period which, by a previous order under this subsection, was substituted for that period)."

(2) The following section is inserted after section 33 of the Children Act 1948—

" Restriction on removal of child from care of voluntary organisation

33A.—(1) Section 3 (8) of this Act shall apply in relation to children who are not in the care of local authorities under section 1 of this Act but who are in voluntary homes or are boarded out, as it applies by virtue of subsection (3A) of the said section 1 to children in the care of the local authority, except that in the case of a child who is not in the care of a local authority the references in subsection (3A) to a local authority shall be construed as references to the voluntary organisation in whose care the child is.

(2) For the purposes of this section—
    (a) a child is boarded out if he is boarded out, by the voluntary organisation in whose care he is, with foster parents to live in their home as a member of their family;
    (b) " voluntary home " includes a controlled community home and an assisted community home.".

57. The following section is substituted for section 2 of the Children Act 1948.

" **Assumption by local authority of parental rights and duties**

2.—(1) Subject to the provisions of this Part of this Act, if it appears to a local authority in relation to any child who is in their care under the foregoing section—

(*a*) that his parents are dead and he has no guardian or custodian; or

(*b*) that a parent of his—

    (i) has abandoned him, or

    (ii) suffers from some permanent disability rendering him incapable of caring for the child, or

    (iii) while not falling within sub-paragraph (ii) of this paragraph, suffers from a mental disorder (within the meaning of the Mental Health Act 1959), which renders him unfit to have the care of the child, or

    (iv) is of such habits or mode of life as to be unfit to have the care of the child, or

    (v) has so consistently failed without reasonable cause to discharge the obligations of a parent as to be unfit to have the care of the child; or

(*c*) that a resolution under paragraph (*b*) of this subsection is in force in relation to one parent of the child who is, or is likely to become, a member of the household comprising the child and his other parent; or

(*d*) that throughout the three years preceding the passing of the resolution the child has been in the care of a local authority under the foregoing section, or partly in the care of a local authority and partly in the care of a voluntary organisation, the local authority may resolve that there shall vest in them the parental rights and duties with respect to that child, and, if the rights and duties were vested in the parent on whose account the resolution was passed jointly with another person, they shall also be vested in the local authority jointly with that other person.

(2) In the case of a resolution passed under paragraph (*b*), (*c*) or (*d*) of subsection (1) of this section, unless the person whose parental rights and duties have under the resolution vested in the local authority has consented in writing to the passing of the resolution, the local authority, if that person's whereabouts are known to them, shall forthwith after the passing of the resolution serve on him notice in writing of the passing thereof.

(3) Every notice served by a local authority under subsection (2) of this section shall inform the person on whom the notice is served of his right to object to the resolution and the effect of any objection made by him.

(4) If, not later than one month after notice is served on a person under subsection (2) of this section, he serves a counter-notice in writing on the local authority objecting to the resolution, the resolution shall, subject to the provisions of subsection (5) of this section, lapse on the expiry of fourteen days from the service of the counter-notice.

(5) Where a counter-notice has been served on a local authority under subsection (4) of this section, the authority may not later than fourteen days after the receipt by them of the counter-notice complain to a juvenile court having jurisdiction in the area of the authority, and in that event the resolution shall not lapse until the determination

of the complaint; and the court may on the hearing of that complaint order that the resolution shall not lapse by reason of the counter-notice:

Provided that the court shall not so order unless satisfied—

(a) that the grounds mentioned in subsection (1) of this section on which the local authority purported to pass the resolution were made out, and

(b) that at the time of the hearing there continued to be grounds on which a resolution under subsection (1) of this section could be founded, and

(c) that it is in the interests of the child to do so.

(6) While a resolution passed under subsection (1) (b), (c) or (d) of this section is in force with respect to a child, section 1 (3) of this Act shall not apply in relation to the person who, but for the resolution, would have the parental rights and duties in relation to the child.

(7) Any notice under this section (including a counter-notice) may be served by post, so however that a notice served by a local authority under subsection (2) of this section shall not be duly served by post unless it is sent by registered post or recorded delivery service.

(8) A resolution under this section shall cease to have effect if—

(a) the child is adopted;

(b) an order in respect of the child is made under section 14 or 25 of the Children Act 1975; or

(c) a guardian of the child is appointed under section 5 of the Guardianship of Minors Act 1971.

(9) Where, after a child has been received into the care of a local authority under the foregoing section, the whereabouts of any parent of his have remained unknown for twelve months, then, for the purposes of this section, the parent shall be deemed to have abandoned the child.

(10) The Secretary of State may by order a draft of which has been approved by each House of Parliament amend subsection (1) (d) of this section to substitute a different period for the period mentioned in that paragraph (or the period which, by a previous order under this subsection, was substituted for that period).

(11) In this section—

" parent ", except in subsection (1) (a), includes a guardian or custodian;

" parental rights and duties ", in relation to a particular child, means all rights and duties which by law the mother and father have in relation to a legitimate child and his property except the right to consent or refuse to consent to the making of an application under section 14 of the Children Act 1975 and the right to agree or refuse to agree to the making of an adoption order or an order under section 25 of that Act ".

Supplementary provisions relating to care proceedings

58. In the Children Act 1948, the following sections are inserted after section 4—

" Appeal to the High Court

4A. An appeal shall lie to the High Court from the making by a juvenile court of an order under section 2 (5) or section 4 (3) of this Act (orders confirming or terminating local authority resolutions under section 2 (1) of this Act), or from the refusal by a juvenile court to make such an order.

Guardians ad litem and reports in care proceedings

4B.—(1) In any proceedings under section 2 (5) or 4 (3) or 4A of this Act, a juvenile court or the High Court may, where it considers it necessary in order to safeguard the interests of the child to whom the proceedings relate, by order make the child a party to the proceedings and appoint, subject to rules of court, a guardian ad litem of the child for the purposes of the proceedings.

(2) A guardian ad litem appointed in pursuance of this section shall be under a duty to safeguard the interests of the child in the manner prescribed by rules of court.

(3) Section 6 of the Guardianship Act 1973 shall apply in relation to complaints under section 2 (5) or 4 (3) of this Act as it applies in relation to applications under section 3 (3) of the said Act of 1973.".

59. [*See Children Act 1948, s. 12, for the substitutions made by this section.*]

Children in care of voluntary organisations in England and Wales
Transfer of parental rights and duties to voluntary organisations

60.—(1) Where it appears to a local authority as respects a child in the care of a voluntary organisation which is an incorporated body—

(*a*) that the child is not in the care of any local authority; and

(*b*) that a condition specified in section 2 (1) of the Children Act 1948 is satisfied; and

(*c*) that it is necessary in the interests of the welfare of the child for the parental rights and duties to be vested in the organisation.

the authority may, subject to subsections (5) and (6), resolve that there shall vest in the organisation the parental rights and duties with respect to that child.

(2) While a resolution under this section is in force the parental rights and duties shall vest in the organisation in whose care the child is when the resolution is passed.

(3) If, immediately before the resolution is passed, the parental rights and duties are vested in the parent in relation to whom the resolution is passed jointly with any other person, then on the passing of the resolution the parental rights and duties shall vest jointly in that other person and the organisation in whose care the child is.

(4) In determining, for the purposes of subsection (1) of this section, whether the condition specified in section 2 (1) (*b*) (i) of the Children Act 1948 is satisfied, if the whereabouts of any parent of the child have remained unknown for twelve months, that parent shall be deemed to have abandoned the child.

(5) A resolution under subsection (1) may not be passed by a local authority in respect of any child unless—

(*a*) the child is living in the area of the authority either in a voluntary home or with foster parents with whom he has been boarded by the organisation in whose care he is; and

(*b*) that organisation has requested the authority to pass the resolution.

(6) The parental rights and duties which may vest in an organisation by virtue of this section do not include the right to consent or refuse to consent to the making of an application under section 14 and the right to agree or refuse to agree to the making of an adoption order or an order under section 25; and regulations made under section 33 (1) of the Children Act 1948 shall apply to the emigration of a child notwithstanding that the parental rights and duties relating to the child are vested in the voluntary organisation.

(7) Subsection (8) of section 2 of the Children Act 1948 shall apply in relation to a resolution under subsection (1) as if it were a resolution under the said section 2.

Duty of local authority to assume parental rights and duties

61.—(1) If it appears to a local authority, having regard to the interests of the welfare of a child living within their area, the parental rights and duties with respect to whom are by virtue of a resolution under section 60 vested in a voluntary organisation, that it is necessary that the parental rights and duties should no longer be vested in the organisation, the local authority shall resolve that there shall vest in them the parental rights and duties relating to the child.

(2) The local authority shall within seven days of passing a resolution under subsection (1) by notice in writing inform the organisation and each parent, guardian or custodian of the child whose whereabouts are known to them that the resolution has been passed.

Effect of resolutions under sections 60 and 61

62.—(1) A resolution under subsection (1) of section 60 shall cease to have effect on the passing of a resolution under subsection (1) of section 61.

(2) Section 6 of the Children Act 1948 shall have effect in relation to a resolution under subsection (1) of section 60 as it has effect in relation to a resolution under section 2 of that Act.

(3) A resolution under subsection (1) of section 61 shall be deemed to be a resolution under section 2 of the Children Act 1948 except that sections 2 (2) to (7) and 4 (3) of that Act shall not apply.

Appeals by parents etc.

63.—(1) Subsections (2) to (5) and (7) of section 2 of the Children Act 1948 shall apply to a resolution under section 60 as they apply to a resolution under the said section 2, with the substitution for the reference in subsection (2) to the vesting of parental rights and duties in the local authority of a reference to the vesting of parental rights and duties in the voluntary organisation.

(2) An appeal may be made—
- (a) where the complaint relates to a resolution under section 60, by a person deprived of parental rights and duties by the resolution, or
- (b) where the complaint relates to a resolution under section 61, by a person who but for that resolution and an earlier resolution under section 60 would have parental rights and duties,

to a juvenile court having jurisdiction in the area of the authority which passed the resolution, on the ground that—
- (i) there was no ground for the making of the resolution, or
- (ii) that the resolution should in the interests of the child be determined.

(3) An appeal shall lie to the High Court against the decision of a juvenile court under this section.

(4) Section 4B of the Children Act 1948 shall apply in relation to proceedings under this section.

Conflict of interest between parent and child

Addition of new sections to Children and Young Persons Act 1969

64. The following heading and sections are inserted after section 32 of the Children and Young Persons Act 1969—

" *Conflict of interest between parent and child or young person*

Conflict of interest between parent and child or young person

32A.—(1) If before or in the course of proceedings in respect of a child or young person—

(a) in pursuance of section 1 of this Act, or

(b) on an application under section 15 (1) of this Act for the discharge of a relevant supervision order or a supervision order made under section 21 (2) of this Act on the discharge of a relevant care order; or

(c) on an application under section 21 (2) of this Act for the discharge of a relevant care order or a care order made under section 15 (1) of this Act on the discharge of a relevant supervision order; or

(d) on an appeal to the Crown Court under section 2 (12) of this Act, or

(e) on an appeal to the Crown Court under section 16 (8) of this Act against the dismissal of an application for the discharge of a relevant supervision order or against a care order made under section 15 (1) on the discharge of—

(i) a relevant supervision order; or

(ii) a supervision order made under section 21 (2) on the discharge of a relevant care order; or

(f) on an appeal to the Crown Court under section 21 (4) of this Act against the dismissal of an application for the discharge of a relevant care order or against a supervision order made under section 21 (2) on the discharge of—

(i) a relevant care order; or

(ii) a care order made under section 15 (1) on the discharge of a relevant supervision order,

it appears to the court that there is or may be a conflict, on any matter relevant to the proceedings, between the interests of the child or young person and those of his parent or guardian, the court may order that in relation to the proceedings the parent or guardian is not to be treated as representing the child or young person or as otherwise authorised to act on his behalf.

(2) If an application such as is referred to in subsection (1) (b) or (c) of this section is unopposed, the court, unless satisfied that to do so is not necessary for safeguarding the interests of the child or young person, shall order that in relation to proceedings on the application no parent or guardian of his shall be treated as representing him or as otherwise authorised to act on his behalf; but where the application was made by a parent or guardian on his behalf the order shall not invalidate the application.

(3) Where an order is made under subsection (1) or (2) of this section for the purposes of proceedings on an application within subsection (1) (a), (b) or (c) of this section, that order shall also have effect for the purposes of any appeal to the Crown Court arising out of those proceedings.

(4) The power of the court to make orders for the purposes of an application within subsection (1) (a), (b) or (c) of this section shall also be exercisable, before the hearing of the application, by a single justice.

(5) In this section—

' relevant care order ' means a care order made under section 1 of this Act;

'relevant supervision order' means a supervision order made under section 1 of this Act.

Safeguarding of interests of child or young person where section 32A order made

32B.—(1) Where the court makes an order under section 32A (2) of this Act the court, unless satisfied that to do so is not necessary for safeguarding the interests of the child or young person, shall in accordance with rules of court appoint a guardian ad litem of the child or young person for the purposes of the proceedings.

In this subsection 'court' includes a single justice.

(2) Rules of court shall provide for the appointment of a guardian ad litem of the child or young person for the purposes of any proceedings to which an order under section 32A (1) of this Act relates.

(3) A guardian ad litem appointed in pursuance of this section shall be under a duty to safeguard the interests of the child or young person in the manner prescribed by rules of court."

Legal aid for parents where order made under new section 32A of 1969 Act

65. In section 28 (power to order legal aid to be given) of the Legal Aid Act 1974—

(*a*) in subsection (1), for " subsections (3) and (6) " there is substituted " subsections (3), (6) and (6A) ", and

(*b*) the following subsection is inserted after subsection (6)—

" (6A) Where a court makes an order under section 32A of the Children and Young Persons Act 1969 affecting the parent or guardian of a person in relation to any proceedings, it may order that the parent or guardian shall be given legal aid for the purpose of taking such part in the proceedings as may be allowed by rules of court.

In this subsection ' guardian ' has the same meaning as in the Children and Young Persons Act 1933."

Safeguarding of interests of children before children's hearings etc. in Scotland

66. In the Social Work (Scotland) Act 1968 the following section is inserted after section 34—

" Safeguarding of interests of children before children's hearings etc.

34A.—(1) In any proceedings—

(*a*) before a children's hearing;

(*b*) before the sheriff on an application under section 42 (2) (*c*) of this Act;

(*c*) before the sheriff on an appeal under section 49 or 51 of this Act,

the chairman (in the case of proceedings referred to in paragraph (*a*) above) or the sheriff (in any other case)—

(i) shall consider whether it is necessary for the purpose of safeguarding the interests of the child in the proceedings, because there is or may be a conflict, on any matter relevant to the proceedings, between the interests of the child and those of his parent, to appoint a person to act for that purpose; and

(ii) without prejudice to any existing power to appoint a person to represent the interests of the child, may, if he thinks fit, appoint a person to act for the purpose specified in paragraph (i) above.

(2) The power to make rules under—
: (*a*) section 35 (4) of this Act,
: (*b*) section 32 of the Sheriff Courts (Scotland) Act 1971,

shall include power to make rules providing for—
: (i) the procedure in relation to the disposal of matters arising under this section;
: (ii) appointment under subsection (1) of this section, the functions of a person so appointed and any right of such person to information relating to the proceedings in question.

(3) The expenses of a person appointed under subsection (1) of this section shall—
: (*a*) in so far as reasonably incurred by him in safeguarding the interests of the child in the proceedings, and
: (*b*) except in so far as otherwise defrayed in terms of regulations made under section 103 (2) of the Children Act 1975,

be borne by the local authority for whose area the children's panel from which the relevant children's hearing has been constituted is formed.

(4) For the purposes of subsection (3) of this section, ' relevant children's hearing ' means—
: (*a*) in the case of proceedings referred to in subsection (1) (*a*) of this section, the children's hearing;
: (*b*) in the case of proceedings referred to in subsection (1) (*b*) of this section, the children's hearing who have directed the application;
: (*c*) in the case of proceedings referred to in subsection (1) (*c*) of this section, the children's hearing whose decision is being appealed against."

Absence from care and children in need of secure accommodation

Recovery of children in care of local authorities

67.—(1) This section applies to a child—
: (*a*) who is in the care of a local authority under section 1 of the Children Act 1948; and
: (*b*) with respect to who there is in force a resolution under section 2 of that Act; and
: (*c*) who—
:: (i) has run away from accommodation provided for him by the local authority under Part II of the said Act; or
:: (ii) has been taken away from such accommodation contrary to section 3 (8) of the said Act; or
:: (iii) has not been returned to the local authority as required by a notice served under section 49 of the Children and Young Persons Act 1963 on a person under whose charge and control the child was, in accordance with section 13 (2) of the said Act of 1948, allowed to be.

(2) If a justice of the peace is satisfied by information on oath that there are reasonable grounds for believing that a person specified in the information can produce the child to whom this section applies, he may issue a summons directed to the person so specified and requiring him to attend and produce the child before a magistrates' court acting for the same petty sessions area as the justice.

(3) Without prejudice to the powers under subsection (2) above, if a justice of the peace is satisfied by information on oath that there are reasonable grounds for believing that a child to whom this section applies is in premises specified in the information, he may issue a search warrant

authorising a person named in the warrant, being an officer of the local
authority in whose care the child is, to search the premises for the child;
and if the child is found, he shall be placed in such accommodation as
the local authority may provide for him under Part II of the Children
Act 1948.

(4) A person who, without reasonable excuse, fails to comply with a
summons under subsection (2) shall, without prejudice to any liability
apart from this subsection, be guilty of an offence and liable on summary
conviction to a fine not exceeding £100.

Extension of powers under section 32 of Children and Young Persons Act 1969

68.—(1) Section 32 of the Children and Young Persons Act 1969
(detention of absentees) shall have effect subject to the following
provisions of this section.

(2) In subsection (1) of the said section 32, paragraph (*b*) shall cease
to have effect.

(3) After subsection (1) of the said section 32, there is inserted the
following subsection:—

" (1A) If a child or young person is absent from a place of safety
to which he has been taken in pursuance of section 2 (5), 16 (3) or
28 of this Act without the consent of—

(*a*) the person who made the arrangements for his detention in
the place of safety in pursuance of the said section 2 (5) or
16 (3), or

(*b*) the person on whose application an authorisation relating to
the child or young person has been issued under the said
section 28,

he may be arrested by a constable anywhere in the United Kingdom
or the Channel Islands without a warrant, and shall, if so arrested,
be conducted to the place of safety at the expense of the person
referred to in paragraph (*a*) or (*b*) (as the case may be) of this
subsection."

(4) In subsection (2) of the said section 32, after the words " subsection (1) " there are inserted the words " or (1A) ", and for the words
" twenty pounds " there is substituted the word " £100 ".

(5) After the said subsection (2), the following subsections are
inserted—

" (2A) Without prejudice to its powers under subsection (2) of
this section, a magistrates' court (within the meaning of that subsection) may, if it is satisfied by information on oath that there are
reasonable grounds for believing that a person who is absent as
mentioned in subsection (1) or (1A) of this section is in premises
specified in the information, issue a search warrant authorising a
constable to search the premises for that person.

(2B) A court shall not issue a summons or search warrant under
subsection (2) or (2A) of this section in any case where the person
who is absent is a person to whom subsection (1A) of this section
applies, unless the information referred to in the said subsection (2)
or (2A) is given by the person referred to in subsection (1A) (*a*) or (*b*)
(as the case may be) of this section."

(6) In subsection (3) of the said section 32, for the words " one
hundred pounds " there is substituted the word " £400 ".

(7) In subsection (4) of the said section 32, the words " subsection
(1) " there are substituted the words " subsections (1), (1A) and (2A) ",
and for the words " that subsection " there are substituted the words
" subsection (1)."

Certificates of unruly character

69. The court shall not certify under section 22 (5) or section 23 (2) or (3) of the Children and Young Persons Act 1969 (committals to remand centres or prison) that a child is of so unruly a character that he cannot safely be committed to the care of a local authority unless the conditions prescribed by order made by the Secretary of State are satisfied in relation to that child.

In this section, " court " includes a justice.

Children of unruly character in Scotland

70. The following provisions of the Criminal Procedure (Scotland) Act 1975 (which relate to children of unruly character) shall be amended in the manner specified in paragraphs (*a*) to (*c*) below—

(*a*) in sections 23 (1) (*b*), 24 (1), 297 (1) and 329 (1) (*b*) of the said Act of 1975 the following words are added at the end—

" ; but the court shall not so certify a child unless such conditions as the Secretary of State may by order made by statutory instrument prescribe are satisfied in relation to the child.";

(*b*) in sections 23 (3) and 329 (3) of the said Act of 1975 the following words are added at the end—

" ; but a commitment shall not be so revoked unless such conditions as the Secretary of State may by order made by statutory instrument prescribe are satisfied in relation to the said person.";

(*c*) in sections 24 (2) and 297 (2) of the said Act of 1975 the following words are added at the end—

"; but a commitment shall not be so revoked unless such conditions as the Secretary of State may by order made by statutory instrument prescribe are satisfied in relation to the child.".

71. [*See Children and Young Persons Act 1969, s. 64, for the substitutions made by this section.*]

Grants in respect of secure accommodation for children in Scotland

72. The following section is inserted after section 59 of the Social Work (Scotland) Act 1968—

" Grants in respect of secure accommodation for children

59A.—(1) The Secretary of State may make to a local authority grants of such amount and subject to such conditions as he may with the consent of the Treasury determine in respect of expenditure incurred by the authority in—

(*a*) providing;

(*b*) joining with another local authority in providing; or

(*c*) contributing by way of grant under section 10 (3) of this Act to the provision by a voluntary organisation of,

secure accommodation in residential establishments.

(2) The conditions subject to which grants are made under subsection (1) of this section may include conditions for securing the repayment in whole or in part of such grants.

(3) In this section " secure accommodation " means accommodation provided for the purpose of restricting the liberty of children.".

Further amendments of Social Work (Scotland) Act 1968

Amendment of s. 15 of Social Work (Scotland) Act 1968

73. In section 15 of the Social Work (Scotland) Act 1968 the following subsections are inserted after subsection (3)—

" (3A) Subsection (8) (penalty for taking away a child in care etc.) of section 17 of this Act shall apply to a child in the care of a local authority under this section, notwithstanding that no resolution is in force under section 16 of this Act with respect to the child, if he has been in the care of that local authority throughout the preceding six months; and for the purposes of the application of paragraph (*b*) of that subsection in such a case a parent or guardian of the child shall not be taken to have lawful authority to take him away:

Provided that that subsection shall not be virtue of this subsection apply in relation to an act done—

(*a*) with the consent of the local authority, or

(*b*) by a parent or guardian of the child who has given the local authority not less than 28 days' notice of his intention to do it.

(3B) The Secretary of State may by order, a draft of which has been approved by each House of Parliament, amend subsection (3A) of this section by substituting a different period for the period of 28 days or of six months mentioned in that subsection (or for the period which by a previous order under this subsection, was substituted for that period).".

Substitution of s. 16 of Social Work (Scotland) Act 1968

74. The following section is substituted for section 16 of the Social Work (Scotland) Act 1968—

" **Resolution by local authority in respect of assumption and vesting of parental rights and powers**

16.—(1) Subject to the provisions of this Part of this Act, a local authority may resolve—

(*a*) that there shall vest in them the relevant parental rights and powers with respect to any child who is in their care under section 15 of this Act; or

(*b*) that there shall vest in a voluntary organisation which is an incorporated body, or a trust within the meaning of section 2 (*a*) of the Trusts (Scotland) Act 1921, the relevant parental rights and powers with respect to any child who is in the care of that organisation,

if it appears to the local authority—

(i) that the parents of the child are dead and that he has no guardian; or

(ii) that there exists in respect of a parent or guardian of the child (the said parent or guardian being hereafter in this Part of this Act referred to as the person on whose account the resolution was passed) any of the circumstances specified in subsection (2) of this section; or

(iii) that a resolution under this subsection is in force in terms of sub-paragraph (ii) above in relation to one parent of the child and that parent is, or is likely to become, a member of the household comprising the child and his other parent; or

(iv) that throughout the three years preceding the passing of the resolution the child has been in the care of a local authority under section 15 of this Act, or in the care of a voluntary organisation or partly the one and partly the other.

(2) The circumstances referred to in sub-paragraph (ii) of sub-section (1) of this section are that the person on whose account the resolution was passed—

(*a*) has abandoned the child; or

(*b*) suffers from some permanent disability rendering him incapable of caring for the child; or

(*c*) while not falling within paragraph (*b*) of this subsection, suffers from a mental disorder (within the meaning of the Mental Health (Scotland) Act 1960) which renders him unfit to have the care of the child; or

(*d*) is of such habits or mode of life as to be unfit to have the care of the child; or

(*e*) has so persistently failed without reasonable cause to discharge the obligations of a parent or guardian as to be unfit to have the care of the child.

(3) In this section " the relevant parental rights and powers " means all the rights and powers in relation to the child (other than the right to consent or refuse to consent to the making of an application under section 14 or 25 of the Children Act 1975 and the right to agree or refuse to agree to the making of an adoption order)—

(*a*) where the resolution was passed by virtue of circumstances specified in sub-paragraph (i) of subsection (1) of this section, which the deceased parents would have if they were still living;

(*b*) where the resolution was passed by virtue of circumstances specified in sub-paragraph (ii) of that subsection, of the person on whose account the resolution was passed;

(*c*) where the resolution was passed by virtue of circumstances specified in sub-paragraph (iii) of that subsection, of the parent other than the one on whose account the previous resolution was passed;

(*d*) where the resolution was passed by virtue of circumstances specified in sub-paragraph (iv) of that subsection, of the parents or guardian of the child.

(4) A local authority shall not pass a resolution under paragraph (*b*) of subsection (1) of this section unless—

(*a*) it is satisfied that the child is not in the care of any local authority under any enactment; and

(*b*) it is satisfied that it is necessary in the interests of the welfare of the child for the parental rights and powers to be vested in the voluntary organisation; and

(*c*) the child is living in the area of the local authority either in a residential establishment or with foster parents with whom he has been boarded out by the voluntary organisation in whose care he is; and

(*d*) that organisation has requested the local authority to pass the resolution.

(5) In the case of a resolution passed under subsection (1) of this section by virtue of circumstances specified in sub-paragraph (ii), (iii) or (iv) thereof, unless the person whose parental rights and powers have under the resolution vested in the local authority or in the voluntary organisation as the case may be, has consented in writing to the passing of the resolution, the local authority, if that person's whereabouts are known to them, shall forthwith after the passing of the resolution serve on him notice in writing of the passing thereof.

(6) Every notice served by a local authority under subsection (5) of this section shall inform the person on whom the notice is served

of his right to object to the resolution and of the effect of any objection made by him.

(7) If, not later than one month after notice is served on a person under subsection (5) of this section, he serves a counter-notice in writing on the local authority objecting to the resolution, the resolution shall, subject to the provisions of subsection (8) of this section, lapse on the expiry of fourteen days from the service of the counter-notice.

(8) Where a counter-notice has been served on a local authority under subsection (7) of this section, the authority may, not later than fourteen days after the receipt by them of the counter-notice, make a summary application in respect thereto to the sheriff having jurisdiction in the area of the authority, and in that event the resolution shall not lapse until the determination of the application; and the sheriff may, on the hearing of the application, order that the resolution shall not lapse by reason of the service of the counter-notice:

Provided that the sheriff shall not so order unless satisfied—

    (a) that it is in the interests of the child to do so; and

    (b) that the grounds mentioned in subsection (1) of this section on which the local authority purported to pass the resolution were made out; and

    (c) that at the time of the hearing there continued to be grounds on which a resolution under subsection (1) of this section could be founded.

(9) While a resolution passed under subsection (1) of this section by virtue of circumstances specified in sub-paragraph (ii), (iii) or (iv) thereof is in force with respect to a child, that part of subsection (3) of section 15 of this Act from the words " and nothing in this section shall authorise " onwards shall not apply in relation to the person who, but for the resolution, would have the relevant parental rights and powers in relation to the child.

(10) Any notice under this section (including a counter-notice) may be served by post, but a notice served by a local authority under subsection (5) of this section shall not be duly served by post unless it is sent by registered post or recorded delivery service.

(11) A resolution under this section shall cease to have effect if—

    (a) the child becomes the subject of an adoption order within the meaning of Schedule 2 to the Children Act 1975; or

    (b) an order in respect of the child is made under section 14 or section 25 of the Children Act 1975; or

    (c) a person is appointed, under section 4 (2A) of the Guardianship of Infants Act 1925, to be the guardian of the child; or

    (d) it is a resolution under paragraph (b) of subsection (1) of this section and a resolution is passed under subsection (1) of section 16A of this Act in respect of the child.

(12) If the whereabouts of any parent or guardian of a child have remained unknown for twelve months, and throughout that period the child has been in the care of a local authority under section 15 of this Act, or in the care of a voluntary organisation, or partly the one and partly the other, then for the purposes of this section that parent or guardian shall be deemed to have abandoned the child.

(13) The Secretary of State may by order, a draft of which has been approved by each House of Parliament, amend sub-paragraph (iv) of subsection (1) of this section to substitute a different period for the period of three years mentioned in that subparagraph (or for the

period which, by a previous order under this subsection, was substituted for that period).''.

**Duty of local authority in Scotland to assume parental rights and powers vested
in a voluntary organisation**

75. The following section is inserted after section 16 of the Social
Work (Scotland) Act 1968—

"Duty of local authority to assume parental rights and powers vested in a voluntary organisation

16A.—(1) If it appears to a local authority, having regard to the
interests of the welfare of a child living within their area, the parental
rights and powers in respect of whom are by virtue of a resolution
under section 16 (1) (*b*) of this Act (hereafter in this section referred
to as " the earlier resolution ") vested in a voluntary organisation,
that it is necessary that the said parental rights and powers should no
longer be vested in the organisation, the local authority shall resolve
that the said parental rights and powers shall vest in them; and the
said parental rights and powers shall so vest from the date of the
resolution under this subsection.

(2) The local authority shall, within seven days of passing a
resolution under subsection (1) of this section, by notice in writing
inform—

(*a*) the organisation who but for that resolution; and

(*b*) any person, in so far as that person's whereabouts are known
to them, who, but for that resolution and the earlier resolution,
would have the parental rights and powers in respect of the child, of
the passing thereof.

(3) On a summary application being made for the determining of a
resolution under subsection (1) of this section by a person who but for
that resolution and the earlier resolution would have the parental
rights and powers in respect of the child, the sheriff having jurisdiction
where the applicant resides may order that—

(*a*) the resolution under subsection (1) of this section shall continue
to have effect; or

(*b*) the resolution under subsection (1) of this section shall cease to
have effect and that the earlier resolution shall again take
effect; or

(*c*) the resolution under subsection (1) of this section shall cease to
have effect and that the parental rights and powers in respect
of the child shall again vest in the applicant; or

(*d*) the resolution under subsection (1) of this section shall continue
to have effect, but that either for a fixed period or until the
sheriff, or if the order so provides, the local authority, otherwise directs, the local authority shall allow the care of the child
to be taken over by, and the child to be under the control of,
the applicant.

(4) In hearing an application under subsection (3) of this section
the sheriff may consider whether there was any ground for the making
of the earlier resolution, and if he is satisfied that there was no ground
for the making of that earlier resolution he shall make an order under
subsection (3) (*c*) of this section.

(5) In this section " the parental rights and powers " means all
the rights and powers in relation to the child which in accordance with
the earlier resolution were vested in the voluntary organisation.

(6) While a resolution under subsection (1) of this section is in
force with respect to a child, the child shall be deemed to have

been received into and to be in the care of the local authority by virtue of section 15 of this Act, and subsections (2) to (5) of that section shall apply accordingly; except that where the earlier resolution was passed by virtue of circumstances specified in sub-paragraph (ii), (iii) or (iv) of subsection (1) of section 16 of this Act, that part of subsection (3) of section 15 of this Act from the words " and nothing in this section shall authorise " onwards shall not apply in relation to the person who but for the earlier resolution and the resolution under subsection (1) of this section, would have the parental rights and powers in relation to the child.

(7) Subsection (11) (a), (b) and (c) of section 16, subsections (3) and (4) to (9) of section 17 and subsections (1), 2), (4) and (4A) of section 18 of this Act shall apply to a resolution under this section as they apply to a resolution under section 16 (1) (a) of this Act.

(8) A notice served by a local authority under subsection (2) of this section shall not be duly served by post unless it is sent by registered post or recorded delivery service.".

Return of children taken away in breach of section 17 (8) or (9) of Social Work (Scotland) Act 1968

76. In section 17 of the Social Work (Scotland) Act 1968 (effect of assumption of parental rights) the following subsection is inserted after subsection (9)—

" (10) Where an offence under subsection (8) or (9) of this section has been or is believed to have been committed, a constable, or any person authorised by any court or by any justice of the peace, may take and return the child to the local authority or voluntary organisation in whom are vested the parental rights and powers relating to the child.".

Making of adoption orders where local authority or voluntary organisations have parental rights

77. In section 18 of the Social Work (Scotland) Act 1968 the following subsection is inserted after subsection (4)—

" (4A) A court may entertain an application under—
    (a) section 8 of the Children Act 1975 for an adoption order in respect of a child;
    (b) section 14 of the Children Act 1975 for an order declaring a child free for adoption;
    (c) section 25 of the Children Act 1975 for an order vesting the parental rights and duties relating to a child;
notwithstanding that, by virtue of a resolution under section 16 of this Act, a local authority or a voluntary organisation have parental rights with respect to him.".

Safeguarding of interests of children in proceedings in Scotland relating to the assumption of parental rights

78. In the Social Work (Scotland) Act 1968 the following section is inserted after section 18—

" **Safeguarding of interests of children in proceedings relating to the assumption of parental rights**

18A.—(1) In any proceedings under section 16 (8), 16A (3) or 18 (3) of this Act, the sheriff—
    (a) shall consider whether it is necessary to appoint a person for

the purpose of safeguarding the interests of the child in the proceedings; and

(b) without prejudice to any existing power to appoint a person to represent the interests of the child, may, if he thinks fit, appoint a person to act for the purpose specified in paragraph (a) above.

(2) The power to make rules under section 32 of the Sheriff Courts (Scotland) Act 1971 shall include power to make rules providing for—

(a) the procedure in relation to the disposal of matters arising under this section;

(b) appointment under subsection (1) of this section, the functions of a person so appointed and any right of such a person to information relating to the proceedings in question.".

Amendment of section 20 of Social Work (Scotland) Act

79. The following subsection is substituted for subsection (1) of section 20 of the Social Work (Scotland) Act 1968—

" (1) Where a child is in the care of a local authority under any enactment, the local authority shall, in reaching any decision relating to the child, give first consideration to the need to safeguard and promote the welfare of the child throughout his childhood; and shall so far as practicable ascertain the wishes and feelings of the child regarding the decision and give due consideration to them, having regard to his age and understanding.".

Review of case of child in care in Scotland

80. In the Social Work (Scotland) Act 1968 the following section is inserted after section 20—

" Review of children in care

20A.—(1) Without prejudice to their general duty under section 20 (1) of this Act, it shall be the duty of a local authority who have at any time had a child in their care throughout the preceding six months and have not during that period held a review of his case, to review his case as soon as is practicable after the expiration of that period and, if a supervision requirement is in force with respect to him, the local authority shall consider in the course of the review whether to refer his case to their reporter for review of that requirement by a children's hearing.

(2) The Secretary of State may by regulations—

(a) amend subsection (1) of this section by—

(i) substituting a different period for the period of six months mentioned in that subsection (or for any period which, by previous regulations under this sub-section, was substituted for that period);

(ii) specifying different periods in respect of the first review under that subsection occurring after a child has been taken into care, and in respect of subsequent such reviews;

(b) make provision as to the manner in which cases are to be reviewed under this section;

(c) make provision as to the considerations to which the local authority are to have regard in reviewing cases under this section.".

Restriction on removal of child from care of voluntary organisation

81. The following section is inserted after section 25 of the Social Work (Scotland) Act 1968—

" Restriction on removal of child from care of voluntary organisation

25A.—(1) Section 17 (8) of this Act shall apply in relation to a child who is not in the care of a local authority under section 15 of this Act but who is in the care of a voluntary organisation, as it applies by virtue of subsection (3A) of the said section 15 to a child in the care of a local authority except that, in the case of a child who is not in the care of a local authority, references in subsection (3A) to a local authority shall be construed as references to the voluntary organisation in whose care the child is.

(2) For the purposes of this section, a child is in the care of a voluntary organisation if the voluntary organisation is providing accommodation for the child in a residential establishment or has boarded out the child.".

Power of reporters to conduct proceedings under the Social Work (Scotland) Act 1968

82. The following section is inserted after section 36 of the Social Work (Scotland) Act 1968—

" Power of reporters to conduct proceedings before a sheriff

36A. The Secretary of State and the Lord Advocate may, by regulations—

(a) empowers officers or any officer or class of officers appointed under section 36 of this Act, whether or not they are advocates or solicitors, to conduct before a sheriff—

(i) any proceedings which, under this Act are heard by the sheriff in chambers;

(ii) any application under section 37 or 40 of this Act in relation to a warrant;

(b) prescribe such requirements as they think fit as to qualifications, training or experience necessary for any officer to be so empowered.".

Amendment of section 37 of Social Work (Scotland) Act 1968

83. In section 37 of the Social Work (Scotland) Act 1968—

(a) the following subsection is inserted after subsection (1)—

" (1A) Where a local authority receive information suggesting that a child may be in need of compulsory measures of care, they shall—

(a) cause enquiries to be made into the case unless they are satisfied that such enquiries are unnecessary; and

(b) if it appears to them that the child may be in need of compulsory measures of care, give to the reporter such information about the child as they may have been able to discover.";

(b) for subsection (2) there is substituted—

" (2) A constable or any person authorised by any court or by any justice of the peace may take to a place of safety any child—

(a) in respect of whom any of the offences mentioned in Schedule 1 to the Criminal Procedure (Scotland) Act 1975 has been or is believed to have been committed; or

(b) who is a member of the same household as a child in respect of whom such an offence has been or is believed to have been committed; or

    (*c*) who is, or is likely to become, a member of the same
household as a person who has committed or is
believed to have committed such an offence; or

    (*d*) in respect of whom an offence under section 21 (1) of
the Children and Young Persons (Scotland) Act
1937 has been or is believed to have been committed;
or

    (*e*) who is likely to be caused unnecessary suffering or
serious impairment of health because there is, or is
believed to be, in respect of the child a lack of
parental care,

and any child so taken to a place of safety or any child who
has taken refuge in a place of safety may be detained there
until arrangements can be made for him to be brought before
a children's hearing under the following provisions of this
Part of this Act; and, where a child is so detained, the
constable or the person authorised as aforesaid or the
occupier of the place of safety shall forthwith inform the
reporter of the case.";

   (*c*) in subsection (5), after " renewed " there is inserted " by a
children's hearing ";

   (*d*) the following subsections are inserted after subsection (5)—

" (5A) Where a warrant has been renewed under subsection (5) of this section but it appears to the reporter—

    (*a*) that the children's hearing will not be able to dispose
of the child's case before the expiry of the period of
detention required by the warrant as renewed; and

    (*b*) that further detention of the child is necessary in
the child's own interest,

the reporter may apply to the sheriff for a warrant requiring
the child to be detained in a place of safety for such a period
not exceeding twenty-one days as may be necessary and the
sheriff may issue such a warrant if he is satisfied that such
detention is necessary in the child's own interest.

(5B) On cause shown a warrant authorising detention
under subsection (5A) of this section may be renewed by the
sheriff on one occasion only, for the period mentioned in
that subsection on the application of the reporter.".

Amendment of section 40 of Social Work (Scotland) Act 1968

84. In section 40 of the Social Work (Scotland) Act 1968—

   (*a*) for subsection (7) there is substituted—

" (7) Where a children's hearing before whom a child
is brought are unable to dispose of his case and—

    (*a*) have reason to believe that the child may not attend
at any hearing of his case, or at any proceedings
arising from the case or may fail to comply with a
requirement under section 43 (4) of this Act; or

    (*b*) are satisfied that detention of the child is necessary
in his own interest,

they may issue a warrant requiring the child to be detained
in a place of safety for such a period not exceeding twenty-
one days as may be necessary.";

   (*b*) for subsection (8) there is substituted—

" (8) On cause shown a warrant authorising detention
under subsection (7) of this section may be renewed by a
children's hearing on one occasion only, for the period

582

mentioned in that subsection, on the application of the reporter.";

(*c*) the following subsections are inserted after subsection (8)—

" (8A) Where a warrant has been renewed under subsection (8) of this section but it appears to the reporter—

(*a*) that the children's hearing will not be able to dispose of the child's case before the expiry of the period of detention required by the warrant as renewed; and

(*b*) that further detention of the child is necessary in the child's own interest,

the reporter may apply to the sheriff for a warrant requiring the child to be detained in a place of safety for such a period not exceeding twenty-one days as may be necessary, and the sheriff may issue such a warrant if he is satisfied that such detention is necessary in the child's own interest.

(8B) On cause shown, a warrant authorising detention under subsection (8A) of this section may be renewed by the sheriff on one occasion only, for the period mentioned in that subsection, on the application of the reporter.".

PART IV

FURTHER AMENDMENTS OF LAW OF ENGLAND AND WALES

Explanation of concepts

Parental rights and duties

85.—(1) In this Act, unless the context otherwise requires, " the parental rights and duties " means as respects a particular child (whether legitimate or not), all the rights and duties which by law the mother and father have in relation to a legitimate child and his property; and references to a parental right or duty shall be construed accordingly and shall include a right of access and any other element included in a right or duty.

(2) Subject to section 1 (2) of the Guardianship Act 1973 (which relates to separation agreements between husband and wife), a person cannot surrender or transfer to another any parental right or duty he has as respects a child.

(3) Where two or more persons have a parental right or duty jointly, any one of them may exercise or perform it in any manner without the other or others if the other or, as the case may be, one or more of the others have not signified disapproval of its exercise or performance in that manner.

(4) From the death of a person who has a parental right or duty jointly with one other person, or jointly with two or more other persons, that other person has the right or duty exclusively or, as the case may be, those other persons have it jointly.

(5) Where subsection (4) does not apply on the death of a person who has a parental right or duty, that right or duty lapses, but without prejudice to its acquisition by another person at any time under any enactment.

(6) Subsections (4) and (5) apply in relation to the dissolution of a body corporate as they apply in relation to the death of an individual.

(7) Except as otherwise provided by or under any enactment, while the mother of an illegitimate child is living she has the parental rights and duties exclusively.

Legal custody

86. In this Act, unless the context otherwise requires, " legal custody " means, as respects a child, so much of the parental rights and duties as relate to the person of the child (including the place and manner in which his time is spent); but a person shall not by virtue of having legal custody of a child be entitled to effect or arrange for his emigration from the United Kingdom unless he is a parent or guardian of the child.

Actual custody

87.—(1) A person has actual custody of a child if he has actual possession of his person, whether or not that possession is shared with one or more other persons.

(2) While a person not having legal custody of a child has actual custody of the child he has the like duties in relation to the child as a custodian would have by virtue of his legal custody.

(3) In this Act, unless the context otherwise requires, references to the person with whom a child has his home refer to the person who, disregarding absence of the child at a hospital or boarding school and any other temporary absence, has actual custody of the child.

Child in care of voluntary organisation

88. A child is in the care of a voluntary organisation if—
    (*a*) the organisation has actual custody of him, or
    (*b*) having had actual custody of him, the organisation has transferred that custody to an individual who does not have legal custody of him.

Amendment of Interpretation Act 1889

89.—(1) In the Interpretation Act 1889 after section 19 there is inserted the following section—

" **Meaning of expressions relating to children**

19A.—(1) In any Act passed after the Children Act 1975, unless the contrary intention appears—
    (*a*) the expression " the parental rights and duties ",
    (*b*) the expression " legal custody " (as respects a child), and
    (*c*) references to the person with whom a child has his home,
shall be construed in accordance with Part IV of the Children Act 1975.

(2) This section does not extend to Scotland or Northern Ireland."

Reports in guardianship and matrimonial proceedings

90. [*See Guardianship Act 1973, s. 6, for the substitutions made by this section.*]

91. [*See Matrimonial Proceedings (Magistrates' Courts) Act 1960, s. 4, for the substitutions made by this section.*]

Registration of births

Registration of births of abandoned children

92. The following section is inserted after section 3 of the Births and Deaths Registration Act 1953—

" Registration of births of abandoned children

3A.—(1) Where the place and date of birth of a child who was abandoned are unknown to, and cannot be ascertained by, the person who has charge of the child, that person may apply to the Registrar General for the child's birth to be registered under this section.

(2) On an application under this section the Registrar General shall enter in a register maintained at the General Register Office—

(a) as the child's place of birth, if the child was found by the applicant or by any person from whom (directly or indirectly) the applicant took charge of the child, the registration district and sub-district where the child was found, or, in any other case, where the child was abandoned;

(b) as the child's date of birth, the date which, having regard to such evidence as is produced to him, appears to him to be the most likely date of birth of the child, and

(c) such other particulars as may be prescribed.

(3) The Registrar General shall not register a child's birth under this section if—

(a) he is satisfied that the child was not born in England or Wales; or

(b) the child has been adopted in pursuance of a court order made in the United Kingdom, the Isle of Man or the Channel Islands; or

(c) subject to subsection (5) below, the child's birth is known to have been previously registered under this Act.

(4) If no entry can be traced in any register of births relating to a person who has attained the age of 18 and has not been adopted as aforesaid, that person may apply to the Register General for his birth to be registered under this section—

(5) On the application of—

(a) a person having the charge of a child whose birth had been registered under this Act by virtue of the proviso to section 1 of this Act (as originally enacted), or

(b) any such child who has attained the age of 18 years,

the Registrar General shall re-register the birth of the child under this section, and shall direct the officer having custody of the register of births in which the entry relating to the child was previously made to enter in the margin of the register a reference to the re-registration of the birth."

Registration of father of illegitimate child

93.—(1) At the end of paragraph (b) of section 10 of the Births and Deaths Registration Act of 1953 (which makes provision for the registration of fathers of illegitimate children) there is added " or

(c) at the request of the mother (which shall be made in writing) on production of—

(i) a certified copy of an order made under section 4 of the Affiliation Proceedings Act 1957 naming that person as the putative father of the child, and

(ii) if the child has attained the age of 16 years, the written consent of the child to the registration of that person as his father."

(2) After the said section 10 there is inserted the following section—

" Re-registration of births of illegitimate children

10A.—(1) Where the birth of an illegitimate child has been

registered under this Act but no person has been registered as the child's father, the registrar shall re-register the birth so as to show a person as the father—

(a) at the joint request of the mother and of that person; or

(b) at the request of the mother on production of—

(i) a declaration in the prescribed form made by the mother stating that that person is the father of the child; and

(ii) A statutory declaration made by that person acknowledging himself to be the father of the child; or

(c) at the request of the mother (which shall be made in writing) on production of—

(i) a certified copy of an order made under section 4 of the Affiliation Proceedings Act 1957 naming that person as the putative father of that child, and

(ii) if the child has attained the age of 16 years, the written consent of the child to the registration of that person as his father;

but no birth shall be re-registered under this section except in the prescribed manner and with the authority of the Registrar General.

(2) On the re-registration of a birth under this section—

(a) the registrar and the mother shall sign the register;

(b) in the case of a request under paragraph (a) of subsection (1) of this section, the other person making the request shall also sign the register; and

(c) if the re-registration takes place more than three months after the birth, the superintendent registrar shall also sign the register.".

(3) In section 9 of the said Act of 1953 (which enables information required to be given to the registrar to be given to other persons) after subsection (3) there are added the following subsections—

" (4) A request made under section 10 of this Act may be included in a declaration under subsection (1) of this section, and, if the request is made under paragraph (b) or (c) of that section, the documents required by that paragraph to be produced shall be produced to the officer in whose presence the declaration is made and sent by him with the declaration to the registrar.

(5) A request made under section 10A of this Act instead of being made to the registrar may be made by making and signing in the presence of and delivering to a prescribed officer a statement in the prescribed form and producing to the officer any documents required to be produced by that section, and—

(a) the officer shall send the request together with those documents, if any, to the registrar who shall with the authority of the Registrar General re-register the birth as if the request had been made to him; and

(b) the person or persons who sign the statement shall be deemed to have signed the register as required by subsection (2) of that section.".

Extent of Part IV

Extent of Part IV

94. This Part does not extend to Scotland.

Part V

Miscellaneous and Supplemental

Foster children

Visiting of foster children

95.—(1) In section 1 of the Children Act 1958 (visiting of foster children), the words " so far as appears to the authority to be appropriate " shall cease to have effect, and for the words " from time to time " there are substituted the words " in accordance with regulations made under section 2A of this Act ".

(2) In section 1A of the Children Act 1958 (visiting of foster children in Scotland) the words " where the local authority consider such a course to be necessary or expedient for the purposes of this section," shall cease to have effect, and for the words " from time to time " there are substituted the words " in accordance with regulations made under section 2A of this Act.".

(3) The following section is inserted in the said Act after section 2—

" Visits to foster children

2A.—(1) The Secretary of State may make regulations requiring foster children in a local authority's area to be visited by an officer of the local authority on specified occasions or within specified periods of time.

(2) Every person who is maintaining a foster child within the area of a local authority on the date on which regulations made under subsection (1) of this section come into operation, and who before that date has not given notice in respect of the child to the local authority under section 3 (1) of this Act, shall within eight weeks of that date give written notice that he is maintaining the child to the local authority.

(3) Regulations under this section shall be made by statutory instrument which shall be subject to annulment in pursuance of a resolution of either House of Parliament.".

(4) In section 3 of the said Act, as it applies to England and Wales, (duty of persons maintaining foster children to notify local authority)—

(a) in subsection (5A), for the words " one or more foster children " there are substituted the words " a foster child ", and for the words " foster children " and " any foster children " there are substituted the words " that foster child ";

(b) in subsection (5B) for the words " foster children " there are substituted the words " a foster child ", and for the words " any of them as a " there is substituted the word " that "; and

(c) the following subsection is added at the end—

" (8) Subsection (2A) of this section shall cease to have effect on the date regulations made under section 2A of this Act come into operation.".

Notification by parents

96.—(1) The following section is inserted in the Children Act 1958 after section 3—

" Notification by parents

3A.—(1) The Secretary of State may by regulations made by statutory instrument make provision for requiring parents whose children are or are going to be maintained as foster children to give

587

to the local authority for the area where the children are, or are going to be, living as foster children, such information about the fostering as may be specified in the regulations.

(2) Regulations under this section—

> (*a*) may include such incidental and supplementary provisions as the Secretary of State thinks fit;
>
> (*b*) shall be subject to annulment in pursuance of a resolution of either House of Parliament.".

(2) In section 14 of the said Act (offences), in subsection (1) (*a*), after the words " this Part of this Act " there are inserted the words " or under regulations made under section 3A of this Act ".

Advertisements relating to foster children

97.—(1) In section 37 of the Children Act 1958 the following subsections are inserted after subsection (1)—

" (1A) The Secretary of State may by regulations prohibit the parent or guardian of any child from publishing or causing to be published an advertisement indicating that foster parents are sought for the child.

(1B) The Secretary of State may by regulations prohibit—

> (*a*) a member of a class of persons specified in the regulations, or
>
> (*b*) a person other than a person, or other than a member of a class of persons, specified in the regulations,

from publishing or causing to be published any advertisement indicating that he is willing to undertake, or to arrange for, the care and maintenance of a child.

(1C) Regulations made under this section—

> (*a*) may make different provision for different cases or classes of cases, and
>
> (*b*) may exclude certain cases or classes of cases,

and shall be made by statutory instrument subject to annulment in pursuance of a resolution of either House of Parliament.".

(2) In subsection (2) of the said section 37, after the words " this section " there are inserted the words " or of regulations made under this section ".

Inquiries
Inquiries in England and Wales

98.—(1) The Secretary of State may cause an inquiry to be held into any matter relating to—

> (*a*) the functions of the social services committee of a local authority, in so far as those functions relate to children;
>
> (*b*) the functions of an adoption agency;
>
> (*c*) the functions of a voluntary organisation in so far as those functions relate to voluntary homes;
>
> (*d*) a home maintained by the Secretary of State for the accommodation of children who are in the care of local authorities and are in need of the particular facilities and services provided in the home;
>
> (*e*) the detention of a child under section 53 of the Children and Young Persons Act 1933.

(2) The Secretary of State may, before an inquiry is commenced, direct that it shall be held in private, but where no such direction has been given, the person holding the inquiry may if he thinks fit hold it or any part of it in private.

(3) Subsections (2) to (5) of section 250 of the Local Government Act 1972 (powers in relation to local inquiries) shall apply in relation to an inquiry under this section as they apply in relation to a local inquiry under that section.

(4) In this section—

" functions " includes powers and duties which a person has otherwise than by virtue of any enactment;

" voluntary home " means a home or other institution for the boarding, care and maintenance of poor children which is supported wholly or partly by voluntary contributions, but does not include a mental nursing home or residential home for mentally disordered persons within the meaning of Part III of the Mental Health Act 1959.

(5) This section does not apply to Scotland.

Inquiries in Scotland

99.—(1) In Scotland the Secretary of State may cause an inquiry to be held into any matter relating to—

(a) the functions of a local authority under the Social Work (Scotland) Act 1968 in so far as the matter relates to children;

(b) the functions of a local authority under the enactments specified in paragraph (a) of section 1 (4) and paragraphs (b) to (e) and (h) of section 2 (2) of the Social Work (Scotland) Act 1968;

(c) the functions of an adoption society;

(d) the functions of a voluntary organisation in so far as those functions relate to establishments to which sections 61 to 68 of the Social Work (Scotland) Act 1968 apply and in so far as the matter relates to children; or

(e) the detention of a child under—

(i) section 57 or 58A of the Children and Young Persons (Scotland) Act 1937; or

(ii) section 206 or 413 of the Criminal Procedure (Scotland) Act 1975.

(2) The Secretary of State may, before an inquiry is commenced, direct that it shall be held in private, but where no such direction has been given, the person holding the inquiry may if he thinks fit hold it or any part of it in private.

(3) Subsections (2) to (8) of section 210 of the Local Government (Scotland) Act 1973 (powers in relation to local inquiries) shall apply in relation to an inquiry under this section as they apply in relation to a local inquiry under that section.

(4) In this section " functions " includes powers and duties exercisable otherwise than by virtue of any enactment.

Supplemental

Courts

100.—(1) In this Act " authorised court ", as respects an application for an order relating to a child, shall be construed as follows.

(2) If the child is in England or Wales when the application is made, the following are authorised courts—

(a) the High Court:

(b) the county court within whose district the child is and, in the case of an application under section 14, any county court within whose district a parent or guardian of the child is;

(c) any other county court prescribed by rules made under section 102 of the County Courts Act 1959;

(*d*) a magistrates' court within whose area the child is and, in the case of an application under section 14, a magistrates' court within whose area a parent or guardian of the child is.

(3) If the child is in Scotland when the application is made, the following are authorised courts—

(*a*) the Court of Session;

(*b*) the sheriff court of the sheriffdom within which the child is.

(4) If, in the case of an application for an adoption order or an order under section 14, the child is not in Great Britain when the application is made, the following are authorised courts—

(*a*) the High Court;

(*b*) the Court of Session.

(5) In the case of a Convention adoption order paragraphs (*b*), (*c*) and (*d*) of subsection (2) or, as the case may be, paragraph (*b*) of subsection (3) do not apply.

(6) In the case of an order under section 25, paragraph (*d*) of subsection (2) does not apply.

(7) Subsection (2) applies in the case of an application for an order under section 34, 35 or 38 relating to a child who is subject to a custodianship order whether or not the child is in England or Wales and for the purposes of such an application the following are also authorised courts—

(*a*) the court which made the custodianship order and, where that court is a magistrates' court, any other magistrates' court acting for the same petty session area;

(*b*) the county court within whose district the applicant is;

(*c*) a magistrates' court within whose area the applicant is;

(*d*) where the application is made under section 35 and the child's mother or father or custodian is the petitioner or respondent in proceedings for a decree of divorce, nullity or judicial separation which are pending in a court in England or Wales, that court.

(8) Subsection (2) does not apply in the case of an application under section 30 or 42 but for the purposes of such an application the following are authorised courts—

(*a*) if there is pending in respect of the child an application for an adoption order or an order under section 14 or a custodianship order, the court in which that application is pending;

(*b*) in any other case, the High Court, the county court within whose district the applicant lives and the magistrates' court within whose area the applicant lives.

(9) Subsections (3) and (8) do not apply in the case of an application under section 30 in Scotland but for the purposes of such an application the following are authorised courts—

(*a*) if there is pending in respect of the child an application for—

(i) an adoption order; or

(ii) an order under section 14,

the court in which that application is pending;

(*b*) in any other case—

(i) the Court of Session;

(ii) the sheriff court of the sheriffdom within which the applicant resides.

Appeals etc.

101.—(1) Where any application has been made under this Act to a county court, the High Court may, at the instance of any party to the application, order the application to be removed to the High Court and there proceeded with on such terms as to costs at it thinks proper.

(2) Subject to subsection (3), where on an application to a magistrates' court under this Act the court makes or refuses to make an order, an appeal shall lie to the High Court.

(3) Where an application is made to a magistrates' court under this Act, and the court considers that the matter is one which would more conveniently be dealt with by the High Court, the magistrates' court shall refuse to make an order, and in that case no appeal shall lie to the High Court.

Evidence of agreement and consent

102.—(1) Any agreement or consent which is required by Part I, except section 24 (6), or Part II to be given to the making of any order or application for an order may be given in writing, and, if the document signifying the agreement or consent is—

    (a) in the case of an adoption order or an application for an order under section 14, witnessed in accordance with rules, or

    (b) in the case of an application made under Part II, witnessed in accordance with rules of court,

it shall be admissible in evidence without further proof of the signature of the person by whom it was executed.

(2) A document signifying such agreement or consent which purports to be witnessed in accordance with rules or, as the case may be, with rules of court shall be presumed to be so witnessed, and to have been executed and witnessed on the date and at the place specified in the document, unless the contrary is proved.

(3) In the application of this section to Scotland—

    (a) for " made under Part II " there is substituted " to which Part II applies ";

    (b) for " admissible in evidence " there is substituted " sufficient evidence "; and

    (c) for " rules of court " there is substituted " act of sederunt ".

Panel for guardians ad litem and reporting officers

103.—(1) The Secretary of State may by regulations make provision for the establishment of a panel of persons from whom—

    (a) guardians ad litem and reporting officers may in accordance with rules or rules of court be appointed for the purposes of—

        (i) section 20 of this Act;

        (ii) section 32B of the Children and Young Persons Act 1969;

        (iii) section 4B of the Children Act 1948;

    (b) persons may be appointed for the purposes of section 18A or 34A of the Social Work (Scotland) Act 1968.

(2) Regulations under subsection (1) may provide for the expenses incurred by members of the panel to be defrayed by local authorities.

(3) In relation to Scotland, the reference in subsection (1) to guardians ad litem shall be construed as a reference to curators ad litem.

Saving for powers of High Court

104. Nothing in this Act shall restrict or affect the jurisdiction of the High Court to appoint or remove guardians, or otherwise in respect of children.

Periodic review of Act

105. The Secretary of State shall, within three years of the first of the dates appointed by order by the Secretary of State under section

108 (2) and, thereafter, every five years lay before Parliament a report on the operation of those sections of the Act which are in force at that time; and the Secretary of State shall institute such research as is necessary to provide the information for these reports.

Regulations and orders

106.—(1) Where a power to make regulations or orders is exercisable by the Secretary of State by virtue of this Act, regulations or orders made in the exercise of that power shall be made by statutory instrument and may—

(a) make different provision in relation to different cases or classes of case, and

(b) exclude certain cases or classes of case.

(2) A statutory instrument containing regulations made by the Secretary of State under section 103 shall be subject to annulment in pursuance of a resolution of either House of Parliament.

(3) Any power conferred on the Secretary of State by this Act to make orders includes a power to vary or revoke an order so made.

Interpretation

107.—(1) In this Act, unless the context otherwise requires—

" adoption order " means an order under section 8 (1);

" adoption society " has the same meaning as in the 1958 Act;

" approved adoption society " means an adoption society approved under Part I;

" area ", in relation to a magistrates' court, means the commission area (within the meaning of section 1 of the Administration of Justice Act 1973) for which the court is appointed;

" authorised court " shall be construed in accordance with section 100;

" British adoption order " means an adoption order, or any provision for the adoption of a child effected under the law of Northern Ireland or any British territory outside the United Kingdom;

" British territory " means, for the purposes of any provision of this Act, any of the following countries, that is to say, the United Kingdom, the Channel Islands, the Isle of Man and a colony, being a country designated for the purposes of that provision by order of the Secretary of State or, if no country is so designated, any of those countries;

" child ", except where used to express a relationship, means a person who has not attained the age of 18;

" the Convention " means the Convention relating to the adoption of children concluded at The Hague on 15th November 1965 and signed on behalf of the United Kingdom on that date;

" Convention adoption order " means an adoption order made as mentioned in section 24 (1);

" Convention country " means any country outside British territory, being a country for the time being designated by an order of the Secretary of State as a country in which, in his opinion, the Convention is in force;

" guardian " means—

(a) a person appointed by deed or will in accordance with the provisions of the Guardianship of Infants Acts 1886 and 1925 or the Guardianship of Minors Act 1971 or by a court of competent jurisdiction to be the guardian of the child, and

(b) in relation to the adoption of an illegitimate child, includes the father where he has custody of the child by virtue of an order under section 9 of the Guardianship of Minors Act 1971, or under section 2 of the Illegitimate Children (Scotland) Act 1930;

" home " shall be construed in accordance with section 87 (3);

" local authority " means in relation to England and Wales the council of a county (other than a metropolitan county), a metropolitan district, a London borough or the Common Council of the City of London;

" notice " means a notice in writing;

" relative " has the same meaning as in the 1958 Act;

" rules " means, in England and Wales, rules made under section 9 (3) of the 1958 Act or made by virtue of section 9 (4) of the 1958 Act under section 15 of the Justices of the Peace Act 1949;

" the 1958 Act " means the Adoption Act 1958;

" United Kingdom national " means, for the purposes of any provision of this Act, a citizen of the United Kingdom and Colonies satisfying such conditions, if any, as the Secretary of State may by order specify for the purposes of that provision;

" voluntary organisation " means a body, other than a public or local authority, the activities of which are not carried on for profit.

(2) In this Act, in relation to Scotland, unless the context otherwise requires—

" actual custody " means care and possession;

" legal custody " means custody;

" local authority " means a regional or islands council; and

" rules " means rules made by act of sederunt.

(3) Except so far as the context otherwise requires, any reference in this Act to an enactment shall be construed as a reference to that enactment as amended by or under any other enactment, including this Act.

(4) In this Act, except where otherwise indicated—

(a) a reference to a numbered Part, section or Schedule is a reference to the Part or section of, or the Schedule to, this Act so numbered, and

(b) a reference in a section to a numbered subsection is a reference to the subsection of that section so numbered, and

(c) a reference in a section, subsection or Schedule to a numbered paragraph is a reference to the paragraph of that section, subsection or Schedule so numbered.

Amendments, repeals, commencement and transitory provisions

108.—(1) Subject to the following provisions of this section—

(a) the enactments specified in Schedule 3 shall have effect subject to the amendments specified in that Schedule (being minor amendments or amendments consequential on the preceding provisions of this Act), and

(b) the enactments specified in Schedule 4 are repealed to the extent shown in column 3 of that Schedule.

(2) This Act, except the provisions specified in subsections (3) and (4), shall come into force on such date as the Secretary of State may by order appoint and different dates may be appointed for, or for different purposes of, different provisions.

(3) Sections 71, 72 and 82, this section, section 109 and paragraph 57 of Schedule 3 shall come into force on the passing of this Act.

(4) The following provisions of this Act shall come into force on 1st January 1976—

    (*a*) sections 3, 8 (9) and (10), 13, 59, 83 to 91, 94, 98, 99, 100 and 103 to 107;

    (*b*) Schedules 1 and 2;

    (*c*) in Schedule 3, paragraphs 1, 2, 3, 4, 6, 8, 9, 13 (6), 15, 17, 18, 19, 20, 21 (1) (2) and (4), 22 to 25, 27 (*b*), 29, 33, 34 (*b*), 35, 36 (*b*), 38, 39 (*c*) (*d*) and (*e*), 40, 43, 48, 49, 51 (*a*), 52 (*f*) (ii) and (*g*) (ii), 54, 55, 58 to 63, 65 to 70, 75 (3), 77, 78, 81 and 83;

    (*d*) Parts I, II and III of Schedule 4.

(5) Until the date appointed under subsection (2) for sections 4 to 7, in this Act and in the 1958 Act " adoption agency " means a local authority or a registered adoption society within the meaning of the 1958 Act.

(6) Until the date so appointed for section 12, section 5 (1) of the 1958 Act shall, in relation to an application made after 31st December 1975 for an adoption order, have effect with the addition at the end of paragraph (*b*) of the following words " or

    (*c*) has seriously ill-treated the child and that (whether because of the ill-treatment or for other reasons) the rehabilitation of the child within the household of that person is unlikely."

(7) Until the date so appointed for section 18, section 21A of the Children and Young Persons Act 1969 shall have effect as if for references to section 25 there were substituted references to section 53 of the 1958 Act.

(8) An order under subsection (2) may make such transitional provision as appears to the Secretary of State to be necessary or expedient in connection with the provisions thereby brought into force, including such adaptations of those provisions or any provision of this Act then in force or any provision of the 1958 Act as appear to him to be necessary or expedient in consequence of the partial operation of this Act.

Short title and extent

109.—(1) This Act may be cited as the Children Act 1975.

(2) This Act, except—

    (*a*) section 68;

    (*b*) paragraphs 10, 11 and 63 of Schedule 3; and

    (*c*) Schedule 4 in so far as it repeals—

        (i) the words " or adoption " in section 9 (5) of the Adoption Act 1968, and

        (ii) the references in that Act to section 19 of the Adoption Act 1958,

does not extend to Northern Ireland.

(3) Subsection (1) of section 68 extends to the Channel Islands.

SCHEDULES

                         SCHEDULE 1

STATUS CONFERRED BY ADOPTION OR LEGITIMATION IN ENGLAND AND WALES

PART I

INTERPRETATION

1.—(1) This Part applies for the construction of this Schedule, except where the context otherwise requires.

(2) " Adoption " means adoption—
- (*a*) by an adoption order as defined in section 107,
- (*b*) by an adoption order made under the 1958 Act or the Adoption Act 1950 or any enactment repealed by the Adoption Act 1950,
- (*c*) by an order made in Northern Ireland, the Isle of Man or in any of the Channel Islands,
- (*d*) which is an overseas adoption as defined by section 4 (3) of the Adoption Act 1968, or
- (*e*) which is an adoption recognised by the law of England and Wales, and effected under the law of any other country,

and cognate expressions shall be construed accordingly.

(3) " Legitimation " means—
- (*a*) legitimation under section 1 of the Legitimacy Act 1926,
- (*b*) legitimation within section 8 of that Act (legitimation by extraneous law), or
- (*c*) legitimation (whether or not by virtue of subsequent marriage of the parents) recognised by the law of England and Wales, and effected under the law of any other country,

and cognate expressions shall be construed accordingly.

(4) These definitions of adoption and legitimation include, where the context admits, those effected before the passing of this Act, and the date of an adoption effected by an order is the date of the making of the order.

(5) " Existing ", in relation to any enactment or other instrument, means one passed or made before 1st January 1976 (and whether or not before the passing of this Act).

(6) The death of the testator is the date at which a will or codicil is to be regarded as made.

Dispositions of property

2.—(1) In this Schedule—
" disposition " includes the conferring of a power of appointment and any other disposition of an interest in or right over property;
" power of appointment " includes any discretionary power to transfer a beneficial interest in property without the furnishing of valuable consideration.

(2) This Schedule applies to an oral disposition of property as if contained in an instrument made when the disposition was made.

PART II

ADOPTION ORDERS

Status conferred by adoption

3.—(1) An adopted child shall be treated in law—
- (*a*) where the adopters are a married couple, as if he had been born as a child of the marriage (whether or not he was in fact born after the marriage was solemnized) ;
- (*b*) in any other case, as if he had been born to the adopter in wedlock (but not as a child of any actual marriage of the adopter).

(2) An adopted child shall be treated in law as if he were not the child of any person other than the adopters or adopter.

(3) It is hereby declared that this paragraph prevents an adopted child from being illegitimate.

(4) This paragraph has effect—
- (*a*) in the case of an adoption before 1st January 1976, from that date, and
- (*b*) in the case of any other adoption, from the date of the adoption.

(5) Subject to the provisions of this Part, this paragraph applies for the construction of enactments or instruments passed or made before the adoption or later, and so applies subject to any contrary indication.

(6) Subject to the provisions of this Part, this paragraph has effect as respects things done, or events occurring, after the adoption, or after 31st December 1975, whichever is the later.

Vocabulary

4. A relationship existing by virtue of paragraph 3 may be referred to as an adoptive relationship, and—

   (a) a male adopter may be referred to as the adoptive father;

   (b) a female adopter may be referred to as the adoptive mother;

   (c) any other relative of any degree under an adoptive relationship may be referred to as an adoptive relative of that degree,

but this paragraph does not prevent the term "parent", or any other term not qualified by the word "adoptive", being treated as including an adoptive relative.

Instruments and enactments concerning property

5.—(1) Paragraph 3—

   (a) does not apply to an existing instrument or enactment so far as it contains a disposition of property, and

   (b) does not apply to any public general Act in its application to any disposition of property in an existing instrument or enactment.

(2) The repeal by this Act of sections 16 and 17 of the 1958 Act, and of provisions containing references to those sections, does not affect their application in relation to a disposition of property effected by an existing instrument.

(3) For the purposes of this paragraph, and of paragraph 6, provisions of the law of intestate succession applicable to the estate of a deceased person shall be treated as if contained in an instrument executed by him (while of full capacity) immediately before his death.

6.—(1) Subject to any contrary indication, the rules of construction contained in this paragraph apply to any instrument, other than an existing instrument, so far as it contains a disposition of property.

(2) In applying paragraph 3 (1) to a disposition which depends on the date of birth of a child or children of the adoptive parent or parents, the disposition shall be construed as if—

   (a) the adopted child had been born on the date of adoption,

   (b) two or more children adopted on the same date had been born on that date in the order of their actual births,

but this does not affect any reference to the age of a child.

(3) Examples of phrases in wills on which sub-paragraph (2) can operate are—

   1. Children of A "living at my death or born afterwards".

   2. Children of A "living at my death or born afterwards before any one of such children for the time being in existence attains a vested interest, and who attains the age of 21 years".

   3. As in example 1 or 2, but referring to grandchildren of A, instead of children of A.

   4. A for life "until he has a child", and then to his child or children.

Note. Sub-paragraph (2) will not affect the reference to the age of 21 years in example 2.

(4) Paragraph 3 (2) does not prejudice any interest vested in possession in the adopted child before the adoption, or any interest expectant (whether immediately or not) upon an interest so vested.

(5) Where it is necessary to determine for the purposes of a disposition of property effected by an instrument whether a woman can have a child, it shall be presumed that once a woman has attained the age of fifty-five she will not adopt a child after execution of the instrument, and notwithstanding paragraph 3 if she does so the child shall not be treated as her child or as the child of her spouse (if any) for the purposes of the instrument.

(6) In this paragraph "instrument" includes a private Act settling property, but not any other enactment.

(7) Paragraph 3 (6) has effect subject to this paragraph.

Other enactments and instruments

7.—(1) Paragraph 3 does not apply for the purposes of the table of kindred and affinity in Schedule 1 to the Marriage Act 1949 or sections 10 and 11 (incest) of the Sexual Offences Act 1956.

(2) Paragraph 3 does not apply for the purposes of any provision of—

   (a) the British Nationality Acts 1948 to 1965,

   (b) the Immigration Act 1971,

(*c*) any instrument having effect under an enactment within paragraph (*a*) or (*b*), or

(*d*) any other provision of the law for the time being in force which determines citizenship of the United Kingdom and Colonies.

(3) Paragraph 3 shall not prevent a person being treated as a near relative of a deceased person for the purposes of section 32 of the Social Security Act 1975 (payment of death grant), if apart from paragraph 3 he would be so treated.

(4) Paragraph 3 does not apply for the purposes of section 70 (3) (*b*) or section 73 (2) of the Social Security Act 1975 (payment of industrial death benefit to or in respect of an illegitimate child of the deceased and the child's mother).

(5) Subject to regulations made under section 72 of the Social Security Act 1975 (entitlement of certain relatives of deceased to industrial death benefit), paragraph 3 shall not affect the entitlement to an industrial death benefit of a person who would, apart from paragraph 3, be treated as a relative of a deceased person for the purposes of the said section 72.

Pensions

8. Paragraph 3 (2) does not affect entitlement to a pension which is payable to or for the benefit of a child and is in payment at the time of his adoption.

Adoption of child by natural parents

9. In the case of a child adopted by one of its natural parents as sole adoptive parent, paragraph 3 (2) has no effect as respects entitlement to property depending on relationship to that parent, or as respects anything else depending on that relationship.

Peerages, etc.

10. An adoption does not affect the descent of any peerage or dignity or title of honour.

Insurance

11. Where a child is adopted whose natural parent has effected an insurance with a friendly society or a collecting society or an industrial insurance company for the payment on the death of the child of money for funeral expenses, the rights and liabilities under the policy shall by virtue of the adoption be transferred to the adoptive parents who shall for the purposes of the enactments relating to such societies and companies be treated as the person who took out the policy.

PART III

LEGITIMATION

Instruments concerning property

12.—(1) Subject to any contrary indication, the rules of construction contained in this paragraph apply to any instrument, other than an existing instrument, so far as the instrument contains a disposition of property.

(2) For the purposes of this paragraph, provisions of the law of intestate succession applicable to the estate of a deceased person shall be treated as if contained in an instrument executed by him (while of full capacity) immediately before his death.

(3) A legitimated person, and any other person, shall be entitled to take any interest as if the legitimated person had been born legitimate.

(4) A disposition which depends on the date of birth of a child or children of the parent or parents shall be construed as if—

(*a*) a legitimated child had been born on the date of legitimation,

(*b*) two or more children legitimated on the same date had been born on that date in the order of their actual births,

but this does not affect any reference to the age of a child.

(5) Examples of phrases in wills on which sub-paragraph (4) can operate are set out in paragraph 6 (3).

(6) If an illegitimate person, or a person adopted by one of his natural parents, dies (before the passing of this Act or later) and—

(a) his parents subsequently marry, and

(b) the deceased would, if living at the time of the marriage, have become a legitimated person,

section 1 (1) of the Legitimacy Act 1926 and this paragraph shall apply for the construction of the instrument so far as it relates to the taking of interests by, or in succession to, his spouse, children and remoter issue as if he was legitimated at the date of the marriage.

(7) In this paragraph "instrument" includes a private Act settling property, but not any other enactment.

(8) Section 1 (1) of the Legitimacy Act 1926 has effect subject to the provisions of this paragraph.

(9) Part II of Schedule 4, which repeals enactments superseded by this paragraph, has effect as respects any instrument, other than an existing instrument.

Legitimation of adopted child

13.—(1) Paragraph 3 does not prevent an adopted child being legitimated under the Legitimacy Act 1926 if either natural parent is the sole adoptive parent.

(2) Where an adopted child (with a sole adoptive parent) is legitimated—

(a) paragraph 3 (2) shall not apply after the legitimation to the natural relationship with the other natural parent, and

(b) revocation of the adoption order in consequence of the legitimation shall not affect Part II as it applies to any instrument made before the date of legitimation.

PART IV

SUPPLEMENTAL

Dispositions depending on date of birth

14.—(1) Where a disposition depends on the date of birth of a child who was born illegitimate and who—

(a) is adopted by one of the natural parents as sole adoptive parent, or

(b) is legitimated (or, if deceased, is treated as legitimated),

paragraph 6 (2) and paragraph 12 (4) do not affect entitlement under Part II of the Family Law Reform Act 1969 (illegitimate children).

(2) Where a disposition depends on the date of birth of an adopted child who is legitimated (or, if deceased, is treated as legitimated), paragraph 12 (4) does not affect entitlement by virtue of paragraph 6 (2).

(3) This paragraph applies for example where—

(a) a testator dies in 1976 bequeathing a legacy to his eldest grandchild living at a specified time,

(b) his daughter has an illegitimate child in 1977 who is the first grandchild,

(c) his married son has a child in 1978,

(d) subsequently the illegitimate child is adopted by the mother as sole adoptive parent or is legitimated,

and in all those cases the daughter's child remains the eldest grandchild of the testator throughout.

Protection of trustees and personal representatives

15.—(1) A trustee or personal representative is not under a duty, by virtue of the law relating to trusts or the administration of estates, to enquire, before conveying or distributing any property, whether—

(a) any adoption has been effected or revoked, or

(b) any person is illegitimate, or is adopted by one of his natural parents, and could be legitimated (or if deceased be treated as legitimated),

if that fact could affect entitlement to the property.

(2) A trustee or personal representative shall not be liable to any person by reason of a conveyance or distribution of the property made without regard to any such fact if he has not received notice of the fact before the conveyance or distribution.

(3) This paragraph does not prejudice the right of a person to follow the property, or any property representing it, into the hands of another person, other than a purchaser, who has received it.

Property devolving with peerages, etc.

16.—(1) This Schedule shall not affect the devolution of any property limited (expressly or not) to devolve (as nearly as the law permits) along with any peerage or dignity or title of honour.

(2) This paragraph applies only if and so far as a contrary intention is not expressed in the instrument, and shall have effect subject to the terms of the instrument.

Entails

17. It is hereby declared that references in this Schedule to dispositions of property include references to a disposition by the creation of an entailed interest.

PART V

EXTENT

18. This Schedule does not apply to Scotland.

Section 8
SCHEDULE 2

STATUS CONFERRED IN SCOTLAND BY ADOPTION

General

1.—(1) In Scotland, a child who is the subject of an adoption order shall, subject to the provisions of this Schedule, be treated in law—

(a) where the adopters are a married couple, as if he had been born as a legitimate child of the marriage (whether or not he was in fact born after the marriage was constituted);

(b) in any other case, as if he had been born as a legitimate child of the adopter (but not as a child of any actual marriage of the adopter),

and as if he were not the child of any person other than the adopters or adopter.

(2) Where an illegitimate child has been adopted by one of his natural parents as sole adoptive parent and the adopter thereafter marries the other natural parent, sub-paragraph (1) shall not affect any enactment or rule of law whereby, by virtue of the marriage, the child is rendered the legitimate child of both natural parents.

(3) Sub-paragraph (1) does not apply in determining the prohibited degrees of consanguinity and affinity in respect of the law relating to marriage or in respect of the crime of incest, except that, on the making of an adoption order, the adopter and the child shall be deemed, for all time coming, to be within the said prohibited degrees in respect of the law relating to marriage.

(4) Sub-paragraph (1) does not apply for the purposes of any provision of—

(a) the British Nationality Act 1948 to 1965,

(b) the Immigration Act 1971,

(c) any instrument having effect under an enactment within paragraph (a) or (b), or

(d) any other law for the time being in force which determines citizenship of the United Kingdom and Colonies.

(5) This paragraph has effect—

(a) in the case of an adoption before 1st January 1976, from that date, and

(b) in the case of any other adoption, from the date of the adoption.

(6) Subject to the provisions of this Schedule, this paragraph applies for the construction of any enactments or instruments passed or made before or after the commencement of this Act so far as the context admits.

(7) Subject to the provisions of this Schedule, this paragraph does not affect things done or events occurring before the adoption or, where the adoption took place before 1st January 1976, before that date.

Pensions

2. The provision in paragraph 1 (1) whereby a child who is the subject of an adoption order is to be treated in law as if he were not the child of any person other

599

than the adopters or adopter shall not affect entitlement to a pension which is payable to, or for the benefit of, the child and is in payment at the time of his adoption.

Insurance

3. Where a child is adopted whose natural parent has effected an insurance with a friendly society or a collecting society or an industrial insurance company for the payment on the death of the child of money for funeral expenses, the rights and liabilities under the policy shall by virtue of the adoption be transferred to the adoptive parents who shall for the purposes of the enactments relating to such societies and companies be treated as the person who took out the policy.

Social Security

4.—(1) Paragraph 1 shall not prevent a person being treated as a near relative of a deceased person for the purposes of section 32 of the Social Security Act 1975 (payment of death grant), if apart from paragraph 1 he would be so treated.

(2) Paragraph 1 does not apply for the purposes of section 70 (3) (*b*) or section 73 (2) of the Social Security Act 1975 (payment of industrial death benefit to or in respect of an illegitimate child of the deceased and the child's mother).

(3) Subject to regulations made under section 72 of the Social Security Act 1975 (entitlement of certain relatives of deceased to industrial death benefit), paragraph 1 shall not affect the entitlement to an industrial death benefit of a person who would, apart from paragraph 1, be treated as a relative of a deceased person for the purposes of the said section 72.

Succession and Property

5.—(1) Paragraph 1 does not affect the existing law relating to adopted persons in respect of—

(*a*) the succession to a deceased person (whether testate or intestate), and

(*b*) the disposal of property by virtue of any inter vivos deed.

(2) In section 23 of the Succession (Scotland) Act 1964 (adopted person to be treated for purposes of succession, etc., as child of adopter)—

(*a*) in subsection (3) (property devolving along with a title or honour, etc.), after " this section " there is inserted " or in the Children Act 1975 ";

(*b*) in subsection (5) (meaning of " adoption order "), for the words from " an order " to " Northern Ireland " there are substituted the words—

" (*a*) an adoption order under the Children Act 1975;

(*b*) an adoption order under the Adoption Act 1958 or the Adoption Act 1950 or any enactment repealed by the Adoption Act 1950;

(*c*) an order effecting an adoption made in Northern Ireland, the Isle of Man or any of the Channel Islands;

(*d*) an " overseas adoption " as defined in section 4 (3) of the Adoption Act 1968; or

(*e*) any other adoption recognised by the law of Scotland;

(whether the order took effect before or after the commencement of this Act) ; ".

(3) In section 24 of the said Act of 1964 (provisions supplementary to section 23), after subsection (1) there is inserted the following subsection—

" (1A) Where, in relation to any purpose specified in section 23 (1) of this Act, any right is conferred or any obligation is imposed, whether by operation of law or under any deed coming into operation after the commencement of the Children Act 1975, by reference to the relative seniority of the members of a class of persons, then, without prejudice to any entitlement under Part I of the Law Reform (Miscellaneous Provisions) (Scotland) Act 1968 of an illegitimate child who is adopted by one of his parents,

(*a*) any member of that class who is an adopted person shall rank as if he had been born on the date of his adoption, and

(*b*) if two or more members of the class are adopted persons whose dates of adoption are the same, they shall rank as between themselves in accordance with their respective times of birth.".

(4) In section 37 (1) of the said Act of 1964 (exclusion from Act of matters relating to titles, etc.), after " nothing in this Act " there is inserted " or (as respects paragraph (*a*) of this subsection) in the Children Act 1975 ".

Adoption and Legitimation

6.—(1) In section 26 of the Adoption Act 1958, after subsection (1) there is inserted the following subsection—

" (1A) Subsection (1) above does not apply to Scotland, and where the natural parents of an illegitimate child, one of whom has adopted him in Scotland, have subsequently married each other, the court by which the adoption order was made may, on the application of any of the parties concerned, revoke that order.".

(2) Section 1 of the Legitimation (Scotland) Act 1968, (requirements and effects of legitimation) is renumbered subsection (1) and at the end there is added the following subsection—

" (2) Subsection (1) above shall apply in relation to an illegitimate person who has been adopted by one of his natural parents as sole adoptive parent, where the adopter thereafter marries the other natural parent, as it applies in relation to any illegitimate person, to the effect of rendering that person the legitimate child of both natural parents; and in this Act " illegitimate ", " legitimated " and cognate expressions shall be construed accordingly.".

(3) In section 6 (2) of the said Act of 1968, for the words from " of an adoption order " to " 1958 " there are substituted the words " (under this section or otherwise) of any adoption order within the meaning of Schedule 2 to the Children Act 1975, in consequence of the marriage of the parents of the adopted person to each other ".

Interpretation

7. In this Schedule, " adoption order " means—
   (a) an adoption order as defined in section 107 ;
   (b) an adoption order under the 1958 Act or the Adoption Act 1950 or any enactment repealed by the Adoption Act 1950 ;
   (c) an order effecting an adoption made in Northern Ireland, the Isle of Man or any of the Channel Islands ;
   (d) an " overseas adoption " as defined in section 4 (3) of the Adoption Act 1968 ; or
   (e) any other adoption recognised by the law of Scotland ;
(whether the order took effect before or after the commencement of this Act) ; and cognate expressions shall be construed accordingly.

Section 108   SCHEDULE 3 [2]

MINOR AND CONSEQUENTIAL AMENDMENTS

Children and Young Persons Act 1933 (23 and 24 Geo. 5 c. 12)

1. [*See s.* 1 (1) (2) *of that Act.*]

Children and Young Persons (Scotland) Act 1937 (c. 37)

2. In section 12 (1) (b) for the words " twenty-five pounds " there is substituted " £400 ".

Education Act 1944 (c. 31)

3. In section 106, the following subsection is substituted for subsection (4)—
   " (4) In this section ' guardian ' means the person having legal custody of the child or young person, as defined by section 86 of the Children Act 1975."

Children Act 1948 (c. 43)

4. [*See s.* 3 (8) *of that Act.*]

5. In section 4—
   (a) In subsection (3) (a) after the words " parent or guardian " there are inserted the words " or custodian " ;
   (b) for subsection (3) (b) there is substituted—

[2] Those amending provisions already in force at the date of going to press have been given effect in the appropriate places in the Acts concerned. A cross-reference only is retained in this Schedule.

F.L.S.—20

" (b) in the case of a resolution passed by virtue of paragraph (b), (c) or (d)
of subsection (1) of the said section 2, by the person who, but for the
resolution, would have the parental rights and duties in relation to the
child,".

6. [*See s.* 43 (1) *of that Act.*]

Marriage Act 1949 (c. 76)

7. In section 3 (1), after the words "shall be required" there are inserted the
words "unless the infant is subject to a custodianship order, when the consent of the
custodian and, where the custodian is the husband or wife of a parent of the infant,
of that parent shall be required".

8. [*See Sched.* 1, *Pt. I, to that Act.*]

9. [*See para.* 2 (*b*) *of Sched.* 2 *to that Act.*]

Maintenance Orders Act 1950 (c. 37)

10. In section 15, after the words "Maintenance Orders (Reciprocal Enforcement)
Act 1972" there are inserted the words "or sections 33 to 45 of the Children Act
1975".

11. In section 16 (2) (*a*), after sub-paragraph (v) there are inserted the
following sub-paragraphs—
" (vi) section 4 of the Affiliation Proceedings Act 1957 on an application
made under section 45 of the Children Act 1975;
(vii) section 34 (1) (*b*) of the Children Act 1975; ".

Magistrates' Courts Act 1952 (c. 55)

12. In section 56 (1) (meaning of "domestic proceedings"), the following
paragraph is inserted after paragraph (*e*)—
" (*f*) under the Adoption Act 1958 or Part I or II of the Children Act 1975 ",
and there are added at the end the following words "or proceedings on an
information ".

Births and Deaths Registration Act 1953 (c. 20)

13.—(1) For "living new-born child" in each place where it occurs, except
sections 6, 7, 8, 34 (3) and 36, there is substituted "still-born child".

(2) In section 1 (2) after paragraph (*d*) there is added—
" (*e*) in the case of a still-born child found exposed, the person who found
the child."

(3) In section 14 (1) (*a*) after "section 10" there is inserted "or 10A".

(4) In section 30 after subsection (1) there is inserted the following subsection—
" (1A) The Registrar General shall cause an index to be made and kept in
the General Register Office of the entries in the register kept by him under section
3A of this Act."

(5) In section 34—
(*a*) in subsection (2) after paragraph (*c*) there is added the following
paragraph—
" (*d*) in relation to the re-registration of a birth under section 9 (5)
of this Act ";
(*b*) in subsection (3) after "new-born child" there is inserted "or still-born
child ".

(6) In section 41—
(*a*) after the definition of "disposal" there is inserted the following
definition—
"'father', in relation to an adopted child, means the child's natural
father; ";
(*b*) after the definition of "the Minister" there is inserted the following
definition—
"'mother', in relation to an adopted child, means the child's natural
mother; ".

Affiliation Proceedings Act 1957 (c. 55)

14. In section 5 (2) there is inserted at the end the following paragraph—
" (*e*) section 45 of the Children Act 1975 (which enables the custodian of a

child to apply for an affiliation order under this Act within three years after the making of the custodianship order).".

Housing Act 1957 (*c.* 56)

15. In Schedule 2, in paragraph 4 (7) for the words "any illegitimate son or daughter, and any adopted son or daughter" there are substituted the words "and any illegitimate son or daughter".

Children Act 1958 (6 & 7 *Eliz.* 2 *c.* 65)

16. In section 2, as it applies in England and Wales,—
   (*a*) in subsection (1), after the word "guardian" there is inserted the word "custodian";
   (*b*) in subsection (4A),—
      (i) for the words "registered adoption society as is referred to in Part II of the Adoption Act 1958" there are substituted the words "adoption society approved under Part I of the Children Act 1975", and
      (ii) for the words "that Act" there are substituted the words "the Adoption Act 1958".

17. In section 2 as it applies to Scotland, after subsection (4) there is inserted the following subsection—
   "(4A) A child is not a foster child for the purposes of this Part of this Act while he is placed in the care and possession of a person who proposes to adopt him under arrangements made by such an adoption agency as is referred to in Part I of the Children Act 1975 or while he is a protected child within the meaning of Part IV of the Adoption Act 1958."

18. [*See s.* 6 *of that Act.*]

19. [*See s.* 14 (2) *of that Act.*]

20. [*See s.* 37 (2) *of that Act.*]

Adoption Act 1958 (7 & 8 *Eliz.* 2 *c.* 5)

21.—(1) For "Adoption Rules" in each place where it occurs there is substituted "rules".
   (2) For "infant" and "infants" in each place where they occur there are respectively substituted "child" and "children".
   (3) For "registered adoption society" in each place where it occurs there is substituted "approved adoption society".
   (4) For "care and possession" in each place where it occurs there is substituted "actual custody".

22. [*See s.* 9 (3) *of that Act.*]

23. [*See s.* 11 (2) *of that Act.*]

24. [*See s.* 21 (1) *of that Act.*]

25. [*See s.* 23 (1) *of that Act.*]

26. In section 26 (2) after the words "adoption order" there are inserted the words "other than a Convention adoption order".

27. In section 32—
   (*a*) the following subsections are substituted for subsection (1)—
      "(1) The Secretary of State may by regulations prohibit unincorporated bodies from applying for approval under section 4 of the Children Act 1975 (Approval of adoption societies); and he shall not approve any unincorporated body whose application is contrary to regulations made under this subsection.
      (1A) The Secretary of State may make regulations for any purpose relating to the exercise of its functions by an approved adoption society.";
   (*b*) [*See subs.* (2) *of that section.*]
   (*c*) the following subsection is added after subsection (3)—
      "(4) Regulations under this section may make different provisions in relation to different cases or classes of cases and may exclude certain cases or classes of cases."

28. In section 33—
   (*a*) in subsection (1)—
      (i) for "registered by the authority under this Part of this Act" there is substituted "approved under Part I of the Children Act 1975";
      (ii) for "the exercise of" to the end there is substituted "its own information or that of the Secretary of State";
   (*b*) in subsection (2), for "by statutory declaration" there is substituted "in a manner specified in the notice".

29. [*See s.* 35 (6) *of that Act.*]

30. In section 36—
   (*a*) in subsection (1) for the words "subsection (2) of section 3 of this Act" there are substituted the words "section 18 (1) of the Children Act 1975"; and
   (*b*) for subsection (3), there is substituted the following—
      "(3) A local authority which receives such notice as aforesaid in respect of a child whom the authority know to be in the care of another local authority shall, not more than seven days after the receipt of the notice, inform that other authority in writing that they have received the notice."

31. In section 37—
   (*a*) in subsection (1) for the words "subsection (2) of section 3 of this Act" there are substituted the words "section 18 (1) of the Children Act 1975";
   (*b*) the following subsections are substituted for subsection (4)—
      "(4) A protected child ceases to be a protected child—
         (*a*) on the appointment of a guardian for him under the Guardianship of Minors Act 1971;
         (*b*) on the notification to the local authority for the area where the child has his home that the application for an adoption order has been withdrawn;
         (*c*) on the making of any of the following orders in respect of the child—
            (i) an adoption order;
            (ii) an order under section 17 of the Children Act 1975;
            (iii) a custodianship order;
            (iv) an order under section 42, 43 or 44 of the Matrimonial Causes Act 1973; or
         (*d*) on his attaining the age of 18,
      whichever first occurs.
      (4A) In relation to Scotland—
         (*a*) subsection (4) does not apply; and
         (*b*) a protected child ceases to be a protected child when—
            (i) the application for an adoption order lapses or is withdrawn;
            (ii) the application for an adoption order is granted or otherwise determined;
            (iii) an order is made awarding custody of the child;
            (iv) an order is made appointing a guardian of the child; or
            (v) the child attains the age of 18.".

32. In section 40 (6) for the words from the beginning to "that is to say" there are substituted the following words "The particulars referred to in subsection (4) of this section are".

33. [*See s.* 44 (2) *of that Act.*]

34. In section 50—
   (*a*) in subsection (1), in paragraph (*b*), for "any consent" there is substituted "any agreement or consent";
   (*b*) [*See subs.* (2) *of that section.*]
   (*c*) in subsection (3), for "adoption society" there is substituted "approved adoption society".

35. [*See s.* 51 (2) *of that Act.*]

36. In section 52 (1)—
   (a) for the words "fifty-three of this Act" there are substituted the words "twenty-five of the Children Act 1975"; and
   (b) [See that section.]

37. In section 55, after the words "this Act" there are inserted the words "or Part I of the Children Act 1975".

38. [See s. 56 of that Act.]

39. In section 57 (1)—
   (a) for the definition of "adoption order" there is substituted "'adoption order' means an order under section 1 of this Act or section 8 (1) of the Children Act 1975;",
   (b) there are inserted after the definition of "adoption society" the words "'approved adoption society' means an adoption society approved under Part I of the Children Act 1975;",
   (c) after the definition of "body of persons" there are inserted the following definitions—
       "'child', except where used to express a relationship, means a person who has not attained the age of 18;
       'Convention adoption order' has the same meaning as in the Children Act 1975;",
   (d) for the definition of "guardian" there is substituted "'guardian' means—
       (a) a person appointed by deed or will in accordance with the provisions of the Guardianship of Infants Acts 1886 and 1925 or the Guardianship of Minors Act 1971 or by a court of competent jurisdiction to be the guardian of the child, and
       (b) in the case of an illegitimate child, includes the father where he has custody of the child by virtue of an order under section 9 of the Guardianship of Minors Act 1971, or under section 2 of the Illegitimate Children (Scotland) Act 1930;",
   (e) after the definition of "relative" there is inserted the following definition—
       "'voluntary organisation' means a body other than a public or local authority the activities of which are not carried on for profit."

40. After section 57 (1) there is inserted—
   "(1A) In this Act, in relation to Scotland, unless the context otherwise requires 'actual custody' means care and possession.".

County Courts Act 1959 (c. 22)

41. In section 109 (2) the following paragraph is inserted after paragraph (g)—
   "(h) any proceedings under the Guardianship of Minors Acts 1971 and 1973 or the Children Act 1975."

Children and Young Persons Act 1963 (c. 37)

42. In section 49 (1), for the words "twenty pounds" there are substituted the words "£100".

Perpetuities and Accumulations Act 1964 (c. 55)

43. In section 4, the following subsection is inserted at the end—
   "(7) For the avoidance of doubt it is hereby declared that a question arising under section 3 of this Act or subsection (1) (a) above of whether a disposition would be void apart from this section is to be determined as if subsection (6) above had been a separate section of this Act."

Adoption Act 1964 (c. 57)

44. In section 1, the following subsection is substituted for subsection (5)—
   "(5) Section 8 (3) and (4) of, and paragraph 11 of Schedule 1 and paragraph 3 of Schedule 2 to, the Children Act 1975 apply in relation to a child who is the subject of an order which is similar to an order under section 25 of that Act and is made (whether before or after this subsection has effect) in

Northern Ireland, the Isle of Man or any of the Channel Islands, as they apply in relation to a child who is the subject of an adoption order."

45. In section 3 (3)—
 (a) for the words " section 53 of the said Act of 1958 " there are substituted the words " section 25 of the Children Act 1975 ";
 (b) for the words from " the word ' Provisionally' '" to the end of the subsection there are substituted the words " the words ' Proposed Foreign Adoption' or, as the case may require, ' Proposed Foreign Re-adoption' followed by the name, in brackets, of the country in which the order was made."

Health Services and Public Health Act 1968 (*c.* 46)

46. For section 64 (3) (*a*) there is substituted—
 " (*a*) ' the relevant enactments ' means—
 (i) Parts III and IV of the Children and Young Persons Act 1933,
 (ii) the National Health Service Act 1946,
 (iii) Part III of the National Assistance Act 1948,
 (iv) the Children Act 1948,
 (v) the Adoption Act 1958,
 (vi) the Children Act 1958,
 (vii) section 9 of the Mental Health Act 1959,
 (viii) section 10 of the Mental Health Act 1959, so far as it relates to cases mentioned in paragraph (*a*) of that section,
 (ix) section 2 (1) (*f*) of the Matrimonial Proceedings (Magistrates' Courts) Act 1960,
 (x) the Children and Young Persons Act 1963, except Part II and section 56,
 (xi) this Act,
 (xii) the Adoption Act 1968,
 (xiii) section 7 (4) of the Family Law Reform Act 1969,
 (xiv) the Children and Young Persons Act 1969, except so far as it relates to any voluntary home designated as mentioned in section 39 (1) of that Act as a controlled or assisted community home,
 (xv) section 43 of the Matrimonial Causes Act 1973,
 (xvi) the National Health Service Reorganisation Act 1973,
 (xvii) the Children Act 1975."

47. For section 65 (3) (*b*) there is substituted—
 " (*b*) ' the relevant enactments ' means—
 (i) Parts III and IV of the Children and Young Persons Act 1933,
 (ii) Part III of the National Health Service Act 1946,
 (iii) Part III of the National Assistance Act 1948,
 (iv) the Children Act 1948,
 (v) the Adoption Act 1958,
 (vi) section 3 of the Disabled Persons (Employment) Act 1958,
 (vii) the Children Act 1958,
 (viii) section 9 of the Mental Health Act 1959,
 (ix) section 10 of the Mental Health Act 1959, so far as it relates to cases mentioned in paragraph (*a*) of that section,
 (x) section 2 (1) (*f*) of the Matrimonial Proceedings (Magistrates' Courts) Act 1960,
 (xi) the Children and Young Persons Act 1963, except Part II and section 56,
 (xii) this Act,
 (xiii) the Adoption Act 1968,
 (xiv) section 7 (4) of the Family Law Reform Act 1969,
 (xv) the Children and Young Persons Act 1969,
 (xvi) section 43 of the Matrimonial Causes Act 1973,
 (xvii) the National Health Service Reorganisation Act 1973,
 (xviii) the Children Act 1975."

Social Work (Scotland) Act 1968 (*c.* 49)

48. In section 2 (2) (functions of the social work committee), the following paragraph is inserted after paragraph (*g*)—
 " (*h*) the Children Act 1975,".

49. For section 5 (2) there is substituted—

" (2) The Secretary of State may make regulations in relation to—

(a) the performance of the functions assigned to local authorities by this Act;

(b) the activities of voluntary organisations in so far as those activities are concerned with the like purposes;

(c) the performance of the functions referred to social work committees under section 2 (2) (b) to (e) and (h) of this Act;

(d) the performance of the functions transferred to local authorities by section 1 (4) (a) of this Act.".

50. In section 6 (1) (b), after sub-paragraph (ii) there is inserted the following sub-paragraph—

" (iii) a child who has been placed for adoption by an adoption agency (within the meaning of section 1 of the Children Act 1975) ; ".

51. In section 10—

(a) in subsection (1), for the words from " with his functions " to the end there is substituted " with—

(a) his functions;

(b) the functions of local authorities,

under this Act or under the enactments specified in paragraph (a) of section 1 (4) and paragraphs (b) to (e) and (h) of section 2 (2) of this Act, in circumstances where it appears to the Secretary of State that such grants or loans should be made.";

(b) after subsection (3) there is inserted—

" (3A) In subsection (3) above, " voluntary organisation the sole or primary object of which is to promote social welfare " includes an adoption society approved under Part I of the Children Act 1975.".

52. In section 17—

(a) in subsection (3), for " section 16 " there is substituted " section 16 (1) (a) " and after " local authority " there is inserted " , in whom are vested in accordance with the resolution the parental rights and powers in respect of a child,";

(b) the following subsection is inserted after subsection (3)—

" (3A) A resolution under section 16 (1) (b) of this Act shall not prevent the voluntary organisation, in whom are vested in accordance with the resolution the parental rights and powers in respect of a child, from allowing, either for a fixed period or until the voluntary organisation otherwise determine, the care of the child to be taken over by, and the child to be under the control of, a parent, guardian, relative or friend in any case where it appears to the voluntary organisation to be for the benefit of the child.";

(c) in subsection (4), for " section 16 " there is substituted " section 16 (1) (a) ";

(d) in subsection (6), for the words " the said section 16 " there is substituted " section 16 of this Act ";

(e) in subsection (7), after the words " local authority " there are inserted the words " or a voluntary organisation ";

(f) in subsection (8)—

(i) for the words " to whom this section applies " there is substituted " , in respect of whom a resolution under section 16 of this Act is in effect,"; and

(ii) for the words " fifty pounds " there is substituted " £400 ";

(g) in subsection (9)—

(i) for the words " where a local authority have, in accordance with subsection (3) of this section, allowed " there is substituted—

" Where—

(a) a local authority have, in accordance with subsection (3) of this section; or

(b) a voluntary organisation have, in accordance with subsection (3A) of this section,

allowed ";

(ii) for the words " fifty pounds " there is substituted " £400 ".

53. In section 18—

(a) in subsection (2), for " section 16 " there is substituted " section 16 (1) (a) ";

607

(*b*) in subsection (3)—

(i) in paragraph (*a*), for " paragraph (*a*) " there is substituted
" sub-paragraph (i) ";

(ii) for paragraph (*b*) there is substituted " (*b*) in the case of a
resolution passed by virtue of circumstances specified in sub-paragraph
(ii), (iii), or (iv) of subsection (1) of the said section 16, by the
person who, but for the resolution, would have the parental rights and
powers in relation to the child,";

(iii) after the words " otherwise direct, the local authority " there
are inserted the words ", and any voluntary organisation having
parental rights and powers with respect to the child,";

(*c*) in subsection (4), after the words " local authority " there are inserted the
words " or voluntary organisation ".

54. In section 32 (2)—

(*a*) for paragraphs (*b*) and (*c*) there is substituted—

" (*b*) he is falling into bad associations or is exposed to moral
danger; or

(*c*) lack of parental care is likely to cause him unnecessary
suffering or seriously to impair his health or development; or ";

(*b*) in paragraph (*d*), for the words " Children and Young Persons (Scotland)
Act 1937 " there is substituted " Criminal Procedure (Scotland) Act
1975 ";

(*c*) after paragraph (*d*) there is inserted—

" (*dd*) the child is, or is likely to become, a member of the same
household as a person who has committed any of the offences mentioned
in Schedule 1 to the Criminal Procedure (Scotland) Act 1975; or ".

55. In section 35 (5) (*a*) at the end there is inserted " and to such other persons
as may be prescribed;".

56. In section 44 (5), after " 20 ", there is inserted " 20A.".

57. In section 49 (3) for the words " The sheriff may examine the reporter and "
there is substituted—

" The reporter, whether or not he is conducting the proceedings before the
sheriff, may be examined by the sheriff; and the sheriff may examine ".

58. In section 69—

(*a*) in subsection (1), at the end there are added the following words—
"; and a court, if satisfied that there are reasonable grounds for believing
that the child is within any premises, may grant a search warrant
authorising a constable to search those premises for the child.".

(*b*) for subsection (5) there is substituted—

" (5) In this and the next following section any reference—

(*a*) to a child absconding includes a reference to his being unlawfully taken
away;

(*b*) to a child absconding from a place or from the control of a person
includes a reference to his absconding while being taken to, or awaiting
being taken to, that place or that person as the case may be.".

59. In section 70, at the end there are added the following words—
"; and a court, if satisfied that there are reasonable grounds for believing
that the child is within any premises, may grant a search warrant authorising
a constable to search those premises for the child.".

60. In section 71, for the words " one hundred pounds " there is substituted
" £400 ".

Adoption Act 1968 (*c.* 53)

61. [*See s.* 8 (2) *of that Act.*]

62. [*See s.* 8 (5) *of that Act.*]

63. [*See s.* 9 (5) *of that Act.*]

64. In section 11 (1)—

(*a*) for the definition of " adoption order " there is substituted the following
definition—

" " adoption order " means an order made under section 8 of the
Children Act 1975 as a Convention adoption order;";

(b) in the definition of " specified order " for the words " section 1 of this Act " there are substituted the words " sections 8 (1) and 24 of the Children Act 1975 ".

65. [*See s.* 12 (2) *of that Act.*]

Housing Act 1969 (c. 33)

66. In section 86 (2) for the words " any illegitimate son or daughter and any adopted son or daughter " there are substituted the words " and any illegitimate son or daughter ".

Children and Young Persons Act 1969 (c. 54)

67. [*See s.* 1 (2) *of that Act.*]

68. [*See s.* 11A *of that Act.*]

69. [*See s.* 21 *of that Act.*]

70. [*See s.* 21A *of that Act.*]

71. In section 27—
(a) in subsection (3), for the words " their general duty aforesaid " there are substituted the words " their general duty under section 12 (1) of the Children Act 1948 ";
(b) the following subsections are substituted for subsection (4)—
" (4) Without prejudice to their general duty under the said section 12, it shall be the duty of a local authority to review the case of each child in their care in accordance with regulations made under the following subsection.
(5) The Secretary of State may by regulations make provision as to—
(a) the manner in which cases are to be reviewed under this section;
(b) the considerations to which the local authority are to have regard in reviewing cases under this section; and
(c) the time when a child's case is first to be reviewed and the frequency of subsequent reviews under this section."

72. In section 58 (1), the following paragraph is inserted after paragraph (b)—
" (bb) premises in which a child is living with a person other than his parent, guardian, relative or custodian, with whom he has been placed by an adoption agency (within the meaning of section 1 of the Children Act 1975); ".

Administration of Justice Act 1970 (c. 31)

73.—(1) In Schedule 1—
(a) after " *Appellate Business* " there is inserted the following paragraph—
" Proceedings on appeal under section 4A of the Children Act 1948; ";
(b) at the end there is inserted the following paragraph—
" Proceedings on appeal under the Children Act 1975 ".
(2) In Schedule 8—
(a) in paragraph 5, after the words " Social Security Act 1966 " there are inserted the words " or section 45 of the Children Act 1975 ";
(b) after paragraph 11, there is inserted the following paragraph—
" 12. An order under section 34 (1) (b) of the Children Act 1975 (payments of maintenance in respect of a child to his custodian).".

Local Authority Social Services Act 1970 (c. 42)

74. In Schedule 1—
(a) at the end of the entry relating to the Adoption Act 1958 there are added the following words " Counselling services for adopted persons ";
(b) the following is inserted at the end—
" Children Act 1975 (c. 72)
Part I ... Maintenance of Adoption Service; function of local authority as adoption agency; applications for orders freeing children for adoption; inquiries carried out by local authorities in adoption cases.

Children Act 1975

Part II ... Application by local authority for revocation of custodianship order; inquiries carried out by local authority in
custodianship cases.".

Guardianship of Minors Act 1971 (c. 3)

75.—(1) In section 9—
    (a) in subsection (2) for " any person (whether or not one of the parents) "
there is substituted " one of the parents " and the words " or either of
the parents " are repealed;
    (b) in subsection (3), the proviso is repealed;
    (c) in subsection (4), the words from " or (before or after the death of either
parent) " to the end are repealed;
    (d) the following subsections are inserted after subsection (4)—
        " (5) An order shall not be made under subsection (1) of this
section giving custody to a person other than the mother or father.
        (6) An order shall not be made under subsection (1) of this section
at any time when the minor is free for adoption (within the meaning
of section 12 (6) of the Children Act 1975) ".
(2) In section 13 (2), after the words " order for the payment of money " there
are inserted the words " made by a magistrates' court ".
(3) [See s. 16 of that Act.]

Attachment of Earnings Act 1971 (c. 32)

76. In Schedule 1—
    (a) in paragraph 6, after the words " Social Security Act 1966 " there are
inserted the words " or section 45 of the Children Act 1975 ";
    (b) after paragraph 11, there is inserted the following paragraph—
        " 12. An order under section 34 (1) (b) of the Children Act 1975
(payments of maintenance in respect of a child to his custodian)."

Parliamentary and Other Pensions Act 1972 (c. 48)

77. In section 15 (6), for the words " a stepchild or adopted child " there are
substituted the words " or a stepchild ".

Matrimonial Causes Act 1973 (c. 18)

78. [See s. 44 (1) of that Act.]

79. In section 50 (1), at the end of paragraph (e) there are inserted the following
words—
    " or
    (f) proceedings to which section 100 (7) (d) of the Children Act 1975 applies
(certain applications for revocation and variation of custodianship etc.
orders) ; ".

Guardianship Act 1973 (c. 29)

80.—(1) In section 4 (3) for the words from " the following provisions " to the
end there are substituted the following words " sections 12 (2) and 13 of the
Guardianship of Minors Act 1971 shall apply as if the order made under section 2
of this Act were an order under section 9 of the Guardianship of Minors Act 1971."
(2) After section 4 (3) there is inserted the following subsection—
    " (3A) An order under section 2 (2) (b) or (3) above relating to a minor
may be varied or discharged by a subsequent order made on the application of
either parent or after the death of either parent on the application of any
guardian under the Guardianship of Minors Act 1971 or on the application of
the local authority to whose care the minor was committed by the order under
section 2 (2) (b)."

81. [See s. 6 (1) of that Act.]

Legal Aid Act 1974 (c. 4)

82. In Schedule 1—
    (a) for paragraph 3 (d), there is substituted—
        " (d) proceedings in which the making of an order under Part I of
the Children Act 1975 is opposed by any party to the proceedings; ";

(b) the following paragraphs are inserted after paragraph 3 (e)—
" (f) proceedings under Part II of the Children Act 1975;
(g) proceedings under section 63 (2) of the Children Act 1975 ".

Housing Act 1974 (c. 44)

83. In section 129 (4), for the words " any illegitimate son or daughter and any adopted son or daughter " there are substituted the words " and any illegitimate son or daughter ".

Section 108

SCHEDULE 4

FURTHER REPEALS

[*The repeals contained in Parts I–III of this Schedule, being already in force, have been given effect in the appropriate places in the Acts concerned.*]

PART IV

ADOPTION ORDERS

Chapter	Short Title	Extent of Repeal
7 & 8 Eliz. 2. c. 5.	Adoption Act 1958.	Sections 1 and 2. Sections 4 and 5. Section 7 (1) (a) and (c) and (3). Section 9 (1) and (5). Section 10. Section 11 (1) and (3). Section 12. Section 21 (2).
1966 c. 19.	Law Reform (Miscellaneous Provisions) (Scotland) Act 1966.	Section 4.
1971 c. 3.	Guardianship of Minors Act 1971.	Section 16 (2).

These repeals take effect on the date section 8 (1) comes into force.

PART V

CHILDREN IN CARE OF LOCAL AUTHORITIES

Chapter	Short Title	Extent of Repeal
10 & 11 Geo. 6. c. 43.	Children Act 1948.	Section 3 (1) and (2).
7 & 8 Eliz. 2. c. 5.	Adoption Act 1958.	Section 15 (4) and (5).
7 & 8 Eliz. 2. c. 72.	Mental Health Act 1959.	In Schedule 7, the entry relating to the Children Act 1948.
1963 c. 37.	Children and Young Persons Act 1963.	Section 48.
1968 c. 49.	Social Work (Scotland) Act 1968.	Section 17 (1) and (2). In section 18 (4) the words " but where on such an application the court appoints a guardian the resolution shall cease to have effect ".
1971 c. 3.	Guardianship of Minors Act 1971.	In section 5 (2) the words from " but where " to the end.

These repeals take effect on the date sections 57 and 74 come into force.

PART VI

REGISTRATION OF BIRTHS

Chapter	Short Title	Extent of Repeal
1953 c. 20.	Births and Deaths Registration Act 1953.	In section 3, the words " and of any person in whose charge the child may be placed " and the proviso. In section 6, the words " or finding " and in that section and in section 7 the words " or from the date when any living new-born child is found exposed ". In section 8, the words " or, in the case of a living new-born child found exposed, from the date of the finding ". In section 36 (*a*), the words " or any living new born child ".
1969 c. 46.	Family Law Reform Act 1969.	Section 27 (2), (3), (4) and (5).

These repeals take effect on the date section 92 comes into force.

PART VII

ADOPTION AGENCIES

Chapter	Short Title	Extent of Repeal
7 & 8 Eliz. 2. c. 5.	Adoption Act 1958.	Section 28 (2). Sections 30 and 31. In section 32 (3) the words from " children " to the end. In section 57 (1) the definitions of " charitable association " and " registered adoption society ". Schedule 3.
1970 c. 42.	Local Authority Social Services Act 1970.	In column 2 of Schedule 1, the words " Making etc. arrangements for the adoption of children; regulation of adoption societies.".

These repeals take effect on the date section 4 comes into force.

PART VIII

ADOPTION: EVIDENCE OF AGREEMENT & GUARDIANS AD LITEM

Chapter	Short Title	Extent of Repeal
7 & 8 Eliz. 2. c. 5.	Adoption Act 1958.	Section 6. Section 9 (7) and (8). Section 11 (4) and (5).

These repeals take effect on the date section 20 comes into force.

PART IX

INQUIRIES ETC. BY ADOPTION AGENCIES

Chapter	Short Title	Extent of Repeal
7 & 8 Eliz. 2. c. 5.	Adoption Act 1958.	Section 3. Section 8. Section 53. In section 57 (1), the definition of " Compulsory School age ".

These repeals take effect on the date section 18 comes into force.

PART X

GRANTS ETC. FOR VOLUNTARY ORGANISATIONS

Chapter	Short Title	Extent of Repeal
10 & 11 Geo. 6. c. 43. 1969 c. 54.	Children Act 1948. Children and Young Persons Act 1969.	Section 45 (2). Section 46. Section 65 (2).

These repeals take effect on the date paragraphs 46 and 47 of Schedule 3 come into force.

PART XI

PROTECTED CHILDREN

Chapter	Short Title	Extent of Repeal
7 & 8 Eliz. 2. c. 5.	Adoption Act 1958.	In section 37 (1), paragraph (*a*), the words " of the person first mentioned in paragraph (*a*) of this subsection or, as the case may be," and the words " but is not a foster child within the meaning of Part I of the Children Act 1958 ". Section 37 (2) and (5). Section 40 (1), (2) and (3). Sections 41 and 42. In section 43 (1), the words from " or in contravention " to " of this Act ".

These repeals take effect on the date paragraph 31 of Schedule 3 comes into force.

PART XII

CUSTODIANSHIP

Chapter	Short Title	Extent of Repeal
1973 c. 29.	Guardianship Act 1973.	In section 2, in subsection (2) (*b*), the words " or to any other individual " and in subsection (4) (*a*) the words " or to any person given the custody of the minor ". In section 3 (3), the words from " or (before " to " section 9 (1) of that Act " and the words from " and section 16 (5) " to the end.

These repeals take effect on the date section 33 comes into force.

INDEX

Index

CUSTODIANSHIP ORDER—*cont.*
  restriction on removal of child,
    559–560
  revocation, 556–557
  variation of, 556–557

CUSTODY, 554–565
  actual, definition, 584
  adoption, before, 188
  child's religious education, 6
  conduct of parent, and, 6
  custodianship order. *See* CUSTODIAN-
    SHIP ORDER.
  guardianship, and, 412
  illegitimate children, 215
  jurisdiction of English summary courts,
    135
  jurisdiction of sheriff, 136
  legal, definition, 584
  orders for, 411–413
  parent, definition of, 6–7
  person, definition of, 6–7
  production of child, 6
  repayment of costs of bringing up
    child, 6
  Scotland, in, 561–565

DEATH,
  amounts disposable on, without repre-
    sentation, 257
    power to provide for further
      increase, 259
  proof of, family allowances and, 263

DEBT,
  wife, of, liability of husband, abolition
    of, 59

DEFINITIONS,
  actual custody, 584
  adoption, 595
  adoption society, 210
  apprentice, 265
  authorised chapel, 128–129
  authorised court, 589–590
  beneficiary, 533
  blood sample, 313
  blood test, 313
  British territory, 592
  care order, 335–336
  child, 56, 89, 371, 472, 592
  child in care of voluntary organisation,
    584
  child, in section 33 of Wills Act
    1837...309
  child of the family, 472
  collecting officer, 147
  compulsory school age, 89
  contribution order, 89–90
  dependant, 232
  disposition, 167, 595
  domestic proceedings, 153
  drug addict, 232
  earnings, 430
  foster child, 178–179, 360
  guardian, 56, 90, 211, 592–593
  habitual drunkard, 232
  interim order, 335–336
  issue, in section 33 of Wills Act
    1837...309
  legal custody, 584
  legal guardian, 56
  legitimation, 595

DEFINITIONS—*cont.*
  local authorities, 84, 371
  local education authority, 90
  maintenance order, 13
  net estate, 524–525, 533
  parent, 6–7, 90
  parental rights and duties, 583
  parents or guardian, 73
  person, 6–7
  place of safety, 57, 211
  power of appointment, 595
  property, 167
  protected child, 204–205, 360
  single woman, 409
  superintendent registrar, 122
  voluntary home, 51–52, 79, 90
  voluntary organisation, 90, 593
  will, 167
  young person, 57, 371

DELICT,
  proceedings between husband and
    wife, 235–236

DEPENDANT,
  definition, 232

DEPOSITION,
  child, by, 42–43
    admissibility, 43

DETENTION,
  absentees, of, 346–347
  child or young person, of, 342–347

DISPOSITION,
  definition, 167

DIVORCE, 266–267
  agreements or arrangements, con-
    sideration by court, 445–446
  ancillary relief, 454
  children, and, 465–468
  co-respondent, relief for, 450
  facts raising presumption of break-
    down of marriage, 442–444
  financial provision, 450–465
  five-year separation cases, grave
    hardship to respondent, and, 445
  grounds for, 442–443
  judicial separation, and, 444–445
  matrimonial home, right of occupation,
    and, 287–288
  no financial relief granted, provision
    as to, 529
  non-judicial, 510
  non-recognition by third country no
    bar to re-marriage, 438
  overseas, recognition of, 436–437
    cross-proceedings, 437
    grounds for, 437
    proof of facts, 437
  proceedings after decree nisi, 446–447
  Queen's Proctor, intervention of, 446
  recognition of, 436–439
    exemptions from, 438–439
    existing rules to continue in force,
      437–438
  reconciliation, and, 445
  remarriage of divorced persons, 266
  restrictions on petitions within three
    years of marriage, 444
  void or voidable decree, validation of,
    476

DOMESTIC PROCEEDINGS,
  definition, 153

620

Index